CARING FOR OUR CHILDREN

National Health and Safety Performance Standards:
Guidelines for Out-of-Home Child Care

Second Edition

A Joint Collaborative Project of

American Academy of Pediatrics
141 Northwest Point Blvd.
Elk Grove Village, IL 60007-1098

American Public Health Association
800 I I Street, N.W.
Washington, DC 20001-3710

National Resource Center for Health and Safety in Child Care
University of Colorado Health Sciences Center at Fitzsimons
Campus Mail Stop F541, PO Box 6508
Aurora, CO 80045-0508

Support for this project was provided by the
Maternal and Child Health Bureau,
Health Resources and Services Administration,
Department of Health and Human Services
(Cooperative Agreement # U93 MC 00098)

ISBN 1-58110-079-5 (American Academy of Pediatrics)
     0-9715682-0-0 (National Resource Center for Health and Safety
                        in Child Care)

Printed and bound in the United States of America
        Design: Jeff Calderone, Kathy Duran, David Merten
        Typesetting: Jeff Calderone, David Merten

TABLE OF CONTENTS

ACKNOWLEDGMENTS

The National Resource Center for Health and Safety in Child Care would like to acknowledge the outstanding contributions of all persons and organizations involved in the revision of *Caring for Our Children: National Health and Safety Performance Standards: Guidelines for Out-of-Home Child Care Programs. Second Edition.* The collaboration of the American Academy of Pediatrics, the American Public Health Association, and the Maternal and Child Health Bureau provided a wide scope of technical expertise from their constituents in the creation of this project. The subject-specific Technical Panels as listed provided the majority of the content and resources. Over 100 organizations were asked to review and validate the accuracy of the content and contribute additional expertise where applicable. The individuals representing these organizations are listed in "Additional Contributors". This broad collaboration and review from the best minds in the field has led to a more comprehensive and useful tool.

In a project of such scope, many individuals provide valuable input to the end product. We would like to acknowledge those individuals whose names may have been omitted.

Steering Committee

Susan S. Aronson, MD, FAAP
Co-Chair, American Academy of Pediatrics, PA

Albert Chang, MD, MPH, FAAP
Co-Chair, American Public Health Association, CA

Phyllis E. Stubbs-Wynn, MD, MPH
Department of Health and Human Services, Health Resources and Services Administration, Maternal and Child Health Bureau, DC

Marilyn J. Krajicek, EdD, RN, FAAN
Director, National Resource Center for Health and Safety in Child Care, CO

Barbara U. Hamilton, MA
Assistant Director, National Resource Center for Health and Safety in Child Care, CO

Technical Panel Chairs and Members

Children With Special Needs
Herbert J. Cohen, MD, FAAP, Chair,
  Bronx, NY
Rebecca Fewell, PhD, Miami, FL
Ruth Kaminer, MD, FAAP, Bronx, NY
Lillian Kornhaber, RPT, Bronx, NY
Peggy Pizzo, MEd, Boston, MA
Anne Riley, RN, Iowa City, IA
Sarah Schoen, MA, OT, Bronx, NY
Nancy Tarshis, MA, CCC/SP, Bronx, NY

Environmental Quality
Steven B. Eng, MPH, RPHI, Chair,
  BC, Canada
Robert E. Brewster, RS, MPA, Wheaton, IL
Lowest Jefferson, Olympia, WA
Shannan Lile, RS, Arlington, TX
Lori Saltzman, Bethesda, MD
Richard K. Snaman, REHS/RS, Arlington, VA
Elizabeth Zanowiak, Washington, DC

General Health
Selma Deitch, MD, MPH, FAAP, Chair,
  Manchester, NH
Joan H. Ascheim, MSN, Concord, NH
Karen Donoghue, RN, Manchester, NH
Steven Grandgeorge, MD, FAAP, Bedford, NH
Richard Nordgren, MD, Lebanon, NH
Carole Treen, Manchester, NH
Mary Jane Wallner, Concord, NH

Health and Safety Organization and Administration
Patricia Schloesser, MD, Chair, Topeka, KS
Chris Ross-Baze, MSW, Topeka, KS
Ed Ehlinger, MD, Minneapolis, MN
Karen E. Kroh, BA, Harrisburg, PA
Shirley Norris, MA, Topeka, KS
Peggy Scally, RN, Lawrence, KS
Maureen Whitman, MN, Portland, OR

Health Concerns Related to Social Environment and Child Development
Albert J. Solnit, MD, FAAP, Chair, New Haven, CT
Jean Adnopoz, MPH, New Haven, CT
Angela Crowley, PhD, APRN, CS, PNP New Haven, CT
Cynthia Farrar, New Haven, CT
Lola Nash, MA, New Haven, CT
June Sale, Los Angeles, CA
Kathryn Young, PhD, Riverside, CT

Infectious Diseases
Larry Pickering, MD, FAAP, Chair, Atlanta, GA
Ralph L. Cordell, PhD, Atlanta, GA
Leigh G. Donowitz, MD, FAAP, Charlottesville, VA
Fred Henderson, MD, Chapel Hill, NC
Pauline D. Koch, MS, Wilmington, DE
Dennis L. Murray, MD, FAAP, Augusta, GA
Robert F. Pass, MD, FAAP, Birmingham, AL
James M. Poole, MD, FAAP, Raleigh, NC

Injury Prevention
Albert Chang, MD, MPH, FAAP, Chair, San Diego, CA
Abbey Alkon, RN, MPH, PhD, Berkeley, CA
Letty Lie, RN, MPH, Minneapolis, MN
Cheryl Neverman, MS, Washington, DC
Joyce Rezin, RN, MS, PNP, San Diego, CA
Ellen R. Schmidt, MS, OTR, Washington, DC

Nutrition
Catherine Cowell, PhD, Chair, New York, NY
Maryrose J. Baiano, MS, DD, Dobbs Ferry, NY
Donna Blum, MS, RD, Alexandria, VA
Robin Brocato, MHS, Washington, DC
Annie Carr, MS, RD, Atlanta, GA
Ofelia Dirige, PhD, RD, San Diego, CA
Darby Eliades Graves, MPH, RD, Albany, OR
Janet Guidry, MPH, RD, New Orleans, LA
Brenda Lisa, MS, RD, Alexandria, VA
Mildred Monroe, MS, RD, LD, Atlanta, GA
Suzanne Rigby, MS, RD, Alexandria, VA
Susan Schlosser, MS, RD, Chappaqua, NY
Ruth Shrock, MS, RD, Columbus, OH
Denise Sofka, MPH, RD, Rockville, MD
Frances Vines, MS, RD, Dallas, TX

Prevention and Management of Child Abuse
David Chadwick, MD, FAAP, Co-Chair, San Diego, CA,
Carole Jenny, MD, FAAP, Co-Chair, Providence, RI
Deborah E. Lowen, MD, FAAP, Stratford, NJ
Patti K. Rosquist, MD, FAAP, Denver, CO
Charles J. Schubert, MD, FAAP, Cincinnati, OH
Sara E. Schuh, MD, FAAP, Charleston, SC
John R. Stirling, Jr., MD, FAAP, Vancouver, WA
Susan Reichert, MD, FAAP, Bend, OR

Staff Health
Iris Graville, RN, MN, Chair, Lopez Island, WA
Judy Calder, RN, BSN, Berkley, CA
Julianne Crevatin, MPH, Seattle, WA
Susan Eckelt, CDA, Tulsa, OK
Rene Gratz, PhD, Milwaukee, WA
Jan Gross, RN, BSN, Greenbank, WA
Karen Liberanti, RN, BSN, Tempe, AZ
Lynn Manfredi/Petitt, BS, Atlanta, GA
Daria Miller, Sunnyside, WA
Lynn White, BA, Conyers, GA

Lead Organizations Review Groups

American Academy of Pediatrics
Laura Aird, MS, Elk Grove Village, IL
Scott Allen, Chicago, IL
Sophie J. Balk, MD, FAAP, Bronx, NY
Dana M. Brazdziunas, MD, FAAP, Maywood, IL
Eileen Casey, MS, Elk Grove Village, IL
Peter A. Gorski, MD, MPA, FAAP, Boston, MA
Lawrence M. Gartner, MD, FAAP, Valley Center, CA
Peter Michael Miller, MD, MPH, FAAP, San Anselmo, CA
Jody R. Murph, MD, MS, FAAP, Iowa City, IA
Sheryl Nelson, MS, Elk Grove Village, IL
S. Donald Palmer, MD, FAAP, Sylacauga, AL
James M. Poole, MD, FAAP, Raleigh, NC
Judy Romano, MD, FAAP, Wheeling, WV
Jay Selcow, MD, FAAP, West Hartford, CT
Alicia Siston, MS, MPH, Elk Grove Village, IL
Howard R. Spivak, MD, FAAP, Boston, MA
Burton Willis, MD, FAAP, Fountain Valley, CA

American Public Health Association

Jonathan B. Kotch, MD, MPH, FAAP,
  Chapel Hill, NC
Ellen T. Meyer, Washington, DC
Larry R. Olsen, DrPH, MPH, SHES, Towson, MD
Mary B. Tierney, MD, Washington, DC
Billie Weiss, MPH, Los Angeles, CA

U.S. Department of Health and Human Services
Child Care Bureau
Moniquin Huggins, Washington, DC

Maternal and Child Health Bureau
Phyllis Stubbs-Wynn, MD, MPH, Rockville, MD
Yolanda Baker, Rockville, MD
Stephanie Bryn, MPH, Rockville, MD
David E. Heppel, MD, FAAP, Rockville, MD
Merle G. McPherson, MD, MPH, Rockville, MD
Kerry Nesseler, RN, MS, Rockville, MD
Mary Overpeck, DrPH, Rockville, MD
John Rossetti, DDS, MPH, Rockville, MD

National Resource Center for Health and Safety in Child Care* Project Team

Marilyn Krajicek, EdD, RN, FAAN - Director
Jennifer Beezley, RN, BA - Co-editor,
  Former Research Assistant
Jeff Calderone, MBA - Former Research Assistant
Shannon Collins, RN, BSN, MSCIS - Health Consultant
Susan Epstein, - Editor
Jeryl Feeley, ND, RN - Former Research Assistant
William Freud, MBA - Assistant Vice Chancellor -
  Information Systems, University of Colorado Health
  Sciences Center
Barbara Hamilton, MA - Assistant Director
Rachel Haynes, ND, CPNP, MSN - Research Assistant
David Merten, BS - Research Assistant
Ruth Neil, PhD, RN - Former Project Coordinator
Patricia Petch, BSc - Former Research Assistant
Elisabeth Rosenberg, BS - Program Assistant
Virginia Torrey, BA - Program Specialist
Joy Wu, PhD - Fellow

* Based at the University of Colorado Health Sciences
Center School of Nursing.

Additional Contributors

Duane Alexander, MD, FAAP
National Institute of Child Health and Human
Development, MD

Sandra Anseth, RN
North Dakota State Department of Health, ND

Sheri Azer, MA
Wheelock College Institute for Leadership and
Career Initiative, MA

Stan Bienick, BSW
Cherokee Center for Family Services, NC

Heidi Bishop, BS
United States Department of Agriculture, VA

Donna Blum-Kemelor, MS, RD, LD
United States Department of Agriculture, VA

Jo Ann Bolick, MA, CPNP, APN
Arkansas Department of Health, AR

John A. Bogert, DDS
American Academy of Pediatric Dentistry, IL

J. Patrick Byrne
National Association for Regulatory
Administration, NJ

Elaine Carr
Community & Family Health Services, AZ

Gloria V. Chen, RN, MBA
Georgia Division of Public Health, Office of Infant
and Child Health, GA

Judy Collins, MS
National Association for Regulatory
Administration, OK

Susan M. Conrath, PhD, MPH
Environmental Protection Agency, DC

Ralph Cordell, PhD
Centers For Disease Control and Prevention, GA

Ron Coté, PE
National Fire Protection Association, MA

Jane Cotler, RN, MS, CSN
Colorado Department of Public Health and
Environment, CO

Jane Coury, MSN, RN
Formerly with Maternal and Child Health Bureau,
PHS/Health Resources and Services
Administration, MD

Angela Crowley, PhD, APRN, CS, PNP
National Association of Pediatric Nurse
Practitioners, CT

Steve Davis, MD
Kentucky Department of Public Health, KY

Butch DeFillippo, MA Rec Admin, CPSI, CPRP
PlaySafe, LLC Recreational Consulting &
Services, NM

Katherine Duchen-Smith, RN, MS, CPNP
National Association of Pediatric Nurse
Practitioners, CO

Susan Eckelt, CDA
National Association for Family Child Care, OK

Lynn T. Elliott, RN, MS
Florida Department of Health, FL

Maria Gil De Lamadrid, JD
Child Care Law Center, CA

Melinda Green
National Black Child Development Institute, DC

Scott Groginsky
National Conference of State Legislatures, CO

Peggy Haack
Center for the Child Care Workforce, DC

Bruce Hershfield
Child Welfare League of America, DC

Dawn Higley, RN, MS, CPNP
Formerly with Utah Department of Health, UT

Kay Hollestelle
The Children's Foundation, DC

Gail Johnson, RN, MS
Formerly with National Association for Sick Child
Day Care, VA

Pauline D. Koch, MS
National Association for Regulatory
Administration, DE

Phil Koshkin
Office of Licensing Child Care Administration, MD

Jonathan B. Kotch, MD, MPH, FAAP
National Training Institute for Child Care Health
Consultants, NC

Karen E. Kroh, BA
National Association for Regulatory Administration, PA

Christopher A. Kus, MD, MPH, FAAP
New York State Department of Health, NY

Marlene Lee, BSN, RN
Maternal and Child Health Branch, Hawaii
Department of Health, HI

Linda Likins
National Association Child Care Resource and
Referral Agencies, Inc, PA

Marjorie J. Long, Esq., CO

Doris Luckenbill, RN, CSN
National Association of School Nurses, Inc, ME

Deborah Markenson, MS, RD
Missouri Department of Health, Nutrition & Child
Care Programs, MO

Paul F. Marmen, MEd, EMT
Oklahoma Emergency Medical Services for
Children, OK

Virginia Marx, AS
National Association of Pediatric Nurse
Practitioners, NJ

Tameron Mitchell, RD, MPH
California Department of Health Services, Primary
Care and Family Health Division, CA

Gwen Morgan, MS
Wheelock College Institute for Leadership and
Career Initiative, MA

Jim O'Brien, PhD
Head Start Bureau, DC

Kathleen Eaton Paterson, RN, MPH
Formerly with Vermont Department of Health, VT

Susan Ponemon
United States Department of Agriculture, VA

Paul S. Rusinko
Maternal and Child Health Bureau, MD

William A. Rutala, PhD
University of North Carolina, NC

Mary Schucker, CPNP, MSN, RN, CRNP
National Association of Pediatric Nurse
Practitioners, PA

Phyllis Sherard, MPA
Wyoming Department of Health, WY

Wendelin Slusser, MD, FAAP, CA

Linda Smith
Formerly with United States Department of
Defense, VA

Karen Sokal-Gutierrez, MD, MPH, FAAP, CA

Patricia M. Spahr, MA
National Association for the Education of Young
Children, DC

Steven B. Steinhoff
Association of Food and Drug Officials, PA

Linda Stern
Child Care Division, Oregon Department of
Employment, OR

Carolynne Stevens, MA
National Association for Regulatory
Administration, VA

Sandy Sullivan
Formerly with The Clorox Company, DC

Jeanette S. Tanos, RN, MHR
Guam Department of Public Health and Social
Services, Guam

Barbara Thompson, MS
United States Department of Defense, VA

Donna Thompson, PhD
National Program for Playground Safety, IA

Joan Turetsky
United States Department of Agriculture, VA

Elaine Tyrrell, MS
U.S. Consumer Product Safety Commission, MD

Lynn White, BA
National Child Care Association, GA

Karen Williams, PhD
University of Wyoming, WY

Judith Wright
Nevada State Health Division, NV

Susan Zamecnik, MEd
National Association for Regulatory
Administration, VT

Robin Zelno
Formerly with American Society for Testing and
Materials, PA

This edition of *Caring for Our Children: National Health
and Safety Performance Standards: Guidelines for Out-of
Home Child Care Programs* was based on the first edition.
For this reason the contributors of the second edition
would like to acknowledge those involved in the cre-
ation of the first edition and their location at the time
of publishing. They are: Olivia Alegre-Ipanag, MD, MPH;
Madeline Appell, MA, New York, NY; Arthur L. Banks,
RS, Washington, DC; Glenda Bean, AR; David Beard,
MSW, Austin, TX; G. Scott Biebink, MD, Minneapolis,
MN; Judy Blanding, MSN, San Jose, CA; Helen Blank, BS,
Washington, DC; Janice Boase, RN, Seattle, WA; Joyce
Borgmeyer, IA; Elizabeth Brannon, MS, RD, Rockville,
MD; Janet Braunstein, RN, MPH, Halifax, NS; Seido
Baba Brodbeck, MPH; Albert H. Brunswasser, MPH,
MBA, Pittsburgh, PA; Mojdeh Bruss, MPH, RD, Albu-
querque, NM; Susan Campbell, MPH; Bria Chakofsky,
RN, Seattle, WA; Barbara Chernofsky, La Mesa, CA;
Norris Class, MS, Topeka, KS; Brenda Coakley, MA,
Washington, DC; Steven Cochi, MD, Atlanta, GA; Judy
Coughlan, RN, Auburn, NY; Martha Daley, Denver, CO;
Dee Cuney, MEd, Napa, CA; Sheila Dobbin, MSW, Bos-
ton, MA; Barry Fidel, MSW, Olympia, WA; David Finkel-
hor, PhD, Durham, NH; Leslie Fisher, MPH, Albany, NY;
Patricia Fosarelli, MD, Baltimore, MD; Judith Garrard,
PhD, Minneapolis, MN; Emily M. Gates, MD, Jackson-
ville, FL; Helene Gayle, MD, MPH, Atlanta, GA; Andrea
Gielen, MPH, Baltimore, MD; Benjamin Gitterman, MD,
CO; David Goff, PE, MS, Hamden, CT; Stacey Graville,
RN, MN, Bellingham, WA; Elmer Green, DDS, MPH,
Albany, NY; Steven Hadler, MD, Atlanta, GA; Meredith
Harris-Copp, EdD, Boston, MA; Terry S. Hatch, MD,
Champaign-Urbana, IL; Debra Hawks Peabody, MPH;
Maxine Hayes, MD, Olympia, WA; Deborah Jackson;
Nancy Ellen Jones, PNP, DrPH, New York, NY; Karen
Juola, Topeka, KS; Dennis O. Juranek, DVM, MSc,
Atlanta, GA; Brearley B. Karsch, MS, RD, Philadelphia,
PA; Kay Kent, RN, Lawrence, KS; George Kupfer, MS,
Ann Arbor, MI; Edgar O. Ledbetter, MD, Elk Grove

Village, IL; Dr. Darryl Leong, IA; Robert Lettelier, NH; Kee MacFarlane, MSW, Los Angeles, CA; Kathleen Malloy, MD, MPH, Martinez, CA; Pamela Mangu, MA, Washington, DC; Valerie Marr, OK; Mary Ann Mateo, Pine Hills, NM; Jack L. Mayer, MD, New York, NY; Marcia K. McDonnell, MN, CANP, Atlanta, GA; Erick W. Mood, MPH, New Haven, CT; Bliss Moore, MPH, RS, Olympia, WA; Randolph S. Moore, MA; Linda Morgan, MD, Lynn, MA; Geraldine Norris, RN, MS, Washington, DC; Mary Ann O'Connor, MA, Hanover, NH; Michael Osterholm, PhD, Minneapolis, MN; Karen Patjens, BA, Tacoma, WA; Georges Peter, MD, Providence, RI; Margaret Phillips, EdD, RD, Rockville, MD; Patricia M. Pierce, PhD, Gainesville, FL; Ann Prendergast, MPH, RD, Rockville, MD; Chris Pressey-Murray, Hanover, NH; Sally Provence, MD, New Haven, CT; Linda Randolph, MD, PHP, Albany, NY; Thomas A. Reardon, RS, Pasadena, CA; Sally Reid, Esq, Dedham, MA; Cheri Robertson, Temecula, CA; Martha Rodgers, MD, Atlanta, GA; Cris Ros-Dukler, TX; Carol W. Runyan, PhD, Chapel Hill, NC; Susan Russell, MS, Chapel Hill, NC; Hector Sanchez, MSW, Washington, DC; Marion N. Scarborough, MPH, RD, Jacksonville, FL; Lawrence Schonberger, MD, MPH, Atlanta, GA; Ellen Schroth, RS, Washington, DC; Ethel Seiderman, MA, Fairfax, CA; Robert Shane, PhD, Wynnewood, PA; Cecil Sheps, MD, MPH, Chapel Hill, NC; Sam Sheps, MD, Vancouver, BC, Canada; Sallye Skipper Blake, EdS, Montgomery, AL; Patricia St. Clair, RN, ScD, Seattle, WA; Jeanne Stellman, PhD, Brooklyn, NY; George Sterne, MD, New Orleans, LA; Siubhan Stevens, San Jose, CA; Carol S. Stevenson, JD, San Franscico, CA; Jack Thompson, Seattle, WA; Jon Tillingheist, OK; Rosemary Totten, BA, CDA, Tacoma, WA; Elaine Trate, Burke, VA; Key Vaughn, RS, Austin, TX; Cynthia Vlasich, RN, Washington, DC; Patricia Wagner, EdD, Brooklyn, NY; Helen Wallace, MD, MPH, San Diego, CA; Aileen Whitfill, Arlington, VA; Mark Widome, MD, MPH, Hershey, PA; Patricia Wise, RN, MEd, Holyoke, MA; Harry Wright, Jr, MD, MPH, Los Angeles, CA; Clotilde Zayas, MA, New York, NY.

INTRODUCTION

In 1992, the American Public Health Association (APHA) and the American Academy of Pediatrics (AAP) jointly published *Caring for Our Children:.National Health and Safety Performance Standards: Guidelines for Out-of-Home Child Care Programs.*[1] The publication was the product of a 5-year national project funded by the U.S. Department of Health and Human Services Maternal and Child Health Bureau (MCHB), Health Resources and Services Administration. This comprehensive set of health and safety standards was a response to many years of effort by advocates for quality child care. In 1976, Aronson and Pizzo recommended development and use of national health and safety standards as part of a report to Congress in association with the *Federal Interagency Day Care Requirements* (FIDCR) *Appropriateness Study.*[1] In the years that followed, experts repeatedly reaffirmed the need for these standards. For example, while the work to prepare *Caring for Our Children* was underway, the National Research Council's report, *Who Cares for America's Children? Child Care Policy for the 1990s* called for uniform national child care standards.[2] It is a privilege to introduce the reader, in the year 2001, to the second edition of *Caring for Our Children.* We will discuss why a new edition was deemed necessary, describe the process of revision, and highlight some of the changes in the new standards.

The 1992 publication anticipated the new edition when it noted (that) "as new knowledge and innovative practices evolve, the standards themselves should be modified or updated."[3] In the years since the first edition was published, the interest in and the enrollment of young children in early childhood education programs has increased not only in the United States but also in other nations in the world. The continuing requests for the hard copy version and documented use of the electronic version shows considerable interest by both a national and an international audience. Thus, the use of the standards since 1992 documents the value of the standards and validates the use of resources required to keep the standards up-to-date. *Caring for Our Children* has been a yardstick

for measuring what has been done and what still needs to be done, as well as a technical manual on how to do it.

The Maternal and Child Health Bureau's funding, in 1995, of a National Resource Center for Health and Safety in Child Care (NRC) at the University of Colorado Health Sciences Center School of Nursing supported the work to produce the new edition. The work plan included the following strategies:

1) Enjoin as many of the experts as possible who contributed to the first edition to participate in the revision effort;
2) Seek additional input from a national constituency of individuals and associations with vital interest in the health and safety of children in out-of-home care;
3) Strive for national consensus through an iterative process of debate and discussion;
4) Obtain approval and endorsement from the original developers, AAP, APHA, and the MCHB.

The revision of the standards for the second edition of *Caring for Our Children* was an extensive process. The 10 technical panels focused on their particular subject matter areas, after which time their recommendations were merged into a single set of recommended standards and widely reviewed by representatives of all stakeholders with an interest in child care, including parents. The final document represents a consensus of the various disciplines involved with child care, with the largest contribution of factual content coming from experts in health and safety.

The second edition benefited from the contribution of 55 newly engaged experts as well as that of a core group of veterans. The two co-chairs of the Steering Committee (Susan S. Aronson, MD, FAAP, and Albert Chang, MD, MPH, FAAP), eight of the 10 Technical Panel chairs, and the MCHB federal project officer (Phyllis Stubbs-Wynn, MD, MPH) were veterans from the first edition. Twenty-two out of 75 members of the Technical Panels were also veterans. Review and comments were received from 100 individuals from 65 stakeholder organizations representing providers, child care advocates, health professionals, safety specialists, early childhood educators, regulators, and federal, military, and state agencies. A complete listing of the Steering Committee, Technical Panel members, and Stakeholder Organizations appears on the Acknowledgment pages.

The process of revising the standards and the consensus building was organized in stages:
1) Technical Panel Chairs recruited members to their panels and reviewed the standards from the first edition. They removed standards that were no longer applicable or out-of-date, identified those that were still applicable (in their original or in a revised form), and formulated new standards that were deemed appropriate and necessary.
2) Telephone conference calls were convened among technical panel chairs to bring consensus on standards that bridge several technical areas.
3) A draft of these revised standards was sent to a national and state constituency of stakeholders for their comments and suggestions.
4) This feedback was subsequently reviewed and considered by the technical panels (often more than one) and a decision was made to further revise or not to revise a standard. It should be noted that the national review brought many important points of view and new information for additional discussion and debate.
5) The edited standards were then sent to designated review committees of the AAP and the APHA. The funding agency, MCHB, also conducted a concurrent review. Final copy was approved by the Steering Committee representing the three organizations and the NRC.

The second edition contains eight chapters of 659 *standards* and a ninth chapter of 48 *recommendations* for licensing and community agencies and organizations. We have made the following significant content and format changes in the second edition:
• New and revised standards in all areas, such as sleep position of infants related to SIDS studies and playground equipment specifications;

• Integration of standards that are relevant to children with special needs, as well as to all children, throughout the document to promote inclusion;
• A two-column format to increase readability and eliminate empty space;
• Merged and consolidated standards (from 981 standards and recommendations to 707 standards and recommendations);
• Expansion of the rationale and comment sections;
• Updated references;
• Incorporation of former appendices into appropriate standards;
• A more activist posture in standards pertaining to training requirements (for providers), health education activities (for providers, children, and parents), and management of acute illness (such as respiratory infections) and chronic illness (such as asthma).

See Appendix A for the guiding principles used in writing these standards.

In projects of this scope and magnitude, the end product is only as good as the persons who participate in the effort. It is hard to enumerate in this introduction the countless hours of dedication and effort from contributors and reviewers. The project owes each of them a huge debt of gratitude. Their reward will come when high-quality child care services become available to all children and their families!

Overlap with Requirements of Other Organizations

We recognize that many organizations have requirements and recommendations that apply to out-of-home child care. For example, the National Association for the Education of Young Children (NAEYC) publishes requirements for developmentally appropriate practice and accreditation of child care centers; Head Start follows Performance Standards; the AAP has many standards related to child health; the Child Welfare League of America has requirements for child care service; the U.S. Department of Defense has standards for military child care; the National Fire Protection Association has standards for fire safety in child care settings. The Child Care Bureau (CCB) administers the Child Care and Development Fund (CCDF) which provides funds to states, territories, and tribes to assist low-income families, families receiving temporary public assistance, and those transitioning from public assistance in obtaining child care so that they can work or attend training/education. Child care providers serving children funded by CCDF must meet basic health and safety requirements set by states and tribes. All of these are valuable resources, as are many excellent state publications. By addressing health and safety as an integrated component of child care, *Caring for Our Children* complements these other child care requirements and recommendations.

The concept of limiting child:staff ratio and group size exemplifies this overlap. The NAEYC emphasizes the need for low infant:staff ratios for very young children to facilitate developmentally appropriate, warm, trusting and reciprocal relationships. Having a few infants whose care is entrusted to a limited number of adults in a setting where the overall numbers of interactions is controlled by a small group size and a primary caregiving relationship helps develop the child's trust and ability to make emotional attachments. Also, sufficient and specific staff assignments are essential so caregivers know the status of each baby at all times; to be sure that the baby is safe, to be able to evacuate that child and other children in the group in case of fire or other facility emergency, as well as to have sufficient time to practice and track health and safety routines, such as feedings and diaper changing for each child. Caregivers in group child care settings perform the same demanding work as parents of twins, triplets, or quadruplets.

Health involves more than the absence of illness and injury. To stay healthy, children depend on adults to make healthy choices for them and to teach them to make such choices for themselves over the course of a lifetime. Child development addresses physical growth and the development in many areas: gross and fine motor skills, language, emotional balance, cognitive capacity, and personal-social skills. Thus, health and safety issues overlap with those considered part of early childhood education and mental health. Such overlap is inevitable and indeed desirable.

Continuing Improvement

Standards are never static. Each year the knowledge base increases, and new scientific findings become available. New areas of concern and interest arise. These standards will assist citizens who are involved in the continuing work of standards improvement at every level: in child care practice, in regulatory administration, and in the professional performance of the relevant disciplines.

Each of these areas affects the others in the ongoing process of improving the way we meet the needs of children. Possibly the most important use of these standards will be to raise the level of understanding among the general public about what those needs are, and to contribute to a greater willingness to commit more resources to achieve quality child care where children can grow and develop in a healthy and safe environment.

Albert Chang MD, MPH, FAAP
Susan S. Aronson MD, FAAP
Co-Chairs, Steering Committee

REFERENCES:

[1] USHEW, Office of the Assistant Secretary for Planning and Evaluation. *Policy Issues in Day care: Summaries of 21 Papers.* pp 109-115. 1977.

[2] National Research Council, National Academy of Sciences. *Who Cares for America's Children? Child Care Policy in the 1990s.* Washington DC, 1990.

[3] American Public Health Association and American Academy of Pediatrics. *Caring for Our Children. National Health and Safety Performance Standards: Guidelines for Out-of-Home Child Care Programs.* Washington, DC, 1992.

DEFINITIONS

We have defined many terms in the Glossary found on page 479. Some of these are so important to the user that we are emphasizing them here as well.

Types of requirements: Three terms describe different types of requirements have been carried forward from the 1992 edition:

- A *standard* is a statement that defines a goal of practice. It differs from a recommendation or a guideline in that it carries great incentive for universal compliance. It differs from a regulation in that compliance is not necessarily required for legal operation. It usually is legitimized or validated based on scientific or epidemiological data, or when this evidence is lacking, it represents the widely agreed upon, state-of-the-art, high-quality level of practice.

  The agency, program, or health practitioner that does not meet the standard may incur disapproval or sanctions from within or outside the organization. Thus, a standard is the strongest criteria for practice set by a health organization or association. For example, many manufacturers advertise that their products meet ASTM standards as evidence to the consumer of safety, while those products that cannot meet the standards are sold without such labeling to undiscerning purchasers. In *Caring for Our Children*, specific standards define the frequency of visits to child care facilities and qualifications of health consultants to such facilities. Some states have adopted or even exceeded parts of these standards in their regulations, but many more have not done so. Facilities that use a health consultant, as specified in Standards 1.040 through 1.044, could be expected to be of higher quality than those that do not.

- A *recommendation* is a statement of practice that potentially provides a health benefit to the population served. An organization or a group of individuals with expertise or broad experience in the subject matter usually initiates it. It may originate within the group or be solicited by

individuals outside the organization. A recommendation is not binding on the practitioner; that is, there is no obligation to carry it out. A statement may be issued as recommendation because it addresses a fairly new topic or issue, because scientific supporting evidence may not yet exist, or because the practice may not yet enjoy widespread acceptance by the members of the organization or by the intended audience for the recommendation.

  For example, in Chapter 9 of *Caring for Our Children*, Recommendation 9.004 suggests that States should adopt uniform categories and definitions for use in their own licensing that cover the types of facilities addressed by the standards. While it is recognized that each State might differ in the specific definitions of services they choose to use, the recommendation says that each State should be sure that the sum of their licensing effort should address all the types of service specified in the standards.

- A *guideline* is a statement of advice or instruction pertaining to practice. Like a recommendation, it originates in an organization with acknowledged professional standing. Although it may be unsolicited, a guideline is developed in response to a stated request or perceived need for such advice or instruction. For example, the American Academy of Pediatrics (AAP) has a guideline for the elements required to make the diagnosis of Attention-Deficit/Hyperactivity Disorder.

- A *regulation* takes a previous recommendation or guideline and makes it a requirement for legal operation. A regulation originates in an agency with either governmental or official authority and has the power of law. Such authority is usually accompanied by an enforcement activity. Examples of regulations are: State regulations pertaining to health and safety requirements for caregivers and children in a licensed child care center, and immunizations required for participation in group care. The components of the regulation, of course, will vary by topic addressed as well as by area of jurisdiction (e.g., municipality or state). Because a regulation prescribes a practice that every agency or program must comply with, it usually is the minimum or the floor below which no agency or program should operate.

Types of facilities: Child care offers developmental care and education for children who live at home with their families. Several types of facilities are covered by the general definition of child care. Although States vary greatly in their legal definitions, overall, there is a generally understood definition for child care facilities. Much overlap and confusion of terms still exists in defining child care facilities. Although the needs of children do not differ from one setting to another, the declared intent of different types of facilities may differ. Thus, facilities that operate part-day, in the evening, during the traditional work day and work week, or during a specific part of the year may call themselves by different names. These standards recognize that while children's needs do not differ in any of these settings, the way children's needs are met may differ by whether the facility is in a residence or a non-residence and whether the child is expected to have a longer or only a very short-term arrangement for care. Thus, we have designated the type of facility to which each standard applies using the following definitions:

- A *Small Family Child Care Home* provides care and education for up to six children at one time, including the preschool children of the caregiver, in a residence that is usually, but not necessarily, the home of the caregiver. The key elements are that this type of care takes place in a setting that is used both for child care and as a residence (often simultaneously) and that the total number of children is limited to a maximum of six at any one time. Family members or other helpers may be involved in assisting the caregiver, but often, there is only one caregiver present at any one time.

- A *Large Family Child Care Home* provides care and education for between 7 and 12 children at a time, including the preschool children of the caregiver, in a residence that is usually, but not necessarily, the home of one of the caregivers. Staffing of this facility involves one or more

qualified adult assistants so that the requirements specified in the child:staff ratio and group size standard are met. The key element that distinguishes this type of facility is the combined use of the premises as a residence and for child care (often simultaneously) and that the number of children in care requires more than one caregiver present at any one time.

- A *Center* is a facility that provides care and education to any number of children in a nonresidential setting, or 13 or more children in any setting, if the facility is open on a regular basis. To distinguish a child care center from drop-in facility, a center usually provides care for some children for more than 30 days per year per child. In many cases, summer camps operate for more 30 days per year per child and, in fact, provide center-based child care.

- A *Drop-in-Facility* provides care for fewer than 30 days per year per child either on a consecutive or intermittent basis or on a regular basis, but for a series of different children.

- A *School-Age Child Care Facility* offers activities to children before and after school, during vacations, and on non-school days set aside for such activities as teachers' in-service programs.

- A *Facility for Children with Special Needs* provides specialized care and education for children who cannot be accommodated in a setting with typically developing children.

- A *Facility for Ill Children* provides care for one or more children who are temporarily excluded from care in their regular child care setting. Their condition does not require parental care but they cannot participate in the regular program at their usual source of child care, require more staff time than can be offered in their usual setting without putting the other children at risk, or have a condition that poses a risk for the adults or children in their usual child care facility. Such facilities for ill children are of two types:

- An *Integrated or Small Group Care Facility for Ill Children* provides care that has been approved by the licensing agency in a facility that cares for well children and is authorized to include up to six ill children.

- A *Special Facility for Ill Children* cares only for ill children or cares for more than six ill children at a time.

Age groups: Although we recognize that designated age groups and developmental levels must be used flexibly to meet the needs of individual children, many of the standards are applicable to specific age and developmental categories. The following categories are used in *Caring for Our Children.*

Develop-mental Stage	Age	Functional Definition (By Developmental Level)
Infant	0-12 months	Birth to ambulation
Toddler	13-35 months	Ambulation to accomplishment of self-care routines such as use of the toilet
Pre-schooler	36-50 months	From achievement of self-care routines to entry into regular school
School-Age Child	5-12 years	Entry into regular school, including kindergarten through 6th grade

Format and Language Level

In Chapters 1 through 8, the reader will find the scientific reference and/or epidemiological evidence for the standard in the rationale section of each standard. The rationale explains the intent of and the need for the standard. Where no scientific evidence for a standard is available, the standard is based on the best available professional consensus. If such a professional consensus has been pub-

lished elsewhere, that reference is cited. References for the rationales are at the end of each chapter. Thus, the rationales both justify the standard and serve as an educational tool. The Comments section includes other explanatory information relevant to the standard, such as applicability of the standard and, in some cases, suggested ways to measure compliance with the standard. Although this document reflects the best information available at the time of publication, like the first edition, this second edition will need updating from time to time to reflect changes in knowledge affecting child care.

Because the standards have many users with differing backgrounds and need for reference material, we ask readers of *Caring for Our Children* to accept some inconvenience when their purpose might be better met by a different format. The electronic version will help users to search for key words and concepts that might be addressed in a variety of places in the document. Although the standards have not been written from the perspective of a single use, we expect that many of the standards will be used as licensing requirements. Therefore, to the extent possible, the wording of the standards has been written to be measurable and enforceable. Also, measurability is important for performance standards in a contractual relationship between a provider of service and a funding source. Concrete and specific language helps caregivers and facilities put the standards into practice. Where a standard is difficult to measure, we have provided guidance to make the requirement as specific as possible. For some readers, the wording of some standards may seem highly technical; they will need to have that standard interpreted by specialists. Whenever feasible, we have written the standards to be understood by readers from a wide variety of backgrounds.

Users of the Standards

The intended users of the standards include many who contribute to the well-being of children. Each has a unique viewpoint. For many of the users, access to the Internet version of the publication will be useful. For those who need a full print document, the hard copy will be preferable. Many will want to use both versions for different purposes. For example, the electronic search of the Internet version helps identify all points in the standards that address a particular topic. The hard copy is easily used where Internet access is unavailable. The intended users include:

- Health professionals
- Trainers
- Regulators
- Child Care Providers
- Academics and Researchers

All of the standards are attainable. Some may have already been attained in individual settings; others can be implemented over time. For example, any organization that funds child care should, in our opinion, adopt these standards as funding requirements and should set a payment rate that covers the cost of meeting them.

The following are some of the ways in which *Caring for Our Children* may be used:

1. ***As guidance material for administrators and caregivers:*** Anyone operating a child care facility on any level needs information on good practice. These standards will inform:
    - Administrators at all levels, from those who operate a chain of centers to caregivers in small family child care homes
    - Caregivers
    - Those who teach courses to caregivers.

2. ***As a reference for consultants:*** Public health professionals, pediatricians, and others provide consultation to caregivers. This role requires knowledge that goes beyond traditional patient-centered pediatrics or public health approaches. Many local and state health departments have developed child care guidance material that public health nurses, sanitarians, and nutritionists, among others, use in consulting with caregivers. This document will help support and update such guidance material.

3. ***As guidance to citizens' groups in states revising their licensing requirements:*** Because licensing has the force of law, caregivers and facilities must meet any requirements set by licensing agencies. Resource limitations may delay full implementation of some of the standards. To address such limitations, the Maternal and Child Health Bureau funded a project to set priorities among the standards based on their association with the prevention of disease, disability and death (morbidity and mortality). The publication of this subset of the first edition of *Caring for Our Children* was called *Stepping Stones to Using Caring for Our Children*. Where resource constraints require focused implementation, the updated standards that correspond with *Stepping Stones* should be the first implemented. A similar process must be used to look at the new standards that first appear in the second edition.

4. ***As guidance material to State Departments of Education (DOEs) and local school administration:*** Some public schools and private schools offer programs for 4-year-olds and even younger children. A few schools provide infant programs. Licensing requirements for child care seldom cover public and private school systems. Few States have written standards for such programs when they are operated by schools. Many school codes fail to adequately address child handwashing, location of bathrooms, child:staff ratios and group size, teacher qualifications for working with preschool children, and injury prevention. As state DOEs begin to write standards for school-operated child care and preschool facilities, and as principals begin to implement good practice in early childhood and child care facilities, this guidance material will help.

5. ***As guidance material for funding of sub-sidized facilities:*** Most States and localities provide child care services for income-eligible families through purchase-of-service contracts and individual vendor/voucher mechanisms. Public interest in purchasing child development services for at-risk children has increased, largely due to dissemination of research about the key role played by early childhood experience in the development of the brain. Welfare-to-work policies have increased attention to the use of non-parental child care by the poor that parallels increased interest in child care for middle and upper class families as more women in all groups are participating in the labor force.

   Many communities offer subsidized child care/developmental services for children with special needs. Schools and other agencies are setting up specialized arrangements to serve children with special needs, sometimes paying for children with special needs to be included in local community child care settings with typically developing children. When States and localities purchase child care services, the standards offer guidance not only on the level of service to expect, but also a way to estimate the corresponding level of funding to meet such requirements for children with special needs.

6. ***As guidance material to other national private organizations that write standards:*** Several other national organizations have expressed their strong interest in child care by writing standards for accreditation or guidance for the field. Both the first and second editions of *Caring for Our Children* draw on the expertise of these other organizations in developing the standards. Reciprocally, the work done on these standards should be equally useful to other organizations.

7. ***As guidance material for parents and the general public:*** Parents need consumer information to choose quality child care for their children. By drawing on the standards, organizations that serve parents can train their staff and develop educational materials that provide credentialed advice for parents. For example, resource and referral counselors, community health professionals, and social workers will be able to use *Caring for Our Children* as a reference for their work with parents, the general public, and the media.

Relationship of the Standards to Laws, Ordinances, and Regulations

The members of the technical panels could not annotate the standards to address local laws, ordinances, and regulations. Many of these legal requirements are out-of-date or have a different intent from that addressed by the standards. Users of this document should check legal requirements that may apply to facilities in particular locales. Where conflicts are noted, we recommend further work at the local level to resolve such conflicts.

In general, child care is regulated by at least three different legal entities or jurisdictions. The first is the building code jurisdiction. Building inspectors enforce building codes to protect life and property in all buildings, not just child care facilities. Some of the recommended standards should be written into state or local building codes, rather than into the licensing requirements.

The second major legal entity that regulates child care is the health system. A number of different codes are intended to prevent the spread of disease in restaurants, hospitals, and other institutions where hazards and risky practices might exist. Many of these health codes are not specific to child care; however, specific provisions for child care might be found in a health code. Some of the provisions in the recommended standards might be appropriate for incorporation into a health code.

The third legal jurisdiction applied to child care is child care licensing. Usually, before a child care operator receives a license, the operator must obtain approvals from health and building safety authorities. Sometimes a standard is not included as a child care licensing requirement because it is covered in another code. Sometimes, however, it is not covered in any code. Since children need full protection, the issues addressed in this document should be addressed in some aspect of public policy, and consistently addressed within a community. In an effective regulatory system, different inspectors do not try to regulate the same thing. Advocates should decide which codes to review in making sure that these standards are addressed appropriately in their regulatory systems. Although the licensing requirements are most usually affected, it may be more appropriate to revise the health or building codes to include certain standards and it may be necessary to negotiate conflicts among applicable codes.

CHAPTER 1

Staffing

1.1 CHILD:STAFF RATIO AND GROUP SIZE

STANDARD 1.001
RATIOS FOR SMALL FAMILY CHILD CARE HOMES

The small family child care home provider child:staff ratios shall conform to the following table:

If the small family child care home provider has no children under two years of age in care,	**then** the small family child care home provider may have 1-6 children over two years of age in care
If the small family child care home provider has 1 child under two years of age in care,	**then** the small family child care home provider may have 1-3 children over two years of age in care
If the small family child care home provider has 2 children under two years of age in care,	**then** the small family child care home provider may have no children over two years of age in care

The small family child care home provider's own children shall be included in the child:staff ratio.

RATIONALE: Although child:staff ratios alone do not predict the quality of care, direct warm social interaction between adults and children is more common and more likely with lower child:staff ratios. Care - givers must be recognized as performing a job for groups of children that parents of twins, triplets, or quadruplets would rarely be left to handle alone. In child care, these children do not come from the same family and must learn a set of common rules that may differ from expectations in their own homes.

Low child:staff ratios are most critical for infants and young toddlers (0 to 24 months) (1). Infant development and caregiving quality improves when group size and child:staff ratios are smaller (2). Improved verbal

interactions are correlated with lower child:staff ratios (3). For 3- and 4-year old children, the size of the group is even more important than ratios. The recommended group size and child:staff ratio allow 3- to 5- year old children to have continuing adult support and guidance while encouraging independent, self-initiated play and other activities (4).

The National Fire Protection Association (NFPA) requires in the *NFPA-101 Life Safety Code* that small family child care homes serve no more than 2 clients incapable of self-preservation (6).

COMMENTS: Some states are setting limits on the number of school-age children that are allowed to be cared for in small family child care homes, e.g., two school-age children in addition to the maximum number allowed for infants/preschool children. No data are available to support using a different ratio where school-age children are in family child care homes. Since school-age children require focused caregiver time and attention for supervision and adult-child interaction, this standard applies the same ratio to all children over two years of age. The family child care provider must be able to have a positive relationship and provide guidance for each child in care.

Unscheduled inspections encourage compliance with this standard.

For more information regarding brain development in children in child care, see STANDARD 1.010.

TYPE OF FACILITY: *Small Family Child Care Home*

STANDARD 1.002
RATIOS FOR LARGE FAMILY CHILD CARE HOMES AND CENTERS

Child:staff ratios in centers and large family child care homes shall be maintained as follows during all hours of operation, including transport and nap times:

During nap time, at least one adult shall be physically present in the same space as the children.

Age	Maximum Child:Staff Ratio	Maximum Group Size
Birth - 12 mos.	3:1	6
13 - 30 mos.	4:1	8
31 - 35 mos.	5:1	10
3-year-olds	7:1	14
4-year-olds	8:1	16
5-year-olds	8:1	16
6 - 8-year-olds	10:1	20
9 - 12-year-olds	12:1	24

Other adults who are included in the child:staff ratio need not be in the same space with the children when all the children are napping. However, in case of emergency, these adults shall be on the same floor and shall have no barrier to their coming to help immediately. The caregiver who is in the same space with the children shall be able to summon these adults without leaving the children.

When there are mixed age groups in the same room, the child:staff ratio and group size shall be consistent with the age of most of the children when no infants or toddlers are in the mixed age group. When infants or toddlers are in the mixed age group, the child:staff ratio and group size for infants and toddlers shall be maintained. In large family child care homes with two or more caregivers caring for no more than 12 children, no more than three children younger than 2 years of age shall be in care.

RATIONALE: These child:staff ratios are within the range of recommendations for each age group that the National Association for the Education of Young Children (NAEYC) uses in its accreditation program (5). The NAEYC recommends a range that assumes the director and staff are highly trained and, by virtue of the accreditation process, has determined a staffing pattern that enables effective staff function. The standard for child:staff ratios in this document uses a single desired ratio, rather than a range, for each age group. In some cases, these child:staff ratios and group sizes are the more stringent ratios and group

sizes recommended in the National Research Council's report, *Who Cares for America's Children? Child Care Policy for the 1990s* (1). According to the National Research Council, child:staff ratios and group size are two of the four most important areas to be addressed in national standards.

Children with special health care needs may require additional staff on-site, depending on their special need and extent of disability (1).

Low child:staff ratios for non-ambulatory children are essential for fire safety. The National Fire Protection Association, in its *NFPA-101 Life Safety Code*, recommends that no more than three children younger than 2 years of age be cared for in large family child care homes where two staff members are caring for up to 12 children (6).

Children benefit from social interactions with peers. However, larger groups are generally associated with less positive interactions and developmental outcomes. Group size and ratio of children to adults are limited to allow for one to one interaction, intimate knowledge of individual children, and consistent caregiving (7).

Although child:staff ratios alone do not predict the quality of care, direct warm social interaction between adults and children is more common and more likely with lower child:staff ratios. Caregivers must be recognized as performing a job for groups of children that parents of twins, triplets, or quadruplets would rarely be left to handle alone. In child care, these children do not come from the same family and must learn a set of common rules that may differ from expectations in their own homes.

Low child:staff ratios are most critical for infants and young toddlers (0 to 24 months) (1). Infant development and caregiving quality improves when group size and child:staff ratios are smaller (2). Improved verbal interactions are correlated with lower ratios (3). For 3- and 4-year old children, the size of the group is even more important than ratios. The recommended group size and child:staff ratio allow 3- to 5- year old children to have continuing adult support and guidance while encouraging independent, self-initiated play and other activities (4).

In addition, the children's physical safety and sanitation routines require a staff that is not fragmented by excessive demands. Child:staff ratios in child care settings should be sufficiently low to keep staff stress below levels that might result in anger with children. Caring for too many young children, in particular, increases the possibility of stress to the caregiver, and may result in loss of self-control.

Although observation of sleeping children does not require the physical presence of more than one caregiver, the staff needed for an emergency response or evacuation of the children must remain available for this purpose. Nap time may be the best option for regular staff conferences and staff training, but these activities should take place in an area next to the room where the children are sleeping so no barrier will prevent the staff from assisting if emergency evacuation becomes necessary.

COMMENTS: The child:staff ratio indicates the maximum number of children permitted per caregiver (8). These ratios assume that caregivers do not have time-consuming bookkeeping and housekeeping duties, so they are free to provide direct care for children. The ratios do not include other personnel (such as bus drivers) necessary for specialized functions (such as driving a vehicle).

Group size is the number of children assigned to a caregiver or team of caregivers occupying an individual classroom or well-defined space within a larger room (8). The "group" in child care represents the "homeroom" for school-age children. It is the psychological base with which the child identifies and from which the child gains continual guidance and support in various activities. This standard does not prohibit larger numbers of children from joining in collective activities as long as child:staff ratios and the concept of "home room" are maintained.

Unscheduled inspections encourage compliance with this standard.

These standards are based on what children need for quality nurturing care. Those who question whether these ratios are affordable must consider that our efforts to limit costs have resulted in overlooking the basic needs of children and creating a highly stressful

work environment for caregivers. Community resources other than parent fees and a greater public investment in child care are critical to achieving the child:staff ratios and group sizes specified in this standard.

For more information regarding brain development in children in child care, see STANDARD 1.010.

TYPE OF FACILITY: *Center; Large Family Child Care Home*

STANDARD 1.003
RATIOS FOR FACILITIES SERVING CHILDREN WITH SPECIAL HEALTH NEEDS

Facilities enrolling children with special needs shall determine, by an individual assessment of each child's needs, whether the facility requires a lower child:staff ratio.

RATIONALE: The child:staff ratio must allow the needs of the children enrolled to be met. The facility should have sufficient direct care professional staff to provide the required programs and services. Integrated facilities with fewer resources may be able to serve children who need fewer services, and the staffing levels may vary accordingly. Adjustment of the ratio allows for the flexibility needed to meet the child's type and degree of special need. The facility should seek consultation with parents and other professionals regarding the appropriate child:staff ratio and may wish to increase the number of staff members if the child requires significant special assistance.

COMMENTS: These ratios do not include personnel who have other duties that might preclude their involvement in needed supervision while they are performing those duties, such as cooks, maintenance workers, or bus drivers.

TYPE OF FACILITY: *Center; Large Family Child Care Home: Small Family Child Care Home*

STANDARD 1.004
RATIOS DURING TRANSPORTATION

Child:staff ratios established for out-of-home child care shall be maintained on all transportation the facility provides or arranges. The driver shall not be included in the ratio. No child of any age shall be left unattended in a vehicle.

RATIONALE: Children must continue to receive adequate supervision during transport. Placement of a child in a vehicle does not eliminate the need for supervision.

Drivers must not be distracted from safe driving practices by being simultaneously responsible for the supervision of children.

TYPE OF FACILITY: *Center; Large Family Child Care Home; Small Family Child Care Home*

STANDARD 1.005
RATIOS FOR WADING AND SWIMMING

The following child:staff ratios shall apply while children are wading or swimming:

Developmental Levels	Child:Staff Ratio
Infants	1:1
Toddlers	1:1
Preschoolers	4:1
School-age Children	6:1

During any swimming/wading activity involving mixed developmental levels where either an infant or a toddler is present, the ratio shall always be 1 adult to 1 infant/toddler. The required ratio of adults to older children shall be met without including the adults who are required for supervision of infants and/or toddlers. An adult shall remain in direct physical contact with infants at all times during swimming or wading.

RATIONALE: The circumstances surrounding drownings and water-related injuries of young children suggest that requirements and environmental modifications will reduce the risk for this type of injury. Essential elements are close continuous supervision (9), fences and self-locking gates around all swimming/wading pools, hot tubs, and spas, and special safety covers on pools when they are not in use (10). Infant swimming programs have led to water intoxication and seizures because infants may swallow excessive water when they are engaged in any submersion activities.

COMMENTS: These ratios do not include personnel who have other duties that might preclude their involvement in supervision during swimming/wading activities while they are performing those duties. Thus, this ratio excludes cooks, maintenance workers, or lifeguards from being counted in the child:staff ratio if they are involved in these specialized duties at the same time. A lifeguard is not counted in the child:staff ratio unless he/she is assigned only to the children in that group.

TYPE OF FACILITY: *Center; Large Family Child Care Home; Small Family Child Care Home*

1.2 LICENSURE/CERTIFICATION OF QUALIFIED INDIVIDUALS

STANDARD 1.006
CHILD CARE CREDENTIAL

Any individual who will be primarily responsible for children in a separate classroom, a group of children, or a small family child care home shall hold an official child care credential as granted by the authorized state agency.

RATIONALE: The supervision of children must be overseen by a person who has experience and education to properly care for them. The qualification of anyone who will be alone with children must be actively assured and not assumed.

TYPE OF FACILITY: *Center; Large Family Child Care Home; Small Family Child Care Home*

1.3 PRESERVICE QUALIFICATIONS AND SPECIAL TRAINING

GENERAL QUALIFICATIONS FOR ALL CAREGIVERS, INCLUDING DIRECTORS, OF ALL TYPES OF FACILITIES

STANDARD 1.007
STAFF RECRUITMENT

Staff recruitment shall be based on a policy of non-discrimination with regard to gender, race, ethnicity, disability, or religion, as required by the Equal Employment Opportunity Act. The policy of non-discrimination shall extend also to sexual orientation. Staff recruitment policies shall adhere to requirements of the Americans with Disabilities Act as it applies to employment. The tasks required for each position shall be defined in writing and the suitability of an applicant shall be measured with regard to the applicant's qualifications and abilities with the tasks required in the role.

RATIONALE: Child care providers must adhere to federal law. In addition, child care providers should model diversity and non-discrimination in their employment practices to enhance the quality of the program and to teach children and parents about diversity and tolerance for individuals on the staff who are competent caregivers with different background and orientation in their private lives.

The goal of the Americans with Disabilities Act (ADA) in employment is to reasonably accommodate applicants and employees with disabilities to provide them equal employment opportunity and to integrate them into the program's staff to the extent feasible, given the individual's limitations. Under the ADA, employers are expected to make reasonable accommodations for persons with disabilities. Some disabilities may be accommodated, whereas others may not allow the person to do essential tasks. The fairest way to address this evaluation is to define the tasks and measure the abilities of applicants to perform them.

COMMENTS: Reasons to deny employment include the following:
1) The applicant or employee is not qualified or is unable to perform the essential functions of the job with or without reasonable accommodations;
2) Accommodation is unreasonable or will result in undue hardship to the program;
3) The applicant's or employee's condition will pose a significant threat to the health or safety of that individual or of other staff members or children.

Accommodations and undue hardship are defined and based on each individual situation.

Caregivers can obtain copies of the Equal Employment Opportunity Act and the American with Disabilities Act from their local public library (11, 12). Facilities should consult with ADA experts through the U.S. Department of Education funded Disability and Business Technical Assistance Centers throughout the country. These centers can be reached by calling 1-800-949-4232 and callers will be routed to the appropriate region.

TYPE OF FACILITY: *Center; Large Family Child Care Home; Small Family Child Care Home*

STANDARD 1.008
REFERENCES AND BACKGROUND CHECKS

Directors of centers and caregivers in large and small family child care homes shall check references and examine employment history and criminal and other appropriate court records (including fingerprinting and checks with state child abuse registries) before employing any staff member (including substitutes), even in states where licensing has not been instituted. Background checks shall be required for all child care providers.

When checking references, prospective employers shall specifically ask about previous convictions with child abuse or child sexual abuse. Failure of the prospective employee to disclose previous convictions of child abuse or child sexual abuse is grounds for dismissal.

Persons who acknowledge being sexually attracted to children or who acknowledge having physically or sexually abused children, or who are known to have committed such acts shall not be hired or allowed to work in the child care facility.

RATIONALE: To ensure their safety and physical and mental health, children must be protected from any risk of abuse. Although few persons will acknowledge past child abuse to another person, the obvious attention directed to the question by the licensing agency or caregiver may discourage some potentially abusive individuals from seeking employment in child care. In addition, the measure is very inexpensive.

COMMENTS: Records of substantiated child abuse are usually kept in state social services departments.

In the State of California, a state supported service for facilitating background checks has been successful in identifying people applying for child care jobs who have a history of previous offenses against children.

Child care centers with multiple caregivers are more likely to protect children from abuse than child care sites where there is only one caregiver. Therefore, this standard must be applied to caregivers who work in isolation.

TYPE OF FACILITY: *Center; Large Family Child Care Home; Small Family Child Care Home*

STANDARD 1.009
PRESERVICE AND ONGOING STAFF TRAINING

In addition to the credentials listed in STANDARD 1.014, prior to employment, a director of a center or a small family child care home network enrolling 30 or more children shall provide documentation of at least 26 clock hours of training in health, psychosocial, and safety issues for out-of-home child care facilities.

Small family child care home providers shall provide documentation of at least 12 hours of training in child development and health management for out-of-home child care facilities prior to initiating operation.

All directors and caregivers shall document receipt of training that revisits the following topics every 3 years:
a) Child development knowledge and best practice, including knowledge about the developmental stages of each child in care;
b) Child care as a support to parents;
c) Parent relations;
d) Ways that communicable diseases are spread;
e) Procedures for preventing the spread of communicable disease, including handwashing, sanitation, diaper changing, food handling, health department notification of reportable diseases, equipment, toy selection and proper washing, sanitizing to reduce the risk for disease and injury, and health issues related to having pets in the facility;
f) Immunization requirements for children and staff, as defined in STANDARD 1.045;
g) Common childhood illnesses and their management, including child care exclusion policies;
h) Organization of the facility to reduce the risks for illness and injury;
i) Teaching child care staff and children about infection control and injury prevention;
j) Staff occupational health and safety practices, such as proper procedures, in accordance with Occupational Safety and Health Administration (OSHA) bloodborne pathogens regulations;
k) Emergency procedures, as defined in STANDARD 3.048 through STANDARD 3.052;
l) Promotion of health in the child care setting, through compliance with STANDARD 3.001 through STANDARD 3.089;
m) Management of a blocked airway, rescue breathing, and other first aid procedures, as required in SSTANDARD 1.026;
n) Recognition and reporting of child abuse in compliance with state laws;
o) Nutrition;
p) Knowledge of medication administration policies and practices;
q) Caring for children with special needs in compliance with the Americans with Disabilities Act (ADA);
r) Behavior management.

RATIONALE: The director of a center or large family child care home or the small family child care home provider is the person accountable for all policies.

Basic entry-level knowledge of health and safety is essential to administer the facility. Caregivers must be knowledgeable about infectious disease because properly implemented health policies can reduce the spread of disease, not only among the children but also among staff members, family members, and in the greater community. Knowledge of injury prevention measures in child care is essential to control known risks. Pediatric first aid training is important because the director or small family child care home provider is fully responsible for all aspects of the health of the children in care.

COMMENTS: The American Academy of Pediatrics (AAP) and the National Association for the Education of Young Children (NAEYC) published a set of videos, based on the first edition of *Caring for Our Children,* that illustrates how to meet the standards in centers and family child care homes. This six-part video series is accompanied by a set of reproducible handouts for training. Other training materials, including videos, workshop curricula, and print materials suitable for training of caregivers, are also available from the AAP and NAEYC. Contact information for the AAP and the NAEYC is located in Appendix BB.

Training in infectious disease control and injury prevention is strongly recommended. This type of training may be obtained from qualified personnel of children's and community hospitals, managed care companies, health agencies, public health departments, pediatric emergency room physicians, or other health professionals in the community.

For more information about training opportunities, contact the AAP, Healthy Child Care America Project, the National Resource Center for Health and Safety in Child Care, or the National Training Institute for Child Care Health Consultants (at the University of North Carolina). Contact information is located in Appendix BB.

TYPE OF FACILITY: *Center; Large Family Child Care Home; Small Family Child Care Home*

STANDARD 1.010
ADDITIONAL QUALIFICATIONS FOR CAREGIVERS SERVING CHILDREN BIRTH TO 35 MONTHS OF AGE

Caregivers shall be prepared to work with infants and toddlers and, when asked, shall be knowledgeable and demonstrate competency in tasks associated with caring for infants and toddlers:
a) Diapering;
b) Bathing;
c) Feeding;
d) Holding;
e) Comforting;
f) Putting babies down to sleep positioned on their backs and on a firm surface to reduce the risk of Sudden Infant Death Syndrome (SIDS);
g) Providing responsive and continuous interpersonal relationships and opportunities for child-initiated activities.

To help manage atypical or disruptive behaviors of children, caregivers, in collaboration with parents, shall seek professional consultation from the child's source of routine health care or a mental health professional.

RATIONALE: The brain development of infants is particularly sensitive to the quality and consistency of interpersonal relationships. Much of the stimulation for brain development comes from the responsive interactions of caregivers and children during daily routines. Children need to be allowed to pursue their interests and encouraged to reach for new skills (13).

COMMENTS: For additional qualifications and responsibilities of teachers for centers and homes serving children from birth to 35 months, see also General Qualifications for All Caregivers, STANDARD 1.007 through STANDARD 1.010; and Training, STANDARD 1.023 through STANDARD 1.036.

TYPE OF FACILITY: *Center; Large Family Child Care Home; Small Family Child Care Home*

STANDARD 1.011
ADDITIONAL QUALIFICATIONS FOR CAREGIVERS SERVING CHILDREN 3 TO 5 YEARS OF AGE

Caregivers shall demonstrate the ability to apply their knowledge and understanding of the following, to children within the program setting:
a) Typical and atypical development of 3- to 5-year-old children;
b) Social and emotional development of children, including children's development of independence and their ability to adapt to their environment and cope with stress;
c) Cognitive, language, early literacy, and mathematics development of children through activities in the classroom;
d) Cultural backgrounds of the children in the facility's care by demonstrating cultural competence through interactions with children and families and through program activities.

To help manage atypical or disruptive behaviors of children, caregivers, in collaboration with parents, shall seek professional consultation from the child's source of routine health care or a mental health professional.

RATIONALE: Three- and 4-year-old children continue to depend on the affection, physical care, intellectual guidance, and emotional support of their teachers (4, 13).

A supportive, nurturing setting that supports a demonstration of feelings and accepts regression as part of development continues to be vital for preschool children. Preschool children need help building a positive self-image, a sense of self as a person of value from a family and a culture of which they are proud. Children should be enabled to view themselves as coping, problem-solving, passionate, expressive individuals.

COMMENTS: For additional qualifications and responsibilities of teachers for centers and homes serving children between 3 and 5 years old, see also General Qualifications for All Caregivers, STANDARD 1.007 through STANDARD 1.011; and Training, STANDARD 1.023 through STANDARD 1.036.

TYPE OF FACILITY: *Center; Large Family Child Care Home; Small Family Child Care Home*

STANDARD 1.012
ADDITIONAL QUALIFICATIONS FOR CAREGIVERS SERVING SCHOOL-AGE CHILDREN

Caregivers shall demonstrate knowledge about and competence with the social and emotional needs and developmental tasks of 5- to 12-year old children, be able to recognize and appropriately manage difficult behaviors, and know how to implement a socially and cognitively enriching program that has been developed with input from parents.

To help manage atypical or disruptive behaviors of children, caregivers, in collaboration with parents, shall seek professional consultation from the child's source of routine health care or a mental health professional.

RATIONALE: A school-age child develops a strong, secure sense of identity through positive experiences with adults and peers (14, 15). An informal, enriching environment that encourages self-paced cultivation of interests and relationships promotes the self-worth of school-age children.

When children display behaviors that are unusual or difficult to manage, caregivers should work with parents to seek a remedy that allows the child to succeed in the child care setting, if possible.

COMMENTS: The first resource for addressing behavior problems is the child's source of routine health care. Support from a mental health professional may be needed. If the child's health provider cannot help or obtain help from a mental health professional, the child care provider and the family may need a mental health consultant to advise about appropriate management of the child. Local mental health agencies or pediatric departments of medical schools may offer help from child psychiatrists, psychologists, other mental health professionals skilled in the issues of early childhood, and pediatricians who have a subspecialty in developmental and behavioral pediatrics.

For additional qualifications and responsibilities of teachers for centers serving school-age children, see also General Qualifications for All Caregivers, STANDARD 1.007through STANDARD 1.012; and Training, STANDARD 1.023 through STANDARD 1.036.

TYPE OF FACILITY: *Center; Large Family Child Care Home; Small Family Child Care Home*

STANDARD 1.013
GENERAL QUALIFICATIONS FOR ALL PERSONNEL OF CENTERS

Staff members shall reflect the cultural, language, and ethnic backgrounds of children enrolled in the program. Centers shall have a plan of action for recruiting and hiring a diverse staff that is representative of the children in the facilities' care.

RATIONALE: Young children's identities cannot be separated from family, culture, and their home language. Children need to see successful role models from their own ethnic and cultural groups and to develop the ability to relate to people who are different from themselves.

COMMENTS: In staff recruiting, the hiring pool should extend beyond the immediate neighborhood of the child's residence or location of the facility, to reflect the diversity of people with whom the child can be expected to have contact as a part of life experience.

TYPE OF FACILITY: *Center*

QUALIFICATIONS OF DIRECTORS OF CENTERS

STANDARD 1.014
GENERAL QUALIFICATIONS OF DIRECTORS

The director of a center enrolling fewer than 60 children shall be at least 21 years old and shall have the following qualifications:

a) A Bachelor's degree in early childhood education, child development, social work, nursing, or other child related field OR a combination of college coursework and experience, including:
   1) A minimum of four courses in child development and early childhood education;
   2) Two years of experience, under qualified supervision, working as a teacher serving the ages and developmental abilities of the children enrolled in the center where the individual will act as the director;
   3) A course in business administration or early childhood administration, or at least 6 months of on the job training in an administrative position;
c) A valid certificate in pediatric first aid, including management of a blocked airway, and rescue breathing, as specified in First Aid and CPR, STANDARD 1.026 through STANDARD 1.028;
d) Knowledge of community resources available to children with special needs and the ability to use these resources to make referrals or achieve interagency coordination;
e) Administrative and management skills in facility operations;
f) Capability in curriculum design;
g) Oral and written communication skills;
h) Demonstrated life experience skills in working with children in more than one setting.

The director of a center enrolling more than 60 children shall have the above and at least 3 years experience as a teacher of children in the age group(s) enrolled in the center where the individual will act as the director, plus at least 6 months experience in administration.

RATIONALE: The director of the facility is the team leader of a small business. Both administrative and child development skills are essential for this individual to manage the facility and set appropriate expectations. College-level coursework has been shown to have a measurable, positive effect on quality child care, whereas experience per se has not (3, 16, 17).

The director of a center plays a pivotal role in ensuring the day-to-day smooth functioning of the facility within the framework of appropriate child development principles and knowledge of family relationships.

The well-being of the children, the confidence of the parents of children in the facility's care, and the high morale and consistent professional growth of the staff depend largely upon the knowledge, skills, and dependable presence of a director who is able to respond to long-range and immediate needs and able to engage staff in decision-making that affects their day-to-day practice. Management skills are important and should be viewed primarily as a means of support for the key role of educational leadership that a director provides. A skilled director should know how to use community resources and to identify specialized personnel to enrich the staff's understanding of behavior and curriculum content. Past experience working in an early childhood setting is essential to running a facility.

Life experience may include experience rearing one's own children or previous personal experience acquired in any child care setting. Work as a hospital aide or at a camp for children with special needs would qualify, as would experience in school settings. This experience, however, must be supplemented by competency-based training to determine and provide whatever new skills are needed to care for children in child care settings.

COMMENTS: The profession of early childhood education is being informed by research on the association of developmental outcomes with specific practices. The exact combination of college coursework and supervised experience is still being developed. For example, the National Association for the Education of Young Children (NAEYC) has published the *Guidelines for Preparation of Early Childhood Professionals* (18). Additional information on the early childhood education profession is available from Wheelock College Institute for Leadership and Career Initiatives. The National Child Care Association (NCCA) has developed a 40-hour curriculum based on administrator competencies (19). Contact information for the NAEYC, the Wheelock College Institute for Leadership and Career Initiatives, and the NCCA is located in Appendix BB.

The qualifications stipulated in the AAP/APHA standards, as well as state and local regulations for administrators of child care facilities that serve typically developing children, may require supplementation because of the special requirements of the populations of children with special needs. The center is one component in a network of services for children with special needs in most communities. Every state participating in Part C of IDEA is required to have a directory of services. Having a directory of services available is useful and could fulfill part of the requirement. Many communities have agencies, such as local resource and referral agencies, that gather information about services available to children with special needs.

For additional information on qualifications for directors of centers, see General Qualifications for All Caregivers, STANDARD 1.007 through STANDARD 1.013; and Training, STANDARD 1.023 through STANDARD 1.036.

TYPE OF FACILITY: *Center*

STANDARD 1.015
MIXED DIRECTOR/TEACHER ROLE

Centers enrolling 30 or more children shall employ a non-teaching director. Centers with fewer than 30 children may employ a director who teaches as well.

RATIONALE: The duties of a director of a facility with more than 30 children do not allow the director to be involved in the classroom in a meaningful way.

COMMENTS: This standard does not prohibit the director from occasional substitute teaching, as long as the substitute teaching is not a regular and significant duty. Occasional substitute teaching may keep the director in touch with the teachers' issues.

TYPE OF FACILITY: *Center*

STANDARD 1.016
DIFFERENTIATED ROLES

Centers shall employ a teaching/caregiving staff for direct work with children in a progression of roles, as listed in descending order of responsibility:
1. Education Coordinators;
2. Lead Teachers;
3. Teachers;
4. Associate Teachers;
5. Assistant Teachers;
6. Aides.

Each role with increased responsibility shall require increased educational qualifications and experience, as well as increased salary.

RATIONALE: A progression of roles enables centers to offer career ladders rather than dead-end jobs. It promotes a mix of college-trained staff with other members of a child's own community who might have entered at the aide level and moved into higher roles through college or on-the-job training.

Professional education and pre-professional inservice training programs provide an opportunity for career progression and can lead to job and pay upgrades and fewer turnovers. Turnover rates in child care positions in 1997 averaged 30% (20).

COMMENTS: Early childhood professional knowledge must be required whether programs are in private centers, public schools, or other settings. The National Association for the Education of Young Children's (NAEYC) National Academy of Early Childhood Programs recommends a multi-level training program that addresses pre-employment educational requirements and continuing education requirements for entry-level assistants, teachers, and administrators. It also establishes a table of qualifications for accredited programs (5). The NAEYC requirements include development of an employee compensation plan to increase salaries and benefits to ensure recruitment and retention of qualified staff and continuity of relationships (18). The NAEYC's recommendations should be consulted in conjunction with the standards in this document.

TYPE OF FACILITY: *Center*

STANDARD 1.017
QUALIFICATIONS OF EDUCATION COORDINATORS, LEAD TEACHERS, AND TEACHERS

Education coordinators, lead teachers, and teachers shall be at least 21 years of age and shall have at least the following education, experience, and skills:
a) A Bachelor's degree in early childhood education, child development, social work, nursing, or other child-related field, or a combination of experience and relevant college coursework;
b) One year or more years of experience, under qualified supervision, working as a teacher serving the ages and developmental abilities of the children in care;
c) On-the-job training to provide a nurturing environment and to meet the child's out-of-home needs;
d) A valid certificate in pediatric first aid, including management of a blocked airway and rescue breathing, as specified in First Aid and CPR, STANDARD 1.026 through STANDARD 1.028;
e) Knowledge of normal child development and early childhood education, as well as knowledge of children who are not developing typically;
f) The ability to respond appropriately to children's needs;
g) The ability to recognize signs of illness and safety hazards;
h) Oral and written communication skills.

Every center, regardless of setting, shall have at least one licensed/certified lead teacher (or mentor teacher) who meets the above requirements working in the child care facility at all times when children are in care.

Additionally, facilities serving children with special needs associated with developmental delay shall have one licensed/certified teacher who is certified in special education.

RATIONALE: Child care that promotes healthy development is based on the developmental needs of infants, toddlers, and preschool children. Caregivers are chosen for their knowledge of, and ability to respond appropriately to, the needs of children of this age generally and the unique characteristics of individual children (2, 7, 12, 18). Both early childhood and special educational experience are useful in a center.

COMMENTS: The profession of early childhood education is being informed by new research on child development practices related to child outcomes. For additional information on qualifications for child care staff, refer to the *Guidelines for Preparation of Early Childhood Professional* from the National Association for the Education of Young Children (NAEYC) (18). Additional information on the early childhood education profession is available from Wheelock College Institute for Leadership and Career Initiatives and the Center for the Child Care Workforce (CCW). Contact information is located in Appendix BB.

TYPE OF FACILITY: *Center*

STANDARD 1.018
QUALIFICATIONS FOR ASSOCIATE TEACHERS, ASSISTANT TEACHERS, AIDES, AND VOLUNTEERS

Associate teachers shall be at least 18 years of age and shall have an Associate's degree in early childhood education or child development, and 6 or more months' of experience in child care.

Assistant teachers shall be at least 18 years of age, have a high school diploma or GED, and participate in on-the-job training, including a structured orientation to the developmental needs of young children and access to consultation, with periodic review, by a supervisory staff member.

Aides and volunteers shall be at least 16 years of age and shall participate in on-the-job training, including a structured orientation to the developmental needs of young children. Aides and volunteers shall not be counted in the child:staff ratio and shall work only under the continual supervision of qualified staff.

Any driver who transports children for a child care program shall be at least 21 years of age.

All associate teachers, assistant teachers, aides, drivers, and volunteers shall possess:

a) The ability to carry out assigned tasks competently under the supervision of another staff member;
b) An understanding of and the ability to respond appropriately to children's needs;
c) Sound judgement;
d) Emotional maturity.

RATIONALE: While volunteers and students can be as young as 16, age 18 is the earliest age of legal consent. Mature leadership is clearly preferable. Age 21 allows for the maturity necessary to meet the responsibilities of managing a center or independently caring for a group of children who are not one's own.

Child care that promotes healthy development is based on the developmental needs of infants, toddlers, and preschool children. Caregivers are chosen for their knowledge of, and ability to respond appropriately to, the general needs of children of this age and the unique characteristics of individual children (2, 7, 12, 18).

Staff training in child development and/or early childhood education is related to positive outcomes for children (10). This training enables the staff to provide children with a variety of learning and social experiences appropriate to the age of the child. Everyone providing service to, or interacting with, children in a center contributes to the child's total experience.

Adequate compensation for skilled workers will not be given priority until the skills required are recognized and valued. Caregiving requires skills to promote development and learning by children whose needs and abilities change at a rapid rate.

COMMENTS: Experience and qualifications used by the Child Development Associate (CDA) program and the National Child Care Association credentialing program (NCCA) and included in degree programs with field placement are valued above didactic teaching alone. Early childhood professional knowledge must be required whether programs are in private centers, public schools, or other settings.

The National Association for the Education of Young Children's (NAEYC) National Academy of Early

Childhood Programs has established a table of qualifications for accredited programs (5).

Caregivers who lack educational qualifications may be employed as continuously supervised personnel while they acquire the necessary educational qualifications if they have personal characteristics, experience, and skills in working with parents and children, and the potential for development on the job or in a training program.

TYPE OF FACILITY: *Center; Large Family Child Care Home*

QUALIFICATIONS FOR CAREGIVERS OF LARGE AND SMALL FAMILY CHILD CARE HOMES

STANDARD 1.019
GENERAL QUALIFICATIONS OF FAMILY CHILD CARE CAREGIVERS

Caregivers in large and small family child care homes shall be at least 21 years of age, hold an official credential as granted by the authorized state agency, meet the general requirements specified in STANDARD 1.007 through STANDARD 1.012, based on ages of the children served, and shall have the following education, experience, and skills;

a) Current accreditation by the National Association for Family Child Care (including entry-level qualifications and participation in required training) and have a college certificate representing a minimum of 3 credit hours of family child care leadership or master caregiver training or hold an Associate's degree in early childhood education or child development;

b) A valid certificate in pediatric first aid, including management of a blocked airway and rescue breathing, as specified in First Aid and CPR, STANDARD 1.026 through STANDARD 1.028;

c) Preservice training in health management in child care, including the ability to recognize signs of illness and safety hazards;

d) Knowledge of normal child development, as well as knowledge of children who are not developing typically;

e) The ability to respond appropriately to children's needs;

f) Oral and written communication skills.

Additionally, large family child care home caregivers shall have at least 1 year of experience, under qualified supervision, serving the ages and developmental abilities of the children in their large family child care home.

Assistants, aides, and volunteers employed by a large family child care home shall meet the qualifications specified in STANDARD 1.018.

RATIONALE: In both large and small family child care homes, staff members must have the education and experience to meet the needs of the children in care. Small family child care home providers often work alone and are solely responsible for the health and safety of small numbers of children in care.

Age 18 is the earliest age of legal consent. Mature leadership is clearly preferable. Age 21 is more likely to be associated with the level of maturity necessary to independently care for a group of children who are not one's own.

The National Association for Family Child Care (NAFCC) has established an accreditation process to enhance the level of quality and professionalism in small family child care (35). Contact information for NAFCC is found in Appendix BB.

COMMENTS: A large family child care home provider caring for more than six children and employing one or more assistants functions as a facility director. An operator of a large family-child-care home should be offered training relevant to the management of a small child care center, including training on providing a quality work environment for employees.

For more information on assessing the work environment of family child care employees, see *Creating Better Family Child Care Jobs: Model Work Standards*, a publication by the Center for the Child Care Workforce (CCW) (21). Contact information for the CCW is located in Appendix BB.

TYPE OF FACILITY: *Large Family Child Care Home; Small Family Child Care Home*

STANDARD 1.020
SUPPORT NETWORKS FOR FAMILY CHILD CARE

Large and small family child care home providers shall have active membership in local or state family child care associations (if such associations exist) or in the National Association for Family Child Care (NAFCC), or belong to a network of family child care home providers that offers ongoing training and information on how to provide quality child care.

RATIONALE: Membership in peer professional organizations shows a commitment to quality child care and also provides a conduit for information to otherwise isolated caregivers. Membership in a family child care association and attendance at meetings indicate the desire to gain new knowledge about how to work with children.

COMMENTS: For more information about family child care associations, contact the National Association for Family Child Care (NAFCC). Contact information is located in Appendix BB.

For additional qualifications and responsibilities of large and small family child care home providers, see General Qualifications for All Caregivers, STANDARD 1.007 through STANDARD 1.012; and Training, STANDARD 1.023 through STANDARD 1.036.

TYPE OF FACILITY: *Large Family Child Care Home; Small Family Child Care Home*

STANDARD 1.021
QUALIFICATIONS FOR HEALTH ADVOCATES

Each facility shall designate a person as health advocate to be responsible for policies and day-to-day issues related to health, development, and safety of individual children, children as a group, staff, and parents. The health advocate shall be the primary parent contact for health concerns, including health-related parent/staff observations, health-related information, and the provision of resources. The health advocate shall also identify children who have no regular source of health care and refer them to a health care provider who offers competent routine child health services.

For centers, the health advocate shall be licensed/certified/credentialed as a director, lead teacher, teacher, or associate teacher, or shall be a health professional, health educator, or social worker who works at the facility on a regular basis (at least weekly).

The health advocate shall have documented training in the following topics that include:
a) Sudden Infant Death Syndrome (SIDS), for facilities caring for infants;
b) Control of infectious diseases, including Standard/Universal Precautions;
c) How to recognize and handle an emergency;
d) Recognition and handling of seizures;
e) Recognition of safety, hazards, and injury prevention interventions;
f) How to help parents, caregivers, and children cope with death, severe injury, and natural or man-made catastrophes;
g) Recognition of child abuse and neglect and knowledge of when to contact a consultant;
h) Organization and implementation of a plan to meet the emergency needs of children with special health needs.

RATIONALE: The effectiveness of an intentionally designated health advocate in improving the quality of performance in a facility has been demonstrated in all types of early childhood settings (22). A designated caregiver with health training is effective in developing an ongoing relationship with the parents and a personal interest in the child (8, 23). Caregivers who are better trained are more able to prevent, recognize, and correct health and safety problems. An internal advocate for issues related to health and safety can help integrate these concerns with other factors involved in formulating facility plans.

COMMENTS: The director should assign the health advocate role to a staff member who seems to have an interest, aptitude and training in this area. This person need not perform all the health and safety tasks in the facility but should serve as the person who raises health and safety concerns. This staff person has designated responsibility for seeing that plans are implemented to ensure a safe and healthful facility (22).

A health advocate is a regular member of the staff of a center or large or small family child care home network, and is not the same as the health consultant recommended in Health Consultants, STANDARD 1.040 through STANDARD 1.044. For small family child care homes, the health advocate will usually be the caregiver. If the health advocate is not the child's caregiver, the health advocate should work with the child's caregiver. The person who is most familiar with the child and the child's family will recognize atypical behavior in the child and support effective communication with parents.

A plan for personal contact with parents should be developed, even though this contact will not be possible daily. A plan for personal contact and documentation of a designated caregiver as health advocate will ensure specific attempts to have the health advocate communicate directly with caregivers and families on health-related matters.

For additional qualifications and responsibilities of health advocates, see Training, STANDARD 1.023 through STANDARD 1.036; and Direct Care and Provisional Staff, STANDARD 1.009 through STANDARD 1.013.

TYPE OF FACILITY: *Center; Large Family Child Care Home; Small Family Child Care Home*

STANDARD 1.022
STAFF WHO CHECK
IMMUNIZATION RECORDS

At least one caregiver shall have knowledge of childhood immunization requirements and shall be responsible for periodically reviewing the children's immunization records to ensure that they are current. The caregiver shall have sufficient knowledge of childhood immunization requirements to be able to review immunization records and determine which immunizations are needed and when they should be given. This person shall be responsible for reviewing each

child's immunization records at least quarterly and for identifying and referring, to their usual source of health care, children in need of additional immunizations.

RATIONALE: Children require frequent immunizations in early childhood. Although children may be current with required immunizations when they enroll, they sometimes miss scheduled immunizations thereafter. Because the risk of vaccine-preventable disease increases in group settings, assuring appropriate immunizations is an essential responsibility in child care.

COMMENTS: For more information on immunizations, see STANDARD 3.005 and STANDARD 3.006.

TYPE OF FACILITY: *Center; Large Family Child Care Home; Small Family Child Care Home*

1.4 TRAINING

ORIENTATION TRAINING

STANDARD 1.023
INITIAL ORIENTATION OF ALL
STAFF

All new full-time and part-time staff shall be oriented to, and demonstrate knowledge of, the items listed below. The director of any center or large family child care home shall provide this training to all newly hired caregivers before they begin to care for children. For centers, the director shall document, for each new staff member, the topics covered and the dates of orientation training. Staff members shall not be expected to take responsibility for any aspect of care for which their orientation and training have not prepared them.

Small family child care home providers shall avail themselves of orientation training offered by the licensing agency, a resource and referral agency, or other such agency. This training shall include evaluation that involves demonstration of the knowledge and skills covered in the training lesson.

The orientation shall address, at a minimum:
a) Regulatory requirements;
b) The goals and philosophy of the facility;
c) The names and ages of the children for whom the caregiver will be responsible, and their specific developmental needs;
d) Any special adaptation(s) of the facility required for a child with special needs for whom the staff member might be responsible at any time;
e) Any special health or nutrition need(s) of the children assigned to the caregiver;
f) The planned program of activities at the facility. See Program of Developmental Activities, STANDARD 2.001 through STANDARD 2.027;
g) Routines and transitions;
h) Acceptable methods of discipline. See Discipline, STANDARD 2.039 through STANDARD 2.043; and Discipline Policy, STANDARD 8.008 through STANDARD 8.010;
i) Policies and practices of the facility about relating to parents. See Parent Relationships, STANDARD 2.044 through STANDARD 2.057;
j) Meal patterns and food handling policies and practices of the facility. See Plans and Policies for Food Handling, Feeding, and Nutrition, STANDARD 8.035 and STANDARD 8.036; Food Service Records, STANDARD 8.074; Nutrition and Food Service, STANDARD 4.001 through STANDARD 4.070;
k) Occupational health hazards for caregivers, including attention to the physical health and emotional demands of the job and special considerations for pregnant caregivers. See Occupational Hazards, STANDARD 1.048; and *Major Occupational Health Hazards,* Appendix B;
l) Emergency health and safety procedures. See Plan for Urgent Medical Care or Threatening Incidents, STANDARD 8.022 and STANDARD 8.023; and Emergency Procedures, STANDARD 3.048 through STANDARD 3.052;
m) General health and safety policies and procedures, including but not limited to the following:
   1) Handwashing techniques and indications for handwashing. See Handwashing, STANDARD 3.020 through STANDARD 3.024;

2) Diapering technique and toilet use, if care is provided to children in diapers and/or children needing help with toilet use, including appropriate diaper disposal and diaper-changing techniques. See Toilet, Diapering, and Bath Areas, STANDARD 5.116 through STANDARD 5.125; Toilet Use, Diapering, and Toilet Learning/Training, STANDARD 3.012 through STANDARD 3.019; Toilet Learning/Training Equipment, Toilets, and Bathrooms, STANDARD 3.029 through STANDARD 3.033;
3) Identifying hazards and injury prevention;
4) Correct food preparation, serving, and storage techniques if employee prepares food. See Food Safety, STANDARD 4.042 through STANDARD 4.060;
5) Knowledge of when to exclude children due to illness and the means of illness transmission;
6) Formula preparation, if formula is handled. See Plans and Policies for Food Handling, Feeding, and Nutrition, STANDARD 8.035 and STANDARD 8.036; and Nutrition for Infants, STANDARD 4.011 through STANDARD 4.021;
7) Standard precautions and other measures to prevent exposure to blood and other body fluids, as well as program policies and procedures in the event of exposure to blood/body fluid. See Prevention of Exposure to Body Fluids, STANDARD 3.026;
n) Recognizing symptoms of illness. See Daily Health Assessment, STANDARD 3.001 and STANDARD 3.002;
o) Teaching health promotion concepts to children and parents as part of the daily care provided to children. See Health Education for Children, STANDARD 2.060 through STANDARD 2.063;
p) Child abuse detection, prevention, and reporting. See Child Abuse and Neglect, STANDARD 3.053 through STANDARD 3.059;
q) Medication administration policies and practices;
r) Putting infants down to sleep positioned on their backs and on a firm surface to reduce the risk of Sudden Infant Death Syndrome (SIDS).

Caregivers shall also receive continuing education each year, as specified in Continuing Education, STANDARD 1.029 through STANDARD 1.036.

RATIONALE: Upon employment, staff members should be able to perform basic sanitizing and emergency procedures. Orientation ensures that all staff members receive specific and basic training for the work they will be doing and become acquainted with their new responsibilities. Orientation programs for new employees should be specific to an individual facility since facilities and the children enrolled vary(30).

Because of frequent staff turnover, directors are obligated to institute orientation programs that protect the health and safety of children and new staff members.

Orientation and ongoing training are especially important for aides and assistant teachers, for whom pre-service educational requirements are limited. Entry into the field at the level of aide or assistant teacher should be attractive and easy for members of the families and cultural groups of the children in care to enter the field. Training ensures that staff members are challenged and stimulated, have access to current knowledge, and have access to education that will qualify them for new roles. Offering a career ladder will attract individuals into the child care field, where labor is in short supply. Ongoing training in one role can become preservice training to qualify for another role.

Health training for child care staff not only protects the children in care, infectious disease control in child care helps to prevent spread of infectious disease in the community. Young children in child care have been shown to be associated with community outbreaks.

COMMENTS: Many states have preservice education and experience qualifications for caregivers by role and function. States are including ongoing health training in their licensing requirements; the broader skills have proved important and necessary to teachers in part-day and full-day programs alike. Both full-day and part-day programs require competence in all facets of child development, not just the learning components.

Child care staff members are important figures in the lives of the young children in their care and in the wellbeing of families and the community. In the future, all training for child care staff should include more attention to health issues.

Training in conflict resolution is encouraged. Child abuse includes also children's abuse of their peers. Staff should learn how to handle conflict resolution among the children and among themselves, as well as modeling examples of conflict resolution from which children can learn.

Colleges and accrediting bodies should examine teacher preparation guidelines and substantially increase the health content of early childhood professional preparation.

For definitions of Standard precautions, Transmission-based precautions, Universal precautions, see Glossary.

TYPE OF FACILITY: *Center; Large Family Child Care Home; Small Family Child Care Home*

STANDARD 1.024
ORIENTATION FOR CARE OF CHILDREN WITH SPECIAL HEALTH NEEDS

When a child care facility enrolls a child with special needs, the facility shall ensure that staff members have been oriented in understanding that child's special needs and ways of working with that child in a group setting.

Caregivers in small family child care homes, who care for a child with special needs, shall meet with the parents and a health care worker involved with the child (if the parent has provided prior, informed, written consent) about the child's special needs and how these needs may affect his/her developmental progression or play with other children.

In addition to Orientation Training, STANDARD 1.023, the staff in child care facilities shall have orientation training based on the special needs of children in their care. This training may include, but is not limited to, the following topics:

a) Positioning for feeding and handling techniques of children with physical disabilities;
b) Proper use and care of the individual child's adaptive equipment, including how to recognize defective equipment and to notify parents that repairs are needed;
c) How different disabilities affect the child's ability to participate in group activities;
d) Methods of helping the child with special needs to participate in the facility's programs;
e) Role modeling, peer socialization, and interaction;
f) Behavior modification techniques, positive rewards for children, promotion of self-esteem, and other techniques for managing difficult behavior;
g) Grouping of children by skill levels, taking into account the child's age and developmental level;
h) Intervention for children with special health care problems;
i) Communication needs.

RATIONALE: A basic understanding of developmental disabilities and special care requirements of any child in care is a fundamental part of any orientation for new employees. Training is an essential component to ensure that staff members develop and maintain the needed skills. A comprehensive curriculum is required to ensure quality services. However, lack of specialized training for staff does not constitute grounds for exclusion of children with disabilities.

Staff members need information about how to help children use adaptive equipment properly. Staff members need to understand how and why various items are used and how to check for malfunctions. If a problem occurs with adaptive equipment, the staff must recognize the problem and inform the parent so that the parent can notify the health care or equipment provider of the problem and request that it be remedied. While the parent is responsible for arranging for correction of equipment problems, child care staff must be able to observe and report the problem to the parent.

COMMENTS: These training topics are generally applicable to all personnel serving children with special needs and apply to these facilities. The

curriculum may vary depending on the type of facility, classifications of disabilities of the children in the facility, and ages of the children. The staff is assumed to have the training described in Orientation Training, STANDARD 1.023, including child growth and development. These additional topics will extend their basic knowledge and skills to help them work more effectively with children who have special needs and their families. Caregivers should have a basic knowledge of special needs, supplemented by specialized training for children with special needs. The types of children with special needs served should influence the selection of the specialized training. The number of hours offered in any inservice training program should be determined by the staff's experience and professional background.

Service plans in small family child care homes may require a modified implementation plan. The option of child care in small family child care homes for children with special needs must include special requirements.

Training and other technical assistance can be obtained from the following:

a) The state-designated lead agency responsible for implementing IDEA;
b) American Academy of Pediatrics (AAP);
c) American Nurses' Association (ANA);
d) State and community nursing associations;
e) National therapy associations;
f) Local resource and referral agencies;
g) Federally funded, University Centers for Excellence in Developmental Disabilities Education, Research, and Service programs for individuals with developmental disabilities;
h) Other colleges and universities with expertise in training others to work with children who have special needs;
i) Community-based organizations serving people with disabilities (Easter Seals, American Diabetes Association, American Lung Association, etc.).

The parent is responsible for solving equipment problems unless the parent requests that the child care facility remedy the problem directly and the staff agrees to do it.

TYPE OF FACILITY: *Center; Large Family Child Care Home; Small Family Child Care Home*

TYPE OF FACILITY: *Center; Large Family Child Care Home; Small Family Child Care Home*

STANDARD 1.025
ORIENTATION DURING INITIAL EMPLOYMENT

During the first 3 months of employment, the director of a center or the caregiver in a large family home shall document, for all full-time and part-time staff members, additional orientation in, and the employees' satisfactory knowledge of, the following topics:

a) Recognition of symptoms of illness and correct documentation procedures for recording symptoms of illness. This shall include the ability to perform a daily health assessment of children to determine whether any are ill and, if so, whether a child who is ill should be excluded from the facility;

b) Exclusion and readmission procedures and policies;

c) Cleaning and sanitation procedures and policies;

d) Procedures for administering medication to children and for documenting medication administered to children;

e) Procedures for notifying parents or legal guardians of a communicable disease occurring in children or staff within the facility;

f) Procedures and policies for notifying public health officials about an outbreak of disease or the occurrence of a reportable disease.

Before being assigned to tasks that involve identifying and responding to illness, staff members shall receive orientation training on these topics. Small family child care home providers shall not commence operation before receiving orientation on these topics.

RATIONALE: Children are ill frequently. Staff members responsible for child care must be able to recognize illness, carry out the measures required to prevent the spread of communicable diseases, and handle ill children appropriately.

COMMENTS: See also Daily Health Assessment, STANDARD 3.001 and STANDARD 3.002.

FIRST AID AND CPR

STANDARD 1.026
FIRST AID TRAINING FOR STAFF

The director of a center and a large family child care home and the caregiver in a small family child care home shall ensure that all staff members involved in providing direct care have training in pediatric first aid, including management of a blocked airway and rescue breathing, as specified in STANDARD 1.027.

At least one staff person who has successfully completed training in pediatric first aid, as specified in STANDARD 1.027, shall be in attendance at all times and in all places where children are in care. Instances in which at least one staff member shall be certified in CPR include when children are involved in swimming and wading and when at least one child is known to have a specific special health need as determined by that child's physician (such as cardiac arrhythmia) that makes the child more likely than a typical child to require cardiac resuscitation. In each case of a child with a special health need, the child care provider shall ask the child's physician whether caregivers with skills in the management of a blocked airway and rescue breathing will suffice, or whether caregivers require skills in cardiac resuscitation to meet the particular health needs of the child. Records of successful completion of training in pediatric first aid, as specified in STANDARD 1.027, shall be maintained in the files of the facility.

RATIONALE: To ensure the health and safety of children in a child care setting, someone who is qualified to respond to common life-threatening emergencies must be in attendance at all times. A staff trained in pediatric first aid, including management of a blocked airway and rescue breathing, coupled with a facility that has been designed or modified to ensure the safety of children, can mitigate the consequences of injury and reduce the potential for death from life-threatening conditions. Knowledge of pediatric first aid, including management of a blocked airway and rescue breathing, and the confidence to use these skills, are critically important to the outcome of an emergency situation.

The need for cardiac resuscitation is rare. Children who have specific cardiac problems, such as cardiac arrhythmia, or children who are drowning in cold water, require cardiac resuscitation. Except in these two instances, cessation of cardiac function does not occur until respiratory failure causes irreversible and devastating brain damage. Therefore, except in these two instances, caregivers require respiratory resuscitation skills, not CPR skills.

Small family child care home providers often work alone and are solely responsible for the health and safety of children in care. They must have the necessary skills to manage any emergency while caring for all the children in the group.

In a study of incidence of injuries in centers, first aid was sufficient treatment for the majority of incidents (25). In a survey of over 2,000 child care programs in North Carolina, 16% had used first aid for choking, 2.3% had used rescue breathing, and only 1% had used CPR during the preceding 36 months of the survey. The authors of this report felt that maintaining CPR training and certification was difficult and probably not cost-effective (37). Minor injuries are common. For emergency situations that require attention from a health professional, first aid procedures can be taken to control the situation until a medical professional can provide definitive care.

Documentation of current certification in the facility assists in implementing and in monitoring for proof of compliance.

COMMENTS: Preparation of the first edition of this document included an extensive discussion of whether the staff should have cardiac resuscitation skills for children.

Many people use the term "CPR" as shorthand for resuscitation and rescue skills. In discussions with the American Academy of Pediatrics' liaison to the American Heart Association pediatric resuscitation committee, this issue was discussed again during the preparation of this edition of the Standards, with the

same conclusion related to limited circumstances where CPR training should be required. Ongoing education about the difference between training in pediatric first aid that includes management of a blocked airway and rescue breathing and training in CPR will be necessary because of the public's familiarity with and use of the term "CPR."

CPR training for cardiac resuscitation involves specific courses focused on pulmonary and cardiac resuscitation, not first aid for other, more common injuries. Evaluations of retention of the techniques taught in CPR courses reportedly reveals poor recall within months after completion. The time and other resources required to provide pediatric CPR training could be better spent on learning first aid, including management of a blocked airway and rescue breathing, and other types of training. CPR training for management of adult cardiac emergencies is valuable and appropriate as a staff and community health goal, but as described above, such training is not a standard of practice for routine child care.

For each child with a special health need, the child care health form should have a check-off box or a request for notification about whether caregivers with skills in management of a blocked airway and rescue breathing will suffice, or does the child have a greater risk than a typical child to require cardiac resuscitation. This proactive approach will alert the child's clinician to consider the need for caregivers to acquire cardiac resuscitation skills on a case-by-case basis. If the child's clinician indicates that the child's condition might require that caregivers provide cardiac resuscitation, CPR training should be required for staff who care for the child. Instead of CPR training for all staff in child care, this focused approach is more likely to insure the safety of the few children for whom CPR might be required.

For additional information on first aid and CPR, see STANDARD 2.027, on pediatric first aid training requirements; STANDARD 1.028, which requires staff to have CPR training for activities involving swimming or wading; and RECOMMENDATION 9.038 through RECOMMENDATION 9.040, on state and local training and technical assistance.

TYPE OF FACILITY: *Center; Large Family Child Care Home; Small Family Child Care Home*

STANDARD 1.027
TOPICS COVERED IN FIRST AID TRAINING

Management of a blocked airway and rescue breathing comprise two of the core elements of pediatric first aid training. In addition, the course must present an overview of the Emergency Medical Services (EMS), accessing EMS, safety at the scene, and isolation of body substances, and the first aid instruction that is offered shall include, but not be limited to, recognition and first response of pediatric emergency management in a child care setting of the following situations:

a) Abrasions and lacerations;
b) Bleeding, including nosebleeds;
c) Burns;
d) Fainting;
e) Poisoning, including swallowed, contact, and inhaled;
f) Puncture wounds, including splinters;
g) Injuries, including insect, animal, and human bites;
h) Shock;
i) Convulsions or nonconvulsive seizures;
j) Musculoskeletal injury (such as sprains, fractures);
k) Dental and mouth injuries;
l) Head injuries;
m) Allergic reactions, including information about when auto-injected epinephrine might be required;
n) Eye injuries;
o) Loss of consciousness;
p) Electric shock;
q) Drowning;
r) Heat-related injuries, including heat exhaustion/heat stroke;
s) Cold injuries;
t) Moving and positioning injured/ill persons;
u) Management of a blocked airway and rescue breathing for infants and children with return demonstration by the learner;
v) Illness-related emergencies (such as stiff neck, inexplicable confusion, sudden onset of blood-red or purple rash, severe pain, temperature of 105 degrees F or higher, or looking/acting severely ill);
w) Standard Precautions;
x) Organizing and implementing a plan to meet an emergency for any child with a special health care need;
y) Addressing the needs of the other children in the group while managing emergencies in a child care setting.

RATIONALE: First aid for children in the child care setting requires a more child-specific approach than standard adult-oriented first aid offers. To ensure the health and safety of children in a child care setting, someone who is qualified to respond to common injuries and life-threatening emergencies must be in attendance at all times. A staff trained in pediatric first aid, including management of a blocked airway and rescue breathing, coupled with a facility that has been designed or modified to ensure the safety of children, can reduce the potential for death and disability. Knowledge of pediatric first aid, including management of a blocked airway and rescue breathing, and the confidence to use these skills, are critically important to the outcome of an emergency situation.

Small family child care home providers often work alone and are solely responsible for the health and safety of children in care. Such providers must have pediatric first aid competence.

COMMENTS: Usually, other children will have to be supervised while the injury is managed. Parental notification and communication with emergency medical services must be carefully planned. First aid information can be obtained from the American Academy of Pediatrics (AAP) and the American Heart Association (AHA). Contact information for the AAP and the AHA is located in Appendix BB.

For discussion of the need for training in CPR, see STANDARD 1.026.

TYPE OF FACILITY: *Center; Large Family Child Care Home; Small Family Child Care Home*

STANDARD 1.028
CPR TRAINING FOR SWIMMING AND WADING

Facilities that have a swimming pool or use a water-filled wading pool shall require that at least one staff member with current documentation of successful completion of training in infant and child (pediatric) CPR (Cardiopulmonary Resuscitation) shall be on duty at all times during business hours.

At least one of the caregivers, volunteers, or other adults who is counted in the child:staff ratio for wading and swimming shall have documentation of successful completion of training in basic water safety and infant and child CPR according to the criteria of the American Red Cross or the American Heart Association.

For small family child care homes, the person trained in water safety and CPR shall be the caregiver. Written verification of successful completion of CPR and lifesaving training, water safety instructions, and emergency procedures shall be kept on file.

RATIONALE: Drowning involves cessation of breathing and rarely requires cardiac resuscitation of salvageable victims. Nevertheless, because of the increased risk for cardiopulmonary arrest related to wading and swimming, the facility should have personnel trained to provide CPR and to deal promptly with a life-threatening drowning emergency. During drowning, cold exposure provides the possibility of protection of the brain from irreversible damage associated with respiratory and cardiac arrest. Children drown in as little as 2 inches of water. The difference between a life and death situation is the submersion time. Thirty seconds can make a difference. The timely administration of resuscitation efforts by a care-giver trained in water safety and CPR is critical. Studies have shown that prompt rescue and the presence of a trained resuscitator at the site can save about 30% of the victims without significant neurological consequences.

COMMENTS: See also Safety Rules for Swimming/Wading Pools, STANDARD 5.215; and Water Safety, STANDARD 3.045 through STANDARD 3.047. For information on the child:staff ratio for wading and swimming, see STANDARD 1.005.

TYPE OF FACILITY: *Center; Large Family Child Care Home; Small Family Child Care Home*

CONTINUING EDUCATION

STANDARD 1.029
CONTINUING EDUCATION FOR DIRECTORS AND CAREGIVERS IN CENTERS AND LARGE FAMILY CHILD CARE HOMES

All directors and caregivers of centers and large family child care homes shall successfully complete at least 30 clock hours per year of continuing education in the first year of employment, 16 clock hours of which shall be in child development programming and 14 of which shall be in child health, safety, and staff health. In the second and each of the following years of employment at a facility, all directors and caregivers shall successfully complete at least 24 clock hours of continuing education based on individual competency needs and any special needs of the children in their care, 16 hours of which shall be in child development programming and 8 hours of which shall be in child health, safety, and staff health.

The effectiveness of training shall be assessed by change in performance following participation in training.

RATIONALE: Because of the nature of their caregiving tasks, caregivers must attain multifaceted knowledge and skills. Child health and employee health are integral to any education/training curriculum and program management plan. Planning and evaluation of training should be based on performance of the staff member(s) involved. Too often, staff members make training choices based on what they like to learn about (their "wants") and not the areas in which their performance should be improved (their "needs"). Participation in training does not ensure that the participant will master the information and skills offered in the training experience. Therefore, successful completion, not just participation, must be assessed.

In addition to low child:staff ratio, group size, age mix of children, and stability of caregiver, the training/education of caregivers is a specific indicator of child care quality (20). Most skilled roles require training related to the functions and responsibilities the role requires. Staff members who are better trained are better able to prevent, recognize, and correct health and safety problems. The number of training hours recommended in this standard reflects the central focus of caregivers on child development, health, and safety.

The National Association for the Education of Young Children (NAEYC), a leading organization in child care and early childhood education, recommends annual training based on the needs of the program and the preservice qualifications of staff. Training should address the following areas:
a) Health and safety;
b) Child growth and development;
c) Nutrition;
d) Planning learning activities;
e) Guidance and discipline techniques;
f) Linkages with community services;
g) Communication and relations with families;
h) Detection of child abuse;
i) Advocacy for early childhood programs;
j) Professional issues (18).

There are few illnesses for which children should be excluded from child care. Decisions about management of ill children are facilitated by skill in assessing the extent to which the behavior suggesting illness requires special management (30). Continuing education on managing communicable diseases helps prepare caregivers to make these decisions. All caregivers should be trained to prevent, assess, and treat injuries common in child care settings and to comfort an injured child.

COMMENTS: Tools for assessment of training needs are part of the accreditation self-study tools available from the NAEYC, the National Association for Family Child Care (NAFCC) and the National Child Care Association (NCCA). Contact information is located in Appendix BB. Successful completion of training can be measured by a performance test at the end of

training and by ongoing evaluation of performance on the job.

Resources for training on health issues include:
• State and local health departments (especially the public health nursing department);
• Resource and referral agencies;
• State and local chapters of:
  - American Academy of Pediatrics (AAP);
  - American Academy of Family Physicians (AAFP);
  - American Nurses' Association (ANA);
  - Visiting Nurse Association (VNA);
  - National Association of Pediatric Nurse Practitioners (NAPNAP);
  - National Association for the Education of Young Children (NAEYC);
  - National Association for Family Child Care (NAFCC);
  - National Training Institute for Child Health Consultants;
  - Emergency Medical Services for Children (EMSC) National Resource Center.

For nutrition training, facilities should check to be sure that the nutritionist, who provides advice, has experience with, and knowledge of, food service issues in the child care setting. Most state maternal and child health departments have a Nutrition Specialist on staff. If this Nutrition Specialist has knowledge and experience in child care, facilities might negotiate for this individual to serve or identify someone to serve as a consultant and trainer for the facility.

Many resources are available for nutrition specialists who can provide training in food service and nutrition. See Appendix C, for qualifications of nutrition specialists. Some resources to contact include:
• Local, county, and state health departments;
• State university and college nutrition departments;
• Home economists at utility companies;
• State affiliates of the American Dietetic
• Association;
• State and regional affiliates of the American Public Health Association;
• The American Association of Family and Consumer Services;
• National Resource Center for Health and Safety in Child Care;
• Registered dietitian at a hospital;

- High school home economics teachers;
- The Dairy Council;
- The local American Heart Association affiliate;
- The local Cancer Society;
- The Society for Nutrition Education;
- The local Cooperative Extension office.

Nutrition education resources may be obtained from the Food and Nutrition Information Center. Contact information is located in Appendix BB. The staff's continuing education in nutrition may be supplemented by periodic newsletters and/or literature or audiovisual materials prepared or recommended by the Nutrition Specialist. See Appendix C, for information on qualifications for nutrition specialists.

Caregivers should have a basic knowledge of special needs, supplemented by specialized training for children with special needs. The type of special needs of the children in care should influence the selection of the training topics. The number of hours offered in any inservice training program should be determined by the experience and professional background of the staff, which is best achieved through a regular staff conference mechanism.

Financial support and accessibility to training programs requires attention to facilitate compliance with this standard. Many states are using federal funds from the Child Care and Development Block Grant to improve access, quality, and affordability of training for early care and education professionals. Home study, video courses, workshops, training newsletters, telecommunications, and lectures can be used to meet the training hours requirement, as can training conducted on site at the child care facility. Completion of training may be documented by self-declaration or by submitting self-tests. Although on-site training can be costly, it may be a more effective approach than participation in training at a remote location.

See also Technical Assistance and Consultation to Caregivers and Families, RECOMMENDATION 9.030 and RECOMMENDATION 9.036; and Training, RECOMMENDATION 9.038 through RECOMMENDATION 9.040. See STANDARD 1.052 and STANDARD 1.055, on performance evaluation related to continuing education.

TYPE OF FACILITY: *Center; Large Family Child Care Home*

STANDARD 1.030
CONTINUING EDUCATION FOR SMALL FAMILY CHILD CARE HOME PROVIDERS

Small family child care home providers shall have at least 24 clock hours of continuing education in areas determined by self-assessment and, where possible, by a performance review of a skilled mentor or peer reviewer.

RATIONALE: In addition to low child:staff ratio, group size, age mix of children, and stability of caregiver, the training/education of caregivers is a specific indicator of child care quality (20). Most skilled roles require training related to the functions and responsibilities the role requires. Caregivers who are better trained are better able to prevent, recognize, and correct health and safety problems.

Because of the nature of their caregiving tasks, caregivers must attain multifaceted knowledge and skills. Child health and employee health are integral to any education/training curriculum and program management plan. Planning and evaluation of training should be based on performance of the child care provider. Too often, caregivers make training choices based on what they like to learn about (their "wants") and not the areas in which their performance should be improved (their "needs").

Small family child care home providers often work alone and are solely responsible for the health and safety of small numbers of children in care. Peer review is part of the process for accreditation of family child care. Self-evaluation may not identify training needs or focus on areas in which the caregiver is particularly interested and may be skilled already.

COMMENTS: The content of continuing education for small family child care home providers may include the following topics:
a) Child growth and development;
b) Infant care;
c) Recognizing and managing minor illness;

d) Managing the care of children who require the special procedures listed in Standard 3.063;

e) Business aspects of the small family child care home;

f) Planning developmentally appropriate activities in mixed age groupings;

g) Nutrition for children in the context of preparing nutritious meals for the family;

h) Acceptable methods of discipline;

i) Organizing the home for child care;

j) Preventing unintentional injuries in the home;

k) Available community services;

l) Detecting, preventing, and reporting child abuse;

m) Advocacy skills;

n) Pediatric first aid, including management of a blocked airway and rescue breathing. See STANDARD 1.026 and STANDARD 1.027;

o) CPR (if the caregiver takes care of children with special needs or has a swimming/wading pool). See STANDARD 1.028;

p) Methods of effective communication with children and parents;

q) Mental health;

r) Evacuation drill procedures, as specified in Evacuation Plan, Drills, and Closings, STANDARD 8.024 through 8.027;

s) Occupational health hazards. See Occupational Hazards, STANDARD 1.048; and *Major Occupational Health Hazards*, Appendix B;

t) Death, dying, and the grief cycle;

u) SIDS risk-reduction practices.

In-home training alternatives to group training for small family child care home providers are available, such as distance courses on the Internet, listening to audiotapes or viewing videotapes with self-checklists. These training alternatives provide more flexibility for providers who are remote from central training locations or have difficulty arranging coverage for their child care duties to attend training. Nevertheless, gathering family child care home providers for training when possible provides a break from the isolation of their work and promotes networking and support. Satellite training via down links at local extension service sites, high schools, and community colleges scheduled at convenient evening or weekend times is another way to mix quality training with local availability and some networking.

TYPE OF FACILITY: *Small Family Child Care Home*

STANDARD 1.031
TRAINING OF STAFF WHO HANDLE FOOD

All staff members with food handling responsibilities shall obtain training in food service. The director of a center or a large family child care home or the designated supervisor for food service shall obtain certification equivalent to the Food Service Manager's Protection (Sanitation) certificate.

RATIONALE: Outbreaks of foodborne illness have occurred in many settings, including child care facilities. Some of these outbreaks have led to fatalities and severe disabilities. Young children are particularly susceptible to foodborne illness. Because large centers serve more meals daily than many restaurants do, the supervisors of food handlers in these settings should have successfully completed food service certification, and the food handlers in these settings should have successfully completed courses on appropriate food handling.

COMMENTS: Sponsors of the Child and Adult Care Food Program provide this training for some small family child care home providers. For training in food handling, contact the regional office of the Food and Drug Administration, health departments, or the delegate agencies that handle nutrition and environmental health inspection programs. Contact information is located in located in Appendix BB. Other sources are US Department of Agriculture (USDA) publications, family child care associations, resource and referrals, and licensing agencies.

TYPE OF FACILITY: *Center; Large Family Child Care Home; Small Family Child Care Home*

STANDARD 1.032
CHILD ABUSE EDUCATION

Caregivers shall use child abuse prevention education materials provided by the licensing agency, state and national organizations, or from other community agencies such as local branches of the National Committee to Prevent Child Abuse, to educate and establish child abuse prevention and recognition measures for the children, caregivers, and parents. The education and prevention shall address physical, sexual, and psychological or emotional abuse, injury prevention, the dangers of shaking infants and toddlers, as well as signs and symptoms of sexually transmitted diseases. Child care directors and head teachers shall participate in training to recognize visible signs of child abuse, including pattern marks, bruises in unusual locations, pattern or immersion burns, shaken baby syndrome, and behaviors suggesting sexual abuse. They shall know how to refer children with vaginal, penile, or rectal discharge or bleeding to their health provider. A child care provider shall refer the child to the local child protection agency for any reasonable suspicion of child abuse or neglect.

Caregivers shall be trained in compliance with their state's child abuse reporting laws.

RATIONALE: Centers and large and small family child care homes are strategic locations in which to distribute materials for the prevention of abuse and also for indicators of sexually transmitted diseases. The medical diagnosis of child physical and sexual abuse is complex. However, education about the physical manifestations of abuse can increase the number of appropriate referrals to physicians and child protection agencies.

COMMENTS: All caregivers should learn about the mandated reporting requirements for caregivers, the process for follow-up after making a report, and the protection and exposure of mandated reporters under the state's child abuse law. States and child care providers will select appropriate material from the many available media that can be used in child abuse prevention activities.

Child abuse materials designed for medical audiences may not be suitable for child care training because the photographs in them contain shocking images. Selective use of photographs that help caregivers recognize signs of physical abuse, however, is appropriate.

Resources are available from the American Academy of Pediatrics, the National Clearinghouse on Child Abuse and Neglect Information, and the National

Committee for Prevention of Child Abuse. Contact information is located in Appendix BB.

TYPE OF FACILITY: *Center; Large Family Child Care Home; Small Family Child Care Home*

STANDARD 1.033
TRAINING ON OCCUPATIONAL RISK RELATED TO HANDLING BODY FLUIDS

The director of a center or a large family child care home caregiver shall ensure that all staff members who are at risk of occupational exposure to blood or other blood-containing body fluids will be offered hepatitis B immunizations and will receive annual training in Standard Precautions. Training shall be consistent with applicable standards of the Occupational Safety and Health Administration (OSHA Standard 29 CFR 1910.1030, "Occupational Exposure to Bloodborne Pathogens") and local occupational health requirements and shall include, but not be limited to:
a) Modes of transmission of bloodborne pathogens;
b) Standard Precautions;
c) Hepatitis B vaccine, pre-exposure, or post-exposure within 24 hours;
d) Program policies and procedures regarding exposure to blood/body fluid;
e) Reporting procedures under the exposure control plan to ensure that all first-aid incidents involving exposure are reported to the employer before the end of the work shift during which the incident occurs.

RATIONALE: Providing first aid in situations where blood is present is an intrinsic part of a caregiver's job. Split lips, scraped knees and other minor injuries associated with bleeding are common in child care. Regarding the applicability of the OSHA standard to child care, Patricia K. Clark, Director of the Directorate of Compliance Assistance stated:

"One of the central provisions of the OSHA standard on bloodborne pathogens is that employers are responsible for determining which job classifications or specific tasks and procedures are reasonably anticipated to result in worker contact with blood or other

potentially infectious materials (OPIM). The standard relates coverage to occupational exposure, regardless of where that exposure may occur, since the risk of infection with bloodborne pathogens is dependent on the likelihood of exposure to blood or OPIM regardless of the particular job title or place of employment. If it is determined that a child care worker has occupational exposure, as defined by the standard, then that employee is covered by all sections of the standard including training, vaccination, personal protective equipment, and so forth."

Child care workers who are designated as responsible for rendering first aid or medical assistance as part of their job duties are covered by the scope of this standard.

COMMENTS: OSHA has model exposure control plan materials for use by child care facilities. Using the model exposure control plan materials, child care providers can prepare a plan to comply with the OSHA requirements. The model plan materials are available from regional offices of OSHA. Contact information for OSHA is located in Appendix BB.

TYPE OF FACILITY: *Center; Large Family Child Care Home*

STANDARD 1.034
TRAINING RECORD

The director of a center or a large family child care home shall provide and maintain documentation of training received by, or provided for, staff. For centers, the date of the training, the number of hours, the names of staff participants, the name(s) and qualification(s) of the trainer(s), and the content of the training (both orientation and continuing education) shall be recorded in each staff person's file or in a separate training file.

Small family child care home providers shall keep a written record of training acquired.

RATIONALE: The training record shall be used to assess each employee's need for additional training and to provide regulators with a tool to monitor compliance. Continuing education with course credit shall be recorded and the records made available to

staff members to document their applications for licenses/certificates or for license upgrading (26).

In many states, small family child care home providers are required to keep records of training.

COMMENTS: Colleges issue transcripts, workshops can issue certificates, and facility administrators can maintain individual training logs.

TYPE OF FACILITY: *Center; Large Family Child Care Home; Small Family Child Care Home*

STANDARD 1.035
RELEASED TIME AND
EDUCATIONAL LEAVE

A center, large family child care home or a support agency for a network of small family child care homes shall make provisions for paid, released time for staff to participate in required training during work hours, or reimburse staff for time spent attending training outside of regular work hours. Any hours worked in excess of 40 hours in a week shall be paid at time and a half.

RATIONALE: Most caregivers work long hours and most are poorly paid (20). Using personal time for education required as a condition of employment is an unfair expectation until compensation for work done in child care is much more equitable. Many child care workers also work at other jobs to make a living wage and would miss income from their other jobs, or would incur stress in their family life if they had to take time outside of child care hours to participate in work-related training.

COMMENTS: Education in child care often takes place when the participant is not released from other work-related duties, such as answering phones or caring for children. Providing substitutes and released time during work hours for such training is likely to enhance the effectiveness of training.

Large family child care homes employ staff in the same way as centers, except for size and location in a residence. For small family child care home providers, released time and compensation while engaged in training can be arranged only if the small family child

care home provider is part of a support network that makes such arrangements. This standard does not apply to small family child care home providers independent of networks.

The Fair Labor Standard Act mandates payment of time and a half for all hours worked in excess of 40 hours in a week.

TYPE OF FACILITY: *Center, Large Family Child Care Homes, Small Family Child Care Homes*

STANDARD 1.036
PAYMENT FOR CONTINUING EDUCATION

Directors of centers and large family child care homes shall arrange for continuing education that is paid for by the government, by charitable organizations, or by the facility, rather than by the employee. Small family child care home providers shall avail themselves of training opportunities offered in their communities.

RATIONALE: Caregivers often make low wages and may not be able to pay for mandated training. A majority of child care workers earn close to or less than the minimum wage (20).

TYPE OF FACILITY: *Center; Large Family Child Care Home; Small Family Child Care Home*

1.5 SUBSTITUTES

STANDARD 1.037
EMPLOYMENT OF SUBSTITUTES

Substitutes shall be employed to ensure that child:staff ratios (as specified in Child:Staff Ratio and Group Size, STANDARD 1.001 through STANDARD 1.005) are maintained at all times. Substitutes and volunteers must meet the requirements specified in General Qualifications for All Caregivers, STANDARD 1.007 through STANDARD 1.013. Those without licenses/certificates shall work under direct supervision and shall not be alone with a group of children.

A substitute shall have the same clearances as the provider including criminal record check, child abuse history, and medical assessment.

RATIONALE: The risk to children from care by unqualified caregivers is the same whether the caregiver is a paid substitute or a volunteer.

Substitutes should be free from communicable diseases.

COMMENTS: Substitutes are difficult to find, especially at the last minute. Planning for a competent substitute pool is essential for child care operation. Requiring substitutes for small family child care homes to have first aid certification, which includes management of a blocked airway and rescue breathing, forces these caregivers to close during the times they cannot cover with a competent substitute. Since closing a child care home has a negative impact on the families and children they serve, systems should be developed to provide qualified alternative homes or substitutes for family child care home providers.

The lack of back-up for family child care home providers is an inherent liability in this type of care. The problem is somewhat ameliorated when family child care home providers who do not operate at full capacity every day can provide back-up care for children enrolled with other family child care home providers. Parents and children should be familiar with these alternative arrangements. Few family child care home providers are comfortable with having a stranger, even a qualified substitute, come into their home to provide alternative care in the setting most familiar to the child. Parents who use family child care must be sure they have suitable alternative care for situations in which the child's usual caregiver cannot provide the service.

See also Qualifications of Large and Small Family Child Care Home Providers, STANDARD 1.019 and STANDARD 1.020; Staff Health, STANDARD 1.045; and Licensure/Certification of Qualified Individuals, STANDARD 1.006.

TYPE OF FACILITY: *Center; Large Family Child Care Home*

STANDARD 1.038
ORIENTATION OF SUBSTITUTES FOR CENTERS AND LARGE FAMILY CHILD CARE HOMES

The director of any center or large family child care home shall provide orientation training to newly hired substitutes. This training shall include the opportunity for an evaluation and a repeat demonstration of the training lesson. In centers, this orientation training shall be documented. All substitutes shall be oriented to, and demonstrate competence in, the tasks for which they will be responsible. All substitute caregivers, during the first week of employment, shall be oriented to, and shall demonstrate competence in at least the following items:

a) The names of the children for whom the caregiver will be responsible, and their specific developmental needs;

b) Any special health or nutrition need(s) of the children assigned to the caregiver;

c) The planned program of activities at the facility. See Program of Activities, STANDARD 8.042 and STANDARD 8.043; and Program of Developmental Activities, STANDARD 2.001 through STANDARD 2.027;

d) Routines and transitions;

e) Acceptable methods of discipline. See Discipline, STANDARD 2.039 through STANDARD 2.043;

f) Meal patterns and food handling policies of the facility. See Plans and Policies for Food Handling, Feeding, and Nutrition, STANDARD 8.035 and STANDARD 8.036, Food Service Records, STANDARD 8.074, and Nutrition and Food Service, STANDARD 4.001 through STANDARD 4.070;

g) Emergency health and safety procedures. See Plan for Urgent Medical Care or Threatening Incidents, STANDARD 8.022 and STANDARD 8.023; and Emergency Procedures, STANDARD 3.048 through STANDARD 3.052;

h) General health policies and procedures as appropriate for the ages of the children cared for, including but not limited to the following:

1) Handwashing techniques, including indications for handwashing. See Handwashing, STANDARD 3.020 through STANDARD 3.023;

2) Diapering technique, if care is provided to children in diapers, including appropriate diaper disposal and diaper changing techniques. See Toilet, Diapering, and Bath Areas, STANDARD 5.116 through STANDARD 5.125; Toileting, Diapering, and Toilet Learning/Training, STANDARD 3.012 through STANDARD 3.019; Sanitation, Disinfection, and Maintenance of Toilet Learning/Training Equipment, Toilets, and Bathrooms, STANDARD 3.029 through STANDARD 3.033;

3) The practice of putting infants down to sleep positioned on their backs and on a firm surface to reduce the risk of Sudden Infant Death Syndrome, as well as general nap time routines for all ages. See STANDARD 3.008 and STANDARD 5.144 through STANDARD 5.146;

4) Correct food preparation and storage techniques, if employee prepares food. See Plans and Policies for Food Handling, Feeding, and Nutrition, STANDARD 8.035 and STANDARD 8.036 and Food Safety, STANDARD 4.050 through STANDARD 4.059;

5) Formula preparation if formula is handled. See Nutrition for Infants, STANDARD 4.016 through STANDARD 4.019;

6) Proper use of gloves in compliance with Occupational Safety and Health Administration (OSHA) bloodborne pathogens regulations. See STANDARD 3.026 and Appendix D, on proper gloving procedures;

7) Injury Prevention and Safety.

RATIONALE: Upon employment, staff members shall be able to carry out the duties assigned to them. Because facilities and the children enrolled in them vary, orientation programs for new employees that address the health and safety of the children enrolled as well as employees' health and safety concerns specific to the site, can be most productive (24). Because of frequent staff turnover, centers and large family child care homes must institute orientation programs as needed that protect the health and safety of children and new staff.

TYPE OF FACILITY: *Center; Large Family Child Care Home*

STANDARD 1.039
ORIENTATION FOR SUBSTITUTES FOR SMALL FAMILY CHILD CARE HOMES

A short-term substitute caregiver in a small family child care home shall be oriented on the first day of employment to emergency response practices, including how to call for emergency medical assistance, how to reach parents or emergency contacts, how to arrange for transfer to medical care, and the evacuation plan.

RATIONALE: Upon employment, staff members should be able to carry out the duties assigned to them. Because facilities and the children enrolled in them vary, orientation programs for new employees that address the health and safety of the children enrolled as well as employees' health and safety concerns specific to the site, can be most productive (24).

COMMENTS: Substitute caregivers must possess current CPR if the small family-child-care home has a swimming/wading pool and first aid certification which includes management of a blocked airway and rescue breathing. See First Aid and CPR, STANDARD 1.026 through STANDARD 1.028.

For more information on emergencies, see Plan for Urgent Medical Care or Threatening Incidents, STANDARD 8.022 and STANDARD 8.023; and Evacuation Plan, Drills, and Closings, STANDARD 8.024 through STANDARD 8.027.

TYPE OF FACILITY: *Small Family Child Care Home*

1.6 HEALTH CONSULTANTS

STANDARD 1.040
USE OF CHILD CARE HEALTH CONSULTANTS

Each center, large family child care home, and small family child care home network shall use the services of a health consultant qualified to provide advice for child care as defined in STANDARD 1.041. Centers and large and small family child care home providers shall avail themselves of community resources established for health consultation to child care.

RATIONALE: Few child care staff are trained as health professionals and few health professionals have training about the community child care programs. When physical, mental, social, or health concerns are raised for the child or for the family, they should be addressed appropriately, often through consultation with or referral to resources available in the community.

Caregivers need to use health consultants in a variety of fields (such as physical and mental health care, nutrition, environmental safety and injury prevention, oral health care, and developmental disabilities). Health consultants should have specific training in the child care setting (31). Such training is more widely available through efforts such as state programs implementing the Healthy Child Care America Campaign, and national support funded by the Maternal and Child Health Bureau, Health Resources and Services Administration, including the National Resource Center for Health and Safety in Child Care, the national staff of the Healthy Child Care America Campaign at the American Academy of Pediatrics and the National Training Institute for Child Care Health Consultants. Contact information is located in Appendix BB.

In states where health consultation is mandatory, compliance is nearly universal (32).

COMMENTS: A health consultant should be a health professional who has an interest in and experience with children, has knowledge of resources and regulations, and is comfortable linking health resources with facilities that provide primarily education and social services. State regulatory agencies should maintain or contract for the maintenance of a registry of health consultant resources in the community. For example, in Pennsylvania, the PA Chapter of the American Academy of Pediatrics (AAP) maintains and provides training and support for health professionals in such a registry under contracts with the child care regulatory agency and the state department of health. Additional registries are being developed by the National Resource Center for Health and Safety in Child Care,

Healthy Child Care America Campaign from the Maternal and Child Health Bureau, Health Resources and Services Administration, and the National Training Institute for Child Care Health Consultants. Child care health consultants may be employed by public or non-profit agencies such as health departments or resource and referral agencies, other health institutions, or may work as independent health consultants. Caregivers also should not overlook health professionals with pediatric and health consultant experience who are parents of children enrolled in their facility. However, involving parents as health consultants requires caution to avoid crossing boundaries of confidentiality and conflict of interest. To foster access to and accountability of health consultants, some form of compensation should be offered.

TYPE OF FACILITY: *Center; Large Family Child Care Home; Small Family Child Care Home*

STANDARD 1.041
KNOWLEDGE AND SKILLS OF CHILD CARE HEALTH CONSULTANTS

A facility shall have a health consultant who is a health professional with training and experience as a child care health consultant. Graduate students in a discipline related to child health shall be acceptable as child care health consultants supervised by faculty knowledgeable in child care. A child care health consultant shall either have the full knowledge base and skills required for this role, or arrange to partner with other health professionals who can provide the necessary knowledge and skills.

The knowledge base of the child care health consultant (personally or by involving other health professionals) shall include:
a)   National health and safety standards for out-of-home child care;
b)   How child care facilities conduct their day-to-day operations;
c)   Child care licensing requirements;
d)   Disease reporting requirements for child care providers;
e)   Immunizations for children;
f)   Immunizations for child care providers;
g)   Injury prevention for children;

h)   Staff health, including occupational health risks for child care providers;
i)   Oral health for children;
j)   Nutrition for children;
k)   Inclusion of children with special health needs in child care;
l)   Recognition and reporting requirements for child abuse and neglect;
m)   Community health and mental health resources for child and parent health.

The skills of the child care health consultant shall include the ability to perform or arrange for performance of the following activities:
a)   Teaching child care providers about health and safety issues;
b)   Teaching parents about health and safety issues;
c)   Assessing child care providers' needs for health and safety training;
d)   Assessing parents' needs for health and safety training;
e)   Meeting on-site with child care providers about health and safety;
f)   Providing telephone advice to child care providers about health and safety;
g)   Providing referrals to community services;
h)   Developing or updating policies and procedures for child care facilities;
i)   Reviewing health records of children;
j)   Reviewing health records of child care providers;
k)   Helping to manage the care of children with special health care needs;
l)   Consulting with a child's health professional about medication;
m)   Interpreting standards or regulations and providing technical advice, separate and apart from the enforcement role of a regulation inspector.

Although the child care health consultant may have a dual role, such as providing direct care to some of the children or serving as a regulation inspector, these roles shall not be mixed with the child care health consultation role.

The child care health consultant shall have contact with the facility's administrative authority, the staff, and the parents in the facility. The administrative authority shall review, respond to, and implement the child care health consultant's recommendations. The child care health consultant shall review

and approve the written health policies used by center-based facilities.

Programs with a significant number of non-English-speaking families shall seek a child care health consultant who is culturally sensitive and knowledgeable about community health resources for the parents' native culture and languages.

RATIONALE: The specific health and safety consultation needs for an individual facility depend on the characteristics of that facility (31). All facilities should have an overall child care health consultation.

The special circumstances of group care may not be part of the health professional's usual education. Therefore, child care providers should seek health consultants who have the necessary specialized training or experience. Such training is more readily available now as described in the previous standard.

To be effective, a child care health consultant should know the available resources in the community and should engage in a partnership with the administrative authority for the facility, the staff, and parents in the consultative and policy-setting process. Setting health and safety policies in cooperation with the staff, parents, health professionals, and public health authorities will help ensure successful implementation of a quality program (30).

Health professionals who serve as child care health consultants do not always have a public health perspective or the full range of knowledge and skills required. Therefore, public health professionals and other health professionals with appropriate training and skills should serve as a resource to inform those who work in the private sector or whose health professional expertise is specialized and lacking in broader knowledge and skills that may be required. For example, while a sanitarian may provide excellent health consultation on hygiene and infectious disease control, another health professional may need to be consulted about medication administration or playground safety. A Certified Playground Safety Inspector would be able to provide consultation about gross motor play hazards, and would not likely be able to provide sound advice about food safety and nutrition.

COMMENTS: The policies and procedures reviewed for approval by child care health consultants should include, but not be limited to, the following:
    a) Admission and readmission after illness, including inclusion/exclusion criteria;
    b) Health evaluation and observation procedures on intake, including physical assessment of the child and other criteria used to determine the appropriateness of a child's attendance;
    c) Plans for health care and management of children with communicable diseases;
    d) Plans for surveillance and management of illnesses, injuries, and problems that arise in the care of children;
    e) Plans for caregiver training and for communication with parents and health care providers;
    f) Policies regarding nutrition, nutrition education, and oral health;
    g) Plans for the inclusion of children with special health needs;
    h) Emergency plans;
    i) Safety assessment of facility playground;
    j) Policies regarding staff health and safety;
    k) Policies for administration of medication.

See Identifiable Governing Body/Accountable Individual, STANDARD 8.001 through STANDARD 8.003, for additional information regarding administrative authority.

TYPE OF FACILITY: *Center; Large Family Child Care Home; Small Family Child Care Home*

STANDARD 1.042
SPECIALIZED CONSULTATION FOR FACILITIES SERVING CHILDREN WITH DISABILITIES

When children at the facility include those with developmental delay or disabilities, the staff or documented consultants shall include any of the following, with prior informed, written parental consent and as appropriate to each child's needs:
a)   A physician;
b)   A registered dietitian;
c)   A registered nurse or pediatric nurse practitioner;
d)   A psychologist;

e) A physical therapist;
f) An occupational therapist;
g) A speech pathologist;
h) A respiratory therapist;
i) A social worker;
j) A parent of a child with special needs;
k) The child care provider.

RATIONALE: The range of professionals needed may vary with the facility, but the listed professionals should be available as consultants when needed. These professionals need not be on staff at the facility, but may simply be available when needed through a variety of arrangements, including contracts, agreements, and affiliations. The parent's participation and written consent in the native language of the parent, including Braille/sign language, is required to include outside consultants.

TYPE OF FACILITY: *Center; Large Family Child Care Home; Small Family Child Care Home*

STANDARD 1.043
FREQUENCY OF CHILD CARE
HEALTH CONSULTATION VISITS

The health consultant shall visit each facility as needed to review and give advice on the facility's health component. Center-based facilities that serve any child younger than 2 years of age shall be visited at least once a month by a health professional with general knowledge and skills in child health and safety. Center-based facilities that are not open at least 5 days a week or that serve only children 2 years of age or older shall be visited at least quarterly, on a schedule that meets the needs of the composite group of children. Small and large family child care homes shall be visited at least annually. Written documentation of health consultant visits shall be maintained at the facility.

RATIONALE: Almost everything that goes on in a facility and almost everything about the facility itself affects the health of the children it serves (29). Infants are particularly vulnerable to injuries, infections, and psychological harm. Their rapid changes in behavior make regular and frequent visits by the health consultant extremely important. In facilities where health and safety problems or a high turnover of staff occurs,

more frequent visits by the health consultant should be arranged.

COMMENTS: For health consultants to facilities serving children with special needs, see STANDARD 1.003, STANDARD 1.042, and STANDARD 1.044. For health consultants serving special facilities for children who are ill, see STANDARD 3.075. For nutrition staffing and consultation, see STANDARD 4.026 and STANDARD 4.027. For additional information on health consultants, see Health Consultation, STANDARD 8.020; Consultation Records, STANDARD 8.073, on documentation of health consultant training and visits; and Consultants, RECOMMENDATION 9.033 and RECOMMENDATION 9.034.

TYPE OF FACILITY: *Center; Large Family Child Care Home; Small Family Child Care Home*

STANDARD 1.044
REGISTERED NURSES TO PROVIDE
MEDICAL TREATMENT

Child care facilities shall arrange for a registered nurse to provide staff training and ongoing supervision of the health needs and practices of staff and children and to ensure appropriate administration of medication and prescribed medical treatment if an individual assessment of a child reveals that such services are required.

RATIONALE: An on-site health care professional must be available to assess and manage the needs of children who require medical assistance.

COMMENTS: Small family child care home providers may arrange for the services of a registered nurse on an as-needed consultative basis.

TYPE OF FACILITY: *Center; Large Family Child Care Home; Small Family Child Care Home*

1.7 STAFF HEALTH

If a staff member has no contact with the children, or with anything that the children come into contact with, Standards in Section 1.7 Staff Health do not apply to that staff member.

STANDARD 1.045
PREEMPLOYMENT AND ONGOING ADULT HEALTH APPRAISALS, INCLUDING IMMUNIZATION

All paid and volunteer staff members who work more than 40 hours per month shall have a health appraisal before their first involvement in child care work. Health appraisals shall be required every 2 years thereafter, unless the staff member's health provider recommends that this be done more frequently. If a child care provider works also at a different child care facility, a new health appraisal shall be required if there is a question about the results of the previous health appraisal, 2 years have elapsed since the previous health appraisal, or signs of ill health appear. People who work less than 40 hours per month shall be encouraged to have a health appraisal. The appraisal shall identify any accommodations required of the facility for the staff person to function in his or her assigned position. A statement from the health care provider that an appraisal covering the listed areas was completed, and details about any findings that require accommodation shall be on file at the facility.

Health appraisals for paid and volunteer staff members who work more than 40 hours per month shall include at a minimum:
a) Health history;
b) Physical exam;
c) Dental exam;
d) Vision and hearing screening;
e) The results and appropriate follow-up of a tuberculosis (Tb) screening using the Mantoux intradermal skin test, one-step procedure. See STANDARD 6.014;
f) A review and certification of up-to-date immune status (measles, mumps, rubella, diphtheria, tetanus, polio, varicella, influenza, pneumonia, hepatitis A, and hepatitis B) (24). See

Immunizations, STANDARD 3.005 through STANDARD 3.007;
g) A review of occupational health concerns based on the performance of the essential functions of the job. See Occupational Hazards, STANDARD 1.048; and *Major Occupational Health Hazards*, Appendix B;
h) Assessment of risk from exposure to common childhood infections, such as parvovirus, CMV, and chickenpox (24, 28);
i) Assessment of orthopedic, psychological, neurological, or sensory limitations or communicable diseases that require accommodations or modifications for the person to perform tasks that typical adults can do.

All adults who reside in a family child care home who are considered to be at high risk for Tb, and all adults who work less than 40 hours in any month in child care shall have completed Tb screening as specified in STANDARD 6.014. Adults who are considered at high risk for Tb include those who are foreign-born, have a history of homelessness, are HIV-infected, have contact with a prison population, or have contact with someone who has active Tb.

The Tb test of staff members with previously negative skin tests shall not be repeated on a regular basis unless required by the local or state health department. A record of test results and appropriate follow-up evaluation shall be on file in the facility.

All adults who work in child care shall be encouraged to have a full health appraisal.

RATIONALE: Under the Americans with Disabilities Act (ADA), employers are expected to make reasonable accommodations for persons with disabilities. Under ADA, accommodations are based on an individual case by case situation. Undue hardship is defined also on a case by case basis.

Since detection of Tuberculosis using screening of healthy individuals has a low yield compared with screening of contacts of known cases of tuberculosis, routine repeated screening of healthy individuals with previously negative skin tests is not a reasonable use of resources. Since local circumstances and risks of exposure may vary, this recommendation should be subject to modification by local or state health authorities.

Even for young, healthy adults, care of children increases the risk of developing medical problems that can affect the adult's ability to perform on the job. For the protection of the children and adult staff members, a 2-year health appraisal should be considered as minimal surveillance.

Dental decay is transmissible. Bacteria which contribute to dental decay can be transmitted from care - givers to infants. Individuals with active tooth decay are more likely to transmit this bacteria to the children in their care.

COMMENTS: To focus the evaluation by the health professional, child care facilities should provide the job description or list of activities that the staff person is expected to perform. Unless the job description defines the duties of the role specifically, under federal law the facility may be required to adjust the activities of that person. For example, child care facilities typically require the following activities of caregivers:
a) Moving quickly to supervise and assist young children;
b) Lifting children, equipment, and supplies;
c) Sitting on the floor and on child-sized furniture;
d) Washing hands frequently;
e) Eating the same food as that served to the children (unless the staff member has dietary restrictions);
f) Hearing and seeing at a distance required for playground supervision or driving;
g) Being absent from work for illness no more often than the typical adult, to provide continuity of caregiving relationships for children in child care.

NAEYC's *Healthy Young Children: A Manual for Programs* provides models for an assessment by a health professional. See also *Model Child Care Health Policies,* available from National Association for the Education of Young Children (NAEYC) and from the American Academy of Pediatrics (AAP). Contact information located in Appendix BB.

Concern about the cost of health exams (particularly when many caregivers do not receive health benefits and earn minimum wage) is a barrier to meeting this standard. When staff members need hepatitis B immunization to meet OSHA requirements, the cost of this immunization may or may not be covered under a managed care contract. If not, the cost of health supervision (such as immunizations, dental and health exams) must be covered as part of the employee's preparation for work in the child care setting by the prospective employee or the employer. Child care workers are among those for whom annual influenza vaccination should be strongly considered.

Facilities should consult with ADA experts through the U.S. Department of Education funded Disability and Business Technical Assistance Centers throughout the country. These centers can be reached by calling 1-800-949-4232 and callers are routed to the appropriate region.

Also see STANDARD 1.045, STANDARD 6.014 and STANDARD 6.015. For a sample child care staff health assessment form, see Appendix E.

TYPE OF FACILITY: *Center; Large Family Child Care Home; Small Family Child Care Home*

STANDARD 1.046
DAILY STAFF HEALTH ASSESSMENT

On a daily basis, the administrator of the facility or caregiver shall assess (visually and verbally) staff members, substitutes, and volunteers for obvious signs of ill health. Staff members, substitutes, and volunteers shall be responsible for reporting immediately to their supervisor any injuries or illnesses they experience at the facility or elsewhere, especially those that might affect their health or the health and safety of the children. It is the responsibility of the administration, not the ill or injured staff member, to arrange for a substitute provider.

RATIONALE: Sometimes adults report to work when feeling ill or become ill during the day but believe it is their responsibility to stay. The administrator's or care-giver's assessment may prevent the spread of illness.

COMMENTS: Administrators and caregivers need guidelines to ensure proper application of this standard. For a demonstration of how to implement this standard, see the video series, *Caring for Our Children*, available from National Association for the Education of Young Children (NAEYC) and the American Academy of Pediatrics (AAP) (34). Contact information is located in Appendix BB.

TYPE OF FACILITY: *Center; Large Family Child Care Home; Small Family Child Care Home*

STANDARD 1.047
HEALTH LIMITATIONS OF STAFF

Staff and volunteers must have a health care provider's release to return to work in the following situations:
a) When they have experienced conditions that may affect their ability to do their job or require an accommodation to prevent illness or injury in child care work related to their conditions (such as pregnancy, specific injuries, or infectious diseases);
b) After serious or prolonged illness;
c) When their condition or health could affect promotion or reassignment to another role;
d) Before return from a job-related injury;
e) If there are workers' compensation issues or if the facility is at risk of liability related to the employee's or volunteer's health problem;
f) When there is suspicion of a communicable disease.

If a staff member is found to be unable to perform the activities required for the job because of health limitations, the staff person's duties shall be limited or modified until the health condition resolves or employment is terminated because the facility can prove that it would be an undue hardship to accommodate the staff member with the disability.

RATIONALE: Under the Americans with Disabilities Act (ADA), employers are expected to make reasonable accommodations for persons with disabilities. Under ADA, accommodations are based on an individual case by case situation. Undue hardship is defined also on a case by case basis.

COMMENTS: Facilities should consult with ADA experts through the U.S. Department of Education

funded Disability and Business Technical Assistance Centers throughout the country. These centers can be reached by calling 1-800-949-4232 and callers are routed to the appropriate region.

For additional information on health limitations of staff members, see STANDARD 6.030, for staff with acute or chronic hepatitis B (HBV); and STANDARD 6.036, for staff with asymptomatic HIV.

TYPE OF FACILITY: *Center; Large Family Child Care Home*

STANDARD 1.048
OCCUPATIONAL HAZARDS

The center's written personnel policies shall address the major occupational health hazards for workers in child care settings. Special health concerns of pregnant providers shall be carefully evaluated, and up-to-date information regarding occupational hazards for pregnant providers shall be made available to them and other workers. The occupational hazards including those regarding pregnant workers listed in Appendix B (*Major Occupational Health Hazards*) shall be referenced and used in evaluations by providers and supervisors.

RATIONALE: Employees must be aware of the risks to which they are exposed so they can weigh those risks and take countermeasures. As a workforce composed primarily of women of childbearing age, pregnancy is common among providers in child care settings. In a study of child care personnel, one quarter of the study's sample reported becoming pregnant since beginning work in child care, with higher pregnancy rates for directors (33%) and family home providers (36%) than for center staff (15%) (33, 36).

TYPE OF FACILITY: *Center; Large Family Child Care Home*

STANDARD 1.049
STRESS

The following measures to lessen stress for the staff shall be implemented to the maximum extent possible:
a) Wages and benefits that fairly compensate the skills, knowledge, and performance required of caregivers, at the levels of wages and benefits paid for other jobs that require comparable skills, knowledge, and performance;
b) Job security;
c) Training to improve skills and hazard recognition;
d) Stress management and reduction training;
e) Regular work breaks;
f) Appropriate child:staff ratios;
g) Liability insurance for caregivers;
h) Staff lounge separate from child care area;
i) The use of sound-absorbing materials;
j) Regular performance reviews which, in addition to addressing any areas requiring improvement, provide constructive feedback, individualized encouragement and appreciation for aspects of the job well performed;
k) Stated provisions for back-up staff, for example, to allow caregivers to take necessary time off when ill without compromising the function of the center or incurring personal negative consequences from the employer. This back-up shall also include a stated plan to be implemented in the event a staff member needs to have a short, but relatively immediate break away from the children.

RATIONALE: One of the best indicators of quality child care is consistent staff with low turnover rates. The National Child Care Staffing Study found that staff turnover increased from 26% in 1992 to 31% in 1997 (20). Despite having higher levels of formal education than the average American worker, a large percentage of teaching staff members earn an average $5.15 an hour (20).

Stress reduction measures (particularly adequate wages) are essential to decrease staff turnover and thereby promote quality care (20). The health, welfare, and safety of adult workers in child care determine their ability to provide care for the children. Serious physical abuse usually occurs when the caregiver is under high stress. Regular breaks with substitutes should be available when the caregiver cannot continue to provide care.

Sound-absorbing materials, break times, and a separate lounge allow for respite from noise and from non-auditory stress. Unwanted sound, or noise, can be damaging to hearing as well as to psychosocial well-being. The stress effects of noise will aggravate other stress factors present in the facility. Lack of adequate sound reduction measures in the facility can force the caregiver to speak at levels above those normally used for conversation, and thus may increase the risk of throat irritation. When caregivers raise their voices to be heard, the children tend to raise theirs, escalating the problem.

COMMENTS: Documentation of implementation of such measures shall be on file in the facility. Injury-preventive and hygienic activities recommended for the children also protect the staff.

See Child:Staff Ratio and Group Size, STANDARD 1.001 through STANDARD 1.005.

TYPE OF FACILITY: *Center*

INFECTIOUS DISEASES/INJURIES

See STANDARD 8.010, on staff injuries from acts of aggression by children; STANDARD 3.070 through STANDARD 3.080, on caring for ill children; STANDARD 5.080, on prevention of back injuries; Toilet, Diapering, and Bath Areas, STANDARD 5.116 through STANDARD 5.125; Toileting and Diapering, STANDARD 3.012 through STANDARD 3.019; and Sanitation, Disinfection, and Maintenance of Toilet Learning/Training Equipment, Toilets, and Bathrooms, STANDARD 3.029 through STANDARD 3.033; and Infectious Diseases, STANDARD 6.001 through STANDARD 6.039.

ENVIRONMENTAL EXPOSURES

See Toxic Substances, STANDARD 5.100 through STANDARD 5.111.

1.8 STAFF BENEFITS

STANDARD 1.050
BASIC BENEFITS

The following basic benefits shall be offered to staff:
a) Affordable health insurance;
b) Sick leave;
c) Vacation leave;
d) Social Security or other retirement plan;
e) Workers' compensation;
f) Holidays;
g) Personal leave;
h) Educational benefits;
i) Family, parental and medical leave.

Centers and large family child care homes shall have written policies that detail these benefits of employees at the facility.

RATIONALE: The quality and continuity of the care-giving workforce is the main determining factor of the quality of care. Nurturing the nurturers is essential to prevent burnout and promote retention. Fair labor practices should apply to child care as well as other work settings. Child care workers should be considered as worthy of benefits as workers in other careers.

Medical coverage should include the cost of the health appraisals and immunizations required of child care workers, and care for the increased incidence of communicable disease and stress-related conditions in this work setting.

Sick leave is important to minimize the spread of communicable diseases and maintain the health of staff members. Sick leave promotes recovery from illness and thereby decreases the further spread or recurrence of illness.

Other benefits contribute to higher morale and less staff turnover, and thus promote quality child care. Lack of benefits is a major reason reported for high turnover of child care staff (20).

The potential for acquiring injuries and infections when caring for young children is a health and safety hazard for child care workers. Information abounds about the risk of infectious disease for children in child care settings. Children are reservoirs for many infectious agents. Staff members come into close and frequent contact with children and their excretions and secretions and are vulnerable to these illnesses. In addition, many child care workers are women who are planning a pregnancy or who are pregnant, and they may be vulnerable to potentially serious effects of infection on the outcome of pregnancy.

COMMENTS: Staff benefits may be appropriately addressed in center personnel policies and in state and federal labor standards. Not all the material that has to be addressed in these policies is appropriate for state child care licensing requirements. Having facilities acknowledge which benefits they do provide will help enhance the general awareness of staff benefits among child care workers and other concerned parties. Currently, this standard is difficult for many facilities to achieve, but new federal programs and shared access to small business benefit packages will help. Many options are available for providing leave benefits and education reimbursements, ranging from partial to full employer contribution, based on time employed with the facility.

Providers should be encouraged to have health insurance. Health benefits can include full coverage, partial coverage (at least 75% employer paid), or merely access to group rates. Some local or state child care associations offer reduced group rates for health insurance for child care facilities and individual providers.

See also Personnel Policies, STANDARD 8.044.

TYPE OF FACILITY: *Center; Large Family Child Care Home; Small Family Child Care Home*

1.9 PERFORMANCE EVALUATION

STANDARD 1.051
STAFF FAMILIARITY WITH FACILITY POLICIES, PLANS AND PROCEDURES

All caregivers shall be familiar with the provisions of the facility's policies, plans, and procedures, as described in Administration, STANDARD 8.001 through STANDARD 8.079. The compliance with these policies, plans, and procedures shall be used in staff performance evaluations and documented in the personnel file.

RATIONALE: Written policies, plans and procedures provide a means of staff orientation and evaluation essential to the operation of any organization.

TYPE OF FACILITY: *Center; Large Family Child Care Home*

STANDARD 1.052
EMPLOYEE EVALUATION

For each employee, there shall be a written annual self-evaluation, a performance review from the personnel supervisor, and a continuing education plan based on the needs assessment, described in STANDARD 1.029 through STANDARD 1.033 and STANDARD 1.055.

RATIONALE: A system for evaluation of employees is a basic component of any personnel policy.

COMMENTS: Formal evaluation is not a substitute for continuing feedback on day-to-day performance. Compliance with this standard may be determined by licensing requirements set by the state and local regulatory processes.

TYPE OF FACILITY: *Center; Large Family Child Care Home*

STANDARD 1.053
STAFF ENDORSEMENT OF DISCIPLINE POLICY

All caregivers shall sign an agreement on the discipline policy, as specified in STANDARD 8.008 through STANDARD 8.010.

RATIONALE: Caregivers are more likely to avoid abusive practices if they are well-informed about effective, non-abusive methods for managing children's behaviors. Positive methods of discipline create a constructive and supportive social group and reduce incidents of aggression.

TYPE OF FACILITY: *Center; Large Family Child Care Home*

STANDARD 1.054
MONTHLY OBSERVATION OF STAFF

Monthly observation of staff shall include an evaluation of each member's adherence to the policies and procedures of the facility with respect to sanitation, hygiene, and management of communicable diseases. Routine, direct observation of employees is the best way to evaluate hygiene and safety practices.

RATIONALE: Ongoing observation is an effective tool to evaluate consistency of staff adherence to program policies and procedures. It also serves to identify areas for additional orientation and training.

COMMENTS: The use of videotaping of the interactions of child care providers with children, among other activities, for purposes of employee evaluation, quality assurance, marketing, education and research is recognized as useful and desirable, but is not required. Desirable interactions can be encouraged and undesirable ones avoided as a result of videotaping. Providers can utilize videotapes as a tool for the reassurance of parents.

TYPE OF FACILITY: *Center; Large Family Child Care Home*

STANDARD 1.055
ANNUAL STAFF COMPETENCY EVALUATION

The competency of personnel and their continuing education needs shall be assessed annually through a systematic process and shall be documented.

RATIONALE: Staff members who are well trained are better able to prevent, recognize, and correct health and safety problems (27).

COMMENTS: Compliance with this standard may be determined by licensing requirements set by the state and local regulatory processes, and by state and local funding requirements, or by accrediting bodies. In some states, a central Child Development Personnel Registry may track and certify the qualifications of staff.

TYPE OF FACILITY: *Center*

STANDARD 1.056
CORRECTIVE ACTION FOR LACK OF COMPETENCY

When a staff member of a center, large family child care home, or small family child care network does not meet the minimum competency level, that employee shall work with the employer to develop a plan to assist the person in achieving the necessary skills. The plan shall include a timeline for completion and consequences if it is not achieved.

RATIONALE: A system for evaluation and a plan to promote continued development are essential to assist staff to meet performance requirements. Children must be protected from incompetent caregiving.

COMMENTS: The minimum competency level is related to the director's assessment of the caregiver's performance.

For additional information on performance evaluation, see also Personnel Records, STANDARD 8.058.

TYPE OF FACILITY: *Center; Large Family Child Care Home; Small Family Child Care Home*

STANDARD 1.057
HANDLING COMPLAINTS ABOUT CHILD CARE PROVIDERS

When complaints are made to licensing or referral agencies about child care providers, the providers shall receive formal notice of the complaint and the resulting action, if any. Providers shall maintain records of such complaints, and make them available to parents on request, and post a notice of how to contact the state agency responsible for maintaining complaint records.

RATIONALE: Parents seeking child care should know if previous complaints have been made, particularly if the complaint is substantiated. Parents can then evaluate whether or not the complaint is valid, and whether the complaint has been adequately addressed and necessary changes have been made.

COMMENTS: This policy requires program development by licensing agencies.

TYPE OF FACILITY: *Center; Large Family Child Care Home; Small Family Child Care Home*

REFERENCES

1. National Research Council. *Who Care for America's Children? Child Care Policy in the 1990's.* Washington, DC: National Academy Press; 1990.

2. National Institute of Child Health and Human Development (NICHD) Early Child Care Research Network. Characteristics of infant child care: factors contributing to positive caregiving. *Early Child Res Q.* 1996;11:269-306.

3. Roupp R, Travers J, Glantz R, et al. *Children at the Center: Final Report of the National Day Care Study.* Vol 1. Cambridge, Mass: Abt Associates; 1979.

4. National Institute of Child Health and Human Development (NICHD) Early Child Care Research Network. Child Outcomes When Child Center Classes Meet Recommended Standards for Quality. *Am J Public Health.* 1999;89:1072-77.

5. National Association for the Education of Young Children (NAEYC). *Accreditation and Criteria Procedures of the National Academy of Early Childhood Programs.* Washington, DC: NAEYC; 1998.

6. National Fire Protection Association (NFPA). *NFPA 101 Life Safety Code 2000 Edition.* Quincy, Mass: NFPA; 2000.

7. Bredekamp S, Copple C, eds. *Developmentally Appropriate Practice in Early Childhood Programs.* Rev ed. Washington, DC: National Association for the Education of Young Children (NAEYC); 1997.

8. Deitch S, ed. *Health in Day Care: A Manual for Health Care Professionals.* Elk Grove Village, Ill: American Academy of Pediatrics; 1987.

9. American Academy of Pediatrics. Drowning in infants, children and adolescents. *Pediatrics.* 1993;92:292-4.

10. Consumer Product Safety Commission (CPSC). *Safety Barrier Guidelines for House Pools.* Washington, DC: CPSC; 1994:362.

11. Equal Employment Opportunity Act, 42 USC § 2000 (1972).

12. American with Disabilities Act, 3 USC § 421 (1990).

13. Shore R. *Rethinking the Brain: New Insights into Early Development.* New York, NY: Families and Work Institute; 1997.

14. Posner JK, Vandele DL. After-school activities and the development of low income urban children: a longitudinal study. *Dev Psychol.* 1999;35:868-79.

15. Rosenthal R, Vandele DL. Quality of care at school-age child care programs: replicatable features, observed experiences, child perspectives, and parent perspectives. *Child Dev.* 1996;67:2434-5.

16. Howes C. Children's experiences in center-based child care as a function of teacher background and adult:child ratio. *Merrill-Palmer Q.* 1997;43:404-24.

17. Helburn S, ed. *Cost, Quality and Child Outcomes in Child Care Centers.* Denver, Colo: University of Colorado at Denver; 1995.

18. National Association for the Education of Young Children (NAEYC), Division of Early Childhood Council for Exceptional Children and National Board for Professional Teaching Standards. *Guidelines for Preparation of Early Childhood Professionals.* Washington, DC: NAEYC; 1996.

19. National Early Childhood Program Accreditation Commission, Inc. *National Early Childhood Program Accreditation, 1996.* Conyers, Ga: National Early Childhood Program Accreditation Commission, Inc; 1997.

20. Whitebrook M, Howes C, Phillips D. *Worthy Work, Unlivable Wages: The National Child Care Staffing Study, 1988-1997.* Washington, DC: Center for the Child Care Workforce; 1998.

21. Center for Child Care Workforce. *Creating Better Family Child Care Jobs: Model Work Standards.* Washington, DC: Center for Child Care Workforce; 1999.

22. Uline MS. Health promotion and injury prevention in a child development center. *J Pediatr Nurs.* 1997;12:148-54.

23. Kendrick AS, Kaufmann R, Messenger KP, eds. *Healthy Young Children: A Manual for Programs.* Washington, DC: National Association for the Education of Young Children; 1991.

24. Hale CM, Polder JA. *The ABC's of Safe and Healthy Child Care: A Handbook for Child Care Providers.* Atlanta, Ga: Centers for Disease Control and Prevention; 1997.

25. Gun W, Pinsky P, Sacks J, et al. Injury and poisoning in out-of-home child care and home care. *Amer J Dis Child.* 1991:779-81.

26. Azer S, Eldred D. *Training Requirements in Child Care Licensing Regulations.* Boston, Mass: Center for Career Development in Early Care and Education; 1998.

27. Owens C. *Rights in the Workplace: A Guide for Child Care Teachers.* Washington, DC: Worker Option Resource Center; 1997.

28. Holmes SJ, Morrow AL, Pickering LK. Child care practices and effects of social change on the epidemiology of infectious diseases and antibiotic resistance. *Epidemiol Rev.* 1996;18:100-28.

29. Thacker SB, Addiss DG, Goodman RA, et al. Infectious diseases and injuries in child day care: opportunities for healthier children. *JAMA.* 1993;269(21):2734-5.

30. Crowley AA. Health services in child care day care centers: a survey. *J Pediatr Health Care.* 1990;4(5):252-9.

31. London F. Nurse in day care. *Adv Clin Care.* 1990;5(2):14-5.

32. American Red Cross. *Health and Safety Services: Child Care Course.* Available at: *www.siteone.com/redcross/hscourses/fs3116.htm.* Accessed November 26, 2000.

33. Crowley AA. Child care health consultation: the Connecticut experience. *Matern Child Health J.* 2000;4(1):67-75.

34. Gratz RR, Claffey A. Adult health in child care: health status, behaviors and concerns of teachers, directors and family care providers. *Early Child Res Q.* 1996;11:243-267.

35. American Academy of Pediatrics (AAP). *Caring for Our Children Video Series.* Elk Grove Village, Ill: AAP; 1996.

36. Wheelock College, The Family Child Care Accreditation Project. *Quality Standards for the National Association of Family Child Care (NAFCC) Accreditation.* Des Moines, Iowa: NAFCC; 1999.

37. Gratz R, Boulton P. Health considerations for pregnant child care staff. *J Pediatr Health Care.* 1994;8:18-26.

38. Stevens, PB, Dunn, KA. Use of cardiopulmonary resuscitation by North Carolina day care providers. *J School Health.* 1994;64:381-383.

CHAPTER 2

Program: Activities for Healthy Development

2.1 PROGRAM OF DEVELOPMENTAL ACTIVITIES

GENERAL PROGRAM ACTIVITIES

STANDARD 2.001
WRITTEN DAILY ACTIVITY PLAN AND STATEMENT OF PRINCIPLES

Facilities shall establish and implement a written, planned program of daily activities based on the child's individual development at each stage of early childhood. The objective of the program of daily activities shall be to foster incremental developmental progress.

Centers shall develop a written statement of principles that sets out the basic elements from which the daily program is to be built. An annual review of the written statement of principles guiding program development shall engage all staff. The elements to be included are those specified in the current edition of *Caring for Our Children, the National Health and Safety Performance Standards: Guidelines for Out-of-Home Child Care Programs*.

RATIONALE: Reviews of children's performance after attending out-of-home child care indicate that children attending facilities with well-developed curricula achieve appropriate levels of development (1, 2).

Early childhood specialists agree on the:
a) Inseparability of cognitive, physical, emotional, and social development;
b) Influence of the child's health on all these areas;
c) Central importance of continuity of affectionate care;
d) Relevance of the phase or stage concept;
e) Importance of action (including play) as a mode of learning (3).

Those who provide child care and education must be clear about the curriculum they are implementing.

All facilities need a written description of the planned program of daily activities so staff and parents can have a common understanding and ability to compare the program's actual performance to the stated intent. Child care is a "delivery of service" involving a contractual relationship between the provider and the consumer. A written plan helps to define the service and contributes to specific and responsible operations that are conducive to sound child development and safety practices and to positive consumer relations. In centers, because more than two child care staff members are involved in operating the facility, a written statement of principles helps achieve consensus about the basic elements from which all staff will plan the daily program. Caregivers need to be properly trained to develop and implement an effective plan.

Plans can ensure that some thought goes into programming for children. They also allow for monitoring and accountability. A written plan can provide a basis for staff orientation.

COMMENTS: The *NAEYC Accreditation Criteria and Procedures*, the National Association for Family Child Care (NAFCC) accreditation standards and the National Child Care Association (NCCA) standards can serve as resources. Contact information for the National Association for the Education of Young Children (NAEYC), NAFCC, and NCCA is located in Appendix BB.

TYPE OF FACILITY: *Center; Large Family Child Care Home; Small Family Child Care Home*

STANDARD 2.002
PROGRAM OF ACTIVITIES INCLUDING SPECIAL INTERVENTIONS

Facilities shall have a Program of Activities to include special interventions for children with any special restriction(s) of activities.

RATIONALE: All care facilities benefit from a regular activity schedule. For the child with special needs, an individualized education program or an individualized family service plan is required by the IDEA. The child's plan for care in an inclusive setting shall include activities with the other children at the facility as part of the child's regularly scheduled activities.

COMMENTS: Children with special needs will be participating in activities, adapted to their abilities, with peers, but may have some separately scheduled activities that may be required to implement the child's Individualized Education Program (IEP).

TYPE OF FACILITY: *Center; Large Family Child Care Home; Small Family Child Care Home*

STANDARD 2.003
CONTENT OF FACILITY ACTIVITIES

The facility's activities shall include:
a) Both structured and unstructured times;
b) Both teacher-directed and child-initiated experiences;
c) Family involvement activities.

RATIONALE: A planned but flexible program that allows children to make decisions about their activities fosters independence and creative expression. The facility shall implement its program effectively.

TYPE OF FACILITY: *Center; Large Family Child Care Home; Small Family Child Care Home*

STANDARD 2.004
HELPING FAMILIES COPE WITH SEPARATION

The staff of the facility shall help the child and parents cope with the experience of separation and loss.

For the child, this shall be accomplished by:
a) Encouraging parents to spend time in the facility with the child;
b) Enabling the child to bring to child care tangible reminders of home/family (such as a favorite toy or a picture of self and parent);
c) Helping the child to play out themes of separation and reunion;
d) Frequently exchanging information between the child's parents and caregivers, including activities and routine care information;
e) Reassuring the child about the parent's return;
f) Ensuring that the caregiver(s) are consistent both within the parts of a day and across days.

For the parents, this shall be accomplished by:
a) Validating their feelings as a universal human experience;
b) Providing parents with information about the positive effects for children of high quality facilities with strong parent participation;
c) Encouraging parents to discuss their feelings;
d) Providing parents with evidence, such as photographs, that their child is being cared for and is enjoying the activities of the facility.

RATIONALE: In childhood, some separation experiences facilitate psychological growth by mobilizing new approaches for learning and adaptation. Other separations are painful and traumatic. The way in which influential adults provide support and understanding, or fail to do so, will shape the child's experience (4).

Many parents who prefer to care for their young children only at home may have no other option than to place their children in out-of-home child care before 6 weeks of age, because many employers do not provide parental leave. In most other industrialized countries (such as France, Sweden, Norway, Finland, Denmark, and Holland) family leave with pay is available for a minimum of 6 months and can be taken by either mother or father or in some combination. Some parents prefer combining out-of-home child care with parental care to provide good experiences for their children and support for other family members to function most effectively. Whether parents view out-of-home child care as a necessary accommodation to undesired circumstances or a benefit for their family, parents and their children need help from the child care staff to accommodate the transitions between home and out-of-home settings.

Many parents experience pain at separation. For most parents, the younger their child and the less experience they have had with sharing the care of their children with others, the more intense their pain at separation.

COMMENTS: Depending on the child's developmental stage, the impact of separation on the child and parent will vary. Child care facilities should understand and communicate this variation to parents and work with parents to plan developmentally

appropriate coping strategies for use at home and in the child care setting. For example, a child at 18 to 24 months of age is particularly vulnerable to separation stress. Entry into child care at this age may trigger behavior problems, such as difficulty sleeping. Even for the child who has adapted well to a child care arrangement before this developmental stage, such difficulties can occur as the child continues in care and enters this developmental stage. For younger children, who are working on understanding object permanence (usually around 9 to 12 months of age), parents who sneak out after bringing their children to the child care facility may create some level of anxiety in the child throughout the day. Sneaking away leaves the child unable to discern when someone the child trusts will leave without warning.

TYPE OF FACILITY: *Center; Large Family Child Care Home; Small Family Child Care Home*

STANDARD 2.005
TOILET LEARNING/TRAINING

The facility shall develop and implement a plan that teaches each child how and when to use the toilet. Toilet learning/training, when initiated, shall follow a prescribed, sequential plan that is developed and coordinated with the parent's plan for implementation in the home environment and shall be based on the child's developmental level rather than chronological age.

To help children achieve bowel and bladder control, caregivers shall enable children to take an active role in using the toilet when they are physically able to do so and when parents support their children's learning to use the toilet. Caregivers shall take into account the preferences and customs of the child's family.

For children who have not yet learned to use the toilet, the facility shall defer toilet learning/training until the child's family is ready to support this learning and the child demonstrates:

a) An understanding of the concept of cause and effect;
b) An ability to communicate;
c) The physical ability to remain dry for up to 2 hours.

For school-age children, toilet learning/training shall include frequent opportunities to use the toilet and an emphasis on appropriate handwashing after using the toilet.

Children with special needs may require specific instructions or precautions.

RATIONALE: A child's achievement of motor and intellectual or developmental skills may be advanced or delayed, depending on the child's abilities, primary disability, or combination of disabilities. The child may not be socially or emotionally ready to learn how to use the toilet, despite the emergence of other skills. Caregivers should enable children to take an active part in controlling the functions of their bodies in a manner that gives them a sense of pride and confidence (27, 28).

Toilet learning/training is achieved more rapidly once a child is toilet scheduled and demands from adults across environments are consistent. The family may not be prepared, at the time, to extend this learning/ training into the home environment.

School-age children may not respond when their bodies signal a need to use the toilet because they are involved in activities or embarrassed about needing to use the toilet. Holding back stool or urine can lead to constipation and urinary tract problems. Also, unless reminded, many children forget to wash their hands after toileting.

COMMENTS: The area of toilet learning/training for children with special needs is difficult because there are no age-related, disability-specific rules to follow. As a result, support and counseling for parents and caregivers are required to help them deal with this issue. Some children with multiple disabilities do not demonstrate any requisite skills other than being dry for a few hours. Establishing a toilet routine may be the first step toward learning to use the toilet and at the same time improving hygiene and skin care.

Cultural expectations of toilet learning/training need to be recognized and respected.

For more information on toilet learning/training, see *Tiolet Training/Learning: Guideline for Parents*, available

from the American Academy of Pediatrics (AAP). Contact information is located in Appendix BB.

See also Toilets and Toilet Training Equipment, STANDARD 5.116 through STANDARD 5.124; and Sanitation, Disinfection, and Maintenance of Toilet Learning/Training Equipment, Toilets, and Bathrooms, STANDARD 3.029 through STANDARD 3.033.

TYPE OF FACILITY: *Center; Large Family Child Care Home; Small Family Child Care Home*

STANDARD 2.006
COMMUNICATION IN NATIVE LANGUAGE

At least one member of the staff shall be able to communicate in the native language of the parents and children, or the facility shall work with parents to arrange for a translator to communicate with parents and children.

RATIONALE: The future development of the child depends on his/her command of language (5). Richness of language increases as a result of experiences as well as through the child's verbal interaction with adults and peers. Basic communication with parents and children requires an ability to speak their language.

TYPE OF FACILITY: *Center; Large Family Child Care Home; Small Family Child Care Home*

STANDARD 2.007
DIVERSITY IN ENROLLMENT AND CURRICULUM

Facilities shall work to increase understanding of cultural, ethnic, and other differences by enrolling children who reflect the cultural and ethnic diversity of the community and by providing cultural curricula that engages children and teaches multicultural learning activities.

RATIONALE: Children who participate in programs that reflect and show respect for the cultural diversity of their communities learn to understand and value

cultural diversity. This learning in early childhood enables their healthy participation in a democratic pluralistic society throughout life (6, 7, 8). By facilitating the expression of cultural development or ethnic identity and by encouraging familiarity with different groups and practices through ordinary interaction and activities integrated into a developmentally appropriate curriculum, a facility can foster children's ability to relate to people who are different from themselves, their sense of possibility, and their ability to succeed in a diverse society, while also promoting feelings of belonging and identification with a tradition.

COMMENTS: The facility might celebrate holidays and other events of the cultural and ethnic groups in the community to provide opportunities to introduce children to a range of customs and beliefs. Materials, displays, and learning activities must represent the cultural heritage of the children and the staff to instill a sense of pride and positive feelings of identification in all children and staff members. In order to enroll a diverse group, the facility should market its services in a culturally sensitive way and should make sincere efforts to employ staff members that represent the culture of the children and their families. Children need to see members of their own community in positions of influence in the services they use.

TYPE OF FACILITY: *Center; Large Family Child Care Home; Small Family Child Care Home*

STANDARD 2.008
VERBAL INTERACTION

The child care facility shall assure that each child has at least one speaking adult person who engages the child in verbal exchanges linked to daily events and experiences. To encourage the development of language, the caregiver shall demonstrate skillful verbal communication and interaction with the child.
*   For infants, these interactions shall include
*   responses to, and encouragement of, soft infant sounds, as well as naming of objects by the caregiver.
*   For toddlers, the interactions shall include naming of objects and actions and supporting, but not forcing, the child to do the same.

• For preschool and school-age children, inter-actions shall include respectful listening and responses to what the child has to say, ampli-fying and clarifying the child's intent.

RATIONALE: Conversation with adults is one of the main channels through which children learn about themselves, others, and the world in which they live. While adults speaking to children teach the children facts and relay information, the social and emotional communications and the atmosphere of the exchange are equally important. Reciprocity of expression, response, the initiation and enrichment of dialogue are hallmarks of the social function and significance of the conversations (9, 10, 11, 25).

The future development of the child depends on his/her command of language (5). Richness of the child's language increases as it is nurtured by verbal interac-tions and learning experiences with adults and peers. Basic communication with parents and children requires an ability to speak their language.

TYPE OF FACILITY: *Center; Large Family Child Care Home; Small Family Child Care Home*

STANDARD 2.009
PLAYING OUTDOORS

Children shall play outdoors daily when weather and air quality conditions do not pose a significant health risk. Outdoor play for infants may include riding in a carriage or stroller; however, infants shall be offered opportunities for gross motor play outdoors, as well.

Weather that poses a significant health risk shall include wind chill at or below 15 degrees F and heat index at or above 90 degrees F, as identified by the National Weather Service.

Air quality conditions that pose a significant health risk shall be identified by announcements from local health authorities or through ozone (smog) alerts. Such air quality conditions shall require that children remain indoors where air conditioners ventilate indoor air to the outdoors. Children with respiratory health problems such as asthma shall not play outdoors when local health authorities

announce that the air quality is approaching unhealthy levels.

Children shall be protected from the sun by using shade, sun-protective clothing, and sunscreen with UVB-ray and UVA-ray protection of SPF-15 or higher, with permission as described in STAN-DARD 3.081, during outdoor play. Before pro-longed physical activity in warm weather, children shall be well-hydrated and shall be encouraged to drink water during the activity. In warm weather, children's clothing shall be light-colored, light-weight, and limited to one layer of absorbent material to facilitate the evaporation of sweat. Children shall wear sun-protective clothing, such as hats, long-sleeved shirts and pants, when playing outdoors between the hours of 10 AM and 2 PM.

In cold weather, children's clothing shall be layered and dry. Caregivers shall check children's extremi-ties for maintenance of normal color and warmth at least every 15 minutes when children are out-doors in cold weather.

RATIONALE: Outdoor play is not only an opportu-nity for learning in a different environment; it also provides many health benefits. Generally, infectious disease organisms are less concentrated in outdoor air than indoor air. Light exposure of the skin to sun-light promotes the production of Vitamin D that growing children require. Open spaces in outdoor areas, even those confined to screened rooftops in urban play spaces encourage children to develop gross motor skills and fine motor play in ways that are difficult to duplicate indoors. Nevertheless, some weather conditions make outdoor play hazardous.

Caregivers must protect children from adverse weather and air quality. Wind chill conditions that pose a risk of frostbite as well as heat and humidity that pose a significant risk of heat-related illness are defined by the National Weather Service and are announced routinely. The federal government has established health standards for a number of air pol-lutants. Child care providers must use this informa-tion appropriately.

Heat-induced illness and cold injury are preventable. Children have greater surface area-to-body mass ratio than adults. Therefore, children do not adapt to extremes of temperature as effectively as adults when exposed to a high climatic heat stress or to cold. Children produce more metabolic heat per mass unit than adults when walking or running. They also have a lower sweating capacity and cannot dissipate body heat by evaporation as effectively (87).

COMMENTS: The Iowa Department of Public Health, Healthy Child Care Iowa has prepared a convenient color-coded guide for child care providers to use to determine which weather conditions are comfortable for outdoor play, which require caution, and which are dangerous. This guide is available on the website for the Iowa Department of Public Health at http://www.idph.state.ia.us/fch/fam-serv/HCCI/products/weatherwatch.pdf. The federal Clean Air Act requires that the Environmental Protection Agency (EPA) establish ambient air quality health standards. Most local health departments monitor weather and air quality in their jurisdiction and make appropriate announcements.

To access the latest weather information and warnings, contact the National Weather Service. Contact information is located in Appendix BB.

See STANDARD 3.081 for information on requirements for applying sunscreen.

TYPE OF FACILITY: *Center; Large Family Child Care Home; Small Family Child Care Home*

PROGRAM ACTIVITIES FROM BIRTH TO 35 MONTHS

STANDARD 2.010
PERSONAL CAREGIVER RELATIONSHIPS FOR INFANTS AND TODDLERS

Opportunities shall be provided for each child to develop a personal and affectionate relationship with, and attachment to, that child's parents and one or a small number of caregivers whose care for and responsiveness to the child ensure relief of distress, experiences of comfort and stimulation, and satisfaction of the need for a personal relationship. The facility shall limit the number of care-

givers who interact with any one infant to no more than three caregivers in a given day and no more than five caregivers across the period that the child is an infant in child care. The caregivers shall:
a) Hold and comfort children who are upset;
b) Engage in social interchanges such as smiling, talking, touching, singing, and eating;
c) Be play partners as well as protectors;
d) Attune to children's feelings and reflect them back.

RATIONALE: Trustworthy adults who give of themselves as they provide care and learning experiences play a key role in a child's development as an active, self-knowing, self-respecting, thinking, feeling, and loving person (9). Limiting the number of adults with whom an infant interacts fosters reciprocal understanding of communication cues that are unique to each child. This leads to a sense of trust of the adult by the infant that the infant's needs will be understood and met promptly (88, 89). Studies of infant behavior show that infants have difficulty forming trusting relationships in settings where many adults interact with a child, e.g., in hospitalization of infants when shifts of adults provide care. This difficulty occurs even if each of the many adults are very caring in their interaction with the child. Assigning a consistent caregiver to an eight-hour shift in such settings has been observed to help. This limits the number of different adults with whom the child interacts in a three to 24-hour period (90, 91).

COMMENTS: Kissing, hugging, holding, and cuddling infants and children are expressions of wholesome love that should be encouraged. Caregivers should be advised that it is all right to demonstrate affection for children of both sexes. At all times, caregivers should respect the wishes of children, regardless of their ages, with regard to physical contact and their comfort or discomfort with it. Caregivers should avoid even "friendly contact" (such as touching the shoulder or arm) with a child if the child is uncomfortable with it. This is especially true of school-age children (12).

TYPE OF FACILITY: *Center; Large Family Child Care Home; Small Family Child Care Home*

STANDARD 2.011
INTERACTIONS WITH INFANTS AND TODDLERS

Caregivers shall talk, listen to, and otherwise interact with young infants as they feed, change, and cuddle them.

RATIONALE: Richness of language increases by nurturing it through verbal interactions between the child and adults and peers. Adults' speech is one of the main channels through which children learn about themselves, others, and the world in which they live. While adults speaking to children teach the children facts, the social and emotional communications and the atmosphere of the exchange are equally important. Reciprocity of expression, response, the initiation and enrichment of dialogue are hallmarks of the social function and significance of the conversations (9, 10, 11, 25).

The future development of the child depends on his/her command of language (5). Richness of language increases as it is nurtured by verbal interactions of the child with adults and peers. Basic communication with parents and children requires an ability to speak their language.

COMMENTS: Live, real-time interaction with caregivers is preferred. For example, caregivers' naming objects or singing rhymes to all children supports language development. Children's stories and poems presented on recordings with a fixed speed for sing-along can actually interfere with a child's ability to participate in the singing or recitation. The pace will be too fast for some children, and the activity will have to be repeated for the child to learn it.

TYPE OF FACILITY: *Center; Large Family Child Care Home; Small Family Child Care Home*

STANDARD 2.012
SPACE AND ACTIVITY TO SUPPORT LEARNING OF INFANTS AND TODDLERS

The facility shall provide a safe and clean space, both indoors and outdoors, and colorful material and equipment arranged to support learning. The facility shall provide opportunities for the child to act upon the environment by experiencing age-appropriate obstacles, frustrations, and risks in order to learn to manage inner feelings and resources, as well as the occurrences and demands of the outer world. The facility shall provide opportunities for play that:
- Lessen the child's anxiety and help the child adapt to reality and resolve conflicts;
- Enable the child to explore the real world;
- Help the child practice resolving conflicts;
- Use symbols (words, numbers, and letters);
- Manipulate objects;
- Exercise physical skills;
- Encourage language development;
- Foster self-expression;
- Strengthen the child's identity as a member of a family and a cultural community.

RATIONALE: Opportunities to be an active learner are vitally important for the development of motor competence and awareness of one's own body and person, the development of sensory motor intelligence, the ability and motivation to use physical and mental initiative, and feelings of mastery and successful coping. Coping involves original, imaginative, and innovative behavior as well as previously learned strategies.

Learning to resolve conflicts constructively in childhood is essential in preventing violence later in life (13, 14). A physical and social environment that offers opportunities for active mastery and coping enhances the child's adaptive abilities (15, 16). The importance of play for developing cognitive skills, for maintaining an affective and intellectual equilibrium, and for creating and testing new capacities is well recognized. Play involves a balance of action and symbolization, and of feeling and thinking (17, 18, 19).

For more information regarding appropriate play materials for young children, see *Which Toy for Which Child: A Consumer's Guide for Selecting Suitable Toys* from the U.S. Consumer Product Safety Commission (CPSC) and *The Right Stuff for Children Birth to 8: Selecting Play Materials to Support Development* from National Association for the Education of Young Children (NAEYC). Contact information for the CPSC and the NAEYC is located in Appendix BB.

TYPE OF FACILITY: *Center; Large Family Child Care Home; Small Family Child Care Home*

STANDARD 2.013
SEPARATION OF INFANTS AND TODDLERS FROM OLDER CHILDREN

Except in family style, small, closed groups of mixed aged children, infants and toddlers younger than 3 years of age shall be cared for in a closed room(s) that separates them from older children.

In facilities caring for three or more children younger than 3 years of age, activities that bring children younger than 3 years of age in contact with older children shall be prohibited, unless the younger children already have regular contact with the older children as part of a group or because of pooling of children during early morning arrivals or late afternoon departures.

Caregivers of infants shall not be responsible for the care of older children who are not a part of the infants' closed child care group.

Groups of infants shall receive care in closed room(s) that separate them from other groups of infants and older children.

RATIONALE: Infants need quiet, calm environments, away from the stimulation of older children and other groups. Younger infants should be cared for in rooms separate from the more boisterous toddlers. In addition to these developmental needs of infants, separation is important for reasons of disease prevention. Rates of hospitalization for all forms of acute infectious respiratory tract diseases are highest during the first year of life, indicating that respiratory tract illness becomes less severe as the child gets older. Therefore, infants should be a focus for interventions to reduce the incidence of respiratory tract diseases.

COMMENTS: This separation of younger children from older children ideally should be implemented in all facilities but may be less feasible in small or large family child care homes. Although a group of children of different ages receiving care together from one or two caregivers may increase this risk of transmission of infection among members of the group, the developmental and curricular advantage of mixed age groupings may offset this risk.

Separation of groups of children by low partitions that divide a single common space without sound attenuation or control of interactions among the caregivers who are working with different groups is not acceptable. This arrangement essentially combines the separate smaller groups into a large group. When partitions are used, they must control interaction between groups and control sound transmission. The acoustic controls should limit significant transmission of sound from one group's activity into other group environments.

TYPE OF FACILITY: *Center*

PROGRAM ACTIVITIES FOR 3- TO 5-YEAR-OLDS

STANDARD 2.014
PERSONAL CAREGIVER RELATIONSHIPS FOR 3- TO 5-YEAR-OLDS

Facilities shall provide opportunities for each child to build long-term, trusting relationships with a few caring caregivers by limiting the number of adults the facility permits to care for any one child in child care to a maximum of 8 adults in a given year and no more than 3 in a day.

RATIONALE: Children learn best from adults who know and respect them; who act as guides, facilitators, and supporters of a rich learning environment; and with whom they have established a trusting relationship (20, 21). When the facility allows too many adults to be involved in the child's care, the child does not develop a reciprocal, sustained, responsive, trusting relationship with any of them.

Children should have continuous friendly and trusting relationships with several caregivers who are reasonably consistent within the child care facility. Young children can extract from these relationships a sense of themselves with a capacity for forming trusting relationships and self-esteem. Relationships are fragmented by rapid staff turnover or if the child is frequently moved from one child care facility to another.

COMMENTS: Compliance should be measured by staff and parent interviews. Turnover of staff lowers the quality of the facility. High quality facilities maintain low turnover through their wage policies, training and support for staff (22).

TYPE OF FACILITY: *Center; Large Family Child Care Home; Small Family Child Care Home*

STANDARD 2.015
OPPORTUNITIES FOR LEARNING FOR 3- TO 5-YEAR-OLDS

Facilities shall provide opportunities for children to observe, explore, order and reorder, make mistakes and find solutions, and move from the concrete to the abstract in learning.

RATIONALE: The most meaningful learning has its source in the child's self-initiated activities. The learning environment that supports individual differences, learning styles, abilities, and cultural values fosters confidence and curiosity in learners (20, 21).

TYPE OF FACILITY: *Center; Large Family Child Care Home; Small Family Child Care Home*

STANDARD 2.016
SELECTION OF EQUIPMENT FOR 3- TO 5-YEAR-OLDS

The facility shall select, for both indoor and outdoor play, developmentally appropriate equipment, for safety, for its ability to provide large and small motor experiences, and for its adaptability to serve many different ideas, functions, and forms of creative expression.

RATIONALE: An aesthetic, orderly, appropriately stimulating, child-oriented environment contributes to the preschooler's sense of well-being and control (23).

COMMENTS: See also Play Equipment, STANDARD 5.081 through STANDARD 5.092.

TYPE OF FACILITY: *Center; Large Family Child Care Home; Small Family Child Care Home*

STANDARD 2.017
EXPRESSIVE ACTIVITIES FOR 3- TO 5-YEAR-OLDS

Caregivers shall encourage and enhance expressive activities that include play, painting, drawing, story telling, music, singing, dancing, and dramatic play.

RATIONALE: Expressive activities are vehicles for socialization, conflict resolution, and language development. They are, in addition, vital energizers and organizers for cognitive development. Stifling the preschooler's need to play damages a natural integration of thinking and feeling (24).

TYPE OF FACILITY: *Center; Large Family Child Care Home; Small Family Child Care Home*

STANDARD 2.018
FOSTERING COOPERATION OF 3- TO 5-YEAR-OLDS

Facilities shall foster a cooperative rather than a competitive atmosphere.

RATIONALE: As 3-, 4-, and 5-year-olds play and work together, they shift from almost total dependence on the adult to seeking support from peers. The rules and responsibilities of a well-functioning group help children of this age to internalize impulse control and to become increasingly responsible for managing their behavior. A dynamic curriculum designed to include the ideas and values of a broad socioeconomic group of children will promote socialization. The inevitable clashes and disagreements are more easily resolved when there is a positive influence of the group on each child (19).

COMMENTS: Encouraging verbal skills and attentiveness to the needs of individuals and the group as a whole supports a cooperative atmosphere.

TYPE OF FACILITY: *Center; Large Family Child Care Home; Small Family Child Care Home*

STANDARD 2.019
FOSTERING LANGUAGE DEVELOPMENT OF 3- TO 5-YEAR-OLDS

The facility shall be rich in first-hand experiences that offer opportunities for language development. Facilities shall also have an abundance of books of fantasy, fiction, and nonfiction, and provide chances for the children to relate stories. Caregivers shall foster language development by:
a)   Speaking with children rather than at them;
b)   Encouraging children to talk with each other by helping them to listen and respond;
c)   Giving children models of verbal expression;
d)   Reading books about the child's culture and history, which would serve to help the child develop a sense of self;
e)   Listening respectfully when children speak.

RATIONALE: Language reflects and shapes thinking. A curriculum created to match preschoolers' needs and interests enhances language skills. First-hand experiences encourage children to talk with each other and with adults, to seek, develop, and use increasingly more complex vocabulary, and to use language to express thinking, feeling, and curiosity (10, 25).

COMMENTS: Compliance should be measured by structured observation. Examples of verbal encouragement of verbal expression are: "Ask Johnny if you may play with him"; "Tell him you don't like being hit"; "Tell Sara what you saw downtown yesterday"; "Tell Mommy about what you and Johnny played this morning." These encouraging statements should be followed by respectful listening, without pressuring the child to speak.

TYPE OF FACILITY: *Center; Large Family Child Care Home; Small Family Child Care Home*

STANDARD 2.020
BODY MASTERY FOR 3- TO 5-YEAR-OLDS

The facility shall offer children opportunities to learn about their bodies and how their bodies function in the context of socializing with others. Caregivers shall support the children in their curiosity and body mastery, consistent with parental expectations and cultural preferences. Body mastery includes feeding oneself, learning how to use the toilet, running, skipping, climbing, balan-cing, playing with peers, displaying affection, and using and manipulating space.

Autoerotic or masturbatory activity shall be ignored unless it is excessive, interferes with other activities, or is noticed by other children, in which case the caregiver shall make a brief non-judgmental comment that touching of private body parts feels good, but is usually done in a private place. After making such a comment, the caregiver shall offer friendly assistance in going on to other activities.

RATIONALE: Achieving the pleasure and gratification of feeling physically competent on a voluntary basis is a basic component of developing self-esteem and the ability to socialize with adults and other children inside and outside the family (12, 15, 16, 20, 21, 24, 26).

TYPE OF FACILITY: *Center; Large Family Child Care Home; Small Family Child Care Home*

STANDARD 2.021
HEALTH, NUTRITION AND SAFETY AWARENESS FOR 3- TO 5-YEAR-OLDS

Facilities shall address health, nutrition, and safety awareness as an integral part of the overall program.

Child care centers shall have written program plans addressing the health and/or nutrition, and safety aspects of each formally structured activity documented in the written curriculum.

RATIONALE: The curriculum that best meets the needs of preschool children is one in which the daily events of living together provide the raw materials for an integrated approach. Young children learn better through experiencing an activity and observing behavior than through didactic training (80). There may be a reciprocal relationship between learning and play so that play experiences are closely related to learning (17, 18). Children can accept and enforce rules about health and safety when they have personal experience of why these rules were created.

TYPE OF FACILITY: *Center; Large Family Child Care Home; Small Family Child Care Home*

PROGRAM ACTIVITIES FOR SCHOOL-AGE CHILDREN

STANDARD 2.022
SUPERVISED SCHOOL-AGE ACTIVITIES

The facility shall have a program of supervised activities designed especially for school-age children, to include:
a) Free choice of play;
b) Opportunities to develop physical fitness through a program of focused activity;
c) Opportunities for concentration, alone or in a group;
d) Time to read or do homework;
e) Opportunities to be creative, to explore the arts, sciences, and social studies, and to solve problems;
f) Opportunities for community service experience (museums, library, leadership development, senior citizen homes, etc.);
g) Opportunities for adult-supervised skill-building and self-development groups, such as scouts, team sports, and club activities (as transportation, distance, and parental permission allow).

RATIONALE: Programs organized for older children after school or during vacation time should meet the needs of these children for recreation, responsible completion of school work, expanding their interests, learning cultural sensitivity, exploring community resources, and practicing pro-social skills (31, 32).

COMMENTS: For more information on school-age standards, see The *NSACA Standards for Quality School-Age Care*, available from the National School-Age Care Alliance (NSACA). Contact information is located in Appendix BB.

TYPE OF FACILITY: *Center; Large Family Child Care Home; Small Family Child Care Home*

STANDARD 2.023
SPACE FOR SCHOOL-AGE ACTIVITY

The facility shall provide a space for indoor and outdoor activities for children in school-age child care.

RATIONALE: A safe and secure environment that fosters the growing independence of school-age children is essential for their development (33, 34).

TYPE OF FACILITY: *Center; Large Family Child Care Home; Small Family Child Care Home*

STANDARD 2.024
DEVELOPING RELATIONSHIPS FOR SCHOOL-AGE CHILDREN

The facility shall offer opportunities to school-age children for developing trusting,, supportive relationships with the staff and with peers.

RATIONALE: Although school-age children need more independent experiences, they continue to need the guidance and support of adults. Peer relationships take on increasing importance for this age group.

TYPE OF FACILITY: *Center; Large Family Child Care Home; Small Family Child Care Home*

STANDARD 2.025
PLANNING ACTIVITIES FOR SCHOOL-AGE CHILDREN

The facility shall offer a program based on the needs and interests of the age group, as well as of the individuals within it. Children shall participate in planning the program activities.

RATIONALE: A child care facility for school-age children should provide an enriching contrast to the formal school program. Facilities that offer a wide range of activities (such as team sports, cooking, dramatics, art, music, crafts, games, open time, quiet time, use of community resources) allow children to explore new interests and relationships.

TYPE OF FACILITY: *Center; Large Family Child Care Home; Small Family Child Care Home*

STANDARD 2.026
COMMUNITY OUTREACH FOR SCHOOL-AGE CHILDREN

The facility shall provide opportunities for and engage with community outreach and involvement of school-age children, such as field trips and community improvement projects.

RATIONALE: As the world of the school-age child encompasses the larger community, facility activities should reflect this stage of development. Field trips and other opportunities to explore the community should enrich the child's experience.

TYPE OF FACILITY: *Center; Large Family Child Care Home; Small Family Child Care Home*

STANDARD 2.027
COMMUNICATION BETWEEN CHILD CARE AND SCHOOL

Facilities that accept school-age children directly from school shall devise a system of communication with the child's school teacher.

RATIONALE: Activities that have gone on during the day may be important in anticipating and understanding children's after-school behavior. The connection between children's school learning experience and their out-of-school activities is important.

COMMENTS: This communication may be facilitated by providing a notebook that is passed between the child care facility and child's teacher. The child's teacher and a staff member from the facility should meet at least once to exchange telephone numbers and to offer a contact in the event relevant information needs to be shared.

TYPE OF FACILITY: *Center; Large Family Child Care Home; Small Family Child Care Home*

2.2 SUPERVISION

STANDARD 2.028
METHODS OF SUPERVISION

Caregivers shall directly supervise infants, toddlers, and preschool children by sight and hearing at all times, even when the children are in sleeping areas. Caregivers shall not be on one floor level of the building, while children are on another floor.

School-age children shall be permitted to participate in activities off the premises with written approval by a parent and by the caregiver.

Caregivers shall regularly count children on a scheduled basis, at every transition, and whenever leaving one area and arriving at another, to confirm the safe whereabouts of every child at all times.

Developmentally appropriate child:staff ratios shall be met during all hours of operation, including indoor and outdoor play and field trips, following precautions for specific areas and equipment. No center-based facility shall operate with fewer than two staff members if more than six children are in care, even if the group otherwise meets the child:staff ratio. Although centers often downsize the number of staff for the early arrival and late

departure times, another adult must be present to help in the event of an emergency. The supervision policies of centers and large family child care homes shall be written policies.

RATIONALE: Supervision is basic to the prevention of harm. Parents have a contract with caregivers to supervise their children. To be available for supervision or rescue in an emergency, an adult must be able to hear and see the children. In case of fire, a supervising adult should not need to climb stairs or use a ramp or an elevator. These changes in elevation usually become unusable because they are the pathways for smoke.

Children who are presumed to be sleeping might be awake and in need of adult attention. Risk-taking behavior must be detected; and illness, fear, or other stressful behavior must be managed.

Children like to test their skills and abilities. This is particularly noticeable around playground equipment. Even if the highest safety standards for playground layout, design and surfacing are met, serious injuries can happen if children are left unsupervised. Adults who are involved, aware, and appreciative of young children's behaviors are in the best position to safeguard their well-being. Active and positive supervision involves:
a) Knowing each child's abilities;
b) Establishing clear and simple safety rules;
c) Being aware of potential safety hazards;
d) Standing in a strategic position;
e) Scanning play activities and circulating;
f) Focusing on the positive rather than the negative to teach a child what is safe for the child and other children.

Children should be protected against sexual abuse by limiting situations in which a caregiver, other adult, or an older child is left alone with a child in care without another adult present. See STANDARD 3.059, for additional information regarding safe physical layouts for child care facilities.

Many instances have been reported where a child has hidden when the group was moving to another location, or where the child wandered off when a door was opened for another purpose. Regular counting of

children will alert the staff to begin a search before the child gets too far or into trouble.

Counting children routinely is without substitute in assuring that a child has not slipped into an unobserved location.

COMMENTS: Caregivers should record the count on an attendance sheet or on a pocket card, along with notations of any children joining or leaving the group. Caregivers should do the counts before the group leaves an area and when the group enters a new area. The facility should assign and reassign counting responsibility as needed to maintain a counting routine. Facilities might consider counting systems such as using a reminder tone on a watch or musical clock that sounds at timed intervals (about every 15 minutes) to help the staff remember to count.

Older preschool children and school-age children may use toilet facilities without direct visual observation.

The staff should assess the setting to ascertain how the ability to see and hear child activities might be improved. The use of devices such as convex mirrors to assure visibility around corners, and baby monitors for older preschool and school-age children, who use the toilet by themselves, may be considered. Facilities might also consider the use of surveillance devices or systems placed strategically in areas where they might contribute further to child safety. In addition, these systems are beneficial because they can allow parents to observe the facility; and caregivers can use them as support in the event of an accusation of abuse.

Planning must include advance assignments to maintain appropriate staffing. Sufficient staff must be maintained to evacuate the children safely in case of emergency. Compliance with proper child:staff ratios should be measured by structured observation, by counting caregivers and children in each group at varied times of the day, and by reviewing written policies.

For additional information on supervision, see STANDARD 5.117, on children using toilet learning/ training equipment.

TYPE OF FACILITY: *Center; Large Family Child Care Home; Small Family Child Care Home*

2.3 TRANSPORTATION

STANDARD 2.029
COMPETENCE AND TRAINING OF TRANSPORTATION STAFF

At least one adult who accompanies or drives children for field trips and out-of-facility activities shall receive training by a professional knowledgeable about child development and procedures to ensure the safety of all children. The caregiver shall hold a valid pediatric first aid certificate, including rescue breathing and management of blocked airways, as specified in First Aid and CPR, STANDARD 1.026 through STANDARD 1.028.

All drivers, passenger monitors, chaperones, and assistants shall receive instructions in safety precautions. If transportation is provided, these instructions shall include:
a) Use of developmentally appropriate safety restraints;
b) Proper placement of the child in the motor vehicle;
c) Handling of emergency situations. If a child has a chronic medical condition that could result in an emergency (such as asthma, diabetes, seizures), the driver or chaperone shall have written instructions including parent emergency contacts, child summary health information, special needs, and treatment plans, and shall be trained to;
   1) Recognize the signs of a medical emergency;
   2) Know emergency procedures to follow;
   3) Have on-hand, any emergency supplies or medications necessary;
d) Map and appropriate route to emergency facility;
e) Defensive driving;
f) Child supervision during transport, including never leaving a child unattended in a vehicle.

The receipt of such instructions shall be documented in a personnel record for any paid staff or volunteer who participates in field trips or transportation activities. Child:staff ratios shall be maintained on field trips and during transport, as specified in STANDARD 1.001 through STANDARD 1.005.

RATIONALE: Injuries are more likely to occur when a child's surroundings or routine changes. Activities outside the facility may pose increased risk for injury. When children are excited or busy playing in unfamiliar areas, they are more likely to forget safety measures unless they are closely supervised at all times.

Children have died from heat stress from being left unattended in closed vehicles. Temperatures in hot cars can reach dangerous levels within 15 minutes (35).

Adults cannot be assumed to be knowledgeable about the various developmental levels or special needs of children. Training by someone with appropriate knowledge and experience is needed to appropriately address these issues.

COMMENTS: When field trips are planned, it is recommended that the sites should be visited by child care staff in advance of the actual field trip to ensure that the site is accessible for the children with special needs. This standard also applies when caregivers are walking with children to and from a destination.

TYPE OF FACILITY: *Center; Large Family Child Care Home; Small Family Child Care Home*

STANDARD 2.030
QUALIFICATIONS FOR DRIVERS

Any driver who transports children for a child care program shall be at least 21 years of age and shall have:
a) A valid driver's license that authorizes the driver to operate the vehicle being driven;
b) Evidence of a safe driving record for more than five years, with no crashes where a citation was issued;
c) No record of substance abuse or conviction for crimes of violence or child abuse;
d) No alcohol or other drugs associated with impaired ability to drive within 12 hours prior to transporting children. Drivers shall ensure that any prescription drugs taken will not impair their ability to drive;
e) No criminal record of crimes against or involving children, child neglect or abuse, or any crime of violence.

The driver's license number, vehicle insurance information, and verification of current state vehicle inspection shall be on file in the facility.

The center director shall require drug testing when noncompliance with the restriction on the use of alcohol or other drugs is suspected.

RATIONALE: Driving children is a significant responsibility. Child care programs must assure that anyone who drives the children is competent to drive the vehicle being driven.

COMMENTS: The driver should advise the health care provider of his/her job and question whether it is safe to drive children while on medication(s) prescribed. Compliance can be measured by testing blood or urine levels for drugs. Refusal to permit such testing should preclude continued employment.

TYPE OF FACILITY: *Center; Large Family Child Care Home; Small Family Child Care Home*

STANDARD 2.031
ROUTE TO EMERGENCY MEDICAL FACILITY

Any driver who transports children for a child care program shall keep instructions for the quickest route to the nearest hospital from any point on the route in the vehicle.

RATIONALE: Driving children is a significant responsibility. Child care programs must assure that anyone who transports children can obtain emergency care promptly.

TYPE OF FACILITY: *Center; Large Family Child Care Home; Small Family Child Care Home*

STANDARD 2.032
DROP-OFF AND PICK-UP POINTS

The facility shall have, and communicate to staff and parents, a plan for safe, supervised drop-off and pick-up points and pedestrian crosswalks in the vicinity of the facility. The plan shall require

drop-off and pick-up only at the curb or at an off-street location protected from traffic. The facility shall assure that any adult who supervises drop-off and loading can see and assure that children are clear of the perimeter of all vehicles before any vehicle moves.

RATIONALE: Injuries and fatalities have occurred during the loading and unloading process, especially in situations where vans or school buses are used to transport children.

COMMENTS: The child care provider should examine the parking area and determine the safest way to drop off and pick up children. Plans for loading and unloading should be discussed with the children, families, caregivers, and drivers.

TYPE OF FACILITY: *Center; Large Family Child Care Home; Small Family Child Care Home*

STANDARD 2.033
VEHICLE SAFETY RESTRAINTS

When children are driven in a motor vehicle other than a bus, school bus, or a bus operated by a common carrier, the following shall apply:
- A child shall be transported only if the child is fastened in an approved developmentally appropriate safety seat, seat belt, or harness appropriate to the child's weight, and the restraint is installed and used in accordance with the manufacturers' instructions for the car seat and the motor vehicle. Each child must have an individual seat belt and be positioned in the vehicle in accordance with the requirements for the safe use of air bags in the back seat;
- A child under the age of 4 shall be transported only if the child is securely fastened in a developmentally appropriate child passenger restraint system that meets the federal motor vehicle safety standards contained in the Code of Federal Regulations, Title 49, Section 571.213, and this compliance is so indicated on the safety restraint device;
- If small buses or vans have safety restraints installed, children weighing over 40 pounds shall have access to belt-positioning booster

seats with lap and shoulder belts. Children weighing under 40 pounds shall use car safety seats;

• Vehicles shall accommodate the placement of wheelchairs with four tie-downs affixed according to the manufactures' instructions in a forward-facing direction. The wheelchair occupant shall be secured by a three-point tie restraint during transport.

RATIONALE: Safety restraints are effective in reducing death and injury when they are used properly. The best car safety seat is one that fits in the vehicle being used, fits the child being transported, has never been in a crash, and is used correctly every time. The use of restraint devices while riding in a vehicle reduces the likelihood of a passenger's suffering serious injury or death if the vehicle is involved in a crash. The use of child safety seats reduces risk of death by 71% for children less than 1 year of age and by 54% for children ages 1-4 (36).

It is reasonable to require that the license holder ensure that the child be placed in restraint devices that conform to state and federal laws. The standard does not apply when children are being transported in vehicles not routinely or commonly equipped with restraints. The standard, however, does clarify that it is the responsibility of the caregiver to ensure that children are fastened in a restraint system. Federal law applies only to vehicles equipped with factory-installed seat belts after 1967.

The provision of mandatory restraints, regardless of the driver or age of the vehicle, is necessary to ensure children's health and safety. The use of safety restraints and choice of positioning in the vehicle is determined by close inspection of the manufacturer's instructions for seat restraints and for the vehicle.

At all times, vehicles should be ready to transport children who must ride in wheelchairs (38, 39). Manufacturers' specifications should be followed to assure that safety requirements are met.

COMMENTS: When school buses meet current standards for the transport of school-age children, containment design features help protect children from injury, although the use of seat belts would provide additional protection. To obtain the Code of Federal Regulations, contact the Superintendent of Documents. Contact information is located in Appendix BB.

Many issues are involved in fitting the wide variety of safety restraints into the many different types of motor vehicles. Positioning children in relation to air bags in the vehicle adds a further complication. If the instructions for the safety restraint and for the motor vehicle do not make clear what should be done, contact the National Highway and Transportation Safety Administration (NHTSA) Auto Safety Hotline for more information. Contact information is located in Appendix BB.

Parents and others who transport young children should be aware that incompatibility problems between the design of the car safety seat, vehicle seat, and the seat belt system can be life-threatening and can be avoided by:

• Reading the vehicle owner's manual and child restraint device instructions carefully;
• Testing the car safety seat for a safe snug fit in the vehicle;
• Having the car seat installation checked by a certified car seat technician at an approved car seat check station in the community;
• Remembering that the rear vehicle seat is the safest place for a child of any age to ride.

TYPE OF FACILITY: *Center; Large Family Child Care Home; Small Family Child Care Home*

STANDARD 2.034
TRAVEL TIME

Children shall not be transported for more than 1 hour per one-way trip on a routine basis.

RATIONALE: It is unreasonable to expect young children to remain confined and seated in a transportation device for a period exceeding 1 hour. Commuting is tiring in general, and particularly difficult if the child spends many hours in child care. The time period may need to be lessened for infants or children with special health needs.

Exceptions for a special field trip may be allowed, but these exceptions should occur infrequently and allow for rest and stretch stops during the trip.

TYPE OF FACILITY: *Center; Large Family Child Care Home; Small Family Child Care Home*

STANDARD 2.035
NO SMOKING IN VEHICLES

There shall be no smoking in the vehicles used by the facility at any time.

In each vehicle from a center, a "NO SMOKING" sign shall be posted.

RATIONALE: Children in confined spaces, e.g., closed vehicles, should not be exposed to secondhand smoke, particularly children with respiratory problems. Exposure to smoke and smoke fumes could trigger increased respiratory difficulties.

COMMENTS: Compliance can be measured by interviewing drivers and inspecting vehicles for evidence of smoking.

TYPE OF FACILITY: *Center; Large Family Child Care Home; Small Family Child Care Home*

STANDARD 2.036
DISTRACTIONS WHILE DRIVING

The driver shall not play the radio or CD player loudly or use ear phones to listen to music or other distracting sounds while children are in the vehicles operated by the facility. Cellular phones shall be used only when the vehicle is stopped and in emergency situations only.

In each vehicle from a center, a sign shall be posted stating "NO LOUD RADIOS, TAPES, OR CDS".

RATIONALE: Loud noise interferes with normal conversation and may be especially disturbing to children with central nervous system abnormalities. It is also distracting to the driver and the passenger monitor or assistant attending the children in the vehicle.

COMMENTS: A driver's use of a portable radio, tape, or CD player with earphones is unacceptable.

TYPE OF FACILITY: *Center; Large Family Child Care Home; Small Family Child Care Home*

STANDARD 2.037
CHILD BEHAVIOR DURING TRANSPORTATION

Children, as both passengers and pedestrians, shall be instructed in safe transportation behavior with terms and concepts appropriate for their age and stage of development.

RATIONALE: Teaching passenger safety to children reduces injury from motor vehicle crashes to young children (40). Young children need to develop skills that will aid them in assuming responsibility for their own health and safety, and these skills can be developed through health education implemented during the early years (37, 41).

COMMENTS: Curricula and materials can be obtained from state departments of transportation, the American Automobile Association (AAA), the American Academy of Pediatrics (AAP), the American Red Cross, and the National Association for the Education of Young Children (NAEYC). Contact information is located in Appendix BB.

TYPE OF FACILITY: *Center; Large Family Child Care Home; Small Family Child Care Home*

STANDARD 2.038
EMERGENCY SUPPLIES FOR FIELD TRIPS

First aid kits shall be taken on field trips, as specified in STANDARD 5.093. Cellular phones shall be taken on field trips for use in emergency situations.

RATIONALE: The ability to communicate for help in an emergency situation while traveling is critical to the safety of children in a vehicle.

TYPE OF FACILITY: *Center; Large Family Child Care Home; Small Family Child Care Home*

2.4 DISCIPLINE

STANDARD 2.039
DISCIPLINE MEASURES

Discipline shall include positive guidance, re-direction, and setting clear-cut limits that foster the child's ability to become self-disciplined. Disciplinary measures shall be clear and under-standable to the child, shall be consistent, and shall be explained to the child before and at the time of any disciplinary action.

Caregivers shall guide children to develop self-control and orderly conduct in relationships with peers and adults. Caregivers shall show children positive alternatives rather than just telling children "no." Caregivers shall care for children without resorting to physical punishment or abusive language. Caregivers shall acknowledge and model desired behavior.

For children 3 or over, facilities shall selectively use "time out" only to enable the child to regain con-trol of himself or herself. The caregiver shall keep the child within visual contact. The caregiver shall take into account the child's developmental stage, tolerances, and ability to learn from "time out."

Expectations for children's behavior shall be writ-ten and shared with families and children of appro-priate age.

RATIONALE: The word "discipline" originates from a Latin root that implies learning and education. The modern dictionary defines discipline as: "training that develops self-control, character, or orderliness and efficiency." Unfortunately, common usage has corrupted the word so that many consider discipline as synonymous with punishment, most particularly corporal punishment (52, 85). Discipline is most effective when it is consistent, reinforces desired behaviors, and offers natural and logical consequences for negative behaviors. Research studies find that corporal punishment has limited effectiveness and potentially hurtful side effects (53-57).

Children have to be given understandable guidelines for their behavior if they are to develop internal con-trol of their actions. The aim is to develop personal standards in self-discipline, not to enforce a set of institutional rules.

COMMENTS: Discipline should be an ongoing process to help children develop inner control so they can manage their own behavior in a socially approved manner. Positive discipline may include brief, supervised separation from the group, or withdrawal of privileges, such as playtime with other children. Natural consequences are effective and useful if not associated with injury (for example, when a child misuses and breaks a toy, the toy does not work any more). Logical consequences of an action (such as not being able to play in the sandbox for a time as a consequence of throwing sand) are also effective methods of positive discipline.

"Time out" should not be used with infants and tod-dlers, as they are too young to cognitively understand this consequence (44). Certain children learn from time out. Time out should be used consistently, for an appropriate duration, not excessively. For more details on the effective use of "time out", see the American Academy of Pediatrics *Guidance for Effective Discipline* (44). Also see *The Magic Years* by Selma H. Fraiberg, published by Charles Scribner's Sons. Con-tact information is located in Appendix BB.

For additional requirements related to discipline, see also Management and Health Policy and Statement of Services, STANDARD 8.004 and STANDARD 8.005, on signed parent agreements; Discipline Policy, STANDARD 8.008 through STANDARD 8.010, on dealing with acts of aggression and fighting by children; Posting Documents, STANDARD 8.077, on posting discipline policies; and Child Abuse and Neglect, STANDARD 3.053 through STANDARD 3.059.

TYPE OF FACILITY: *Center; Large Family Child Care Home; Small Family Child Care Home*

STANDARD 2.040
HANDLING PHYSICAL AGGRESSION

The facility shall use the teaching method described in STANDARD 2.039 immediately when it is important to show that aggressive physical behavior toward staff members or children is unacceptable. Caregivers shall intervene immediately when children become physically aggressive.

RATIONALE: Children in out-of-home care in the United States have demonstrated more aggressive behavior than children reared at home or children in facilities in other countries. Children mimic adult behavior; adults who demonstrate loud or violent behavior serve as models for children (45). Caregiver intervention protects children and encourages them to exhibit more acceptable behavior (47).

COMMENTS: Children could assist in the rule-making to develop this sense of responsibility.

TYPE OF FACILITY: *Center; Large Family Child Care Home; Small Family Child Care Home*

STANDARD 2.041
DISPENSING DISCIPLINE IN EQUITABLE MANNER

Disciplinary practices that the facility establishes shall be dispensed in an equitable manner and shall be designed to encourage children to be fair, to respect property, and to assume personal responsibility and responsibility for others.

RATIONALE: To foster social development, a facility should have a clearly defined code of behavior that applies equally to all children and a disciplinary policy to support it. Because not everyone shares the same opinion about what is "right," caregivers should explain to new caregivers and to parents the behavioral goals and disciplinary methods established for the facility. It is important for staff members to be consistent in their approach, and the best results are achieved with family cooperation. Child care administrators and caregivers can facilitate good behavior by creating an environment responsive to the children's needs. A good "fit" between the

temperament of the caregiver and the child always helps (48).

TYPE OF FACILITY: *Center; Large Family Child Care Home; Small Family Child Care Home*

STANDARD 2.042
PROHIBITED CAREGIVER BEHAVIORS

The following behaviors shall be prohibited in all child care settings and by all caregivers:
a) Corporal punishment, including beating, hitting, spanking, shaking, pinching, excessive exercise, exposure to extreme temperatures, and other measures producing physical pain;
b) Withdrawal or the threat of withdrawal of food, or forcing of food, rest, or bathroom opportunities;
c) Abusive or profane language or verbal abuse, threats, or derogatory remarks about the child or child's family;
d) Any form of public or private humiliation, including threats of physical punishment;
e) Any form of emotional abuse, including rejecting, terrorizing, ignoring, isolating, or corrupting a child;
f) Binding or tying to restrict movement, such as in a car seat (except when travelling); or enclosing in a confined space such as a closet, locked room, box, or similar cubicle.

RATIONALE: Corporal punishment may be physical abuse or may easily become abusive. Emotional abuse can be extremely harmful to children, but, unlike physical or sexual abuse, it is not adequately defined in most state child abuse reporting laws. Corporal punishment is clearly prohibited in small family child care homes and centers in the majority of states (49-51). Research links corporal punishment with negative effects such as later criminal behavior and impairment of learning (53-57).

Factors supporting prohibition of certain methods of punishment include current child development theory and practice, legal aspects (namely, that a caregiver does not foster a relationship with the child in place of the parents), and increasing liability suits. The American Academy of Pediatrics (AAP) is opposed to

the use of corporal punishment (44). Physicians, educators, and caregivers should neither inflict nor sanction corporal punishment (56).

COMMENTS: Appropriate alternatives to corporal punishment vary as children grow and develop. As infants become more mobile, the caregiver must create a safe space and impose limitations by encouraging activities that distract them from harmful situations. Brief verbal expressions of disapproval help prepare infants and toddlers for later use of reasoning. However, the caregiver cannot expect infants and toddlers to be controlled by verbal reprimands. Preschoolers have begun to develop an understanding of rules and can be expected to understand "time out" (out-of-group activity) under adult supervision as a consequence for undesirable behavior. School-age children begin to develop a sense of personal responsibility and self-control and will recognize the removal of privileges (such as loss of participation in an activity) (44).

TYPE OF FACILITY: *Center; Large Family Child Care Home; Small Family Child Care Home*

STANDARD 2.043
USING PHYSICAL RESTRAINT

When a child's behavior makes it necessary, for his own or others' protection, to restrain the child, the most desirable method of restraint is holding the child by another person as gently as possible to accomplish the restraint. Children shall not be physically restrained longer than necessary to control the situation. No bonds, ties, or straps shall be employed to restrain young children.

Children shall not be given medicines, drugs, or herbal or folk remedies that will affect their behavior except as prescribed by their health care provider and with specific written instructions from their health care provider for use of the medicine.

The decision to restrain the child shall be made by the staff person with the most experience in child care and shall only be made for extreme circumstances. Training in the use of any form of physical restraint shall be provided by persons with extensive child care experience including experience with children who have required restraint.

RATIONALE: Undue physical restraint, especially with bonds, ties, or straps can be abusive, as can the use of medications or drugs to control children's behavior.

COMMENTS: For Medication Policy, see STANDARD 8.021 and STANDARD 3.081 through STANDARD 3.083.

TYPE OF FACILITY: *Center; Large Family Child Care Home; Small Family Child Care Home*

2.5 PARENT RELATIONSHIPS

GENERAL

STANDARD 2.044
MUTUAL RESPONSIBILITY OF
PARENTS AND STAFF

There shall be a reciprocal responsibility of the family and child care staff to observe, participate, and be trained in the care that each child requires.

All aspects of child care programs shall be designed to facilitate parental input and involvement. Involved, non-custodial parents shall have access to the same developmental and behavioral information given to the custodial parent, if they have joint legal custody, permission by court order, or written consent from the custodial parent.

Caregivers shall informally share with parents daily information about their child's needs and activities.

RATIONALE: This plan will help achieve the important goal of carryover of facility components from the child care setting to the child's home environment. The child's learning of new skills is a continuous process occurring both at home and in child care.

Research, practice, and accumulated wisdom attest to the crucially important influence of children's

relationships with those closest to them. Children's experience in child care will be most beneficial when parents and caregivers develop feelings of mutual respect and trust. In such a situation, children feel a continuity of affection and concern, which facilitates their adjustment to separation and use of the facility.

An ongoing source of stress for an infant or a young child is the separation from those they love and depend upon. Of the various programmatic elements in the facility that can help to alleviate that stress, by far the most important is the comfort in knowing that parents and caregivers know the children and their needs and wishes, are in close contact with each other, and can respond in ways that enable children to deal with separation.

The encouragement and involvement of parents in the social and cognitive leaps of preschoolers provide parents with the confidence vital to their sense of competence. Communication should be sensitive to ethnic and cultural practices. See STANDARD 2.006 through STANDARD 2.008. The parent/caregiver partnership models positive adult behavior for school-age children and demonstrates a mutual concern for the child's well-being (15, 58-70).

In families where the parents are separated, it is usually in the child's best interest for both parents to be involved in the child's care, and informed about the child's progress and problems in care. However, it is generally up to the courts to decide who has legal custody of the child. Child care providers should comply with court orders and written consent from the parent with legal authority, and not try to make the determination themselves regarding the best interests of the child.

TYPE OF FACILITY: *Center; Large Family Child Care Home; Small Family Child Care Home*

STANDARD 2.045
PARENT-TO-PARENT
COMMUNICATION

The facility shall give consenting parents a list of names and phone numbers of other consenting

parents whose children attend the same facility. The list shall include an annotation encouraging parents whose children attend the same facility to communicate with one another about the service. The facility shall update the list at least annually.

RATIONALE: Encouraging parents' communication is simple, inexpensive, and beneficial. Such communication may include the exchange of positive aspects of the facility and positive knowledge about children's peers. If parents communicate with each other, they can share concerns about the behavior of a specific caregiver and can identify patterns of action suggestive of abuse.

TYPE OF FACILITY: *Center; Large Family Child Care Home; Small Family Child Care Home*

STANDARD 2.046
PARENT VISITS

Caregivers shall inform all parents that they may visit the site at any time when their child is there, and that, under normal circumstances, they will be admitted without delay. This open-door policy shall be part of the "admission agreement" or other contract between the parent and the caregiver, if they have custody, joint custody, permission by court order, or written consent from the custodial parent. Parents are welcomed and encouraged to speak freely to staff about concerns and suggestions.

RATIONALE: This provision may be the single most important method for preventing the abuse of children in child care. Requiring unrestricted access of parents to their children is essential to preventing the abuse of children in child care (71, 72). When access is restricted, areas observable by the parents may not reflect the care the children actually receive.

COMMENTS: Child care providers should not attempt to handle on their own an unstable (for example, intoxicated) parent who wants to be admitted but whose behavior poses a risk to the children. Child care providers should consult local police or the local child protection agency about their recommendations for how staff can obtain support from law

enforcement authorities to avoid incurring increased by improperly refusing to release a child.

Parents can be interviewed to see if the open-door policy is enthusiastically implemented.

For additional information on parent relationships in general, see STANDARD 2.050through STANDARD 2.054; see STANDARD 2.006, on primary language of the parents. For information regarding complaint procedures, see STANDARD 2.052. See Management and Health Policy and Statement of Services, STANDARD 8.004 and STANDARD 8.005, for more information on admission agreements.

TYPE OF FACILITY: *Center; Large Family Child Care Home; Small Family Child Care Home*

REGULAR COMMUNICATION

STANDARD 2.047
PARENT CONFERENCES

Along with short informal daily conversations between parents and caregivers, planned communication (for example, parent conferences) shall be scheduled with at least one parent of every child in care:
a) To review the child's development and adjustment to care;
b) To reach agreement on appropriate, nonviolent, disciplinary measures;
c) To discuss the child's strengths, specific health issues, and concerns such as persistent behavior problems, developmental delays, special needs, overweight, underweight, or eating or sleeping problems.

At these planned conferences a caregiver shall review with the parent the child's health report and the health record to identify medical and developmental issues that require follow-up or adjustment of the facility.

Each review shall be documented in the child's facility health record with the signature of the parent and the staff reviewer. These planned conferences shall occur:
a) As part of the intake process;

b) At each health update interval;
c) On a calendar basis, scheduled according to the child's age:
   1) Every 6 months for children under 6 years of age;
   2) Every year for children 6 years of age and older;
d) Whenever new information is added to the child's facility health record.

Additional conferences shall be scheduled if the parent or caregiver has a concern at any time about a particular child. Any concern about a child's health or development shall not be delayed until a scheduled conference date.

Notes about these planned communications shall be maintained in each child's record at the facility and shall be available for review.

RATIONALE: Parents and caregivers alike should be aware of, and should have arrived at, an agreement concerning each other's beliefs and knowledge about how to deal with children. Reviewing the health record with parents ensures correct information and can be a valuable teaching and motivational tool (73). It can also be a staff learning experience, through insight gained from parents on a child's special circumstances.

A health history is the basis for meeting the child's health, mental, and social needs in the child care setting (73). Review of the health record can be a valuable educational tool for parents, through better understanding of the health report and immunization requirements (73). A goal of out-of-home care of infants and children is to identify parents who are in need of instruction so they can provide preventive health/nutrition care at a critical time during the child's growth and development. It is in the child's best interest that the staff communicates with parents about the child's needs and progress. Parent support groups and parent involvement at every level of facility planning and delivery are usually beneficial to the children, parents, and staff. Communication among parents whose children attend the same facility helps the parents to share useful information and to be mutually supportive.

Both parents and caregivers have essential rights in helping to shape the kind of child care service their children receive.

COMMENTS: The need for follow-up on needed intervention increases when an understanding of the need and motivation for the intervention has been achieved through personal contact. A health history is most useful if the health advocate (see Qualifications of Health Advocates, STANDARD 1.021) personally reviews the records and updates the parents. A health history ensures that all information needed to care for the child is available to the appropriate staff member. Special instructions, such as diet, can be copied for everyday use. Compliance can be assessed by reviewing the records of these planned communications.

Parents who use child care services should be regarded as active participants and partners in facilities that meet their needs as well as their children's. Compliance can be measured by interviewing parents and staff.

See Plan for Child Health Services, STANDARD 8.013 through STANDARD 8.017, on health assessment; and STANDARD 3.004, on nutrition assessment and follow-up. See STANDARD 8.046 through STANDARD 8.051, for more information on health reports; and see STANDARD 8.051 and STANDARD 8.052, for more information on health records.

TYPE OF FACILITY: *Center; Large Family Child Care Home; Small Family Child Care Home*

STANDARD 2.048
DESIGNATED STAFF FOR PARENT CONTACT

The facility shall assign a specific staff member to each parent to ensure contact between the designated staff member and parent that may take place at the beginning and end of the day or when a parent drops in. In small family child care homes, this contact will be with the child care provider.

The contact shall consist of:

a) Discussions between the parent and staff member regarding observations of the child (including health issues);
b) Providing an opportunity for the parents to observe the child's playmates and surroundings.

RATIONALE: A designated staff member with health training is helpful in developing a personal interest in the child and maintaining an ongoing relationship with the parent(s) (74, 75). A plan for personal contact and documentation of a designated staff person will ensure specific attempts to communicate directly with families about health-related matters.

COMMENTS: The facility should have a plan for personal contact with parents, even though contact may not be possible on a daily basis. Compliance can be documented by spot observations or self-reporting. In larger facilities, the designated staff person might be the "health advocate." See Qualifications of Health Advocates, STANDARD 1.021.

For additional information on regular communication, see also STANDARD 8.043, on transition contacts with parents.

TYPE OF FACILITY: *Center; Large Family Child Care Home; Small Family Child Care Home*

LOG FOR INFANTS, TODDLERS, AND PRESCHOOLERS

STANDARD 2.049
DAILY LOG

For infants, toddlers, and preschoolers, the facility shall have a method, such as a daily log or notebook entry, whereby parents and staff can exchange observations, concerns, and comments.

RATIONALE: Notebooks can substitute, in part, for direct parent contact, when the latter is not possible (66). Notebooks also can be an effective means for parents to express their concerns and wishes when they might feel intimidated in a face-to-face "con-

ference" setting. Notebooks can be educational for parents by pointing out concerns or the need for special considerations in the child care setting, and by including health information or resources as appropriate.

COMMENTS: The staff should maintain a daily log at the facility for review by staff and parents; the parent can carry the notebook to and from the facility.

Alternative methods (regular phone contact, daily face-to-face conversation, and the like) might be more effective for parents or caregivers who have difficulty with written communication.

TYPE OF FACILITY: *Center; Large Family Child Care Home; Small Family Child Care Home*

PARENTAL INVOLVEMENT

STANDARD 2.050
SEEKING PARENT INPUT

Each caregiver shall, at least twice a year, seek the views of parents about the strengths and needs of the facility. Caregivers shall honor parents' requests for more frequent reviews.

RATIONALE: This standard strengthens the recognition by parent and caregiver alike that parents have essential rights in helping to shape the kind of child care service their children receive.

COMMENTS: Small and large family child care homes should have group meetings of all parents once or twice a year. This standard avoids mention of procedures that are inappropriate to small family child care, as it does not require any explicit mechanism (such as a parent advisory council) for obtaining or offering parental input. Individual or group meetings with parents would suffice to meet this standard. Seeking consumer input is a cornerstone of facility planning and evaluation.

TYPE OF FACILITY: *Center; Large Family Child Care Home; Small Family Child Care Home*

STANDARD 2.051
SUPPORT SERVICES FOR PARENTS

Centers shall establish parent groups and parent support services. Centers shall document these services and shall include intra-agency activities or other community support group offerings. The caregiver shall record parental participation in these on-site activities in the facility record.

RATIONALE: Parental involvement at every level of program planning and delivery and parent support groups are elements that are usually beneficial to the children, parents, and staff of the facility. The parent association group facilitates mutual understanding between the center and parents. Parental involvement also helps to broaden parents' knowledge of administration of the facility and develops and enhances advocacy efforts.

COMMENTS: Parent meetings within a facility are useful means of communication that supplement mailings and indirect contacts.

TYPE OF FACILITY: *Center*

STANDARD 2.052
PARENT COMPLAINT PROCEDURES

Facilities shall have in place complaint procedures to jointly resolve with parents any problems that may arise. Arrangements for the resolutions shall be documented. Centers shall develop mechanisms for holding formal and informal meetings between staff and groups of parents.

RATIONALE: Coordination between the facility and the parents is essential to promote their respective child care roles and to avoid confusion or conflicts surrounding values. In addition to routine meetings, special meetings can deal with crises and unique problems.

COMMENTS: These meetings could identify facility needs, assist in developing resources, and recommend facility and policy changes to the governing body. See Identifiable Governing Body/Accountable Individual, STANDARD 8.001 through STANDARD 8.003. It is most helpful to document the proceedings of these meetings to facilitate future communications and to ensure continuity of service delivery. Facility-sponsored activities could take place outside facility hours.

TYPE OF FACILITY: *Center; Large Family Child Care Home; Small Family Child Care Home*

STANDARD 2.053
PARENT CONSENT

The facility shall require parental consent and participation when significant decisions involving a child's services are made and during the process of formal evaluation of a child.

Parents shall be explicitly invited to:
a) Participate in discussions of the results of their child's evaluations and the relationship of their child's needs to the caregivers' ability to serve that child appropriately;
b) Give alternative perspectives;
c) Share their expectations and goals for their child and have these expectations and goals integrated with any plan for their child.

The facility shall document parents' presence at these meetings and invitations to attend.

If the parents do not attend the assessment, the caregiver shall inform the parents of the results, and offer an opportunity for discussion.

RATIONALE: To provide services effectively, facilities must recognize parents' observations and reports about the child and their expectations for the child, as well as the family's need of child care services. A marked discrepancy between professional and parental observations of, or expectations for, a child necessitates further discussion and development of a consensus on a plan of action.

Parents need to have accurate information about their children. An evaluation of a child is complete only when the facility has discussed the information with the parent. The caregiver should explain the results to parents honestly, but sensitively, without using technical jargon (64).

COMMENTS: Parents need to be included in the process of shaping decisions about their children, e.g., adding, deleting, or changing a service.

Efforts should be made to provide notification of meetings in the primary language of the parents.

Efforts to schedule meetings at times convenient to parents should be encouraged. Those conducting an evaluation, and when subsequently discussing the findings with the family, should consider parents' input. Parents have both the motive and the legal right to be included in decision-making and to seek other opinions.

A second, independent opinion can be offered to the family to confirm the original evaluation, but extensive "shopping" for a more desirable or favorable opinion should be discouraged.

TYPE OF FACILITY: *Center; Large Family Child Care Home; Small Family Child Care Home*

HEALTH INFORMATION SHARING

STANDARD 2.054
PARENTS' INFORMATION ON THEIR CHILD'S HEALTH AND BEHAVIOR

The facility shall ask parents for information regarding the child's health and behavioral status upon registration or if there has been an extended gap in the child's attendance at the facility.

RATIONALE: Admission of children without this information will leave the center unprepared to deal with daily and emergent health needs of the child, other children, and staff if there is a question of communicability of disease.

COMMENTS: Some parents may resist providing this information. If so, the caregiver should invite them to view this exchange of information as an opportunity to express their own concerns about the facility. For information on inclusion/exclusion/dismissal policy, see STANDARD 3.065 through STANDARD 3.069.

TYPE OF FACILITY: *Center; Large Family Child Care Home; Small Family Child Care Home*

USE OF COMMUNITY HEALTH RESOURCES

STANDARD 2.055
FAMILY SOURCE OF HEALTH CARE

The facility shall help families who have no regular health care provider to locate a resource that can meet their needs.

RATIONALE: Primary care and preventive health services for children and adults will assist the parents' ability to support their children's healthy growth and development and can identify problems early for intervention. Health services should be comprehensive and range from preventive activities (such as immunizations, injury prevention, diet changes for good nutrition and for allergies) to acute treatments (such as skin problems, ear infections, behavioral issues) to more complicated matters (such as evaluation and referral for potential chronic health problems, hearing, neuromuscular issues).

COMMENTS: Linking families to the health care system (such as a well-child clinic, public health department, private physician, or health insurance programs for which they or the child might be eligible) is a primary prevention goal. Child care providers can assist families to obtain information about their child's eligibility for their state Children's Health Insurance Program (CHIP) and access to a medical home. As a last resort, the family should know what emergency room is closest to their home. Emergency rooms are not designed to provide primary, preventive health care for children or adults. Every state has a Maternal and Child Health helpline where parents can call for help in finding out about how to pay for child health care and how to locate a source of primary care for their children and for themselves. The regional offices of the Maternal and Child Health Bureau, Health Resources and Services Administration (HRSA) of the U.S. Department of Health and Human Services can provide the helpline

numbers for the states in their region. Additional resources include child care resource and referral agencies, county health departments, EPSDT programs, hospital pediatric departments and county medical societies.
See also STANDARD 8.015, on the family's health care provider.

TYPE OF FACILITY: *Center; Large Family Child Care Home; Small Family Child Care Home*

STANDARD 2.056
COMMUNITY HUMAN SERVICE RESOURCES INFORMATION

The facility shall make available to parents and staff information about human service resources in the community.

RATIONALE: To meet the individual needs of the families, community resources should be identified and the information made available to families. Families' primary and trusted source of information about community resources may be the child care provider. Daily contacts with families give child care providers unique opportunities to support family needs.

COMMENTS: Local resource and referral agencies, mental health services, social services, community health centers, hospitals, private physicians, public health nurses, Head Start, clinic groups, the American Red Cross, public schools, early intervention programs, and county extension services are but a few examples of potential resources. Parents and care-givers will be more aware of these community resources when the child care facility calls their attention to them. The facility can do this by providing information on how to access resource directories and helpline numbers and by inviting personnel from community agencies to participate in staff and parent meetings, or "open houses."

Information on how to access resource directories or helpline numbers can also be obtained from resource and referral agencies, child care consultants in some states, health advocates in center-based programs, and in public health departments.

TYPE OF FACILITY: *Center; Large Family Child Care Home; Small Family Child Care Home*

STANDARD 2.057
ENABLING PARENTS AS CHILD ADVOCATES

Child care providers shall inform parents about programs and sources of information that will improve parents' capability as advocates for the children's needs. When the facility does not directly offer applicable services, the child care provider shall refer parents to agencies with experience in working with the needs of their children. Facilities shall document any referrals in writing.

RATIONALE: Applicable referrals will make parents more effective advocates for their children's needs.

COMMENTS: Information should be shared with parents in the parents' primary language and with sensitivity to the parents' ethnic and cultural practices.

Advocacy training can be provided by a service provider or an outside agency. In the case of a child with special needs, the family can be referred to agencies involved with special needs. For additional information on parental participation, see Parental Involvement, STANDARD 2.050through STANDARD 2.053, and Health Information Sharing, STANDARD 2.054.

TYPE OF FACILITY: *Center; Large Family Child Care Home; Small Family Child Care Home*

STANDARD 2.058
ON-SITE SERVICES FOR CHILDREN WITH SPECIAL HEALTH NEEDS

Child care providers shall be aware of all on-site services, including the following service providers, that may be of use for children in care:
a) Special clinics the child may attend, including sessions with medical specialists and registered dieticians;
b) Special therapists for the child (such as occupational, physical, speech, nutrition);

c) Counselors, therapists, or mental health service providers for parents (such as social workers, psychologists, psychiatrists).

All care providers shall provide written documentation of the services rendered in the primary language of the parent. Information shall be exchanged only with the prior written, informed consent of the parent.

RATIONALE: Knowing who is treating the child and coordinating services with these individuals is vital to program implementation. There should be a liaison with special clinics for specific disabilities and illnesses when children are seen for consultation at these units. Services provided onsite at the facility should be coordinated with those offered at another site (77, 78).

COMMENTS: Although information is best related in writing, telephone contacts are also helpful. Confidentiality should be respected both with written and verbal communication. Regular contacts between professionals working with the child and family served by the child care facility improve coordination of care, minimize confusion for the family and prevent duplication. Caregivers, however, must strictly adhere to guidelines concerning confidentiality. Documentation of special therapy is necessary for monitoring purposes. These therapies may be provided by private therapists or by clinics or centers specializing in such services. Some social and psychological data may have to be exchanged within the limits of discretion and confidentiality.

TYPE OF FACILITY: *Center; Large Family Child Care Home; Small Family Child Care*

STANDARD 2.059
COMMUNICATION FROM SPECIALISTS

Providers who come into the facility to furnish special services to a child shall also communicate at each visit with the caregiver at the facility who is responsible for sharing information with the parent. These providers may include, but are not limited to, physicians, registered nurses, occupational therapists, physical therapists, speech

therapists, educational therapists, and registered dietitians. The discussions shall be documented in the child's written record.

RATIONALE: Therapeutic services must be coordinated with the child's general education program and with the parents and caregivers so everyone understands the child's needs. To be most useful, the providers must share the therapeutic techniques with the caregivers and parents and integrate them into the child's daily routines, not just at therapy sessions. Parental consent to share some information may be necessary.

COMMENTS: See Child Records, 8.046 through 8.052, for information regarding child health records.

TYPE OF FACILITY: *Center; Large Family Child Care Home; Small Family Child Care Home*

2.6 HEALTH EDUCATION

HEALTH EDUCATION FOR CHILDREN

STANDARD 2.060
HEALTH EDUCATION ACTIVITIES

Caregivers shall talk about healthy behaviors while they carry out routine daily activities. Activities shall be accompanied by words of encouragement and praise for achievement.

Facilities shall use developmentally appropriate health education materials in the children's activities and shall also share these with the families whenever possible.

All health education activities shall be geared to the child's developmental age and shall take into account individual personalities and interests.

RATIONALE: This is an important way to demonstrate and reinforce health behaviors of caregivers and children alike. The effectiveness of health education is enhanced when shared between the provider and the parent (79).

Young children learn better through experiencing an activity and observing behavior than through didactic training (80). Learning and play have a reciprocal relationship; play experiences are closely related to learning (17, 18).

COMMENTS: Caregivers are important in the lives of the young children in care. They should be educated and supported to be able to interact optimally with children in their care. Compliance shall be documented by observation. Consultation can be sought from a certified health education specialist. The American Association for Health Education (AAHE) and the National Commission for Health Education Credentialing, Inc. (NCCHEC) provide information on this specialty. Contact information for the AAHE and NCCHEC is located in Appendix BB.

An extensive education program to make such experiential learning possible must be supported by strong community resources in the form of both consultation and materials from sources such as the health department, nutrition councils, and so forth. Suggestions for topics and methods of presentation are widely available. Examples include, but are not limited to, crossing streets safely, car seat safety, latch key programs, health risks from secondhand smoke, and tooth brushing. *Risk Watch* is a prepared curriculum from the National Fire Protection Association (NFPA) offering comprehensive injury prevention strategies for children in preschool through eighth grade. Contact information for the NFPA is located in Appendix BB.

TYPE OF FACILITY: *Center; Large Family Child Care Home; Small Family Child Care Home*

STANDARD 2.061
HEALTH EDUCATION TOPICS

Health education for children and staff shall include physical, oral, mental/emotional, nutritional, and social health and shall be integrated daily in the program of activities, to include such topics as:
a) Body awareness;
b) Families (including cultural heritage);
c) Personal/social skills;
d) Expression of feelings;
e) Self-esteem;
f) Nutrition;
g) Personal hygiene;
h) Safety (such as home, vehicular care seats and belts, playground, bicycle, fire, and firearms);
i) Conflict management and violence prevention;
j) First aid;
k) Physical health;
l) Handwashing;
m) Awareness of special needs;
n) Importance of rest and sleep;
o) Fitness;
p) Oral health;
q) Health risks of secondhand smoke;
r) Taking medications;
s) Dialing 911 for emergencies.

RATIONALE: For young children, health and education are inseparable. Children learn about health and safety by experiencing risk taking and risk control, fostered by adults who are involved with them. Whenever opportunities for learning arise; facilities should integrate education to promote healthy behaviors. Health education should be seen not as a structured curriculum, but as a daily component of the planned program that is part of child development. Certified health education specialists are a good resource for this instruction. The American Association for Health Education (AAHE), the National Commission for Health Education Credentialing, Inc. (NCCHEC), and the State and Territorial Injury Prevention Directors' Association (STIPDA) provide information on this specialty. Contact information for the AAHE, NCCHEC, and STIPDA is located in Appendix BB.

TYPE OF FACILITY: *Center; Large Family Child Care Home; Small Family Child Care Home*

STANDARD 2.062
GENDER AND SEXUALITY

The facility shall prepare caregivers to appropriately discuss with the children anatomical facts related to gender identity and sexuality differences.

RATIONALE: Open discussions among adults concerning childhood sexuality increase their comfort with the subject. The adults' comfort may reduce children's anxiety about sexuality.

COMMENTS: Developing a common approach to matters involving young children, sexuality and gender identity is not always easy because the views of facility administrators, caregivers, parents, and community leaders do not always coincide (53).

TYPE OF FACILITY: *Center; Large Family Child Care Home; Small Family Child Care Home*

STANDARD 2.063
STAFF MODELING OF HEALTHY BEHAVIOR

The facility shall require all staff members to model healthy behaviors and attitudes in their contact with children in the facility, including eating nutritious foods, complying with no tobacco use policies, and handwashing protocols.

RATIONALE: Modeling is an effective way of confirming that a behavior is one to be imitated.

COMMENTS: Modeling healthy behavior and attitudes can be specified in the plan as compliance with no tobacco use policies, handwashing protocols, and so forth.

See Policy on Smoking, Tobacco Use, Prohibited Substances, and Firearms, STANDARD 8.038 and STANDARD 8.039. See also Hygiene, STANDARD 3.012 through STANDARD 3.019, on handwashing protocols.

TYPE OF FACILITY: *Center; Large Family Child Care Home; Small Family Child Care Home*

HEALTH EDUCATION FOR STAFF

HEALTH EDUCATION FOR PARENTS

STANDARD 2.064
HEALTH EDUCATION TOPICS FOR STAFF

Health education for staff shall include physical, oral, mental/emotional, nutritional, and social health of children. At a minimum, the topics shall include those listed in STANDARD 2.061.

RATIONALE: Children learn about health and safety by experiencing risk taking and risk control, fostered and managed by adults. Whenever opportunities for learning arise, facilities should integrate health education to promote healthy behaviors. Health education should be seen not as a structured curriculum, but instead, as a daily component of the planned program that is part of child development.

COMMENTS: Community resources could provide written health-related materials. Consultation can be sought from a certified health education specialist. Small and large family child care home providers can cover physical, oral, mental, and social health on an informal basis, as the small size of the homes and the varied ages of the enrollees preclude a "curriculum" per se.

The American Association for Health Education (AAHE) and the National Commission for Health Education Credentialing, Inc. (NCCHEC) provide information on certified health education specialists. Contact information for the AAHE and NCCHEC is located in Appendix BB. For additional information on health education for staff, see also Training, STANDARD 1.023 through STANDARD 1.036, for a comprehensive description of staff training topics. See Health Education for Children for topics, STANDARD 2.061.

TYPE OF FACILITY: *Center; Large Family Child Care Home; Small Family Child Care Home*

STANDARD 2.065
OPPORTUNITIES FOR HEALTH EDUCATION OF PARENTS

Parents shall be given opportunities to observe staff members modeling healthy behavior and facilitating child development. Parents shall also have opportunities to ask questions and to describe how effective the modeling has been.

RATIONALE: Modeling can be an effective educational tool (37,44).

COMMENTS: By providing a one-way observation area or other opportunities for parents to learn by example, the facility can avoid intimidating parents.

TYPE OF FACILITY: *Center; Large Family Child Care Home; Small Family Child Care Home*

STANDARD 2.066
METHODS FOR HEALTH EDUCATION OF PARENTS

The facility shall schedule regular health education programs for parents, designed to meet the unique characteristics of the enrolled families. These programs may be in a variety of forms including open-house meetings with guest speakers, opportunities for discussion, newsletters, a video lending library, children's projects, health and safety fact sheets. The facility shall offer health education programs and information on a regular basis.

RATIONALE: Health education of all those who participate in the child care setting in any way is an integrated approach to ensure child care health and safety. The incorporation of healthy behaviors is accomplished by consistency between home and child care settings. If done using established adult learning techniques that are sensitive to ethnic and cultural practices, didactic teaching can be effective for educating parents. If not done well, there is a danger of demeaning parents and making them feel less, rather than more, capable (82, 83).

COMMENTS: Even small family-child-care homes can plan for these meetings. Frequently, the parents who might benefit most do not attend. Severe time constraints on many families may preclude their participation.

Community resources that may provide help with these programs include:
a) The Women, Infants and Children (WIC) Supplemental Food Program;
b) Medical and dental societies;
c) Departments of social services;
d) Mental health, drug, and alcohol programs;
e) Child development specialists;
f) Public health departments;
g) SAFE KIDS coalitions;
h) Local safety councils;
i) Certified health education specialists;
j) Parent education organizations;
k) Midwifery and birthing centers;
l) Visiting Nurse Associations.

The American Association for Health Education (AAHE) and the National Commission for Health Education Credentialing, Inc. (NCCHEC) provide information on certified health education specialists. Contact information for the AAHE and NCCHEC is located in Appendix BB.

TYPE OF FACILITY: *Center; Large Family Child Care Home; Small Family Child Care Home*

STANDARD 2.067
PARENT EDUCATION PLAN

The content of a parent education plan shall be individualized to meet each family's needs and shall be sensitive to cultural values and beliefs. Written material, at a minimum, shall address the most important health and safety issues for all age groups served, shall be in a language understood by families, and may include the topics listed in

STANDARD 2.061, with special emphasis on the following:
a) Safety (such as home, community, playground, firearm, vehicular, or bicycle);
b Oral health promotion and disease prevention;
c) Value of healthy lifestyle choices (such as exercise, nutrition, avoidance of substance abuse and tobacco use);
d) Importance of well child care (such as immunizations, hearing/vision screening, monitoring growth and development);
e) Child development;
f) Parental health (such as pregnancy care, substance abuse prevention, smoking cessation, HIV/AIDS prevention, stress management, or subjects of concern to the parent);
g) Domestic violence;
h) Conflict management and violence prevention;
i) Prevention and management of infectious disease, including the need for parents of infants in child care to adopt some handwashing and diapering procedures (as done in child care) for the parents' protection as well as for the protection of the other children and adults in the family;
j) Child behavior (normal and problematic);
k) Handling emergencies/first aid;
l) Child advocacy skills;
m) Special needs.

Health education for parents shall utilize principles of adult learning to maximize the potential for parents to learn about key concepts. Facilities shall utilize opportunities for learning, such as the case of an illness present in the facility, to inform parents about illness and prevention strategies.

The staff shall introduce seasonal topics when they are relevant to the health and safety of parents and children.

RATIONALE: Adults learn best when they are motivated, comfortable, and respected, when they can immediately apply what they have learned, and when multiple learning strategies are used. Individualized content and approaches are needed for successful intervention. Parent attitudes, beliefs, fears, and educational and socioeconomic levels all should be given consideration in planning and conducting parent education (81, 82). Parental behavior can be modified by education. Parents should be involved closely with the facility. If done well, didactic teaching can be effective

for educating parents. If not done well, there is a danger of demeaning parents and making them feel less, rather than more, capable (81, 82).

The concept of parent control and empowerment is key to successful parent education in the child care setting. Support and education for parents lead to better parenting abilities.

Knowing the family will help the health advocate. See Qualifications of Health Advocates, STANDARD 1.021, to determine content and method of the parent education plan. Specific attention should be paid to the parents' need for support and consultation or help with resources for their own problems. If the facility suggests a referral or resource, this should be documented in the child's record. Specifics of what the parent shared need not be recorded.

COMMENTS: Community resources could provide written health-related materials. Small and large family child care home providers can cover physical, oral, mental, and social health on an informal basis, as the small size of the homes and the varied ages of the enrollees preclude a "curriculum" per se. School-age child care facilities do not need to incorporate child health education into their programs, as enrollees receive this information in school.

TYPE OF FACILITY: *Center; Large Family Child Care Home; Small Family Child Care Home*

REFERENCES

1. Colker LJ, et al. Curriculum for infants and toddlers: who needs it? *Child Care Infor Exch.* 1996;112:74-78.

2. Smith AB. Quality programs that care and educate. *Child Educ.* 1996;72:330-336.

3. Dimidijian VJ, ed. *Play's Place in Public Education for Young Children.* Washington, DC: National Education Association (NEA) Early Childhood Education (NEA); 1992. NEA's Early Childhood Education Series.

4. Blecher-Sass H. Good-byes can build trust. *Young Child.* 1997;52:12-14.

5. Moerk EL. The guided acquisition of first language skills. *Adv Appl Dev Psychol.* 2000;20:248.

6. Wardle F. Meeting the needs of multicultural and multiethnic children in early childhood settings. *Early Child Educ J.* 1998;26:7-11.

7. Ramsey PG. *Teaching and Learning in a Diverse World: Multicultural Education for Young Children.* 2nd ed. New York, NY: Teachers College Press; 1998.

8. Ramsey PG. Growing up with the contradictions of race and class. Research in review. *Young Child.* 1995;50:18-22.

9. Baron N, Schrank LW. *Children Learning Language: How Adults Can Help.* Lake Zurich, Ill: Learning Seed; 1997.

10. Szanton ES, ed. *Creating Child-Centered Programs for Infants and Toddlers, Birth to 3 Year Olds, Step by Step: A Program for Children and Families.* New York, NY: Children's Resources International, Inc.; 1997.

11. Kontos S, Wilcox-Herzog A. Teachers' interactions with children: why are they so important? Research in review. *Young Child.* 1997;52:4-12.

12. Botkin D, et al. Children's affectionate behavior: gender differences. *Early Educ Dev.* 1991;2(4):270-86.

13. Massey MS. *Early Childhood Violence Prevention: ERIC Digest.* Champaign,Ill: ERIC Clearinghouse on Elementary and Early Childhood Education; 1998.

14. Levin DE. *Teaching Young Children in Violent Times: Building a Peaceable Classroom. A Preschool-Grade 3 Violence Prevention and Conflict Resolution Guide.* Cambridge, Mass: Educators for Social Responsibility; 1994.

15. Mayr T, Ulich M. Children's well-being in day care centres: an exploratory empirical study. *Int J Early Years Educ.* 1999;7(3):229-39.

16. Cartwright S. Group trips: an invitation to cooperative learning. *Child Care Infor Exch.* 1998;124: 95-7.

17. Evaldson A, Corsaro WA. Play and games in the peer cultures of preschool and preadolescent children: an interpretative approach. *Childhood.* 1998;5:377-402.

18. Petersen EA. The amazing benefits of play. *Child Fam.* 1998;17:7-8.

19. Pica R. Beyond physical development: why young children need to move. *Young Child.* 1997;52:4-11.

20. Rodd, J. *Understanding Young Children's Behavior: A Guide for Early Childhood Professionals.* New York, NY: Teacher's College Press; 1996.

21. Greenberg, P. *Character Development: Encouraging Self-esteem & Self-discipline in Infants, Toddlers and Two-Year-Olds.* Washington, DC: National Association for the Education of Young Children; 1991.

22. Whitebook M, Bellm D. *Taking on Turnover: An Action Guide for Child Care Center Teachers and Directors.* Washington, DC: Center for the Child Care Workforce; 1998.

23. Torelli L, Durrett C. Landscape for learning: the impact of classroom design on infants and toddlers. *Early Child News.* 1996;8:12-17.

24. Cooney M, et al. From hitting to tattling to communication and negotiation: the young child's stages of socialization. *Early Child Educ J.* 1996;24:23-27.

25. Snow CE, Burns SM, Griffin, P. Language and literacy environments in preschools. *ERIC Digest.* 1999;ED 426818.

26. Dodge DT, et al. *Caring for Infants and Toddlers: A Supervised Self-Instructional Training Program.* Vol 2. Washington, DC: Teaching Strategies, Inc; 1991.

27. Stephens K. Toilet training: children step up to independence. *Child Care Infor Exch.* 1999;125:76-80.

28. Honig AS. Toilet learning. *Day Care Early Educ.* 1993;21:6-9.

29. Matthews D. Action based learning environments. *Soc Stud Rev.* 1993;23:17-20.

30. Meyerhoff MK. *The Power of Play: A Discussion about Early Childhood Education.* Lindenhurst, Ill: Epicenter Inc.; 1998.

31. Coltin L. *Enriching Children's Out-of-School Time: ERIC Digest.* Champaign, Ill: ERIC Clearinghouse on Elementary and Early Childhood Education; 1999.

32. Fashola OS. Implementing effective after-school programs. *Here's How.* 1999;17(3):1-4.

33. Greenspan, SL. Building children's minds: early childhood development for a better future. *Our Child.* 1997:23(4), 6-10.

34. Maxwell LE. Designing early childhood education environments: a partnership between architect and educator. *Educ Facility Planner.* 1996;33(4):15-17.

35. Gibbs LI., Lawrence DW, Kohn MA. Heat exposure in an enclosed automobile. *J La State Med Soc.* 1995;147:545-6.

36. The National Safe Kids Campaign. *Motor Vehicle Occupant Injury Fact Sheet.* Washington DC: National Safe Kids Campaign; 1999. Available at: www.safekids.org/fact99/mv99.html. Accessed November 30, 2000.

37. Lehman GR, Geller ES. Participative education for children: an effective approach to increase safety belt use. *J Appl Behav Anal.* 1990;23(2):219-25.

38. The Rehabilitation Act, 29 USC §701 (1973).

39. Mawdsley RD. Transporting students with disabilities. *Sch Bus Aff.* 1998;64(12):22-24.

40. Windome MD, ed. *Injury Prevention and Control for Children and Youth.* 3rd ed. Elk Village Grove, Ill: American Academy of Pediatrics; 1997.

41. Kane WM, Herrera KE. *Safety Is No Accident: Children's Activities in Injury Prevention.* Santa Cruz, Calif: ETR Associates; 1993.

42. Elliot T, Wiley DC. Assessing healthy behavior recognition in preschool, head start children. *J Health Educ.* 1996;27(5):294-99.

43. Christensen AM, et al. Teaching pairs of preschoolers with disabilities to seek adult assistance in response to simulated injuries: acquisition and promotion of observational learning. *Educ Treat Child.* 1996;19(1):3-18.

44. American Academy of Pediatrics (AAP). Guidance for effective discipline. *Pediatrics.* 1998;101:723-728.

45. Acting against violence--a response for children. Beginnings workshop. *Child Care Info Exch.* 1995;102:33-56.

46. Truxal MR. *Increasing Teacher/Parent Awareness of Developmentally Appropriate Movies for 3-6 Year Olds through Use of a Rating Scale.* New York, NY: EDRS; 1994.

47. Rush KL. Caregiver-child interactions and early literacy development of preschool children from low-income environments. *Topics Early Child Educ.* 1999;19(1):3-14.

48. Allhusen VD, Cochran MM. *Infants' Attachment Behaviors With Their Day Care Providers.* New York, NY: EDRS; 1991.

49. The Children's Foundation. *Family Child Care Licensing Study, 2000.* Washington, DC: Author; 2000.

50. Azer S, Eldred D. *Training Requirements in Child Care Licensing Regulations.* Boston, Mass: Center for Career

Development in Early Care and Education, Wheelock College; 1998.

51. Meadows A, ed. *Caring for America's Children.* Washington, DC: National Academy of Sciences & National Research Council; 1991.

52. Hodgkin, R. Why the "gentle smack" should go: Policy review. *Child Soc.* 1997;11(3):201-04.

53. Straus MA, et al. Spanking by parents and subsequent antisocial behavior of children. *Arch Pediatr Adolesc Med.* 1997;151:761-67.

54. Deater-Deckard K, et al. Physical discipline among African American and European American mothers: links to children's externalizing behaviors. *Dev Psychol.* 1996;32(6):1065-72.

55. Weiss B, et al. Some consequences of early harsh discipline: child aggression and a maladaptive social information processing style. *Child Dev.* 1992;63(6):1321-35.

56. American Academy of Pediatrics. The short and long-term consequences of corporal punishment. *Pediatrics.* 1996;98(4 Pt 2):803-860.

57. American Academy of Pediatrics. Policy Statement: *Corporal Punishment in Schools (RE9207). Pediatrics.* 1991; 88:173.

58. Marshall NL. *Empowering Low-Income Parents: The Role of Child Care.* Boston, Mass: EDRS; 1991.

59. Greenman J. Parent partnerships: what they don't teach you can hurt. *Child Care Infor Exch.* 1998;124:78-82.

60. Shores E J. *A Call to Action: Family Involvement as a Critical Component of Teacher Education Programs.* Tallahassee, Fla: Southeastern Regional Vision for Education; 1998.

61. Establishing a Sucessful Family Daycare Home: A Resource Guide for Providers. Boston, Mass: Massachusetts State Office for Children; 1990.

62. Tijus CA, et al. The impact of parental involvement on the quality of day care centers. *Int J Early Years Educ.* 1997;5(1):7-20.

63. Jones R. Producing a school newsletter parents will read. *Child Care Infor Exch.* 1996;107:91-3.

64. O'Connor S, et al. ASQ: Assessing School Age Child Care Quality. Wellesly, Mass: Center for Research on Women; 1996.

65. Powell DR. Reweaving parents back into the fabric of early childhood programs: research in review. *Young Child.* 1998;53(5):60-67.

66. Miller SH, et al. Family support in early education and child care settings: making a case for both principles and practices. *Child Today.* 1995;23(4):26-9.

67. Dombro AL. Sharing the care: what every provider and parent needs to know. *Child Today.* 1995;23(4):22-25.

68. Larner M. *Linking Family Support and Early Childhood Programs: Issues, Experiences, Opportunities: Best Practices Project.* Chicago, Ill: Family Resource Coalition; 1995:1-40.

69. Endsley RC, et al. Parent involvement and quality day care in proprietary centers. *J Res Child Educ.* 1993;7(2):53-61.

70. Fagan J. Mother and father involvement in day care centers serving infants and young toddlers. *Early Child Dev Care.* 1994;103:95-101.

71. *Caregivers of Young Children: Preventing and Responding to Child Maltreatment.* Rev ed. McLean, Va: Circle, Inc.; 1992. The user manual series.

72. Baglin CA, Bender M. eds. *Handbook on Quality Child Care for Young Children: Setting Standards and Resources.* San Diego, Calif: Singular Publishing Group; 1994.

73. Aronson S. *Model Child Care Health Policies.* 3rd ed. Bryn Mawr, Pa: American Academy of Pediatrics, Pennsylvania Chapter; 1997.

74. Kendrick AS, Kaufmann R, Messenger KP, eds. *Healthy Young Children: A Manual for Programs.* Washington, DC: National Association for the Education of Young Children; 1995.

75. Nalle MA. Health education in child care: opportunities and challenges. *Health Educ J Eta Sigma Gamma.* 1996; 27(2):5-11.

76. American Academy of Pediatrics. Surveillance of pediatric HIV infection: policy statement. *Pediatrics.* 1998;101(2):315-319.

77. Kelly JF, Booth CL. Child care for infants with special needs: issues and applications. *Inf Young Child.* 1999;12(1):26-33.

78. Bruder MB. A collaborative model to increase the capacity of child care providers to include young children with disabilities. *J Early Intervent.* 1998;21(2):177-86.

79. Holmes M, et al. Promising Partnerships: How to Develop Successful Partnerships in Your Community. Alexandria, Va: National Head Start Association; 1996.

80. Fleer M. ed. *Play Through Profiles: Profiles Through Play.* Watson, Australia: Australian Early Childhood Association Inc.; 1996.

81. Gonzalez-Mena J. When values collide: exploring a cross cultural issue. *Child Care Infor Exch.* 1996;108:30-32.

82. Hendricks C, Russell M, Smith CJ. Staying healthy: strategies for helping parents ensure their children's health and well being. *Child Fam.* 1997;16(4):10-17.

83. Hendricks CM. *Young Children on the Grow: Health, Activity and Education in the Preschool Setting.* Washington, DC: ERIC Clearinghouse on Teacher Education; 1992. Teacher Education Mongraph No. 13.

84. American Academy of Pediatrics. Selecting and using the most appropriate car safety seats for children. *Guidelines for Counseling Parents and Pediatricians.* 1996;97(5):761-2.

85. Fraiberg SH. *The Magic Years.* New York, NY: Charles Scribner's Sons; 1959.

86. Klinich, KD, et al. *Study of Older Child Restraint/ Booster Seat Fit and NASS Injury Analysis.* East Liberty, OH: National Highway Traffic Safety Administration, Vehicle Research and Test Center; 1994.

87. American Academy of Pediatrics. Climatic heat stress and the exercising child and adolescent. *Pediatrics.* 2000; 106: 158-9.

88. Kassidy J, Shaver, P, eds. *Handbook of Attachment: Theory, Research and Clinical Applications.* New York, NY: Guilford Press, 1999: 671-687.

89. Provence, S, Lipton, R. *Infants in Institutions.* New York, NY: International Universities Press, 1962: 55-128.

90. Solnit, AJ. Aggression: a view of theory building in psychoanalysis. *Journal of the American Psychoanalytic Association* 1972; 20:3.

91. Gopnik, A, Meltzoff, AN, Kuhl, PK. *The Scientist in the Crib: Minds, Brains, and How Children Learn.* New York, NY: William Morrow and Co., 1999: 49, 202.

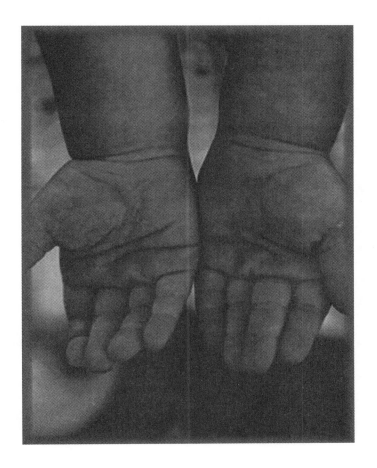

CHAPTER 3

Health Promotion and Protection in Child Care

3.1 HEALTH PROMOTION IN CHILD CARE

DAILY HEALTH CHECK

STANDARD 3.001
CONDUCT OF DAILY HEALTH CHECK

Every day, a trained staff member shall conduct a health check of each child. This health check shall be conducted as soon as possible after the child enters the child care facility and whenever a change occurs while that child is in care. The health check shall address:
a) Changes in behavior (such as lethargy or drowsiness) or appearance from behaviors observed during the previous day's attendance;
b) Skin rashes, itchy skin, itchy scalp, or (during a lice outbreak) nits;
c) If there is a change in the child's behavior or appearance, elevated body temperature, determined by taking the child's temperature;
d) Complaints of pain or of not feeling well;
e) Other signs or symptoms of illness (such as drainage from eyes, vomiting, diarrhea, and so on);
f) Reported illness or injury in child or family members since last date of attendance.

The facility shall gain information necessary to complete the daily health check by direct observation of the child, by querying the parent or legal guardian, and, where applicable, by conversation with the child.

RATIONALE: Daily intake procedures to appraise each child's health and to ascertain recent illness or injury in the child and family reduce the transmission of communicable diseases in child care settings and enable the caregivers to plan for necessary care while the child is in care at the facility.

COMMENTS: This assessment should be performed in a relaxed and comfortable manner that respects the family's culture as well as the child's body and feelings. The health consultant (see Health Consultants, STANDARD 1.040 through STANDARD 1.043) should train the caregiver(s) in conducting a health check, using a checklist. See Appendix F, for a sample symptom record. See Appendix G, for American Academy of Pediatrics' *Recommended Childhood Immunization Schedule*. Contact information is located in Appendix BB.

Assessment by querying the parent should be at the time of transfer of care from the parent to the facility. If this happens outside the facility (when the child is put on a bus or in a car pool, for example), the facility should use some means of communication, such as written notes, checklists, conversations between bus drivers and parents, and daily log books.

See STANDARD 3.068, regarding exclusion from child care.

TYPE OF FACILITY: *Center; Large Family Child Care Home; Small Family Child Care Home*

STANDARD 3.002
DOCUMENTATION OF THE DAILY HEALTH CHECK

The facility shall keep, for at least 3 months, a written record of concerns it identifies for each child during the daily health checks.

RATIONALE: Although the vast majority of communicable diseases of concern in child care have incubation periods of less than 21 days, lags in reporting, non-apparent infections, and the slow-to-develop nature of some outbreaks suggest keeping data for 3 months.

COMMENTS: For additional information on daily health assessment, see also Incidence Logs of Illness, Injury, and Other Problems, STANDARD 8.061 through STANDARD 8.064 and Child Records, STANDARD 8.046 through STANDARD 8.052.

TYPE OF FACILITY: *Center; Large Family Child Care Home*

PREVENTIVE HEALTH SERVICES

STANDARD 3.003
ROUTINE HEALTH SUPERVISION

The facility shall require that the children have routine health supervision by the child's health provider, according to the standards of the American Academy of Pediatrics (AAP). Such health supervision includes routine screening tests, immunizations, and documentation and plotting on standard growth (if younger than 24 months of age) graphs of height and weight assessment and head circumference.

School health services are acceptable to meet this standard if they meet the AAP's standards for school-age children and if the results of such examinations are shared with the child care provider as well as with the school health system. With parental consent, pertinent health information shall be exchanged among the child's routine source of health care and all participants in the child's care, including any school health program involved in the care of the child.

RATIONALE: Provision of routine preventive health services helps detect disease when it is most treatable and through immunization, to prevent diseases for which effective vaccines are available. When children are receiving care that involves the school health system, such care should be coordinated by exchange of information with parental permission among the school health system, the child's usual source of health care, and the child care provider so that all participants in the child's care are aware of the child's health status and follow a common care plan.

The plotting of height and weight measurements by health care providers or school health personnel on a reference growth chart will show how children are growing over time and how they compare with other children of the same chronological age and sex (1). Growth charts are based on data from national probability samples representative of children in the general population. Their use by health care providers will direct the child care provider's attention to unusual body size, which may be a result of disease or

poor nutrition that requires modification of feeding practices in the child care setting (2).

COMMENTS: Some infants and toddlers identified as showing signs of neglect and failure to thrive because of lack of food or inconsistent feeding practices are enrolled in facilities for both promotional and preventive health services. Periodic and accurate height and weight measurements that are plotted and interpreted by a person who is competent in performing these tasks provide an easily obtainable indicator of health status. If such measurements are made in the child care facility, the data from the measurements should be shared by the facility with everyone involved in the child's care, including parents, caregivers, and the child's health care provider. The health consultant can provide staff training on growth assessment. See Health Consultants, STANDARD 1.040 through STANDARD 1.043.

See Appendix H, for *Recommendations for Preventive Pediatric Health Care*. See STANDARD 3.004, on follow-up for nutrition and growth problems and nutrition assessment data; and STANDARD 8.047 through STANDARD 8.052, on files to be kept for each child in care.

TYPE OF FACILITY: *Center; Large Family Child Care Home; Small Family Child Care Home*

STANDARD 3.004
ASSESSMENT AND PLANNING OF NUTRITION FOR INDIVIDUAL CHILDREN

Nutrition assessment data (such as growth and anemia screening) shall be an integral part of the routine health supervision documented in the health record. Communication shall occur with a health care provider on how to meet the nutritional needs of children found to be at risk for nutritional problems.

RATIONALE: Children who need special nutrition intervention or dietary modification of child care feeding routines because of growth problems must be identified so that preventive health/nutrition care can be provided at a critical time during growth and development.

TYPE OF FACILITY: *Center; Large Family Child Care Home; Small Family Child Care Home*

IMMUNIZATIONS

STANDARD 3.005
IMMUNIZATION DOCUMENTATION

The facility shall require that all children enrolling in child care provide written documentation of immunizations appropriate for the child's age. Infants, toddlers, older children, and adolescents shall be immunized as specified in the *Recommended Childhood Immunization Schedule* developed by the American Academy of Pediatrics (AAP), the Advisory Committee on Immunization Practice of the Centers for Disease Control and Prevention (CDC), and the American Academy of Family Practice (AAFP) (AA). See Appendix G. Children whose immunizations are late or not given according to the schedule shall be immunized as recommended by the American Academy of Pediatrics (3)

Because of frequent changes, an updated schedule is published by the AAP every January and shall be consulted for current information (4).

RATIONALE: Routine immunization at the appropriate age is the best means of preventing vaccine-preventable diseases. Laws requiring the age-appropriate immunization of children attending licensed facilities exist in almost all states. Parents of children who attend unlicensed child care should be encouraged to comply with the *Recommended Childhood Immunization Schedule* for infants and children. See Appendix G.

Immunization is particularly important for children in child care because preschool-aged children currently have the highest age-specific incidence of many vaccine-preventable diseases (specifically, measles, pertussis, rubella, varicella, and *Haemophilus influenzae* type b disease).

COMMENTS: In addition to publication in print, as shown in Appendix G, the current *Recommended Childhood Immunization Schedule* is posted on the web site of the American Academy of Pediatrics: www.aap.org/; and the web site of the Centers for Disease Control and Prevention: www.cdc.gov/.

TYPE OF FACILITY: *Center; Large Family Child Care Home; Small Family Child Care Home*

STANDARD 3.006
UNDER-IMMUNIZED CHILDREN

If immunizations are not to be administered because of a medical condition, a statement from the child's health care provider documenting the reason why the child is exempt from the immunization requirement shall be on file.

If immunizations are not given because of parents' religious beliefs, a waiver signed by the parent shall be on file. If a child who is not immunized is in care, the parents must be notified of the risk of the spread of preventable diseases.

Children who have not received their age-appropriate immunizations prior to enrollment and do not have documented religious or medical exemptions from routine childhood immunizations shall show evidence of an appointment for immunizations. The immunization series shall be initiated within one month and completed according to the *Recommended Childhood Immunization Schedule* from the American Academy of Pediatrics (AAP). See Appendix G.

If a vaccine-preventable disease to which children are susceptible occurs in the facility, unimmunized children shall be excluded for the duration of possible exposure or until the age-appropriate immunizations have been completed (whichever comes first).

RATIONALE: Routine immunization at the appropriate age is the best means of preventing vaccine-preventable diseases. Laws requiring the age-appropriate immunization of children attending licensed facilities exist in all states (73). Parents of children who attend unlicensed child care should be encouraged to comply with the *Recommended*

Childhood Immunization Schedule from the American Academy of Pediatrics (AAP) for infants and children. See Appendix G.

The exclusion of an unimmunized child from the facility in the event of an outbreak of a vaccine-preventable disease protects the health of that unimmunized child.

COMMENTS: A sample statement excluding a child from immunizations is: "This is to inform you that [NAME] should not be immunized with [VACCINE] because of [CONDITION, such as immunosuppression]. [SIGNED], [PHYSICIAN] [DATE]"

See Appendix G, for the *Recommended Childhood Immunization Schedule* from the AAP.

TYPE OF FACILITY: *Center; Large Family Child Care Home; Small Family Child Care Home*

STANDARD 3.007
IMMUNIZATION OF CHILD CARE PROVIDERS

Child care providers shall be current for all immunizations routinely recommended for adults by the Advisory Committee on Immunization Practices (ACIP) of the Centers for Disease Control and Prevention (CDC). All child care providers shall have:
a) Completed a primary series for tetanus and diphtheria, and shall receive boosters every 10 years;
b) Been immunized or certified immune by a health care provider against measles, mumps, rubella, poliomyelitis, varicella (chickenpox), and hepatitis B following guidelines of the ACIP (2, 4).

Additionally, influenza immunization is recommended for people 50 years of age and older and pneumococcal polysaccharide vaccine is recommended for people 65 years of age or older.

If a staff member is not appropriately immunized for medical or religious reasons, the child care facility shall require documentation of the reason, in writing.

RATIONALE: Vaccine-preventable infections of adults represent a continuing cause of morbidity and mortality and source of transmission of infectious organisms. Vaccines, which are safe and effective in preventing these diseases, need to be used in adults to minimize disease and to eliminate potential sources of transmission (4, 5)

COMMENTS: For additional information on adult immunization, contact the Centers for Disease Control and Prevention (CDC) or visit the CDC website at www.cdc.gov/. Contact information is located in Appendix BB.

For additional information on vaccine-preventable diseases, see Health Plan for Child Health Services, STANDARD 8.013 through STANDARD 8.017; for additional immunization standards, Pre-employment Staff Health Appraisal, STANDARD 1.045.

TYPE OF FACILITY: *Center; Large Family Child Care Home; Small Family Child Care Home*

SLEEP

STANDARD 3.008
SCHEDULED REST PERIODS AND SLEEP ARRANGEMENTS

The facility shall provide an opportunity for, but shall not require, sleep and rest. The facility shall make available a regular rest period for school-aged children, if the child desires. For children who are unable to sleep, the facility shall provide time and space for quiet play.

Unless the child has a note from a physician specifying otherwise, infants shall be placed in a supine (back) position for sleeping to lower the risks of Sudden Infant Death Syndrome (SIDS). Soft surfaces and gas-trapping objects such as pillows, quilts, sheepskins, soft bumpers or waterbeds shall not be placed under or with an infant for sleeping. When infants can easily turn over from the supine to the prone position, they shall be put down to sleep on their back, but allowed to adopt whatever position they prefer for sleep.

Unless a doctor specifies the need for a positioning device that restricts movement within the child's bed, such devices shall not be used.

RATIONALE: Conditions conducive to sleep and rest for younger children include a consistent caregiver, a routine quiet place, and a regular time for rest (6). Most preschool children in all-day care benefit from scheduled periods of rest. This rest may take the form of actual napping, a quiet time, or a change of pace between activities. The times of naps will affect behavior at home (8). The supine (back) position presents the least risk of SIDS (7, 8). Once infants develop the motor skills to move from their back to their side or stomach it is safe to put them to sleep on their backs and allow them to adapt to whatever position makes them comfortable. Repositioning sleeping infants onto their backs is not recommended once the child has learned to turn over easily from supine (back) to prone (front). If a child has an illness or a disability that predisposes the child to airway obstruction in the back sleeping position, parents should give the child care provider a physician's note specifying the need for prone sleeping and any other special arrangements required for that child.

COMMENTS: In the young infant, favorable conditions for sleep and rest include being dry, well-fed, and comfortable. A school-age child care facility should make available board games and other forms of quiet play. The 1996 update to the statement prepared by the AAP Task Force on Infant Positioning and SIDS details the rationale for preferential back-positioning when caregivers put children down to sleep. Infants who are back-sleepers at home, but are put to sleep in the prone position in child care settings, have a higher risk of SIDS (7). A certain amount of "tummy time" while the child is awake and observed helps muscle development and reduces the tendency for back positioning to flatten the back of the head (8). Additional resources are available from the National SIDS Resource Center and the Back to Sleep Campaign or from the local or state health department. Contact information is located in Appendix BB.

See STANDARD 5.146, for additional information on appropriate bedding to reduce the risk of SIDS. See STANDARD 1.023 and STANDARD 1.038, regarding child care provider training on SIDS. See also STANDARD 3.089, regarding dealing with SIDS deaths.

TYPE OF FACILITY: *Center; Large Family Child Care Home; Small Family Child Care Home*

STANDARD 3.009
UNSCHEDULED ACCESS TO REST AREAS

All children shall have access to rest or nap areas whenever the child desires to rest. These rest or nap areas shall be set up to reduce distraction or disturbance from other activities. All facilities shall provide for rest areas for children who need to rest off schedule, including children who become ill, at least until the child leaves the facility for care elsewhere.

RATIONALE: Any child, especially children who are ill, may need more opportunity for rest or quiet activities.

COMMENTS: See also STANDARD 3.008, on additional sleep requirements.

TYPE OF FACILITY: *Center; Large Family Child Care Home; Small Family Child Care Home*

ORAL HEALTH

STANDARD 3.010
ROUTINE ORAL HYGIENE ACTIVITIES

Caregivers shall promote the habit of regular tooth brushing. All children with teeth shall brush or have their teeth brushed at least once during the hours the child is in child care. Using a size-appropriate brush and a small amount of fluoride toothpaste, the caregiver shall either brush the child's teeth or supervise as the child brushes his/her own teeth. The younger the child the more the caregiver needs to be involved. After feeding, an infant's teeth and gums shall be wiped with a moist cloth to remove any remaining liquid that coats the teeth and gums and which turns to plaque causing tooth decay. Very few preschool-age children have the hand-eye coordination or the fine motor skills necessary to complete the complex process of tooth brushing. The caregiver shall be able to evaluate each child's motor activity and to teach the child the correct method of tooth brushing when the child is capable of doing this activity. The caregiver shall monitor the tooth brushing activity and thoroughly brush the child's teeth after the child has finished brushing.

The cavity-causing effect of frequent exposure to food shall be reduced by offering the children rinsing water after snacks when brushing is not possible.

RATIONALE: Regular tooth brushing with fluoride toothpaste and flossing is encouraged to reinforce oral health habits and prevent gingivitis and tooth decay. Good oral hygiene is as important for a six-month-old child with one tooth as it is for a six-year-old with many teeth. Tooth brushing at least once a day reduces build-up of decay-causing plaque. The development of tooth decay-producing plaque begins when an infant's first tooth appears in his/her mouth. Tooth decay cannot form without this plaque or the acid-producing bacteria in a child's mouth. The ability to do a good job brushing the teeth is a learned skill, improved by practice. Tooth brushing and flossing activities at home may not suffice to learn this skill or accomplish the necessary plaque removal, especially when children eat most of their meals and snacks during a full day in child care.

COMMENTS: The caregiver should use a layer of fluoride toothpaste (about ¼ to ½ the size of a pea for children under three years of age and a pea-sized amount for children over three years of age) and rinse well. Fluoride is the single most effective way to prevent tooth decay. Brushing of teeth with fluoridated toothpaste is the most efficient way to apply fluoride to the teeth. Children under 3 years of age may swallow toothpaste that contains fluoride. If children swallow more than recommended amounts of fluoride toothpaste, they are at risk for fluorosis, a condition caused by excessive levels of fluoride intake.

The children can also rinse and spit out after a snack if their teeth have already been brushed after a meal. Rinsing with water helps to remove food particles from teeth and may prevent cavities. A sink is not necessary to accomplish tooth brushing in child care. Each child can use a cup of water for tooth brushing. The child should wet the brush in the cup, take a rinsing drink, and then spit into the cup.

For information on toothbrush storage, see STANDARD 5.095 and STANDARD 5.151. For additional information on oral health, see also STANDARD 3.011; and STANDARD 8.046 through STANDARD 8.052, on child records.

TYPE OF FACILITY: *Center; Large Family Child Care Home; Small Family Child Care Home*

STANDARD 3.011
ORAL HEALTH EDUCATION

All children with teeth shall have oral hygiene as a part of their daily activity. Those two years and older shall have developmentally appropriate oral health education that includes information on what plaque is, the process of dental caries development, and the importance of good oral hygiene behaviors. School-age children shall receive additional information including the preventive use of fluoride, dental sealants, mouth guards, and the importance of healthy eating behaviors and regularly scheduled dental visits. Older children shall be informed about the effect of tobacco products on their oral health and additional reasons for avoidance.

RATIONALE: Studies have reported that the oral health of participants improved as a result of educational programs (9, 10).

COMMENTS: Child care providers are encouraged to advise parents that the following ages for preventive and early intervention dental services and education are suggested:

• Dental visits, evaluation for systemic fluoride therapy at six months of age, and professionally applied topical fluoride treatments for high risk children;

- First dental visit whenever there is a question of an oral health problem, but no later than 3 years of age;
- Dental sealants generally at 6 or 7 years of age for first permanent molars, and for primary molars if deep pits and grooves or other high risk factors are present.

When possible, child care providers should provide education for parents on good oral hygiene practices and avoidance of behaviors that increase the risk of early childhood caries, such as inappropriate use of a bottle and frequent consumption of carbohydrate-rich foods.

Local dental health professionals can facilitate compliance with these activities by offering education and training for the child care staff and providing oral health presentations for the children and parents.

See Health Education, STANDARD 2.060 through STANDARD 2.064.

TYPE OF FACILITY: *Center*

3.2 HYGIENE

TOILETING AND DIAPERING

STANDARD 3.012
TYPE OF DIAPERS

Diapers worn by children shall be able to contain urine and stool and minimize fecal contamination of the children, caregivers, environmental surfaces, and objects in the child care setting. Only disposable diapers with absorbent gelling material or carboxymethyl cellulose may be used unless the child has a medical reason that does not permit the use of disposable diapers (such as allergic reactions). When children cannot use disposable diapers for a medical reason, the reason shall be documented by the child's health care provider.

When cloth diapers are used, the diaper shall have an absorbent inner lining completely contained within an outer covering made of waterproof material that prevents the escape of feces and urine. The outer covering and inner lining shall be changed together at the same time as a unit and shall not be reused unless both are cleaned and disinfected, washed, and either chemically disinfected or heat dried at 165 degrees F or more. No rinsing or dumping of the contents of the diaper shall be performed at the child care facility.

RATIONALE: Gastrointestinal tract disease caused by bacteria, viruses, parasites, and hepatitis A virus infection of the liver are spread from infected persons through fecal contamination of objects in the environment and hands of caregivers and children. Procedures that reduce fecal contamination, such as minimal handling of soiled diapers and clothing, handwashing, proper personal hygiene, and fecal containment in diapered children control the spread of these diseases. Diapering practices that require increased manipulation of the diaper and waterproof covering, particularly reuse of the covering before it is cleaned and disinfected, present increased opportunities for fecal contamination of the caregivers' hands, the child, and consequently, objects and surfaces in the environment. Environmental contamination has been associated with increased diarrheal rates in child care facilities (11). Fecal contamination in the center environment may be less when paper diapers are used than when cloth diapers worn with pull-on waterproof pants are used (14). When clothes are worn over either paper or cloth diapers with pull-on waterproof pants, there is a reduction in contamination (11, 14).

Diaper dermatitis occurs frequently in diapered children. Diapering practices that reduce the frequency and severity of diaper dermatitis will require less application of skin creams, ointments, and drug treatments, thereby decreasing the likelihood for fecal contamination of caregivers' hands. Most common diaper dermatitis represents an irritant contact dermatitis; the source of irritation is prolonged contact of the skin with urine, feces, or both (11). The action of fecal digestive enzymes on urinary urea and the resulting production of ammonia make the diapered area more alkaline, which has been shown to damage skin (11, 12). Damaged skin is more susceptible to other biological, chemical, and physical insults that can cause or aggravate diaper dermatitis (11). Frequency and severity of diaper dermatitis are lower when diapers are changed more often, regardless of the diaper used (11). The use of modern disposable diapers with absorbent gelling material or carboxymethyl cellulose has been associated with less frequent and severe diaper dermatitis in some children than with the use of cloth diapers and pull-on pants made of a waterproof material (14).

COMMENTS: Several types of diapers or diapering systems are currently available: disposable paper diapers, reusable cloth diapers worn with pull-on waterproof pants, reusable cloth diapers worn with a modern front closure waterproof cover, and single unit reusable diaper systems with an inner cotton lining attached to an outer waterproof covering. Two types of diapers meet the physical requirements of the standard: modern disposable paper diapers, with absorbent gelling material or carboxymethyl cellulose, and single unit reusable diaper systems, with an inner cotton lining attached to an outer waterproof covering. A third type, reusable cloth diapers worn with a modern front closure waterproof cover, meet the standard only:
1) If the cloth diaper and cover are removed simultaneously as a unit and are not removed as two separate pieces, and;
2) If the cloth diaper and outer cover are not reused until both are cleaned and disinfected.

Reusable cloth diapers worn either without a covering or with pull-on pants made of waterproof material do not meet the physical requirements of the standard and are not recommended in facilities. Whichever diapering system is used in the facility, clothes should be worn over diapers while the child is in the facility. Rigorous protocols should be implemented for diaper handling and changing, personal hygiene, and environmental decontamination. While single unit reusable diaper systems, with an inner cloth lining attached to an outer waterproof covering, and reusable cloth diapers, worn with a modern front closure waterproof cover, meet the physical criteria of this standard (if used as described), they have not been evaluated for their ability to reduce fecal contamination, or for their association with diaper dermatitis. Moreover, it has not been demonstrated

that the waterproof covering materials remain waterproof with repeated cleaning and disinfecting. If these reusable diaper products are used in child care, the user should determine the waterproof characteristics of the covering material at frequent intervals.

For additional information on decreasing contamination when diapering, see also STANDARD 3.014; Handwashing, STANDARD 3.020 through STANDARD 3.024; and Sanitation, Disinfection, and Maintenance of Handwashing Sinks, STANDARD 3.029.

TYPE OF FACILITY: *Center; Large Family Child Care Home; Small Family Child Care Home*

STANDARD 3.013
CHECKING FOR THE NEED TO CHANGE DIAPERS

Diapers shall be checked for wetness and feces at least hourly, visually inspected at least every two hours, and whenever the child indicates discomfort or exhibits behavior that suggests a soiled or wet diaper. Diapers shall be changed when they are found to be wet or soiled.

RATIONALE: Frequency and severity of diaper dermatitis are lower when diapers are changed more often, regardless of the type of diaper used (11). Diaper dermatitis occurs frequently in diapered children. Most common diaper dermatitis represents an irritant contact dermatitis; the source of irritation is prolonged contact of the skin with urine, feces, or both (12). The action of fecal digestive enzymes on urinary urea and the resulting production of ammonia make the diapered area more alkaline, which has been shown to damage skin (11, 12). Damaged skin is more susceptible to other biological, chemical, and physical insults that can cause or aggravate diaper dermatitis (12).

Modern disposable diapers can be checked for wetness by feeling the diaper through the clothing and fecal contents can be assessed by smell. Nonetheless, since these methods of checking may be inaccurate, the diaper should be opened and checked visually at least every two hours. Even though modern disposable diapers can continue to absorb moisture for an extended period of time when they are wet, they should be changed after two hours of wearing if they are found to be wet. This prevents rubbing of wet surfaces against the skin, a major cause of diaper dermatitis.

TYPE OF FACILITY: *Center; Large Family Child Care Home; Small Family Child Care Home*

STANDARD 3.014
DIAPER CHANGE PROCEDURE

The following diaper changing procedure shall be posted in the changing area, shall be followed for all diaper changes, and shall be used as part of staff evaluation of caregivers who do diaper changing. Child caregivers shall never leave a child alone on a table or countertop, even for an instant. A safety strap or harness shall not be used on the diaper changing table. If an emergency arises, caregivers shall put the child on the floor or take the child with them.

Step 1: Get organized. Before you bring the child to the diaper changing area, wash your hands, gather and bring what you need to the diaper changing table:
- Non-absorbent paper liner large enough to cover the changing surface from the child's shoulders to beyond the child's feet;
- Fresh diaper, clean clothes (if you need them);
- Wipes for cleaning the child's genitalia and buttocks removed from the container or dispensed so the container will not be touched during diaper changing;
- A plastic bag for any soiled clothes;
- Disposable gloves, if you plan to use them (put gloves on before handling soiled clothing or diapers);
- A thick application of any diaper cream (when appropriate) removed from the container to a piece of disposable material such as facial or toilet tissue.

Step 2: Carry the child to the changing table, keeping soiled clothing away from you and any surfaces you cannot easily clean and sanitize after the change.
- Always keep a hand on the child;

- If the child's feet cannot be kept out of the diaper or from contact with soiled skin during the changing process, remove the child's shoes and socks so the child does not contaminate these surfaces with stool or urine during the diaper changing;
- Put soiled clothes in a plastic bag and securely tie the plastic bag to send the soiled clothes home.

Step 3: Clean the child's diaper area.
- Place the child on the diaper change surface and unfasten the diaper but leave the soiled diaper under the child.
- If safety pins are used, close each pin immediately once it is removed and keep pins out of the child's reach. Never hold pins in your mouth.
- Lift the child's legs as needed to use disposable wipes to clean the skin on the child's genitalia and buttocks. Remove stool and urine from front to back and use a fresh wipe each time. Put the soiled wipes into the soiled diaper or directly into a plastic-lined, hands-free covered can.

Step 4: Remove the soiled diaper without contaminating any surface not already in contact with stool or urine.
- Fold the soiled surface of the diaper inward.
- Put soiled disposable diapers in a covered, plastic-lined, hands-free covered can. If reusable cloth diapers are used, put the soiled cloth diaper and its contents (without emptying or rinsing) in a plastic bag or into a plastic-lined, hands-free covered can to give to parents or laundry service.
- If gloves were used, remove them using the proper technique (see Appendix D) and put them into a plastic-lined, hands-free covered can.
- Whether or not gloves were used, use a disposable wipe to clean the surfaces of the caregiver's hands and another to clean the child's hands, and put the wipes into the plastic-lined, hands-free covered can.
- Check for spills under the child. If there are any, use the paper that extends under the child's feet to fold over the disposable paper so a fresh, unsoiled paper surface is now under the child's buttocks.

Step 5: Put on a clean diaper and dress the child.
* Slide a fresh diaper under the child.
* Use a facial or toilet tissue to apply any necessary diaper creams, discarding the tissue in a covered, plastic-lined, hands-free covered can.
* Note and plan to report any skin problems such as redness, skin cracks, or bleeding.
* Fasten the diaper. If pins are used, place your hand between the child and the diaper when inserting the pin.

Step 6: Wash the child's hands and return the child to a supervised area.
* Use soap and water, no less than 60 degrees F and no more than 120 degrees F, at a sink to wash the child's hands, if you can.
* If a child is too heavy to hold for handwashing or cannot stand at the sink, use commercial disposable diaper wipes or follow this procedure:
    * Wipe the child's hands with a damp paper towel moistened with a drop of liquid soap.
    * Wipe the child's hands with a paper towel wet with clear water.
    * Dry the child's hands with a paper towel.

Step 7: Clean and sanitize the diaper-changing surface.
* Dispose of the disposable paper liner used on the diaper changing surface in a plastic-lined, hands-free covered can.
* Clean any visible soil from the changing surface with detergent and water; rinse with water.
* Wet the entire changing surface with the sanitizing solution (e.g. spray a sanitizing bleach solution of 1/4 cup of household liquid chlorine bleach in one gallon of tap water, mixed fresh daily)(3).
* Put away the spray bottle of sanitizer. If the recommended bleach dilution is sprayed as a sanitizer on the surface, leave it in contact with the surface for at least 2 minutes. The surface can be left to air dry or can be wiped dry after 2 minutes of contact with the bleach solution.

Step 8: Wash your hands according to the procedure in STANDARD 3.021 and record the diaper change in the child's daily log.
* In the daily log, record what was in the diaper and any problems (such as a loose stool, an unusual odor, blood in the stool, or any skin irritation). Report as necessary (16).

RATIONALE: The procedure for diaper changing is designed to reduce the contamination of surfaces that will later come in contact with uncontaminated surfaces such as hands, furnishings, and floors. Posting the multi-step procedure may help caregivers maintain the routine.

Assembling all necessary supplies before bringing the child to the changing area will ensure the child's safety and make the change more efficient. Taking the supplies out of their containers and leaving the containers in their storage places reduces the likelihood that the storage containers will become contaminated during diaper changing and subsequently spread disease.

Commonly, caregivers do not use disposable paper that is large enough to cover the area likely to be contaminated during diaper changing. If the paper is large enough, there will be less need to remove visible soil from surfaces later and there will be enough paper to fold up so the soiled surface is not in contact with clean surfaces while dressing the child.

If the child's foot coverings are not removed during diaper changing, and the child kicks during the diaper changing procedure, the foot coverings can become contaminated and subsequently spread contamination throughout the child care area.

If the child's clean buttocks are put down on a soiled surface, the child's skin can be resoiled.

Children's hands often stray into the diaper area (the area of the child's body covered by diaper) during the diapering process and can then transfer fecal organisms to the environment. Washing the child's hands will reduce the number or organisms carried into the environment in this way. Infectious organisms are present on the skin and diaper even though they are not seen. To reduce the contamination of clean surfaces, caregivers should use a commercial diaper wipe to wipe their hands after removing the gloves or, if no gloves were used, before proceeding to handle the clean diaper and the clothing. Although handwashing is much more effective than using wipes for either the child's or the caregiver's hands there is a significant risk of injury from losing control of the child on the diaper table if handwashing is attempted at this point. Therefore using a wipe for the child's and caregiver's hands while the caregiver is holding the child is a reasonable compromise.

Although gloves are not necessary for diaper changing, they may reduce contamination of the caregiver's hands and reduce the presence of infectious disease agents under the fingernails and from the hand surfaces. Even if gloves are used, caregivers must wash their hands after each child's diaper changing to prevent the spread of disease-causing agents. Gloves can provide a protective barrier, but they offer little protection beyond that achieved by good handwashing. To achieve maximum benefit from use of the gloves, the caregiver must remove the gloves properly after cleaning the child's genitalia and buttocks and removing the soiled diaper. Otherwise, the contaminated gloves will spread infectious disease agents to the clean surfaces as the child is dressed with a clean diaper and clothing. Note that sensitivity to latex is a growing problem. If caregivers or children who are sensitive to latex are present in the facility, gloves must be made of vinyl or some other substance that does not contain or cross-react with latex. See Appendix D, for proper technique for removing gloves.

Prior to using a bleach solution to sanitize, clean any visible soil from the surface with a detergent and rinse well with water. By itself, bleach is not a good cleaning agent. Two minutes of contact with a solution of ¼ cup household liquid chlorine bleach in one gallon of tap water prepared fresh daily is an effective method of surface-sanitizing of environmental surfaces and other inanimate objects that have first been thoroughly cleaned of organic soil (19, 20, 34). Domestic bleach is sold in the conventional strength of 5.25% hypochlorite and a more recently marketed "ultra" bleach product that contains 6% hypochlorite solution. The recommended 1:64 dilution of 1/4 cup of domestic bleach to 1 gallon of water (or 1 tablespoon to 1 quart of water) produces a solution that contains 500-800 parts per million of available chlorine. Unpublished tests by Chlorox shows 2 minutes of contact on a visibly clean surface that has been coated with a spray of a 1:64 dilution of

household bleach, kills most disease-causing organisms on that surface. Air-drying is fine, since chlorine evaporates when the solution dries. If the surface is to be wiped dry, wait for the 2 minute contact time to elapse first. Industrially prepared detergent-sanitizer solutions or detergent cleaning, rinsing and application of a non-bleach sanitizer is acceptable as long as these products are non-toxic for children and are used according to the manufacturer's instructions.

Always assume that the outside of the spray bottle of sanitizing solution is contaminated. Therefore, the spray bottle should be put away before handwashing (the last and essential part of every diaper change).

COMMENTS: The procedure outlined here is an updated version of that found in *Keeping Healthy:Parents, Teachers, and Children* available from the National Association for the Education of Young Children (NAEYC). The recommended procedure is based on extensive experience observing and teaching diaper changing technique to caregivers. This procedure is demonstrated step-by-step in the video series, *Caring for Our Children*, also available from the NAEYC and the American Academy of Pediatrics (AAP). Contact information is located in Appendix BB.

TYPE OF FACILITY: *Center; Large Family Child Care Home; Small Family Child Care Home*

STANDARD 3.015
USE OF A DIAPER CHANGING AREA

Children shall be diapered or have soiled under-wear changed in the diaper changing area.

RATIONALE: The use of a separate area for diaper changing or changing of soiled underwear reduces contamination of other parts of the child care environment (15).

COMMENTS: See also Diaper Changing Areas, STANDARD 5.132.

TYPE OF FACILITY: *Center; Large Family Child Care Home; Small Family Child Care Home*

STANDARD 3.016
ACCESS TO DIAPER CHANGING AREA

Children shall be discouraged from remaining in or entering the diaper changing area. The contaminated surfaces of waste containers shall not be accessible to children.

RATIONALE: Children cannot be expected to avoid contact with contaminated surfaces in the diaper changing area. They should be in this area only for diaper changing and be protected as much as possible from contact with contaminated surfaces.

TYPE OF FACILITY: *Center; Large Family Child Care Home; Small Family Child Care Home*

STANDARD 3.017
USE OF DIAPER CHANGING SURFACE

Diaper changing shall not be conducted on surfaces used for other purposes, especially not on any counter that is used during food preparation or mealtimes.

RATIONALE: Using diaper changing surfaces for any other use increases the likelihood of contamination and spreading of infectious disease agents.

TYPE OF FACILITY: *Center; Large Family Child Care Home; Small Family Child Care Home*

STANDARD 3.018
HANDLING CLOTH DIAPERS

If cloth diapers are used, soiled cloth diapers and/or soiled training pants shall never be rinsed or carried through the child care area to place the fecal contents in a toilet. Reusable diapers shall be laundered by a commercial diaper service approved by the health department or, if laundered by the caregiver, in a manner that meets the approval of the health department. Soiled cloth diapers shall be stored in a labeled container with a tight-fitting lid provided by an accredited commercial diaper service, or in a sealed plastic bag for removal from the facility by an individual child's family. The sealed plastic bag shall be sent home with the child at the end of the day. The containers or sealed diaper bags of soiled cloth diapers shall not be accessible to any child.

RATIONALE: Containing and minimizing the handling of soiled diapers so they do not contaminate other surfaces is essential to prevent the spread of infectious disease. Putting stool into a toilet in the child care facility increases the likelihood that other surfaces will be contaminated during the disposal. There is no reason to use the toilet for stool if disposable diapers are being used. If laundered diapers are involved, the stool can be dumped at the time the diapers are laundered. Commercial diaper laundries use a procedure that separates solid components from the diapers and does not require prior dumping of feces into the toilet.

COMMENTS: For more information on cloth diapers, see STANDARD 3.012.

TYPE OF FACILITY: *Center; Large Family Child Care Home; Small Family Child Care Home*

STANDARD 3.019
MAINTENANCE OF CHANGING TABLES

Changing tables shall be nonporous, kept in good repair, and cleaned and sanitized after each use to remove visible soil, followed by wetting with an approved sanitizing solution.

RATIONALE: Many communicable diseases can be prevented through appropriate hygiene, sanitation, and disinfection procedures. It is difficult, if not impossible to sanitize porous surfaces, broken edges, and surfaces that cannot be completely cleaned. Bacterial cultures of environmental surfaces in child care facilities have shown fecal contamination, which has been used to gauge the adequacy of sanitation and hygiene measures practiced at the facility (17).
COMMENTS: Caregivers should be reminded that many sanitizers leave residues that can cause skin irritation or other symptoms. Users of all sanitizers except bleach should rinse the surface with clear

water, after proper contact time. Rinsing after using bleach is unnecessary, as the chlorine in the solution evaporates, leaving only a residue of water.

A sprayed solution of ¼ cup of household liquid chlorine bleach to 1 gallon of water requires 2 minutes of contact time to kill the usual load of common infectious agents found in feces (3, 19). Prior to using a bleach solution to sanitize, clean any visible soil from the surface with a detergent and rinse well with water. By itself, bleach is not a good cleaning agent. Two minutes of contact with a solution of ¼ cup household liquid chlorine bleach in one gallon of tap water prepared fresh daily is an effective method of surface-sanitizing of environmental surfaces and other inanimate objects that have first been thoroughly cleaned of organic soil (19, 20, 34). Domestic bleach is sold in the conventional strength of 5.25% hypochlorite and a more recently marketed "ultra" bleach product that contains 6% hypochlorite solution. The recommended 1:64 dilution of 1/4 cup of domestic bleach to 1 gallon of water (or 1 tablespoon to 1 quart of water) produces a solution that contains 500-800 parts per million of available chlorine. Unpublished tests by Chlorox shows 2 minutes of contact on a visibly clean surface that has been coated with a spray of a 1:64 dilution of household bleach, kills most disease-causing organisms on that surface. Air-drying is fine, since chlorine evaporates when the solution dries. If the surface is to be wiped dry, wait for the 2 minute contact time to elapse first. Industrially prepared detergent-sanitizer solutions or detergent cleaning, rinsing and application of a non-bleach sanitizer is acceptable as long as these products are non-toxic for children and are used according to the manufacturer's instructions.

Select a sanitizer that will kill vegetative bacteria, fungi, and viruses. The product must be registered by the U.S. Environmental Protection Agency (EPA) for use as a sanitizer. Prepare and use all products according to label directions for sanitizing, except bleach used in a spray application. The spray application of bleach solution has been tested but has not been reviewed by EPA for commercial labeling. See Appendix I, for *Selecting an Appropriate Sanitizer* (18).

TYPE OF FACILITY: *Center; Large Family Child Care Home; Small Family Child Care Home*

HANDWASHING

STANDARD 3.020
SITUATIONS THAT REQUIRE HANDWASHING

All staff, volunteers, and children shall follow the procedure in STANDARD 3.021 for handwashing at the following times:
a) Upon arrival for the day or when moving from one child care group to another;
b) Before and after:
  • Eating, handling food, or feeding a child;
  • Giving medication;
  • Playing in water that is used by more than one person.
c) After:
  • Diapering;
  • Using the toilet or helping a child use a toilet;
  • Handling bodily fluid (mucus, blood, vomit), from sneezing, wiping and blowing noses, from mouths, or from sores;
  • Handling uncooked food, especially raw meat and poultry;
  • Handling pets and other animals;
  • Playing in sandboxes;
  • Cleaning or handling the garbage.

RATIONALE: Handwashing is the most important way to reduce the spread of infection. Many studies have shown that unwashed or improperly washed hands are the primary carriers of infections. Deficiencies in handwashing have contributed to many outbreaks of diarrhea among children and caregivers in child care centers (21).

In child care centers that have implemented a handwashing training program, the incidence of diarrheal illness has decreased by 50% (22). One study found that handwashing helped to reduce colds when frequent and proper handwashing practices were incorporated into a child care center's curriculum (22, 23, 24).

Good handwashing after playing in sandboxes will help prevent ingesting zoonotic parasites that could be present in contaminated sand and soil (26).

Thorough handwashing with soap for at least 10 seconds using comfortably warm, running water, (no less than 60 degrees F and no more than 120 degrees F) removes organisms from the skin and allows them to be rinsed away (25). Handwashing is effective in preventing transmission of disease.

Washing hands after eating is especially important for children who eat with their hands, to decrease the amount of saliva (which may contain organisms) on their hands. Illnesses may be spread in a variety of ways:
a) In human waste (urine, stool);
b) In body fluids (saliva, nasal discharge, secretions from open injuries; eye discharge, blood);
c) Cuts or skin sores;
d) By direct skin-to-skin contact;
e) By touching an object that has germs on it;
f) In drops of water, such as those produced by sneezing and coughing, that travel through the air.

Since many infected people carry communicable diseases without having symptoms and many are contagious before they experience a symptom, staff members need to protect themselves and the children they serve by carrying out hygienic procedures on a routine basis (24).

Animals, including pets, are a source of infection for people, and people may be a source of infection for animals (27).

TYPE OF FACILITY: *Center; Large Family Child Care Home; Small Family Child Care Home*

STANDARD 3.021
HANDWASHING PROCEDURE

Children and staff members shall wash their hands using the following method:
a) Check to be sure a clean, disposable paper (or single-use cloth) towel is available.

b) Turn on warm water, no less than 60 degrees F and no more than 120 degrees F, to a comfortable temperature.
c) Moisten hands with water and apply liquid soap to hands.
d) Rub hands together vigorously until a soapy lather appears, and continue for at least 10 seconds. Rub areas between fingers, around nailbeds, under fingernails, jewelry, and back of hands.
e) Rinse hands under running water, no less than 60 degrees F and no more than 120 degrees F, until they are free of soap and dirt. Leave the water running while drying hands.
f) Dry hands with the clean, disposable paper or single use cloth towel.
g) If taps do not shut off automatically, turn taps off with a disposable paper or single use cloth towel.
h) Throw the disposable paper towel into a lined trash container; or place single-use cloth towels in the laundry hamper; or hang individually labeled cloth towels to dry. Use hand lotion to prevent chapping of hands, if desired.

RATIONALE: Running water over the hands removes soil, including infection-causing organisms. Wetting the hands before applying soap helps to create a lather that can loosen soil. The soap lather loosens soil and brings it into solution on the surface of the skin. Rinsing the lather off into a sink removes the soil from the hands that the soap brought into solution. Warm water, no less than 60 degrees F and no more than 120 degrees F, is more comfortable than cold water; using warm water promotes adequate rinsing during handwashing (25).

Children and staff members should use liquid soap. Although adequately drained bar soap has not been incriminated in transmission of bacteria; bar soaps sitting in water have been shown to be heavily contaminated with *Pseudomonas* and other bacteria. Many children do not have the dexterity to handle a bar of soap. Many adults and children do not take the time to rinse the soil they have applied to the soap bar before putting down the soap bar.

By using a paper towel to turn off the water faucet, people who have just completed handwashing prevent recontamination of their hands.

COMMENTS: Premoistened cleansing towlettes do not effectively clean hands and should not be used as a substitute for washing hands with soap and running water. When running water is unavailable, such as during an outing, towlettes may be used as a temporary measure until hands can be washed under running water. Antibacterial soaps may be used but are not required.

Water basins should not be used as an alternative to running water. If running water from an approved central plumbing source is unavailable, the staff should use a large container fitted with a spigot and fill it daily with a supply of safe water to run water over the hands, which are held above a water basin as a temporary measure. Camp sinks and portable commercial sinks with foot or hand pumps dispense water as for a plumbed sink and are satisfactory if filled with fresh water daily. The staff should clean and disinfect the water reservoir container and water catch basin daily. Outbreaks of disease have been linked to shared wash water and wash basins.

Single-use towels can be used. Shared cloth towels can transmit infectious disease. Even though a child may use a cloth towel that is solely for that child's use, preventing shared use of towels is difficult. Disposable towels prevent this problem, but once used, must be discarded. Many communicable diseases can be prevented through appropriate hygiene and sanitation. Taps that turn off automatically or those that can be turned off without using hands avoid the recontamination problem.

The use of cloth roller towels is not recommended for the following reasons:
a) Children often use cloth roll dispensers improperly, resulting in more than one child using the same section of towel.
b) Incidents of accidental strangulation have been reported (oral communication, U.S. Consumer Product Safety Commission Data Office, September 2000).

For additional information, see *Keeping Healthy*, available from the National Association for the Education of Young Children (NAEYC) and *The ABC's of Safe and Healthy Child Care* available from the

Centers for Disease Control and Prevention (CDC). Contact information located in Appendix BB.

TYPE OF FACILITY: *Center; Large Family Child Care Home; Small Family Child Care Home*

STANDARD 3.022
ASSISTING CHILDREN WITH HANDWASHING

Caregivers shall provide assistance with handwashing at a sink for infants who can be safely cradled in one arm and for children who can stand but not wash their hands independently. A child who can stand shall either use a child-size sink or stand on a safety step at a height at which the child's hands can hang freely under the running water. After assisting the child with handwashing, the staff member shall wash his or her own hands.

If a child is unable to stand and is too heavy to hold safely to wash the hands at the sink, caregivers shall use the following method:
• Wipe the child's hands with a damp paper towel moistened with a drop of liquid soap. Then discard the towel.
• Wipe the child's hands with a clean, wet, paper towel until the hands are free of soap. Then discard the towel.
• Dry the child's hands with a clean paper towel.

RATIONALE: Encouraging and teaching children good handwashing practices must be done in a safe manner. Washing the hands of infants helps reduce the spread of infection, and washing under water is best.

TYPE OF FACILITY: *Center; Large Family Child Care Home; Small Family Child Care Home*

STANDARD 3.023
TRAINING AND MONITORING FOR HANDWASHING

The facility shall ensure that staff members and children who are developmentally able to learn personal hygiene are instructed in, and monitored on, the use of running water, soap, and single-use or disposable towels in handwashing, as specified in STANDARD 3.021.

RATIONALE: Education of the staff regarding hand-washing and other cleaning procedures can reduce the occurrence of illness in the group of children in care (21, 23).

Staff training and monitoring have been shown to reduce the spread of infections of the gastrointestinal tract (often with diarrhea) or liver (28-31).

- In a study of four centers, staff training in hygiene combined with close monitoring of staff compliance was associated with a significant decrease in infant-toddler diarrhea (28).
- In another study, periodic evaluation of caregivers trained in hygiene was associated with significant improvement in the practices under study. Training combined with evaluation was associated with additional significant improvement (29).
- In a study of 12 centers, continuous surveillance without training was associated with a significant decrease in diarrheal illness during the course of longitudinal study. One-time staff training without subsequent monitoring did not result in additional decreases (31).
- A similar decline in diarrhea rates during the course of surveillance without training was observed in a longitudinal study of 52 centers (30).

These studies suggest that training combined with outside monitoring of child care practices can modify staff behavior as well as the occurrence of disease. Involving the children in similar education can be expected to improve the effectiveness of staff training in controlling the spread of infectious disease.

TYPE OF FACILITY: *Center; Large Family Child Care Home; Small Family Child Care Home*

NOSE-BLOWING

STANDARD 3.024
PROCEDURE FOR NASAL
SECRETIONS

Staff members and children shall blow or wipe their noses with disposable, one-use tissues and then discard them in a plastic-lined, covered, hands-free trash container. After blowing the nose,

they shall wash their hands, as specified in STANDARD 3.021 and STANDARD 3.022.

RATIONALE: Handwashing is the most important way to reduce the spread of infection. Many studies have shown that unwashed or improperly washed hands are the primary carriers of infections.

TYPE OF FACILITY: *Center; Large Family Child Care Home; Small Family Child Care Home*

EXPOSURE TO BODY FLUIDS

STANDARD 3.025
CUTS AND SCRAPES

Cuts or sores that are leaking body fluids shall be covered with a dry dressing to avoid contamination of surfaces in child care. The caregiver shall wear gloves if there is to be any contact with a wound.

If an individual has a cut or sore that is leaking a body fluid that cannot be contained or cannot be covered with a dry dressing, that person shall be excluded from the facility until the cut or sore is scabbed over or healed.

RATIONALE: Touching a contaminated object or surface may spread infectious organisms. Body fluids may contain infectious organisms.

Gloves can provide a protective barrier against infectious diseases that may be carried in body fluids.

COMMENTS: Covering sores on lips and on eyes is difficult. Dry scabs are best left open to the air. See STANDARD 3.069, for information regarding staff herpes simplex (cold sores).

TYPE OF FACILITY: *Center; Large Family Child Care Home; Small Family Child Care Home*

STANDARD 3.026
PREVENTION OF EXPOSURE TO BLOOD AND BODILY FLUIDS

Child care facilities shall adopt a modified version of Standard Precautions developed for use in hospitals by The Centers for Disease Control and Prevention as defined in this standard and as may be recommended by the Centers for Disease Control and Prevention for child care settings in the future. This modified version of Standard Precautions shall be used to handle potential exposure to blood, including the blood-containing body fluids and tissue discharges, and to handle other potentially infectious fluids.

In child care settings, exceptions to Standard Precautions as defined by the Centers for Disease Control and Prevention for hospital settings shall include:
a) Use of non-porous gloves is optional unless blood or blood containing body fluids may be involved. Gloves are not required for feeding human milk or cleaning up of spills of human milk.
b) Gowns and masks are not required.
c) Sufficient barriers include materials such as disposable diaper table paper that is moisture resistant, and non-porous gloves.

The staff shall be educated regarding routine precautions to prevent transmission of blood-borne pathogens before beginning to work in the facility and at least annually thereafter. The staff training shall comply with requirements of the Occupational Safety and Health Administration (OSHA), where applicable.

Procedures for Standard Precautions shall include:
a) Surfaces that may come in contact with potentially infectious body fluids must be disposable or of a material that can be sanitized. Use of materials that can be sterilized is not required.
b) The staff shall use barriers and techniques that:
1) Minimize potential contact of mucous membranes or openings in skin to blood or other potentially infectious body fluids and tissue discharges and
2) Reduce the spread of infectious material within the child care facility.
Such techniques include avoiding touching surfaces with potentially contaminated materials unless those surfaces are sanitized before further contact occurs with them by other objects or individuals.
c) When spills of body fluids, urine, feces, blood, saliva, nasal discharge, eye discharge, injury or tissue discharges, and human milk occur, these spills shall be cleaned up immediately, and further managed as follows:
1) For spills of vomit, urine, human milk, and feces, all floors, walls, bathrooms, tabletops, toys, kitchen counter tops, and diaper-changing tables in contact shall be cleaned and sanitized as for the procedure for diaper changing tables in STANDARD 3.014, Step 7.;
2) For spills of blood or other potentially infectious body fluids, including injury and tissue discharges, the area shall be cleaned and sanitized. Care shall be taken to avoid splashing any contaminated materials onto any mucus membrane (eyes, nose, mouth);
3) Blood-contaminated material and diapers shall be disposed of in a plastic bag with a secure tie.
4) Floors, rugs and carpeting that have been contaminated by body fluids shall be cleaned by blotting to remove the fluid as quickly as possible, then sanitized by spot-cleaning with a detergent-disinfectant, and shampooing, or steam-cleaning the contaminated surface.

RATIONALE: Some children and adults may unknowingly be infected with HIV or other infectious agents, such as hepatitis B virus, as these agents may be present in blood or body fluids (19, 28). Thus, the staff in all facilities should adopt Standard Precautions for all blood spills. Bacteria and viruses carried in the blood, such as hepatitis B, pose a small but specific risk in the child care setting (11). Blood and body fluids containing blood (such as watery discharges from injuries) pose the highest potential risk, because bloody body fluids contain the highest concentration of viruses. In addition, hepatitis B virus can survive in dried state in the environment for at least a week and perhaps even longer. Some other body fluids such as saliva contaminated with blood or blood-associated fluids may contain live virus (such as hepatitis B virus) but at lower concentrations than are found in blood itself. Other body fluids, including urine and feces, do not pose a risk with these bloodborne diseases unless they are visibly contaminated with blood, although these fluids do pose a risk with other infectious diseases.

Gloves are used mainly when people knowingly contact or suspect they may contact blood or blood-containing body fluids, including blood-containing tissue or injury discharges. These fluids may contain the viruses that transmit HIV, hepatitis B, and hepatitis C. While human milk (breast milk) can be contaminated with blood from a cracked nipple, the risk of transmission of infection to caregivers who are feeding expressed human milk is very low. Wearing of gloves to feed or clean up spills of expressed human milk is unnecessary, but caregivers with open cuts on their hands should avoid getting expressed human milk on their hands, especially if they have any open skin or sores on their hands.

During the preparation of the 2nd edition of Caring for Our Children, the Steering Committee consulted several experts on the issue of precautions required for handling of human milk. Published policies confirm a clear consensus that gloves are not required for feeding human milk. Although the issue of use of gloves for clean up of human milk spills has not been addressed in previously published policies or in peer-reviewed literature, the Steering Committee could find no persuasive evidence that the risk involved in cleaning up spills is sufficient to require the use of gloves for human milk spills in child care settings.

Touching a contaminated object or surface may spread illnesses. Many types of infectious germs may be contained in human waste (urine, feces) and body fluids (saliva, nasal discharge, tissue and injury discharges, eye discharges, blood). Because many infected people carry communicable diseases without having symptoms, and many are contagious before they experience a symptom, staff members need to protect themselves and the children they serve by carrying out sanitation procedures on a routine basis. Education of the staff regarding cleaning procedures can reduce the occurrence of illness in the group of children with whom they work (19, 28).

Prior to using a bleach solution to sanitize, clean any visible soil from the surface with a detergent and rinse well with water. By itself, bleach is not a good cleaning agent. Two minutes of contact with a solution of ¼

cup household liquid chlorine bleach in one gallon of tap water prepared fresh daily is an effective method of surface-sanitizing of environmental surfaces and other inanimate objects that have first been thoroughly cleaned of organic soil (19, 20, 34). Domestic bleach is sold in the conventional strength of 5.25% hypochlorite and a more recently marketed "ultra" bleach product that contains 6% hypochlorite solution. The recommended 1:64 dilution of 1/4 cup of domestic bleach to 1 gallon of water (or 1 tablespoon to 1 quart of water) produces a solution that contains 500-800 parts per million of available chlorine. Unpublished tests by Chlorox shows 2 minutes of contact on a visibly clean surface that has been coated with a spray of a 1:64 dilution of household bleach, kills most disease-causing organisms on that surface. Air-drying is fine, since chlorine evaporates when the solution dries. If the surface is to be wiped dry, wait for the 2 minute contact time to elapse first. Industrially prepared detergent-sanitizer solutions or detergent cleaning, rinsing and application of a non-bleach sanitizer is acceptable as long as these products are non-toxic for children and are used according to the manufacturer's instructions.

Cleaning and sanitizing rugs and carpeting that have been contaminated by body fluids is challenging. Extracting as much of the contaminating material as possible before it penetrates the surface to lower layers helps to minimize this challenge. Cleaning and sanitizing the surface without damaging it requires use of special cleaning agents designed for use on rugs, or steam cleaning.

Requirements of the OSHA for a facility plan and annual training of staff members who may be exposed to blood as a condition of their employment apply to child care workers who are employees.

COMMENTS: The Region III office of OSHA developed a model plan for child care facilities. Filling in the blanks in this model plan is easier than starting from scratch to write a conforming plan. The sanctions for failing to comply with OSHA requirements can be costly, both in fines and in health consequences. Child care providers should take the necessary steps to meet OSHA requirements.

Regional offices of OSHA are listed with other federal agencies in the telephone directory.

Either single-use disposable gloves or utility gloves should be used. Single-use disposable gloves should be used only once and then discarded immediately without being handled. If utility gloves are used, they should be cleaned after every use with soap and water and then dipped in bleach solution up to the wrist. The gloves should then be taken off and hung to dry. The utility gloves should be worn, not handled, during this cleaning and sanitizing procedure.

Staff who wear gloves must be mindful that the wearing of gloves does not prevent contamination of their hands or of surfaces touched with contaminated gloved hands. Handwashing and sanitizing of contaminated surfaces is still required even when gloves are used.

For the proper technique for removing gloves, see Appendix D.

TYPE OF FACILITY: *Center; Large Family Child Care Home; Small Family Child Care Home*

STANDARD 3.027
FEEDING OF HUMAN MILK TO ANOTHER MOTHER'S CHILD

If a child has been fed another child's bottle of expressed human milk, this shall be treated as an accidental exposure to a potential HIV-containing body fluid. Providers shall:
a) Inform the parents of the child who was given the wrong bottle that:
   1) Their child was given another child's bottle of expressed human milk;
   2) The risk of transmission of HIV is very small;
   3) They should notify the child's physician of the exposure;
   4) The child should have a baseline test for HIV and a follow-up test six months later.
   5) The mother of the child should have an HIV test immediately and a follow-up test six months later.
b) Inform the mother who expressed the human milk of the bottle switch and ask:

1) If she has ever had an HIV test and, if so, if she would be willing to share the results with the parents of the exposed child;
2) If she does not know if she has ever had an HIV test, if she would be willing to contact her obstetrician and find out, and if she has, share the results with the parents;
3) If she has never had an HIV test, if she would be willing to have one immediately and a follow-up test six months later and share results with the parents;
4) If the mother has had a previous test more than six months prior to the incident, if she would be willing to have a test immediately and a follow-up test six months later and share results with the parents;
5) When the human milk was expressed and how it was handled before being brought to the facility.

RATIONALE: Baseline HIV testing on all parties concerned is necessary to rule out the current existence of the HIV virus. A repeat test at six months after exposure is necessary to ensure that sero-conversion (a previously negative blood test becomes positive), to the HIV virus has not occurred. The mother of the baby who drank the wrong bottle is asked to be tested at baseline and six months to ensure any potential positive tests are not the result of a mother-child exposure. The mother who's expressed breast milk was fed to the baby is encouraged to have a baseline HIV test and then repeated in six months, as a recent exposure to the HIV virus may not be evident on the baseline test.

Instances in which one child is mistakenly fed another child's bottle should be rare if proper procedures are used; more common occurrence is for one child to feed from a bottle that another child has dropped or that was put down. Risk of HIV transmission from expressed human milk that another child has drunk is believed to be low because:
a) In the United States, women who are HIV-positive and aware of that fact are advised not to breastfeed their infants;
b) Compounds present in human milk act, together with time and cold temperatures, to destroy the HIV present in expressed human milk (34, 35).

COMMENTS: While the risk of HIV transmission through human milk is low, it is still a concern. There is probably an even greater risk of transmitting hepatitis B, hepatitis C, or CMV (cytomegalovirus).

HIV testing may not account for a potential exposure to the virus from the time in between the previous test and the exposure. An infant should be tested up to 9 months after the exposure if the status of the donor mother is unknown. If an infant is exposed to expressed human milk from the wrong mother, that infant should complete the hepatitis B vaccination series, if he/she has not already.

For additional information on human milk, see STANDARD 4.017.

TYPE OF FACILITY: *Center; Large Family Child Care Home; Small Family Child Care Home*

3.3 SANITATION, DISINFECTION, AND MAINTENANCE

STANDARD 3.028
ROUTINE FREQUENCY OF
CLEANING AND SANITATION

The routine frequency of cleaning and sanitation in the facility shall be as indicated in the table below. This frequency shall be increased from baseline routine frequencies whenever there are outbreaks of illness, there is known contamination, visible soil, or when recommended by the health department to control certain infectious diseases. All surfaces, furnishings, and equipment that are not in good repair or that have been contaminated by body fluids shall be taken out of service until they are repaired, cleaned, and, if contaminated, sanitized effectively.

RATIONALE: Since children will touch any surface they can reach (including floors), all surfaces in a child care facility may be contaminated and can spread infectious disease agents. Therefore, all surfaces must be properly sanitized.

Illnesses may be spread in a variety of ways, such as by coughing, sneezing, direct skin-to-skin contact, or touching a contaminated object or surface. Respiratory tract secretions that can contain viruses (including respiratory syncytial virus and rhinovirus) that contaminate environmental surfaces remain infectious for variable periods of time, and infection has been acquired by touching articles and surfaces contaminated with infectious respiratory secretions (33).

Regular and thorough cleaning of rooms prevents the transmission of diseases (17). Many communicable diseases can be prevented through appropriate hygiene and sanitation procedures. Bacterial cultures of environmental surfaces in child care facilities have shown fecal contamination, which has been used to gauge the adequacy of facilities' sanitation and hygiene measures. Therefore, a reasonable effort should be made to clean respiratory secretions from environmental surfaces. However, to continuously maintain tabletops and toys free of contamination from respiratory tract secretions is an unrealistic goal. Meals and snacks are often served on the same tables used for play. Children frequently remove food from their plates and eat directly from the surface of the table. This behavior should be discouraged, and cleaning and sanitizing prior to eating may reduce the risk of transmitting disease.

Mops should be assumed to be contaminated since they are used to remove contamination from other surfaces.

COMMENTS: Levels of fecal coliforms in the environment have been shown to increase during outbreaks of diarrheal illnesses. Increasing the frequency of cleaning and sanitizing may reduce environmental contamination. Doubling the frequency is somewhat arbitrary, and health officials may recommend a more frequent cleaning schedule in certain areas, depending on the nature of the problem. Head gear can be placed in the dryer. Another way to prevent transmission of lice nits is to have children wear disposable shower caps before playing with hats. See *Pediculosis capitis* (head lice), STANDARD 6.038.

The bleach solution used for sanitizing the child care environment is also appropriate for sanitizing mops and rags. Detachable mop heads and reusable rags may be cleaned in a washing machine and dried in a mechanical dryer or hung to dry.

Compliance with these procedures is measured by staff interviews and by observation of practices when contamination occurs. See also STANDARD 3.026, for information regarding exposure to blood and bodily fluids.

For more information on frequency of cleaning and sanitizing, see page 106 for a frequency chart adapted from *Keeping Healthy*, 1999 from the National Association for the Education of Young Children. Contact information is located in Appendix BB.

TYPE OF FACILITY: *Center; Large Family Child Care Home; Small Family Child Care Home*

SANITATION, DISINFECTION, AND MAINTENANCE OF TOILET LEARNING/TRAINING EQUIPMENT, TOILETS, AND BATHROOMS

STANDARD 3.029
POTTY CHAIRS

Use of potty chairs shall be discouraged. If potty chairs are used, they shall be emptied into a toilet, cleaned in a utility sink, sanitized after each use, and stored in the bathroom. After the potty is sanitized, the utility sink shall also be sanitized.

RATIONALE: Sanitary handling of potty chairs is difficult and, therefore, their use in child care facilities is not recommended.

Potty chairs should not be washed in a sink used for washing hands.

COMMENTS: If potty chairs are used, they should be constructed of plastic or similar nonporous synthetic products. Wooden potty chairs should not be used, even if the surface is coated with a finish. The finished

surface of wooden potty chairs is not durable and, therefore, may become difficult to wash and sanitize effectively.

For more information on potty chairs, see STANDARD 5.124.

TYPE OF FACILITY: *Center; Large Family Child Care Home; Small Family Child Care Home*

STANDARD 3.030
EQUIPMENT USED FOR CLEANING AND SANITIZING

Utility gloves and equipment designated for cleaning and sanitizing toilet learning/training equipment and flush toilets shall be used for each cleaning and shall not be used for other cleaning purposes. Utility gloves shall be washed with soapy water and dried after each use.

RATIONALE: Contamination of hands and equipment in a child care room has played a role in the transmission of disease (17).

TYPE OF FACILITY: *Center; Large Family Child Care Home; Small Family Child Care Home*

AREA	CLEAN	SANITIZE	FREQUENCY
Classrooms/Child Care/Food Areas			
Countertops/tabletops, Floors, Door and cabinet handles	X	X	Daily and when soiled.
Food preparation & service surfaces	X	X	Before and after contact with food activity; between preparation of raw and cooked foods.
Carpets and large area rugs	X		Vacuum daily when children are not present. Clean with a carpet cleaning method approved by the local health authority. Clean carpets only when children will not be present until the carpet is dry. Clean carpets at least monthly in infant areas, at least every 3 months in other areas and when soiled.
Small rugs	X		Shake outdoors or vacuum daily. Launder weekly.
Utensils, surfaces and toys that go into the mouth or have been in contact with saliva or other body fluids	X	X	After each child's use, or use disposable, one-time utensils or toys.
Toys that are not contaminated with body fluids. Dress-up clothes not worn on the head. Sheets and pillowcases, individual cloth towels (if used), combs and hairbrushes, wash cloth and machine-washable cloth toys. (None of these items should be shared among children.)	X		Weekly and when visibly soiled.
Blankets, sleeping bags, Cubbies	X		Monthly and when soiled.
Hats	X		After each child's use or use disposable hats that only one child wears.
Cribs and crib mattresses	X		Weekly, before use by a different child, and whenever soiled or wet.
Phone receivers	X	X	Weekly.
Toilet and Diapering Areas			
Handwashing sinks, faucets, surrounding counters, soap dispensers, door knobs	X	X	Daily and when soiled.
Toilet seats, toilet handles, door knobs or cubicle handles, floors	X	X	Daily, or immediately if visibly soiled.
Toilet bowls	X	X	Daily.
Changing tables, potty chairs (Use of potty chairs in child care is discouraged because of high risk of contamination).	X	X	After each child's use.
General Facility			
Mops and cleaning rags	X	X	Before and after a day of use, wash mops and rags in detergent and water, rinse in water, immerse in sanitizing solution, and wring as dry as possible. After cleaning and sanitizing, hang mops and rags to dry.
Waste and diaper containers	X		Daily.
Any surface contaminated with body fluids: saliva, mucus, vomit, urine, stool, or blood	X	X	Immediately, as specified in STANDARD 3.026.

Adapted from *Keeping Healthy*, National Association for the Education of Young Children. 1999.

STANDARD 3.031
RAGS AND DISPOSABLE TOWELS USED FOR CLEANING

Disposable towels shall be preferred for cleaning. If clean reusable rags are used, they shall be laundered separately between uses for cleaning. Disposable towels shall be sealed in a plastic bag and removed to outside garbage. Cloth rags shall be placed in a closed, foot-operated receptacle until laundering.

RATIONALE: Materials used for cleaning become contaminated in the process and must be handled so they do not spread potentially infectious material.

COMMENTS: Sponges generally are contaminated with bacteria and are difficult to clean. Therefore, use of sponges in child care facilities for cleaning purposes is not recommended.

TYPE OF FACILITY: *Center; Large Family Child Care Home; Small Family Child Care Home*

STANDARD 3.032
ODORS

Odors in toilets, bathrooms, diaper changing and other inhabited areas of the facility shall be controlled by ventilation and sanitation. Toilets and bathrooms, janitorial closets, and rooms with utility sinks or where wet mops and chemicals are stored shall be mechanically ventilated to the outdoors with local exhaust mechanical ventilation to control and remove odors. Chemical air fresheners shall not be used.

RATIONALE: Chemical air fresheners may cause nausea or an allergic response in some children. Ventilation and sanitation help control and prevent the spread of disease and contamination.

TYPE OF FACILITY: *Center; Large Family Child Care Home; Small Family Child Care Home*

STANDARD 3.033
WASTE RECEPTACLES

Waste receptacles in toilet rooms shall be kept clean and in good repair, and emptied daily.

RATIONALE: This practice prevents the spread of disease and filth.

COMMENTS: For additional information on sanitation and maintenance of toilet learning/training equipment, toilets, and bathrooms, see also Toilets and Toilet Training Equipment, STANDARD 5.116 through STANDARD 5.125; and for Diaper Changing Areas, see STANDARD 5.132.

TYPE OF FACILITY: *Center; Large Family Child Care Home; Small Family Child Care Home*

SELECTION AND MAINTENANCE OF SURFACES

STANDARD 3.034
SELECTION OF SURFACES AND MATERIALS

Walls, ceilings, floors, furnishings, equipment, and other surfaces shall be suitable to the location and the users. They shall be maintained in good repair, free from visible soil and in a clean condition. Carpets, porous fabrics, and other surfaces that trap soil and potentially contaminated materials shall not be used in toilet rooms, diaper change areas, and areas where food handling occurs.

Areas used by staff or children who have allergies to dust mites or components of furnishings or supplies shall be maintained according to the recommendations of health professionals.

RATIONALE: Carpets and porous fabrics are not appropriate for some areas because they are difficult to clean and sanitize. Disease-causing microorganisms have been isolated from carpets.

Caregivers must remove illness-causing materials. Many allergic children have allergies to dust mites, which are microscopic insects that ingest the tiny particles of skin that people shed normally every day. Dust mites live in carpeting and fabric but can be killed by frequent washing and use of a mechanical, heated dryer. Restricting the use of carpeting and furnishings to types that can be laundered regularly helps. Other children may have allergies to animal products such as those with feathers, fur, or wool. Some may be allergic to latex.

COMMENTS: One way to measure compliance with the standard for cleanliness is to wipe the surface with a clean mop or clean rag, and then insert the mop or rag in cold rinse water. If the surface is clean, no residue will appear in the rinse water.

Disposable gloves are commonly made of latex or vinyl. If latex-sensitive individuals are present in the facility, only vinyl disposable gloves should be used. Other common supplies that contain latex, such as rubber bands, should also be removed from the environment.

As long as their feet are clean, children and adults may be barefoot in the play area.

TYPE OF FACILITY: *Center; Large Family Child Care Home; Small Family Child Care Home*

STANDARD 3.035
SHOES IN INFANT PLAY AREAS

Before walking on surfaces that infants use specifically for play, adults and children shall remove or cover shoes they have worn outside the play area used by that group of infants. These individuals may wear shoes and shoe covers that are used only in the play area for that group of infants.

RATIONALE: When infants play, they touch the surfaces on which they play with their hands, then put their hands in their mouths. Shoes may be conduits of infectious material when people walk on surfaces that are contaminated with disease-causing organisms, then walk in the infant play area.

COMMENTS: Facilities can meet this standard in several ways. The facility can designate contained play surfaces for infant play on which no one walks with shoes. Individuals can wear shoes or slippers that are worn only to walk in the infant play area or they can wear clean cloth or disposable shoe covers over shoes that have been used to walk outside the infant play area.

This standard applies to shoes that have been worn in toilet and diaper changing areas, in the play areas of other groups of children, as well as outdoors. All of these locations are potential sources of contamination for the area where infants are crawling and playing.

TYPE OF FACILITY: *Center; Large Family Child Care Home*

SELECTION, SANITATION, DISINFECTION, AND MAINTENANCE OF TOYS AND OBJECTS

STANDARD 3.036
USE OF TOYS THAT CAN BE WASHED AND SANITIZED

Toys that cannot be washed and sanitized shall not be used. Toys that children have placed in their mouths or that are otherwise contaminated by body secretion or excretion shall be set aside where children cannot access them. They must be set aside until they are washed with water and detergent, rinsed, sanitized, and air-dried by hand or in a mechanical dishwasher that meets the requirements of STANDARD 4.063 through STANDARD 4.065. Play with plastic or play foods shall be closely supervised to prevent shared mouthing of these toys.

Machine washable cloth toys shall be for use by one individual only until these toys are laundered.

Indoor toys shall not be shared between groups of infants or toddlers unless they are washed and sanitized before being moved from one group to the other.

RATIONALE: Contamination of hands, toys and other objects in child care areas has played a role in the transmission of diseases in child care settings (17). All toys can spread disease when children put the toys in their mouths, touch the toys after putting their hands in their mouths during play or eating, or after toileting with inadequate handwashing. Using a mechanical dishwasher is an acceptable labor-saving approach for plastic toys as long as the dishwasher can wash and sanitize the surfaces.

COMMENTS: Small toys with hard surfaces can be set aside for cleaning by putting them into a dish pan labeled "soiled toys." This dish pan can contain soapy water to begin removal of soil, or it can be a dry container used to bring the soiled toys to a toy cleaning area later in the day. Having enough toys to rotate through cleaning makes this method of deferred cleaning possible.

See STANDARD 3.028, for frequency of routine cleaning and sanitizing. For more information regarding appropriate play materials for young children, see STANDARD 2.012.

TYPE OF FACILITY: *Center; Large Family Child Care Home; Small Family Child Care Home*

STANDARD 3.037
OBJECTS INTENDED FOR THE MOUTH

Thermometers, pacifiers, teething toys, and similar objects shall be cleaned and reusable parts shall be sanitized between uses. Pacifiers shall not be shared.

RATIONALE: Contamination of hands, toys and other objects in child care areas has played a role in the transmission of diseases in child care settings (17).

TYPE OF FACILITY: *Center; Large Family Child Care Home; Small Family Child Care Home*

STANDARD 3.038
ROUTINE CHECKS OF PLAY EQUIPMENT

A staff member shall be assigned to check all play equipment at least monthly to ensure that it is safe for children. In addition, the staff shall observe equipment while children are playing on it to ensure that it is safe for children.

RATIONALE: A monthly safety check of all the equipment in the facility as a focused task provides an opportunity to notice wear and tear that requires maintenance. Observations should be made while the children are playing, too, to spot any maintenance problems and correct them as soon as possible.

COMMENTS: Site safety checklists have been developed for this type of periodic audit. The following is an example of an adaptation of such a checklist (71):
* Toys and play equipment have no sharp edges or points, small parts, pinch points, chipped paint, splinters, or loose nuts or bolts.
* All painted toys are free of lead.
* Toys are put away when not in use.
* Toys that are mouthed are washed and sanitized after each use.
* Children are not permitted to play with any type of plastic bag, latex balloon or latex/vinyl gloves.
* Children under 4 years of age are not permitted to have band aids that they can detach and thereby create a potential choking hazard. Gauze and tape should be used for bandaging instead. Unlike band aids, gauze and porous tape rarely form complete airway plugs.
* Toys are too large to fit completely into a child's mouth and have no small, detachable parts to cause choking. No coins, safety pins, or marbles for children under 4 years of age.
* Infants and toddlers are not permitted to eat small objects and foods that may easily cause choking, such as hot dogs, hard candy, seeds, nuts, popcorn, and uncut round foods such as whole grapes and olives.
* Toy chests have air holes and a lid support or have no lid. A lid that slams shut can cause pinching, head injuries, or suffocation.
* Shooting or projectile toys are not present.

- Commercial art materials are stored in their original containers out of children's reach. The manufacturer's label includes a reference to meeting ASTM Standards.
- Rugs, curtains, pillows, blankets, and cloth toys are flame-resistant.
- Sleeping surfaces are firm. Waterbeds and soft bedding materials such as sheepskin, quilts, comforters, pillows, and granular materials (plastic foam beds or pellets) used in beanbags are not accessible to infants.
- Hinges and joints are covered to prevent small fingers from being pinched or caught.
- Protrusions such as nails or bolts are not present.
- Cribs, playpens, and highchairs are away from drapery cords and electrical cords.
- Cribs, playpens, and highchairs are used properly and according to the manufacturer's recommendations for age and weight. Cribs have no corner posts.
- Cribs have slats placed 2-3/8 inches apart or less and have snug-fitting mattresses. Mattresses are set at their lowest settings and sides are locked at their highest settings.
- Toys are not hung across the cribs of infants who can sit up.
- Rattles, pacifiers, or other objects are never hung around an infant's neck.
- Five-gallon buckets are not accessible to infants and toddlers (See STANDARD 3.045).

TYPE OF FACILITY: *Center; Large Family Child Care Home; Small Family Child Care Home*

SELECTION, SANITATION, DISINFECTION, AND MAINTENANCE OF BEDDING

STANDARD 3.039
INDIVIDUAL BEDDING

Bedding (sheets, pillows, blankets, sleeping bags) shall be of a type that can be washed. Each child's bedding shall be kept separate from other children's bedding, on the bed or stored in individually labeled bins, cubbies, or bags. Bedding shall be cleaned according to STANDARD 3.028.

RATIONALE: Lice infestation, scabies, and ringworm are among the most common infectious diseases in child care. Toddlers often nap or sleep on mats or cots and the mats or cots are taken out of storage during nap time, then placed back in storage. Lice, infestations, scabies, ringworm and other diseases can be spread if bedding material that various children use are stored together. Providing bedding for each child and storing each set in individually labeled bins, cubbies, or bags in a manner that separates the personal articles of one individual from those of another will prevent the spread of disease.

TYPE OF FACILITY: *Center; Large Family Child Care Home; Small Family Child Care Home*

STANDARD 3.040
CRIB SURFACES

Cribs and crib mattresses shall have a nonporous, easy-to-wipe surface. All surfaces shall be cleaned as specified in STANDARD 3.028.

RATIONALE: Contamination of hands, toys and other objects in child care areas has played a role in the transmission of diseases in child care settings (17).

COMMENTS: For additional information on sanitation, disinfection, and maintenance of bedding, see also Laundry, STANDARD 5.140 and STANDARD 5.141.

TYPE OF FACILITY: *Center; Large Family Child Care Home; Small Family Child Care Home*

3.4 HEALTH PROTECTION IN CHILD CARE

STANDARD 3.041
TOBACCO USE AND PROHIBITED SUBSTANCES

Tobacco use, alcohol, and illegal drugs shall be prohibited on the premises of the facility at all times.

RATIONALE: Scientific evidence has linked respiratory health risks to secondhand smoke. No children, especially those with respiratory problems, should be exposed to additional risk from the air they breathe. Infants and young children exposed to secondhand smoke are at risk of developing bronchitis, pneumonia, and middle ear infections when they experience common respiratory infections (36-39). Separation of smokers and nonsmokers within the same air space does not eliminate or minimize exposure of nonsmokers to secondhand smoke.

Cigarettes used by adults are the leading cause of ignition of fatal house fires (40-42).

COMMENTS: The age, defenselessness, and lack of discretion of the children under care make this prohibition an absolute requirement.

TYPE OF FACILITY: *Center; Large Family Child Care Home; Small Family Child Care Home*

ANIMALS

STANDARD 3.042
PETS THAT MIGHT HAVE CONTACT WITH CHILDREN

Any pet or animal present at the facility, indoors or outdoors, shall be in good health, show no evidence of carrying any disease, be fully immunized, and be maintained on a flea, tick, and worm control program. A current (time-specified) certificate from a veterinarian shall be on file in the facility, stating that the specific pet meets these conditions.

All contact between animals and children shall be supervised by a caregiver who is close enough to remove the child immediately if the animal shows signs of distress or the child shows signs of treating the animal inappropriately. The caregiver shall instruct children on safe procedures to follow when in close proximity to these animals (for example, not to provoke or startle animals or touch them when they are near their food). Potentially aggressive animals (such as pit bulls) shall not be in the same physical space with the children.

RATIONALE: The risk of injury, infection, and aggravation of allergy from contact between children and animals is significant. The staff must plan carefully when having an animal in the facility and when visiting a zoo or local pet store. Children should be brought into direct contact only with animals known to be friendly and comfortable in the company of children.

Dog bites to children under 4 years of age usually occur at home, and the most common injury sites are the head, face, and neck. Dog bites cause an estimated 600,000 injuries and 10-20 deaths a year (45). Many human illnesses can be acquired from pets (43, 52-53). Many allergic children have symptoms when they are around animals. About 6% of the U.S. population is allergic to animals, and 25% of people being treated for allergies are sensitive to dogs and cats (47).

COMMENTS: Bringing animals and children together has both risks and benefits. Pets teach children about how to be gentle and responsible, about life and death, and about unconditional love. Nevertheless, animals can pose serious health risks.

Facilities must be sure an animal is healthy and a suitable pet to bring into contact with children, as determined by a recent check-up by a veterinarian.

TYPE OF FACILITY: *Center; Large Family Child Care Home; Small Family Child Care Home*

STANDARD 3.043
PROHIBITED PETS

The facility shall not keep or bring in ferrets, turtles, iguanas, lizards or other reptiles, psittacine birds (birds of the parrot family), or any wild or dangerous animals. The facility may consider an exception for reptiles if:
a) The animals are kept behind a glass wall in a tank or container where a child cannot touch the animals or the inside of the tank;
b) The health department grants authority for possession of such animals.

RATIONALE: Animals, including pets, are a source of illness for people, and people may be a source of illness for animals (27, 45). Reptiles may carry salmonella and pose a risk to children who are likely to put unwashed hands in their mouths.

TYPE OF FACILITY: *Center; Large Family Child Care Home; Small Family Child Care Home*

STANDARD 3.044
CARE FOR PETS

The facility shall care for all pets as recommended by the health department. When pets are kept on the premises, the facility shall write and adhere to procedures for their care and maintenance. Proof of current compliance with required pet immunizations shall be signed by a veterinarian and shall be kept on file at the facility.

When animals are kept in the child care facility, the following conditions shall be met:
a) The living quarters of animals shall be enclosed and kept clean of waste to reduce the risk of human contact with this waste;
b) Animal cages shall be of an approved type with removable bottoms and shall be kept clean and sanitary;
c) Animal litter boxes shall not be located in areas accessible to children;
d) All animal litter shall be removed immediately from children's areas and discarded as required by local health authorities;
e) Animal food supplies shall be kept out of reach of children;

f) Live animals and fowl shall be prohibited from food preparation, food storage, and eating areas;
g) Caregivers and children shall wash their hands after handling animals, animal food, or animal wastes, as specified in Handwashing, STANDARD 3.021 through STANDARD 3.024.

RATIONALE: Animals, including pets, are a source of illness for people; likewise, people may be a source of illness for animals (27, 45). Handwashing is the most important way to reduce the spread of infection. Unwashed or improperly washed hands are primary carriers of infections.

Just as food intended for human consumption may become contaminated, a pet's food can become contaminated by standing at room temperature, or by being exposed to animals, insects, or people.

TYPE OF FACILITY: *Center; Large Family Child Care Home; Small Family Child Care Home*

WATER SAFETY

STANDARD 3.045
SUPERVISION NEAR BODIES OF WATER

Children shall not be permitted to play without constant supervision in areas where there is any body of water, including swimming pools, built-in wading pools, tubs, pails, sinks, or toilets, ponds and irrigation ditches.

Children who need assistance with toileting shall not be allowed in toilet or bathroom facilities without direct visual supervision. Children less than 5 years of age shall not be left unattended in a bathtub or shower.

RATIONALE: Small children can drown within 30 seconds, in as little as 2 inches of liquid (44).

In a comprehensive study of drowning and submersion incidents involving children under 5 years of age in Arizona, California, and Florida, the U.S. Consumer Product Safety Commission found that:

a) Submersion incidents involving children usually happen in familiar surroundings;

b) Pool submersions involving children happen quickly. Seventy-seven percent of the victims had been missing from sight for 5 minutes or less;

c) Child drowning is a silent death. Splashing may not occur to alert someone that the child is in trouble.

Each year, approximately 1,500 children under age 20 drown. A national study that examines where drowning most commonly take place concluded that infants are most likely to drown in bathtubs, toddlers are most likely to drown in swimming pools, and older children and adolescents are most likely to drown in freshwater (rivers, lakes, ponds). Researchers from the National Institute of Child Health and Human Development, Johns Hopkins University School of Public Health, the U.S. Consumer Product Safety Commission and the Maternal and Child Health Bureau reviewed more that 1,400 death certificates from 1995. All of the death certificates were for children under 20 years of age who drowned.

While swimming pools pose the greatest risk for toddlers, about one-quarter of drowning among toddlers are in other freshwater sites, such as ponds or lakes. Researchers found that after the age of 10, the risk of drowning in a swimming pool was up to 15 times greater among black males as compared with white males. The reason for this increased risk is unknown. One explanation offered by the study's authors was that the public pools in which black teens swim might be less safe, with fewer lifeguards and more crowded conditions. Or the increased risk could be attributed to a difference in swimming ability, resulting from fewer opportunities for black males to participate in swimming lessons. The study authors conclude that there is a need for multifaceted approach to drowning prevention.

The American Academy of Pediatrics recommends:
•Swimming lessons for all children over the age of 5;
•Constant supervision of infants and young children when they are in the bathtub or around other bodies of water;

•Installation of fencing that separates homes from residential pools;
•Use of personal flotation devices when riding on a boat or playing near a river, lake or ocean;
•Teaching children never to swim alone or without adult supervision;
•Teaching children the dangers of drug and alcohol consumption during aquatic activities;
•Stressing the need for parents and teens to learn cardiopulmonary resuscitation (74).

Deaths and nonfatal injuries have been associated with baby bathtub "supporting ring" devices that are supposed to keep a baby safe in the tub. These rings usually contain three or four legs with suction cups that attach to the bottom of the tub. The suction cups, however, may release suddenly, allowing the bath ring and baby to tip over. A baby also may slip between the legs of the bath ring and become trapped under it. Caregivers must not rely on these devices to keep a baby safe in the bath and must never leave a baby alone in these bath support rings (50, 56).

An estimated 50 infants and toddlers drown each year in buckets containing liquid used for mopping floors and other household chores. Of all buckets, the 5-gallon size presents the greatest hazard to young children because of its tall straight sides and its weight with even just a small amount of liquid. It is nearly impossible for top-heavy infants and toddlers to free themselves when they fall into a 5-gallon bucket head first (48).

The Centers for Disease Control (CDC)-National Center for Injury Prevention and Control recommends that whenever young children are swimming, playing, or bathing in water, an adult should be watching them constantly. The supervising adult should not read, play cards, talk on the telephone, mow the lawn, or do any other distracting activity while watching children (49).

COMMENTS: Flotation devices should never be used as a substitute for supervision. Knowing how to swim does not make a child drown-proof.

The need for constant supervision is of particular concern in dealing with very young children and children with significant motor dysfunction or mental retardation.

See STANDARD 1.005, for information regarding supervision and child:staff ratios during wading and swimming activities. See also Safety Rules for Swimming/Wading Pools, STANDARD 5.215. For fencing water hazards, see STANDARD 5.198.

TYPE OF FACILITY: *Center; Large Family Child Care Home; Small Family Child Care Home*

STANDARD 3.046
BEHAVIOR AROUND A POOL

Caregivers shall prohibit dangerous behavior in or around the pool. Children shall not be permitted to push each other, hold each other under water, or run at poolside. Children shall be instructed to call for help only in a genuine emergency.

RATIONALE: Such behavior is dangerous and will distract caregivers from supervising other children, thereby placing the other children at risk.

TYPE OF FACILITY: *Center; Large Family Child Care Home; Small Family Child Care Home*

STANDARD 3.047
POOL TOYS

Tricycles, wagons, and other non-water toys shall not be permitted on the pool deck. Use of flotation devices shall be prohibited.

RATIONALE: Playing with non-water toys, such as tricycles or wagons, on the pool deck may result in unintentional falls into the water. Reliance on flotation devices may give children false confidence in their ability to protect themselves in deep water. Flotation devices also may promote complacency in caregivers who believe the child is safe.

TYPE OF FACILITY: *Center; Large Family Child Care Home; Small Family Child Care Home*

EMERGENCY PROCEDURES

STANDARD 3.048
EMERGENCY PROCEDURES

When an immediate response is required, the following emergency procedures shall be utilized:
a) First aid shall be employed, and the emergency medical response team shall be called, as indicated;
b) The facility shall implement a plan for emergency transportation to a local hospital or health care facility;
c) The parent or parent's emergency contact person shall be called as soon as practical;
d) A staff member shall accompany the child to the hospital and will stay with the child until the parent or emergency contact person arrives.

RATIONALE: The staff must know the plan for dealing with emergency situations when a child requires immediate care and a parent is not available.

COMMENTS: First aid instructions are provided by the American Academy of Pediatrics (AAP). Contact information for the AAP is located in Appendix BB.

TYPE OF FACILITY: *Center; Large Family Child Care Home; Small Family Child Care Home*

STANDARD 3.049
WRITTEN PLAN FOR MEDICAL
EMERGENCY

Facilities shall have a written plan for immediate management and rapid access to medical care as appropriate to the situation. This plan shall:
a) Describe for each child any special emergency procedures that will be used, if required, by the caregiver or by a physician or registered nurse available to the caregiver;
b) Note any special medical procedures, if required by the child's condition, that will be used or might be required for the child while he/she is in the facility's care, including the possibility of a need for cardiac resuscitation;

c) Include in a separate format, any information to be given to an emergency responder in the event that one must be called to the facility for the child. This information shall include:
   1) Any special information needed by the emergency responder to respond appropriately to the child's condition;
   2) A listing of the child's health care providers in the event of an emergency.

RATIONALE: The medical aspect of caring for children is likely to be the facet of care that caregivers are most poorly equipped to carry out, as their training is usually in early childhood education. The preparation of a written plan (a brief one would suffice) provides and opportunity for caregivers to work out how to deal with routine, urgent, and emergency medical needs.

Children with special needs may need an emergency responder whether it is for an asthma emergency, a cardiac emergency, or any of a number of conditions that put children at risk for emergency response and transport. An individual child's written plan for the first responders will save time and may be critical in the provision of appropriate care of a child in crisis.

COMMENTS: Training and other technical assistance for developing emergency plans can be obtained from the following:
a) American Academy of Pediatrics (AAP);
b) American Nurses' Association (ANA);
c) State and community nursing associations;
d) National therapy associations;
e) Local resource and referral agencies;
f) Federally funded, University Centers for Excellence in Developmental Disabilities Education, Research, and Service, programs for individuals with developmental disabilities;
g) Other colleges and universities with expertise in training others to work with children who have special needs;
h) Community-based organizations serving people with disabilities (Easter Seals, American Diabetes Association, American Lung Association, etc.).
i) Community sources of training in infant/child CPR (American Heart Association, American Red Cross, Emergency Medical Services for Children National Resource Center).

The State-designated lead agency responsible for implementing IDEA may provide additional help.

For additional information regarding emergency plans, see STANDARD 8.022 and STANDARD 8.023. For additional discussion about first aid and CPR, see STANDARD 1.026.

TYPE OF FACILITY: *Center; Large Family Child Care Home; Small Family Child Care Home*

STANDARD 3.050
SYRUP OF IPECAC

Syrup of ipecac shall be available for administration as a vomiting agent, but shall be used only under the direction of the poison control center, a physician, or a nurse practitioner.

RATIONALE: An emetic (vomiting agent), such as syrup of ipecac, limits the absorption of certain toxins. Emetics, however, should not be used without the direction of a physician or a poison control center, because certain toxic substances (petroleum distillates, for example) can damage breathing passages when vomited and aspirated (55).

TYPE OF FACILITY: *Center; Large Family Child Care Home; Small Family Child Care Home*

STANDARD 3.051
USE OF FIRE EXTINGUISHERS

The staff shall demonstrate the ability to locate and operate the Fire extinguishers.

RATIONALE: A fire extinguisher may be used to put out a small fire or to clear an escape path. (57).

COMMENTS: Staff should be trained that the first priority is to remove the children from the facility safely and quickly. Fighting a fire is secondary to the safe exit of the children and staff.

TYPE OF FACILITY: *Center; Large Family Child Care Home; Small Family Child Care Home*

STANDARD 3.052
RESPONSE TO FIRE AND BURNS

Children shall be instructed to STOP, DROP, and ROLL when garments catch fire. Children shall be instructed to crawl on the floor under the smoke. Cool water shall be applied to burns immediately. The injury shall be covered with a loose bandage or clean cloth.

RATIONALE: Running when garments have been ignited will fan the fire. Removing heat from the affected area will prevent continued burning and aggravation of tissue damage. Asphyxiation causes more deaths in house fires than does thermal injury (57).

COMMENTS: For additional information on emergency procedures, see Emergency Plan, STANDARD 8.022 and STANDARD 8.023; and Evacuation Plan and Drills, STANDARD 8.024 through STANDARD 8.027.

TYPE OF FACILITY: *Center; Large Family Child Care Home; Small Family Child Care Home*

CHILD ABUSE AND NEGLECT

STANDARD 3.053
REPORTING SUSPECTED CHILD ABUSE, NEGLECT, EXPLOITATION

The facility shall report to the department of social services, child protective services, or police as required by state and local laws, in any instance where there is reasonable cause to believe that child abuse, neglect, or exploitation may have occurred.

RATIONALE: All states in the United States have laws mandating the reporting of child abuse and neglect to child protection agencies and/or police. Laws about when and to whom to report vary by state. Failure to report abuse is a crime in all states and may lead to legal penalties.

TYPE OF FACILITY: *Center; Large Family Child Care Home; Small Family Child Care Home*

STANDARD 3.054
CONSULTANTS ON CHILD ABUSE AND NEGLECT

Caregivers and health professionals shall establish linkages with physicians, child psychiatrists, nurses, nurse practitioners, physician's assistants, and child protective services who are knowledgeable about child abuse and neglect and are willing to provide them with consultation about suspicious injuries or other circumstances that may indicate abuse or neglect. The names of these consultants shall be available for inspection.

Child care workers are mandated to report suspected child abuse and neglect.

RATIONALE: Many mistakes in reporting can be avoided by working with an experienced consultant before a decision is made about what to do. When the child care worker's level of suspicion is high, a consultation with an outside expert may not be needed, and could delay the initiation of an effective investigation and adequate protection of the child.

COMMENTS: Many health departments will be willing to provide this service. The American Academy of Pediatrics (AAP) can also assist in recruiting and identifying physicians who are skilled in this work. Contact information for the AAP is located in Appendix BB.

See also Health Consultation, STANDARD 8.020; and Health Consultants, STANDARD 1.040 through STANDARD 1.044.

TYPE OF FACILITY: *Center; Large Family Child Care Home; Small Family Child Care Home*

STANDARD 3.055
IMMUNITY OF REPORTERS OF CHILD ABUSE FROM SANCTION

Caregivers who report abuse in the settings where they work shall be immune from discharge, retaliation, or other disciplinary action for that reason alone, unless it is proven that the report was malicious.

RATIONALE: Reports of child abuse in child care settings are made infrequently by workers. Reported cases suggest that sometimes workers are intimidated by superiors in the centers where they work, and for that reason, fail to report abuse (58).

TYPE OF FACILITY: *Center*

STANDARD 3.056
INSTRUCTION AND FORMS FOR STAFF TO RECOGNIZE AND REPORT CHILD ABUSE

Caregivers shall know methods for reducing the risks of child abuse and neglect. They shall know how to recognize common symptoms and signs of child abuse and neglect.

Employees and volunteers in centers shall receive an instruction sheet about child abuse reporting that contains a summary of the state child abuse reporting statute and a statement that they will not be discharged solely because they have made a child abuse report. Some states have specific forms that are required to be completed when abuse is reported or which, though not required, assist mandated reporters in documenting accurate and thorough reports. In those states, facilities shall have such forms on hand and all staff shall be trained in the appropriate use of those forms.

RATIONALE: While caregivers are not expected to be able to definitively diagnose or investigate child abuse, it is important that they be aware of common signs and symptoms of child maltreatment, such as extensive, unexplained bruises and recurrent serious injuries.

Reports of child abuse in child care settings are made infrequently by workers. Reported cases suggest that sometimes workers are intimidated by superiors in the centers where they work, and for that reason, fail to report abuse (58).

COMMENTS: For information on common factors that lead to abuse, see Appendix K, *Clues to Child Abuse and Neglect*, and Appendix L, *Risk Factors for Abuse and/or Neglect*.

TYPE OF FACILITY: *Center; Large Family Child Care Home; Small Family Child Care Home*

STANDARD 3.057
CARE FOR CHILDREN WHO HAVE BEEN ABUSED

Child care providers in facilities where children with behavioral abnormalities related to abuse or neglect are enrolled, shall have access to specialized training and expert advice. The capacity of the child care setting to meet the needs of an abused child shall be assessed, with consultation from experts in the area.

RATIONALE: Abused children are likely to be more needy and to require more individual staff time and attention than children who are not abused.

COMMENTS: A quantitative standard for this case is difficult to establish at present. Centers serving children with a history of abuse-related behavior problems may require more staff.

TYPE OF FACILITY: *Center*

STANDARD 3.058
DEALING WITH CAREGIVER STRESS

Caregivers shall have ways of taking breaks and finding relief at times of high stress (for example, they shall be allowed 15 minutes of break time every four hours, in addition to a lunch break of at least 30 minutes). In addition, there shall be a written plan/policy in place for the situation in which a caregiver recognizes that he/she (or a colleague) is stressed and needs help immediately. The plan shall allow for caregivers who feel they may lose control to have a short, but relatively immediate break away from the children.

RATIONALE: Serious physical abuse usually occurs at a time of high stress for the caregiver.

COMMENTS: For more information on stress management, see STANDARD 1.049.

TYPE OF FACILITY: *Center; Large Family Child Care Home; Small Family Child Care Home*

STANDARD 3.059
FACILITY LAYOUT TO REDUCE RISK OF ABUSE

The physical layout of facilities shall be arranged so that all areas can be viewed by at least one other adult in addition to the caregiver at all times when children are in care. Such a layout reduces the risk of abuse and likelihood of extended periods of time in isolation for individual caregivers with children, especially in areas where children may be partially undressed or in the nude.

Video surveillance equipment, parabolic mirrors, or other devices designed to improve visual access shall be installed to enhance safety for the children.

RATIONALE: The presence of multiple caretakers greatly reduces the risk of serious abusive injury. Abuse tends to occur in privacy and isolation, and especially in toileting areas (58). A significant number of cases of abuse have been found involving young children being diapered in diaper changing areas (58).

COMMENTS: This standard does not mean to disallow privacy for older children who may need privacy for independent toileting.

For more information on bathrooms, see STANDARD 5.116 through STANDARD 5.125.

TYPE OF FACILITY: *Center*

3.5 SPECIAL MEDICAL CONDITIONS IN YOUNG CHILDREN

SEIZURES (INCLUDING EPILEPSY)

STANDARD 3.060
SEIZURE CARE PLAN

The child care facility shall have a seizure care plan and ensure that all caregivers receive training to successfully implement the plan. If a child in care has epilepsy or a history of febrile seizures that are not considered a form of epilepsy, the child's seizure care plan shall include the following:
a) Types of seizures the child has (such as partial, generalized, or unclassified), as well as a description of the manifestation of these types of seizures in this child;
b) The current treatment regimen for this child, including medications, doses, schedule of administration, guidelines, route of administration, and potential side effects for routine and as-needed medications;
c) Restrictions from activities that:
   1) Could be dangerous if the child were to have a seizure during the activity;
   2) Could precipitate a seizure (examples include swimming and falling from a height);
d) Recognizing and providing first aid for a seizure;
e) Guidelines on when emergency medical help should be sought for the child who has epilepsy, such as:
   1) A major convulsive seizure lasting more than 5 minutes;
   2) One seizure after another without waking up between seizures;
   3) The child is completely unresponsive for 20 minutes after the seizure;
f) Documentation in the child's health report that indicates:
   1) Whether the child has had a history of any type of *seizures*;
   2) Whether the child is currently taking medication to control the seizures;
   3) What observations caregivers should make to help the child's clinician adjust the medication;

4) The type and frequency of reported seizures as well as seizures observed in the facility;

g) Plans for support of the child with epilepsy and the child's family.

RATIONALE: A child that has a seizure may not have epilepsy or even a history of seizures. Child care providers should be trained to care for any child who has a seizure. For children with epilepsy, the child care staff should have detailed information and skills to understand the child's health needs and how to meet these needs in the child care setting. Seizures are usually self-limited events. Prolonged seizures, sequential seizures without recovery to a normal status, or remaining unresponsive for 20 minutes after a seizure suggests that the child is in status epilepticus and requires emergency care. The staff must respond appropriately to self-limited seizures and situations that require emergency help.

Epilepsy can be overwhelming for the child and family. The child care staff must offer support in understanding the condition and contribute positively to management of the child.

The child's physician needs reliable information on the number and type of seizures as well as the symptoms that might be side effects of the child's medication so the physician can make appropriate adjustments in the child's therapy.

COMMENTS: This information should be provided by the child's physician. Although children may be sleepy for a period after having a generalized seizure, sending children home after they have recovered from a seizure is unnecessary and should be discouraged, unless specified in the health plan.

The classification system currently used for seizures replaces earlier terminology as follows:
• Grand Mal is now referred to as Generalized Seizure.
• Petit Mal is now referred to as Partial Seizure.

Children with febrile seizures (who are not diagnosed with any form of epilepsy) do not receive anticonvulsant medication. These children usually outgrow this condition.

If the child's parents consent, child care providers should establish a close and continuing liaison with the child's health care provider, especially if the seizures are not well controlled. Sometimes the child's clinicians will monitor the medication prescribed to control seizures by measuring blood samples and sometimes through observations by caregivers and parents. In either case, dosage may have to be adjusted to reduce side effects or provide better control.

TYPE OF FACILITY: *Center; Large Family Child Care Home; Small Family Child Care Home*

STANDARD 3.061
TRAINING FOR STAFF TO HANDLE SEIZURES

Staff members shall be trained in, and shall be prepared to follow, the prescribed procedure when a child has a seizure. These procedures include proper positioning, keeping the airway open, and knowing when and whom to call for medical assistance. All staff members shall be instructed about the relevant side effects of any anti-convulsant medications that children in the facility take and how to observe and report them.

Telephone numbers for emergency care shall be posted, as specified in Posting Documents, STANDARD 8.077.

RATIONALE: Without training, a staff member may panic when a child has a seizure. Without specific procedures, well-intended staff members may not take the steps required to avoid preventable injury during a seizure.

Anti-convulsant medication may affect a child's health and behavior. Observing and reporting these side effects contributes significantly to a health care provider's ability to recommend appropriate modifications in medication.

COMMENTS: The general guidelines for managing seizures apply to children with special needs. Staff members can be trained through initial and ongoing inservice efforts in specific procedures to follow with a child who has a seizure as well as appropriate supervision and movement of the other children present. See Continuing Education, STANDARD 1.029 through STANDARD 1.033.

Changes in health and behavior that may result from medication should be reported to the parent in the parent's native language and with sensitivity to the parent's ethnic and cultural practices. With written parental consent, the caregiver may also share this information with the child's primary health care provider. Useful references concerning seizures and side effects of medications used to control seizures, particularly if a child begins a new medicine while attending the facility, include the following:
a) The child's parent;
b) The child's primary health care provider (if the parents consent to contact between the provider and the child care facility);
c) A pharmacist;
d) A health textbook.

See also Medications, STANDARD 3.081 through STANDARD 3.083; and Medication Policy, STANDARD 8.021.

TYPE OF FACILITY: *Center; Large Family Child Care Home; Small Family Child Care Home*

ASTHMA

STANDARD 3.062
MANAGEMENT OF CHILDREN WITH ASTHMA

When a child who has had a diagnosis of asthma by a health professional attends the child care facility, the following actions shall occur:
a)   Each child with asthma shall have a special care plan prepared for the facility by the child's source of health care, to include:
1)   Written instructions regarding how to avoid the conditions that are known to trigger asthma symptoms for the child;
2)   Indications for treatment of the child's asthma in the child care facility;
3)   Names, doses, and method of administration of any medications, e.g., inhalers, the

child should receive for an acute episode and for ongoing prevention;
4)   When the next update of the special care plan is due;
b)   Based on the child's special care plan, the child's caregivers shall receive training, demonstrate competence in, and implement measures for:
1)   Preventing exposure of the asthmatic child to conditions likely to trigger the child's asthma;
2)   Recognizing the symptoms of asthma;
3)   Treating acute episodes;
c)   Parents and staff shall arrange for the facility to have necessary medications and equipment to manage the child's asthma while the child is at the child care facility;
d)   Properly trained caregivers shall promptly and properly administer prescribed medications according to the training provided and in accordance with the special care plan;
e)   The facility shall notify parents of any change in asthma symptoms when that change occurs. See the *Special Care Plan for a Child with Asthma*, Appendix M;
f)   The facility shall try to reduce these common asthma triggers by:
1)   Encouraging the use of allergen impermeable nap mats or crib/mattress covers;
2)   Prohibiting pets (particularly furred or feathered pets);
3)   Prohibiting smoking inside the facility or on the playground;
4)   Discouraging the use of perfumes, scented cleaning products, and other fumes;
5)   Quickly fixing leaky plumbing or other sources of excess water;
6)   Ensuring frequent vacuuming of carpet and upholstered furniture at times when the children are not present;
7)   Storing all food in airtight containers, cleaning up all food crumbs or spilled liquids, and properly disposing of garbage and trash;
8)   Using integrated pest management techniques to get rid of pests (using the least hazardous treatments first and progressing to more toxic treatments only as necessary);
9)   Keeping children indoors when local weather forecasts predict unhealthy ozone levels or high pollen counts.

RATIONALE: Asthma is common, occurring in 7%-10% of all preschool and school-aged children. Asthma is a major cause of morbidity in childhood, resulting in sleep disturbance, limitations in exercise, absenteeism from child care and school, and hospitalization. Despite increased awareness and knowledge of the problem, asthma remains underdiagnosed and undertreated. Proper diagnosis, treatment, and prevention of exposure to environmental triggers can lessen complications and improve long term outcome. (59)

Respiratory infections are the primary trigger of asthma (especially of severe episodes) in the young child. Because respiratory infections and asthma are common in early childhood, child care providers should expect to serve children with asthma. Respiratory irritants such as secondhand cigarette smoke, fumes, odors, chemicals, excess humidity, and very hot or cold air may also trigger asthma, so children with asthma should be protected from these irritants. In older preschoolers and school-age children, allergens (pets, mold, cockroaches, dust mites) in the child care setting or school may contribute as well. Reducing exposure to potential triggers is important to control symptoms and prevent attacks and also to improve the long-term prognosis.

Prompt and appropriate intervention during an acute episode of asthma is essential to prevent severe or prolonged effects. Many hospitalizations and most deaths from asthma are the result of delayed recognition of the symptoms or delayed and inadequate treatment. In general, when a child with known asthma has symptoms suggesting an acute asthma episode, treatment should begin promptly, according to instructions. In most instances, a delay in treatment is likely to have more negative effects than occasional overtreatment. Children should not have to wait to begin treatment until a parent can arrive to give it.

The physical assessment of some children with asthma can be augmented by use of a peak flow meter. Peak flow meters can only be used with children who are old enough to understand directions for use and able to cooperate. Peak flow readings can help to determine when treatment should be started, even for a child with no signs of distress, when

treatment is helping, and when additional treatment or advice is needed. Staff members must receive training about the purpose, expected response, and possible side effects of medications they are expected to administer. They also must be trained in the proper use of equipment such as inhalers or nebulizers according to the guidelines for medication administration in that state's licensure regulations.

COMMENTS: Asthma is a chronic lung disease caused by an oversensitivity of the bronchial tubes to various stimuli or "triggers." In asthma, the lining of the tubes becomes inflamed and swollen and extra mucus is produced. Muscles surrounding the airways tighten so that the air passages become narrower. Typical symptoms of asthma include coughing, wheezing, tightness in chest, and shortness of breath. The symptoms of asthma can occur together or alone. Often, the only symptom of asthma is chronic or recurrent cough, particularly while sleeping, during activity, or with colds. Asthma is not the only condition that can cause these symptoms but is certainly the most common.

Symptoms can vary from very mild to severe and life threatening. They can be only occasional or continuous. Specific symptoms and warning signs can vary from child to child. Likewise, specific recommendations for treatment are likely to vary. Appropriate treatment depends on the frequency and severity of the symptoms. Accurate assessment by caregivers will aid in establishing the diagnosis and determining long-term management needs.

All of the symptoms of asthma need not be present at one time in any child. Asthma episodes can range from very mild to severe and life threatening. Not all children with asthma have allergies. Sensitivity to triggers may fluctuate over time, so exposure to one or more triggers may not always precipitate an attack. Also, triggers tend to be cumulative; the more a child is exposed to at one time, the more likely is an attack. Indications for notification of parents and physician will vary.

Notify parents if any one of the following is present (46):
a) Symptoms persist despite one dose of prescribed "rescue" medication (especially if symptoms are

bad enough to interfere with sleep, eating, or activity);

b) Two or more doses of "rescue" medication have been needed during the course of a single day for recurrent symptoms;

c) Peak flow remains 50%-80% of normal despite one dose of the prescribed "rescue" medication;

d) Symptoms are severe (see below).

Notify physician/emergency services if any one of the following occurs (46):

a) Child is struggling to breathe, hunches over, or sucks in chest and neck muscles in an attempt to breathe;

b) Child is having difficulty walking or talking because of shortness of breath;

c) Peak flow is less than 50% of normal;

d) Lips or fingernails turn gray or blue.

Additional resources on caring for children with asthma such as the *How Asthma-Friendly is Your Child-Care Setting? Checklist* can be obtained from the National Heart, Lung, and Blood Institute and other useful materials from the Asthma and Allergy Foundation of America. Contact information for these organizations is located in Appendix BB.

TYPE OF FACILITY: *Center; Large Family Child Care Home; Small Family Child Care Home*

SPECIAL ADAPTATIONS

STANDARD 3.063
CARING FOR CHILDREN WHO
REQUIRE MEDICAL PROCEDURES

A facility that enrolls children who require tube feedings, endotrachial suctioning, oxygen, postural drainage, or catheterization daily (unless the child requiring catheterization can perform this function on his/her own) or any other special medical procedures performed routinely, or who might require special procedures on an urgent basis, shall receive a written report from the health care provider who prescribed the special treatment (such as a urologist for catheterization). A facility shall receive a written report from the child's

clinician about any special preparation to perform urgent procedures other than those that might be required for a typical child, such as cardiac resuscitation. This report shall include instructions for performing the procedure, how to receive training in performing the procedure, and what to do and who to notify if complications occur. Training for the child care staff shall be provided by a qualified health care professional in accordance with state practice acts.

RATIONALE: The specialized skills required to implement these procedures are not traditionally taught to educators or educational assistants as part of their academic or practical experience.

COMMENTS: Parents are responsible for supplying the required equipment. The facility should offer staff training and allow sufficient staff time to carry out the necessary procedures. Caring for children who require intermittent catheterization or maintaining supplemental oxygen is not as demanding as it first sounds, but the implication of this standard is that facilities serving children who have complex medical problems need special training and consultation. Without these supports, facilities should not be expected to serve these children.

Before enrolling a child who will need this type of care, child care providers can request and review fact sheets and instructions, and training that includes a return demonstration of competence of caregivers for handling specific procedures. Often, the child's parents or clinicians have these materials and know where training is available. When the specifics are known, caregivers can make a more responsible decision about what would be required to serve the child.

See STANDARD 7.001, regarding facilities serving children with disabilities and other special needs. For additional discussion about first aid and CPR, see STANDARD 1.026.

TYPE OF FACILITY: *Center; Large Family Child Care; Small Family Child Care Home*

3.6 MANAGEMENT OF ILLNESS

STANDARD 3.064
LEVELS OF ILLNESS

The facility shall specify in its policies what severity level(s) of illness the facility can manage and how much and what types of illness will be addressed. The plan of care shall be approved by the facility's health consultant.

- *Severity Level 1* consists of children whose health condition is accompanied by high interest and complete involvement in activity associated with an absence of symptoms of illness (such as children recovering from pink eye, rash, or chickenpox), but who need further recuperation time. Appropriate activities for this level include most of the normal activities for the child's age and developmental level, including both indoor and outdoor play. For full recovery, children at this level need no special care other than medication administration services offered at the facility.
- *Severity Level 2* encompasses children whose health condition is accompanied by a medium activity level because of symptoms (such as children with low-grade fever, children at the beginning of an illness, and children in the early recovery period of an illness). Appropriate activities for this level include crafts, puzzles, table games, fantasy play, and opportunities to move about the room freely.
- *Severity Level 3* is composed of children whose health condition is accompanied by a low activity level because of symptoms that preclude much involvement. Appropriate activities for this level are sleep and rest; light meals and liquids; passive activities such as stories and music; and, for children who need physical comforting, being held and rocked (especially children under 3 years of age).

Individuals and public and private organizations that provide child care for ill children shall develop and adhere to written guidelines for facilities for ill children that are consistent with the administrative procedures and staff policies, as specified in these standards, to reduce the introduction and transmission of communicable disease.

RATIONALE: Children enrolled in child care are of an age that places them at increased risk for acquiring infectious diseases. Many children with illness (particularly mild respiratory tract illness without fever) can continue to attend and participate in activities in their usual facility. Excluding these children from child care is not recommended (3, 60). This perspective is reflected in the standards for excluding children from child care attendance. See Inclusion/Exclusion/Dismissal of Ill Children, STANDARD 3.065 through STANDARD 3.068.

Young children enrolled in facilities have a high incidence of illness (upper respiratory tract infections, otitis media, diarrhea, hepatitis A infections, skin conditions, and asthma) that may not allow them to participate in the usual facility activities. Because many state regulations now require that children with these conditions be excluded from their usual care arrangements several alternative care arrangements have been established, including (61):
a) Care in the child's own home;
b) Care in a small family child care home;
c) Care in the child's own center with special provisions designed for the care of ill children (sometimes called the infirmary model);
d) Care in a separate center that serves only children with illness or temporary conditions.

Clearly, when children with possible communicable diseases are present in the alternative care arrangements, emphasis on preventing further spread of disease is as important as in the usual facilities. In one study, no additional transmission of communicable disease occurred in children attending a sick child care center (62). Prevention of additional cases of communicable disease should be a key objective in these alternative care arrangements for children with minor illness and temporary disability.

Current state regulations concerning exclusion of children from facilities because of illness may be more restrictive than these standards. Some states currently require isolation of a child who becomes ill during the day while attending the facility and for an ill child who is not expected to return to the facility the following day. The most common alternative care arrangement is for a parent of the ill child to stay home from work and care for the child. Some states have established regulations governing child care for sick children (61, 73).

Data are inadequate by which to judge the impact of group care of ill children on their subsequent health and on the health of their families and community. The principles and standards proposed in this manual represent the most current views of pediatric and infectious disease experts on providing this special form of child care. These standards will require revision as new information on disease transmission in these facilities becomes available. The National Association for Sick Child Daycare (NASCD) conducts and sponsors original research on issues related to sick child care and helps establish sick care facilities across the nation. Contact information for the NASCD is located in Appendix BB.

COMMENTS: Technical expertise and guidance can be obtained from the health consultant. See Health Consultants, STANDARD 1.040 through STANDARD 1.043. For additional information on general requirements for special facilities for ill children, see STANDARD 3.070 through STANDARD 3.080. See also Health Department Role, RECOMMENDATION 9.025.

TYPE OF FACILITY: *Center; Large Family Child Care Home; Small Family Child Care Home*

STANDARD 3.065
INCLUSION/EXCLUSION/DISMISSAL OF CHILDREN

The parent, legal guardian, or other person the parent authorizes shall be notified immediately when a child has any sign or symptom that requires exclusion from the facility. The facility shall ask the parents to consult with the child's health care provider. The child care provider shall ask the parents to inform them of the advice received from the health care provider. The advice of the child's health care provider shall be followed by the child care facility.

With the exception of head lice for which exclusion at the end of the day is appropriate, a facility shall temporarily exclude a child or send

the child home as soon as possible if one or more of the following conditions exists:
a) The illness prevents the child from participating comfortably in activities as determined by the child care provider;
b) The illness results in a greater need for care than the child care staff can provide without compromising the health and safety of the other children as determined by the child care provider;
c) The child has any of the following conditions:
   1) Fever, accompanied by behavior changes or other signs or symptoms of illness until medical professional evaluation finds the child able to be included at the facility;
   2) Symptoms and signs of possible severe illness until medical professional evaluation finds the child able to included at the facility. Symptoms and signs of possible severe illness shall include
   • lethargy that is more than expected tiredness,
   • uncontrolled coughing,
   • inexplicable irritability or persistent crying,
   • difficult breathing,
   • wheezing, or
   • other unusual signs for the child;
   3) Diarrhea, defined by more watery stools, decreased form of stool that is not associated with changes of diet, and increased frequency of passing stool, that is not contained by the child's ability to use the toilet. Children with diarrheal illness of infectious origin generally may be allowed to return to child care once the diarrhea resolves, except for children with diarrhea caused by *Salmonella typhi, Shigella* or *E. coli 0157:H7*. For *Salmonella typhi*, 3 negative stool cultures are required. For *Shigella* or *E. coli 0157:H7*, two negative stool cultures are required. Children whose stools remain loose but who, otherwise, seem well and whose stool cultures are negative, need not be excluded. See also Child-Specific Procedures for Enteric (Diarrheal) and Hepatitis A Virus (HAV) Infections, STANDARD 6.023, for additional separation and exclusion information for children with diarrhea; STANDARD 3.066, on separate care for these children;

and STANDARD 3.084 and STANDARD 3.087, on notifying parents;

4) Blood in stools not explainable by dietary change, medication, or hard stools;

5) Vomiting illness (two or more episodes of vomiting in the previous 24 hours) until vomiting resolves or until a health care provider determines that the cause of the vomiting is not contagious and the child is not in danger of dehydration. See also STANDARD 3.066, on separate care for these children;

6) Persistent abdominal pain (continues more than 2 hours) or intermittent pain associated with fever or other signs or symptoms;

7) Mouth sores with drooling, unless a health care provider or health department official determines that the child is noninfectious;

8) Rash with fever or behavior change, until a physician determines that these symptoms do not indicate a communicable disease;

9) Purulent conjunctivitis (defined as pink or red conjunctiva with white or yellow eye discharge), until after treatment has been initiated. In epidemics of nonpurulent pink eye, exclusion shall be required only if the health authority recommends it;

10) Pediculosis (head lice), from the end of the day until after the first treatment. See STANDARD 6.038;

11) Scabies, until after treatment has been completed. See STANDARD 6.037;

12) Tuberculosis, until a health care provider or health official states that the child is on appropriate therapy and can attend child care. See STANDARD 6.014 and STANDARD 6.015;

13) Impetigo, until 24 hours after treatment has been initiated;

14) Strep throat or other streptococcal infection, until 24 hours after initial antibiotic treatment and cessation of fever. See also Group A Streptococcal (GAS) Infection, STANDARD 6.012 and STANDARD 6.013;

15) Varicella-Zoster (Chickenpox), until all sores have dried and crusted (usually 6 days). See also STANDARD 6.019 and STANDARD 6.020;

16) Pertussis, until 5 days of appropriate antibiotic treatment (currently, erythromycin, which is given for 14 consecutive days) has been completed. See STANDARD 6.009 and STANDARD 6.010;

17) Mumps, until 9 days after onset of parotid gland swelling;

18) Hepatitis A virus, until 1 week after onset of illness, jaundice, or as directed by the health department when passive immunoprophylaxis (currently, immune serum globulin) has been administered to appropriate children and staff members. See STANDARD 6.023 through STANDARD 6.026;

19) Measles, until 4 days after onset of rash;

20) Rubella, until 6 days after onset of rash;

21) Unspecified respiratory tract illness, see STANDARD 6.017;

22) Shingles (herpes zoster). See STANDARD 6.020;

23) Herpes simplex, see STANDARD 6.018.

Some states have regulations governing isolation of persons with communicable diseases including some of those listed here. Providers shall contact their health consultant or health department for information regarding isolation of children with diseases such as chickenpox, pertussis, mumps, hepatitis A, measles, rubella, and tuberculosis (3). If different health care professionals give conflicting opinions about the need to exclude an ill child on the basis of the risk of transmission of infection to other children, the health department shall make the determination.

The child care provider shall make the decision about whether a child meets or does not meet the exclusion criteria for participation and the child's need for care relative to the staff's ability to provide care. If parents and the child care staff disagree, and the reason for exclusion relates to the child's ability to participate or the caregiver's ability to provide care for the other children, the child care provider shall not be required by a parent to accept responsibility for the care of the child during the period in which the child meets the providers's criteria for exclusion.

RATIONALE: Short term exclusion of children with many mild infectious diseases is likely to have only a minor impact on the incidence of infection among other children in the group. Thus, when formulating exclusion policies, it is reasonable to focus on the needs and behavior of the ill child and the ability of the staff in the out-of-home child care setting to meet those needs without compromising the care of other children in the group (32).

As states update their regulations, the trend has been to be much more specific about what diseases or conditions should be excluded, and what can be included. Isolation of a child in a child care setting is not an effective way to prevent the spread of disease, and is only used in certain circumstances, such as when an excluded child whose illness is considered to be contagious, who has not already exposed the child care group, and is waiting to be transported home, or when an included child needs a less stimulating environment than the child's usual care setting. Most ill children will rest in any setting if they are tired.

Fever is defined as an elevation of body temperature above normal. Oral temperatures above 101 degrees F, rectal temperatures above 102 degrees F, or axillary (armpit) temperatures above 100 degrees F usually are considered to be above normal in children. Children's temperatures may be elevated for a variety of reasons, all of which may not indicate serious illness or warrant exclusion from child care. For instance, a child's over exertion in a hot dry climate may produce a fever. Generally, children should be excluded whenever fever is accompanied by behavior changes, signs, or symptoms of illness that require parental evaluation of their illness and need for care.

Because very young infants may have serious illnesses without much change in behavior in the early stages of illness, rectal temperatures above 101 degrees F or axillary (armpit) temperatures above 100 degrees F without behavioral change is considered to be significant in infants 8 weeks of age and younger and a reason to seek immediate medical professional care for these young infants. Although health care professionals worry most about children under 8 weeks of age who have fever, concern for fever in infants under 4 months of age provides a wide margin of safety. No age standard for fever is included, but prudent practice would be to seek medical evaluation for infants under 4 months of age who have an unexplained fever. An infant under 4 months of age with a fever on the day following an immunization would not be considered to have an unexplained

temperature elevation and need not be excluded as long as the child is acting normally. The presence of fever alone has little relevance to the spread of disease and should not disallow a child's participation in child care. A small proportion of childhood illness with fever is caused by life-threatening diseases, such as meningitis. Except for very young infants, serious illnesses with fever are associated with recognizable behavior change. Facilities should inform parents promptly when their child is found to have a fever or behavior change in child care.

The presence of diarrhea, particularly in diapered children and the presence of vomiting increase the likelihood of exposing other children to the infectious agents that cause these illnesses. It may not be reasonable to routinely culture children who have fever and diarrhea. In some outbreak settings, however, identifying infected children and excluding or treating them may be necessary. Because these infections are easily transmitted and can be severe, exclusion of children with diarrhea because of *Shigella* and *E. coli 0157:H7* is recommended until two stool cultures are negative and exclusion of children with diarrhea because of *Salmonella typhi* is recommended until three stool cultures are negative. For *Salmonella* species other than *S.typhi* stool cultures are not required from asymptomatic individuals (3).

Vomiting with symptoms such as lethargy and/or dry skin or mucous membranes, or reduced urine output, may indicate dehydration. A child with these symptoms should be evaluated medically (63). A child who vomits should be observed carefully for other signs of illness and for dehydration. If dehydration is not present, the child may continue to attend the facility.

If a child with abdominal pain is drowsy, irritable, and unhappy, has no appetite, and is unwilling to participate in usual activities, the child should be seen by that child's health care provider. Abdominal pain may be associated with viral, bacterial, or parasitic gastrointestinal tract illness, which is contagious, or with food poisoning. It also may be a manifestation of another disease or illness such as kidney disease. If the pain is severe or persistent, the child should be referred for medical evaluation.

Any rash that has open, weeping wounds and/or is not healing should be evaluated medically.

Not all conjunctivitis is infectious. Some is caused by allergies, or by chemical irritation (such as after swimming). Infectious nonpurulent conjunctivitis usually is accompanied by a clear, watery eye discharge, without fever, eye pain, or redness of the eyelid. This type of conjunctivitis usually can be managed without excluding a child from a facility, as in the case of children with mild infection of the respiratory tract. Such a child, however, might require exclusion if a responsible health department authority, the child's health care provider, or the facility's health consultant (see Health Consultants, STANDARD 1.040 through STANDARD 1.043) determines that the child's conjunctivitis was contributing to transmission of the infection within or outside the facility.

Purulent conjunctivitis is defined as pink or red conjunctiva with white or yellow eye discharge, often with matted eyelids after sleep, and including eye pain or redness of the eyelids or skin surrounding the eye. This type of conjunctivitis is more often caused by a bacterial infection, which may require antibiotic treatment. Children with purulent conjunctivitis, therefore, should be excluded until the child's health care provider has examined the child and cleared him or her for readmission to the facility, with or without treatment.

Lice and scabies are highly contagious, and all parents should be notified to watch for signs of infestation (3, 64). However, children discovered with lice need not be removed until the end of the day and may return after the first treatment.

Chickenpox, measles, rubella, mumps, and pertussis are highly communicable illnesses for which routine exclusion of infected children is warranted. Excluding children with treatable illnesses until appropriate treatment has reduced the risk of transmission is also appropriate.

A child may be included in the regular facility and his or her activities may be modified if the child is comfortable and the facility has enough caregivers to accommodate the adaptation. No child should be forced to participate in activities when in ill health. Exclusion/dismissal should be for the comfort and safety of both the ill child and the rest of the children in the group, if the facility cannot meet the ill child's needs (62).

Parents and the child care staff may disagree about whether a child meets or does not meet the exclusion criteria. If the reason for exclusion relates to the child's ability to participate or the caregiver's ability to provide care for the other children, the child care provider is entitled to make this decision and cannot be forced by a parent to accept responsibility for the care of an ill child. The parent is neither in a position to assess the factors involved in care of the group, nor legally able to transfer responsibility for the care of the child to an unwilling caregiver. If the reason for exclusion relates to a decision about whether the child has a communicable disease that poses a risk to the other children in the group, different health care professionals in the community might give conflicting opinions. In these cases, the health department has the legal authority to make a determination.

COMMENTS: For all infectious diseases for which treatment has been initiated, continuing to include the child in care after treatment has been initiated should be conditional on completing the prescribed course of therapy and clinical improvement of the child's illness. When measles, rubella, mumps, invasive *H. influenzae* disease, or pertussis are diagnosed for a child in the facility, children in the facility who are not immunized for the disease must be excluded if they are exposed.

The lay term "pink eye" is used interchangeably with purulent conjunctivitis and nonpurulent conjunctivitis. The infectious characteristics of purulent and nonpurulent conjunctivitis, however, are quite different. As indicated in the rationale, not all pink eye (conjunctivitis) is infectious.
If the caregiver is unable to contact the parent, medical advice should be sought until the parents can be located.

Diarrhea is considered resolved when the child seems well and has resumed a pre-illness stool pattern, or when the child seems well and has developed a new, but regular pattern of non-watery bowel movements for more than a week, even if this new pattern is more frequent and loose bowel movements than was usual for the child before the diarrhea episode.

Oral temperatures should not be taken on children younger than 4 years of age unless a digital thermometer can be used successfully. Rectal temperature or aural (ear) equivalent to rectal temperature shall be taken only by persons with specific training in this technique. Instructions on how to take a child's temperature and a sample symptom record are provided in *Healthy Young Children*, available from the National Association for the Education of Young Children (NAEYC). See a sample symptom record in Appendix F. See Appendix N, for *Situations That Require Medical Attention Right Away*. Protocols for managing illness are provided in the *Child Care Health Handbook*, available from the Seattle King County Department of Public Health. Contact information for the organizations listed is located in Appendix BB.

TYPE OF FACILITY: *Center; Large Family Child Care Home; Small Family Child Care Home*

STANDARD 3.066
SEPARATION OF EXCLUDED
CHILDREN FROM THE GROUP

A child with uncontrolled vomiting or diarrhea or any other illness that requires that the child be sent home from the facility shall be provided care separate from the other children, with extra attention to hygiene and sanitation, until the child's parent arrives to remove the child.

RATIONALE: Uncontrolled vomiting and acute diarrhea often are caused by bacteria, viruses or parasites that can be found in vomit or stool. Until the cause of the episode is known and because organisms can be spread from infected persons to susceptible contacts, children with uncontrolled vomiting or diarrhea should not be in contact with other children in the child care facility. To minimize the spread of infection to others, the child shall be provided care separate from other children until the child leaves the facility. In addition, these children

often are too ill to participate comfortably in program activities.

COMMENTS: For additional information on the inclusion, exclusion, and dismissal of children from child care, see STANDARD 3.065.

TYPE OF FACILITY: *Center; Large Family Child Care Home; Small Family Child Care Home*

STANDARD 3.067
OUTBREAK CONTROL

During the course of an identified outbreak of any communicable illness at the facility, a child shall be excluded if the health department official or health care provider suspects that the child is contributing to transmission of the illness at the facility. The child shall be readmitted when the health department official or health care provider who made the initial determination decides that the risk of transmission is no longer present.

RATIONALE: Secondary spread of infectious disease has been proven to occur in child care. Control of outbreaks of infectious diseases in child care may include age appropriate immunization, antibiotic prophylaxis, observing well children for signs and symptoms of disease and ensuring that children do not spread organisms which may sustain an outbreak. Removal of children known or suspected of contributing to an outbreak will help to limit transmission of the disease by preventing the development of new cases of the disease.

TYPE OF FACILITY: *Center; Large Family Child Care Home; Small Family Child Care Home*

STANDARD 3.068
CONDITIONS THAT DO NOT
REQUIRE EXCLUSION

Certain conditions do not constitute a reason for automatically denying admission to, or sending a child home from child care, unless the child would be excluded by the criteria in STANDARD 3.068 or the child is suspected by a health department authority to contribute to transmission of the illness at the facility. These conditions that do not require exclusion include:

a) Presence of bacteria or viruses in urine or feces in the absence of illness symptoms, like diarrhea. Exceptions include children infected with highly contagious organisms capable of causing serious illness such as *E. coli 0157:H7, Shigella,* or *Salmonella typhi.* Children with *E. coli 0157:H7 or Shigella* shall be excluded from child care until two stool cultures are negative and they are cleared to return by local health department officials. Children with *Salmonella typhi* shall be excluded from child care until three stool cultures are negative and they are cleared to return by local health department officials;

b) Nonpurulent conjunctivitis, defined as pink conjunctiva with a clear, watery eye discharge and without fever, eye pain, or eyelid redness;

c) Rash without fever and without behavior changes;

d) CMV infection, as described in STANDARD 6.021 and STANDARD 6.022;

e) Hepatitis B virus carrier state, provided that children who carry HBV chronically have no behavioral or medical risk factors, such as unusually aggressive behavior (biting, frequent scratching), generalized dermatitis, or bleeding problems;

f) HIV infection, provided that the health, neurologic development, behavior, and immune status of an HIV-infected child are appropriate as determined on a case-by-case basis by qualified health professionals, including the child's health care provider, who are able to evaluate whether the child will receive optimal care in the specific facility being considered and whether that child poses a potential threat to others;

g) Parvovirus B19 infection in a person with a normal immune system.

RATIONALE: Excluding children with many mild infectious diseases is likely to have only a minor impact on the incidence of infection among other children in the group and the staff (32). Thus, when formulating exclusion policies, it is reasonable to focus on the needs and behavior of the ill child and the ability of staff in the out-of-home child care setting to meet those needs without compromising the care of other children in the group (32).

COMMENTS: The lay term pink eye is used interchangeably to describe purulent and nonpurulent conjunctivitis. The infectious characteristics of purulent and nonpurulent conjunctivitis, however, are quite different. For more information on the difference between purulent and nonpurulent conjunctivitis, see STANDARD 3.068, on conjunctivitis.

For additional information on child inclusion, exclusion, and dismissal, see STANDARD 6.003 on exclusion during antibiotic treatment of *Haemophilus influenzae* type b (Hib); STANDARD 6.008, on exclusion during antibiotic treatment of meningococcal infection; STANDARD 6.011, on exclusion during antibiotic treatment of pertussis; STANDARD 6.034 on excluding children with an immune system that does not function properly to prevent infection.

TYPE OF FACILITY: *Center; Large Family Child Care Home; Small Family Child Care Home*

STANDARD 3.069
STAFF EXCLUSION FOR ILLNESS

Please note that if a staff member has no contact with the children, or with anything with which the children come into contact, this standard does not apply to that staff member.

A facility shall not deny admission to or send home a staff member or substitute with illness unless one or more of the following conditions exists (65). The staff member shall be excluded as follows:

a) Chickenpox, until all lesions have dried and crusted, which usually occurs by 6 days;

b) Shingles, only if the lesions cannot be covered by clothing or a dressing until the lesions have crusted;

c) Rash with fever or joint pain, until diagnosed not to be measles or rubella;

d) Measles, until 4 days after onset of the rash (if the staff member or substitute is immunocompetent);

e) Rubella, until 6 days after onset of rash;

f) Diarrheal illness, three or more episodes of diarrhea during the previous 24 hours or blood in stools, until diarrhea resolves; if *E.coli 0157:H7* or *Shigella* is isolated, until diarrhea resolves and two stool cultures are negative;

g) Vomiting illness, two or more episodes of vomiting during the previous 24 hours, until vomiting resolves or is determined to result from noncommunicable conditions such as pregnancy or a digestive disorder;

h) Hepatitis A virus, until 1 week after onset or as directed by the health department when immunoglobulin has been given to appropriate children and staff in the facility;

i) Pertussis, until after 5 days of appropriate antibiotic therapy (which is to be given for a total of 14 days) and until disease preventive measures, including preventive antibiotics and vaccines for children and staff who have been in contact with children infected with pertussis, have been implemented;

j) Skin infection (such as impetigo), until 24 hours after treatment has been initiated;

k) Tuberculosis, until noninfectious and cleared by a health department official;

l) Strep throat or other streptococcal infection, until 24 hours after initial antibiotic treatment and end of fever;

m) Head lice, from the end of the day of discovery until after the first treatment;

n) Scabies, until after treatment has been completed;

o) Purulent conjunctivitis, defined as pink or red conjunctiva with white or yellow eye discharge, often with matted eyelids after sleep, and including eye pain or redness of the eyelids or skin surrounding the eye, until 24 hours after treatment has been initiated;

p) *Haemophilus influenzae* type b (Hib), prophylaxis, until antibiotic treatment has been initiated;

q) Meningococcal infection, until all staff members, for whom antibiotic prophylaxis has been recommended, have been treated. See STANDARD 6.006 through STANDARD 6.008;

r) Respiratory illness, if the illness limits the staff member's ability to provide an acceptable level of child care and compromises the health and safety of the children.

Child care providers who have herpes cold sores shall not be excluded from the child care facility, but shall:

1) Cover and not touch their lesions;

2) Carefully observe handwashing policies;

3) Refrain from kissing or nuzzling infants or children, especially children with dermatitis.

RATIONALE: Adults are as capable of spreading infectious disease as children are. See also the Rationale for Child Inclusion/Exclusion/Dismissal, STANDARD 3.065.

COMMENTS: Other management procedures should be followed as stated in Child Inclusion/Exclusion/Dismissal, STANDARD 3.065. For additional information on infectious disease, see STANDARD 6.001through STANDARD 6.039.

TYPE OF FACILITY: *Center; Large Family Child Care Home; Small Family Child Care Home*

CARING FOR ILL CHILDREN

STANDARD 3.070
SPACE REQUIREMENTS FOR CARE OF ILL CHILDREN

Environmental space utilized for the care of children who are ill with infectious diseases and cannot receive care in their usual child care group shall meet all requirements for well children and include the following additional requirements:

a) If the program for ill children is in the same facility as the well-child program, well children shall not use or share furniture, fixtures, equipment, or supplies designated for use with ill children unless it has been cleaned and sanitized before use by well children;

b) Indoor space that the facility uses for ill children, including hallways, bathrooms, and kitchens, shall be separate from indoor space used with well children; this reduces the likelihood of mixing supplies, toys, and equipment. The facility may use a single kitchen for ill and well children if the kitchen is staffed by a cook who has no child care responsibilities other than food preparation and who does not handle soiled dishes and utensils until after food preparation and food service are completed for any meal;

c) Children whose symptoms indicate infections of the gastrointestinal tract (often with diarrhea) or liver, who receive care in special facilities for ill children shall receive this care in a space separate from other children with other illnesses to reduce the likelihood of disease being transmitted between children by limiting child-to-child interaction, separating staff responsibilities, and not mixing supplies, toys, and equipment;

d) If the facility cares for children with chickenpox, these children shall receive care in a separate room that is ventilated externally.

e) Each child care room shall have a handwashing sink that can provide a steady stream of water, no less than 60 degrees F and no more than 120 degrees F, at least for 10 seconds. Soap and disposable paper towels shall be available at the handwashing sink at all times.

f) Each room where children who wear diapers receive care shall have its own diaper changing area adjacent to a handwashing sink.

RATIONALE: Transmission of infectious diseases in child care settings may be influenced by the design, construction, and maintenance of the physical environment (66). The population that uses centers should in time become less susceptible to chickenpox through immunization. Some children, however, are too young to be routinely immunized and may be susceptible; and, although universal immunization with varicella vaccine is recommended, full compliance with the recommendation has not been achieved. Chickenpox is readily spread by airborne droplets (3). With implementation of universal use of varicella vaccine, the incidence of varicella in child care facilities will be reduced (3).

Handwashing sinks should be stationed in each room, to promote handwashing and also to give the care-givers an opportunity for continuous supervision of the other children in care when washing their hands. The sink must deliver a consistent flow of water for 10 seconds so that the user does not need to touch the faucet handles.

Diaper changing areas should be adjacent to sinks to foster cleanliness and also to enable caregivers to provide continuous supervision of other children in care.

COMMENTS: Some facilities have staffed get well rooms typically caring for fewer than six ill children.

TYPE OF FACILITY: *Center; Large Family Child Care Home; Small Family Child Care Home*

STANDARD 3.071
QUALIFICATIONS OF DIRECTORS OF FACILITIES THAT CARE FOR ILL CHILDREN

The director of a facility that cares for ill children shall have the following minimum qualifications, in addition to the general qualifications described in Qualifications of Directors of Centers, STANDARD 1.007 through STANDARD 1.014:

a) At least 40 hours of training in prevention and control of communicable diseases and care of ill children, including subjects listed in STANDARD 3.073;

b) At least 2 prior years of satisfactory performance as a director of a regular facility;

c) At least 12 credit hours of college-level training in child development or early childhood education.

RATIONALE: The director shall be college-prepared in early childhood education and have taken college-level courses in illness prevention and control, since the director is the person responsible for establishing the facility's policies and procedures and for meeting the training needs of new staff members.

TYPE OF FACILITY: *Center*

STANDARD 3.072
PROGRAM REQUIREMENTS FOR FACILITIES THAT CARE FOR ILL CHILDREN

Any facility that offers care for the ill child of any age shall:

a) Provide a caregiver who is familiar to the child;

b) Provide care in a place with which the child is familiar and comfortable;

c) Involve a caregiver who has time to give individual care and emotional support, who knows of the child's interests, and who knows of activities that appeal to the age group and to a sick child;

d) Offer a program planned in consultation with qualified health care personnel and with ongoing medical direction.

RATIONALE: When children are ill, they are stressed by the illness itself. Unfamiliar places and caregivers add to the stress of illness when a child is sick. Since illness tends to promote regression and dependency, ill children need a person who knows and can respond to the child's cues appropriately.

COMMENTS: Because children are most comfortable in a familiar place with familiar people, the preferred arrangement for ill children will be the child's home or the child's regular child care arrangement, when the child care facility has the resources to adapt to the needs of such children. Acquainting all children in care with the ill child area prior to use may reduce the child's anxiety in the event of illness.

For additional information on the care of ill children, see Reporting Illness, STANDARD 3.086 through STANDARD 3.089, and Health Department Plan, RECOMMENDATION 9.025.

TYPE OF FACILITY: *Center; Large Family Child Care Home; Small Family Child Care Home*

STANDARD 3.073
CAREGIVER QUALIFICATIONS FOR FACILITIES THAT CARE FOR ILL CHILDREN

Each caregiver in a facility that cares for ill children with level 2 or level 3 illness (as defined in STANDARD 3.064) shall have at least 2 years of successful work experience as a caregiver in a regular well-child facility prior to employment in the special facility. In addition, the Level 1 or Level 2 facility shall document, for each caregiver, 20 hours of pre-service orientation training on care of ill children beyond the orientation training specified in Training, STANDARD 1.023 through STANDARD 1.033. This training shall include the following subjects:

a) Pediatric first aid, including management of a blocked airway, rescue breathing, and first aid

for choking. See STANDARD 1.026 through STANDARD 1.028;

b) General infection-control procedures, including:
1) Handwashing;
2) Handling of contaminated items;
3) Use of sanitizing chemicals;
4) Food handling;
5) Washing and sanitizing of toys;
6) Education about methods of disease transmission.

c) Care of children with common mild childhood illnesses, including:
1) Recognition and documentation of signs and symptoms of illness;
2) Administration and recording of medications;
3) Temperature taking;
4) Nutrition of ill children;
5) Communication with parents of ill children;
6) Knowledge of immunization requirements;
7) When and how to call for medical assistance or notify the health department of communicable diseases;
8) Emergency procedures. See STANDARD 3.048 through STANDARD 3.052;

d) Child development activities for children who are ill;

e) Orientation to the facility and its policies.

This training shall be documented in the staff personnel files, and compliance with the content of training routinely evaluated. Based on these evaluations, the training on care of ill children shall be updated with a minimum of 6 hours of annual training for individuals who continue to provide care to ill children.

RATIONALE: Because meeting the physical and psychological needs of ill children requires a higher level of skill and understanding than caring for well children, a commitment to children and an understanding of their general needs is essential. Work experience will help the caregiver develop these skills. States that have developed rules regulating facilities have recognized the need for training in illness prevention and control and management of medical emergencies. First and foremost, people working with children should have an understanding of children and should create an environment for children that is developmentally appropriate, healthful, and safe at all times. Therefore, staff members caring for ill children in special facilities or in a get well room in a regular center should meet the staff qualifications that are applied to child care facilities generally.

Child care providers have to be prepared for handling illness and must understand their scope of work. Special training is required of teachers who work in special facilities for ill children because the director and the caregivers are dealing with communicable diseases and need to know how to prevent the spread of infection. Each caregiver should have training to decrease the risk of transmitting disease. The potential for medical emergencies as a result of illness is greater in facilities for ill children than in regular well-child facilities, so these facilities have to be prepared.

COMMENTS: States that have developed rules regulating facilities have recognized the need for training in illness prevention and control, aseptic technique, and management of medical emergencies.

See RECOMMENDATION 9.025, on health department assistance in developing this training.

TYPE OF FACILITY: *Center; Large Family Child Care Home; Small Family Child Care Home*

STANDARD 3.074
CHILD-STAFF RATIOS FOR FACILITIES THAT CARE FOR ILL CHILDREN

Each facility for ill children shall maintain a child-to-staff ratio no greater than the following:

Age of Children	Child to Staff Ratio
2-24 months	3 children to 1 staff member
25-71 months	4 children to 1 staff member
72 months and older	6 children to 1 staff member

RATIONALE: No studies are available to substantiate appropriate staffing levels. Most staffing requirements that state licensing authorities develop are stated in terms of number of staff members required to remove children from a building quickly in the event of fire or other emergency. The expert consensus is that ill children require more intensive and personalized care; therefore, the lowest ratios used per age group seem appropriate.

COMMENTS: These ratios do not include other personnel (such as bus drivers) necessary for specialized functions (such as transportation).

TYPE OF FACILITY: *Center; Large Family Child Care Home; Small Family Child Care Home*

STANDARD 3.075
HEALTH CONSULTANTS FOR FACILITIES THAT CARE FOR ILL CHILDREN

Each special facility that provides care for ill children shall use the services of a health consultant for ongoing consultation on overall operation and development of written policies relating to health care. The health consultant (see STANDARD 1.040 through STANDARD 1.044) shall have training and experience with pediatric health issues.

The facility shall involve the consultant in development and/or implementation, review, and sign-off of the written policies and procedures for managing specific illnesses. The facility staff and the consultant shall review and update the written policies annually.

The facility shall assign the health consultant the responsibility for reviewing written policies and procedures for the following:
a) Admission and readmission after illness, including inclusion/exclusion criteria;
b) Health evaluation procedures on intake, including physical assessment of the child and other criteria used to determine the appropriateness of a child's attendance;
c) Plans for health care and for managing children with communicable diseases;

d) Plans for surveillance of illnesses that are admissible and problems that arise in the care of children with illness;

e) Plans for staff training and communication with parents and health care providers;

f) Plans for injury prevention;

g) Situations that require medical care within an hour.

RATIONALE: Appropriate involvement of health consultants is especially important for facilities that care for ill children. Facilities should use the expertise of health professionals to design and provide a child care environment with sufficient staff and facilities to meet the needs of ill children (32, 70). The best interests of the child and family must be given primary consideration in the care of ill children. Consultation by physicians, especially pediatricians, is critical in planning facilities for the care of ill children (25).

COMMENTS: Caregivers should seek the services of a health consultant through state and local professional organizations, such as:

a) Local chapters of the American Academy of Pediatrics (AAP);

b) American Nurses Association (ANA);

c) Visiting Nurse Association (VNA);

d) American Academy of Family Physicians;

e) National Association of Pediatric Nurse Practitioners (NAPNAP);

f) National Association for the Education of Young Children (NAEYC);

g) National Association for Family Child Care;

h) Emergency Medical Services for Children (EMSC) National Resource Center;

i) National Training Institute for Child Care Health Consultants;

j) State or local health department (especially public health nursing, communicable disease, and epidemiology departments).

Caregivers also should not overlook health professionals with appropriate pediatric experience who are parents of children enrolled in their facility. A health professional (community health nurse, for example) may provide consultation, as a volunteer, or paid via a stipend, hourly rate, or honorarium. If a parent provides health consultation, conflicts of interest must be addressed in advance.

For additional information on health consultants, see also Health Consultation, STANDARD 8.020; Consultation Records, STANDARD 8.073, on documentation of health consultant visits; Health Consultants, STANDARD 1.040 and STANDARD 1.044, on general health consultant qualifications and responsibilities; and, STANDARD 3.072, on health consultants for special facilities for ill children.

TYPE OF FACILITY: *Center; Large Family Child Care Home; Small Family Child Care Home*

STANDARD 3.076
LICENSING OF FACILITIES THAT CARE FOR ILL CHILDREN

Special facilities that care for ill children shall be required to comply with specific licensing requirements, which shall address the unique regulatory needs of service to children with illness cared for in out-of-home settings.

RATIONALE: Facilities for ill children generally are required to meet the licensing requirements that apply to all facilities of a specific type, for example, small or large family child care homes or centers. Additional requirements should apply when ill children will be in care.

COMMENTS: For additional information on licensing special facilities for ill children, see also Regulatory Policy, RECOMMENDATION 9.001 through RECOMMENDATION 9.003, on licensing requirements.

TYPE OF FACILITY: *Center; Large Family Child Care Home; Small Family Child Care Home*

STANDARD 3.077
INFORMATION REQUIRED FOR ILL CHILDREN

For each day of care in a special facility that provides care for ill children, the caregiver shall have the following information on each child:

a) The child's specific diagnosis and the individual providing the diagnosis (physician, parent or legal guardian);
b) Current status of the illness, including potential for contagion, diet, activity level, and duration of illness;
c) Health care, diet, allergies (particularly to foods or medication), and medication plan, including appropriate release forms to obtain emergency health care and administer medication;
d) Communication with the parent on the child's progress;
e) Name, address, and telephone number of the child's source of primary health care;
f) Communication with the child's primary health care provider.

RATIONALE: The caregiver must have child-specific information to provide optimum care for each ill child and to make appropriate decisions regarding whether to include or exclude a given child. The caregiver must have contact information for the child's source of primary health care to assist with the management of any situation that arises.

COMMENTS: Too often, parents who are not with the child contact the child's source of health care to seek advice. The parent is relaying secondhand information and cannot answer questions that must be addressed by the caregiver who is with the child at the time. These three-way conversations are frustrating and can lead to inappropriate advice.

For school-age children, documentation of the care of the child during the illness should be provided to the parent to deliver to the school health program upon the child's return to school. Coordination with the child's source of health care and school health program facilitates the overall care of the child.

TYPE OF FACILITY: *Center; Large Family Child Care Home; Small Family Child Care Home*

STANDARD 3.078
INCLUSION AND EXCLUSION OF CHILDREN FROM FACILITIES THAT SERVE ILL CHILDREN

Facilities that care for ill children who have conditions that require additional attention from the caregiver shall arrange for or ask the health consultant to arrange for a clinical health evaluation, by a licensed health care professional, for each child who is admitted to the facility. These facilities shall include children with conditions listed in STANDARD 3.065 if their policies and plans address the management of these conditions, except for the following conditions which require exclusion from all types of child care facilities that are not medical care institutions (such as hospitals or skilled nursing facilities):
a) Fever and a stiff neck, lethargy, irritability, or persistent crying;
b) Diarrhea (three or more loose stools in an 8-hour period or more stools compared to the child's normal pattern, with more stool water or less form) and one or more of the following:
　1) Signs of dehydration;
　2) Blood or mucus in the stool, unless at least one stool culture demonstrates absence of *Shigella, Salmonella, Campylobacter,* and *E. coli 0157:H7.* See STANDARD 3.065 and STANDARD 6.023;
　3) Diarrhea attributable to *Salmonella, Campylobacter,* or *Giardia* except that a child with diarrhea attributable to *Campylobacter* or *Giardia* may be readmitted 24 hours after treatment has been initiated if cleared by the child's physician;
c) Diarrhea attributable to *Shigella* and *E. coli 0157:H7,* until diarrhea resolves and two stool cultures taken 48 hours apart are negative (29);
d) Vomiting three or more times, or signs of dehydration;
e) Contagious stages of pertussis, measles, mumps, chickenpox, rubella, or diphtheria, unless the child is appropriately isolated from children with other illnesses and cared for only with children having the same illness;
f) Untreated infestation of scabies or head lice;
g) Untreated tuberculosis;
h) Undiagnosed rash;

i) Abdominal pain that is intermittent or persistent;
j) Difficulty in breathing;
k) Lethargy such that the child does not play;
l) Undiagnosed jaundice (yellow skin and whites of eyes);
m) Other conditions as may be determined by the director or health consultant.

RATIONALE: These signs may indicate a significant systemic infection that requires professional medical management and parental care. Because diarrheal illness caused by *Shigella, E. coli 0157:H7, Salmonella, Campylobacter, Cryptosporidium*, rotavirus and other enteric viruses, and *Giardia lamblia* may spread from child to child or from child to staff, children and staff with these infections, when accompanied by diarrhea, should be excluded from child care.

Antibiotic therapy of *Campylobacter* may not alter symptoms, but it does decrease shedding of the organism and, therefore, lowers the infectivity of these children. Antibiotic therapy for salmonella gastroenteritis is generally not recommended unless diarrhea is severe, sepsis is present, or the child has a specific underlying medical condition that makes this illness problematic. Therefore, most children with Salmonella gastroenteritis will not be treated with antibiotics and should not be included in regular or special child care until the diarrheal illness has resolved. *Shigella* and *E. coli 0157:H7* both can produce severe illness and, therefore, exclusion recommendations are more stringent.

COMMENTS: For additional information regarding health consultants, see STANDARD 1.040 through STANDARD 1.044.

TYPE OF FACILITY: *Center; Large Family Child Care Home; Small Family Child Care Home*

STANDARD 3.079
EXCEPTIONS TO REQUIRED EXCLUSION OF CHILDREN FROM FACILITIES THAT CARE FOR ILL CHILDREN

A facility may care for children with symptoms requiring exclusion provided that the licensing authority has given approval of the facility, written plans describing symptoms and conditions that are admissible, and procedures for daily care. In jurisdictions that lack regulations and licensing capacity for facilities that care for ill children, the local health authority shall review these plans and procedures annually in an advisory capacity.

RATIONALE: This standard ensures that child care facilities are continually reviewed by an appropriate state authority and that facilities maintain appropriate standards in caring for ill children.

COMMENTS: See also RECOMMENDATION 9.005, for information on written plans for the inclusion and exclusion of ill children.

TYPE OF FACILITY: *Center; Large Family Child Care Home; Small Family Child Care Home*

STANDARD 3.080
PLAY EQUIPMENT IN FACILITIES THAT CARE FOR ILL CHILDREN

In a facility that cares for ill children, a varied supply of play equipment and materials shall be available that stimulate an ill child's interest and involvement and provide a match between an ill child's level of development and condition of health or illness, as defined by the facility's health consultant (see Health Consultants, STANDARD 1.040 through STANDARD 1.044) and the child's health care provider.

RATIONALE: Frequent mild illness is a normal condition of childhood, and the activity level of ill children is age dependent. Ill children, like well children, need to engage inn activities that are suitable to their age and developmental level and consistent with their state of health or illness and their accompanying level of interest or responsiveness.

A low level of responsiveness in the school-age child usually leads to sleeping and resting for much of the day, requiring a minimum of activities and stimulation. Infants, toddlers, and preschool-age children tend to be unable to rest for such long periods of time, and therefore require more attention from the caregiver in terms of providing activities and guidance.

TYPE OF FACILITY: *Center; Large Family Child Care Home; Small Family Child Care Home*

MEDICATIONS

STANDARD 3.081
PERMISSIBLE ADMINISTRATION OF MEDICATION

The administration of medicines at the facility shall be limited to:
a) Prescribed medications ordered by a health care provider for a specific child, with written permission of the parent or legal guardian;
b) Nonprescription (over-the-counter) medications recommended by a health care provider for a specific child or for a specific circumstance for any child in the facility, with written permission of the parent or legal guardian.

RATIONALE: Before assuming responsibility for administration of medicine, facilities must have clear, accurate instruction and medical confirmation of the child's need for medication while in the facility. Caregivers should not be involved in inappropriate use of drugs based solely on a parent's desire to give the child medication. Parents are victims of their own desire to do something for self-limited illnesses and the vigorous advertisement for many over-the-counter medications, including acetaminophen and combinations of antihistamines and decongestants as cold remedies.

Overuse of medications has been confirmed by results of the National Center for Health Statistics' survey of the incidence of medicated respiratory tract infection, which showed that 29.5% of children under 5 years of age in the survey were reported by their parents to have received a medication for a

respiratory tract illness in the 2 weeks before the interview (69).

Decongestants and antihistamines have been shown to prolong the retention of secretions in the middle ear rather than helping children get well. No existing evidence reports that decongestants or antihistamines, alone or in combination, prevent middle ear infections; therefore, the use of such medications for common colds is not recommended (68).

COMMENTS: A health care provider can write a standing order for a commonly used nonprescription medication (such as acetaminophen or sunscreen) that defines when the medication should be used for any child in the facility. For example: "With parental consent, children who are older than 4 months of age may receive acetaminophen when their body temperature exceeds 101 degrees F, according to the dose schedule and instructions provided by the manufacturer of the acetaminophen," or "With parental consent, children may have sunscreen applied to exposed skin, except eyelids, 30 minutes before exposure to the sun and every 2 hours while in the sun. Sunscreen preparations shall be applied according to the instructions provided by the manufacturer."

Parents should always be notified in every instance when medication is used. Telephone instructions from a health care provider are acceptable if the caregiver fully documents them and if the parent initiates the request for health care provider instruction. Advance notification of the parent (before medication is given) is ideal but may not be appropriate if a child needs medication urgently (such as to stop an allergic reaction) or when contacting the parent will unreasonably delay appropriate care.

Safeguards against liability for accepting telephone instructions for medication administration should be checked with an attorney. Nonprescription medications should be given according to the manufacturers' instructions unless a health care provider provides written instructions otherwise. A sample form for parental consent to administer medication is in *Healthy Young Children*, from the National Association for the Education of Young Children (NAEYC). Contact information is located in Appendix BB.

TYPE OF FACILITY: *Center; Large Family Child Care Home; Small Family Child Care Home*

TYPE OF FACILITY: *Center; Large Family Child Care Home; Small Family Child Care Home*

STANDARD 3.082
LABELING AND STORAGE OF MEDICATIONS

Any prescribed medication brought into the facility by the parent, legal guardian, or responsible relative of a child shall be dated, and shall be kept in the original container. The container shall be labeled by a pharmacist with:
a)   The child's first and last names;
b)   The date the prescription was filled;
c)   The name of the health care provider who wrote the prescription, the medication's expiration date;
d)   The manufacturer's instructions or prescription label with specific, legible instructions for administration, storage, and disposal;
e)   The name and strength of the medication.

Over-the-counter medications shall be kept in the original container as sold by the manufacturer, labeled by the parent, with the child's name and specific instructions given by the child's health professional for administration.

All medications, refrigerated or unrefrigerated, shall have child-resistant caps, shall be kept in an organized fashion, shall be stored away from food at the proper temperature, and shall be inaccessible to children. Medication shall not be used beyond the date of expiration.

RATIONALE: Before assuming responsibility for administration of medicine, facilities must have clear, accurate instruction and medical confirmation of the child's need for medication while in the facility.

Child-resistant safety packaging was shown to decrease among children aged 0-4 years, while poisonings from unregulated products increased for this age group (67).

COMMENTS: A small lock box can be kept in the refrigerator to hold medications.

STANDARD 3.083
TRAINING OF CAREGIVERS TO ADMINISTER MEDICATION

Any caregiver who administers medication shall be trained to:
a)   Check that the name of the child on the medication and the child receiving the medication are the same;
b)   Read and understand the label/prescription directions in relation to the measured dose, frequency, and other circumstances relative to administration (such as in relation to meals);
c)   Administer the medication according to the prescribed methods and the prescribed dose;
d)   Observe and report any side effects from medications;
e)   Document the administration of each dose by the time and the amount given.

RATIONALE: Caregivers need to be aware of what medication the child is receiving, who prescribed the medicine and when, and what the known reactions or side effects may be if a child has a negative reaction to the medicine (72). A child's reaction to medication occasionally is extreme enough to initiate the protocol developed for emergencies. The medication record is especially important if medications are frequently prescribed or if long-term medications are being used. See *Model Child Care Health Policies* from the American Academy of Pediatrics (AAP) and the National Association for the Education of Young Children (NAEYC). Contact information for the AAP and the NAEYC is located in Appendix BB.

COMMENTS: For additional information on medications, see STANDARD 8.021 and STANDARD 8.051.

TYPE OF FACILITY: *Center; Large Family Child Care Home; Small Family Child Care Home*

NOTIFICATION OF PARENTS

STANDARD 3.084
PROCEDURE FOR PARENT NOTIFICATION ABOUT EXPOSURE OF CHILDREN TO COMMUNICABLE DISEASE

The center director or large or small family home child caregiver shall follow the recommendations of these standards, the facility's health consultant, or the local health authority regarding notification of parents of children who attend the facility about exposure of their child to a communicable disease. When notification is recommended, it shall be oral or written and shall include the following information:
a) The diagnosed disease to which the child was exposed, whether there is one case or an out-break, and the nature of the exposure (such as a child in same room or facility);
b) Signs and symptoms of the disease that the parent should watch for in the child;
c) Mode of transmission for the disease;
d) Period of communicability and how long to watch for signs and symptoms of the disease;
e) Disease-prevention measures recommended by the health department (if appropriate);
f) Control measures implemented at the facility;

The notice shall not identify the child who has the communicable disease.

> RATIONALE: Effective control and prevention of infectious diseases in child care depends on affirmative relationships between parents, caregivers, public health authorities, and primary health care providers.

> COMMENTS: For a sample letter to parents notifying them of illness of their child or other enrolled children, see *Healthy Young Children*, available from the National Association for the Education of Young Children (NAEYC). Contact information is located in Appendix BB.

> TYPE OF FACILITY: *Center; Large Family Child Care Home; Small Family Child Care Home*

STANDARD 3.085
COMMUNICABLE DISEASES THAT REQUIRE PARENT NOTIFICATION

In cooperation with the health department, the facility or the health department shall inform parents of other children who attend the facility that their child may have been exposed at the facility to the following diseases or conditions:
a) *Neisseria meningitidis* (meningitis). See STANDARD 6.006 through STANDARD 6.008;
b) Pertussis. See STANDARD 6.009 through STANDARD 6.011;
c) Streptococcal infections. See Group A Streptococcal (GAS) Infection, STANDARD 6.012 and STANDARD 6.013;
d) Varicella-Zoster (Chickenpox) Virus. See STANDARD 6.019 through STANDARD 6.020;
e) Skin infections (head lice, scabies, and ringworm). See STANDARD 6.037 through STANDARD 6.039;
f) Infections of the gastrointestinal tract (often with diarrhea) and hepatitis A virus (HAV). See STANDARD 6.023 through STANDARD 6.026;
g) *Haemophilus influenzae* type B (Hib). See STANDARD 6.001 through STANDARD 6.003;
h) Parvovirus B19 (fifth disease). See STANDARD 6.016;
i) Measles;
j) Tuberculosis. See STANDARD 6.014 and STANDARD 6.015.

> RATIONALE: Early identification and treatment of infectious diseases are important in minimizing associated morbidity and mortality as well as further reducing transmission. Notification of parents will permit them to discuss with their child's health provider the implications of the exposure and to closely observe their child for early signs and symptoms of illness.

> COMMENTS: For a sample letter to parents notifying them of illness of their child or other enrolled children, see *Healthy Young Children*, available from the National Association for the Education of Young Children (NAEYC). Contact information located in Appendix BB.

For notification of the Health Department, see Reporting Illness, STANDARD 3.086 through STANDARD 3.089. See also Health Department Plan and Role, RECOMMENDATION 9.025; on the health department's responsibility in communicable diseases.

TYPE OF FACILITY: *Center; Large Family Child Care Home; Small Family Child Care Home*

REPORTING ILLNESS AND DEATH

STANDARD 3.086
NOTIFICATION OF THE FACILITY ABOUT COMMUNICABLE DISEASE OR OTHER PROBLEMS BY PARENTS

Upon registration of each child, the facility shall inform parents that parents must notify the facility within 24 hours after their child or any member of the immediate household has developed a known or suspected communicable disease as required by the health department. When the child has a disease requiring exclusion or dismissal, the parents shall inform the facility of the diagnosis.

The facility shall encourage parents to inform the caregivers of any other problems which may affect the child's behavior.

> RATIONALE: This requirement will facilitate prompt reporting of disease and enable the caregiver to provide better care. Disease surveillance and reporting to local health authorities are crucial to preventing and controlling diseases in the child care setting. The major purpose of surveillance is to allow early detection of disease and prompt implementation of control measures.

> Ascertaining whether an ill child is attending a facility is important when evaluating childhood illnesses. Ascertaining whether an adult with illness is working in a facility or is a parent of a child attending a facility is important when considering infectious diseases that are more commonly manifested in adults. Cases of illness in family member such as infections of the gastrointestinal tract (with diarrhea), or infections of

the liver may necessitate questioning about possible illness in the child attending child care. Testing the child for infection may be needed as a protective measure. Information concerning communicable disease in a child care attendee, staff member, or household contact should be communicated to public health authorities, to the child care director, and to the child's parents.

COMMENTS: See Child Inclusion/Exclusion/ Dismissal, STANDARD 3.065 through STANDARD 3.068, for information regarding the exclusion or dismissal of children from a child care facility.

TYPE OF FACILITY: *Center; Large Family Child Care Home; Small Family Child Care Home*

STANDARD 3.087
LIST OF EXCLUDABLE AND REPORTABLE CONDITIONS FOR PARENTS

The facility shall give to each parent a written list of conditions for which exclusion and dismissal are required, as specified in STANDARD 3.065 (25).

For the following conditions, the caregiver shall ask parents to have the child evaluated by a health care provider. The advice of the health care provider shall be documented for the child care provider in the following situations:
a)   The child has any of the following conditions: fever, lethargy, irritability, persistent crying, difficult breathing, or other manifestations of possible severe illness;
b)   The child has diarrhea with blood or mucus in the stool(s);
c)   The child has E. coli O157:H7, Shigella or Salmonella infection;
d)   The child has mouth sores associated with drooling;
e)   The child has a rash with fever and behavioral change;
f)   The child has purulent conjunctivitis;
g)   The child has tuberculosis;
h)   The child vomits 2 or more times during the previous 24 hours;
i)   The child has impetigo;
j)   The child has streptococcal pharyngitis;
k)   The child has scabies;

l) The child has pertussis;
m) The child has hepatitis A virus infection.

The facility shall have a list of reportable diseases provided by the health department and shall provide a copy to each parent.

> RATIONALE: Vomiting with symptoms such as lethargy and/or dry skin or mucous membranes or reduced urine output, may indicate dehydration, and the child should be medically evaluated. Diarrhea with fever or other symptoms usually indicates infection. Blood and/or mucus may indicate shigellosis or infection with *E. coli 0157:H7*, which should be treated (3).

> Effective control and prevention of infectious diseases in child care depend on affirmative relationships between parents, caregivers, health departments, and primary health care providers.

> COMMENTS: If there is more than one case of vomiting in the facility, it may indicate contagious illness or food poisoning.

> If a child with abdominal pain is drowsy, irritable, and unhappy, has no appetite, and is unwilling to participate in usual activities, the child should be seen by that child's health care provider. Abdominal pain may be associated with viral, bacterial, or parasitic gastrointestinal tract illness, which is contagious, or with food poisoning. It also may be a manifestation of another disease or illness such as kidney disease. If the pain is severe or persistent, the child should be referred for medical consultation (by telephone, if necessary).

> If the caregiver is unable to contact the parent, medical advice should be sought until the parents can be located.

> The facility should post the health department's list of communicable diseases as a reference. The facility shall inform parents that they may be required to report communicable diseases to the health department.

> For additional information on reporting illness, see also Disease Surveillance of Enteric (Diarrheal) and

Hepatitis A Virus Infections, STANDARD 6.025, on reporting hepatitis B; Health Department Plan, RECOMMENDATION 9.025, on child records.

See also *Situations that Require Medical Attention Right Away*, Appendix N.

TYPE OF FACILITY: *Center; Large Family Child Care Home; Small Family Child Care Home*

STANDARD 3.088
WRITTEN POLICY FOR REPORTING ILLNESS TO THE HEALTH DEPARTMENT

The facility shall have a written policy that complies with the state's reporting requirements for ill children. All communicable diseases shall be reported to the health department. The facility shall have the telephone number of the responsible health authority to whom confirmed or suspected cases of these diseases, or outbreaks of other communicable diseases, shall be reported, and shall designate a staff member as responsible for reporting the disease.

> RATIONALE: Reporting to the health department provides the department with knowledge of illnesses within the community and ability to offer preventive measures to children and families exposed to the outbreak of a disease.

TYPE OF FACILITY: *Center; Large Family Child Care Home; Small Family Child Care Home*

STANDARD 3.089
DEATH (SIDS AND OTHER)

If a facility experiences the death of a child, the following shall be done:
a) If the child dies while at the facility:
    1) Immediately notify emergency medical personnel;
    2) Immediately notify the child's parents;
    3) Notify the Licensing agency;
    4) Provide age appropriate information for children and parents;

b) For a suspected Sudden Infant Death
Syndrome (SIDS) death or other unexplained
deaths:
1) Seek support and information from local,
state, or national SIDS resources;
2) Provide SIDS information to the parents of
the other children in the facility;
3) Provide age-appropriate information to
the other children in the facility;
c) If the child dies while not at the facility:
1) Provide age-appropriate information for
children and parents;
2) Make resources for support available to
parents and children.
d) Release specific information about the
circumstances of the child's death that the
child's family agrees the facility may share.

RATIONALE: The licensing agency and a SIDS
program can offer support and counseling to
caregivers. Following the steps described in the
Standard would constitute prudent action (7).
Accurate information given to the other parents and
children will help them understand the event and
facilitate their support of the caregiver.

COMMENTS: It is important that caregivers are
knowledgeable about SIDS and that they take proper
steps so that they are not falsely accused of child
abuse. For information regarding preventive care and
proper sleep position, see STANDARD 3.008. For
information and support, contact the National SIDS
Resource Center. Contact information is located in
Appendix BB.

TYPE OF FACILITY: *Center; Large Family Child Care
Home; Small Family Child Care Home*

REFERENCES

1. Paige DM. *Clinical Nutrition.* 2nd ed. St. Louis, Mo: Mosby Yearbook Inc.; 1988.

2. American Academy of Pediatrics. *Pediatric Nutrition Handbook.* 4th ed. Elk Grove, Ill: American Academy of Pediatrics; 1998.

3. American Academy of Pediatrics, Committee on Infectious Diseases. *Red book 2000: Report of the committee on infectious diseases.* Elk Grove Village, Ill: American Academy of Pediatrics; 2000.

4. American Academy of Pediatrics, Committee on Infectious Disease. Recommended childhood immunization schedule - United States, January - December 2001. *Pediatrics.* 2001;107:202-204.

5. Advisory Committee on Immunization Practices (ACIP). Immunization of health-care workers. *Mor Mortal Wkly Rev CDC Surveill Summ.* 1997;46(RR18).

6. Deitch S, ed. *Health in Day Care: A Manual for Health Professionals.* Elk Grove Village, Ill: American Academy of Pediatrics; 1987.

7. Moon RY, Patel KM, Shaefer SJM. Sudden infant death syndrome in child care settings. *Pediatrics.* 2000;106(2),295-300.

8. American Academy of Pediatrics Task Force on Infant Feeding and SIDS. Changing concepts of sudden infant death syndrome: implications for infant sleeping environment and sleep position. *Pediatrics.* 2000;105(3);650-656.

9. Ogasawara T, Watanabe T, Kasahara H. Readiness for toothbrushing of young children. *ASDC J Dent Child.* 1992;59(5),353-359.

10. Kallestal C, Wang NJ, Persen PE, Arnadottir IB. Caries-preventive methods used for children and adolescents in Denmark, Iceland, Norway, and Sweden. *Community Dent Oral Epidemiol.* 1999;27(2),144-151.

11. Van R, Morrow AL, Reves RR, et al. Environmental contamination in child day care centers. *Am J Epidemiol.* 1991;133:460-470.

12. Gorski, PA. Toilet training guidelines: day care providers-the role of the day care provider in toilet training. *Pediatrics.* 1999;103(suppl 6, pt 2):1367-1368.

13. Fox JA, ed. Diaper rash. *Prim Health Care Child.* 1997;593-594.

14. Kubiak M, Kressner B, Raynor W, Davis J, Syverson RE. Comparison of stool containment in cloth and single-use diapers using a simulated infant feces. *Pediatrics.* 1993;91(3);632-636.

15. Aronson SS. The ideal diaper-changing station. *Child Care Info Exch.* 1999;130:92-93.

16. *Keeping Healthy: Parents, Teachers, and Children.* Washington, DC: National Association for the Education of Young Children, 1999.

17. *The ABC's of safe and healthy child care: a handbook for child care providers.* Washington DC: Centers for Disease Control and Prevention; 1996.

18. *Well Being: A Guide to Promote the Physical Health, Safety and Emotional Well-Being of Children in Child Care Centres and Family Day Care Homes.* 2nd ed. Toronto, Ontario: Canadian Paediatric Society; 1996.

19. Rutala WA, Weber DJ. Uses of inorganic hypochlorite (bleach) in health-care facilities. *Clin Microbiol.* 1997;10:597-610.

20. Weber DJ, Barbee SL, Sobsey MD, Rutula WA. The effect of blood on the antiviral activity of sodium hypochlorite, a phenolic, and a quaternary ammonium compound. *Infect Control and Hosp Epidemiol.* 1999;20:821-827.

21. Hawks D, Ascheim J, Giebink GS, Graville S, Solnit AJ. Science, prevention, and practice VII: improving child day care, a concurrent summary of the American Public Health Association/American Academy of Pediatrics national health and safety guidelines for child-care programs; featured standards and implementation. *Pediatrics.* 1994;95(6);1110-1112.

22. Soto JC, Guy M, Belanger L. Science, prevention and practice II: preventing infectious diseases, abstracts on handwashing and infection control in day-care centers. *Pediatrics.* 1994;94(6);1030.

23. Roberts L, Mapp E, Smith W, Jorm L, Pate M, Douglas RM, McGilchrist C. Effect of infection control measures on the frequency of upper respiratory infection in child care: a randomized, controlled trial. *Pediatrics.* 2000;105(suppl 4, Pt 1);738-742.

24. Niffenegger JP. Proper handwashing promotes wellness in child care. *J Pediatr Health Care.* 1997;11:26-31.

25. Donowitz LG, ed. *Infection Control in the Child Care Center and Preschool.* 2nd ed. Baltimore, Md: Williams & Wilkins. 1996;18-19,68.

26. Palmer SR, Soulsby L, Simpson DIH, eds. *Zoonoses: Biology, Clinical Practice, and Public Health Control.* New York, NY: Oxford University Press; 1998.

27. Weinberg AN, Weber DJ, eds. Animal associated human infections. *Infect Dis Clin North Am.* 1991;5:1-175,649-731.

28. Black RE, Dykes AC, Anderson KE. Handwashing to prevent diarrhea in day care centers. *Am J Epidemiol.* 1981;113:445-451.

29. Roberts L, Jorm L, Patel M, et al. Effect of infection control measures on the frequency of diarrhea episodes in child care: a randomized, controlled trial. *Pediatrics.* 2000:105(4):743-746.

30. Carabin H, Gyorkos TW, Soto JC, et al. Effectiveness of a training program in reducing infections in toddlers attending day care centers. *Epidemiol.* 1999;10:219-27.

31. Bartlett AV, Jarvis RA, Ross V, et al. Diarrheal illness among infants and toddlers in day care centers: effects of active surveillance and staff training without subsequent monitoring. *Am J Epidemiol.* 1988;127:808-817.

32. Churchill RB, Pickering LK. Infection control challenges in child care centers. *Infect Dis Clin North Am.* 1997;11:347-65.

33. Butz AM, Fosarelli P, Dick D, et al. Prevalence of rotavirus on high-risk fomites in day-care facilities. *Pediatrics.* 1993;92:202-5.

34. Van de Perre P, Simonon A, Hitimana, et al. Infective and anti-infective properties of breastmilk from HIV-1-infected women. *Lancet.* 1993;341(8850):914-8.

35. Newburg DS, Viscidi RP, Ruff A, Yolken RH. A human milk factor inhibits binding of human immunodeficiency virus to the CD4 receptor. *Pediatr Res.* 1992;31(1):22-8.

36. Schwartz J, Timonen KL, Pekkanen J. Respiratory effects of environmental tobacco smoke in a panel study of asthmatic and symptomatic children. *Am J Resp Crit Care Med.* 2000;161:802-6.

37. Stenstrom R, Bernard PA, Ben-Simhon H. Exposure to environmental tobacco smoke as a risk factor for recurrent acute otitis media in children under the age of five years. *Inter J Pediatr Otorhinolaryngol.* 1993;27(2):127-36.

38. Pershagen G. Accumulating evidence on health hazards of passive smoking. *Acta Paediatr.* 1999;88(5):490-2.

39. Gergen PJ, Fowler JA, Maurer KR, et al. The burden of environmental tobacco smoke exposure on the respiratory health of children 2 months through 5 years of age in the United States: third national health and nutritional examination survey, 1988 to 1994. *Pediatrics.* 1998;101(2):E8.

40. Runyan CW, Bangdiwala SI, Linzer MA, et al. Risk factors for fatal residential fires. *N Eng J Med.* 1992;327:856-63.

41. Brigham PA, Mcguire A. Progress towards a fire-safe cigarette. *J Public Health Policy.* 1995;16(4):433-9.

42. Ballard JE, Koepsell TD, Rivara F. Association of smoking and alcohol drinking with residential fire injuries. *Am J Epidemiol.* 1992;135:26-34.

43. Gandhi RR, Liebman MA, Stafford BL, Stafford PW. Dog bite injuries in children: a preliminary survey. *Am Surg.* 1999;65(9):863-4.

44. American Academy of Pediatrics. Drowning in infants, children and adolescents. *Pediatrics.* 1993;92(2):292-294.

45. Aronson S. Pets and kids. *Child Care Infor Exch.* 1997;82-83.

46. US Environmental Protection Agency (EPA). Asthma and Allergy Foundation of America: New England Chapter. *Asthma-friendly Child Care: A Checklist for Parents and Providers.* Washington, DC: EPA; 2000.

47. Nelson HS. Allergen and irritant control: importance and implementation. *Clin Cornerstone.* 1998;1:57-68.

48. US Consumer Product Safety Commission (CPSC). *Infants and Toddlers Can Drown in 5-Gallon Buckets.* Washington, DC: CPSC; 1994:5006.

49. US Consumer Product Safety Commission (CPSC). *CPSC Reminds Pool Owners that Barriers, Supervision Prevent Drowning.* Washington, DC: CPSC; 1997:97-152.

50. US Consumer Product Safety Commission (CPSC). *Drowning Hazard with Baby "Supporting Ring" Devices.* Washington, DC: CPSC; 1994:5084.

51. US Consumer Product Safety Commission (CPSC). *Safety Barrier Guidelines for Home Pools.* Washington, DC: CPSC; 1994:362.

52. Quinlan KP, Sacks JJ. Hospitalizations for dog bite injuries. [letter]. *JAMA.* 1999;281(3):232-3.

53. Weiss HB, Friedman DI, Coben JH. Incidence of dog bite injuries treated in emergency departments. *JAMA.* 1998;279(1):51-3.

54. From the Centers for Disease Control and Prevention: Dog-bite-related fatalities--United States, 1995-1996. *JAMA.* 1997;278(4):278-9.

55. Krenzelok EP, McGuigan M, Lheur P. Position statement: ipecac syrup--American Academy of Clinical Toxicology; European Association of Poison Centres and Clinical Toxicologists. *J Toxicol Clin Toxicol.* 1997;35:699-709.

56. Rauchschwalbe R, Brenner RA, Gordon S. The role of bathtub seats and rings in infant drowning deaths. *Pediatrics.* 1997;100:e1.

57. Committee on Injury and Poison Prevention: Reducing the number of deaths and injuries from residential fires. *Pediatrics.* 2000;105:1355-1357.

58. Goldman R. An educational perspective on abuse. In: Goldman R, Gargiulo R, eds. *Children at Risk: An Interdisciplinary Approach to Child Abuse and Neglect.* Austin, Tex: Pro-Ed; 1990:37-72.

59. Asthma mortality and hospitalization among children and young adults - United States, 1980-1993. *Mor Mortal Wkly Rev CDC Surveill Summ.* 1996;45;350-353.

60. Cordell RL, Solomon SL, Hale CM. Exclusion of mildly ill children from out-of-home child care facilities. *Infect Med.* 1996;13:45-58.

61. The Bureau of National Affairs (BNA). *Expecting the Unexpected: Sick and Emergency Child Care.* Washington, DC: BNA; 1992. Special Report Series on Work and Family, No. 53.

62. McDonald KL, White KA, Heiser JL, et al. Lack of detected increased risk of subsequent illness for children attending a sick-child day care center. *Pediatr Infect Dis J.* 1991;9:15

63. American Academy of Pediatrics, Provisional Committee on Quality Improvement, Subcommittee on Acute Gastroenteritis. Practice parameter: the management of acute gastroenteritis in young children. *Pediatrics.* 1996;97:424-33.

64. Sargent SJ, Martin JT. Scabies outbreak in a day care center. *Pediatrics.* 1994;94(suppl):1012.

65. Reves RR, Pickering LK. Impact of child day care on infectious diseases in adults. *Infect Dis Clin North Amer.* 1992;6:239-50.

66. Staes C, Balk S, Ford K, Passantino RJ, Torrice A. Environmental factors to consider when designing and maintaining a child's day-care environment. *Pediatrics.* 1994;94(suppl):1048-50.

67. Lembershy RB, Nichols MH, King WD. Effectiveness of child-resistant packaging on toxin procurement in young poisoning victims. *Vet Hum Toxicol.* 1996;38:380-3.

68. Sagraves R, Maish W, Kameshka A. Update of otitis media, part 2: treatment. *Am Pharm.* 1993;NS33:29-35.

69. Barden LS, Dowell SF, Schwartz B, et al. Current attitudes regarding use of antimicrobial agents: results from physician's and parents' focus group discussion. *Clin Pediatr.* 1998;37:665-71.

70. Crowley AA. Child care health consultation: the Connecticut experience. *Matern Child Health J.* 2000;4(1):67-75.

71. US Consumer Product Safety Commission (CPSC). *For Kids' Sake: Think Toy Safety.* Atlanta, Ga: CPSC; 1995:281. Available at: http://www.cpsc.gov/cpscpub/pubs/281.html. Accessed November 20, 2000.

72. *Guidelines for School Medication Administration. Part I: Administrative Policies and Procedures, Part II: An Instructional Program for Training School Personnel to Give Medication.* 3rd ed. Denver, Colo: Colorado State Board of Nursing; 1999.

73. *Child Care Center Licensing Study, 2000.* Washington, DC: The Children's Foundation; 2000.

74. Brenner RA, Trumble AC, Smith, GS, Kessler EP, Overpeck, MD. Where children drown, United States, 1995. *Pediatrics* 2001; 108:85-89.

CHAPTER 4

Nutrition and Food Service

4.1 INTRODUCTION

One of the basic responsibilities of every parent and caregiver is to provide nourishing food that is clean, safe and developmentally appropriate for children. Children need freely available, clean drinking water too. Feeding should occur in a relaxed and pleasant environment that fosters healthy digestion and pro social behavior. Food provides energy and nutrients needed by infants and children during a critical period when they grow and develop more rapidly than at any other time.

Human milk, the most natural and beneficial first food, sets the stage for an infant to establish a human relationship. These first feeding experiences foster attachment and bonding, while the infant is nurtured by the mother or primary caretaker. From the first feeding after birth, the process begins of the infant responding to and identifying with the mother during breastfeeding or with the primary caregiver when bottle fed. Each subsequent feeding reinforces human relationships and attitudes about food and eating by the child. The infant learns to associate the food offered with the parent or caregiver, which together forms a feeding/eating dynamic.

As new foods are introduced, children learn to self-feed concurrently with the attainment of physical growth, physiological readiness, and the development of motor coordination, cognitive and social skills. This period is an opportune time for children to learn more about the world around them by expressions of independence. Children pick and choose from different kinds and combinations of foods offered. Eating jags are to be expected as evidence of growth and self-feeding. Family homes and out-of-home care settings have many opportunities to guide and support sound eating habits and food learning experiences for children.

Early food and eating experiences are the foundation for the formation of attitudes about food, eating behavior, and consequently, food habits. Sound food habits build on eating and enjoying a variety of healthful foods. Including culturally acceptable family foods is a dietary goal for feeding infants and young children. Current research documents that a balanced diet combined with regular and routine age-appropriate physical activity can reduce the risks of chronic diseases later in life that are related to diet (1). These two essentials - eating healthy foods and engaging in physical activity on a daily basis - promote a healthy beginning during the early years and throughout the life span. *Nutrition and Your Health: Dietary Guidelines for Americans* is designed to support lifestyle behaviors that promote health, including a diet composed of a variety of healthy foods and physical activity (1). See Appendix O, *Food Guide Pyramid*.

4.2 GENERAL REQUIREMENTS

STANDARD 4.001
WRITTEN NUTRITION PLAN

The facility shall provide children nourishing and attractive food according to a written plan, developed by a qualified Child Care Nutrition Specialist. Caregivers, directors, and food service personnel shall share the responsibility for carrying out the plan. The administrator is responsible for implementing the plan but may delegate tasks to caregivers and food service personnel.

The nutrition plan (see STANDARD 8.035) shall include steps to take when problems require rapid response by the staff such as when a child chokes during mealtime. The completed plan shall be on file and accessible to the staff.

If the facility is large enough to justify employment of a full-time Child Care Nutrition Specialist or Child Care Food Service Manager, the facility shall delegate to this person the responsibility for implementing the written plan.

RATIONALE: Nourishing and attractive food is the cornerstone for health, growth, and development as well as developmentally appropriate learning experiences(2-10). Nutrition and feeding are fundamental and required in every facility. Because children grow and develop more rapidly during the first few years of life than at any other time, the child's home and the facility together must provide food that is adequate in amount and type to meet each child's metabolic, growth, and energy needs.

Meals and snacks provide opportunities for observation and conversation, which aid in children's conceptual, sensory, and language development. Professional nutrition staff must be involved along with the rest of the child care staff to assure compliance with nutrition and food service guidelines in larger facilities, including accommodation of children with special health care needs.

The staff must know ahead of time what procedures to follow, as well as their designated roles during an emergency. The plan should be dated and updated when revised.

COMMENTS: *Making Food Healthy and Safe for children* contains practical tips for implementing the standards for culturally diverse groups of infants and children. This publication is cued to the standards in the first edition of *Caring for Our Children*. Until *Making Food Healthy and Safe for Children* is revised, readers should use Appendix CC Conversion Table from 1st Edition to 2nd Edition to link the numbering of its standards with the numbering of the second edition of *Caring for Our Children*. The guidelines in *Making Food Healthy and Safe for Children* are current. This publication is available from the National Maternal and Child Health Clearinghouse. Contact information is located in Appendix BB.

See STANDARD 4.026 and 4.027 and Appendix C (which includes level of responsibility and education and experience), on Child Care Nutrition Specialists and Child Care Food Service Managers. See STANDARD 4.009 on written feeding plans. See also Nutrition Learning Experiences for Children, STANDARD 4.069, for nutrition learning experiences with this plan.

TYPE OF FACILITY: *Center; Large Family Child Care Home; Small Family Child Care Home*

STANDARD 4.002
USE OF USDA - CACFP GUIDELINES

All meals and snacks and their preparation, service, and storage shall meet the requirements for meals of the child care component of the U.S. Department of Agriculture (USDA), Child and Adult Care Food Program (CACFP), and the 7 Code of Federal Regulations (CFR) Part 226.20 (9,10).

RATIONALE: The CACFP regulations, policies, and guidance materials on meal requirements provide the basic guidelines for good nutrition and sanitation practices. Meals and snacks offered to young children should provide a variety of nourishing foods on a frequent basis to meet the nutritional needs of young children (11, 12). Programs not eligible for reimbursement under the regulations of CACFP are encouraged to use the CACFP food guidance. The CACFP guidance for meals and snack patterns ensures that the nutritional needs of infants and children are met based on current scientific knowledge.

COMMENTS: For examples of diets for infants and children, see Appendices P and Q. The staff should use information on the child's growth in developing individual feeding plans. For information on growth data, see STANDARD 3.003.

TYPE OF FACILITY: *Center; Large Family Child Care Home; Small Family Child Care Home*

STANDARD 4.003
MEAL PATTERN

The facility shall ensure the following:
a) Children in care for 8 and fewer hours shall be offered at least one meal and two snacks or two meals and one snack;
b) Children in care more than 8 hours shall be offered at least two meals and two snacks or three snacks and one meal;
c) A nutritious snack shall be offered to all children in midmorning and in midafternoon;
d) Children shall be offered food at intervals at least 2 hours apart and not more than 3 hours apart unless the child is asleep. Some very young infants may need to be fed at shorter intervals than every 2 hours to meet their nutritional needs.

RATIONALE: Young children need to be fed often. Appetite and interest in food varies from one meal or snack to the next. To ensure that the child's daily

nutritional needs are met, small feedings of nourishing food should be scheduled over the course of a day (2, 6, 10). Snacks should be nutritious, as they often are a significant part of a child's daily intake. Children in care for more than 8 hours need additional food, as this period represents a majority of a young child's waking hours.

COMMENTS: Caloric needs vary greatly from one child to another. They may require more food during growth spurts. Some states have regulations indicating suggested times for meals and snacks.

TYPE OF FACILITY: *Center; Large Family Child Care Home; Small Family Child Care Home*

STANDARD 4.004
CATEGORIES OF FOODS

Children in care shall be offered 5 or more servings of a fruit, vegetable, or juice each day. At least one of these servings shall be high in Vitamin C. A fruit, vegetable, or juice high in Vitamin A shall be offered at least three times a week.

RATIONALE: Current dietary guidance recommends at least five servings of fruits and vegetables daily (13). Juice is a means of fulfilling part of this requirement, but shall not be the exclusive offering. To serve fruits and vegetables without focusing on specific nutrients is not sufficient. The child's health, education, and food/nutrition learning experiences must be emphasized. Certain nutrients have been identified that may promote optimum health and may be protective against some disease processes.

COMMENTS: The staff should provide an example to children by eating the same foods and by discussing the food being eaten as part of nutrition education for the children.

TYPE OF FACILITY: *Center; Large Family Child Care Home; Small Family Child Care Home*

STANDARD 4.005
JUICE

The facility shall serve only full-strength (100%) fruit juice from a cup. The facility shall offer juice at specific meals and snacks instead of continuously throughout the day.

RATIONALE: Feeding juice only at specific meals and snacks will reduce acids produced by bacteria in the mouth that cause tooth decay. The frequency of exposure, rather than the quantity of food, is important in determining whether foods cause tooth decay. Although sugar is not the only dietary factor likely to cause tooth decay, it is a major factor in the prevalence of tooth decay (14, 15). Drinks that are called fruit juice drinks or fruit punches contain less than 100% fruit juice and are of a lower nutritional value than 100% fruit juice. Continuous consumption of juice during the day has been associated with a decrease in appetite for other nutritious foods which can result in feeding problems.

COMMENTS: Caregivers, as well as many parents, need to understand and accept the relationship between food eaten and tooth decay. Foods with high sugar content (such as candies or sweetened beverages) should be avoided because they contribute to tooth decay and poor nutrition.

TYPE OF FACILITY: *Center; Large Family Child Care Home; Small Family Child Care Home*

STANDARD 4.006
AVAILABILITY OF DRINKING WATER

Clean, sanitary drinking water shall be readily available throughout the day.

RATIONALE: When children are thirsty between meals and snacks, clean water is the best choice. Offering drinking water is good for hydration and reduces the acid in the mouth, which contribute to early childhood caries. Drinking water during the day will reduce the intake of extra calories (from fruit juice) which are associated with overweight and obesity.

COMMENTS: For drinking water supply in case of emergency, see STANDARD 4.058.

TYPE OF FACILITY: *Center; Large Family Child Care Home; Small Family Child Care Home*

STANDARD 4.007
DIETARY MODIFICATIONS

If dietary modifications are indicated based on a child's medical or special dietary needs, the caregiver shall modify or supplement the child's diet on a case-by-case basis, in consultation with the parents and the Nutrition Specialist, a trained nutrition expert, or the child's usual health care source.

Reasons for modification of the child's diet may be related to allergies, food idiosyncrasies, and other identified feeding issues.

For a child identified with medical special needs for dietary modification or special feeding techniques, written instructions from the child's parent or legal guardian and the child's health care provider shall be provided in the child's record and carried out accordingly. Dietary modifications shall be recorded, as specified in STANDARD 8.050.

These written instructions must identify:
a) The child's special needs;
b) Any dietary restrictions based on the special needs;
c) Any foods to be omitted from the diet and any foods to be substituted;
d) Limitations of life activities;
e) Any other pertinent special needs information.

The Nutrition Specialist shall approve menus that accommodate needed dietary modifications.

RATIONALE: Child care homes and facilities should have explicit and written procedures for dietary modifications or meal substitutes. Dietary modifications for any child, including those with special health care needs, developmental problems of chewing and swallowing food, and food allergies, should be carefully monitored by a trained health professional, coordinated with the rest of the child's health care, and documented in the child's record. Periodic monitoring of dietary modifications or substitutions should provide opportunities to reevaluate the plan to ensure that the child's nutritional needs are met as the child grows and develops.

As a safety and health precaution, the staff should know in advance whether a child has food allergies, tongue thrust, special medical needs related to feeding, or requires nasogastric or gastric tube feedings or special positioning. These situations require individual planning prior to the child's entry into child care and on an ongoing basis (8, 9).

Detailed information on a child's special needs is invaluable to the facility staff in meeting the nutritional needs of that child.

COMMENTS: Close collaboration between the home and the facility is needed for children on special diets Parents may have to provide food on a temporary or permanent basis if the facility, after exploring all community resources, is unable to provide the special diet.

For additional information on the Nutrition Specialist, see STANDARD 4.027.

TYPE OF FACILITY: *Center; Large Family Child Care Home; Small Family Child Care Home*

STANDARD 4.008
WRITTEN MENUS, INTRODUCTION OF NEW FOODS

Facilities shall develop, at least one month in advance, written menus showing all foods to be served during that month and shall make them available to parents. The facility shall date and retain these menus; amended to reflect any changes in the food actually served. Any substitutions shall be of equal nutrient value.

To avoid problems of food sensitivity in very young children, child care providers shall obtain from the child's parents, a list of foods that have already been introduced (without any reaction), and then serve some of these foods to the child. As new foods are introduced, child care providers shall share and discuss these foods with the parents prior to their introduction.

RATIONALE: Planning menus in advance helps to ensure that food will be on hand. Parents need to be informed about food served in the facility to know how to complement it with the food they serve at home. If a child has difficulty with any food served at the facility, parents can address this issue with appropriate staff members. Some regulatory agencies require menus as a part of the licensing and auditing process (2, 6).

COMMENTS: Making the menus available to parents by posting them in a prominent area helps inform parents about proper nutrition. Sample menus and menu planning templates are available from most state health departments, the state extension service, and the Child and Adult Care Food Program. Contact information for the State Administrators of the Child and Adult Care Food Program is located in Appendix BB.

For information on posting menus, see STANDARD 8.077.

TYPE OF FACILITY: *Center; Large Family Child Care Home; Small Family Child Care Home*

STANDARD 4.009
FEEDING PLANS

Before any child enters a child care facility, the facility shall obtain a written history of any special nutrition or feeding needs the child has. The staff shall review this history with the child's parents. If further information is required, along with the parents' written consent, the program may consult with the child's primary health care provider.

The written history of special nutrition or feeding needs shall be used to develop individual feeding plans and, collectively, to develop facility menus. Disciplines related to special nutrition needs, including nursing, speech, and occupational and physical therapy, shall participate when needed and/or when they are available to the facility. With the exception of children on special diets, the general nutrition guidelines for facilities in General Requirements, STANDARD 4.001 through STANDARD 4.010; Nutrition for Infants, STANDARD 4.011 through STANDARD 4.021; Nutri-

tion for Toddlers and Preschoolers, STANDARD 4.022 through STANDARD 4.024; and Nutrition for School-age Children, STANDARD 4.025, shall be applied.

The feeding plan shall include steps to take when a situation arises that requires rapid response by the staff (such as a child's choking during mealtime or a child with a known history of food allergies demonstrating signs and symptoms of anaphylaxis). The completed plan shall be on file and accessible to the staff.

RATIONALE: Children with special needs may have individual requirements relating to diet, swallowing, and similar feeding needs that require the development of an individual plan prior to their entry into the facility.

Many children with special needs have difficulty with feeding, including delayed attainment of basic chewing, swallowing, and independent feeding skills. Food, eating style, utensils, and equipment, including furniture, may have to be adapted to meet the developmental and physical needs of individual children (16).

Staff members must know ahead of time what procedures to follow, as well as their designated roles during an emergency.

Anaphylaxis is a severe, rapid immune response in an allergic individual. This response manifests itself in a collection of symptoms affecting multiple organ systems in the body. The most dangerous symptoms include difficulty breathing and shock. Anaphylaxis is life-threatening and should be considered a medical emergency requiring immediate recognition and treatment (7, 8, 16).

In children, foods are the most common cause of anaphylaxis. Nuts, eggs, milk, and seafood are the most common allergens for food-induced anaphylaxis in children.

COMMENTS: Close collaboration between the home and the facility is necessary for children on special diets. Parents may have to provide food on a temporary or permanent basis if the facility, after exploring all community resources, is unable to provide the special diet.

TYPE OF FACILITY: *Center; Large Family Child Care Home; Small Family Child Care Home*

STANDARD 4.010
CARE FOR CHILDREN WITH FOOD ALLERGIES

When children with food allergies attend the child care facility, the following shall occur:

a) Each child with a food allergy shall have a special care plan prepared for the facility by the child's source of health care, to include:
  1) Written instructions regarding the food(s) to which the child is allergic and steps that need to be taken to avoid that food;
  2) A detailed treatment plan to be implemented in the event of an allergic reaction, including the names, doses, and methods of administration of any medications that the child should receive in the event of a reaction. The plan shall include specific symptoms that would indicate the need to administer one or more medications;

b) Based on the child's special care plan, the child's caregivers shall receive training, demonstrate competence in, and implement measures for:
  1) Preventing exposure to the specific food(s) to which the child is allergic;
  2) Recognizing the symptoms of an allergic reaction;
  3) Treating allergic reactions;

c) Parents and staff shall arrange for the facility to have necessary medications, proper storage of such medications, and the equipment and training to manage the child's food allergy while the child is at the child care facility;

d) Caregivers shall promptly and properly administer prescribed medications in the event of an allergic reaction according to the instructions in the special care plan;

e) The facility shall notify the parents of any suspected allergic reactions, the ingestion of the problem food, or contact with the problem food, even if a reaction did not occur;

f) The facility shall notify the child's physician if the child has required treatment by the facility for a food allergic reaction;

g) The facility shall contact the emergency medical services system immediately whenever epinephrine has been administered;

h) Parents of all children in the child's class shall be advised to avoid any known allergies in class treats or special foods brought into the child care setting.

i) Individual child's food allergies shall be posted prominently in the classroom and/or wherever food is served.

j) On field trips or transport out of the child care setting, the written child care plan for the child with allergies shall be routinely carried.

RATIONALE: Food allergy is common, occurring in between two and eight percent of infants and children (17). Food allergic reactions can range from mild skin or gastrointestinal symptoms to severe, life-threatening reactions with respiratory and/or cardiovascular compromise. Deaths from food allergy are being reported in increasing numbers. A major factor in these deaths has been a delay in the administration of life-saving emergency medication, particularly epinephrine. Intensive efforts to avoid exposure to the offending food(s) are therefore warranted. Detailed care plans and the ability to implement such plans for the treatment of reactions is essential for all food-allergic children (2, 8, 16).

Successful food avoidance requires a cooperative effort that must include the parents, the child, the child's health care provider, and the child care staff. The parents, with the help of the child's health care provider, must provide detailed information on the specific foods to be avoided. In some cases, especially for children with multiple food allergies, the parents may need to take responsibility for providing all the child's food. In other cases, the child care staff may be able to provide safe foods as long as they have been fully educated about effective food avoidance.

Effective food avoidance has several facets. Foods can be listed on an ingredient list under a variety of names, such as milk being listed as casein, caseinate, whey, and lactoglobulin. Food sharing between children must be prevented by careful supervision and repeated instruction to the child about this issue. Accidental exposure may also occur through contact between children or by contact with contaminated surfaces, such as a table on which the food allergen

remains after eating. Some children may have an allergic reaction just from being in proximity to the offending food, without actually ingesting it. Such contact should be minimized by washing children's hands and faces and all surfaces that were in contact with food. In addition, reactions may occur when a food is used as part of an art or craft project, such as the use of peanut butter to make a bird feeder or wheat to make play dough.

Some children with food allergy will have mild reactions and will only need to avoid the problem food(s). Others will need to have an antihistamine or epinephrine available to be used in the event of a reaction. For all children with a history of anaphylaxis, or for those with peanut and/or tree nut allergy (whether or not they have had anaphylaxis), epinephrine should be readily available. This will usually be provided as a pre-measured dose in an auto-injector, such as the Epi-Pen or Epi-Pen Junior. Specific indications for administration of epinephrine should be provided in the detailed care plan. In virtually all cases, Emergency Medical Services (EMS) should be called immediately and children should be transported to the emergency room by ambulance after the administration of epinephrine (8). A single dose of epinephrine wears off in 15 to 20 minutes.

TYPE OF FACILITY: *Center; Large Family Child Care Home; Small Family Child Care Home*

4.3 REQUIREMENTS FOR SPECIAL GROUPS OR AGES OF CHILDREN

NUTRITION FOR INFANTS

STANDARD 4.011 GENERAL PLAN FOR FEEDING INFANTS

At a minimum, meals and snacks the facility provides for infants shall contain the food in the meal and snack patterns shown in Appendix P. Food shall be appropriate for infants' individual nutrition requirements and developmental stages as deter-

mined by written instructions obtained from the child's parent or health care provider.

The facility shall encourage and support breastfeeding. Facilities shall have a designated place set aside for breastfeeding mothers who want to come during work to breastfeed (18-24).

The facility shall offer solid foods and fruit juices to infants 6 months of age and younger only upon the recommendation of the parent and the child's health professional.

RATIONALE: Human milk or iron-fortified formula is the infant's first food and supports rapid growth in both weight and length during the first year of life and beyond. Human milk, as an exclusive food, is best suited to meet the entire nutritional needs of an infant from birth until 6 months of age. Human milk is the best source of milk for infants for at least the first 12 months of age and, thereafter, for as long as mutually desired. Breastfeeding protects infants from many acute and chronic diseases and has advantages for the mother, as well.

Advantages for the infant include reduction of some of the risks that are greater for infants in group care. The advantages of breastfeeding documented by research include reduction in the incidence of diarrhea, lower respiratory disease, otitis media, bacteremia, bacterial meningitis, botulism, urinary tract infections, necrotizing enterocolitis, SIDS, insulin-dependent diabetes, lymphoma, allergic disease, ulcerative colitis, and other chronic digestive diseases (20, 21). Some evidence suggests that breastfeeding is associated with enhanced cognitive development (22, 25). Therefore, human milk is the ideal nutrient source for term and many preterm infants.

Except in the presence of rare genetic diseases, the clear advantage of human milk over any formula should lead to vigorous efforts by child care providers to promote and sustain breastfeeding for mothers who are willing to nurse their babies whenever they can and to pump and supply their milk to the child care facility when direct feeding from the breast is not possible. Even if infants receive formula during the child care day, some breastfeeding or expressed human milk from their mothers is beneficial (24).

Iron-fortified infant formula is the best next to human milk as a food for infant feeding. Supplementation with juice, cereal, and any other foods during the first 4 months of life is unnecessary and, for healthy infants, inappropriate. An adequately nourished infant is more likely to achieve normal physical and mental development, which will have long-term positive consequences on health (7, 8).

TYPE OF FACILITY: *Center; Large Family Child Care Home; Small Family Child Care Home*

STANDARD 4.012
INTRODUCTION OF SOLID FOODS TO INFANTS

In consultation with the child's parent and health care provider, solid foods shall be introduced routinely at no sooner than 6 months of age, as indicated by an individual child's nutritional and developmental needs. Introduction of solids and fruit juices for breastfed infants shall be started at six months of age unless the parent or health provider specifically recommends otherwise. Modification of basic food patterns shall be provided in writing by the child's health care provider.

RATIONALE: Early introduction (prior to 6 months of age) of solid food interferes with the intake of human milk or iron-fortified formula that the infant needs for growth. Solid food given before an infant is developmentally ready may be associated with allergies and digestive problems. For breastfed infants, gradual introduction of iron-fortified foods should occur after 6 months, during which time these foods will complement the human milk. After 4 to 6 months of age, breastfed infants may require an additional source of iron in their diets. Infants who are not exclusively fed human milk should consume iron-fortified formula as the substitute for human milk. Infants on iron-fortified formula have an 8% risk for iron deficiency. Those exclusively breastfed have a 20% risk of iron deficiency by 9 to 12 months of age, and those consuming non fortified formula or whole cow's milk have the a 30% to 40% risk of iron deficiency by 9 to 12 months of age. In the United States, major non milk sources of iron in the infant diet are iron-fortified cereal and meats (8).

The transitional phase of feeding which occurs around 6 months of age is a critical time of development of fine, gross, and oral motor skills. When an infant is able to open her/his mouth, lean forward in anticipation of food offered, close the lips around a spoon, and transfer from front of the tongue to the back and swallow, he/she is ready to eat semi-solid foods. The process of learning a more mature style of eating begins because of physical growth occurring concurrently with social, cultural, sociological, and physiological development. Failure to introduce non-liquid food after 6 months of age may result in difficulties in introducing solid foods later. Variations in readiness for solid foods are common. While this standard states that the introduction of solids should start no sooner than 6 months of age for most infants, caregivers should be prepared to respond to a health care provider's recommendation for introduction of solids as early as 4 months of age for some infants.

Dental decay is transmissible. Bacteria which contribute to dental decay can be transmitted from caregivers to infants. Individuals with active tooth decay are more likely to transmit this bacteria to the children in their care.

COMMENTS: Early introduction of solids and fruit juices can interfere with breastfeeding or formula feeding. Many infants find juices appealing and may be satisfied by the calories in solids so they subsequently drink less human milk or formula (15). When juice is introduced, it should be by cup rather than bottle to decrease the occurrence of dental caries. Infants do not need juice unless their stools become hard from under-hydration or introduction of solids.

Although many people believe that infants sleep better when they start to eat solids, research reported in 1998 shows that longer sleeping periods are developmentally and not nutritionally determined in mid-infancy (8, 9).

A full daily allowance of Vitamin C is found in human milk (25). Most breastfed infants do not require supplemental vitamins. The AAP recommends Vitamin D supplementation for selected groups of infants whose mothers may be Vitamin D deficient or those infants who are not exposed to adequate sunlight (8, 18).

TYPE OF FACILITY: *Center; Large Family Child Care Home; Small Family Child Care Home*

STANDARD 4.013
FEEDING INFANTS ON DEMAND WITH FEEDING BY A CONSISTENT CAREGIVER

Caregivers shall feed infants on demand unless the parent and the child's health care provider gives written instructions otherwise. Whenever possible, the same caregiver shall feed a specific infant for most of that infant's feedings.

RATIONALE: Demand feeding meets the infant's nutritional and emotional needs and provides an immediate response to the infant, which helps ensure trust and feelings of security.

When the same caregiver regularly works with a particular child, that caregiver is more likely to understand that child's cues and to respond appropriately.

COMMENTS: Caregivers should be gentle, patient, sensitive, and reassuring by responding appropriately to the infant's feeding cues. Cues such as opening the mouth, making suckling sounds, and moving the hands at random all send information from an infant to a caregiver. Early relationships between an infant and caregivers involving feeding set the stage for an infant to develop eating patterns for life.

Waiting for an infant to cry to indicate hunger is not necessary or desirable. Nevertheless, feeding children who are alert and interested in interpersonal interaction, but who are not showing signs of hunger, is not appropriate. Cues for hunger or interaction-seeking may vary widely in different infants.

TYPE OF FACILITY: *Center; Large Family Child Care Home; Small Family Child Care Home*

STANDARD 4.014
TECHNIQUES FOR BOTTLE FEEDING

When bottle feeding, caregivers shall either hold infants or feed them sitting up. Infants who are unable to sit shall always be held for bottle feeding. The facility shall not permit infants to have bottles in the crib or to carry bottles with them either during the day or at night.

A caregiver shall not bottle feed more than one infant at a time.

RATIONALE: The manner in which food is given to infants is conducive to the development of sound eating habits for life. Caregivers should promote proper oral hygiene and feeding practices including proper use of the bottle for all infants and toddlers. Bottle propping can cause choking and aspiration and may contribute to long-term health issues, including ear infections (otitis media), orthodontic problems, speech disorders, and psychological problems (8, 14, 18, 22, 26, 27).

Any liquid except plain water can cause early childhood dental caries (8, 14, 18, 22, 26, 27). Early childhood dental caries in primary teeth may hold significant short-term and long-term implications for the child's health (8, 14, 18, 22, 26, 27).

Children are at an increased risk for injury when they walk around with bottle nipples in their mouths. Glass bottles create a safety hazard if the bottle is dropped and broken. Bacteria introduced by saliva makes milk consumed over a period of more than an hour unsuitable and unsafe for consumption. For safety and sanitary reasons, bottles should not be allowed in the crib or bed, whether propped or not.

It is difficult for a caregiver to be aware of and respond to infant feeding cues when feeding more than one infant at a time.

COMMENTS: Caregivers and parents need to understand the relationship between dental caries and the milk or juice in a bottle used as a pacifier.

Caregivers should offer children fluids from a cup as soon as they are developmentally ready. Children may be able to drink from a sippy cup as early as 5 months of age while for others it is later. Weaning a child to drink from a cup is an individual process, which occurs over a wide range of time. The American Academy of Pediatric Dentistry (AAPD) recommends weaning by the child's first birthday.

Use of a bottle or cup in an effort to modify a child's behavior should not be allowed (8, 28).

TYPE OF FACILITY: *Center; Large Family Child Care Home; Small Family Child Care Home*

STANDARD 4.015
FEEDING HUMAN MILK

Expressed human milk shall be placed in a clean and sanitary bottle and nipple that fits tightly to prevent spilling during transport to home or facility. The bottle shall be properly labeled with the infant's name. The bottle shall immediately be stored in the refrigerator on arrival. Expressed human milk shall be discarded if it presents a threat to a baby such as:
* Human milk is in an unsanitary bottle;
* Human milk that has been unrefrigerated for an hour or more;
* A bottle of human milk that has been fed over a period that exceeds an hour from the beginning of the feeding.

RATIONALE: This standard promotes the family's choice and practice of feeding human milk which is familiar to the infant. Child care providers should support and encourage this method of infant feeding because it is best for the infant.

Though human milk has antibacterial components, the bacterial load and the antibacterial component in any individual sample of human milk is unknown. When the infant feeds, the milk is inoculated by the infant's saliva and the bacteria in the infant's mouth. If the infant eats expressed milk from a bottle for periods in excess of an hour, bacteria could overwhelm the antibacterial components in the milk.

COMMENTS: The intent of this standard is to promote, support, and advocate feeding human milk by a mother because of the overwhelming benefits of human milk for infants. Using caution, providers can

safely and properly store expressed human milk transported to the child care facility.

Chilled or frozen human milk may be transported from home to the child care facility in a cooler bag as long as the ambient temperature is below 86 degrees F and the out-of-refrigerator time is less than 2 hours. See STANDARD 3.027 and STANDARD 6.035 for accidental feeding of human milk to another mother's child.

TYPE OF FACILITY: *Center; Large Family Child Care Home; Small Family Child Care Home*

STANDARD 4.016
PREPARING INFANT FORMULA

Formula provided by parents or by the facility shall come in a factory-sealed container. The formula shall be of the same brand that is served at home and shall be of ready-to-feed strength or prepared according to the manufacturer's instructions, using water from a source approved by the health department.

Formula mixed with cereal, fruit juice, or any other foods shall not be served unless the child's source of health care provides written documentation that the child has a medical reason for this type of feeding.

RATIONALE: This standard promotes the feeding of a formula familiar to the infant and supports family feeding practice. By following this standard, the staff is able, when necessary, to prepare formula and feed an infant safely, thereby reducing the risk of inaccuracy or feeding the infant unsanitary formula. Written guidance for both staff and parents must be available to determine when formula provided by parents will not be served as described in the standard above about unsanitary and unsafe formula. If a child has a special health problem, such as reflux, or inability to take in nutrients because of delayed development of feeding skills, the child's health professional should provide a written plan for the staff to follow so that the child is fed appropriately.

COMMENTS: The intent of this standard is to protect a child's health by reducing the risk of unsanitary and unsafe conditions of transporting infant formula prepared at home and brought to the facility.

To make infant formula bottles, the facility does not have to keep more than one container of the same brand and type of formula open at the same time. Parents can contribute their child's share of the formula or a share of the cost for a brand of formula the facility feeds to more than one infant. The bottles must be sanitary, properly prepared and stored, and must be the same brand in child care and at home.

In many communities, the sanitation standard for community water is high enough that tap water could be used, but this may vary from time to time and from community to community. Unless local health authorities recommend otherwise, water should be brought to a rolling boil before being used to make formula from concentrate or powder.

A safe source of water (usually tap water that is prepared fresh daily by being brought to a rolling boil) can be kept at room temperature. This water can be used by adding powdered formula to a bottle of water just before feeding (8, 18, 28). Bottles made in this way from powdered formula do not require refrigeration or warming and are promptly ready for feeding. The caregiver can make up whatever amount the infant seems to need at the time. Staff preparing formula shall thoroughly wash their hands prior to beginning preparation of infant feedings of any type.

Powdered formula is the least expensive type of formula. Providers shall only use the scoop that comes with the can and not interchange the scoop from one product to another, since the volume of the scoop may vary from manufacturer to manufacturer and product to product. Although many infant formulas are made from powder, the liquid preparations are diluted with water at the factory. Concentrated infant formula, not ready-to-feed, must be diluted with water. Sealed, ready-to-feed bottles are easy to use also, but they are the most expensive approach to feeding formula.

Although some children have a medical indication for alternative feeding practices, feeding of solids and fruit beverages in the bottle to the child is often associated with premature feeding of these foods (when the

infant is not developmentally ready for them) (8, 10, 16, 18, 25).

TYPE OF FACILITY: *Center; Large Family Child Care Home; Small Family Child Care Home*

STANDARD 4.017
PREPARATION AND HANDLING OF BOTTLE FEEDING

Only cleaned and sanitized bottles, or their equivalent, and nipples shall be used. All filled containers of human milk shall be of the ready-to-feed type, identified with a label which won't come off in water or handling, bearing the date of collection and child's full name. The filled, labeled containers of human milk shall be kept frozen or refrigerated, and iron-fortified formula shall be refrigerated until immediately before feeding. Any contents remaining after a feeding shall be discarded. Prepared bottles of formula from powder or concentrate or ready-to-feed formula shall be labeled with the child's name and date of preparation, kept refrigerated, and shall be discarded after 48 hours if not used. An open container of ready-to-feed or concentrated formula shall be covered, refrigerated, and discarded after 48 hours if not used.

Unused expressed human milk shall be discarded after 48 hours if refrigerated, or by three months if frozen, and stored in a deep freezer at 0 degrees F. Unused frozen human milk which has been thawed in the refrigerator shall be used within 24 hours. Frozen human milk shall be thawed under running cold water or in the refrigerator.

Human milk from a mother shall be used only with that mother's own child.

A bottle that has been fed over a period that exceeds an hour from the beginning of the feeding or has been unrefrigerated an hour or more shall not be served to an infant.

RATIONALE: Identification of the bottles prevents the potential for cross-infection when the facility is caring for more than one bottle-fed infant (2, 8). Placing human milk in ready-to-feed bottles (including single-use bags in a plastic holder) decreases the potential for exposure and spills. Infants should not be fed a formula different from the one the parents feed

at home or human milk intended for another infant, as even minor differences in formula and the specific components of human milk can cause gastrointestinal upsets and other problems (54).

Bottled formula that has been fed should not be reused because the formula will have been contaminated with saliva and bacteria, which could multiply to spoil the formula before the bottle is refed. This is especially true if the bottle is out of refrigeration for the first feeding for an hour or more and then reheated. Open containers of powdered formula are not safe to use beyond the stated shelf period (8). It is difficult to maintain 0 degrees F consistently in a freezer compartment of a refrigerator or freezer, so caregivers should carefully monitor temperature of freezers used to store human milk using an appropriate working thermometer. Human milk contains components that are damaged by excessive heating during or after thawing from the frozen state (54).

Labels for containers of human milk should be resistant to loss of the name and date when washing and handling. This is especially important when the frozen bottle is thawed in running tap water. There may be several bottles from different mothers being thawed and warmed at the same time in the same place. Frozen milk should never be thawed in a microwave oven.

COMMENTS: See STANDARD 4.018, regarding bottle warming and microwave ovens. STANDARD 3.027 regarding accidental feeding of human milk to another mother's child.

TYPE OF FACILITY: *Center; Large Family Child Care Home; Small Family Child Care Home*

STANDARD 4.018
WARMING BOTTLES AND INFANT FOODS

Bottles and infant foods shall be warmed under running warm tap water or by placing them in a container of water that is no warmer than 120 degrees F Bottles shall not be left in a pot of water to warm for more than 5 minutes. Bottles and infant foods shall not be warmed in a microwave

oven. After warming, bottles shall be mixed gently and the temperature of the milk tested before feeding. Infant foods shall be stirred carefully to distribute the heat evenly. A caregiver shall not hold an infant while removing a bottle or infant food from the container of warm water or while preparing a bottle or stirring infant food that has been warmed in some other way.

If a slow-cooking device, such as a crock pot, is used for warming infant formula, human milk, or infant food, this slow-cooking device shall be out of children's reach, shall contain water at a temperature that does not exceed 120 degrees F. and shall be emptied, sanitized, and refilled with fresh water daily.

RATIONALE: Bottles of formula or human milk that are warmed at room temperature or in warm water for an extended time provide an ideal medium for bacteria to grow. Infants have received burns from hot water dripping from an infant bottle that was removed from a crock pot or by pulling the crock pot down on themselves by a dangling cord. Caution should be exercised to avoid raising the water above a safe level for warming infant formula or infant food. Studies have documented the dangers of using microwave ovens for heating human milk, formula, or food to be fed to infants (29, 55).

Excessive shaking of human milk may damage some of the cellular components that are valuable to the infant, as may excessive heating. Excessive shaking of formula may cause foaming that increases the likelihood of feeding air to the infant.

TYPE OF FACILITY: *Center; Large Family Child Care Home; Small Family Child Care Home*

STANDARD 4.019
CLEANING AND SANITIZING EQUIPMENT USED FOR BOTTLE FEEDING

Bottles, bottle caps, nipples and other equipment used for bottle feeding shall not be reused without first being cleaned and sanitized by washing in a dishwasher or by washing, rinsing and boiling for one minute.

RATIONALE: Infant feeding bottles are contaminated by the child's saliva during feeding. Formula and milk promote growth of bacteria. To avoid contamination of subsequent feedings, bottles, bottle caps, and nipples that are reused should be washed and sanitized.

COMMENTS: Excessive boiling of latex bottle nipples will damage them.

TYPE OF FACILITY: *Center; Large Family Child Care Home; Small Family Child Care Home*

STANDARD 4.020
FEEDING COW'S MILK

The facility shall not serve any cow's milk to infants from birth to 12 months of age and shall serve only whole, pasteurized milk to children between 12 and 24 months of age who are not on formula or human milk. The facility shall not serve skim milk, reconstituted nonfat dry milk, or milk containing 1% or 2% butterfat to any child between 12 and 24 months of age, except with the written direction of a parent and the child's health care provider.

RATIONALE: Low-fat milk does not provide enough calories and nutrients for children from 1 to 2 years of age. If a child seems to be gaining weight excessively, he or she should be referred to the primary health care provider. The American Academy of Pediatrics recommends that whole cow's milk not be used during the first year of life (7, 8, 18, 28, 53).

COMMENTS: This standard is consistent with the recommendation of the American Academy of Pediatrics for feeding children to 2 years of age, when brain development requires a certain amount of fat in the diet. Although obesity can be a problem, it can be controlled by volume of intake and balance with other desirable foods instead of reducing the fat content of milk in children younger than 2 years of age.

TYPE OF FACILITY: *Center; Large Family Child Care Home; Small Family Child Care Home*

STANDARD 4.021
FEEDING SOLID FOODS TO INFANTS

Staff members shall serve commercially packaged baby food from a dish, not directly from a factory-sealed container. They shall serve solid food by spoon only. They shall discard uneaten food in dishes from which they have fed a child. The facility shall wash off all jars of baby food with soap and warm water before opening the jars, and examine the food carefully when removing it from the jar to make sure there are not glass pieces or foreign objects in the food.

Food shall not be shared among children using the same dish or spoon. Unused portions in opened factory-sealed baby food containers or food brought in containers prepared at home shall be stored in the refrigerator and discarded if not consumed after 24 hours of storage. Solid food shall not be fed in a bottle or in an infant feeder unless the child has specific written instructions from a health professional to do so.

RATIONALE: The external surface of a commercial container may be contaminated with disease-causing microorganisms during shipment or storage and may contaminate the food product during feeding. A dish should be cleaned and sanitized before use, thereby reducing the likelihood of surface contamination. Any food brought from home should not be served to other children. This will prevent cross-contamination and reinforce the policy that food sent to the facility is for the designated child only.

Uneaten food should not be put back into its original container for storage because it may contain potentially harmful bacteria from the infant's saliva. Solid food should not be fed in a bottle or an infant feeder apparatus because of the potential for choking. In addition, this method teaches the infant to eat solid foods incorrectly.

COMMENTS: For additional information on nutrition for infants, seeSTANDARD 8.036. See also STANDARD 4.038, on the size of food pieces to serve infants, and STANDARD 4.035 and STANDARD 4.036, on supervision of feeding.

TYPE OF FACILITY: *Center; Large Family Child Care Home; Small Family Child Care Home*

NUTRITION FOR TODDLERS AND PRESCHOOLERS

STANDARD 4.022
MEAL AND SNACK PATTERNS

At a minimum, meals and snacks the facility provides for toddlers and preschoolers shall contain the meal and snack patterns shown for these age groups in Appendix Q.

RATIONALE: During periods of slower growth, the children must eat nutritious foods. With limited appetites and selective eating of toddlers and preschoolers, less nutritious foods can easily displace more nutritious foods from the child's diet.

COMMENTS: A nutritional analysis of the requirements in Appendix Q was conducted to ensure that a snack and lunch meet two-thirds of the Recommended Dietary Allowances (30). Children who are eating more than one snack and one meal may not want all the food offered at any one of these times. On the other hand, toddlers and preschoolers may eat only some meals or some snacks. The amount of food offered to them must be sufficient to meet their needs at that point.

TYPE OF FACILITY: *Center; Large Family Child Care Home; Small Family Child Care Home*

STANDARD 4.023
PORTIONS FOR TODDLERS AND PRESCHOOLERS

The facility shall serve toddlers and preschoolers small-sized portions and shall permit them to have one or more additional servings as needed to meet the needs of the individual child.

RATIONALE: Gradual extension of the diet begun in infancy should continue throughout the preschool period. A child will not eat the same amount each day because appetites vary and food "jags" are common (8, 10-12, 28). If normal variations in eating patterns are accepted without comment, feeding problems usually do not develop. Requiring that a child eat a specified food or amount of food may lead to eating problems. Eating habits established in infancy and early childhood possibly may contribute to problems later in life. Including nutritious snacks in the daily meal plan will help to ensure that the child's nutrient needs are met. The quality of snacks for young children is especially important, and small, frequent feedings are recommended to achieve the total desired daily intake.

COMMENTS: Continuing to meet the child's needs for growth and activity is important. During the second and third years of life, the child grows much less rapidly than during the first year of life.

TYPE OF FACILITY: *Center; Large Family Child Care Home; Small Family Child Care Home*

STANDARD 4.024
ENCOURAGING SELF-FEEDING BY TODDLERS

Caregivers shall encourage toddlers to hold and drink from a cup, to use a spoon, and to use their fingers for self-feeding.

RATIONALE: As children enter the second year of life, they are interested in doing things for themselves. Self-feeding appropriately separates the responsibilities of adults and children. The adult is responsible for providing nutritious food, and the child for deciding how much of it to eat (6, 8, 10, 28, 31). To allow for the proper development of motor skills and eating habits, children need to be allowed to practice learning to feed themselves.

COMMENTS: Foods served should be appropriate to the toddler's developmental ability. For additional information on nutrition for toddlers and preschoolers, see STANDARD 4.014 through STANDARD 4.019, on bottle feeding, STANDARD 4.038, on the size of food pieces to serve toddlers and preschoolers, and STANDARD 4.035 and STANDARD 4.036, on supervision of feeding.

TYPE OF FACILITY: *Center; Large Family Child Care Home; Small Family Child Care Home*

NUTRITION FOR SCHOOL-AGE CHILDREN

STANDARD 4.025
MEAL AND SNACK PATTERNS FOR SCHOOL-AGE CHILDREN

Meals and snacks the facility provides for school-age children, including those in school-age child care facilities, shall contain at a minimum the meal and snack patterns shown for this age group in Appendix Q. Children attending facilities for 2½ or more hours after school need at least one snack.

RATIONALE: The principles of providing adequate, nourishing food for younger children apply to this group as well. This age is characterized by a rapid rate of growth that increases the need for energy and essential nutrients to support optimal growth. Food intake may vary considerably because this is a time when children express strong food likes and dislikes. The quantity and quality of food provided should contribute toward meeting nutritional needs for the day and should not dull the appetite (3, 4, 6, 10, 28).

COMMENTS: A nutritional analysis was conducted of the requirements in Appendix Q, to ensure that a snack and lunch meet two thirds of the Recommended Dietary Allowances (31).

TYPE OF FACILITY: *Center; Large Family Child Care Home; Small Family Child Care Home*

4.4 STAFFING

STANDARD 4.026
FOOD SERVICE STAFF BY TYPE OF FACILITY AND FOOD SERVICE

Each center-based facility shall employ trained staff and provide ongoing supervision and consultation in accordance with individual site needs as determined by the Child Care Nutrition Specialist (see Appendix C). In centers, prior work experience in food service shall be required for the solitary worker responsible for food preparation without the continuous on-site supervision of a food service manager. For facilities operating 6 or more hours a day or preparing and serving food on the premises, the following food service staff requirements shall apply:

SETTING	FOOD SERVICE STAFF
Small and large family child care homes	Caregiver
Centers serving up to 30 children	Full-time child care Food Service Worker (cook)
Centers serving up to 50 children	Full-time child care Food Service Worker (cook) and part-time child care Food Service Aide
Centers serving up to 125 children	Full-time child care Food Service Manager or full-time child care Food Service Worker (cook) and full-time child care Food Service Aide

SETTING	FOOD SERVICE STAFF
Centers serving up to 200 children	Full-time child care Food Service Manager and full-time child care Food Service Worker (cook) and one full-time plus one part-time child care Food Service Aide
Vendor food service	One assigned staff member or one part-time staff member, depending on amount of food service preparation needed after delivery

RATIONALE: Trained personnel working in the food service component of facilities is essential to meet the nutrition standards required in these facilities (6, 10, 28, 31-33). Home cooking experience is not enough when large volumes of food must be served to children and adults. The type of food service, type of equipment, number of children to be fed, location of the facility, and food budget determine the staffing patterns. An adequate number of food service personnel is essential to meet the goals and objectives of the facility and ensure that children are fed according to the facility's daily schedule. If the facility serves only food brought from home, food service staff are needed to oversee the appropriate use of such food if the facility operates for 6 or more hours a day.

COMMENTS: The food service staff may not necessarily consist of full-time or regular staff members but may include some workers hired on a consulting or contractual basis. Resources for food service staff include vocational high school food preparation programs, university and community college food preparation programs, and trade schools that train cooks and chefs.

TYPE OF FACILITY: *Center, Large Family Child Care Home, Small Family Child Care Home*

STANDARD 4.027
CHILD CARE NUTRITION SPECIALIST

A local Child Care Nutrition Specialist (see Appendix C) or food service expert shall be employed to work with the architect or engineer on the design of the parts of the facility involved in food service, to develop and implement the facility's nutrition plan (see STANDARD 8.035) and to prepare the initial food service budget. The nutrition plan encompasses:
a) Kitchen layout;
b) Food procurement, preparation, and service;
c) Staffing;
d) Nutrition education.

When contemplating alterations in the nutrition plan, such as installing a new dishwasher or expanding storage or dining areas, the procedure to be followed shall be the same as for new construction or renovation. The food service expert shall be involved in the decision-making and shall oversee carrying out completion of the plan.

RATIONALE: Efficient and cost-effective food service in a facility begins with a plan and evaluation of the physical components of the facility. Planning for the food service unit includes consideration of location and adequacy of space for receiving, storing, preparing, and serving areas; cleaning up; dish washing; dining areas, plus space for desk, telephone, records, and employee facilities (such as handwashing sinks, toilets, and lockers). All facets must be considered for new or existing sites, including remodeling or renovation of the unit (10-12, 28).

TYPE OF FACILITY: *Center*

4.5 MEAL SERVICE, SEATING, AND SUPERVISION

STANDARD 4.028
DEVELOPMENTALLY APPROPRIATE SEATING AND UTENSILS FOR MEALS

The child care staff shall ensure that children who do not require highchairs are comfortably seated at tables that are between waist and mid-chest level and allow the child's feet to rest on a firm surface while seated for eating.

All furniture and eating utensils that a child care agency/facility uses shall enable children to eat at their best skill level and to increase their eating skill.

RATIONALE: Proper seating while eating reduces the risk of food aspiration and improves comfort in eating (32).

Suitable furniture and utensils provide comfort, enable the children to perform eating tasks they have already mastered, and facilitate the development of skill and coordination in handling food and utensils (10-12, 28).

COMMENTS: Eating utensils should be unbreakable, durable, attractive, and suitable in function, size, and shape for use by children. Dining areas should be clean and cheerful (2, 4, 6, 10, 28).

Compliance is measured by observation of the fit of furniture for children.

TYPE OF FACILITY: *Center; Large Family Child Care Home; Small Family Child Care Home*

STANDARD 4.029
TABLEWARE AND FEEDING UTENSILS

Tableware and feeding utensils shall meet the following requirements:
a) Dishes shall have smooth, hard, glazed surfaces and shall be free from cracks or chips. Sharp-edged plastic utensils intended for use in the mouth or dishes that have sharp or jagged edges shall not be used.
b) Disposable tableware (such as plates, cups, utensils) made of heavy weight paper or food-grade medium weight plastic shall be permitted for single service if they are discarded after use. The facility shall not use Styrofoam tableware for children under 4 years of age.
c) Single-service articles (such as napkins, paper placemats, paper tablecloths, and paper towels) shall be discarded after one use.
d) Washable placemats, bibs, napkins, and tablecloths, if used, shall be laundered or washed, rinsed, and sanitized after each meal. Fabric articles shall be sanitized by being machine-washed and dried after each use.
e) Highchair trays, plates, and all items used in food service that are not disposable shall be washed, rinsed, and sanitized. Tables and highchair trays that are used for eating shall be washed, rinsed, and sanitized just before and right after they are used for eating. Children who eat at tables shall have disposable or washed and sanitized plates for their food.
f) Imported dishes and imported ceramic dishware or pottery shall be certified by the regulatory health authority to meet U.S. standards and to be safe from lead or other heavy metals before they can be used.
g) All surfaces in contact with food shall be lead-free.

RATIONALE: Clean food service utensils, napkins, bibs, and tablecloths prevent the spread of microorganisms that can cause disease. The surfaces that are in contact with food must be sanitary.

Food should not be put directly on the table surface for two reasons. First, even washed and sanitized tables are more likely to be contaminated than disposable plates or washed and sanitized dishes. Second, learning to eat from plates reduces contamination of the table surface when children put down their partially eaten food while they are eating.

Although highchair trays can be considered tables, they function as plates for seated children. The tray should be washed and sanitized in the same way as plates and other food service utensils (2, 6, 10). The use of disposable items eliminates the spread of contamination and disease and fosters safety and injury prevention. Single-service items are usually porous. Items intended for reuse must be capable of being washed, rinsed, and sanitized.

Sharp-edged plastic spoons can cut soft oral tissues, especially when an adult is feeding a child and slides the spoon out of the child's closed mouth. Older children can cut their mouth tissues the same way.

Styrofoam can break into pieces that could become choking hazards for young children.

Imported dishware may be improperly fired and may release toxic levels of lead into food. U.S. government standards prevent the marketing of domestic dishes with lead in their glazes. There is no safe level of lead in dishware.

COMMENTS: Ideally, food should not be placed directly on highchair trays, as studies have shown that highchair trays can be loaded with infectious microorganisms. If the highchair tray is made of plastic, is in good repair, and is free from cracks and crevices, it can be made safe if it is washed and sanitized before placing a child in the chair for feeding and if the tray is washed and sanitized after each child has been fed. Food must not be placed directly on highchair trays made of wood or metal, other than stainless steel, to prevent contamination by infectious microorganisms or toxicity from metals.

If in doubt about whether tableware is safe and sanitary, consult the regulatory health authority or local health department.

TYPE OF FACILITY: *Center; Large Family Child Care Home; Small Family Child Care Home*

STANDARD 4.030
ACTIVITIES THAT ARE
INCOMPATIBLE WITH EATING

The child care staff shall ensure that children do not eat when walking, running, playing, lying down, or riding in vehicles.

RATIONALE: Children should be seated when eating (6, 10, 28, 33). This reduces the risk of aspiration (6, 9, 10-12).

TYPE OF FACILITY: *Center; Large Family Child Care Home; Small Family Child Care Home*

STANDARD 4.031
SOCIALIZATION DURING MEALS

Caregivers shall sit at the table and shall eat the meal or snack with the children. Family style meal service shall be encouraged, except for infants and very young children who require that an adult feeds them. The adult(s) shall encourage social interaction and conversation about the concepts of color, quantity, number, temperature of food, and events of the day. Extra assistance and time shall be provided for slow eaters. Eating should be an enjoyable experience at the facility and at home.

RATIONALE: The presence of an adult or adults, who eat with the children, offers a role model and helps prevent behaviors that increase the possibility of fighting, feeding each other, stuffing food into the mouth, and other negative behaviors. Conversation at the table adds to the pleasant mealtime environment and provides opportunities for informal modeling of appropriate eating behaviors and communication of nutrition education (2, 6, 10, 28). The future development of children depends, to no small extent, on their command of language, and richness of language increases as adults and peers nurture it (28). Family style meals encourage children to serve themselves (10-12, 28). In addition to being nourished by food, eating experiences help infants and young children to establish warm human relationships. When children lack the developmental skills for self-feeding, they will be unable to serve food to themselves. As soon as a

child learns to finger-feed, taking finger foods from a serving plate becomes possible and desirable.

COMMENTS: Compliance is measured by structured observation. Use of small pitchers, a limited number of portions on service plates, and adult assistance to enable children to successfully serve themselves helps to make family style service possible without contamination or waste of food.

See STANDARD 4.069 Plan For Food and Feeding Experience.

TYPE OF FACILITY: *Center; Large Family Child Care Home; Small Family Child Care Home*

STANDARD 4.032
PARTICIPATION OF OLDER CHILDREN AND STAFF IN MEALTIME ACTIVITIES

Both older children and staff shall be actively involved in serving food and other mealtime activities, such as setting and cleaning the table, with provision for staff to supervise and assist children with appropriate handwashing procedures and sanitizing of eating surfaces and utensils to prevent cross contamination.

RATIONALE: Children develop self-help and new motor skills as well as increase their dexterity through this type of involvement. Children require close supervision from staff and adults when they use knives and have contact with food surfaces and food that other children will use.

COMMENTS: Compliance is measured by structured observation.

TYPE OF FACILITY: *Center; Large Family Child Care Home; Small Family Child Care Home*

STANDARD 4.033
EXPERIENCE WITH FAMILIAR AND NEW FOODS

In consultation with the family and child care nutrition specialist, caregivers shall offer children familiar foods that are typical of the child's culture and religious preferences, and shall also introduce a variety of healthful foods that may not be familiar, but meet a child's nutritional needs.

RATIONALE: By learning about new food, children increase their knowledge of the world around them, and the likelihood that they will choose a more varied, better balanced diet in later life. Eating habits and attitudes about food formed in the early years often last a lifetime.

TYPE OF FACILITY: *Center; Large Family Child Care Home; Small Family Child Care Home*

STANDARD 4.034
HOT LIQUIDS AND FOODS

Adults shall not consume hot liquids in child care areas. They shall keep hot liquids and hot foods out of the reach of infants, toddlers, and preschoolers. Adults shall not place hot liquids and foods at the edge of a counter or table, or on a tablecloth that could be yanked down, while the adult is holding or working with a child. Electrical cords from coffee pots shall not be allowed to hang within the reach of children. Food preparers shall position pot handles toward the back of the stove.

RATIONALE: The most common burn in young children is scalding from hot liquids tipped over in the kitchen (34-36).

TYPE OF FACILITY: *Center; Large Family Child Care Home; Small Family Child Care Home*

STANDARD 4.035
NUMBERS OF CHILDREN FED SIMULTANEOUSLY BY ONE ADULT

One adult shall not feed more than one infant or three children who need adult assistance with feeding at the same time.

RATIONALE: Cross-contamination among children whom one adult is feeding simultaneously poses significant risk. In addition, mealtime should be a socializing occasion. Feeding more than three children at the same time necessarily resembles an impersonal production line. It is difficult for the caregiver to be aware of and respond to infant feeding cues when feeding more than one infant at a time. Children with a special need for feeding assistance may need one-on-one supervision.

TYPE OF FACILITY: *Center; Large Family Child Care Home; Small Family Child Care Home*

STANDARD 4.036
LOCATION OF THE ADULT SUPERVISING CHILDREN FEEDING THEMSELVES

Children in mid-infancy who are learning to feed themselves shall be supervised by an adult seated within arm's reach of them at all times while being fed. Children over 12 months of age who can feed themselves shall be supervised by an adult who is seated at the same table or within arm's reach of the child's highchair or feeding table.

RATIONALE: A supervising adult should watch for several common problems that typically occur when children in mid-infancy begin to feed themselves. "Squirreling" of several pieces of food in the mouth increases the likelihood of choking. Supervised eating also promotes the child's safety by discouraging activities that can lead to choking.

TYPE OF FACILITY: *Center; Large Family Child Care Home; Small Family Child Care Home*

STANDARD 4.037
FOOD THAT ARE CHOKING HAZARDS

Caregivers shall not offer to children under 4 years of age foods that are implicated in choking incidents (round, hard, small, thick and sticky, smooth, or slippery). Examples of these foods are hot dogs (whole or sliced into rounds), raw carrot rounds, whole grapes, hard candy, nuts, seeds, raw peas, hard pretzels, chips, peanuts, popcorn, marshmallows, spoonfuls of peanut butter, and chunks of meat larger than can be swallowed whole.

RATIONALE: These are high-risk foods, often implicated in choking incidents (37). Ninety percent of fatal chokings occur in children younger than 4 years of age (6-8, 10-12). Peanuts may block the lower airway. A chunk of hot dog or a whole grape may completely block the upper airway (6-8, 10-12, 38).

COMMENTS: To reduce the risk of choking, menus should reflect the developmental abilities of the age of children served. Lists of high-risk foods should be made available. The presence of molars is a good indication of a healthy child's ability to chew hard foods (such as raw carrot rounds) that are likely to cause choking. Although dried fruits are sometimes mentioned as food hazards, a search of the literature does not identify a single instance when raisins were associated with a lethal choking incident. Because raisins are wrinkled, air likely gets around them, enabling the child's cough to remove them from the airway (37-39).

TYPE OF FACILITY: *Center; Large Family Child Care Home; Small Family Child Care Home*

STANDARD 4.038
PROGRESSION OF EXPERIENCES WITH FOOD TEXTURES

For infants, foods shall be fed which are age and developmentally appropriate. Foods shall progress from pureed to ground to finely mashed to finely chopped as an infant develops. When children are ready for chopped foods, these foods shall be cut into small pieces no larger than $1/4$-inch cubes or

thin slices. For toddlers, foods shall be cut up in small pieces no larger than ½-inch cubes (11, 12, 37).

> RATIONALE: Often, infants and toddlers swallow pieces of food whole without chewing.

> TYPE OF FACILITY: *Center; Large Family Child Care Home; Small Family Child Care Home*

STANDARD 4.039
PROHIBITED USES OF FOOD

Caregivers shall encourage, but not force, children to eat. Caregivers shall not use food as a reward or punishment.

> RATIONALE: Children who are forced to eat or for whom adults use food to modify behavior come to view eating as a tug-of-war and are more likely to develop lasting food dislikes and unhealthy eating behaviors. Offering food as a reward or punishment places undue importance on food and may have negative effects on the child by promoting "clean the plate" responses that may lead to obesity or poor eating behavior (2, 6, 8, 10, 28).

> TYPE OF FACILITY: *Center; Large Family Child Care Home; Small Family Child Care Home*

4.6 FOOD BROUGHT FROM HOME

STANDARD 4.040
SELECTION AND PREPARATION OF FOOD BROUGHT FROM HOME

The parent (or legal guardian) shall provide meals upon written agreement between the parent and the staff. Food brought into the facility shall have a label showing the child's name, the date, and the type of food. Lunches and snacks the parent provides for one child's eating shall not be shared with other children. When foods are brought to the facility from home or elsewhere, these foods shall, to the extent reasonable, be limited to whole fruits (like apples, oranges, or pears) and commer-

cially packaged foods. When whole fruit is not reasonable (such as cantaloupe or watermelon), a written policy shall be in place regarding how the food must be prepared by the adult who is responsible for cutting the fruit for the child. Potentially hazardous and perishable foods shall be refrigerated, as specified in Food Safety, STANDARD 4.050 through STANDARD 4.060, and all foods shall be protected against contamination.

> RATIONALE: Foodborne illness and poisoning from food is a common occurrence when food has not been properly refrigerated and covered. Although many of these illnesses are limited to vomiting and diarrhea, sometimes they are life-threatening. Restricting food sent to the facility to the designated child reduces the risk of food poisoning from unknown procedures used in home preparation and transport. Food brought from home should be nourishing, clean, and safe for a child, and the other children should not be exposed to the unknown risk. The facility has an obligation to ensure that any food shared with other children complies with the food and nutrition guidelines for meals and snacks that the child care facility should observe.

> COMMENTS: Some local health and/or licensing jurisdictions prohibit foods being brought from home.

> TYPE OF FACILITY: *Center; Large Family Child Care Home; Small Family Child Care Home*

STANDARD 4.041
NUTRITIONAL QUALITY OF FOOD BROUGHT FROM HOME

The facility shall provide parents with written guidelines that the facility has established to meet the nutritional requirements of the children in the facility's care and suggested ways parents can assist the facility in meeting these guidelines. The facility shall have food available to supplement a child's food brought from home if the food brought from home is deficient in meeting the child's nutrient requirements. If the food the parent provides consistently does not meet the nutritional or food safety requirements, the facility shall provide the food and refer the parent for consultation to a Child Care Nutrition Specialist (see Appendix C), to the child's primary health care provider, or to

community resources with trained nutritionists/ dietitians (such as WIC, extension services, and health departments).

RATIONALE: The caregiver/facility has a responsibility to follow feeding practices that promote optimum nutrition that supports growth and development in infants, toddlers, and children. Child care providers/ facilities who fail to follow best feeding practices even when parents wish such counter practices to be followed negate their basic responsibility of protecting a child's health, social, and emotional well being.

COMMENTS: See also nutrition requirements in General Requirements, STANDARD 4.001 through STANDARD 4.010, and Requirements for Special Groups of Children, STANDARD 4.011 through STANDARD 4.025. For additional information on food brought from home, see STANDARD 1.031, on training for food handlers.

TYPE OF FACILITY: *Center; Large Family Child Care Home; Small Family Child Care Home*

4.7 KITCHEN AND EQUIPMENT

STANDARD 4.042
FOOD PREPARATION AREA

The food preparation area of the kitchen shall be separate from eating, play, laundry, toilet, and bathroom areas and from areas where animals are permitted, and shall not be used as a passageway while food is being prepared. Food preparation areas shall be separated by a door, gate, counter, or room divider from areas the children use for activities unrelated to food, except in small family child care homes when separation may limit supervision of children.

Infants and toddlers shall not have access to the kitchen in child care centers. Access by older children to the kitchen of centers shall be permitted only when supervised by staff members who have been certified by the Child Care Nutrition Specialist (see Appendix C) or the center director as qualified to follow the facility's sanitation and safety procedures.

In all types of child care facilities, children shall never be in the kitchen unless they are directly supervised by a caregiver. Children of preschoolage and older shall be restricted from access to areas while hot food is being prepared. School-age children may engage in food preparation activities. Parents and other adults shall be permitted to use the kitchen only if they know and follow the food safety rules of the facility. The facility shall check with local health authorities about any additional regulations that apply.

RATIONALE: The presence of children in the kitchen increases the risk of contamination of food as well as injury to children from burns and use of kitchen appliances and cooking techniques that require more skill than could be expected for their developmental level. The most common burn in young children is scalding from hot liquids tipped over in the kitchen (34-36).

The kitchen should be used only by authorized individuals who have met the requirements of the local health authority and who know and follow the food safety rules of the facility so they do not contaminate food and food surfaces for subsequent food-related activities.

TYPE OF FACILITY: *Center; Large Family Child Care Home; Small Family Child Care Home*

STANDARD 4.043
DESIGN OF FOOD SERVICE EQUIPMENT

Food service equipment shall be designed, installed, operated, and maintained according to the manufacturer's instructions and in a way that meets the equivalent performance and health standards of the National Sanitation Foundation or applicable local or State public health authority, or the U. S. Department of Agriculture (USDA) food program and sanitation codes, as determined by the regulatory public health authority.

RATIONALE: The design, installation, operation, and maintenance of food service equipment must follow the manufacturer's instructions and meet the standards for such equipment to ensure that the equipment protects the users from injury and the

consumers of foods prepared with this equipment from foodborne disease (40). The manufacturer's warranty that equipment will meet recognized standards is valid only if the equipment is properly maintained.

COMMENTS: Inspectors with appropriate training should periodically check food service equipment and provide technical assistance to facilities. The local public health department typically conducts such inspections. Manufacturers should attest to their compliance with equipment standards of the National Sanitation Foundation (NSF) and the Code of Federal Regulations, Part 200, Section 354.210 (revised January 1990), USDA Food Safety and Inspection Service. Testing labs such as Underwriters Laboratories (UL) also test food service equipment. Contact information for the NSF, the USDA, and the UL is located in Appendix BB.

Before making a purchase, child care facilities should not only check the warranty but also the maintenance instructions provided by the equipment manufacturer to be sure the required maintenance is feasible, given the facility's resources. If the facility receives inspections from the public health department, the facility may want to consult with them before making a purchase. The facility director or food service staff should retain maintenance instructions and check to be sure that all users of the equipment follow the instructions.

TYPE OF FACILITY: *Center*

STANDARD 4.044
MAINTENANCE OF FOOD SERVICE SURFACES AND EQUIPMENT

All surfaces that come into contact with food, including tables and countertops, as well as floors and shelving in the food preparation area shall be in good repair, free of cracks or crevices, and shall be made of smooth, nonporous material that is kept clean and sanitized. All kitchen equipment shall be clean and shall be maintained in operable condition according to the manufacturer's guidelines for maintenance and operation. The facility shall maintain an inventory of food service equip-

ment that includes the date of purchase, the warranty date, and a history of repairs.

RATIONALE: Cracked or porous materials must be replaced because they trap food and other organic materials in which microorganisms can grow. Harsh scrubbing on these areas tends to create even more areas where organic material can lodge and increase the risk of contamination. Repairs with duct tape, package tapes, and other commonly used materials add surfaces that trap organic materials. Cracked, chipped, or porous materials that can harbor organic material must be replaced.

Food service equipment is designed by the manufacturer for specific types of use. The equipment must be maintained to meet those performance standards or food will become contaminated and spoil. An accurate and ongoing inventory of food service equipment tracks maintenance requirements and can provide important information when a breakdown occurs.

TYPE OF FACILITY: *Center; Large Family Child Care Home; Small Family Child Care Home*

STANDARD 4.045
FOOD PREPARATION SINKS

The sink used for food preparation shall not be used for handwashing or any other purpose. Handwashing sinks and sinks involved in diaper changing shall not be used for food preparation. All food service sinks shall be supplied with hot and cold running water under pressure.

RATIONALE: Separation of sinks used for handwashing or other potentially contaminating activities from those used for food preparation prevents contamination of food. Hot and cold running water are essential for thorough cleaning and sanitizing of equipment and utensils and cleaning of the facility.

COMMENTS: See STANDARD 4.065 for water temperature for cleaning and sanitizing dishes in the absence of a dishwasher and STANDARD 5.040, on hot water at sinks.

TYPE OF FACILITY: *Center; Large Family Child Care Home; Small Family Child Care Home*

STANDARD 4.046
HANDWASHING SINK SEPARATE FROM FOOD ZONES

Centers shall provide a separate handwashing sink in the facility. It shall have an 8-inch-high splash guard or have 18 inches of space between the handwashing sink and any open food zones (such as preparation tables and food sink).

Where continuous water pressure is not available, handwashing sinks shall have at least 30 seconds of continuous flow of water to initiate and complete handwashing.

RATIONALE: Separation of sinks used for handwashing or other potentially contaminating activities from those used for food preparation prevents contamination of food.

Proper handwashing requires a continuous flow of water, no less than 60 degrees F and no more than 120 degrees F, to allow sufficient time for wetting and rinsing the hands.

TYPE OF FACILITY: *Center*

STANDARD 4.047
MAINTAINING SAFE FOOD TEMPERATURES

The facility shall use refrigerators that maintain food temperatures of 40 degrees F or lower in all parts of the food storage areas, and freezers shall maintain temperatures of 0 degrees F or lower in food storage areas.

Thermometers with markings in no more than 2-degree increments shall be provided in all refrigerators, freezers, ovens, and holding areas for hot and cold foods. Thermometers shall be clearly visible, easy to read, and accurate, and shall be kept in working condition and regularly checked.

RATIONALE: Storage of food at proper temperatures minimizes bacterial growth (47).

The use of accurate thermometers to monitor temperatures at which food is cooked and stored helps to ensure food safety. Hot foods must be checked to be sure they reach temperatures that kill microorganisms in that type of food. Cold foods must be checked to see that they are being maintained at temperatures that safely retard the growth of bacteria. Thermometers with larger than 2-degree increments are hard to read accurately.

COMMENTS: Providing thermometers with a dual scale in Fahrenheit and Celsius will avoid making a child care provider convert between the two different temperature scales.

TYPE OF FACILITY: *Center; Large Family Child Care Home; Small Family Child Care Home*

STANDARD 4.048
VENTILATION OVER COOKING SURFACES

In centers using commercial cooking equipment to prepare meals, ventilation shall be equipped with an exhaust system capable of providing a capture velocity of 50 feet per minute 6 inches above the outer edges of the cooking surfaces at the prescribed filter velocities (41).

All gas ranges in centers shall be mechanically vented and fumes filtered prior to discharge to the outside. All vents and filters shall be maintained free of grease build-up and food spatters, and in good repair.

RATIONALE: An exhaust system must properly collects fumes and grease-laden vapors at their source.

Properly maintained vents and filters control odor, fire hazards, and fumes.

COMMENTS: The center should refer to the owner's manual of the exhaust system for a description of capture velocity. Commercial cooking equipment refers to the type of equipment that is typically found in restaurants and other food service businesses.

Proper construction of the exhaust system duct-work assures that grease and other build-up can be easily accessed and cleaned.

If the odor of gas is present when the pilot lights are on, turn off gas and immediately call a qualified gas technician or commercial gas provider. Never use an open flame to locate a gas leak.

TYPE OF FACILITY: *Center*

STANDARD 4.049
MICROWAVE OVENS

Microwave ovens shall be inaccessible to pre-school children. Any microwave oven in use in a child care facility shall be manufactured after October 1971 and shall be in good repair.

RATIONALE: Young children can be burned when their faces come near the heat vent. The issues involved with the safe use of microwave ovens (such as no metal, the right plastic, and steam trapping) make use of this equipment by preschool-age children too risky. Older ovens made before the Federal standard went into effect in October 1971 can expose users or passers-by to microwave radiation.

COMMENTS: If school-age children are allowed to use a microwave oven in the facility, this use should be closely supervised to avoid injury. See STANDARD 4.018 for prohibition of use of microwave ovens to warm infant feedings.

TYPE OF FACILITY: *Center; Large Family Child Care Home; Small Family Child Care Home*

4.8 FOOD SAFETY

STANDARD 4.050
COMPLIANCE WITH USDA FOOD SANITATION STANDARDS, STATE AND LOCAL RULES

The facility shall conform to the applicable portions of the U.S. Food and Drug Administration model food sanitation standards (42) and all applicable state and local food service rules and regulations for centers and small and large family child care homes regarding safe food protection and sanitation practices. If federal model standards and local regulations are in conflict, the health authority with jurisdiction shall determine which requirement the facility must meet.

RATIONALE: Minimum standards for food safety are based on scientific data that demonstrate the conditions required to prevent contamination of food with infectious and toxic substances that cause foodborne illness. Many of these standards have been placed into statutes and therefore must be complied with by law.

Federal, state, and local food safety codes, regulations, and standards may conflict. In these circumstances, the decision of the regulatory health authority should prevail.

COMMENTS: The U. S. Food and Drug Administration's (FDA) *Model Food Code* is a good resource to have on hand. The Food Code is available on the Internet. Contact information is located in Appendix BB.

TYPE OF FACILITY: *Center; Large Family Child Care Home; Small Family Child Care Home*

STANDARD 4.051
STAFF RESTRICTED FROM FOOD HANDLING

No one who has signs or symptoms of illness, including vomiting, diarrhea, and infectious skin sores that cannot be covered, or who potentially or actually is infected with bacteria, viruses or parasites that can be carried in food, shall be responsible for food handling. Plastic gloves, which shall be kept clean and replaced when soiled, shall be used when food is served by hand (11, 12). No one with open or infected injuries shall work in the food preparation area unless the injuries are covered with nonporous (such as latex or vinyl) gloves.

In centers and large family child care homes, staff members who are involved in the process of preparing or handling food shall not change diapers. Staff members who work with diapered children shall not prepare or serve food for older groups of children. When staff members who are caring for infants and toddlers are responsible for changing diapers, they shall handle food only for the infants and toddlers in their groups and only after thoroughly washing their hands. Caregivers who prepare food shall wash their hands carefully before handling food, regardless of whether they change diapers. Plastic gloves shall be used in addition to handwashing. When caregivers must handle food, staffing assignments shall be made to foster completion of the food handling activities by caregivers of older children, or by caregivers of infants and toddlers before the caregiver assumes other caregiving duties for that day.

RATIONALE: Food handlers who are ill can easily communicate their illness to others by contaminating the food they prepare with the infectious agents they are carrying. Frequent and proper handwashing before and after using plastic gloves reduces food contamination (43, 44).

Caregivers who work with infants and toddlers frequently are exposed to feces and to children with infections of the intestines (often with diarrhea) or liver. Education of child care staff regarding handwashing and other cleaning procedures can reduce the occurrence of illness in the group of children with whom they work (43, 44).

The possibility of involving a larger number of people in a foodborne outbreak is greater in child care than in most households. Cooking larger volumes of food requires special caution to avoid contamination of the food with even small amounts of infectious materials. With larger volumes of food, staff must exercise greater diligence to avoid contamination because larger quantities of food take longer to heat or to cool to safe temperatures. Larger volumes of food spend more time in the danger zone of temperatures (between 40 degrees F and 140 degrees F) where more rapid multiplication of microorganisms occurs.

Whenever possible, cooks should not be assigned child care or janitorial duties, so as to reduce the cook's exposure to infectious materials. The cook who is exposed to infectious materials may

subsequently infect the food served in the facility. If a caregiver must cook, letting that caregiver complete the food preparation before assuming caregiver duties (such as wiping noses, diaper changing, or toilet supervision) for that day can minimize the risk.

COMMENTS: Facilities can minimize the need for final preparation in the caregiving areas by careful planning, advance preparation, and serving of foods at safe temperatures.

For additional information on handwashing, see STANDARD 3.021 through STANDARD 3.023.

TYPE OF FACILITY: *Center; Large Family Child Care Home; Small Family Child Care Home*

STANDARD 4.052
PRECAUTIONS FOR A SAFE FOOD SUPPLY

All foods stored, prepared, or served shall be safe for human consumption by observation and smell (10-12). The following precautions shall be observed for a safe food supply:
a) Home-canned food, food from dented, rusted, bulging, or leaking cans, and food from cans without labels shall not be used;
b) Foods shall be inspected daily for spoilage or signs of mold, and foods that are spoiled or moldy shall be discarded;
c) Meat shall be from government-inspected sources or otherwise approved by the governing health authority (44);
d) All dairy products shall be pasteurized and Grade A where applicable;
e) Raw, unpasteurized milk, milk products; unpasteurized fruit juices; and raw or undercooked eggs shall not be used. Freshly squeezed fruit or vegetable juice prepared in the child care facility prepared just prior to serving is permissible;
f) Unless a child's health provider documents a different milk product, children from 12 months to 2 years of age shall be served only whole milk. Children older than 2 years of age shall be served whole, skim, 1%, or 2% milk. If allowed by funding resources, dry milk and milk products may be reconstituted in the facility for cooking purposes only, provided

that they are prepared, refrigerated, and stored in a sanitary manner, labeled with the date of preparation, and used or discarded within 24 hours of preparation;

g) Meat, fish, poultry, milk, and egg products shall be refrigerated or frozen until immediately before use (47);

h) Frozen foods shall be defrosted in the refrigerator, under cold running water, as part of the cooking process, or by using the defrost setting of a microwave oven (47);

i) All fruits and vegetables shall be washed thoroughly with water prior to use (47);

j) Frozen foods shall never be defrosted by leaving them at room temperature or standing in water that is not kept at refrigerator temperature (47).

k) Food shall be served promptly after preparation or cooking or maintained at temperatures of not less than 140 degrees F for hot foods and not more than 40 degrees F for cold foods.

l) All opened moist foods that have not been served shall be dated, covered, and maintained at a temperature of 40 degrees F or lower in the refrigerator or 0 degrees F or lower in the freezer, verified by a working thermometer kept in the refrigerator or freezer.

m) Fully cooked and ready-to-serve hot foods shall be held for no longer than 30 minutes before being served, or covered and refrigerated.

RATIONALE: For children, a small dose of infectious or toxic material can lead to serious illness. Some molds produce toxins that may cause illness or even death (such as aflatoxin or ergot).

Keeping frozen food at 0 degrees F or below, cold food below 40 degrees F and hot food above 140 degrees F prevents bacterial growth (9, 10). Food intended for human consumption can become contaminated if left at room temperature.

Foodborne illnesses from *Salmonella* and *E. coli 0157:H7* have been associated with consumption of contaminated, raw, or undercooked egg products, meat, poultry, and seafood. Children tend to be more susceptible to *E. coli 0157:H7* infections from consumption of undercooked meats, and such infections can lead to kidney failure and death.

Home-canned food and food from dented, rusted, bulging, or leaking cans has an increased risk of containing microorganisms or toxins. Users of unlabeled food cans cannot be sure what is in the can and how long the can has been stored.

Excessive heating of foods results in loss of nutritional content and causes foods to lose appeal by altering color, consistency, texture, and taste.

Caregivers should discourage parents from bringing home-baked items for the children to share as it is difficult to determine the cleanliness of the environment in which the items are baked and transported.

Several states allow the sale of raw milk or milk products. These products have been implicated in outbreaks of salmonellosis, listeriosis, toxoplasmosis, and campylobacteriosis and should never be served in child care facilities (45, 46). Only pasteurized milk and fruit juices should be served. Foods made with uncooked eggs have been involved in a number of outbreaks of *Salmonella* infections. Eggs should be well cooked before being eaten, and only pasteurized eggs or egg substitutes should be used in foods requiring raw eggs.

The American Academy of Pediatrics (AAP) recommends that children from 12 months to 2 years of age receive whole milk or formula. Children 2 years of age and older can drink skim, 1%, or 2% milk (7, 8, 10-12, 18, 28).

Soil particles and contaminants that adhere to fruits and vegetables can cause illness. Therefore, all fruits or vegetables used to make fresh juice at the facility should be washed first.

Thawing frozen foods under conditions that expose any of the food's surfaces to temperatures between 40 and 140 degrees F promotes the growth of bacteria that may cause illness if ingested. Storing perishable foods at safe temperatures in the refrigerator or freezer reduces the rate at which microorganisms in these foods multiply.

COMMENTS: Caregivers should consult with the health department regarding proper cooking temperatures.

The general rule is "keep hot foods hot and cold foods cold-out of the temperature danger zone between 40 degrees F and 140 degrees F." The FDA 1999 Food Code specifies that potentially hazardous foods be refrigerated at 41 degrees F or less. It is easier for caregivers to remember the 40 to 140 degree range than it is to remember a 41 to 140 degree range. Therefore, for practical reasons and since 40 degrees F is within the FDA 1999 Food Code refrigeration temperature range, 40 degrees F is used in this standard. (42, 56)

The use of dairy products fortified with vitamins A and D is recommended (51A).

TYPE OF FACILITY: *Center; Large Family Child Care Home; Small Family Child Care Home*

STANDARD 4.053
LEFTOVERS

Food returned from individual plates and family style serving bowls and platters and unrefrigerated foods into which microorganisms are likely to have been introduced during food preparation or service, shall be discarded.

Unserved food shall be covered promptly for protection from contamination, shall be refrigerated immediately, and shall be used within 24 hours. Hot foods shall be cooled first before they are fully covered in the refrigerator. Prepared perishable foods that have not been maintained at safe temperatures for 2 hours or more shall be discarded.

RATIONALE: Served foods have a high probability of contamination during serving. Bacterial multiplication proceeds rapidly in perishable foods out of refrigeration, as much as doubling the numbers of bacteria every 15 to 20 minutes.

The potential is high for perishable foods (such as those that could have been exposed to bacterial contamination during preparation) that have been out of the refrigerator for more than 2 hours to have substantial loads of bacteria. When such food is stored and served again, it may cause foodborne illness.

COMMENTS: All food, once served or handled outside the food preparation area, should be discarded.

TYPE OF FACILITY: *Center; Large Family Child Care Home; Small Family Child Care Home*

STANDARD 4.054
PREPARATION FOR AND STORAGE OF FOOD IN THE REFRIGERATOR

All food stored in the refrigerator shall be tightly covered, wrapped, or otherwise protected from direct contact with other food. Hot foods to be refrigerated and stored shall be transferred to shallow containers in food layers less than 3 inches deep and refrigerated immediately. These foods shall be covered when cool. Any pre-prepared or leftover foods that are not likely to be served the following day shall be labeled with the date of preparation before being placed in the refrigerator. The basic rule for serving food shall be, "first food in, first food out" (6, 10-12).

In the refrigerator, raw meat, poultry and fish shall be stored below cooked or ready to eat foods.

RATIONALE: Covering food protects it from contamination and keeps other food particles from falling into it. Hot food cools more quickly in a shallow container, thereby decreasing the time when the food would be susceptible to contamination. Foods should be covered only after they have cooled. Leaving hot food uncovered allows it to cool more quickly, thereby decreasing the time when bacteria may be produced.

Labeling of foods will inform the staff about the duration of storage, which foods to use first, and which foods to discard because the period of safe storage has passed.

Storing raw meat, poultry and fish below ready-to-eat foods reduces the possibility that spills or drips from raw animal foods might contaminate ready-to-eat food.

COMMENTS: See Appendix R, for a Food Storage Chart.

TYPE OF FACILITY: *Center; Large Family Child Care Home; Small Family Child Care Home*

STANDARD 4.055
MAINTENANCE OF CLEAN REFRIGERATORS AND FREEZERS

Refrigerators and freezers shall be free of visible spills. The interior surfaces shall be cleaned and sanitized as often as necessary to assure that these appliances are maintained in a clean and sanitary condition.

RATIONALE: During routine use, refrigerators and freezers become soiled by foods stored in them and by handling food and containers as they are being placed in or taken out of them. Without routine cleaning and sanitizing, this soil builds up and creates a place for bacterial growth, with subsequent contamination of stored foods.

TYPE OF FACILITY: *Center; Large Family Child Care Home; Small Family Child Care Home*

STANDARD 4.056
STORAGE OF FOODS NOT REQUIRING REFRIGERATION

Foods not requiring refrigeration shall be stored at least 6 inches above the floor in clean, dry, well-ventilated storerooms or other approved areas (47). Food products shall be stored in such a way (such as in nonporous containers off the floor) as to prevent insects and rodents from entering the products.

RATIONALE: Storage of food off the floor in a safe and sanitary manner helps prevent food contamination and keeps insects and rodents from entering the products. This practice also facilitates cleaning.

COMMENTS: Storing food 6 inches or higher above the floor enables easier cleaning of the floor under the food. Storing food in nonporous containers

prevents contamination of the food by insects, cleaning chemicals, and spills of other foods.

TYPE OF FACILITY: *Center; Large Family Child Care Home; Small Family Child Care Home*

STANDARD 4.057
STORAGE OF DRY BULK FOODS

Dry, bulk foods that are not in their original, unopened containers shall be stored off the floor in clean metal, glass, or food-grade plastic containers with tight-fitting covers. All bulk food containers shall be labeled and dated, and placed out of children's reach. Children shall be permitted to handle household-size food containers during supervised food preparation and cooking activities and when the container holds a single serving of food intended for that child's consumption.

RATIONALE: Food-grade nonporous containers prevent insect infestations and contamination from other foods and cleaning chemicals. By labeling and dating food, the food service staff can rotate the oldest foods to be used next and discard foods that have gone beyond safe storage times. Keeping bulk food containers out of the children's reach prevents contamination and misuse. Young children cannot be expected to have learned safe food handling practices well enough to risk the food supply of others.

TYPE OF FACILITY: *Center*

STANDARD 4.058
SUPPLY OF FOOD AND WATER FOR DISASTERS

In areas where natural disasters (such as earthquakes) occur, a 48 hour supply of food and water shall be kept in stock for each child and staff member (47).

RATIONALE: It may take as long as 48 hours for help to arrive in some areas after a natural disaster of great magnitude.

COMMENTS: A child care facility should consult with their local health authority or local emergency preparedness agency for more information on disaster preparedness.

TYPE OF FACILITY: *Center; Large Family Child Care Home; Small Family Child Care Home*

STANDARD 4.059
STORAGE OF GARBAGE

Garbage shall be placed in containers inaccessible to children and shall be removed from the kitchen daily. The containers shall be labeled and covered with tight fitting lids between deposits.

RATIONALE: This practice minimizes odors, controls insects and rodents, and protects children and premises from contamination.

TYPE OF FACILITY: *Center; Large Family Child Care Home; Small Family Child Care Home*

STANDARD 4.060
STORAGE OF CLEANING AGENTS SEPARATE FROM FOOD

Cleaning agents that must be stored in the same room with food shall be clearly labeled and kept separate from food items in locked cabinets. Cleaning agents shall not be stored on shelves above those holding food items. Cleaning agents and food items shall not be stored on the same shelf. Any storage room or cabinet that contains cleaning agents shall be locked. Poisonous or toxic materials shall remain in their original labeled containers.

RATIONALE: Food products should be stored away from cleaning products to prevent accidental poisoning, potential leakage, and contamination.

COMMENTS: Store cleaning agents below any food items.

TYPE OF FACILITY: *Center; Large Family Child Care Home; Small Family Child Care Home*

4.9 MAINTENANCE

STANDARD 4.061
CLEANING OF FOOD AREAS AND EQUIPMENT

Areas and equipment used for storage, preparation, and service of food shall be kept clean. All of the food preparation, food service, and dining areas shall be cleaned and sanitized before and after use. Food preparation equipment shall be cleaned and sanitized after each use and stored in a clean and sanitary manner, and protected from contamination.

Sponges shall not be used for cleaning and sanitizing. Disposable paper towels or washable cloths that are only used once shall be used. Used cloths shall be stored in a covered container and washed daily.

RATIONALE: Outbreaks of foodborne illness have occurred in child care settings. Many of these communicable diseases can be prevented through appropriate hygiene and sanitation methods. Keeping hands clean reduces soiling of kitchen equipment and supplies. Education of child care staff regarding routine cleaning procedures can reduce the occurrence of illness in the group of children with whom they work (43).

Sponges harbor bacteria and are difficult to completely clean and sanitize between cleaning surface areas.

COMMENTS: "Clean" means free of visible soil. Routine cleaning of kitchen areas should comply with the cleaning schedule provided in Appendix S or local health authority regulations.

TYPE OF FACILITY: *Center; Large Family Child Care Home; Small Family Child Care Home*

STANDARD 4.062
CUTTING BOARDS

Cutting boards shall be made of nonporous material and shall be scrubbed with hot water and detergent and sanitized between uses for different foods or placed in a dishwasher for cleaning and sanitizing. The facility shall not use wooden cutting boards, boards made with wood components, and boards with crevices and cuts.

RATIONALE: Wood boards and boards with cracks and crevices harbor food or organic material that can promote bacterial growth and contaminate the next food cut on the surface.

COMMENTS: Heavy duty plastic and Plexiglas cutting boards can be placed in dishwashers.

TYPE OF FACILITY: *Center; Large Family Child Care Home; Small Family Child Care Home*

STANDARD 4.063
DISHWASHING IN CENTERS

Centers shall provide a three-compartment dishwashing area with dual integral drain boards or an approved dishwasher capable of sanitizing multiuse utensils. If a dishwasher is installed, there shall be at least a two-compartment sink with a spray unit. If a dishwasher or a combination of dish pans and sink compartments that yield the equivalent of a three-compartment sink is not used, paper cups and plates and plastic utensils shall be used and shall be disposed of after every use.

RATIONALE: These are minimum requirements for proper cleaning and sanitizing of dishes and utensils (11, 12).

A three-compartment sink is ideal. If only a single- or double-compartment sink is available, three freestanding dish pans or two sinks and one dish pan may be used as the compartments needed to wash, rinse, and sanitize dishes.

An approved dishwasher is a dishwasher that meets the approval of the regulatory health authority. Dishwashers should be carefully chosen. Depending on the size of the child care center and the food prepared, a household dishwasher may be adequate. Because of the time required to complete a full wash, rinse, and dry cycle, household domestic dishwashers are recommended for centers that do only one load of dishes after a snack or meal. Commercial dishwashers are recommended for centers that have a lot of children.

The length of time to wash dishes in commercial dishwashers is 3 to 4 minutes. Commercial dishwashers that operate at low water temperatures (140 to 150 degrees F) are recommended because they are more energy-efficient. These would be equipped with automatic detergent and sanitizer injectors. When choosing a dishwasher, caregivers can consult with the local health authority to ensure that they meet local health regulations.

COMMENTS: Household dishwashing machines can effectively wash and sanitize dishes and utensils provided that certain conditions are met (52). The three types of household dishwashers are:
a) Those that lack or operate without sanitizing wash or rinse cycles;
b) Those that have sanitizing wash or rinse cycles and a thermostat that senses a temperature of 150 degrees F or higher before the machine advances to the next step in its cycle;
c) Those that have a sanitizing cycle and a thermostat as in (b) but advance to the next step in its cycle after 15 minutes, if the temperature required to operate the thermostat is not reached.

All three types of household dishwashers are capable of producing the cumulative heat factor to meet the National Sanitation Foundation time-temperature standard for commercial, spray-type dishwashing machines. Dishwasher types (a) and (c) are capable of doing so only if the temperature of their inlet water is 155 degrees F or higher.

The temperature of a hot water supply necessary for operating a dishwasher conflicts with what is considered a safe temperature to prevent scalding.

Installing a separate small hot water tank for a dishwasher is one option to consider. See STANDARD 5.040, for additional information on water temperature.

TYPE OF FACILITY: *Center*

STANDARD 4.064
DISHWASHING IN SMALL AND LARGE FAMILY CHILD CARE HOMES

Small and large family child care homes shall provide a three-compartment dishwashing arrangement or a dishwasher. At least a two-compartment sink or a combination of dish pans and sink compartments shall be installed to be used in conjunction with a dishwasher to wash, rinse, and sanitize dishes. The dishwashing machine must incorporate a chemical or heat sanitizing process. If a dishwasher or a three-compartment dishwashing arrangement is not used, paper cups and plates and plastic utensils shall be used and shall be disposed of after every use.

RATIONALE: These are minimum requirements for proper cleaning and sanitizing of dishes and utensils (5, 10). The purpose is to remove food particles and other soil, and to control bacteria.

TYPE OF FACILITY: *Large Family Child Care Home; Small Family Child Care Home*

STANDARD 4.065
METHOD FOR WASHING DISHES BY HAND

If the facility does not use a dishwasher, reusable food service equipment and eating utensils shall be scraped to remove any leftover food, washed thoroughly in hot water containing a detergent solution, rinsed, and then sanitized by one of the following methods:

a) Immersion for at least 2 minutes in a luke-warm (not less than 75 degrees F) chemical sanitizing solution (bleach solution of a least 100 parts per million by mixing 1 1/2 teaspoons of domestic bleach per gallon of water). The sanitized items shall be air-dried; or

b) Or, complete immersion in hot water and maintenance at a temperature of 170 degrees F for not less than 30 seconds. The items shall be air-dried (48, 53, 57).

c) Or, other methods if approved by the health department.

RATIONALE: These procedures provide for proper sanitizing and control of bacteria (6, 10-12).

COMMENTS: To manually sanitize dishes and utensils in hot water at 170 degrees F, a special hot water booster is usually required. To avoid burning the skin while immersing dishes and utensils in this hot water bath, special racks are required. Therefore, if dishes and utensils are being washed by hand, the chemical sanitizer method using household bleach will be a safer choice.

Often, sponges are used in private homes when washing dishes. The structure of natural and artificial sponges provides an environment in which microorganisms thrive. This may contribute to the microbial load in the wash water. Nevertheless, the rinsing and sanitizing process should eliminate any pathogens contributed by a sponge. When possible, a cloth that can be laundered should be used instead of a sponge.

The concentration of bleach used for sanitizing dishes is much more diluted than the concentration recommended for sanitizing surfaces elsewhere in the facility. After washing and rinsing the dishes, the amount of infectious material on the dishes should be small enough so that the 2 minutes of immersion in the bleach solution combined with air-drying will reduce the number of microorganisms to safe levels. The stronger sanitizing solution used for other surfaces in the facility is made by diluting ¼ cup of household liquid chlorine bleach in 1 gallon of water to achieve 500-800 parts per million. Using this 1:64 dilution is acceptable, but stronger than needed to sanitize detergent-cleaned and thoroughly rinsed dishes.

Air-drying of surfaces that have been sanitized using bleach leaves no residue, since chlorine evaporates when the solution dries. However, other sanitizers may need to be rinsed off to remove retained chemical from surfaces.

TYPE OF FACILITY: *Center; Large Family Child Care Home; Small Family Child Care Home*

4.10 MEALS FROM OUTSIDE VENDORS OR CENTRAL KITCHENS

STANDARD 4.066
APPROVED OFF-SITE FOOD SERVICES

Food provided by a central kitchen or vendor to off-site locations shall be obtained from sources approved and inspected by the local health authority.

RATIONALE: This standard ensures that the child care facility receives safe food.

TYPE OF FACILITY: *Center; Large Family Child Care Home; Small Family Child Care Home*

STANDARD 4.067
FOOD SAFETY DURING TRANSPORT

After preparation, food shall be transported promptly in clean, covered, and temperature-controlled containers. Hot foods shall be maintained at temperatures not lower than 140 degrees F, and cold foods shall be maintained at temperatures of 40 degrees F or lower. Hot foods may be allowed to cool before serving to young children as long as the food is cooked to appropriate temperatures and the time at room temperature does not exceed 2 hours. The temperature of foods shall be checked with a working food-grade, metal probe thermometer.

RATIONALE: Served foods have a high probability of becoming contaminated during serving. Bacteria multiply rapidly in perishable foods out of refrigeration, as much as doubling every 15 to 20 minutes.

Foods at 140 degrees are too hot for children's mouths.

A working food-grade, metal probe thermometer will accurately determine when foods are safe for consumption.

COMMENTS: If the temperature of hot foods is well below 140 degrees F when it arrives, the caregiver should review delivery and storage practices and make any changes necessary to maintain proper food temperatures during storage and delivery.

The caregiver shall record food temperatures in a log book to document the pattern of temperature control and spot shifts toward unsafe levels.

TYPE OF FACILITY: *Center; Large Family Child Care Home; Small Family Child Care Home*

STANDARD 4.068
HOLDING OF FOOD PREPARED AT OFF-SITE FOOD SERVICE FACILITIES

Centers receiving food from an off-site food service facility shall have provisions for the proper holding and serving of food and washing of utensils to meet the requirements of the Food and Drug Administration's Model Food Code and the standards approved by the State or local health authority (42).

RATIONALE: Served foods have a high probability of becoming contaminated during serving. Bacteria multiply rapidly in perishable foods out of refrigeration, as much as doubling every 15 to 20 minutes.

COMMENTS: Contact information for the Food and Drug Administration's Food Code is located in Appendix BB.

TYPE OF FACILITY: *Center*

4.11 NUTRITION LEARNING EXPERIENCES AND EDUCATION

STANDARD 4.069
NUTRITION LEARNING EXPERIENCES FOR CHILDREN

The facility shall have a nutrition plan (see STANDARD 4.001 and STANDARD 8.035) that integrates the introduction of food and feeding experiences with facility activities and home feeding. The plan shall include opportunities for children to develop the knowledge and skills necessary to make appropriate food choices.

For centers, this plan shall be a written plan and shall be the shared responsibility of the entire staff, including directors, food service personnel, and parents. The nutrition plan shall be developed with guidance from, and shall be approved by, the Child Care Nutrition Specialist (see Appendix C).

Caregivers shall teach children about the taste and smell of foods. The children shall feel the textures and learn the different colors and shapes of foods. The teaching shall be evident at mealtimes and during curricular activities, without interfering with the pleasure of eating.

RATIONALE: Nourishing and attractive food is a foundation for developmentally appropriate learning experiences and contributes to health and well-being (2-10, 18, 28, 50, 51). Coordinating the learning experiences with the food service staff maximizes effectiveness of the education. In addition to the nutritive value of food, infants and young children are helped, through the act of feeding, to establish warm human relationships. Eating should be an enjoyable experience in the facility and at home.

Nutrition is a vital component of good health. Enjoying and learning about food in childhood promotes good nutrition habits for a lifetime.

COMMENTS: Parents and caregivers should always be encouraged to sit at the table and eat the same food offered to young children as a way to strengthen family style eating which supports child's serving and feeding him or herself. Family style eating requires special training for the food service and child care staff since they need to monitor food served in a group setting. The use of serving utensils shall be encouraged to minimize food handling by children. The presence of an adult at the table with children while they are eating is a way to encourage social interaction and conversation about the food such as its name, color, texture, taste, and concepts such as number, size, and shape; as well as sharing events of the day. The parent or adult can help the slow eater, prevent behaviors that might increase risk of fighting, eating each others food and stuffing food in mouth which might cause choking.

Several community based nutrition resources can help child care providers with the nutrition and food service component of their programs. The key to identifying a qualified nutrition professional is training in pediatric nutrition (normal nutrition, nutrition for children with special needs, dietary modifications) and experience and competency in basic food service systems.

Local resources for nutrition education include:
- Local and state nutritionists in health department in maternal and child health programs and divisions of children with special health care needs;
- Registered dietitians/nutritionists at hospitals;
- WIC and cooperative extension nutritionists;
- School food service personnel;
- State administrators of Child and Adult Care Food Program;
- National School Food Service Management Institute;
- Child Care Nutrition Resource System of the Food and Nutrition Information System (National Agricultural Library, USDA);
- Nutrition consultants with local affiliates of the following organizations:
  - American Dietetic Association;
  - American Public Health Association;
  - Society for Nutrition Education;
  - American Association of Family and Consumer Sciences;
  - Dairy Council;
  - American Heart Association;
  - American Cancer Society;

•American Diabetes Association;
•Professional home economists like teachers and those with consumer organizations;
•Nutrition departments of local colleges and universities.

Contact information for the national organizations is located in Appendix BB.

Compliance is measured by structured observation.

For additional information on nutrition learning experiences for children, see also STANDARD 4.031 through 4.033, on mealtime activities.

TYPE OF FACILITY: *Center; Large Family Child Care Home; Small Family Child Care Home*

STANDARD 4.070
NUTRITION EDUCATION FOR PARENTS

Parents shall be informed of the scope of nutrition learning activities provided in the facility. Nutrition information and education programs shall be conducted at least twice a year under the guidance of the Child Care Nutrition Specialist (see Appendix C), based on a needs assessment for nutrition information and education as perceived by families and staff.

RATIONALE: One goal of a facility is to provide a positive environment for the entire family. Informing parents about nutrition, food, food preparation, and mealtime enhances nutrition and mealtime interactions in the home, which helps to mold a child's food habits and eating behavior (2, 3, 6, 7, 10-12, 28, 51, 52). Nutrition education directed at parents complements and enhances the nutrition education provided to their children.

COMMENTS: The educational programs may be supplemented by periodic newsletters and/or literature.

Several community based nutrition resources can help child care providers with the nutrition and food service component of their programs. The key to identifying a qualified nutrition professional is training in pediatric nutrition (normal nutrition, nutrition for

children with special needs, dietary modifications) and experience and competency in basic food service systems.

Local resources for nutrition education include:
•Local and state nutritionists in health department in maternal and child health programs and divisions of children with special health care needs;
•Registered dietitians/nutritionists at hospitals;
•WIC and cooperative extension nutritionists;
•School food service personnel;
•State administrators of Child and Adult Care Food Program;
•National School Food Service Management Institute;
•Child Care Nutrition Resource System of the Food and Nutrition Information System (National Agricultural Library, USDA);
•Nutrition consultants with local affiliates of the following organizations:
•American Dietetic Association;
•American Public Health Association;
•Society for Nutrition Education;
•American Association of Family and Consumer Sciences;
•Dairy Council;
•American Heart Association;
•American Cancer Society;
•American Diabetes Association;
•Professional home economists like teachers and those with consumer organizations;
•Nutrition departments of local colleges and universities.

Contact information for the national organizations is located in Appendix BB.

TYPE OF FACILITY: *Center; Large Family Child Care Home; Small Family Child Care Home*

REFERENCES

1. US Dept of Agriculture, US Dept of Health and Human Services. *Nutrition and Your Health: Dietary Guidelines for Americans*. Washington, DC: US Dept of Agriculture, US Dept of Health and Human Services; 2000.

2. US Dept of Health and Human Services. *Head Start Program Performance Standards and other Regulations*. Rev ed. Washington, DC: US Dept of Health and Human Services, Administration for Children and Families, Head Start Bureau; 1999.

3. Green M, ed. *Bright Futures: Guidelines for Health Supervision of Infants, Children, and Adolescents*. Arlington, Va: National Center for Education in Maternal and Child Health; 1999.

4. Story M, Holt K, Sofka D, eds. *Bright Futures in Practice: Nutrition*. Arlington, Va: National Center for Education in Maternal and Child Health; 2000.

5. Wardle F, Winegarner N. Nutrition and head start. *Child Today*. 1992;21(I),5-7.

6. Graves DE, Suitor CW, Holt KA, eds. *Making Food Healthy and Safe for Children: How to Meet the National Health and Safety Performance Standards: Guidelines for Out-of-home Child Care Programs*. Arlington, Va: National Center for Education in Maternal and Child Health; 1997.

7. Dietz WH, Stern L, eds. *Guide to Your Child's Nutrition*. Elk Grove Village, Ill: American Academy of Pediatrics; 1998.

8. Kleinman RE, ed. *Pediatric Nutrition Handbook*. 4th ed. Elk Grove Village, Ill: American Academy of Pediatrics; 1998.

9. Lally JR, Griffin A, Fenichel E, Segal M, Szanton E, Weissbourd B. *Caring for Infants and Toddlers in Groups: Developmentally Appropriate Practice*. Arlington, Va: Zero to Three; 1995.

10. Enders, JB. *Food, Nutrition and the Young Child*. New York, NY: Merrill; 1994.

11. US Dept of Agriculture. *Child and Adult Care Food Program: Nutrition Guidance for Child Care Homes*. Washington, DC: US Dept of Agriculture, Family Child Services; 1995.

12. US Dept of Agriculture. *Child and Adult Care Food Program: Nutrition Guidance for Child Care Centers*. Washington, DC: US Dept of Agriculture, Family Child Services; 1995.

13. US Dept of Agriculture. *Food Guide Pyramid for Young Children-A Daily Guide for 2- to 6-Year Olds*. Washington, DC: US Dept of Agriculture, Center for Nutrition Policy and Promotion; 1999.

14. Cassamassimo P, ed. *Bright Futures in Practice: Oral Health*. Arlington, Va: National Center for Education in Maternal and Child Health; 1996.

15. Dennison BA, Rockwell HL, Baker SL. Excess fruit juice consumption by preschool-aged children is associated with short stature and obesity. *Pediatrics*. 1997;99(1):15-22.

16. Samour PQ, Helm KK, Lang CE. *Handbook of Pediatric Nutrition*. 2nd ed. Gaithersburg, Md: Aspen Publishers, Inc.; 1999:86-89, 110-111, 166, 344-345.

17. Burks AW, Stanley JS. Food allergy. *Curr Opin Pediatr.* 1998;10:588-593.

18. *Manual of Clinical Dietetics*. 4th ed. Chicago, Ill: Chicago Dietetic Association and Ill South Suburbs Dietetic Association; 1992.

19. US Dept of Agriculture. *Breastfed Babies Welcome Here!* Washington, DC: US Dept of Agriculture, Food and Nutrition Services; 1993.

20. American Academy of Pediatrics. Breastfeeding and the use of human milk. *Pediatrics,* 1997; 100(6): 1035-1039.

21. Uauy R, DeAndroca I. Human milk and breast feeding for optimal brain development. *J Nutr.*1995; 125 (suppl 8):2218-2280S.

22. Wang YS, Wu SY. The effect of exclusive breast feeding on development and incidence of infection in infants. *J Hum Lactation.* 1996;12:27-30.

23. Quasdt S. Ecology of breast feeding in the US: an applied perspective. *Am J Hum Biol.* 1998;10(2):221-228.

24. Hammosh M. Breast feeding and the working mother. *Pediatrics.* 1996;97:492-498.

25. Lawrence RA. *Breast feeding: a guide for the medical profession.* 4th ed. St. Louis, Mo: Mosby-Year Book, Inc; 1994.

26. American Academy of Pediatric Dentistry. Recommendation for preventive pediatric dental care. *Pediatr Dent.* 1993;15:158-159.

27. American Academy of Pediatric Dentistry. Reference manual 1994-1995. *Pediatr Dent.* 1994;16(7, special issue):1-96.

28. Pipes PL, Trahms CM. *Nutrition in infancy and childhood.* 5th ed. St. Louis, Mo: Mosby-Year Book, Inc.; 1993.

29. Nemethy M, Clore ER. Microwave heating of infant formula and breast milk. *J Pediatr Health Care.* 1990; 4:131-5.

30. National Research Council. *Recommended Dietary Allowances.* 10th ed. Washington, DC: National Academy Press; 1989.

31. American Dietetic Association. Nutrition standards for child care programs. *J Am Diet Assoc.* 1994;94(3):323-326.

32. US Dept of Agriculture. *Quantity Recipes for Child Care Centers.* Washington, DC: US Dept of Agriculture; 1996:FNS-86 rev.

33. US Dept of Agriculture. *Food Buying Guide for Child Nutrition Programs.* Washington, DC: US Dept of Agriculture; 1993:PA-1331.

34. Morrow SE, Smith DL, Cairns BA, et al. Etiology and outcome of pediatric burns. *J Pediatr Surg.* 1996;31(3):329-33.

35. Rieg LS, Jenkins M. Burn injuries in children. *Crit Care Nurs Clin North Am.* 1991;3(3)457-50.

36. Wade J, Purdue GF, Hunt JL. Crawl on your belly like GI Joe...many pediatric burns can be prevented. *JBurn Care Rehabil.* 1990;11(3)261-3.

37. Rimell FL, Thome A Jr, Stool S, et al. Characteristics of objects that cause choking in children. *JAMA.*1995;274:1763-66.

38. Baker SB, Fisher RS. Childhood asphyxiation by choking or suffocation. *JAMA.* 1980;244:1343-46.

39. Harris CS, Baker SP, Smith GA, et al. Childhood asphyxiation by food: a national analysis and overview.*JAMA.* 1984;251(17):2231-35.

40. *Commercial Cooking, Re-thermalization and Powered Hot Food Holding and Transport Equipment.* Ann Harbor, Mich: National Sanitation Foundation; 1997:ANSI/ NSF4-1997.

41. *Heating, Ventilation and Air Conditioning Systems and Application Handbook.* Atlanta, Ga: American Society of Heating Refrigeration and Air Conditioning Engineers; 1987.

42. US Food and Drug Administration. *Model Food Code, 1999.* Springfield, Va: US Food and Drug Administration, National Technical Information Service; 1999.

43. Cowell C, Schlosser S. Food safety in infant and preschool day care. *Top Clin Nutr.* 1998;14(l):9-15.

44. US Dept of Agriculture. Food Safety and Inspection Service. *Keeping Kids Safe: A Guide for Safe Handling and Sanitation for Child Care Providers.* Washington, DC: US Dept of Agriculture; 1996.

45. Potter ME. Unpasteurized milk: the hazards of a health fetish. *JAMA.* 1984;252:2048-52.

46. Sacks JJ. Toxoplasmosis infection associated with raw goat's milk. *JAMA.* 1982;246:1728-32.

47. *Facts about Food and Floods: A Consumer Guide to Food Quality and Safe Handling after a Flood or Power Outage.*

Brochure, Washington, DC: Food Marketing Institutes; 1996.

48. Bryan FL, DeHart GH. Evaluation of household dish-washing machines, for use in small institutions. *J Milk Food Tech.* 1975;38:509-15.

49. Clorox Health Advisory Council. *Simple Solutions for Healthy Child Care.* Oakland, Calif: The Clorox Corporation; 1996:6.

50. William CO, ed. *Pediatric Manual of Clinical Dietetics.* Chicago, Ill: American Dietetic Association; 1998:57.

51. Tamborlane WV, ed. *The Yale Guide to Children's Nutrition.* New Haven, Conn: Yale University Press; 1997:42,48.

52. Brieger, KM. *Cooking up the Pyramid: An Early Childhood Nutrition Curriculum.* Pine Island, NY: Clinical Nutrition Services; 1993.

53. American Academy of Pediatrics, Committee on Nutrition. The use of whole cow's milk in infancy. *Pediatrics.* 1992;89:1105-1109.

54. American Academy of Pediatrics, Work Group on Breastfeeding. Policy statement on breastfeeding. *Pediatrics.* 1997;100:1035.

55. Dixon JJ, Burd DA, Roberts, DG. Severe burns resulting from an exploding teat on a bottle of infant formula milk heated in a microwave oven. *Burns.* 1997;23:268-9.

56. *The ABC's of safe and healthy child care: a handbook for child care providers.* Washington DC: Centers for Disease Control and Prevention; 1996.

57. American Academy of Pediatrics, Committee on Infectious Diseases. *Red book 2000: Report of the committee on infectious diseases.* Elk Grove Village, Ill: American Academy of Pediatrics; 2000.

CHAPTER 5

Facilities, Supplies, Equipment, and Transportation

5.1 OVERALL SPACE AND EQUIPMENT REQUIREMENTS

GENERAL LOCATION, LAYOUT, AND CONSTRUCTION OF THE FACILITY

STANDARD 5.001
LOCATION OF CENTER

A center shall not be located in a private residence unless that portion of the residence is used exclusively for the care of children during the hours of operation.

RATIONALE: Centers in these standards are generally defined as "providing care and education for any number of children in a non- residential setting.". When there are a large number of children in care who may span the age groups of infants, toddlers, preschool and school-age children, special sanitation and design are needed to protect children from injury and prevent transmission of disease. Undivided attention must be given to these purposes during child care operations.

COMMENTS: The portion of a private residence used as a child care facility is variable and unique to each specific situation. If other people will be using the private residence during the child care facility's hours of operation, then the caregiver must arrange the residence so that the activities of these people do not occur in the area designated for child care. See also STANDARD 5.009, for more information on the use and purpose of child care facilities.

TYPE OF FACILITY: *Center*

STANDARD 5.002
INSPECTION OF BUILDINGS

Newly constructed, renovated, remodeled, or altered buildings shall be inspected by a public inspector to assure compliance with applicable building and fire codes before the building can be made accessible to children.

RATIONALE: Building codes are designed to ensure that a new or altered building is safe for occupants.

TYPE OF FACILITY: *Center*

STANDARD 5.003
COMPLIANCE WITH FIRE PREVENTION CODE

Every 12 months, the child care facility shall obtain written documentation to submit to the regulatory licensing authority that the facility complies with a state-approved or nationally recognized Fire Prevention Code. If available, this documentation shall be obtained from a fire prevention official with jurisdiction where the facility is located. Where fire safety inspections or a Fire Prevention Code applicable to child care centers is not available from local authorities, the facility shall arrange for a fire safety inspection by an inspector who is recognized by the National Fire Protection Association (NFPA) and is qualified to conduct such inspections using the *NFPA-101 Life Safety Code*.

RATIONALE: Regular fire safety checks by trained officials will ensure that a licensed child care facility continues to meet all applicable fire safety codes.

TYPE OF FACILITY: *Center*

STANDARD 5.004
ACCESSIBILITY OF FACILITY

The facility shall be accessible for children who use wheel chairs and for other children and adults with motor disabilities, in accordance with Section 504 of the Rehabilitation Act of 1973 and the Americans with Disabilities Act (ADA). Accessibility includes access to buildings, toilets, sinks, drinking fountains, outdoor play areas, and all classroom and therapy areas. Special provisions shall also be made, as needed, for the child with health, vision, or hearing impairment.

RATIONALE: Accessibility has been detailed in full, in Section 504 of the Rehabilitation Act of 1973. It is also a key component of the Americans with

Disabilities Act barring discrimination against anyone with a disability.

COMMENTS: Any facility accepting children with motor disabilities must be accessible to all children served. Small family child care home providers may be limited in their ability to serve such children, but are not precluded from doing so if there is a reasonable degree of compliance with this standard. Not all children with motor disabilities live in fully physically accessible accommodations at home. Nevertheless, access to public and most private facilities is a key to the implementation of the ADA. If toilet learning/training is a relevant activity, the facility may be required to provide adapted toilet equipment in addition to that specified in Toilets and Toilet Learning/Training Equipment, STANDARD 5.117 through STANDARD 5.125

For more information on requirements regarding accessibility, the Americans with Disabilities Act Accessibility Guidelines (ADAAG) and the U.S. Access Board's *Guide to ADA Accessibility Guidelines for Play Areas.* Contact information is located in Appendix BB.

TYPE OF FACILITY: *Center; Large Family Child Care Home; Small Family Child Care Home*

STANDARD 5.005
SITE LOCATION FREE FROM HAZARDS

Facilities shall be located on a well-drained site, free from hazards, in areas protected from:
a) High air pollution;
b) Loud or constant noises;
c) Heavy traffic;
d) Unsafe buildings;
e) Deep excavations;
f) Radiation hazards;
g) Radon hazards;
h) Pits, abandoned wells or other risks of entrapment or inhumation (burial);
i) Any other unsafe or harmful environmental elements.

RATIONALE: This requirement will reduce exposure to conditions that cause injury or adversely affect health. Epidemiological studies indicate a relationship between outdoor air pollution and adverse respiratory effects on children(1). Risk of injury and risk of disease from insects, which breed in poorly drained areas, must be controlled to have a safe facility and outdoor play areas.

Among 471 childhood suffocation deaths in California between 1960 and 1981, 111 were caused by burial beneath earth, sand, or other material (56). Some occurred at construction sites where children were playing, and others occurred at beaches and other remote areas. Children also can fall into wells, pits, and other excavations and can become trapped in refrigerators and other home appliances.

COMMENTS: An environmental audit should be conducted before construction of a new building or renovation of an older building (2). The environmental audit should include assessments of the following:
a) Historical land use, seeking possibility of toxic contamination of soil;
b) The possibility of lead and asbestos in older buildings;
c) Potential sources of infestation, noise, air pollution, and toxic exposures;
d) The location of the playground in relation to infested stagnant water, roadways, industrial emissions, building exhaust outlets, and any other hazards to children.

For information on noise levels, see STANDARD 5.046.

TYPE OF FACILITY: *Center; Large Family Child Care Home; Small Family Child Care Home*

STANDARD 5.006
STRUCTURALLY SOUND FACILITY

Every exterior wall, roof, and foundation shall be structurally sound, weather-tight, and water-tight and shall be finished to control mold, dust, and entry of pests into the child care space.

Every interior floor, wall, and ceiling shall be structurally sound and shall be finished to control exposure of the occupants to levels of toxic fumes, dust, mold, ventilation, heating, lighting, or noise deemed hazardous by local health authorities.

RATIONALE: Children must be protected from hazardous exposures.

COMMENTS: Child care operations often use older buildings or buildings designed for purposes other than child care. Both the design of structures and the lack of maintenance can lead to exposure of children to mold, dust, pests, and toxic materials. "Sick building syndrome" is a term used to describe problems inside structures due to finishing that exposes occupants to hazardous conditions. Environmental health authorities have special training in identification of these potential health risks.

TYPE OF FACILITY: *Center; Large Family Child Care Home; Small Family Child Care Home*

STANDARD 5.007
USE OF BASEMENTS

Finished basements may be used for children 2 years of age and older, if the space is in compliance with STANDARD 5.008 and STANDARD 5.020. Basements shall be:
a) Dry and well ventilated;
b) Well lighted;
c) Maintained at required temperatures and humidity;
d) Free of radon in excess of 4 picocuries per liter of air;
e) Free of friable asbestos.

RATIONALE: Basement areas can be quite habitable and should be usable as long as environmental quality and fire safety is satisfactory.

TYPE OF FACILITY: *Center; Large Family Child Care Home; Small Family Child Care Home*

STANDARD 5.008
BUILDINGS OF WOOD CONSTRUCTION

In buildings of wood construction, children, including infants and toddlers, shall be housed and cared for only on the ground floor, with one exception. Older, preschool-age and school-age children shall be able to use floors other than the ground floor in a building of wood construction that has required exits and care is provided in:
a) A daylight-lit basement with exits that are no more than a half flight high;
b) A tri-level facility with half flights of stairs;
c) A facility that is protected throughout by an automatic sprinkler system, which has its exit stairs enclosed by minimum 1-hour fire barriers with openings in those barriers protected by minimum 1-hour fire doors;
d) Any door encountered along the egress route shall be easy for caregivers and older preschool-age children to open.

RATIONALE: Fire and building safety experts recommend that children, including infants, be permitted above ground level only in certain types of construction.

COMMENTS: Infants and toddlers should always be on the main floor with access directly to the outdoors. Doors along the egress route need to be easy to open. Consult local or state fire safety codes and child care licensing laws.

TYPE OF FACILITY: *Center; Large Family Child Care Home; Small Family Child Care Home*

STANDARD 5.009
UNRELATED BUSINESS IN A CHILD CARE AREA

Child care areas shall not be used for any business or purpose unrelated to child care when children are present in these areas.

RATIONALE: Child care requires child-oriented, child-safe areas where the child's needs are primary.

TYPE OF FACILITY: *Center; Large Family Child Care Home; Small Family Child Care Home*

STANDARD 5.010
OFFICE SPACE

Office space separate from child care areas shall be provided for administration and staff in centers. Children shall not have access to this area unless they are supervised by staff.

RATIONALE: For the efficient and effective operation of a center, office areas where activities incompatible with the care of young children are conducted should be separate from child care areas. These office areas can be expected to contain supplies and equipment that should not be accessible to children. In addition, where records and documents, some of them confidential, are kept, staff should be free from the distractions of child care (3, 4).

Adults need space, too. Care providers, if they are to avoid burnout, need a place to make a phone call, or to sit quietly for a few moments.

TYPE OF FACILITY: *Center*

STANDARD 5.011
SEPARATION OF OPERATIONS
FROM CHILD CARE AREAS

Rooms or spaces that are used for the following activities or operations shall be separated from the child care areas and shall not be encountered along the route of egress:
a)   Commercial-type kitchen;
b)   Boiler, maintenance shop;
c)   Janitor closet;
d)   Laundry;
e)   Woodworking shop;
f)   Flammable or combustible storage;
g)   Painting operation;
h)   Rooms that are used for any purpose involving the presence of toxic substances.

The exit and the fire-resistant separation shall be approved by the appropriate regulatory agencies responsible for building and fire inspections. In small and large family child care homes, a fire-resistant separation shall not be required where the food preparation kitchen contains only a domestic cooking range and the preparation of food does not result in smoke or grease-laden vapors escaping into indoor areas.

RATIONALE: Hazards and toxic substances must be kept separate from space used for child care to prevent children's and staff members' exposure to injury.

Cleaning agents must be inaccessible to children (out of reach and behind locked doors). Food preparation surfaces must not be contaminated by diaper changing procedures. Children must be restricted from access to the stove when cooking surfaces are hot.

Egress must not require travel through hazardous areas.

COMMENTS: In small family child care homes, mixed use of rooms is common. Some combined use of space for food preparation, storage of cleaning equipment and household tools, laundry, and diaper changing require that each space within a room be defined according to its purpose and that exposure of children to hazards be controlled.

TYPE OF FACILITY: *Center; Large Family Child Care Home; Small Family Child Care Home*

STANDARD 5.012
USE OF ROOMS FOR
MULTIPURPOSES

Children may play, eat, and nap in the same room (other than bathrooms, hallways, and closets), if that room is large enough to provide a defined space for each activity while that activity is under way and if the room meets other building requirements. Programming shall be such that the use of the room for one purpose does not interfere with use of the room for other purposes.

RATIONALE: Multipurpose use is permissible as long as bathrooms, exit routes, and uninhabitable spaces are not included in multipurpose activity areas.

COMMENTS: Compliance may be measured by structured observation.

TYPE OF FACILITY: *Center*

OPENINGS

STANDARD 5.013
WEATHER-TIGHTNESS AND
WATER-TIGHTNESS OF OPENINGS

Each window, exterior door, and basement or cellar hatchway shall be weather-tight and water-tight when closed.

RATIONALE: Children's environments must be protected from exposure to moisture, dust, and temperature extremes.

TYPE OF FACILITY: *Center; Large Family Child Care Home; Small Family Child Care Home*

STANDARD 5.014
POSSIBILITY OF EXIT FROM
WINDOWS

All windows in areas used by children under 5 years of age shall be constructed, adapted, or adjusted to limit the exit opening accessible to children to less than 3.5 inches, or be otherwise protected with guards that prevent exit by a child, but that do not block outdoor light. Where such windows are required by building or fire codes to provide for emergency rescue and escape, the windows and guards, if provided, shall be equipped to enable staff to release the guard and open the window fully when escape or rescue is required. Such release shall not require the use of tools or keys.

RATIONALE: This standard is needed to prevent children from falling out of windows. Standards from the U.S. Consumer Product Safety Commission

(CPSC) and the American Society for Testing and Materials (ASTM) require the opening size to be 3.5 inches to prevent the child from getting through or the head from being entrapped. Some children may be able to pass their body through a slightly larger opening but then get stuck and hang from the window opening with their head trapped inside. Caregivers must not depend on screens to keep children from falling out of windows. Windows to be used as fire exits must be immediately accessible.

TYPE OF FACILITY: *Center; Large Family Child Care Home; Small Family Child Care Home*

STANDARD 5.015
SCREENS FOR VENTILATION
OPENINGS

All openings used for ventilation shall be screened against insect entry.

RATIONALE: Screens prevent the entry of insects, which may bite, sting, or carry disease. See STANDARD 5.014 for safety precautions for windows.

TYPE OF FACILITY: *Center; Large Family Child Care Home; Small Family Child Care Home*

STANDARD 5.016
SAFETY GUARDS FOR GLASS
WINDOWS/DOORS

Glass windows and glass door panels within 36 inches of the floor shall have safety guards (such as rails or mesh) or be of safety-grade glass or polymer (such as Lexan) and equipped with a vision strip.

RATIONALE: Glass panels can be invisible to an active child or adult. When a child collides with a glass panel, serious injury can result from the collision impact or the broken glass.

COMMENTS: In areas where glass windows are repeatedly broken, installation of polymer material (Lexan, for example) should be considered. See STANDARD 5.014 for safety precautions for windows.

TYPE OF FACILITY: *Center; Large Family Child Care Home; Small Family Child Care Home*

STANDARD 5.017
FINGER-PINCH PROTECTION DEVICES

Finger-pinch protection devices shall be installed wherever doors are accessible to children. These devices include:
a) Rubber gaskets designed to fit into an inset on the door where the door meets the door jamb and over the opening where the door is hinged;
b) Other types of flexible coverings for the hinged opening;
c) Door closing devices that force the door to close slowly or keep the door from closing fully if it strikes an obstacle.

RATIONALE: Finger-pinch injuries in doors are a significant cause of injury among claims against liability insurance in child care. Installation of inexpensive gaskets, barriers, and closing devices that prevent entrapment of a child's fingers will reduce these injuries.

COMMENTS: Easily installed, inexpensive, and flexible joints for finger-pinch protection are in widespread use in French and Australian child care programs and increasingly in US child care programs. Manufacturers sell rubber gaskets, accordion-pleated plastic, thin strips of flexible plastic, and carpeting fixed to the door and opposing door jamb edge by molding strips. These can be used on the hinge opening and some are designed to fit the closing edge of the door to fill a small gap between the closing edge and door jamb with a yielding material. Adjustable door closing devices are available to slow the rate of door closing. Slowing the door closing rate helps prevent finger pinching in the latch area of the door or abrupt closing of the door against a small child.

TYPE OF FACILITY: *Center; Large Family Child Care Home; Small Family Child Care Home*

STANDARD 5.018
DIRECTIONAL SWING OF INDOOR DOORS

Interior doors from a building area with fewer than 50 persons shall swing in the direction of most frequent travel. Doors from a building area with more than 50 persons and exit enclosure doors shall swing in the direction of egress travel. An exception is that boiler room doors shall swing into the room.

RATIONALE: This standard is to provide easy, quick passage and to prevent injuries. Boiler room doors should swing inward to contain explosions.

The *NFPA-101 Life Safety Code* from the National Fire Protection Association (NFPA), and the model building codes in wide use throughout the United States, require that doors serving an area with 50 or more persons swing in the direction of egress travel (8). This is important because large numbers of persons might push against each other leaving those up against a door without the ability to step back and allow the door to swing back into the room. Contact information for the NFPA is located in Appendix BB.

COMMENTS: Doors in homes usually open inward. The requirement for door swing may be addressed in local building codes.

TYPE OF FACILITY: *Center*

STANDARD 5.019
UNOBSTRUCTED EGRESS

Doorways, exit access paths, and exits shall be free of debris and equipment to allow unobstructed egress travel from inside the child care facility to the outside.

RATIONALE: This provision permits a fast exit in the event of an emergency.

TYPE OF FACILITY: *Center; Large Family Child Care Home; Small Family Child Care Home*

EXITS

STANDARD 5.020
ALTERNATE EXITS AND
EMERGENCY SHELTER

Each building or structure, new or old, shall be provided with a minimum of two exits, at different sides of the building or home, leading to an open space at ground level. If the basement in a small family child care home is being used, one exit must lead directly to the outside. Exits shall be unobstructed, allowing occupants to escape to an outside door or exit stair enclosure in case of fire or other emergency. Each floor above or below ground level used for child care shall have at least two unobstructed exits that lead to an open area at ground level and thereafter to an area that meets safety requirements for a child care indoor or outdoor area where children may remain until their parents can pick them up, if reentry into the facility is not possible.

Entrance and exit routes shall be reviewed and approved by the applicable fire inspector. Exiting shall meet all the requirements of the current edition of the *NFPA-101 Life Safety Code* from the National Fire Protection Association (NFPA).

RATIONALE: Unobstructed exit routes are essential for prompt evacuation. The purpose of having two ways to exit when child care is provided on a floor above or below ground level is to ensure an alternative exit if fire blocks one exit.

COMMENTS: Using an outdoor playground as a safe place to exit to may not always be possible. Some child care facilities do not have a playground located adjacent to the child care building and use local parks as the playground site. Access to these parks may require crossing a street at an intersection with a crosswalk. This would normally be considered safe,

especially in areas of low traffic; however, when sirens go off, a route that otherwise may be considered safe becomes chaotic and dangerous. During evacuation or an emergency, children, as well as staff, become excited and may run into the street when the playground is not fenced and immediately adjacent to the center.

In the event of a fire, staff members and children should be able to get at least 50 feet away from the building or structure. If the children cannot return to their usual building, a suitable shelter containing all items necessary for child care must be available where the children can safely remain until their parents come for them. An evacuation plan should take into consideration all available open areas to which staff and children can safely retreat in an emergency.

For information about the *NFPA-101 Life Safety Code*, contact the National Fire Protection Association. Contact information is located in Appendix BB.

TYPE OF FACILITY: *Center; Large Family Child Care Home; Small Family Child Care Home*

STANDARD 5.021
EVACUATION OF CHILDREN WITH
DISABILITIES

In facilities that include children who have physical disabilities, all exits and steps necessary for evacuation shall have ramps approved by the local building inspector. Children who have ambulatory difficulty, use wheelchairs or other equipment that must be transported with the child (such as an oxygen ventilator) shall be located on the ground floor of the facility or provisions shall be made for efficient emergency evacuation to a safe sheltered area.

RATIONALE: The facility must meet building code standards for the community and also the requirements under the Americans with Disabilities Act (ADA) and their access guidelines. All children must be able to exit the building quickly in case of emergency. Locating children in wheelchairs or those with special equipment on the ground floor may eliminate the need for transporting these children down the stairs during an emergency exit. In buildings where the ground floor cannot be used for such children, arrangements must be made to remove them to a safe location, such as a fire tower stairwell, during an emergency exit.

COMMENTS: Assuring physical access to a facility also requires that a means of evacuation meeting safety standards for exit accommodates any special needs of the children in care.

For additional information on additional access requirements, see STANDARD 5.004 and STANDARD 5.008.

TYPE OF FACILITY: *Center; Large Family Child Care Home; Small Family Child Care Home*

STANDARD 5.022
PATH OF EGRESS

The minimum width of any path of egress shall be 36 inches. An exception is that doors shall provide a minimum clear width of 32 inches. The width of doors shall accommodate wheelchairs and the needs of individuals with physical disabilities.

Where exits are not immediately accessible from an open floor area, safe and continuous passageways, aisles, or corridors leading to every exit shall be maintained and shall be arranged to provide access for each occupant to at least two exits by separate ways of travel. Passageways and corridors shall be kept free of materials and furniture that would prevent clear access.

RATIONALE: Unobstructed access to exits is essential to prompt evacuation. The hallways and door openings must be wide enough to permit easy exit in an emergency. The actual exit is the enclosed stair or the actual door to the outside; doors from most rooms and the travel along a corridor are considered exit access or the path of egress. The *NFPA-101 Life Safety Code* from the National Fire Protection Association permits the usual 36 inches minimum to be reduced to a clear opening of 32 inches for doors (8). This is consistent with ADAAG (Americans with Disabilities Act Accessibility Guidelines) as it affords

enough width for a person in a wheelchair to maneuver through the door opening. Contact information for the NFPA is located in Appendix BB.

TYPE OF FACILITY: *Center*

STANDARD 5.023
LOCKS

The facility shall have no lock or fastening device that prevents free escape from the interior. All door hardware in areas that school-age children use shall be within the reach of the children. In centers, only panic hardware (hardware that can be opened by pressure in the direction of travel) or single-action hardware (hardware that allows a door to open either way but keeps it from swinging back past the center point) shall be permitted on exterior doors.

A double-cylinder deadbolt lock which requires a key to unlock from the inside shall not be permitted on any door along the path of egress from any child care area of a large or small family child care home except the exterior door, and then only if the lock is of a key-capturing type and the key is kept hanging near the door.

If emergency exits lead to potentially unsafe areas for children (such as a busy street), alarms or other signaling devices shall be installed on these exit doors to alert the staff in case a child attempts to leave.

RATIONALE: Children, as well as staff members, must be able to evacuate a building in the event of a fire or other emergency. Nevertheless, the child care provider must assure security from intruders and from unsupervised use of the exit by children.

COMMENTS: Double cylinder deadbolt locks that require a key to unlock the door from the inside are often installed in private homes for added security. In such situations, these dead bolt locks should be present only on exterior doors and should be left in the unlocked position during the hours of child care operation. Locks that prevent opening from the outside, but can be opened without a key from the inside should be used for security during hours of child care

operation. Double cylinder deadbolt locks should not be used on interior doors, such as closets, bathrooms, storage rooms, and bedrooms.

TYPE OF FACILITY: *Center; Large Family Child Care Home*

STANDARD 5.024
LABELED EMERGENCY EXITS

Emergency exits shall be clearly identified and visible at all times during operation of the child care facility. The exits for escape shall be arranged or marked so the path to safety outside is unmistakable.

RATIONALE: As soon as children can learn to recognize exit signs and pathway markings, they will benefit from having these paths of escape clearly marked. Adults who come into the building as visitors need these markings to direct them as well.

TYPE OF FACILITY: *Center*

STANDARD 5.025
ACCESS TO EXITS

An exit to the outside or a common hallway leading to the outside shall be directly accessible from any room. If it is necessary to pass through another room for direct access to the outside, the other room shall not have a barrier or door that can be latched to prevent access through it.

No obstructions shall be placed in the corridors or passageways leading to the exits.

RATIONALE: A room that requires exit through another room to get to an exit path can entrap its occupants when there is a fire or emergency condition if passage can be impeded by a barrier or door that is latched.

An obstruction in the path of exit can lead to entrapment, especially in an emergency situation where groups of people may be exiting together.

TYPE OF FACILITY: *Center; Large Family Child Care Home; Small Family Child Care Home*

FINISHES

STANDARD 5.026
FINISHES OF DOORS, FLOORS AND WALLS

The hand contact and splash areas of doors, and walls shall be covered with a finish that is at least as cleanable as an epoxy finish or enamel paint.

Each bathroom, toilet room, and shower room floor and wall shall be impervious to water up to a height of 5 feet and capable of being kept in a clean and sanitary condition.

RATIONALE: Impervious surfaces for floors and walls prevent deterioration and mold and ensure clean and sanitary surfaces. Surfaces that are easily cleaned facilitate removal of filth and disease-producing germs.

TYPE OF FACILITY: *Center, Large Family Child Care Home; Small Family Child Care Home*

HEATING, COOLING, VENTILATION, AND HOT WATER

STANDARD 5.027
FRESH AIR

As much fresh air as possible shall be provided in rooms that children use. Wherever possible, windows shall be capable of being opened. When windows are not kept open, rooms shall be ventilated, as specified in STANDARD 5.028 through STANDARD 5.032.

RATIONALE: The health and well-being of both the staff and the children can be affected by air quality indoors. The air that people breathe inside a building is contaminated with organisms shared among occupants and sometimes more polluted than the outdoor air. Young children may be affected more than adults by air pollution. Children who spend long hours breathing contaminated or polluted indoor air are more likely to develop respiratory problems, allergies and asthma (10, 11).

Although insulation of a building is important in reducing heating or cooling costs, it is unwise to try to seal the building completely. Air circulation is essential to clear infectious disease agents, odors and toxic substances in the air. Levels of CO_2 are an indicator of the quality of ventilation (7).

TYPE OF FACILITY: *Center; Large Family Child Care Home; Small Family Child Care Home*

STANDARD 5.028
INDOOR TEMPERATURE AND AIR EXCHANGE

A draft-free temperature of 65 degrees F to 75 degrees F shall be maintained at 30% to 50% relative humidity during the winter months. A draft-free temperature of 68 degrees F to 82 degrees F shall be maintained at 30% to 50% humidity during the summer months (9). All rooms that children use shall be heated, cooled, and ventilated to maintain the required temperatures, humidity, and air exchange and to avoid accumulation of odors and fumes. Air exchange shall be a minimum of 15 cubic feet per minute (or 7.5 liters/second) per person of outdoor air.

RATIONALE: These requirements are based on the standards of the American Society of Heating, Refrigerating, and Air Conditioning Engineers (ASHRAE), which take both comfort and health into consideration (9). High humidity can promote growth of mold, mildew, and other biological agents that can cause eye, nose, and throat irritation and may trigger asthma episodes in people with asthma. These precautions are essential to the health and well-being of both the staff and the children. When planning construction of a facility, it is healthier to build windows that open.

COMMENTS: Airflow can be adjusted by using fans and open windows. To promote air circulation,

windows should be opened whenever weather permits or when children are out of an area. Heat loss can be controlled by using a heat-recovery ventilator in the window or in the ventilation system that circulates outdoor air (11).

Simple and inexpensive devices that measure the ambient relative humidity indoors may be purchased in hardware stores or toy stores that specialize in science products.

For further information on air quality, contact ASHRAE, the U.S. Environmental Protection Agency (EPA) Public Information Center, the American Gas Association, the Edison Electric Institue, the American Lung Association, the U.S. Consumer Product Safety Commission (CPSC), and the Safe Building Alliance. Contact information is located in Appendix BB.

TYPE OF FACILITY: *Center; Large Family Child Care Home; Small Family Child Care Home*

STANDARD 5.029
ART MATERIALS AND VENTILATION

Areas where arts and crafts activities are conducted shall be well ventilated. Materials that create toxic fumes or gases shall not be used. Caregivers shall ensure that all art materials are properly cleaned-up and stored in original containers that are fully labeled.

RATIONALE: Children in child care should not be exposed to fumes or gases. Labels are required on art supplies to identify any hazardous ingredients, risks associated with their use, precautions, first aid, and sources of further information.

COMMENTS: Staff should be educated to the possibility that some children may have special vulnerabilities to certain art materials (such as children with asthma or allergies).

TYPE OF FACILITY: *Center; Large Family Child Care Home; Small Family Child Care Home*

STANDARD 5.030
ELECTRIC FANS

Electric fans, if used, shall bear the safety certification mark of a recognized testing laboratory, such as UL (Underwriters Laboratories) or ETL (Electrotechnical Laboratory) and be inaccessible to children.

RATIONALE: Children having access to electric fans might insert objects and otherwise interfere with the safe operation of the fan.

TYPE OF FACILITY: *Center; Large Family Child Care Home; Small Family Child Care Home*

STANDARD 5.031
AIR RECIRCULATION SYSTEMS

Filters on air recirculation systems shall be checked and cleaned or replaced according to the manufacturer's instructions.

RATIONALE: Clogged filters will impede proper air circulation required for heating and ventilation. Filters must be cleaned to prevent airborne transmission of microorganisms.

TYPE OF FACILITY: *Center; Large Family Child Care Home; Small Family Child Care Home*

STANDARD 5.032
HEATING AND VENTILATION EQUIPMENT INSPECTION AND MAINTENANCE

All heating and ventilating equipment shall be inspected before each cooling and heating season by a heating/air conditioning contractor, who shall verify in writing that the equipment is properly installed, cleaned, and maintained to operate efficiently and effectively without emitting chemical or microbiological substances. The system shall be operated in accordance with operating instructions.

RATIONALE: Routinely scheduled inspections and proper operation ensure that equipment is working properly.

COMMENTS: Emissions are measured on a sample of air coming from the heating or ventilating system. This test is done by a professional laboratory based on microscopic and chemical testing. To prevent harmful emissions, the system must be operated strictly in accordance with the operating instructions that the manufacturer warrants safe.

TYPE OF FACILITY: *Center; Large Family Child Care Home; Small Family Child Care Home*

STANDARD 5.033
TYPE AND PLACEMENT OF THERMOMETERS

Thermometers that will not easily break and that do not contain mercury shall be placed on interior walls in every indoor activity area at children's height.

RATIONALE: The temperature of the room can vary between the floor and the ceiling. Because heat rises, the temperature at the level where children are playing can be much cooler than at the usual level of placement of interior thermometers (the standing, eye level of adults) in the room. Mercury, glass, or similar materials in thermometers can cause injury and poisoning of children. Placing a safe thermometer at the children's height allows proper monitoring of temperature where the children are in the room. A thermometer should not break easily if a child or adult bumps into it.

TYPE OF FACILITY: *Center; Large Family Child Care Home; Small Family Child Care Home*

STANDARD 5.034
GAS, OIL OR KEROSENE HEATERS, PORTABLE GAS STOVES AND CHARCOAL GRILLS

Inadequately vented or unvented gas or oil heaters and portable open-flame kerosene space heaters shall be prohibited. Portable gas stoves and charcoal grills shall not be used for space heating or any other indoor purposes.

Heat in units that involve flame shall be vented properly to the outside and shall be supplied with a source of combustion air that meets the manufacturer's installation requirements.

RATIONALE: Improper venting of gas and oil heaters can lead to fire and the poisoning of building occupants. Proper venting can prevent accumulation of carbon monoxide gas inside a building. Carbon monoxide is a colorless, odorless, poisonous gas formed when carbon-containing fuel is not burned completely and can cause asphyxiation. Without a sufficient source of combustion air, heating units that burn fuel with a flame will be inefficient and can produce more toxic by-products.

Kerosene and other open-flame heaters discharge fumes into the living area. The potential for carbon monoxide poisoning from incomplete combustion of fuels exists if there is no proper outside ventilation (12, 13). Other pollutants that heaters can release include nitrogen dioxide, particles, polycyclic aromatic hydrocarbons, and acid aerosols. These chemicals can cause both short-term and chronic respiratory disease. Some space heaters are easily tipped over and do not shut off when tipped over. Many become hot enough to start fires in adjacent objects. Many burns have been caused by contact with space heaters and other hot surfaces.

COMMENTS: When possible, fresh air should be used to supply combustion air.

The local health and fire departments should approve any exceptions to this standard before use. For more information about air pollutants associated with the use of heaters, contact the U.S. Consumer Product Safety Commission (CPSC), the U.S. Environmental Protection Agency (EPA) Public Information Center,

and the Occupational Safety and Health Administration of the U.S. Department of Labor. Contact information is located in Appendix BB.

TYPE OF FACILITY: *Center; Large Family Child Care Home; Small Family Child Care Home*

STANDARD 5.035
ELECTRIC SPACE HEATERS

Electric space heaters shall:
a) Be inaccessible to children and be stable;
b) Have protective covering to keep hands and objects away from the electric heating element;
c) Bear the safety certification mark of a recognized testing laboratory, such as UL (Underwriters Laboratories) or ETL (Electrotechnical Laboratory);
d) Be placed at least 3 feet from curtains, papers, furniture and any flammable object;
e) Be properly vented, as required by the regulatory agency.

RATIONALE: Portable electric space heaters are a common cause of fires and burns resulting from very hot heating elements being too close to flammable objects and people (13).

COMMENTS: To prevent burns and potential fires, space heaters must not be accessible to children. Children can start fires by inserting flammable material near electric heating elements. Curtains, papers, and furniture must be kept away from electric space heaters to avoid potential fires. Some electric space heaters function by heating an oil contained in a heat-radiating portion of the appliance. Even though the electrical heating element is inaccessible in this type of heater, the excessively hot surfaces of the appliance can cause burns.

To prevent burns or potential fires, consideration must be given to the ages and activity levels of children in care and the amount of space in a room. Alternative methods of heating may be safer for children.

If portable electric space heaters are used, electrical circuits must not be overloaded. Portable electric space heaters are usually plugged into a regular 120-volt electric outlet connected to a 15-ampere circuit breaker. These circuit breakers are designed for lights and small appliances. A circuit breaker is an overload switch that prevents the current in a given electric circuit from exceeding the capacity of a line. Fuses perform the same function in older systems. If too many appliances are plugged into a circuit, calling for more power than the capacity of the circuit, the breaker reacts by switching off the circuit. Constantly overloaded electrical circuits can cause electrical fires. An electrical inspector or electrical contractor should be consulted if necessary.

This standard is based on the *Safe Home Checklist* (14).

TYPE OF FACILITY: *Center; Large Family Child Care Home; Small Family Child Care Home*

STANDARD 5.036
INSPECTION OF HEATING SYSTEMS

Heating systems, including heaters, stoves used for heating (or furnaces), stovepipes, and chimneys shall be inspected and cleaned before each heating season by a certified heating contractor, who shall furnish a letter or certificate warranting the heating system to be safe and sound. Documentation of these inspections and certification of safety shall be kept on file in the facility.

RATIONALE: Heating equipment is the second leading cause of ignition in fatal house fires (14). Heating equipment that is kept in good repair is less likely to cause fires.

COMMENTS: All heating equipment is intended to be included in this standard.

TYPE OF FACILITY: *Center; Large Family Child Care Home; Small Family Child Care Home*

STANDARD 5.037
PROTECTIVE SCREEN FOR HEATING EQUIPMENT

A protective screen shall be in place with a stove used for heating, or any heating equipment with high surface temperature located in an occupied area.

RATIONALE: Heating equipment can become very hot when in use, potentially causing significant burns. Protective screens reduce children's accessibility to hot stoves.

TYPE OF FACILITY: *Center; Large Family Child Care Home; Small Family Child Care Home*

STANDARD 5.038
FIREPLACES

Fireplaces and fireplace inserts shall be inaccessible to children. Fireplaces shall be properly drafted and the front opening equipped with a secure and stable protective safety screen. The facility shall provide evidence of cleaning the chimney at least once a year, before the heating season, or as frequently as necessary to prevent excessive build-up of burn residues or smoke products in the chimney. If a fireplace is used when children are present, an adult must be in the same room and the children must be within easy reach of the adult.

RATIONALE: Fireplaces provide access to surfaces hot enough to cause burns. Children should be kept away from fire because their clothing can easily ignite. Children should be kept away from a hot surface because they can be burned simply by touching it. Fireplaces are sources of toxic products of combustion that proper drafting removes. Improperly maintained chimneys can lead to fire and accumulation of toxic fumes. Having an adult present on the same floor but in another room is not sufficient to prevent injuries.

A protective safety screen over the front opening of a fireplace will contain sparks and reduce a child's accessibility to an open flame.

Heating equipment is the second leading cause of ignition of fatal house fires (14). This equipment can become very hot when in use, potentially causing significant burns.

COMMENTS: This standard is consistent with the majority of state and local building and fire codes for fire prevention.

TYPE OF FACILITY: *Center; Large Family Child Care Home; Small Family Child Care Home*

STANDARD 5.039
BARRIERS/GUARDS FOR HEATING UNITS

Heating units, including hot water heating pipes and baseboard heaters with a surface temperature hotter than 110 degrees F, shall be made inaccessible to children by barriers such as guards or other devices.

RATIONALE: A mechanical barrier separating the child from the source of heat can reduce the likelihood of burns (15, 16).

COMMENTS: For additional information on heating, cooling, and ventilation, see Openings, STANDARD 5.027 through STANDARD 5.041.

TYPE OF FACILITY: *Center; Large Family Child Care Home; Small Family Child Care Home*

STANDARD 5.040
WATER HEATING DEVICES AND TEMPERATURES ALLOWED

Facilities shall have water heating facilities that are connected to the water supply system as required by the regulatory authority. These facilities shall be capable of heating water to at least 120 degrees F and shall deliver hot water temperature at sinks used for handwashing, or at plumbing fixtures where the hot water will be in direct contact with children, at a temperature of at least 60 degrees F and not exceeding 120 degrees F. Scald-prevention devices, such as special faucets or thermostatically

controlled valves, shall be permanently installed, if necessary, to provide this temperature of water at the faucet. Where a dishwasher is used, it shall have the capacity to heat water to at least 140 degrees F for the dishwasher (with scald preventing devices limiting water temperature at handwashing sinks to 120 degrees F).

RATIONALE: Tap water burns comprise the leading cause of nonfatal burns (45, 46). Children under 5 years of age are the most frequent victims. Water heated to 130 degrees F takes only 30 seconds to burn the skin. If the water is heated to 120 degrees F, which is only 10 degrees F cooler, it takes 2 minutes to burn the skin (46). That extra 2 minutes could provide enough time to remove the child from the hot water source and avoid a burn.

One study suggested that most child care providers do not know the temperature of their hot water (45). Another study indicated that lowering the temperature of water heaters to 120 degrees F proved satisfactory to consumers (46).

Hot water for washing dishes is required to remove soil and sanitizing the dishes.

COMMENTS: A simple and inexpensive method to ensure that hot water temperatures do not exceed 120 degrees F is to adjust the thermostat setting on the hot water heater, checking the temperature of the water the hot water heater produces, using a thermometer at the point of water delivery. Lowering the temperature of the hot water heater that supplies handwashing sinks will not interfere with the performance of laundry washing machines (since these work well with cold water detergents). However, if a dishwasher is used, a minimum hot water supply temperature of 140 degrees F is usually required by the dishwasher manufacturer, even if the dishwasher has its own booster heater. When providers purchase a dishwasher, the manufacturer's requirements should be followed.

Anti-scald aerators designed to fit on the end of a modern bathroom and kitchen faucets, and anti-scald bathtub spouts, are also available at a reasonable cost. Only devices approved by the American National Standards Institute (ANSI) or the Canadian Standards

Association (CSA) should be considered. A number of other scald-prevention devices are available on the market. Consult a plumbing contractor for details. Contact information for the ANSI and the CSA is located in Appendix BB.

This standard ensures the availability of hot water to facilitate cleaning and sanitation. Hot water is needed to clean and sanitize food utensils adequately and sanitize laundry.

TYPE OF FACILITY: *Center; Large Family Child Care Home; Small Family Child Care Home*

STANDARD 5.041
HUMIDIFIERS AND DEHUMIDIFIERS

If humidifiers or dehumidifiers are used to maintain humidity, as specified in STANDARD 5.028, the facility shall follow the manufacturer's cleaning and maintenance instructions to avoid contamination by microorganisms and discharge of microorganisms and contaminants into the air.

RATIONALE: Humidifiers or dehumidifiers may be required to meet American National Standards Institute (ANSI) and Association of Home Appliance Manufacturers (AHAM) Humidifier Standards and must not introduce additional hazards. Contact information for ANSI and AHAM is located in Appendix BB.

COMMENTS: The benefits of humidifiers are uncertain. Improperly maintained humidifiers may become incubators of biological organisms and increase the risk of disease. Also, increased humidity enhances the survival of dust mites; and many children are allergic to dust mites.

TYPE OF FACILITY: *Center; Large Family Child Care Home; Small Family Child Care Home*

LIGHTING

STANDARD 5.042
LEVELS OF ILLUMINATION

Natural lighting shall be provided in rooms where children work and play for more than two hours at a time. Wherever possible, windows installed at child's eye level shall be provided to introduce natural lighting. All areas of the facility shall have glare-free natural and/or artificial lighting that provides adequate illumination and comfort for facility activities. The following guidelines shall be used for levels of illumination:
a) Reading, painting, and other close work areas: 50 to 100 foot-candles on the work surface;
b) Work and play areas: 30 to 50 foot-candles on the surface;
c) Stairs, walkways, landings, driveways, entrances: at least 20 foot-candles on the surface;
d) Sleeping, napping areas: no more than 5 foot-candles during sleeping or napping.

RATIONALE: These levels of illumination facilitate cleaning, reading, comfort, completion of projects, and safety (17). Too little light, too much glare and confusing shadows are commonly experienced lighting problems. Inadequate artificial lighting has been linked to eyestrain, to headache, and to non-specific symptoms of illness (5).

Natural lighting is the most desirable lighting of all. Windows installed at children's eye level not only provide a source of natural light, they also provide a variety of perceptual experiences of sight, sound, and smell which may serve as learning activities for children and a focus for conversation. The visual stimulation provided by a window is important to a young child's development (5, 6). Natural lighting provided by sky lights exposes children to variations in light during the day that is less perceptually stimulating than eye level windows, but is still preferable to artificial lighting.

A study on school performance shows that elementary school children seem to learn better in classrooms with substantial daylight and the opportunity for natural ventilation (76).

COMMENTS: In rooms that are used for many purposes, providing the ability to turn on and off different banks of lights in a room, or installation of light dimmers, will allow caregivers to adjust lighting levels that are appropriate to the activities that are occurring in the room.

Lighting levels should be reduced during nap times to promote resting or napping behavior in children. However, some degree of illumination must be allowed to ensure that staff can continue to observe children.

See also STANDARD 5.160 for exclusion of window cords long enough to encircle a child's neck and STANDARD 5.115, Additional Indoor Requirements for School-age Children.

For further information, contact the American National Standards Institute/Illuminating Engineers Society. Contact information is located in Appendix BB. Contact the lighting or home service department of the local electric utility company to have foot-candles measured.

TYPE OF FACILITY: *Center; Large Family Child Care Home; Small Family Child Care Home*

STANDARD 5.043
LIGHT FIXTURES INCLUDING
HALOGEN LAMPS

Light fixtures containing shielded or shatterproof bulbs shall be used in food preparation areas and all occupied areas. When portable halogen lamps are provided, they shall be installed securely to prevent them from tipping over, and a safety screen must be installed over the bulb.

RATIONALE: Use of shielded or shatterproof bulbs prevents injury to people and contamination of food. Halogen lamps burn at a temperature of approximately 1200 degrees F and are a potential burn or fire hazard. Halogen lighting provides a more energy-efficient alternative to illuminate a room. Halogen bulbs are incorporated into freestanding lamps. Many of the older-style lamps do not have a protective screen to prevent children from touching the hot bulb or

placing flammable materials on the bulb. Some portable lamps have a design that places the halogen bulb on the top of a tall pole. Although the base of these lamps is relatively heavy in weight, children can easily tip the lamps on their side and cause a potential fire hazard.

COMMENTS: Halogen lamps are also incorporated into light fixtures that are mounted permanently on the ceiling or walls. The fixtures are usually placed out of the reach of children and, if properly installed, should not pose a safety hazard.

TYPE OF FACILITY: *Center; Large Family Child Care Home; Small Family Child Care Home*

STANDARD 5.044
HIGH INTENSITY DISCHARGE
LAMPS, MULTI-VAPOR, AND
MERCURY LAMPS

High intensity discharge lamps, multi-vapor, and mercury lamps shall not be used for lighting the interior of buildings unless provided with special bulbs that self-extinguish if the outer glass envelope is broken.

RATIONALE: Multi-vapor and mercury lamps can be harmful when the outer bulb envelope is broken, causing serious skin burns and eye inflammation.

COMMENTS: High intensity lamps are not appropriate for internal illumination of child care facilities since the level of lighting generated is generally too strong for the size of a typical room and/or generates too much glare.

TYPE OF FACILITY: *Center; Large Family Child Care Home; Small Family Child Care Home*

STANDARD 5.045
EMERGENCY LIGHTING

Emergency lighting approved by the local authority shall be provided in corridors, stairwells, and at building exits. Open flames shall not be provided as emergency lighting in child care facilities.

RATIONALE: Provision of emergency lighting in corridors and stairwells enables safe passage to an emergency exit in the event of an electrical power outage. Open flames such as candles, flares, and lanterns are not safe.

COMMENTS: In many places, daylight hours end while child care is still in session, especially in the fall and winter seasons. If electric power outages are frequent, consideration should be given to providing emergency lighting in each room that is accessible to children. In child care homes, battery-powered household emergency lights that insert into electrical wall outlets (to remain charged) may be sufficient, depending on the location of the electrical outlets in corridors, stairwells and near building exits.

Although candles are sometimes recommended in emergency situations for portable lighting, a flashlight is the preferred type of portable emergency lighting in child care facilities. In some jurisdictions, fixed mounted emergency lighting may be required. Ask the local fire marshal for fire safety code requirements.

TYPE OF FACILITY: *Center; Large Family Child Care Home; Small Family Child Care Home*

NOISE

STANDARD 5.046
NOISE LEVELS

Measures shall be taken in all rooms or areas accommodating children to maintain the decibel (db) level at or below 35 to 40 db for at least 80% of the time as measured by an acoustical engineer or, more practically, by the ability to be clearly heard and understood in a normal conversation without raising one's voice. These measures include acoustical ceiling, carpeting, wall covering, partitions, or draperies, or a combination thereof.

RATIONALE: Excessive sound levels can be damaging to hearing, reduce effective communication, and reduce psychosocial well-being. The level of hearing loss commonly experienced by children with fluid in their middle ear space is 35 db. This level of hearing loss correlates with decreased understanding of language. By inference, this level of ambient noise may interfere with the ability of children to hear well enough to develop language normally.

For those with normal hearing, the stressful effects of noise will, at a minimum, add to, and at a maximum, precipitate other stress factors present in the facility. Exposure to excessive levels of noise may have adverse physiologic effects, such as increasing blood pressure. In addition, uncontrolled noise will continually force the caregiver to speak at levels above those normally used for conversation and may increase the risk of throat irritation. This may be a particularly serious consequence when the caregiver's exposure to infectious agents is considered at the same time.

While carpets can help reduce the level of noise, they can absorb moisture and serve as a place for microorganisms to grow. Consider using area rugs that can be taken up and washed often.

COMMENTS: Noise should be measured according to the *Code of Federal Regulations* (CFR), Title 16, Section 1500.47. To obtain this publication, contact the Superintendent of Documents of the U.S. Government Printing Office. Contact information is located in Appendix BB.

When there is new construction or renovation of a facility, consideration should be given to a design that will reduce noise from outside.

Sound control measures should follow the pertinent American Society for Testing and Materials (ASTM) standards for noise, acoustics, and the like, as indicated below:
- *E477-99 Standard Test Method for Measuring Acoustical and Air Flow Performance of Duct Liner Materials and Prefabricated Silencers*
- *E1042-92 Standard Classification of Acoustically Absorptive Materials Applied by Towel or Spray*
- *E1264-98 Standard Classification of Acoustical Ceiling Products*
- *E1124-97 Standard Test Method for Field Measurement of Sound Power Level by the Two-Surface Method*

•E1007-97 *Standard Test Method for Field Measurement of Tapping Machine Impact Sound Transmission in Floor-Ceiling Assemblies and Associated Structures*

•E1050-98 *Standard Test Method for Impedance and Absorption of Acoustical Materials using a Tube, Two Microphones, and a Digital Frequency Analysis System*

•C384-98 *Standard Test Method for Impedance and Absorption of Acoustical Materials by the Impedance Tube Method*

•E1130-90 *Standard Test Method for Objective Measurement of Speech Privacy in Open Offices using Articulation Index*

•E1014-84 *Standard Guide for Measurement of OutDoor A-Weighted Sound Levels*

•E1041-85 *Standard Test Method for Evaluating Masking Sound in Open Offices*

•E596-96 *Standard Test Method for Laboratory Measurement of Noise Reduction of Sound-Isolating Enclosures*

For further information, contact the American Society for Testing and Materials. Contact information is located in Appendix BB.

TYPE OF FACILITY: *Center; Large Family Child Care Home; Small Family Child Care Home*

ELECTRICAL FIXTURES AND OUTLETS

STANDARD 5.047
ELECTRICAL SERVICE

Facilities shall be supplied with electric service. Outlets and fixtures shall be installed and connected to the source of electric energy in a manner that meets the National Electrical Code, as amended by local electrical codes (if any), and as certified by an electrical code inspector.

RATIONALE: Proper installation of outlets and fixtures helps to prevent injury.

COMMENTS: State or local electrical codes may apply. For further information, see the National Fire Protection Association's (NFPA) *National Electrical Code* and the *NFPA-101 Life Safety Code* from the National Fire Protection Association. Contact information for the NFPA is located in Appendix BB.

TYPE OF FACILITY: *Center; Large Family Child Care Home; Small Family Child Care Home*

STANDARD 5.048
SAFETY COVERS AND SHOCK PROTECTION DEVICES FOR ELECTRICAL OUTLETS

All electrical outlets accessible to children who are not yet of school-age shall have safety covers that are attached to the electrical receptacle by a screw or other means to prevent easy removal by a child. Outlet covers that a child can remove by extraction of a plug from the socket shall not be used. Unless screw-mounted outlet covers are installed to semi-permanently prevent access to the outlet or outlets are of the child-resistant ground-fault circuit-interrupter (GFCI) type, safety covers shall be used that are spring-loaded or have a comparable means to automatically prohibit access to electricity when a plug is removed from the outlet. All newly installed electrical outlets accessible to children shall be protected by GFCI shock protection devices or safety receptacles that require simultaneous contact with both prongs of a plug to access the electricity.

RATIONALE: Preventing children from placing fingers or sticking objects into exposed electrical outlets will prevent electrical shock, electrical burns, and potential fires. Devastating oral injuries occur when young children insert a metal object into an outlet then try to use their teeth to extract the object. The combination of electricity and mouth moisture closes the circuit, leading to serious life-long injury. Young children can remove loose-fitting safety plugs and accidentally swallow them. Also, adults may fail to replace them after using the receptacle.

Currently available receptacle-type GFCIs cost less than $10 each. GFCI receptacles significantly reduce the likelihood of injury but still permit a slight shock.

New installations in areas accessible to children should be of the GFCI type. A slight shock may be fatal to a child with seizure disorder or heart problems, so even GFCI receptacles must be fitted with safety covers to prevent children from gaining access to the electricity.

COMMENTS: One type of outlet cover replaces the outlet face plate with a plate that has a spring-loaded outlet cover, which will stay in place when the receptacle is not in use. For receptacles where the facility does not intend to unplug the appliance, a more permanent cap-type cover that screws into the outlet receptacle is available. Several effective and inexpensive outlet safety devices are available in home hardware and baby stores.

TYPE OF FACILITY: *Center; Large Family Child Care Home; Small Family Child Care Home*

STANDARD 5.049
GROUND-FAULT CIRCUIT-INTERRUPTER FOR OUTLETS NEAR WATER

All electrical outlets located within 6 feet of a sink or other water source must have a ground-fault circuit-interrupter (GFCI), which shall be tested at least once every 3 months using the test button located on the device.

RATIONALE: This provision eliminates shock hazards. A slight shock may be fatal to a child with seizure disorder or heart problems.

COMMENTS: Electrical receptacles of the type often found in bathrooms of new homes have a GFCI built into the receptacle. The GFCI does not necessarily have to be near the sink. An electrical receptacle can be protected by a special type of circuit breaker (which has a built-in ground-fault circuit-interrupter) in the electrical panel. See STANDARD 5.048, for details on outlet covers that prevent even a slight shock from GFCI outlets.

TYPE OF FACILITY: *Center; Large Family Child Care Home; Small Family Child Care Home*

STANDARD 5.050
LOCATION OF ELECTRICAL DEVICES NEAR WATER

No electrical device or apparatus accessible to children shall be located so it could be plugged into an electrical outlet while a person is in contact with a water source, such as a sink, tub, shower area, or swimming/wading pool.

RATIONALE: Contact with a water source while using an electrical device provides a path for electricity through the person who is using the device. This can lead to electrical injury.

TYPE OF FACILITY: *Center; Large Family Child Care Home; Small Family Child Care Home*

STANDARD 5.051
EXTENSION CORDS

The use of extension cords shall be discouraged; however, when used, they shall bear the listing mark of a nationally recognized testing laboratory, such as UL, and shall not be placed through doorways, under carpeting, or across water-source areas. Electrical cords (extension and appliance) shall not be frayed or overloaded.

RATIONALE: Electrical malfunction is a major cause of ignition of fatal house fires (14). The U.S. Consumer Product Safety Commission reports that in 1996 extension cords and other electric cords were the ignition sources of fires that caused 90 deaths and burn injuries of 320 persons (14). Extension cords should not be accessible to children, whether in use or when temporarily not in use but plugged in. There is risk of electric shock to a child who may poke a metal object into the extension cord socket.

TYPE OF FACILITY: *Center; Large Family Child Care Home; Small Family Child Care Home*

STANDARD 5.052
ELECTRICAL CORDS

Electrical cords shall be placed beyond children's reach.

RATIONALE:. Injuries have occurred in child care when children pulled appliances such as tape players down on themselves by pulling on the cord. When children chew on an appliance cord, they can reach the wires and suffer severe disfiguring mouth injuries.

TYPE OF FACILITY: *Center; Large Family Child Care Home; Small Family Child Care Home*

FIRE WARNING SYSTEMS

STANDARD 5.053
SMOKE DETECTION SYSTEMS

In centers with new installations, a smoke detection system (such as hard-wired system detectors with control panel) shall be installed with placement of the smoke detectors in the following areas:
a)   Each story in front of doors to the stairway;
b)   Corridors of all floors;
c)   Lounges and recreation areas;
d)   Sleeping rooms.

In large and small family child care homes, smoke alarms that receive their operating power from the building electrical system shall be installed. Battery-operated smoke alarms shall be permitted provided that the facility demonstrates to the fire inspector that testing, maintenance, and battery replacement programs ensure reliability of power to the smoke alarms and that retrofitting the facility to connect the smoke alarms to the electrical system would be costly and difficult to achieve.

RATIONALE: Because of the large number of children at risk in a center, up-to-date smoke detection system technology is needed. In large and small family child care homes, single-station smoke alarms are acceptable. However, for all new building installations where access to enable necessary wiring is available, smoke alarms should be used that receive their power from the building's electrical system. The hard-wired smoke detectors should be interconnected so that occupants receive instantaneous alarms throughout the facility, not just in the room of origin. Batteries are not reliable enough; battery-operated smoke alarms should be accepted only where connecting smoke detectors to existing wiring would be too difficult and expensive as a retrofitted arrangement.

COMMENTS: Some state and local building codes specify the installation and maintenance of smoke detectors and fire alarm systems. For specific information, see the *NFPA-101 Life Safety Code* and the *NFPA 72 National Fire Alarm Code* from the National Fire Protection Association and from the Building Officials and Code Administrators International (BOCA). Contact information is located in Appendix BB.

TYPE OF FACILITY: *Center; Large Family Child Care Home; Small Family Child Care Home*

STANDARD 5.054
FIRE EXTINGUISHERS

Fire extinguisher(s) shall be installed and maintained. The fire extinguisher shall be of the A-B-C type. Size and number of fire extinguishers shall be determined after a survey by the fire marshal or by an insurance company fire loss prevention representative. Instructions for the use of the fire extinguisher shall be posted on or near the fire extinguisher.

RATIONALE: All fire extinguishers are labeled, using standard symbols, for the classes of fires on which they can be used. A red slash through any of the symbols tells you the extinguisher cannot be used on that class of fire. Class A designates ordinary combustibles such as wood, cloth, and paper. Class B designates flammable liquids such as gasoline, oil, and oil-based paint. Class C designates energized electrical equipment, including wiring, fuse boxes, circuit breakers, machinery and appliances

COMMENTS: Staff should be trained that the first priority is to remove the children from the facility safely and quickly. Fighting a fire is secondary to the safe exit of the children and staff.

TYPE OF FACILITY: *Center; Large Family Child Care Home; Small Family Child Care Home*

PLUMBING AND SANITARY FACILITIES

CLEAN WATER AND PLUMBING

STANDARD 5.055
WATER SUPPLY

Every facility shall be supplied with piped running water under pressure, from a source approved by the Environmental Protection Agency (EPA) and/ or the regulatory health authority, to provide an adequate water supply to every fixture connected to the water supply and drainage system. The water shall be sufficient in quantity and pressure to supply water for cooking, cleaning, drinking, toilets, and outside uses.

When water is supplied by a well or other private source, it shall meet all applicable federal, state, and local public health standards and shall be approved by the regulatory health authority. Any facility not served by a public water supply shall keep on file documentation of approval of the water supply.

RATIONALE: This standard ensures a water supply that is safe and does not spread disease or filth or contain dangerous substances. (18).

COMMENTS: For more information on water supply standards, contact the local health authority or the EPA. Contact information is located in Appendix BB.

TYPE OF FACILITY: *Center; Large Family Child Care Home; Small Family Child Care Home*

STANDARD 5.056
WATER HANDLING AND TREATMENT EQUIPMENT

Newly installed water handling and treatment equipment shall meet applicable National Sanitation Foundation (NSF) standards and shall be inspected and approved by the local public health department or its designee.

RATIONALE: Adherence to NSF standards will help ensure a safe water supply. State and local codes vary, but they generally protect against toxins or sewage entering the water supply.

COMMENTS: Model codes are available from the NSF. Contact information for the NSF is located in Appendix BB.

TYPE OF FACILITY: *Center; Large Family Child Care Home; Small Family Child Care Home*

STANDARD 5.057
CROSS-CONNECTIONS

The facility shall have no cross-connections that could permit contamination of the potable water supply:
a) Backflow preventers, vacuum breakers, or strategic air gaps shall be provided for all boiler units in which chemicals are used. Backflow preventers shall be tested annually;
b) Vacuum breakers shall be installed on all threaded janitorial sink faucets and outdoor/indoor hose bibs;
c) Nonsubmersible, antisiphon ballcocks shall be provided on all flush tank-type toilets.

RATIONALE: Pressure differentials may allow contamination of drinking water if cross-connections or submerged inlets exist. Water must be protected from cross connections with possible sources of contamination.

COMMENTS: Short hoses are often attached to the faucets of janitorial sinks (and laundry sinks) and often extend below the top edge of the basin. The ends of a hose in a janitorial sink and a garden hose attached to an outside hose bibs are often found in a pool of

potentially contaminated water. If the water faucet is not completely closed, a loss of pressure in the water system could result in the contaminated water being drawn up the hose like dirt is drawn into a vacuum cleaner; thus contaminating the drinking water supply.

Vacuum breakers may be installed as part of the plumbing fixture or are available to attach to the end of a faucet of hose bib.

TYPE OF FACILITY: *Center; Large Family Child Care Home; Small Family Child Care Home*

STANDARD 5.058
INSTALLATION OF PIPES AND PLUMBING FIXTURES

Each gas pipe, water pipe, gas-burning fixture, plumbing fixture and apparatus, or any other similar fixture and all connections to water, sewer, or gas lines shall be installed and free from defects, leaks, and obstructions in accordance with the requirements of the state or local regulatory agency for buildings.

RATIONALE: This standard prevents accidents and hazardous and unsanitary conditions.

TYPE OF FACILITY: *Center; Large Family Child Care Home; Small Family Child Care Home*

WATER TESTING

STANDARD 5.059
TESTING OF DRINKING WATER

Drinking water shall be tested by the regulatory health authority no less than once a year for bacteriological quality and no less than once every 3 years for chemical quality. Testing shall be in compliance with procedures established by the National Sanitation Foundation (NSF), or equivalent.

RATIONALE: This standard prevents the use of unsafe water supplies, whether well water or

community-supplied water, the quality of which can vary from time to time.

COMMENTS: Tests could include analyses for radon and gross alpha radiation. The need for these tests is still being researched, but it is recommended that they be done. If well water is used, water should also be tested for nitrates. For infants under 4 months, excessive exposure to nitrates is associated with the development of potentially fatal methemoglobinemia. For more information on water testing, contact the NSF. Contact information for the NSF is located in Appendix BB.

TYPE OF FACILITY: *Center*

STANDARD 5.060
HANDWASHING SINK USING PORTABLE WATER SUPPLY

When plumbing is unavailable to provide a handwashing sink, the facility shall provide a handwashing sink using a portable water supply and a sanitary catch system approved by a local public health department. A mechanism shall be in place to prevent children from gaining access to soiled water or more than one child from washing in the same water.

RATIONALE: No barrier (gloves) or chemical substitute (sanitizer solutions) is as effective as running water. The point of handwashing is defeated if children can gain access to the soiled water. Hand sanitizers do not substitute for handwashing.

COMMENTS: Some suppliers of portable toilets provide a variety of portable sinks. All require filling a container with a source of potable water that flows by gravity or by pumping action during use. All require emptying the catch container into a sanitary system. A large water container with a faucet can be combined with a catch container that is covered with a firmly attached grill to prevent children from getting into the contaminated water. Children must not wash in a communal basin because those who wash in the same water share contamination. Also, see *Healthy Young Children* available from the National Association for the Education of Young Children (NAEYC) for a

diagram of an alternative to running water using a portable (bubbler) tank that has a sink tap and a cabinet. Contact information for the NAEYC is located in Appendix BB.

For additional information on handwashing, see STANDARD 3.020 through STANDARD 5.126. See also Sinks, STANDARD 5.126 through STANDARD 5.128. For information on water temperature, see STANDARD 5.040.

TYPE OF FACILITY: *Center; Large Family Child Care Home; Small Family Child Care Home*

STANDARD 5.061
TESTING FOR LEAD LEVELS IN DRINKING WATER

In both private and public drinking water supplies where interior or service piping or joint seals contain lead or other toxic materials, water shall be evaluated at the beginning of operation and at least every 2 years by the regulatory health authority to determine whether lead levels are safe. The samples shall consist of the first draw of water in the facility after at least a 6-hour lapse in use.

RATIONALE: Drinking water must be safe for consumption. Exposure to toxic levels of lead can cause neurological, behavioral, and developmental problems.

COMMENTS: Running the tap water for 30 to 60 seconds before using it for drinking and cooking will reduce the presence of lead in drinking water supplies where piping or joint seals contain lead.

TYPE OF FACILITY: *Center; Large Family Child Care Home; Small Family Child Care Home*

STANDARD 5.062
WATER TEST RESULTS

All water test results shall be in written form and kept with other required reports and documents in one central location in the facility, ready for immediate viewing by regulatory personnel, or copies submitted as required by the local authority that regulates safe water.

RATIONALE: Licensing staff should be easily able to determine compliance with regulatory requirements. Some regulatory authorities prefer to review copies of water test results available for inspection on site; others that do not provide on-site inspections may prefer to have the reports submitted to them.

COMMENTS: See also Posting Documents, STANDARD 8.077.

TYPE OF FACILITY: *Center; Large Family Child Care Home; Small Family Child Care Home*

STANDARD 5.063
EMERGENCY SAFE DRINKING WATER AND BOTTLED WATER

Emergency safe drinking water shall be supplied during interruption of the regular approved water supply. Bottled water shall be certified as chemically and bacteriologically potable by the health department or its designee.

RATIONALE: Children must have constant access to fresh, potable water if the regular approved supply of drinking water is temporarily interrupted.

TYPE OF FACILITY: *Center; Large Family Child Care Home; Small Family Child Care Home*

SEWAGE, GARBAGE AND PEST CONTROL

STANDARD 5.064
SEWAGE FACILITIES

Sewage facilities shall be provided and inspected in accordance with state and local regulations. Whenever a public sewer is available, the facility shall be connected to it. Where public sewers are not available, a septic tank system or other method approved by the local public health department shall be installed. Raw or treated

wastes shall not be discharged on the surface of the ground.

The wastewater or septic system drainage field shall not be located within the outdoor play area of a child care center licensed for 13 or more children, unless the drainage field has been designed by a sanitation engineer with the presence of an outdoor play area in mind and meets the approval of the local health authority.

The exhaust vent from a wastewater or septic system and drainage field shall not be located within the children's outdoor play area.

RATIONALE: Sewage must not be allowed to contaminate drinking water or ground water. It must be carried from the facility to a place where sanitary treatment equipment is available. Raw sewage is a health hazard and usually has an offensive odor.

The weight of children or the combined weight of children and playground equipment may cause the drainage field to become compacted, resulting in failure of the system. Some structures are anchored in concrete, which adds weight. The legs of some equipment, such as swing sets, can puncture the surface of drainage fields. In areas where frequent rains are coupled with high water tables, poor drainage, and flooding, the surface of drainage fields often becomes contaminated with untreated sewage.

COMMENTS: Whether the presence of an outdoor play area would adversely affect the operation of a wastewater or septic system will depend on the type of playground equipment and method of anchoring, the type of resilient surface placed beneath playground equipment to reduce injury from falls, the soil type where the field would be placed (some soils are more compactable than others), the type of ground cover present (a cover of good grass underlain by a good sandy layer is much better than packed clay or some impermeable or slowly impermeable surface layer), and the design of the drainage field itself.

Consult with your local public health department. The national/international organization representing on-site wastewater/sewage interests is the National On-Site Wastewater Recycling Association, Inc.

(NOWRA). Contact information is located in Appendix BB.

TYPE OF FACILITY: *Center; Large Family Child Care Home; Small Family Child Care Home*

STANDARD 5.065
REMOVAL OF GARBAGE

Garbage and rubbish shall be removed from rooms occupied by children, staff, parents, or volunteers on a daily basis and removed from the premises at least twice weekly or at other frequencies approved by the regulatory health authority.

RATIONALE: This practice provides proper sanitation and protection of health, prevents infestations by rodents, insects, and other pests, and prevents odors and injuries.

COMMENTS: Compliance can be tested by checking for evidence of infestation and odors.

TYPE OF FACILITY: *Center; Large Family Child Care Home; Small Family Child Care Home*

STANDARD 5.066
CONTAINMENT OF GARBAGE

Garbage shall be kept in containers approved by the regulatory health authority. Such containers shall be constructed of durable metal or other types of material, designed and used so wild and domesticated animals and pests do not have access to the contents, and so they do not leak or absorb liquids. Waste containers shall be kept covered with tight-fitting lids or covers when stored.

The facility shall have a sufficient number of waste and diaper containers to hold all of the garbage and diapers that accumulate between periods of removal from the premises. Plastic garbage bag liners shall be used in such containers. Exterior garbage containers shall be stored on an easily cleanable surface.

Garbage areas shall be free of litter and waste that is not contained. Children shall not be allowed access to garbage, waste, and refuse storage areas.

If a compactor is used, the surface shall be graded to a suitable drain, as approved by the regulatory health authority.

RATIONALE: Containers for garbage attract animals and insects. When trash contains organic material, decomposition creates unpleasant odors. Therefore, child care facilities must choose and use garbage containers that control sanitation risks, pests, and offensive odors. Lining the containers with plastic bags reduces the contamination of the container itself and the need to wash the containers which hold a concomitant risk of spreading the contamination into the environment.

TYPE OF FACILITY: *Center; Large Family Child Care Home; Small Family Child Care Home*

STANDARD 5.067
CONTAINMENT OF SOILED DIAPERS

Soiled diapers shall be stored inside the facility in containers separate from other waste. Washable, plastic-lined, tightly covered receptacles, with a firmly fitting cover that does not require touching with contaminated hands or objects, shall be provided, within arm's reach of diaper changing tables, to store soiled diapers. The container for soiled diapers shall be designed to prevent the user from contaminating any exterior surfaces of the container or the user when inserting the soiled diaper. Soiled diapers do not have to be individually bagged before placing them in the container for soiled diapers. Soiled cloth diapers and soiled clothing that are to be sent home with a parent, however, shall be individually bagged.

The following types of diaper containers shall not be used;
a) Those that require the user's hand to push the diaper through a narrow opening;
b) Those with exterior surfaces that must be touched with the hand;

c) Those with exterior surfaces that are likely to be touched with the soiled diaper while the user is discarding the soiled diaper;
d) Those that have lids with handles.

Separate containers shall be used for disposable diapers, cloth diapers (if used), and soiled clothes and linens. All containers shall be inaccessible to children and shall be tall enough to prevent children reaching into the receptacle or from falling headfirst into containers. The containers shall be placed in an area that children cannot enter without close adult supervision.

RATIONALE: Separate, plastic-lined waste receptacles that do not require touching with contaminated hands or objects and that children cannot access, enclose odors within, and prevent children from coming into contact with body fluids. Anything that increases handling increases potential for contamination. Step cans or other hands-free cans with tightly fitted lids provide protection against odor and hand contamination.

Containers for soiled diapers should be of a type that prevents contamination of the exterior surfaces of the receptacle by touching during the diapering procedure.

Separate bagging of each diaper increases the handling and therefore increases the risk of contamination.

COMMENTS: Fecal material and urine should not be mixed with regular trash and garbage. Where possible, soiled disposable diapers should be disposed of as biological waste rather than in the local landfill. In some areas, recycling depots for disposable diapers may be available. The facility should not use the short, poorly made domestic step cans that require caregivers to use their hands to open the lids because the foot pedals don't work. Child care providers will find it worthwhile to invest in commercial-grade step cans of sufficient size to hold the number of soiled diapers the facility collects before someone can remove the contents to an outside trash receptacle. These are the types used by doctor's offices, hospitals, and restaurants. A variety of sizes and types are available from restaurant and medical wholesale suppliers. Other types of hands-free containers can be used as long as the user can place the soiled diaper into the

receptacle without increasing contact of the user's hands and the exterior of the container with the soiled diaper.

For additional information on waste that involves body fluids, diaper storage, and disposal, see STANDARD 3.026.

TYPE OF FACILITY: *Center; Large Family Child Care Home; Small Family Child Care Home*

STANDARD 5.068
LABELING, CLEANING AND DISPOSAL OF WASTE AND DIAPER CONTAINERS

Each waste and diaper container shall be labeled to show its intended contents. These containers shall be cleaned daily to keep them free from build-up of soil and odor. Wastewater from these cleaning operations shall be disposed of by pouring it down a toilet or floor drain. Wastewater shall not be poured onto the ground, into handwashing sinks, laundry sinks, kitchen sinks, or bathtubs.

RATIONALE: This standard prevents noxious odors and spread of disease.

TYPE OF FACILITY: *Center; Large Family Child Care Home; Small Family Child Care Home*

STANDARD 5.069
STORAGE AND DISPOSAL OF INFECTIOUS AND TOXIC WASTES

Infectious and toxic wastes shall be stored separately from other wastes, and shall be disposed of in a manner approved by the regulatory health authority.

RATIONALE: This practice provides for safe storage and disposal of infectious and toxic wastes.

TYPE OF FACILITY: *Center; Large Family Child Care Home; Small Family Child Care Home*

STANDARD 5.070
CONTROL OF ANIMAL WASTE AND PESTS

Areas where children play shall be kept free of animal wastes, insects, infestation by rodents and other pests, and shall not provide shelter to pests.

Whenever the regulatory agency determines that the presence of pests in the area constitutes a health hazard, the facility shall take the necessary actions to exclude, exterminate, or otherwise control such pests on its premises.

All extensive extermination shall be provided by a licensed or certified pest control operator, and only after integrated pest management methods have been exhausted.

RATIONALE: This standard reduces potential health hazards to children caused by the presence of pests. Before considering extensive extermination, other non-chemical pest management methods must be implemented. This will reduce unnecessary exposure of children to chemical pesticides.

Uncovered sand is an invitation for a cat or other animal to defecate or urinate and, therefore, is a source for disease transmission (19). This standard also helps ensure pest control. Refer to STANDARD 5.070 through STANDARD 5.073, and STANDARD 5.202, for control of insects.

COMMENTS: The rationale for this standard is one of several reasons why using sand as an impact-absorbing surface in playgrounds is not a good idea. It is almost impossible to cover such a surface. For additional information on sandboxes, see STANDARD 5.180. For additional information on pest control, see also Openings, on STANDARD 5.013 through STANDARD 5.019; and Insect Breeding Hazards, STANDARD 5.202.

TYPE OF FACILITY: *Center; Large Family Child Care Home; Small Family Child Care Home*

STANDARD 5.071
PROTECTION OF OPENINGS FROM RODENT ENTRY

Each foundation, floor, wall, ceiling, roof, window, exterior door, and basement and cellar hatchway shall be free from openings that would allow rodents to enter. Basement or cellar windows used, or intended to be used, for ventilation, and all other openings to a basement or cellar, shall not permit the entry of rodents.

RATIONALE: This standard prevents access to the interior of the facility by rodents. Rodents can carry disease to humans.

COMMENTS: Heavy-duty steel mesh screen (such as ¼-inch hardware cloth or similar, equally effective protective device) can be used to protect these entry points from access by rodents.

TYPE OF FACILITY: *Center; Large Family Child Care Home; Small Family Child Care Home*

STANDARD 5.072
PROTECTION OF OPENINGS FROM FLIES AND INSECTS

Openings to the outside shall be protected against the entrance of flies and other flying insects by:
a) Outward-opening, self-closing doors;
b) Closed windows;
c) Screening;
d) Air curtains;
e) Other effective and approved means.

RATIONALE: Minimizing the potential for flies and other flying insects from entering the child care environment will help prevent disease transmission, insect bites, and insect stings. House flies breed in excrement, garbage and other waste and have been implicated as mechanical vectors in the spread of disease. Some children can develop severe allergic reactions to insect bites and stings.

TYPE OF FACILITY: *Center; Large Family Child Care Home; Small Family Child Care Home*

STANDARD 5.073
TYPE AND USE OF PESTICIDES AND HERBICIDES

If pesticides are used, natural pesticides that are non-toxic to humans shall be given first consideration.

If chemical pesticides are used, they shall be only those that are registered with the Environmental Protection Agency (EPA), of a type applied by a licensed exterminator, in a manner approved by the EPA. The facility shall have and consult a Material Safety Data Sheet (MSDS) for all toxic chemicals used, and shall be in compliance with the directions provided. General right-of-way pesticides or herbicides, sprayed in the community by others, shall be prohibited on the grounds of a child care facility.

Pesticides shall be stored in their original containers and in a locked room or cabinet accessible only to authorized staff. No restricted-use pesticides shall be stored or used on the premises except by properly licensed persons. Banned pesticides shall not be used.

Pesticides shall be applied in a manner that prevents skin contact and other exposure to children or staff members and minimizes odors in occupied areas.

Notification shall be given to parents and staff before using pesticides, to determine if any child or staff member is sensitive to the product. A member of the child care staff shall directly observe the application to be sure that toxic chemicals applied on surfaces do not constitute a hazard to the children or staff. Pesticides shall be used in strict compliance with the instructions on the label or as otherwise directed or approved by the regulatory authority. No pesticide shall be applied while children are present.

Following the use of pesticides, herbicides, fungicides, or other potentially toxic chemicals, the treated area shall be ventilated for the period recommended on the product label or by a nationally certified regional poison control center before being reoccupied. Tests, recommended by a nationally certified regional poison control center, shall be taken to determine safe levels before reentering the facility.

RATIONALE: Children must be protected from exposure to poisons. To prevent contamination and poisoning, child care staff must be sure that these chemicals are applied by individuals who are certified to do so. Direct observation of pesticide application by child care staff is essential to guide the exterminator away from surfaces that children can touch or mouth and to monitor for drifting of pesticides into these areas. The time of toxic risk exposure is a function of skin contact, the efficiency of the ventilating system, and the volatility of the toxic substance. The long-term effects of toxic substances are unknown. Spraying the grounds of a child care facility exposes children to toxic chemicals.

COMMENTS: Manufacturers of pesticides usually provide product warnings that exposure to these chemicals can be poisonous. Material safety data sheets should be available from a licensed exterminator or the product manufacturer.

Child care staff should ask to see the license of the exterminator and should be certain that the individual who applies the toxic chemicals has personally been trained and preferably, individually licensed. In some states only the owner of an extermination company is required to have this training, and he/she may then employ unskilled workers. Child care staff should ensure that the exterminator is familiar with the pesticide he/she is applying.

Child care operators should contact their state pesticide office and request that their child care facility be added to the state pesticide sensitivity list. When a child care facility is placed on the state pesticide sensitivity list, the child care operator will be notified if there are plans for general pesticide application occurring near the child care facility.

Child care staff and children who have developed sensitivity to pesticides can ask their physician to place them on a state pesticide sensitivity list. The state pesticide sensitivity list is made available to exterminators so that they are aware of people working or being cared for in a geographical area who have sensitivity to pesticides.

For further information about pest control, contact the local health authority or the EPA. Contact information is located in Appendix BB.

TYPE OF FACILITY: *Center; Large Family Child Care Home; Small Family Child Care Home*

STANDARD 5.074
TESTING FOR UNSAFE LEVELS OF TOXIC CHEMICALS

If the facility has been treated with a termiticide or any restricted or prohibited-use pesticide in the last 10 years, ambient measurements shall be taken and tested by an organization certified to make such tests according to Environmental Protection Agency (EPA) instructions to ensure that toxic chemicals are not present in unsafe levels. If the testing finds unsafe levels, children shall not be allowed to use these areas until effective corrective measures have been taken to achieve safe levels.

RATIONALE: Many restricted or banned pesticides have residues that persist for many years. These residues can lead to toxic exposure of children.

COMMENTS: Names of certified organizations that perform such tests can be obtained by contacting the regional office of the EPA. Contact information for the EPA is located in Appendix BB.

TYPE OF FACILITY: *Center; Large Family Child Care Home; Small Family Child Care Home*

GENERAL FURNISHINGS AND EQUIPMENT REQUIREMENTS

STANDARD 5.075
SAFETY OF EQUIPMENT, MATERIALS AND FURNISHINGS

Equipment, materials, furnishings, and play areas shall be sturdy, safe, and in good repair and shall meet the recommendations of the U.S. Consumer

Product Safety Commission (CPSC) for control of the following safety hazards:

a) Openings that could entrap a child's head or limbs;
b) Elevated surfaces that are inadequately guarded;
c) Lack of specified surfacing and fall zones under and around climbable equipment;
d) Mismatched size and design of equipment for the intended users;
e) Insufficient spacing between equipment;
f) Tripping hazards;
g) Components that can pinch, sheer, or crush body tissues;
h) Equipment that is known to be of a hazardous type (such as large animal swings);
i) Sharp points or corners;
j) Splinters;
k) Protruding nails, bolts, or other components that could entangle clothing or snag skin;
l) Loose, rusty parts;
m) Hazardous small parts that may become detached during normal use or reasonably foreseeable abuse of the equipment and that present a choking, aspiration, or ingestion hazard to a child;
n) Flaking paint;
o) Paint that contains lead or other hazardous materials.

RATIONALE: The hazards listed in this standard are those found by the U.S. Consumer Product Safety Commission (CPSC) to be most commonly associated with injury.

COMMENTS: Equipment and furnishings that are not sturdy, safe, or in good repair, may cause falls, entrap a child's head or limbs, or contribute to other injuries. Disrepair may expose objects that are hazardous to children. Freedom from sharp points, corners, or edges shall be judged according to the *Code of Federal Regulations, Title 16, Section 1500.48*, and *Section 1500.49*. Freedom from small parts should be judged according to the *Code of Federal Regulations, Title 16, Part 1501*. To obtain these publications, contact the Superintendent of Documents of the U.S. Government Printing Office. For assistance in interpreting the federal regulations, contact the U. S. Consumer Product Safety Commission (CPSC); the CPSC also has regional offices. Contact information for the

Superintendent of Documents and the CPSC is located in Appendix BB.

This standard is particularly important when equipment and furnishings are old and worn. Used equipment and furnishings should be closely inspected to determine whether they meet this standard before allowing them to be placed in a child care facility. If equipment and furnishings have deteriorated to a state of disrepair, where they are no longer sturdy or safe, they should be removed from all areas of a child care facility to which children have access.

TYPE OF FACILITY: *Center; Large Family Child Care Home; Small Family Child Care Home*

STANDARD 5.076
SIZE OF FURNITURE

Furniture shall be durable and child-sized or adapted for children's use. Tables shall be at waist height of the intended child-user and the child's feet shall be able to reach a firm surface while the child is seated.

RATIONALE: Children cannot safely or comfortably use furnishings that are not sized for their use. When children eat or work at tables that are above the waist, they must reach up to get their food or do their work instead of bringing the food from a lower level to their mouth and having a comfortable arrangement when working to develop their fine-motor skills. When eating, this leads to scooping food into the mouth instead of eating more appropriately. When working, this leads to difficulty succeeding with hand-eye coordination. When children do not have a firm surface on which to rest their feet, they cannot reposition themselves easily if they slip down. This can lead to poor posture and increased risk of choking.

TYPE OF FACILITY: *Center; Large Family Child Care Home; Small Family Child Care Home*

STANDARD 5.077
SURFACES OF EQUIPMENT, FURNITURE, TOYS AND PLAY MATERIALS

Equipment, furnishings, toys, and play materials shall have smooth, nonporous surfaces or washable fabric surfaces that are easy to clean and sanitize, or be disposable.

RATIONALE: Few young children practice good hygiene. Messy play is developmentally appropriate in all age groups, and especially among very young children, the same group that is most susceptible to infectious disease. These factors lead to soiling and contamination of equipment, furnishings, toys, and play materials. To avoid transmission of disease within the group, these materials must be easy to clean and sanitize.

COMMENTS: Toys that can be washed in a mechanical dishwasher that meets the standard for cleaning and sanitizing dishes can save labor, if the facility has a dishwasher. Otherwise, after the children have used them, these toys can be placed in a tub of soapy water to soak until the staff has time to scrub, rinse, and sanitize the surfaces of these items. Except for fabric surfaces, nonporous surfaces are best because porous surfaces can trap organic material and soil. Fabric surfaces that can be laundered provide the softness required in a developmentally appropriate environment for young children. If these fabrics are laundered when soiled, the facility can achieve cleanliness and sanitation. When a material cannot be recycled for safe and sanitary use, it should be discarded.

TYPE OF FACILITY: *Center; Large Family Child Care*

STANDARD 5.078
PLACEMENT OF EQUIPMENT AND FURNISHINGS

Equipment and furnishings shall be placed to help prevent collisions and injuries while meeting the objectives of the curriculum and permitting freedom of movement by the children.

RATIONALE: The placement of furnishings plays a significant role in the way space is used. If the staff places furnishings in such a way that they create large runways, children will run in this area. If the staff places furnishings that children can climb in locations where climbing is unsafe, this adds risk to the environment. Placement of furnishings should address the needs of the children for stimulation and development and at the same time help to prevent collisions and injury.

COMMENTS: To prevent children from falling out of windows, the safest place for chairs and other furniture is away from windows. Chairs and other furnishings that children can easily climb should be kept away from cabinets and shelves to discourage children from climbing to a dangerous height or reaching for something hazardous. See STANDARD 5.014 for safety precautions for windows.

TYPE OF FACILITY: *Center; Large Family Child Care Home; Small Family Child Care Home*

STANDARD 5.079
FLOORS, WALLS, AND CEILINGS

Floors, walls, and ceilings shall be in good repair, and easy to clean when soiled. Only smooth, non porous surfaces shall be permitted in areas that are likely to be contaminated by body fluids or in areas used for activities involving food.

Floors shall be free from cracks, bare concrete, dampness, splinters, sliding rugs, and uncovered telephone jacks or electrical outlets.

Carpeting shall be clean, in good repair, nonflammable, and nontoxic.

RATIONALE: Messy play and activities that lead to soiling of floors and walls is developmentally appropriate in all age groups, but especially among very young children, the same group that is most susceptible to infectious disease. These factors lead to soiling and contamination of floors and walls. A smooth, non porous surface is easier to clean and sanitize and therefore, helps prevent the spread of communicable diseases. To avoid transmission of disease within the

group, and to maintain an environment that supports learning cleanliness as a value, all surfaces should be kept clean.

Cracked or porous floors cannot be kept clean and sanitary. Dampness promotes the growth of mold. Sliding rugs and uncovered telephone jacks or electrical outlets in floors are tripping hazards. Damaged floors, walls or ceilings can expose underlying hazardous structural elements and materials. Surface materials must not pose health, safety, or fire hazards.

COMMENTS: Carpeted floors are not smooth, and therefore, carpeting is not consistent with this standard, except for area carpets for activities that do not involve food or contact with body fluids. Many family child care homes and indoor playrooms of centers use wall-to-wall carpeting on the floor. Although carpeted floors may be more comfortable to walk and play on, smooth floor surfaces provide a better environment for children with allergies.

Washable rugs can be placed on smooth floor surfaces. By using friction backings or underlayment, removable and washable carpeting can be used on smooth floor surfaces safely.

When facilities use carpeting or sound-absorbing materials on walls and ceilings, these materials must not be used in areas where contamination with body fluids or food is likely, because they are difficult to clean. Thus, carpeted walls should not be present around the diaper change areas, in toilet rooms, in food preparation areas, or where food is served.

Also, facilities should exercise caution when using carpeting in child care areas because the fibers, adhesive, and formaldehyde associated with the presence of carpeting can pose health problems.

Obtain *ASTM D2859-96 Standard Test Method for Flammability of Finished Textile Floor Covering Materials,* for flammability of finished materials from American Society for Testing and Materials (ASTM). Contact information for the ASTM is located in Appendix BB. Ask the local fire marshal for fire safety code requirements.

TYPE OF FACILITY: *Center; Large Family Child Care Home; Small Family Child Care Home*

STANDARD 5.080
FACILITY ARRANGEMENTS TO MINIMIZE BACK INJURIES

The child care setting shall be organized to reduce the risk of back injuries for adults provided that such measures do not pose hazards for children or affect the implementation of developmentally appropriate practice. Furnishings and equipment shall enable caregivers to hold and comfort children and enable their activities while minimizing the need for bending and for lifting and carrying heavy children and objects. Caregivers shall not routinely be required to use child-sized chairs, tables, or desks.

RATIONALE: Back strain can arise from adult use of child-sized furniture. Analysis of worker compensation claims shows that employees in the service industries, including child care, have an injury rate as great as or greater than that of workers employed in factories. Back injuries are the leading type of injury (20). Appropriate design of work activities and training of workers can prevent most back injuries. The principles to support these recommendations (see Comments) are standard principles of ergonomics, in which jobs and workplaces are designed to eliminate biomechanical hazards.

In a statewide (Wisconsin) survey of health status, behaviors and concerns, 446 randomly selected early childhood professionals, directors, center teachers, and family providers, reported dramatic changes in frequency of backache and fatigue symptoms since working in child care (21).

COMMENTS: Some approaches to reduce risk are:
a) Adult-height changing tables;
b) Small, stable stepladders, stairs, and similar equipment to enable children to climb to the changing table or other places to which they would otherwise be lifted, without creating a fall hazard;
c) Convenient equipment for moving children, reducing the necessity of carrying them;

d) Adult furniture that eliminates awkward sitting or working positions in all areas where adults work.

This standard is not intended to interfere with child adult interactions or to create hazards for children. Modifications can be made in the environment to minimize hazards and injuries for both children and adults. Adult furniture has to be available at least for break times, staff meetings, etc.

See also Staff Health, STANDARD 1.045 through STANDARD 1.049.

TYPE OF FACILITY: *Center; Large Family Child Care Home; Small Family Child Care Home*

STANDARD 5.081
HIGH CHAIR REQUIREMENTS

High chairs, if used, shall have a wide base and if equipped with a tray, shall have a passive means to prevent a child from slipping down and becoming entrapped between the tray and seat. High chairs shall also be equipped with a safety strap to prevent a child from climbing out of the chair. High chairs shall be labeled or warranted by the manufacturer in documents provided at the time of purchase or verified thereafter by the manufacturer as meeting the American Society for Testing Materials (ASTM) *Standard F404-99a Consumer Safety Specification for High Chairs.*

RATIONALE: This standard is to help prevent falls. *ASTM Standard F404-99a Consumer Safety Specifications for High Chairs* covers:
- Sharp edges
- Locking devices
- Drop tests of the tray
- Disengagement of the tray
- Load and stability of the chair
- Protection from coil springs and scissoring
- Maximum size of holes
- Restraining system tests
- Labeling
- Instructional literature

COMMENTS: The Juvenile Products Manufacturers Association (JPMA) has a testing and certification pro-gram for highchairs, play yards, carriages, strollers, walkers, gates, and expandable enclosures. When purchasing such equipment, consumers can look for labeling that certifies that these products meet the standards. Contact information for the ASTM and JPMA is located in Appendix BB.

TYPE OF FACILITY: *Center; Large Family Child Care Home; Small Family Child Care Home*

STANDARD 5.082
CARRIAGE, STROLLER, GATE, ENCLOSURE, AND PLAY YARD REQUIREMENTS

Each carriage, stroller, gate, enclosure, and play yard used shall meet the corresponding American Society for Testing and Materials (ASTM) standard and shall be so labeled on the equipment.
- Carriages/strollers: *ASTM F833-00 Standard Consumer Safety Performance Specification for Carriages and Strollers*
- Gates/enclosures: *ASTM F1004-00 Consumer Safety Specification for Expansion Gates and Expandable Enclosures*
- Play yards: *ASTM F406-99 Consumer Safety Specification for Play Yards*

RATIONALE: The presence of a certification seal placed on Juvenile Products Manufacturers Association (JPMA) products ensures that the product is in compliance with the requirements of the current safety standard for that product at the time of manufacture. ASTM standards are, by congressional act, accepted as federal safety standards.

COMMENTS: For more information, contact the JPMA or the ASTM. Contact information is located in Appendix BB.

TYPE OF FACILITY: *Center; Large Family Child Care Home; Small Family Child Care Home*

STANDARD 5.083
BABY WALKERS

Baby walkers that the child can move across the floor shall not be used in any type of child care facility.

RATIONALE: The environment of a child staying at child care facility is different than that of a child living in his/her own home. In general, more children are present and caregivers cannot provide one-to-one supervision to a child using a baby walker. Baby walkers are dangerous toys because they move children around too fast and to hazardous areas, such as stairs. The upright position also brings children close to objects that they can pull down onto themselves. Many injuries, some fatal, have been associated with baby walkers.

Parents and caregivers report that children who are not yet able to pull or hold themselves upright seem to enjoy using walkers. Nevertheless, there is no evidence that baby walkers are beneficial to children. A study of twins found that the twin not using the walker walked slightly earlier than the sibling using the walker (22). Baby walkers used with high-risk infants and young children with cerebral palsy promoted undesirable reflexes and did not enable the child to develop normally (22).

Recent evidence indicates that stationary devices may also pose a problem by delaying motor development. In one small study, children who used walkers sat, crawled, and walked later than those who did not use walkers. The effect seemed to last for as long as ten months after the initial use of a walker (26).

Baby walkers are the cause of more injuries than any other baby product. Each year, an estimated 21,300 children under 15 months of age were treated in U.S. hospital emergency rooms for injuries related to baby walkers. The majority of the injuries resulted from falls down stairs. A small number of injuries resulted from tipovers, burns, and other injuries from bumping into or climbing on a walker. Because of increased mobility, a child in an baby walker is at high risk for injury if left unsupervised (23).

Because data indicate a considerable risk of major and minor injury and even death from the use of baby walkers, and because there is no clear benefit from their use, the American Academy of Pediatrics (AAP) has recommended that agencies responsible for licensing child care facilities not permit the use of baby walkers in approved centers. The AAP policy suggests that "stationary activity centers" (play tables with rotating seats) may be a reasonable alternative, but that they have not been on the market long enough to compile data on injury rates (24).

COMMENTS: In some countries, federal regulations have prevented the sale of new walkers since 1989 (5).

Baby walkers that do not have wheels are also potential hazards because children are placed in an upright position, enabling them access to dangerous objects, such as cups of hot beverages or poisonous plants that otherwise might not have been accessible (5).

Baby walkers that are manufactured after June 30, 1997 and are certified by the Juvenile Products Manufacturers Association (JPMA), must conform to the provisions of a voluntary standard *ASTM F977-00 Standard Consumer Safety Performance Specification for Infant Walkers* developed by the U.S. Consumer Product Safety Commission (CPSC), the JPMA, and the American Society for Testing and Materials (ASTM) (25). No studies have been completed to determine the number of injuries caused by walkers manufactured under the provisions of this standard.

A copy of the voluntary standard *ASTM F977-00 Standard Consumer Safety Performance Specification for Infant Walkers* is available from ASTM Customer Service. Resources on infant safety are available from the AAP. Contact information for the ASTM and the AAP is located in Appendix BB.

TYPE OF FACILITY: *Center; Large Family Child Care Home; Small Family Child Care Home*

STANDARD 5.084
AVAILABILITY OF A TELEPHONE

The facility shall provide at least one working non-pay telephone for general and emergency use.

RATIONALE: A telephone must be available to all caregivers in an emergency.

TYPE OF FACILITY: *Center; Large Family Child Care Home; Small Family Child Care Home*

PLAY EQUIPMENT

STANDARD 5.085
PLAY EQUIPMENT REQUIREMENTS

To provide safety and prevent injury, play equipment and materials in the facility shall meet the recommendations of the U.S. Consumer Product Safety Commission (CPSC) and the American Society for Testing and Materials (ASTM) for public playground equipment. Equipment and materials intended for *gross-motor* (active) play shall conform to the recommendations in the U.S. CPSC *Handbook for Public Playground Safety* and the provisions in the *ASTM F1487-98 Consumer Safety Performance Specifications for Playground Equipment for Public Use.*

All play equipment shall be constructed, installed, and made available to the intended users in such a manner that meets the American Society for Testing and Materials (ASTM) standards and the U.S. Consumer Product Safety Commission (CPSC) guidelines, as warranted by the manufacturers recommendations. A playground safety inspector who has been certified by the National Recreation and Park Association (NRPA) shall conduct an inspection of playground plans for new installations. Previously installed playgrounds shall be inspected at least once and whenever changes are made to the equipment or intended users.

Play equipment and materials shall be deemed appropriate to the developmental needs, individual interests, and ages of the children, by a person with at least a master's degree in early childhood education or psychology, or a doctoral degree in

psychiatry, or identified as age-appropriate by a manufacturer's label on the product package. Enough play equipment and materials shall be available to avoid excessive competition and long waits.

Children shall always be supervised when playing on playground equipment.

RATIONALE: Play equipment and toys must be safe, sufficient in quantity for the number of children in care, and developmentally appropriate. Equipment that is sized for larger and more mature children poses challenges that younger, smaller, and less mature children may not be able to meet.

The active play areas of a child care facility are associated with frequent and severe injuries. Many technical design and installation safeguards are addressed in the ASTM and CPSC standards. Manufacturers who guarantee that their equipment meets these standards and provide instructions for use to the purchaser ensure that these technical requirements will be met under threat of product liability. Certified playground safety inspectors receive training from the NPRA in association with the federally funded National Center for Playground Safety (NCPS). Since the training received by certified playground safety inspectors exceeds that of most child care personnel, obtaining a professional inspection to detect playground hazards before they cause injury is highly worthwhile.

COMMENTS: Compliance should be measured by structured observation.

Height limits for play equipment should generally be one foot per year of age of the intended users. In some states, height limitations for playground equipment are:
a) 48 inches for preschoolers (30 months to 5 years of age);
b) 6.5 feet for school-age children (6 through 12 years of age).

Consult with your regulatory health authority for any local or state requirements.

Contact information for the National Recreation and Park Association and the National Program for Playground Safety is located in Appendix BB. To obtain the publications listed above, contact the ASTM or the CPSC. Contact information is located in Appendix BB.

See STANDARD 5.183, regarding appropriate playground surfacing. See STANDARD 2.028, regarding the supervision of children.

TYPE OF FACILITY: *Center; Large Family Child Care Home; Small Family Child Care Home*

STANDARD 5.086:
INACCESSIBILITY OF HAZARDOUS PLAY EQUIPMENT

Any hazardous play equipment shall be made inaccessible to children by barriers, or removed until rendered safe or replaced. The barriers shall not pose any hazard.

RATIONALE: Hazardous equipment must be off-limits until it is removed or repaired, but the barrier itself should not introduce a new hazard.

COMMENTS: Examples of barriers to play equipment that pose a safety hazard are structures (including fences) that children can climb, prickly bushes, and standing bodies of water. Barriers such as plastic orange construction site fencing could be used to block access. While not child proof, it is conspicuous and sends a message that it is there to prevent access to the equipment it surrounds.

TYPE OF FACILITY: *Center; Large Family Child Care Home; Small Family Child Care Home*

STANDARD 5.087
INACCESSIBILITY OF TOYS OR OBJECTS TO CHILDREN UNDER 3 YEARS OF AGE

Small objects, toys, and toy parts available to children under the age of 3 years shall meet the federal small parts standards for toys. The following toys or objects shall not be accessible to children under 3 years of age:

a) Toys or objects with removable parts with a diameter less than 1¼ inch and a length less than 2¼ inches;
b) Balls that are smaller than 1¾ inches in diameter;
c) Toys with sharp points and edges;
d) Plastic bags;
e) Styrofoam objects;
f) Coins;
g) Rubber balloons;
h) Safety pins;
i) Marbles;
j) Other small objects.

RATIONALE: According to the federal government's small parts standard on a safe-size toy for children under 3 years of age, a small part should be at least 1¼ inches in diameter and 2¼ inches long. Any part smaller than this has a potential choking hazard. Injury and fatality from aspiration of small parts is well-documented (27). Eliminating small parts from children's environment will greatly reduce the risk.

COMMENTS: Toys or games intended for use by children 3-5 years of age and that contain small parts should be labeled "CHOKING HAZARD--Small Parts. Not for children under 3." Because choking on small parts occurs throughout the preschool years, small parts should be kept away from children at least up to 4 years of age. Also, children occasionally have choked on toys or toy parts that meet federal standards, so caregivers must constantly be vigilant.

Federal standard that applies is *Code of Federal Regulations, Title 16, Part 1501*, which defines the method for identifying toys and other articles intended for use by children under 3 years of age that present choking, aspiration, or ingestion hazards because of small parts. To obtain this publication, contact the Superintendent of Documents of the U.S. Government Printing Office. Also note the American Society for Testing and Materials (ASTM) *F963-96a, Standard Consumer Safety Specification on Toy Safety*. To obtain this publication, contact the ASTM. Contact information for the Superintendent of Documents and the ASTM is located in Appendix BB.

Practically speaking, objects should not be small enough to fit entirely into a child's mouth.

TYPE OF FACILITY: *Center; Large Family Child Care Home; Small Family Child Care Home*

STANDARD 5.088
CRIB TOYS

Toys or objects hung over an infant in a crib shall be held securely and be of a size and weight that would not injure an infant if the toy or object accidently falls or if the infant pulls up on the object.

Crib gyms that are strung across the crib shall not be used for typically developing children over 5 months of age or children who are able to push up on their hands and knees.

RATIONALE: Falling objects could cause injury to an infant lying in a crib.

The presence of crib gyms presents a potential strangulation hazard for infants who are able to lift their head above the crib surface. These children can fall across the crib gym and not be able to remove themselves from that position.

COMMENTS: Ornamental or small toys are often hung over an infant to provide stimulation. If a toy or object hung above an infant crib has small parts attached to it, ensure that the small parts are well secured to the body of the toy. An infant could accidentally swallow or choke on the small parts if they became dislodged and fell within grasp of the infant.

TYPE OF FACILITY: *Center; Large Family Child Care Home; Small Family Child Care Home*

STANDARD 5.089
BALLOONS

Infants, toddlers, and preschool children shall not be permitted to inflate balloons, suck on or put balloons in their mouths nor have access to uninflated or underinflated balloons. Latex balloons or inflated latex objects that are treated as balloons shall not be permitted in the child care facility.

RATIONALE: Balloons are an aspiration hazard (27). The U.S. Consumer Product Safety Commission (CPSC) reported at least 4 deaths from balloon aspiration with choking in 1998 (27). Aspiration injuries occur from latex balloons or other latex objects treated as balloons, such as inflated latex gloves. Latex gloves are commonly used in child care facilities for diaper changing, but they should not be inflated. When children bite inflated latex balloons or gloves, these objects may break suddenly and blow an obstructing piece of latex into the child's airway.

Under inflated or uninflated balloons of all types could be chewed or sucked and pieces potentially aspirated.

TYPE OF FACILITY: *Center; Large Family Child Care Home; Small Family Child Care Home*

STANDARD 5.090
PROJECTILE TOYS

Projectile toys shall be prohibited.

RATIONALE: These types of toys present high risks for aspiration, eye injuries, and other types of injuries (27).

TYPE OF FACILITY: *Center; Large Family Child Care Home; Small Family Child Care Home*

STANDARD 5.091
WATER PLAY TABLES

Communal, unsupervised water play tables shall be prohibited. Communal water tables shall be permitted, if children are supervised and the following conditions apply:
a)   The water tables shall be filled with fresh potable water immediately before a designated group of children begins a water play activity at the table, or shall be supplied with freely flowing fresh potable water during the play activity;
b)   The basin and toys shall be washed and sanitized before the next group uses the water table or the next water play activity takes place;

c) Only children without cuts, scratches, and sores on their hands, and without colds or runny noses, shall be permitted to use a communal water play table;

d) Children shall wash their hands before and after they use a communal water play table;

e) Caregivers shall ensure that no child drinks water from the water table.

As an alternative to a communal water table, separate basins with fresh water for each child to engage in water play shall be permitted.

RATIONALE: Contamination of hands, toys, and equipment in the room in which play tables are located seems to play a role in the transmission of diseases in child care settings (28, 29). Proper handwashing, supervision of children, and cleaning and sanitizing of the water table will help prevent the transmission of disease.

COMMENTS: The addition of bleach to the water is not recommended to avoid splashing of such solutions around the child care environment.

A better way to use water play tables is to use the table to hold a personal basin of water for each child who is engaged in water play. With this approach, supervision must be provided to be sure children confine their play to their own basin. Wherever a suitable inlet and outlet of water can be arranged, safe communal water play can involve free-flowing potable water by attaching a hose to the table that connects to a source of free-flowing potable water and attaching a hose to the table's drain that connects to a water drain or suitable run-off area.

TYPE OF FACILITY: *Center; Large Family Child Care Home; Small Family Child Care Home*

STANDARD 5.092
RIDING TOYS INCLUDING
TRICYCLES AND SCOOTERS

Tricycles, unpowered scooters, and other riding toys the children use shall:
a) Be spokeless;
b) Be capable of being steered;
c) Be of a size appropriate for the child;

d) Have a low center of gravity;
e) Be in good condition and free of sharp edges or protrusions that may injure the children.

All riders shall wear helmets. Children shall not share helmets unless helmets are made with an interior nonporous lining and easily cleanable straps, so their surfaces can be wiped clean between users. Helmets shall be removed before allowing children to use playground equipment. For unpowered scooters, children shall wear knee and elbow pads in addition to helmets. Children shall use scooters only under close adult supervision.

When not in use, riding toys shall be stored in a location where they will not present a physical obstacle to the children and caregivers. The staff shall inspect riding toys at least monthly for protrusions or rough edges that can lead to injury.

RATIONALE: Riding toys can provide much enjoyment for children. However, because of their high center of gravity and speed, they often cause injuries in young children. Wheels with spokes can potentially cause entrapment injuries. Wearing helmets for tricycle riding teaches children the practice of wearing helmets while using wheeled toys. Children must remove their helmets when they are no longer using a riding toy because the helmet can catch on other playground equipment, possibly leading to strangulation.

The U.S. Consumer Product Safety Commission (CPSC) and Centers for Disease Control and Prevention (CDC) reported in 2000 that 23% of children treated in emergency departments for scooter-related injuries were age 8 or under (79).

COMMENTS: Sharing of bicycle helmets should not significantly contribute to the spread of head lice. Head lice are not able to survive away from humans for more than a few days. Wiping the lining with a damp cloth should remove any lice or nits left inside. More vigorous washing of helmets, using detergents, cleaning chemicals, and sanitizers, is not recommended because these chemicals may cause the physical structure of the impact-absorbing material inside the helmet and the straps used to hold the helmet on the head to deteriorate. Caregivers should be

especially vigilant about wiping out helmets and straps during outbreaks of head lice in child care.

For additional special play equipment requirements for infants, toddlers, and preschoolers, see STANDARD 5.087 through STANDARD 5.089. See also Sanitation and Maintenance of Toys and Objects, STANDARD 3.036 through STANDARD 3.038.

TYPE OF FACILITY: *Center; Large Family Child Care Home; Small Family Child Care Home*

SUPPLIES

STANDARD 5.093
FIRST AID KITS

The facility shall maintain at least one readily available first aid kit wherever children are in care, including one for field trips and outings away from the facility and one to remain at the facility if all the children do not attend the field trip. In addition, a first aid kit shall be in each vehicle that is used to transport children to and from a child care center. Each kit shall be a closed container for storing first aid supplies, accessible to child care staff members at all times but out of reach of children. First aid kits shall be restocked after use, and an inventory shall be conducted at least monthly. The first aid kit shall contain at least the following items:
a) Disposable nonporous gloves;
b) Scissors;
c) Tweezers;
d) A non-glass thermometer to measure a child's temperature;
e) Bandage tape;
f) Sterile gauze pads;
g) Flexible roller gauze;
h) Triangular bandages;
i) Safety pins;
j) Eye dressing;
k) Pen/pencil and note pad;
l) Syrup of ipecac (use only if recommended by the Poison Control Center);
m) Cold pack;
n) Current American Academy of Pediatrics (AAP) standard first aid chart or equivalent first aid guide;

o) Coins for use in a pay phone;
p) Water;
q) Small plastic or metal splints;
r) Liquid soap;
s) Adhesive strip bandages, plastic bags for cloths, gauze, and other materials used in handling blood;
t) Any emergency medication needed for child with special needs;
u) List of emergency phone numbers, parents' home and work phone numbers, and the Poison Control Center phone number.

RATIONALE: Facilities must place emphasis on safeguarding each child and ensuring that the staff members are able to handle emergencies. In a study that reviewed 423 injuries, first aid was sufficient treatment for 84.4% of the injuries (30). The supplies needed for pediatric first aid, including rescue breathing and management of a blocked airway must be available for use where the injury occurs.

COMMENTS: Many centers simply leave a first aid kit in all vehicles used to transport children, regardless of whether the vehicle is used to take a child to or from a center, or for outings. Contact information for the AAP is located in Appendix BB.

TYPE OF FACILITY: *Center; Large Family Child Care Home; Small Family Child Care Home*

STANDARD 5.094
SHARING OF PERSONAL ARTICLES PROHIBITED

Combs, hairbrushes, toothbrushes, personal clothing, bedding, and towels shall not be shared and shall be labeled with the name of the child who uses these objects.

RATIONALE: Respiratory, gastrointestinal, and skin infections (such as lice infestation, scabies, and ringworm) are among the most common infectious diseases in child care. These diseases are transmitted by direct skin-to-skin contact or by sharing personal articles such as combs, brushes, towels, clothing, and bedding. Prohibiting the sharing of personal articles and providing space so that personal items may be stored separately helps prevent these diseases from spreading.

TYPE OF FACILITY: *Center; Large Family Child Care Home; Small Family Child Care Home*

STANDARD 5.095
TOOTHBRUSHES AND
TOOTHPASTE

In facilities where tooth brushing is an activity, each child shall have a personally labeled age-appropriate toothbrush. No sharing or borrowing shall be allowed. After use, toothbrushes shall be stored with the bristles up to air dry in such a way that the toothbrushes cannot contact or drip on each other and the bristles are not in contact with any surface. Racks and devices used to hold toothbrushes for storage shall be labeled and shall be washed and sanitized or replaced whenever they are visibly soiled and after any contamination with blood or body fluids. The toothbrushes shall be replaced every six months, or sooner if the bristles become splayed. When a toothbrush becomes contaminated through contact with another brush or use by more than one child, it shall be discarded and replaced with a new one.

If toothpaste is used, each child shall have his/her own labeled toothpaste tube, or toothpaste from a single tube so that a pea-sized amount is dispensed onto a clean piece of paper or paper cup for each child rather than directly on the toothbrush.

Where children require assistance with brushing, caregivers shall wash their hands thoroughly between brushings for each child. Where a child has bleeding gums, caregivers shall wear gloves when assisting such children with brushing their teeth.

RATIONALE: Toothbrushes and oral fluids that collect in the mouth during tooth brushing are contaminated with infectious agents from the mouth and must not be allowed to serve as a conduit of infection from one individual to another. Individually labeling the toothbrushes will prevent different children from sharing the same toothbrush. As an alternative to racks, children can have individualized, labeled cups

and their brush can be stored bristle-up in their cup. Some bleeding may occur during tooth brushing in children who have inflammation of the gums. Although this situation is not usual, caregivers should protect themselves from exposure to blood in such situations, as required by standard precautions and the Occupational Safety and Health Administration (OSHA) regulations.

COMMENTS: Children can use an individually labeled or disposable cup of water to brush their teeth.

Toothpaste is not necessary since the removal of food and plaque is the primary objective of tooth brushing

Some risk of infection is involved when numerous children brush their teeth into sinks that are not sanitized between uses. In child care settings, the Centers for Disease Control and Prevention (CDC) recommends the hygienic measures described in this standard (31).

TYPE OF FACILITY: *Center; Large Family Child Care Home; Small Family Child Care Home*

STANDARD 5.096
SUPPLIES FOR BATHROOMS AND
HANDWASHING SINKS

Bathrooms and handwashing sinks shall be supplied with:
a) Liquid soap, hand lotion, and paper towels or other hand-drying devices approved by the regulatory health authority, within arm's reach of the user of each sink;
b) Toilet paper, within arm's reach of the user of each toilet.

The facility shall permit the use of only single-use cloth or disposable paper towels. The shared use of a towel shall be prohibited. All tissues and disposable towels shall be discarded into an appropriate waste container after use.

RATIONALE: Lack of supplies discourages necessary handwashing. Cracks in the skin and excessive dryness from frequent handwashing discourage the staff from complying with necessary hygiene and may lead to increased bacterial accumulation on hands. The availability of hand lotion to prevent dryness encourages staff members to wash their hands more often. Supplies must be within arm's reach of the user to prevent contamination of the environment with waste, water, or excretion.

Shared cloth towels can transmit infectious disease. Even though a child may use a cloth towel that is solely for that child's use, preventing shared use of towels is difficult. Disposable towels prevent this problem, but once used, must be discarded. Many communicable diseases can be prevented through appropriate hygiene and sanitation.

COMMENTS: Bar soap shall not be used by children or staff. Liquid soap is widely available, economical, and easily used by staff and children. If anyone is sensitive to the type of product used, a substitute product that accommodates to this special need should be used.

A disposable towel dispenser that dispenses the towel without having to touch the container or the fresh towel supply is better than towel dispensers in which the person must use a lever to get a towel, or handle the towel supply to remove one towel. Some roller devices dispense one towel at a time from a paper towel roll; some commercial dispensers hold either a large roll or a pile of folded towels inside the dispenser, with the towel intended for next use sticking out of the opening of the dispenser.

TYPE OF FACILITY: *Center; Large Family Child Care Home; Small Family Child Care Home*

ADDITIONAL FURNISHINGS AND EQUIPMENT REQUIREMENTS FOR FACILITIES SERVING CHILDREN WITH SPECIAL NEEDS

STANDARD 5.097
THERAPEUTIC AND RECREATIONAL EQUIPMENT

The facility shall have therapeutic and recreational equipment to enhance the educational and developmental progress of children with special needs, to the extent that they can reasonably be furnished.

RATIONALE: Children with special needs may require special equipment of various types. For the individual child, the equipment should be available to meet the goals and methods outlined in the service plan.

COMMENTS: Devices and assisted technology that individual children require is unique to them, based on their own specific needs.

The Americans with Disabilities Act (ADA) does not require personal equipment (such as eyeglasses, wheelchairs, etc.) to be furnished by the child care program.

TYPE OF FACILITY: *Center; Large Family Child Care Home; Small Family Child Care Home*

STANDARD 5.098
SPECIAL ADAPTIVE EQUIPMENT

Special adaptive equipment (such as toys and wheelchair accessibility) for children with special needs shall be provided or arranged for by the facility as part of their reasonable accommodations for the child.

RATIONALE: If a facility serves one or more children with special needs, adaptive equipment necessary for the child's participation in all activities is needed.

COMMENTS: Most adaptive equipment can be designed by making simple adaptation of typically used items such as eating utensils, cups, plates, etc.

Child care providers are not responsible for providing personal equipment (such as hearing aids, eyeglasses, braces, and wheelchairs).

See also Appendix T, *Adaptive Equipment for Children with Special Needs*.

TYPE OF FACILITY: *Center; Large Family Child Care Home; Small Family Child Care Home*

STANDARD 5.099
PROSTHETIC DEVICES

A designated staff member shall check prosthetic devices, including hearing aids, eyeglasses, braces, and wheelchairs, daily to ensure that these appliances are in good working order and have been applied properly.

RATIONALE: Battery-driven devices such as hearing aids require close monitoring because they have a short life and young children require adult assistance to replace the batteries. Eyeglasses scratch and break, as do other assistive appliances.

COMMENTS: The facility should have parents supply extra batteries for hearing aids. Facilities should store and discard the batteries in such a manner that children cannot ingest them. With the parents' permission, the staff may perform minor repairs on equipment but should not attempt major repairs.

Leg braces and /or eyeglasses are not effective if they are not applied correctly to the child.

TYPE OF FACILITY: *Center; Large Family Child Care Home; Small Family Child Care Home*

TOXIC SUBSTANCES

STANDARD 5.100
USE AND STORAGE OF TOXIC SUBSTANCES

The following items shall be used as recommended by the manufacturer and shall be stored in the original labeled containers:
a) Cleaning materials;
b) Detergents;
c) Automatic dishwasher detergents;
d) Aerosol cans;
e) Pesticides;
f) Health and beauty aids;
g) Medications;
h) Lawn care chemicals
i) Other toxic materials.

They shall be used only in a manner that will not contaminate play surfaces, food, or food preparation areas, and that will not constitute a hazard to the children. All chemicals used inside or outside shall be stored in their original containers in a safe and secure manner, well away from food. These chemicals shall be used according to manufacturers' instructions, and in a manner that will not contaminate play surfaces or articles.

When not in actual use, toxic materials shall be kept in a locked room or cabinet, fitted with a child-resistive opening device, inaccessible to children, separate from stored medications and food.

Chemicals used in lawn care treatments shall be limited to those listed for use in areas that can be occupied by children.

RATIONALE: There were 2,475,010 human poison exposures reported in 1997 by 73 poison control centers nationwide, representing an estimated 6% of the U.S. population (32). Children under 6 years of age accounted for the following number of exposures:
• Industrial and Home Personal Care Products: 92,560 exposures
• Insecticides: 22,136 exposures
• Chemicals: 16,215 exposures

- Deodorizers:
  9,557 exposures
- Rodenticides:
  9,406 exposures
- Insecticides with Repellents:
  4,475 exposures

Automatic dishwasher detergent is a common household substance that is extremely corrosive and potentially fatal if ingested. Young children have been known to take automatic dishwasher detergent from the dispenser on the internal surface of the door, and have taken detergent directly from the packet (33, 34).

COMMENTS: Many child-resistant types of closing devices can be installed on doors to prevent young children from accessing poisonous substances. Many of these devices are self-engaging when the door is closed and require an adult hand size or skill to open the door. A locked cabinet or room where children cannot gain access is best if such a barrier is used consistently. If a lock requires conscious action on the user's part, however, the lock may not be used consistently.

Lawn care chemicals may have an impact on children's health. Even when using lawn care chemicals that have EPA approval for use in child care environments, operators of child care facilities must take into consideration the quantity and frequency of lawn care chemicals used, whether the lawn is being used by infants or other children who play near the ground and may contaminate their skin or actually ingest grass with lawn care chemical residue, and whether older children have direct skin contact with the lawn when playing. Preferably, no lawn care chemicals should be used on lawns that are used by children. If lawn care chemicals are used, their use should be kept to a minimum.

TYPE OF FACILITY: *Center; Large Family Child Care Home; Small Family Child Care Home*

STANDARD 5.101
USE OF A POISON CONTROL CENTER

The poison control center shall be called for advice about any exposure to toxic substances, or any ingestion emergency. The advice shall be followed and documented in the facility's files. The caregiver shall tell the poison information specialist and/or physician the following information:
a)   The child's age and sex;
b)   The substance involved;
c)   The estimated amount;
d)   The child's condition;
e)   The time elapsed since ingestion or exposure.

The caregiver shall not induce vomiting unless instructed by the Poison Control Center.

RATIONALE: Toxic substances, when ingested, inhaled, or in contact with skin, may react immediately or slowly, with serious symptoms occurring much later. These symptoms may vary with the type of substance. Some common symptoms include dermatitis, nausea, vomiting, diarrhea, and congestion.

COMMENTS: Any question on possible risks for exposure should be referred to poison control professionals for proper first aid and treatment. Regional poison control centers have access to the latest information on emergency care of the poisoning victim.

TYPE OF FACILITY: *Center; Large Family Child Care Home; Small Family Child Care Home*

STANDARD 5.102
INFORMING STAFF REGARDING PRESENCE OF TOXIC SUBSTANCES

Employers shall provide child care workers with hazard information, as required by the Occupational Safety and Health Administration (OSHA), about the presence of toxic substances such as asbestos, formaldehyde, or hazardous chemicals in use in the facility. This information shall include identification of the ingredients of art materials and sanitizing products. Where nontoxic substitutes are available, these nontoxic substitutes shall be used instead of toxic chemicals.

RATIONALE: These precautions are essential to the health and well-being of the staff and the children alike. Federal agencies have stated that the quality of indoor air is more of a problem than that of outdoor air. Indoor air pollution is thus a potential occupational health hazard for child care workers, particularly because of potential for exposure to infectious and chemical agents at the same time. In addition, many cleaning products and art materials contain ingredients that may be toxic. Regulations require employers to make the complete identity of these materials known to users. Because nontoxic substitutes are available for virtually all necessary products, exchanging them for toxic products is required.

COMMENTS: Employers may contact the local building safety inspection authority for information about toxic substances in the building. The U.S. Department of Labor, which oversees OSHA, is responsible for protection of workers and is listed in the phone book of all large cities. Because standards change frequently, the facility should seek the latest standards from the Environmental Protection Agency (EPA). Information on toxic substances in the environment is available from the EPA. Material Safety Data Sheets (MSDS) are a good source of information. For information on consumer products and art materials, contact the U.S. Consumer Product Safety Commission (CPSC). Contact information is located in Appendix BB.

TYPE OF FACILITY: *Center; Large Family Child Care Home*

STANDARD 5.103
RADON CONCENTRATIONS

Radon concentrations inside a home or building used for child care shall be less than 4 picocuries per liter of air.

RATIONALE: Radon is a colorless, odorless, radioactive gas that occurs naturally. It can be found in soil, water, building materials, and natural gas. Radon from the soil is the main cause of radon problems.

When radon gas is inhaled, it can damage lung tissue and lead to lung cancer. Radon levels can be easily measured to determine if acceptable levels have been exceeded. Various methods are available to reduce radon in a building.

COMMENTS: For material and information on radon, contact the Environmental Protection Agency (EPA). Contact information for the EPA is located in Appendix BB.

TYPE OF FACILITY: *Center; Large Family Child Care Home; Small Family Child Care Home*

STANDARD 5.104
PREVENTING EXPOSURE TO ASBESTOS OR OTHER FRIABLE MATERIALS

Any asbestos, fiberglass, or other friable material or any material that is in a dangerous condition found within a facility or on the grounds of the facility shall be removed. Asbestos removal shall be done by a contractor certified to remove, encapsulate, or enclose asbestos in accordance with existing regulations of the Environmental Protection Agency (EPA). No children shall be present until the removal and cleanup of the hazardous condition have been completed.

Pipe and boiler insulation shall be sampled and examined in an accredited laboratory for the presence of asbestos in a friable or potentially dangerous condition.

Nonfriable asbestos shall be identified to prevent disturbance and/or exposure during remodeling or future activities.

RATIONALE: Removal of significant hazards will protect the staff, children, and families who use the facility. Asbestos dust and fibers that are inhaled and reach the lungs can cause lung disease. The requirement for asbestos is based on the National Asbestos School Hazard Abatement Act of 1984 and U.S. Consumer Product Safety Commission (CPSC) guidelines.

COMMENTS: Asbestos that is in a friable condition means that it is easily crumbled. For more information

regarding asbestos and applicable EPA regulations, contact regional offices of the EPA. Contact information is located in Appendix BB.

TYPE OF FACILITY: *Center; Large Family Child Care Home; Small Family Child Care Home*

STANDARD 5.105
PROPER USE OF ARTS AND CRAFTS MATERIALS

Only arts and crafts materials that are labeled nontoxic in accordance with the Labeling of Hazardous Art Material Act (LHAMA), 15 U.S C. 1277 and the American Society for Testing and Materials (ASTM) *D4236-94 Standard Practice for Labeling Art Materials for Chronic Health Hazards* shall be used in the child care facility. The facility shall prohibit use of old or donated materials with potentially harmful ingredients.

Caregivers shall closely supervise all children using art materials and shall make sure art materials are properly cleaned up and stored in original containers that are fully labeled. Caregivers shall have emergency protocols in place in the event of an injury, poisoning, or allergic reaction. When using these materials, children and staff shall not be eating or drinking.

RATIONALE: This standard prevents contamination and injury. Labels are required on art supplies to identify any hazardous ingredients, risks associated with their use, precautions, first aid, and sources of further information (35).

COMMENTS. For information on safe art materials contact the Art and Creative Materials Institute, the ASTM, and the U.S. Consumer Product Safety Commission. Contact information is located in Appendix BB.

TYPE OF FACILITY: *Center; Large Family Child Care Home; Small Family Child Care Home*

STANDARD 5.106
PROHIBITION OF POISONOUS SUBSTANCES AND PLANTS

Poisonous or potentially harmful substances and plants shall be prohibited in any part of a child care facility that is accessible to children. All substances not known to be nontoxic shall be identified and checked by name with the local poison control center to determine safe use.

RATIONALE: Plants are among the most common household substances that children ingest. Contact dermatitis is also a concern. Determining the toxicity of every commercially available household plant is difficult. A more reasonable approach is to keep any unknown plant and other potentially poisonous substances out of the environment that children use. All outside plants and their leaves, fruit, and stems should also be considered potentially toxic (36). Many plants are essentially nontoxic when ingested in small to modest quantities. These nontoxic plants are preferable for use in child care facilities.

COMMENTS: Plants can be placed behind a glass enclosure to keep children from touching the plant. Cuttings, trimmings, and leaves from potentially harmful plants must be disposed of safely so children do not have access to them.

For nontoxic, frequently ingested products and plants, see the American Academy of Pediatrics' (AAP) *Handbook of Common Poisonings in Children.* Contact information for the AAP is located in Appendix BB. See Appendix U, for a list of poisonous and safe plants.

TYPE OF FACILITY: *Center; Large Family Child Care Home: Small Family Child Care Home*

STANDARD 5.107
PROHIBITION OF SPECIFIC CHEMICALS

The use of the following shall be prohibited:
a) Incense;
b) Moth crystals or moth balls;
c) Chemical air fresheners that:

1) Contain ingredients on the Environmental Protection Agency's (EPA) toxic chemicals lists;
2) Are not approved as safe by the regulatory health authority.

RATIONALE: Many chemicals are sold to cover up noxious odors or ward off pests. Many of these chemicals are hazardous. As an alternative, child care providers should dilute noxious odors through cleaning and ventilation, and control pests using nontoxic methods.

COMMENTS: Contact the EPA Regional offices listed in the federal agency section of the telephone directory for assistance, or contact any nationally certified regional poison control center. Contact information for the EPA is located in Appendix BB.

TYPE OF FACILITY: *Center; Large Family Child Care Home; Small Family Child Care Home*

STANDARD 5.108
VENTILATION OF RECENTLY CARPETED OR PANELED AREAS

Doors and windows shall be opened for 48-72 hours in areas that have been recently carpeted or paneled using adhesives. Window fans, room air conditioners, or other means to exhaust emission to the outdoors shall be used.

RATIONALE: Adhesives that contain toxic materials can cause significant symptoms in occupants of buildings where these materials are used.

COMMENTS: Airing the room for 48-72 hours is a minimum recommended period of time. Depending on the degree of air circulation and the rate of introducing fresh air into the room, additional ventilation time may be required. For more information on "safe" levels of home indoor air pollutants, contact the Environmental Protection Agency (EPA) or the U.S. Consumer Product Safety Commission (CPSC). Contact information is located in Appendix BB.

TYPE OF FACILITY: *Center; Large Family Child Care Home; Small Family Child Care Home*

STANDARD 5.109
PROHIBITION OF MATERIALS EMITTING TOXIC SUBSTANCES

Insulation or other materials that contain elements that may emit toxic substances over recommended levels in the child care environment shall not be used in facilities. If existing structures contain such materials, the facility shall be monitored regularly to ensure a safe environment as specified by the regulatory agency.

RATIONALE: Children and caregivers must not be exposed to toxic substances. Some insulation and building materials such as urea foam insulation and particle board can emit formaldehyde gas, a respiratory and eye irritant (38).

COMMENTS: Regional offices of the Environmental Protection Agency (EPA) can be contacted for advice. Contact information is located in Appendix BB.
TYPE OF FACILITY: *Center; Large Family Child Care Home; Small Family Child Care Home*

STANDARD 5.110
TESTING FOR LEAD

Any surface and the grounds around and under surfaces that children use at a child care facility, including dirt and grassy areas shall be tested for excessive lead in a location designated by the health department. Painted play equipment and imported vinyl mini-blinds shall be evaluated for the presence of lead. If they are found to have toxic levels, corrective action shall be taken to prevent exposure to lead at this facility. Only nontoxic paints shall be used.

In all centers, both exterior and interior surfaces covered by paint with lead levels of 0.06% and above, and accessible to children, shall be removed by a safe chemical or physical means or made inaccessible to children, regardless of the condition of the surface.

In large and small family child care homes, flaking or deteriorating lead-based paint on interior or exterior surfaces, equipment, or toys accessible to preschool-age children shall be removed or abated according to health department regulations.

Where lead paint is removed, the surface shall be refinished with lead-free paint or nontoxic material. Sanding, scraping, or burning of high-lead surfaces shall be prohibited. Children and pregnant women shall not be present during abatement activities.

RATIONALE: Ingestion of lead paint can result in high levels of lead in the blood, which affects the central nervous system and can cause mental retardation (38). Paint and other surface coating materials should comply with lead content provisions of the *Code of Federal Regulations, Title 16, Part 1303*.

Some imported vinyl mini-blinds contain lead and can deteriorate from exposure to sunlight and heat and form lead dust on the surface of the blinds (39). The U.S. Consumer Product Safety Commission (CPSC) recommends that consumers with children 6 years of age and younger remove old vinyl mini-blinds and replace them with new mini-blinds made without added lead or with alternative window coverings. For more information on mini-blinds, contact the CPSC. Contact information is located in Appendix BB.

Lead is a neurotoxicant. Even at low levels of exposure, lead can cause reduction in a child's IQ and attention span, and result in reading and learning disabilities, hyperactivity, and behavioral difficulties. Lead poisoning has no "cure." These effects cannot be reversed once the damage is done, affecting a child's ability to learn, succeed in school, and function later in life. Other symptoms of low levels of lead in a child's body are subtle behavioral changes, irritability, low appetite, weight loss, sleep disturbances, shortened attention span.

COMMENTS: Paints made before 1978 may contain lead. If there is any doubt about the presence of lead in existing paint, contact the health department for information regarding testing. Lead is used to make paint last longer. The amount of lead in paint was reduced in 1950 and further reduced again in 1978. Houses built before 1950 likely contain lead paint, and houses built after 1950 have less lead in the paint. House paint sold today has little or no lead. Lead is prohibited in contemporary paints. Lead-based paint is the most common source of lead poisoning in children.

In buildings where lead has been removed from the surfaces, lead paint may have contaminated surrounding soil. Therefore, the soil in play areas around these buildings should be tested. Outdoor play equipment was commonly painted with lead-based paints, too. These structures and the soil around them should be checked if they are not known to be lead-free.

The danger from lead paint depends on:
a) Amount of lead in the painted surface;
b) Condition of the paint;
c) Amount of paint that gets into the child.

Children 9 months through 5 years of age are at the greatest risk for lead poisoning. Most children with lead poisoning do not look or act sick. A blood lead test is the only way to know if children are being lead poisoned. Children should have a test result below 10 ug/dL.

A booklet called *Protect Your Family from Lead in Your Home* is available from the Environmental Protection Agency (EPA), the U.S. CPSC, and U.S. Department of Housing and Urban Development (HUD). The EPA also has a pamphlet, called *Finding a Qualified Lead Professional for Your Home*, that provides information on how to identify qualified lead inspectors and risk assessors. For further information on lead poisoning, contact the EPA or the National Lead Information Center. Contact information is located in Appendix BB.

TYPE OF FACILITY: *Center; Large Family Child Care Home; Small Family Child Care Home*

STANDARD 5.111
CONSTRUCTION AND REMODELING DURING HOURS OF OPERATION

Construction, remodeling, or alterations of structures during child care operations shall be isolated from areas where children are present and done in a manner that will prevent hazards or unsafe conditions (such as fumes, dust, and safety hazards).

RATIONALE: Children should be protected from activities and equipment associated with construction and renovation of the facility that may cause injury or illness.

COMMENTS: Ideally, construction and renovation work should be done when the facility is not in operation and when there are no children present. Many facilities arrange to schedule such work on weekends. If this is not possible, temporary barriers can be constructed to restrict access of children to those areas under construction. A plastic vapor barrier sheet could be temporarily hung to prevent dust and fumes from drifting into those areas where children are present.

TYPE OF FACILITY: *Center; Large Family Child Care Home; Small Family Child Care Home*

5.2 SPACE AND EQUIPMENT IN DESIGNATED AREAS

PLAY INDOORS

STANDARD 5.112
SPACE REQUIRED PER CHILD

In general, the designated area for children's activities shall contain a minimum of 35 square feet of usable floor space per child (or compensating for typical furnishings and equipment being present, 50 square feet measured on the inside, wall-to-wall dimensions) (40). In addition, the following shall apply when the indicated, specific types of children are in care:
a) For children with special needs who are 2 to 12 years of age, the minimum usable floor space in a classroom or playroom shall be 40 square feet;
b) When play and sleep areas for infants, toddlers, or preschool-age children are in the same room, a minimum of 35 square feet of usable floor space per child shall be provided except during periods when the children are using their rest equipment. During sleep periods, the space shall be sufficient to provide spacing between children using rest

equipment, according to STANDARD 5.142 through STANDARD 5.144.

These spaces are exclusive of food preparation areas of the kitchen, bathrooms, toilets, areas for the care of ill children, offices, staff rooms, corridors, hallways, stairways, closets, lockers, laundry, furnace rooms, cabinets, and storage shelving spaces.

RATIONALE: Child behavior tends to be more constructive when sufficient space is organized to promote developmentally appropriate skills. Crowding has been shown to be associated with increased risk of developing upper respiratory infections (41). Also, having sufficient space will reduce the risk of injury from simultaneous activities.

Children with special needs may require more space than typically developing children. Toddlers need more room than infants because of their high activity level, which is associated with a greater risk of infection in this age group. In practice, the 35 square feet of available play space per child has been found to correspond with 50 square feet measured wall-to-wall with the usual furnishings and equipment.

TYPE OF FACILITY: *Center; Large Family Child Care Home; Small Family Child Care Home*

STANDARD 5.113
UNUSABLE SPACE

The floor area beneath ceilings less than 7 feet 6 inches above the floor shall not be counted in determining compliance with the space requirements specified in STANDARD 5.112. Areas that children do not inhabit or use shall not be counted when determining compliance with the above space requirements.

RATIONALE: Ceiling height must be adequate, in addition to floor dimensions, to provide a volume of air that does not quickly concentrate infectious disease or noxious fumes. Ceiling height must be adequate for caregivers to supervise and reach children who require assistance.

COMMENTS: For additional indoor play requirements, see also STANDARD 5.116 on location of toilet and handwashing facilities near indoor play areas; and STANDARD 5.163, on indoor space being used to meet outdoor play space requirements.

TYPE OF FACILITY: *Center; Large Family Child Care Home; Small Family Child Care Home*

STANDARD 5.114
EXCLUSION OF OLDER CHILDREN FROM ROOMS AND AREAS FOR INFANTS AND TODDLERS

In centers, infants and toddlers younger than 3 years of age shall be cared for in rooms that are separate from those used by older children, as specified in STANDARD 2.013.

In all types of facilities, infant and toddler crawling and floor-play areas shall be protected from general walkways and areas that older children use for play.

RATIONALE: Infants need quiet, calm environments, away from the stimulation of older children. Younger infants should be cared for in rooms separate from the more boisterous toddlers. In addition to these developmental needs of infants, separation is important for reasons of disease prevention. Rates of hospitalization for all forms of acute infectious respiratory tract diseases are highest during the first year of life, indicating that respiratory tract illness becomes less severe as the child gets older. Therefore, infants should be a focus for interventions to reduce the incidence of respiratory tract disease. Since most respiratory infections are spread from older children or adults to infants, exposure of infants to older children should be restricted to limit exposure of infants to respiratory tract viruses and bacteria.

While use of separate rooms to care for infants and toddlers is neither possible nor desirable to achieve appropriate supervision in family child care homes, infants and toddlers spend a lot of time on the floor and would likely suffer or cause injury if they were moving around on floor areas that older children or adults were using as general walkways and play areas.

TYPE OF FACILITY: *Center; Large Family Child Care Home; Small Family Child Care Home*

STANDARD 5.115
AREAS FOR SCHOOL-AGE CHILDREN

When school-age children are in care for periods that exceed 2 hours after school, a separate area away from areas for younger children shall be available for school-age children to do homework. Areas used for this purpose shall have:
a) Table space;
b) Chairs;
c) Adequate ventilation;
d) Lighting of 40 to 50 foot-candles in the room;
e) Lighting of 50 to 100 foot-candles on the surface used as a desk.

RATIONALE: School-age children need a quiet space to do homework so they are not forced to work against the demands for attention that younger children pose (7). In family child care homes such an area might be within the same room and separated by a room dividing arrangement of furniture.

COMMENTS: See also Lighting, STANDARD 5.042.

TYPE OF FACILITY: *Center; Large Family Child Care Home; Small Family Child Care Home*

TOILET AND HANDWASHING AREAS

STANDARD 5.116
GENERAL REQUIREMENTS FOR TOILET AND HANDWASHING AREAS

Clean toilet and handwashing facilities shall be within 40 feet of the closest part of all indoor and outdoor play areas that children use.

Toilets shall be located on the same floor as, and next to, the sleeping areas.

RATIONALE: Young children use the toilet frequently and they cannot wait long when they have to use the toilet. Therefore, young children must be able to get to toilet facilities quickly.

Toilet facilities close to sleeping areas allow sleepy children to be close to the toilet.

TYPE OF FACILITY: *Center; Large Family Child Care Home; Small Family Child Care Home*

STANDARD 5.117
LOCATION OF TOILETS

Toilets shall be located in rooms separate from those used for cooking or eating. If toilets are not on the same floor as the child care area and within sight or hearing of a caregiver, an adult shall accompany children younger than 5 years of age to and from the toilet area.

RATIONALE: This standard is to prevent contamination of food and to eliminate unpleasant odors from the food areas. Supervision and assistance are necessary for young children.

COMMENTS: Compliance is monitored by observation.

TYPE OF FACILITY: *Center; Large Family Child Care Home; Small Family Child Care Home*

STANDARD 5.118
ABILITY TO OPEN TOILET ROOM DOORS

Children shall be able to easily open every toilet room door from the inside, and caregivers shall be able to easily open toilet-room doors from the outside if adult assistance is required.

RATIONALE: Doors that can be opened easily will prevent entrapment.

COMMENTS: Inside latches that children can easily manage will allow the child to arrange for privacy when using the toilet. Whatever latch or lock is avail-

able for use, however, must be of a type that the staff can easily open from the outside in case a child requires adult assistance.

TYPE OF FACILITY: *Center; Large Family Child Care Home; Small Family Child Care Home*

STANDARD 5.119
PREVENTING ENTRY TO TOILET ROOMS BY TODDLERS

Toilet rooms shall have barriers that prevent entry by toddlers who are unattended. Toddlers shall be supervised by sight and sound at all times.

RATIONALE: Toddlers can drown in toilet bowls, play in the excrement, or otherwise engage in potentially injurious behavior if they are not supervised in toilet rooms.

TYPE OF FACILITY: *Center; Large Family Child Care Home; Small Family Child Care Home*

STANDARD 5.120
TOILET AREAS FOR CHILDREN 6 YEARS OR OLDER

In centers, males and females who are 6 years of age and older shall have separate and private toilet facilities.

RATIONALE: Although cultures differ in privacy needs, sex-separated toileting among people who are not relatives is the norm for adults. Children should be allowed the opportunity to practice modesty when independent toileting behavior is well established in the majority of the group. By 6 years of age, most children can use the toilet by themselves (42).

TYPE OF FACILITY: *Center*

STANDARD 5.121
CHEMICAL TOILETS

Chemical toilets shall not be used in child care facilities unless they are provided as a temporary

measure in the event that the facility's normal plumbed toilets are not functioning. In the event that chemical toilets may be required on a temporary basis, the child care operator shall seek approval from the regulatory health agency.

RATIONALE: Chemical toilets can pose a safety hazard to young children. Young children climbing on the toilet seat could accidentally fall through the opening and into the chemical that is contained in the waste receptacle.

TYPE OF FACILITY: *Center; Large Family Child Care Home; Small Family Child Care Home*

STANDARD 5.122
RATIOS OF TOILETS, URINALS AND HAND SINKS TO CHILDREN

Toilets, urinals, and hand sinks, easily accessible for use and supervision, shall be provided in the following ratios:
- 1:10 for toddlers and preschool-age children
- 1:15 for school-age children.

When the number of children in the ratio is exceeded by one, an additional fixture shall be required. These numbers shall be subject to the following minimums:
a) A minimum of one sink and one flush toilet for 10 or fewer toddlers and preschool-age children using toilets;
b) A minimum of one sink and one flush toilet for 15 or fewer school-age children using toilets;
c) A minimum of two sinks and two flush toilets for 16 to 30 children using toilets;
d) A minimum of one sink and one flush toilet for each additional 15 children.

For toddlers and preschoolers, the maximum toilet height shall be 11 inches, and maximum height for hand sinks shall be 22 inches. Urinals shall not exceed 30% of the total required toilet fixtures and shall be used by one child at a time. For school-age children, standard height toilet, urinal, and hand sink fixtures are appropriate.

RATIONALE: When children use urinals, more than one child should not use the urinal at the same time.

The environment can become contaminated more easily with multiple simultaneous users because at least one of the children must assume an off-center position in relationship to the fixture during voiding.

Young children use the toilet frequently and cannot wait long when they have to use the toilet. The ratio of 1:10 is based on best professional experience of early childhood educators who are facility operators. This ratio also limits the group that will be sharing facilities (and infections).

COMMENTS: A ratio of 1 toilet to every 10 children may not be sufficient if only one toilet is accessible to each group of 10, so a minimum of 2 toilets per group is preferable when the group size approaches 10. However, a large toilet room with many toilets used by several groups is less desirable than several small toilet rooms assigned to specific groups, because of the opportunities such a large room offers for transmitting infectious disease agents.

When providing bathroom fixtures for a mixed group of preschool and school-age children, requiring a school-age child to use bathroom fixtures designed for preschoolers may negatively impact the self-esteem of the school-age child.

TYPE OF FACILITY: *Center; Large Family Child Care Home*

STANDARD 5.123
NONFLUSHING TOILET EQUIPMENT FOR TOILET LEARNING/TRAINING

Nonflushing equipment in toilet learning/training shall not be counted as toilets in the toilet:child ratio.

RATIONALE: Nonflushing toilet equipment is a significant sanitation hazard and does not supplant the need for flushing toilet equipment for children who can use the toilet.

COMMENTS: Nonflushing toilets include potty chairs.

TYPE OF FACILITY: *Center; Large Family Child Care Home; Small Family Child Care Home*

TYPE OF FACILITY: *Center; Large Family Child Care Home; Small Family Child Care Home*

STANDARD 5.124
TOILET LEARNING/TRAINING EQUIPMENT

Equipment used for toilet learning/training shall be provided for children who are learning to use the toilet. Child-sized toilets or safe and cleanable step aids and modified toilet seats (where adult-sized toilets are present) shall be used in facilities. Nonflushing toilets (potty chairs) shall be strongly discouraged.

If child-sized toilets, step aids, or modified toilet seats cannot be used, non-flushing toilets (potty chairs) meeting the following criteria shall be provided for toddlers, preschoolers, and children with disabilities who require them. Potty chairs shall be:
a) Easily cleaned and sanitized;
b) Used only in a bathroom area;
c) Used over a surface that is impervious to moisture;
d) Out of reach of toilets or other potty chairs;
e) Cleaned and sanitized after each use in a sink used only for cleaning and sanitizing potty chairs.

Equipment used for toilet learning/training shall be accessible to children only under direct supervision.

RATIONALE: Child-sized toilets that are flushable, steps, and modified toilet seats provide for easier maintenance. Sanitary handling of potty chairs is difficult. Flushing toilets are superior to any type of device that exposes the staff to contact with feces or urine. Many communicable diseases can be prevented through appropriate hygiene and sanitation methods. Surveys of environmental surfaces in child care settings have demonstrated evidence of fecal contamination. Fecal contamination has been used to gauge the adequacy of sanitation and hygiene.

COMMENTS: Low toilets with appropriate seats are preferable to nonflushing potty chairs.

STANDARD 5.125
WASTE RECEPTACLES IN TOILET ROOMS

Toilet rooms shall have at least one waste receptacle with a foot-pedal operated lid.

RATIONALE: In toilet rooms, users may need to dispose of waste that is contaminated with body fluids. Sanitary disposal of this material requires a lidded container that does not have to be handled to be opened.

COMMENTS: For additional information on general requirements for toilet, diapering, and bath, see also Sanitation, Disinfection and Maintenance of Toilet Learning/Training Equipment, Toilets, and Bathrooms, STANDARD 3.029 through STANDARD 3.033.

TYPE OF FACILITY: *Center*

SINKS

STANDARD 5.126
HANDWASHING SINKS

A handwashing sink shall be accessible without barriers (such as doors) to each child care area. In areas for infants, toddlers, and preschoolers, the sink shall be located so the caregiver may visually supervise the group of children while carrying out routine handwashing or having children wash their hands. Sinks shall be placed at the child's height or be equipped with a stable step platform to make the sink available to children. If a platform is used, it shall have slip-proof steps and platform surface. Also, each sink shall be equipped so that the user has access to:
a) Water, at a temperature at least 60 and no hotter than 120 degrees F;
b) A foot-pedal operated, electric-eye operated, open, self-closing, slow-closing, or metering faucet that provides a flow of water for at

least 30 seconds without the need to reactivate the faucet;
c) A supply of handcleansing liquid soap;
d) Disposable single-use cloth or paper towels or a heated-air hand-drying device with heat guards to prevent contact with surfaces that get hotter than 110 degrees F.

A steam tap or a water tap that provides hot water that is hotter than 120 degrees F may not be used at a handwashing sink.

RATIONALE: Transmission of many communicable diseases can be prevented through handwashing. To facilitate routine handwashing at the many appropriate times, sinks must be close at hand and permit caregivers to provide continuous supervision while they wash their hands. The location, access, and supporting supplies to enable adequate handwashing are important to the successful integration of this key routine. Foot-pedaled operated or electric-eye operated handwashing sinks and liquid soap dispensers are preferable because they minimize hand contamination during and after handwashing. The flow of water must continue long enough for the user to wet the skin surface, get soap, lather for at least 10 seconds, and rinse completely.

Comfortably warm water helps to release soil from hand surfaces and provides comfort for the person who is washing the hands. When the water is too cold or too hot for comfort, the person is less likely to wet and rinse long enough to lather and wash off soil. Having a steam tap or a super-heated hot water tap available at a handwashing sink poses a significant risk of scald burns.

COMMENTS: Shared access to soap and disposable towels at more than one sink is acceptable if the location of these is fully accessible to each person. There is no evidence that antibacterial soap reduces the incidence of illness among children in child care. For more information about heating water and preventing burns, see STANDARD 5.040. See STANDARD 4.045 through STANDARD 4.046, for sinks used for food preparation and handwashing sinks in food preparation areas.

TYPE OF FACILITY: *Center*

STANDARD 5.127 PROHIBITED USES OF HANDWASHING SINKS

Handwashing sinks shall not be used for rinsing soiled clothing or for cleaning equipment that is used for toileting.

RATIONALE: The sink used to wash/rinse soiled clothing or equipment used for toileting becomes contaminated during this process and can be a source of transmission of disease to those who wash their hands in that sink.

TYPE OF FACILITY: *Center; Large Family Child Care Home*

STANDARD 5.128 MOP SINKS

Centers with more than 30 children shall have a mop sink. Large and small family child-care homes shall have a means of obtaining clean water for mopping and disposing of it in a toilet or in a sink used only for such purposes.

RATIONALE: Handwashing and food preparation sinks must not be contaminated by wastewater. Contamination of hands, toys, and equipment in the room plays a role in the transmission of diseases in child care settings (28, 29).

COMMENTS: For additional information on sinks, see also STANDARD 5.060 on the use of a water supply when plumbing is unavailable, and information on kitchen sinks, STANDARD 4.045 through STANDARD 4.046.

TYPE OF FACILITY: *Center; Large Family Child Care Home; Small Family Child Care Home*

DIAPER CHANGING AREAS

STANDARD 5.129
DIAPER CHANGING TABLES

The facility shall have at least one diaper changing table per infant group or toddler group to allow sufficient time for changing diapers and for cleaning and sanitizing between children. Diaper changing tables and sinks shall be used only by the children in the group whose routine care is provided together throughout their time in child care. The facility shall not permit shared use of diaper changing tables and sinks by more than one group.

RATIONALE: Diaper changing requires time, as does cleaning the changing surfaces. When caregivers from different groups use the same diaper changing surface, disease spreads more easily from group to group. Child care facilities should not put the diaper changing tables and sinks in a buffer zone between two classrooms, because doing so effectively joins the groups from the perspective of cross-contamination.

COMMENTS: See STANDARD 1.001 and STANDARD 1.002, on supervision according to group size. See also STANDARD 5.132 for more information on diaper changing areas.

TYPE OF FACILITY: *Center; Large Family Child Care Home*

STANDARD 5.130
HANDWASHING SINKS FOR DIAPER CHANGING AREAS IN CENTERS

Handwashing sinks in centers shall be provided within arm's reach of the caregiver to diaper changing tables and toilets. A minimum of one handwashing sink shall be available for every two changing tables. Where infants and toddlers are in care, sinks and diaper changing tables shall be assigned for use to a specific group of children and used only by children and adults who are in the assigned group as defined by STANDARD 5.129. Handwashing sinks shall not be used for bathing or removing smeared fecal material.

RATIONALE: Sinks must be close to where the diapering takes place to avoid transfer of contaminants to other surfaces en route to washing the hands of staff and children. Having sinks close by will help prevent the spread of contaminants and disease.

When sinks are shared by multiple groups, cross-contamination occurs. Many child care centers put the diaper changing tables and sinks in a buffer zone between two classrooms, effectively joining the groups through cross-contamination.

COMMENTS: Shared access to soap and disposable towels at more than one sink is acceptable if the location of these is fully accessible to each person.

See also STANDARD 5.132, for more information on diaper changing areas.

TYPE OF FACILITY: *Center*

STANDARD 5.131
HANDWASHING SINKS FOR DIAPER CHANGING AREAS IN HOMES

Handwashing sinks in large and small family child care homes shall be supplied for diaper changing, as specified in STANDARD 5.130, except that they shall be within 10 feet of the changing table if the diapering area cannot be set up so the sink is adjacent to the changing table. If diapered toddlers and preschool-age children are in care, a stepstool shall be available at the handwashing sink, as specified in STANDARD 5.126, so smaller children can stand at the sink to wash their hands. Handwashing sinks shall not be used for bathing or removing smeared fecal material.

RATIONALE: When children from more than one family are in care, the diaper changing area should be arranged to be as close as possible to a non-food sink to avoid fecal-oral transmission of infection. Most home bathrooms can be adapted for diapering by putting two or all of the legs of a diaper changing table in the tub or, in the worst case, in the room adjacent to the bathroom.

Sinks must be close to where the diapering takes place to avoid transfer of contaminants to other surfaces en route to washing the hands of staff and children. Having sinks close by will help prevent the spread of contaminants and disease.

COMMENTS: See also STANDARD 5.132, for more information on diaper changing areas.

TYPE OF FACILITY: *Large Family Child Care Home; Small Family Child Care Home*

STANDARD 5.132
LOCATION AND SETUP OF DIAPER CHANGING AREAS

The changing area shall not be located in food preparation areas and shall not be used for temporary placement of food or utensils or for serving of food. Food and drinking utensils shall not be washed in these sinks. Changing areas and food preparation areas shall be physically separated.

The diaper changing area shall be set up so that no other surface or supply container is contaminated during diaper changing. Bulk supplies shall not be stored on or brought to the diaper changing surface. Instead, the diapers, wipes, gloves, a thick layer of diaper cream on a piece of disposable paper, a plastic bag for soiled clothes, and disposable paper to cover the table in the amount needed for a specific diaper change will be removed from the bulk container or storage location and placed on or near the diaper changing surface before bringing the child to the diaper changing area.

Conveniently located, washable, plastic lined, tightly covered, hands free receptacles, shall be provided for soiled cloths and linen containing body fluids.

Where only one staff member is available to supervise a group of children, the diaper changing table shall be positioned to allow the staff member to maintain constant sight and sound supervision of children.

RATIONALE: The separation of diaper changing areas and food preparation areas prevents transmission of disease.

Bringing storage containers to the diaper changing table is likely to result in their contamination during the diaper changing process. When these containers stay on the table or are replaced in a storage location, they become conduits for transmitting disease agents. Bringing to the table only the amount of each supply that will be consumed in that specific diaper changing will prevent contamination of diapering supplies and the environment. Diaper changing areas should be designed to prevent contamination during the diaper changing process (43).

Hands free receptacles prevent environmental contamination so the children do not come into contact with disease-bearing body fluids.

Often, only one staff person is supervising children when a child has to be changed. Orienting the diaper change table so the staff member can maintain direct observation of all children in the room allows adequate supervision.

COMMENTS: See also containment of soiled diapers STANDARD 5.067.

TYPE OF FACILITY: *Center; Large Family Child Care Home; Small Family Child Care Home*

STANDARD 5.133
CHANGING TABLE REQUIREMENTS

Changing tables shall meet the following requirements:
a) Have impervious, nonabsorbent, smooth surfaces that do not trap soil and are easily sanitized;
b) Be sturdy;
c) Be at a convenient height for use by caregivers (between 28 and 32 inches high);
d) Be equipped with railings or barriers that extend at least 6 inches above the change surface.

RATIONALE: This standard is designed to prevent disease transmission and accidental falls and to provide safety measures during diapering. Commercial diaper change tables vary as much as 10 inches in height. Many standard-height 36" counters are used as the diaper change area. When a railing or barrier is attached, shorter staff members cannot change diapers without standing on a step.

Back injury is the most common cause of occupational injury for child care providers. Using changing tables that are sized for caregiver comfort and convenience can help prevent back injury (43). Railings of 2 inches or less in height have been observed in some diaper change areas and when combined with a moisture-impervious diaper changing pad approximately 1 inch thick, render the railing ineffective. A change table height of 28 inches to 32 inches (standard table height) plus a 6-inch barrier will reduce back strain on staff members and provide a safe barrier to prevent children from falling off the change table.

Data from the U.S. Consumer Product Safety Commission (CPSC) shows that falls are a serious hazard associated with baby changing tables (44). Safety straps on changing tables are provided to prevent falls but they trap soil and they are not easily sanitized. Therefore, diaper changing tables should not have safety straps.

COMMENTS: An impervious surface is defined as a smooth surface that does not absorb liquid or retain soil. While changing a child, the adult must hold onto the child at all times. The activity of diaper changing should be used as an opportunity for adult interaction with the child whose diaper is being changed.

TYPE OF FACILITY: *Center; Large Family Child Care Home; Small Family Child Care Home*

BATHTUBS AND SHOWERS

STANDARD 5.134
RATIO AND LOCATION OF BATHTUBS AND SHOWERS

The facility shall have one bathtub or shower for every six children receiving overnight care. If the facility is caring for infants, it shall have age-appropriate bathing facilities for them. Bathtubs and showers, when required or used as part of the daily program, shall be located within the facility or in an approved building immediately adjacent to it.

RATIONALE: A sufficient number of age appropriate bathing tubs and showers must be available to permit separate bathing for every child.

COMMENTS: Assuming that each bath takes 10 to 15 minutes, a ratio of one tub to six children with time to wash the tub between children means that bathing would require about 1½ hours.

TYPE OF FACILITY: *Center; Large Family Child Care Home; Small Family Child Care Home*

STANDARD 5.135
SAFETY OF BATHTUBS AND SHOWERS

All bathing facilities shall have a conveniently located grab bar that is mounted at a height appropriate for a child to use. Nonskid surfaces shall be provided in all tubs and showers. Bathtubs shall be equipped with a mechanism to guarantee that drains are kept open at all times, except during supervised use.

RATIONALE: Falls in tubs are a well-documented source of injury according to the National Electronic Injury Surveillance System (NASS) data collected by the U.S. Consumer Product Safety Commission (CPSC). Grab bars and nonslip surfaces reduce this risk. Drowning and falls in bathtubs are also a significant cause of injury for young children and children with disabilities. An open drain will prevent a pool of water from forming if a child turns on a water faucet and, therefore, will prevent a potential drowning situation.

COMMENTS: For further information on NASS, contact the U.S. Consumer Product Safety Commission (CPSC). Contact information is located in Appendix BB.

TYPE OF FACILITY: *Center*

KITCHEN

See Kitchen and Equipment, STANDARD 4.042 through STANDARD 4.049.

DRINKING WATER

STANDARD 5.136
ACCESSIBILITY OF DRINKING WATER

Drinking water, dispensed in drinking fountains or by single service cups, shall be accessible to children indoors and outdoors.

RATIONALE: Access to water provides for fluid maintenance essential to body health. The water must be protected from contamination to avoid the spread of disease.

COMMENTS: See STANDARD 4.006, for more information on drinking water.

TYPE OF FACILITY: *Center; Large Family Child Care Home; Small Family Child Care Home*

STANDARD 5.137
DRINKING FOUNTAINS

Drinking fountains shall have an angled jet and orifice guard above the rim of the fountain. The pressure shall be regulated so the water stream does not contact the orifice or splash on the floor, but shall rise at least 2 inches above the orifice guard.

At least 18 inches of space shall be provided between a drinking fountain and any kind of towel dispenser.

RATIONALE: Access to water provides for fluid maintenance essential to body health. The water must be protected from contamination to avoid the spread of disease. Space between a drinking fountain and sink or towel dispenser helps prevent contamination of the drinking fountain by organisms being splashed or deposited during handwashing.

COMMENTS: For further information, contact the Environmental Protection Agency (EPA). Contact information is located in Appendix BB.

TYPE OF FACILITY: *Center*

STANDARD 5.138
LEAD CONTENT OF WATER FROM DRINKING FOUNTAINS

Drinking fountains shall be checked to ensure that they are not contributing high levels of lead to the water, as defined by the *Code of Federal Regulations, Parts 141-143*, and by the 1988 Lead Contamination Control Act as amended.

RATIONALE: Drinking water must be safe for consumption. Exposure to toxic levels of lead can cause neural damage and developmental problems.

COMMENTS: Running the tap water for 30 to 60 seconds before using if for drinking and cooking will reduce the presence of lead in drinking water supplies where piping or joint seals contain lead. For further guidance on drinking water, contact the Environmental Protection Agency (EPA). To obtain the *Code of Federal Regulations, Parts 141-143*, contact the Superintendent of Documents. Contact information is located in Appendix BB.

TYPE OF FACILITY: *Center; Large Family Child Care Home; Small Family Child Care Home*

STANDARD 5.139
SINGLE SERVICE CUPS

Single service cups shall be dispensed by staff or in a cup dispenser approved by the regulatory health authority. Single service cups shall not be reused.

RATIONALE: Reusing cups, even by the same person, leads to growth of organisms in the cup between uses.

TYPE OF FACILITY: *Center*

LAUNDRY

STANDARD 5.140
LAUNDRY SERVICE AND EQUIPMENT

Each center shall have a mechanical washing machine and dryer on site or shall contract with a laundry service. Where laundry equipment is used in a large or small family child care home (or the large or small family child care home provider uses a laundromat), the equipment shall comply with STANDARD 5.141.

RATIONALE: Bedding and towels that are not thoroughly cleaned pose a health threat to users of these items.

TYPE OF FACILITY: *Center; Large Family Child Care Home; Small Family Child Care Home*

STANDARD 5.141
LOCATION OF LAUNDRY AND TEMPERATURE

Laundry equipment shall be located in an area separate and secure from the kitchen and child care areas. The water temperature for the laundry shall be maintained above 140 degrees F unless one of the following conditions exists:
a) The product labeled by the manufacturer as a sanitizer is applied according to the manufacturer's instructions, in which case the temperature shall be as specified by the manufacturer of the product;
b) A dryer is used, that the manufacturer attests heats the clothes above 140 degrees F;
c) The clothes are completely ironed (47).

Dryers shall be vented to the outside. Dryer hoses and vent connections shall be checked periodically for proper alignment and connection. If a commercial laundry service is used, its performance shall at least meet or exceed the requirements listed above.

RATIONALE: Chemical sanitizers are temperature-dependent. Ironing or heating the clothing above 140 degrees F will sanitize. Bent dryer hoses can cause lint

to catch in dryer, which is a potential fire hazard. Disconnected dryer hoses will vent lint, dust, and particles indoors, which may cause respiratory problems.

TYPE OF FACILITY: *Center*

SLEEPING AND REST AREAS

STANDARD 5.142
MULTIPLE USE OF ROOMS

Play, dining, and napping may be carried on in the same area (exclusive of diaper changing areas, toilet rooms, kitchens, hallways, and closets), provided that:
a) The room is of sufficient size to have a defined area for each of the activities allowed there at the time the activity is under way;
b) The room meets other building requirements;
c) Programming is such that use of the room for one purpose does not interfere with use of the room for other purposes.

RATIONALE: Except for toilet and diaper changing areas, which must have no other use, the use of common space for different activities for children facilitates close supervision of a group of children, some of whom may be involved simultaneously in more than one of the activities listed in the standard.

COMMENTS: Compliance is measured by direct observation.

TYPE OF FACILITY: *Center; Large Family Child Care Home; Small Family Child Care Home*

STANDARD 5.143
SPACE FOR INFANT SLEEPING ROOMS

Separate sleeping rooms for infants shall have a minimum of 30 square feet of space per child.

RATIONALE: This requirement helps to prevent injury and provides sufficient space for activities.

TYPE OF FACILITY: *Center; Large Family Child Care Home; Small Family Child Care Home*

STANDARD 5.144
SLEEPING EQUIPMENT AND SUPPLIES

Facilities shall have an individual crib, cot, sleeping bag, bed, mat, or pad with clean linen for each child who spends more than 4 hours a day at the facility. No child shall simultaneously share a bed or bedding with another child. Beds and bedding shall be washed between uses if used by different children. Regardless of age group, bed linens shall not be used as rest equipment in place of cots, beds, pads, or similar approved equipment. Bed linens used under children on cots, cribs, futons, and playpens shall be tight-fitting.

When pads are used, they shall be enclosed in washable covers and shall be long enough so the child's head or feet do not rest off the pad. Mats and cots shall be covered with a waterproof material that can be easily washed and sanitized. Plastic bags or loose plastic material shall not be used as a covering.

No child shall sleep on a bare, uncovered surface. Seasonally appropriate covering, such as sheets or blankets that are sufficient to maintain adequate warmth, shall be available and shall be used by each child below school-age. Pillows shall not be used for infants. If pillows are used by toddlers and older children, pillows shall be assigned to a child and used by that child only while he/she is enrolled in the facility.

Pads and sleeping bags shall not be placed directly on any floor that is cooler than 65 degrees F, when children are resting. Cribs, cots, sleeping bags, beds, mats, or pads shall be placed at least 3 feet apart, unless screens separate them. If screens are provided, arrangements shall permit the staff to observe and have immediate access to each child.

Children under the age of 1 shall sleep on a sleep surface, as specified in SSTANDARD 5.146.

The sleeping surfaces of one child's rest equipment shall not come in contact with the sleeping sur-

faces of another child's rest equipment during storage.

RATIONALE: Separate sleeping and resting, even for siblings, reduces the spread of disease from one child to another.

Because respiratory infections are transmitted by large droplets of respiratory secretions, a minimum distance of 3 feet should be maintained between cots, cribs, sleeping bags beds, mats, or pads used for resting or sleeping. Maintaining a 3-foot distance between cots in military barracks limits the transmission of group A streptococcal (GAS) infections (48). It is reasonable to assume that this spacing will reduce the likelihood of transmission of other respiratory disease agents spread by large droplets and will be effective in controlling the spread of infectious disease in the child care environment. A space of 3 feet between cribs, cots, sleeping bags, beds, mats, or pads also will also provide access by the staff to a child in case of emergency. If the facility uses screens to separate the children, their use must not hinder observation of children by staff or access to children in an emergency.

Lice infestation, scabies, and ringworm are among the most common infectious diseases in child care. These diseases are transmitted by direct skin to skin contact or by the sharing of personal articles such as combs, brushes, towels, clothing, and bedding. Prohibiting the sharing of personal articles helps prevent the spread of these diseases.

The use of tight fitting bed linens prevents suffocation and strangling. Pillows pose a suffocation risk for infants.

Children under 1 year of age should sleep in a crib or be otherwise protected from injury while they sleep.

From time to time, children drool, spit up, or spread other body fluids on their sleeping surfaces. Using cleanable, waterproof, nonabsorbent coverings enables the staff to wash and sanitize the sleeping surfaces. Plastic bags may contribute to suffocation if the material clings to the child's face.

COMMENTS: Although children freely interact and can contaminate each other while awake, reducing the transmission of infectious disease agents on large airborne droplets during sleep periods will reduce the dose of such agents to which the child is exposed overall. Research on the benefits of separation during sleeping in child care, similar to the study of young adults in military barracks, is lacking. Nevertheless, these young adults are together during waking hours also, so using this study as an analogous situation is reasonable. In small family child care homes, the caregiver should consider the home to be a business during child care hours and is expected to abide by regulatory expectations that may not apply outside of child care hours. Therefore, child siblings related to the caregiver may not sleep in the same bed during the hours of operation.

Caregivers may ask parents to provide bedding that will be sent home at least weekly for washing.

Pillows need not be used for older children.

Many child care providers find that placing children in alternate positions so that one child's head is across from the other's feet reduces interaction and promotes settling during rest periods. This positioning may be beneficial in reducing transmission of infectious agents as well.

Canvas cots are generally not safe for infants and toddlers. The end caps require constant replacement and the cots are a cutting/pinching hazard when end caps are not in place. Although some cots are covered by canvas material that is moisture-absorbent, a variety of cots with a washable sleeping surface are designed to be safe for children.

For more information on sleep position for infants, see STANDARD 3.008. For information on the dangers of window cords near cribs and bedding, see STANDARD 5.160.

TYPE OF FACILITY: *Center; Large Family Child Care Home; Small Family Child Care Home*

STANDARD 5.145
CRIBS

Cribs shall be made of wood, metal, or plastic and shall have secure latching devices. They shall have slats spaced no more than 2-3/8 inches apart, with a mattress fitted so that no more than two fingers can fit between the mattress and the crib side in the lowest position. The minimum height from the top of the mattress to the top of the crib rail shall be 20 inches in the highest position. Drop-side latches shall securely hold sides in the raised position, and the child in the crib shall not be able to reach them. Cribs shall not be used with the drop side down. The crib shall not have cornerpost extensions (over 1/16 inch). The crib shall have no cutout openings in the head board or footboard structure in which a child's head could become entrapped. The mattress support system shall not be easily dislodged from any point of the crib by an upward force from underneath the crib. All crib hardware shall be securely tightened and checked regularly. All cribs shall meet the American Society for Testing Materials (ASTM) *F1169-99 Standard Specification for Full Size Baby Crib, F966-00 Standard Consumer Safety Specifications for Full-Size and Non-Full-Size Baby Crib Corner Post Extensions,* and the Code of Federal Regulations *16 CFR 1508 Requirements for Full-Size Baby Cribs* and *16 CFR 1509 Requirements for Non-Full-Size Baby Cribs.*

RATIONALE: Children have strangled because their shoulder or neck became caught in a gap between slats or between mattress and crib side that was too wide. Cornerposts present a potential for clothing entanglement and strangulation (49). Asphyxial crib death from wedging the head or neck in parts of the crib and accidental hanging by a necklace or clothing over a cornerpost have been well-documented (50).

U.S. Consumer Product Safety Commission (CPSC) crib safety standards went into effect in 1974 and were upgraded in 1982. In 2000, voluntary standards regarding corner posts are in place. Refer to the *ASTM F966-00 Standard Consumer Safety Specification for Full-Size and Non-Full-Size Baby Crib Corner Post Extensions.* Still, thousands of older cribs are in use or in attic storage and could be used by the next generation of children. Cribs should not be used with the side down, as children may fall out. The mattress support system must not be easily dislodged from any point of the crib by an upward force from underneath the crib. All four mattress support hangers must be held securely in place. The failure of even one hanger can cause the mattress to sag in the corner and pose an entrapment hazard.

COMMENTS: If portable cribs and those that are not full size are substituted for regular full-sized cribs, they must be maintained in the condition that meets the *ASTM Standard F1822-97 Consumer Safety Specification for Non-Full-Size Baby Cribs.* Portable cribs are designed so they may be folded or collapsed, with or without disassembly. Although portable cribs are not designed to withstand the wear and tear of normal full-sized cribs, they may provide more flexibility for programs that vary the number of infants in care from time to time.

Cribs with big wheels (8 inches wide) are preferred in child care settings with ramps, as they are advantageous during fire evacuation of children. Contact information for ASTM and CPSC is located in Appendix BB.

TYPE OF FACILITY: *Center; Large Family Child Care Home; Small Family Child Care Home*

STANDARD 5.146
INFANT SLEEPING POSITION
EQUIPMENT AND SUPPLIES

Infants under 12 months of age shall be placed on their backs on a firm mattress, mat or pad manufactured for sale in the United States as infant sleeping equipment, for sleep. The mattress, mat, or pad shall either be tightly fitted in furniture manufactured for sale in the United States as infant sleeping equipment or placed where the child cannot fall to a lower surface while resting. If no containing structure is used, the child shall be protected from access to hazards in the sleeping area. Waterbeds, sofas, soft mattresses, pillows, and other soft surfaces shall be prohibited as infant sleeping surfaces. All pillows, quilts, comforters, sheepskins, stuffed toys, and other soft products shall be removed from the crib. If a blanket is used, the infant shall be placed at the foot of the crib with a thin blanket tucked around the crib mattress, reaching only as far as the infant's chest.

The infant's head shall remain uncovered during sleep.

RATIONALE: Placing infants to sleep on their backs instead of their stomachs has been associated with a dramatic decrease in deaths from Sudden Infant Death Syndrome (SIDS). Infants have been found dead on their stomachs with their faces, noses, and mouths covered by soft bedding, such as pillows, quilts, comforters, and sheepskins. However, some infants have been found dead with their heads covered by soft bedding even while sleeping on their backs (51).

Mattresses, mats and pads may be used in a way that does not expose the child to the risk of injury from entrapment or falls. If the mattress, mat or pad is not contained in a crib or similar furniture manufactured for sale in the United States for sleeping of infants, the child's sleeping arrangement must prevent the child from gaining access to hazards. See STANDARD 5.145 regarding requirements and American Society for Testing Materials (ASTM) standards for cribs. Furniture made by someone who does not follow the safety standards may unwittingly expose the child to hazards.

COMMENTS: Consider using a sleeper or other sleep clothing as an alternative to blankets, using no other covering.

TYPE OF FACILITY: *Center; Large Family Child Care Home; Small Family Child Care Home*

STANDARD 5.147
FUTONS

Child-sized futons shall be used only if they meet the following requirements:
a) Not on a frame;
b) Easily cleanable;
c) Encased in a tight-fitting waterproof cover;
d) Meet all other standards in Sleeping, STANDARD 5.142 through STANDARD 5.148.

RATIONALE: Frames pose an entrapment hazard. Futons that are easy to clean can be kept sanitary. Supervision is necessary to maintain adequate spacing of futons and ensure that bedding is not shared, thereby reducing transmission of infectious diseases and keeping children out of traffic areas.

TYPE OF FACILITY: *Center; Large Family Child Care Home; Small Family Child Care Home*

STANDARD 5.148
BUNK BEDS

Children younger than 6 years of age shall not use the upper levels of double-deck beds (or "bunk beds"). Bunk beds must conform to the *U.S. Consumer Product Safety Commission (CPSC) Facts Document #071, Bunk Beds* and the American Society for Testing and Materials (ASTM) *F1427-96 Standard Consumer Safety Specification for Bunk Beds.*

RATIONALE: Falls and entrapment between mattress and guardrails, bed structure and wall, or between slats from bunk beds are a well-documented cause of injury in young children.

COMMENTS: Consult the CPSC, the manufacturer's label, or the consumer safety information provided by the American Furniture Manufacturer's Association (AFMA) for advice. Contact information for the CPSC, the ASTM, and the AFMA is located in Appendix BB.

TYPE OF FACILITY: *Center; Large Family Child Care Home; Small Family Child Care Home*

AREAS FOR SPECIAL THERAPIES AND INJURED OR ILL CHILDREN

STANDARD 5.149
SPACE FOR ILL CHILD

Each facility shall have a separate room or designated area within a room for the temporary or ongoing care of a child who needs to be separated from the group because of injury or illness. This room or area shall be located so the child may be supervised. Toilet and lavatory

facilities shall be readily accessible. If the child under care is suspected of having a communicable disease, all equipment the child uses shall be cleaned and sanitized after use. This room or area may be used for other purposes when it is not needed for the separation and care of a child or if the uses do not conflict.

RATIONALE: Children who are injured or ill may need to be separated from other children to provide for rest and to minimize the spread of potential infectious disease. Toilet and lavatory facilities must be readily available to permit frequent handwashing and provide rapid access in the event of vomiting or diarrhea to avoid contaminating the environment. Handwashing sinks should be stationed in each room not only to provide the opportunity to maintain cleanliness but also to permit the caregiver to maintain continuous supervision of the other children in care.

COMMENTS: Separate rooms need not be used for mild illness since children may consider isolation as a form of punishment. For additional information on caring for injured or ill children, see STANDARD 3.072 though STANDARD 3.080; and STANDARD 8.011 and STANDARD 8.012. See STANDARD 3.066, for situations that require separation or isolation.

TYPE OF FACILITY: *Center; Large Family Child Care Home; Small Family Child Care Home*

STANDARD 5.150
SPACE FOR THERAPY SERVICES

In addition to accessible classrooms, in facilities where some but fewer than 15 children need occupational or physical therapy and some but fewer than 20 children need individual speech therapy, centers shall provide a quiet, private, accessible area within the child care facility for therapy. No other activities shall take place in this area at the time therapy is being provided.

Family child care homes and facilities integrating children who need therapy services shall receive these services in a space that is separate and private during the time the child is receiving therapy.

Additional space may be needed for equipment according to a child's needs.

RATIONALE: Quiet, private space is necessary for physical, occupational, and speech therapies. Most caregivers also indicate that the other children in the facility are disrupted less if the therapies are provided in a separate area. For speech therapy, in particular, working with the child in a quiet location is especially important. Privacy is better for the child and the therapist, and this arrangement is also less distracting to the other children. Nevertheless, child care providers should attempt to incorporate therapeutic principles into the child's general child care activities. Doing so will achieve maximum benefit for the child receiving therapy and promote understanding on the part of the child's peers and caregivers about how to address the child's disability when the therapist is not present.

TYPE OF FACILITY: *Center; Large Family Child Care Home; Small Family Child Care Home*

STORAGE OF CLOTHING, SUPPLIES, AND EQUIPMENT

STANDARD 5.151
STORAGE AND LABELING OF PERSONAL ARTICLES

The facility shall provide separate storage areas for each child's and staff member's personal articles and clothing. Personal effects and clothing shall be labeled with the child's name. Bedding shall be labeled with the child's name and stored separately for each child.

If children use the following items at the child care facility, those items shall be stored in separate, clean containers and shall be labeled with the child's name:
a)   Individual cloth towels for bathing purposes;
b)   Toothbrushes;
c)   Washcloths;
d)   Combs and brushes.

Toothbrushes, towels, and washcloths shall be dry so they can be stored.

RATIONALE: This standard prevents the spread of organisms that cause disease and promotes organization of a child's personal possessions. Lice infestation, scabies, and ringworm are among the most common infectious diseases in child care. Body lice can crawl from one coat collar or hood to another when hooks allow children's clothing to touch each other when hanging. These diseases can be transmitted by direct skin-to-skin contact or by the sharing of personal articles such as combs, brushes, towels, clothing, and bedding. Providing space so personal items may be stored separately helps to prevent the spread of these diseases.

COMMENTS: See also STANDARD 5.144, for additional information on separate bedding.

TYPE OF FACILITY: *Center; Large Family Child Care Home; Small Family Child Care Home*

STANDARD 5.152
STORAGE FOR ADAPTIVE EQUIPMENT

The facility shall provide storage space for all adaptive equipment (such as equipment for physical therapy, occupational therapy, or adaptive physical education) separate and apart from classroom floor space. The storage space shall be easily accessible to the staff. Equipment shall be stored safely and in an organized way.

RATIONALE: Frequently, storing adaptive equipment is a problem in centers. This equipment should be stored outside of classroom space to maximize floor space and minimize distracting clutter.

TYPE OF FACILITY: *Center*

STANDARD 5.153
COAT HOOKS/CUBICLES

Coat hooks shall be spaced so coats will not touch each other, or individual cubicles or lockers of the child's height shall be provided for storing children's clothing and personal possessions.

RATIONALE: Lice infestation, scabies, and ringworm are among the most common infectious diseases in child care. These diseases are transmitted through direct skin-to-skin contact or by sharing personal articles such as combs, brushes, towels, clothing, and bedding. Providing space so personal items may be stored separately helps prevent spread of these diseases.

COMMENTS: Whenever possible, coat hooks should not be placed at children's eye level because of potential risk of injury to eyes.

TYPE OF FACILITY: *Center; Large Family Child Care Home; Small Family Child Care Home*

STANDARD 5.154
STORAGE OF PLAY AND TEACHING EQUIPMENT AND SUPPLIES

The facility shall provide and use space to store play and teaching equipment, supplies, records and files, cots, mats, and bedding.

RATIONALE: This practice enhances safety and provides a good example of an orderly environment.

TYPE OF FACILITY: *Center; Large Family Child Care Home; Small Family Child Care Home*

STANDARD 5.155
STORAGE FOR SOILED AND CLEAN LINENS

Child care facilities shall provide separate storage areas for soiled linen and clean linen.

RATIONALE: This practice discourages contamination of clean areas and children with soiled and contaminated linen. Providing separate storage areas reduces fire load and helps contain fire, if spontaneous combustion occurs in soiled linens.

TYPE OF FACILITY: *Center; Large Family Child Care Home; Small Family Child Care Home*

STANDARD 5.156
CLOSET DOOR LATCHES

Closet doors accessible to children shall have an internal release for any latch so a child inside the closet can open the door.

RATIONALE: Closet doors that can be opened from the inside prevent entrapment.

TYPE OF FACILITY: *Center; Large Family Child Care Home; Small Family Child Care Home*

STANDARD 5.157
INACCESSIBILITY MATCHES AND LIGHTERS

Matches and lighters shall not be accessible to children.

RATIONALE: Eight percent of residential fire deaths are attributed to children playing with matches, cigarette lighters, and other ignition sources (14).

TYPE OF FACILITY: *Center; Large Family Child Care Home; Small Family Child Care Home*

STANDARD 5.158
STORAGE OF FLAMMABLE MATERIALS

Gasoline and other flammable materials shall be stored in a separate building, away from the children.

RATIONALE: Flammable materials are involved in most non-house fire flash burn admissions to burn units among boys 6 to 16 years of age (52). These materials are also involved in unintentional ingestion by children.

TYPE OF FACILITY: *Center; Large Family Child Care Home; Small Family Child Care Home*

STANDARD 5.159
STORAGE OF PLASTIC BAGS

Plastic bags, whether intended for storage, trash, diaper disposal, or any other purpose, shall be stored out of reach of children.

RATIONALE: Plastic bags have been recognized for many years as a cause of suffocation. Warnings regarding this risk are printed on diaper-pail bags, dry-cleaning bags, and so forth. Baker and Fisher (53) found that 4 of 22 deaths by suffocation in Maryland between 1970 and 1978 involved plastic bags. Plastic bags were the most frequent cause of childhood suffocation in their study.

TYPE OF FACILITY: *Center; Large Family Child Care Home; Small Family Child Care Home*

STANDARD 5.160
INACCESSIBILITY OF STRINGS AND CORDS

Strings and cords (such as those that are parts of toys and those found on window coverings) long enough to encircle a child's neck shall not be accessible to children in child care.

Pacifiers attached to strings or ribbons shall not be placed around infants' necks or attached to infants' clothing.

Hood and neck strings from all children's outerwear, including jackets and sweatshirts, shall be removed. Drawstrings on the waist or bottom of garments shall not extend more than 3 inches outside the garment when it is fully expanded. These strings shall have no knots or toggles on the free ends. The drawstring shall be sewn to the garment at its midpoint so the string cannot be pulled out through one side.

RATIONALE: Window covering cords are frequently associated with strangulation of children under five years of age (54). Younger victims, usually between 10 to 15 months of age, can become entangled in cords from window coverings near their cribs. Older children, usually between 2 to 4 years of age, become entangled in cords while climbing on furniture to look out of windows.

Cords and ribbons tied to pacifiers can become tightly twisted, or can catch on crib cornerposts or other protrusions, causing strangulation.

Clothing strings on children's clothing can catch on playground equipment and strangle children. From January 1995 through January 1999 the U.S. Consumer Product Safety Commission (CPSC) reported 22 deaths and 48 non-fatal incidents involving the entanglement of children's clothing drawstrings (55).

COMMENTS: Children's outerwear that has alternative closures (such as snaps, buttons, velcro, and elastic) are recommended.

It is advisable that caregivers avoid wearing necklaces or clothing with drawstrings that could cause entanglement.

For additional information regarding the prevention of strangulation from strings on toys, window coverings, clothing contact the U.S CPSC. Contact information for the CPSC is located in Appendix BB.

TYPE OF FACILITY: *Center; Large Family Child Care Home; Small Family Child Care Home*

STANDARD 5.161
FIREARMS

Centers shall not have any firearms, pellet or BB guns (loaded or unloaded), darts, bows and arrows, cap pistols, or objects manufactured for play as toy guns within the premises at any time. If present in a small or large family child care home, these items must be unloaded, equipped with child protective devices, and kept under lock and key in areas inaccessible to the children. Parents shall be informed about this policy.

RATIONALE: The potential for injury to and death of young children due to firearms is becoming increasingly apparent. These items shall not be accessible to children in a facility (57).

COMMENTS: Compliance is monitored via inspection.

TYPE OF FACILITY: *Center; Large Family Child Care Home; Small Family Child Care Home*

5.3 ACTIVE PLAY INDOOR AND OUTDOOR AREAS

LAYOUT, LOCATION, AND SIZE OF ACTIVE PLAY INDOOR AND OUTDOOR AREAS

STANDARD 5.162
SIZE AND LOCATION OF OUTDOOR PLAY AREA

The facility shall be equipped with an outdoor play area that directly adjoins the indoor facilities or that can be reached by a route that is free of hazards and is no farther than 1/8-mile from the facility. The playground shall comprise a minimum of 75 square feet for each child using the playground at any one time.

The following exceptions to the space requirements shall apply:
a) A minimum of 33 square feet of accessible outdoor play space is required for each infant;
b) A minimum of 50 square feet of accessible outdoor play space is required for each child from 18 to 24 months of age.

RATIONALE: Play areas must be sufficient to allow freedom of movement without collisions among active children. The space allocations and exceptions are based on early childhood and playground professionals' experience.

COMMENTS: See also STANDARD 5.164, regarding the number of children that must be accommodated on an outdoor play area at any one time. If the play area is an off-site playground, see STANDARD 5.196.

TYPE OF FACILITY: *Center*

STANDARD 5.163
SIZE AND REQUIREMENTS OF INDOOR PLAY AREA

If a facility has less than 75 square feet of accessible outdoor space per child or provides active play space indoors for other reasons, a large indoor activity room that meets the requirement for 75 square feet per child may be used if it meets the following requirements:
a) It provides for types of activities equivalent to those performed in an outdoor play space;
b) The area is ventilated with fresh, temperate air at a minimum of 5 cubic feet per minute per occupant when open windows are not possible;
c) The surfaces and finishes are shock-absorbing, as required for outdoor installations in STANDARD 5.183;
d) The play equipment meets the requirements for outdoor installation as stated in STANDARD 5.170 through STANDARD 5.175, STANDARD 5.181 through STANDARD 5.189.

RATIONALE: This standard provides facilities located in inner-city areas with an alternative that allows gross motor play when outdoor spaces are unavailable or unusable. Gross motor play must provide an experience like outdoor play, with safe and healthful environmental conditions that match the benefits of outdoor play as closely as possible. These spaces may be interior if ventilation is adequate to prevent undue concentration of organisms and odors.

COMMENTS: Every ventilating contractor has a meter to measure the rate of airflow. Before indoor areas are used for gross motor activity, a heating and air conditioning contractor should be called in to make airflow measurements.

TYPE OF FACILITY: *Center*

STANDARD 5.164
CAPACITY OF OUTDOOR PLAY AREA

The total outdoor play area shall accommodate at least 33% of the licensed capacity at one time.

RATIONALE: Staggered scheduling can be used to accommodate all the children over the course of 2 to 3 hours. Every young child should have the opportunity for gross motor play at least once and preferably twice a day.

TYPE OF FACILITY: *Center*

STANDARD 5.165
ROOFTOPS AS PLAY AREAS

A rooftop used as a play area shall be enclosed with a fence not less than 6 feet high, and the bottom edge shall be no more than 3 ½ inches from the base. The fence shall be designed to prevent children from climbing it. An approved fire escape shall lead from the roof to an open space at the ground level that meets the safety standards for outdoor play areas.

RATIONALE: Rooftop spaces used for play must have safeguards to prevent children from falling off.

COMMENTS: See also Exits, STANDARD 5.020 through STANDARD 5.025.

TYPE OF FACILITY: *Center*

STANDARD 5.166
ELEVATED PLAY AREAS

Elevated play areas that have been created using a retaining wall shall have a guardrail or fence running along the top of the retaining wall.

If the exposed side of the retaining wall is higher than 2 feet, a fence not less than 6 feet high shall be installed. The bottom edge of the fence shall be no more than 3 ½ inches from the base. The fence shall be designed to prevent children from climbing

it (58). If the height of the exposed side of the retaining wall is 2 feet or lower, a guardrail shall be installed.

RATIONALE: This standard is intended to prevent injuries. Children falling from elevated play areas may suffer fatal head injuries.

COMMENTS: If the exposed side of the retaining wall is less than 2 feet high, additional safety can be provided by placing impact absorbing material at the base of the exposed side of the retaining wall. See Appendix V, for information on depth required for tested shock-absorbing surfacing materials for use under playground equipment.

For a list of recommended absorbing materials, see the *U.S. Consumer Product Safety Commission's Handbook for Public Playground Safety* and the American Society for Testing and Materials (ASTM) *F1487-98 Standard Consumer Safety Performance Specifications for Playground Equipment for Public Use.* Contact information for the CPSC and the ASTM is located in Appendix BB.

TYPE OF FACILITY: *Center; Large Family Child Care Home; Small Family Child Care Home*

STANDARD 5.167
LOCATION OF SATELLITE DISHES

A satellite dish shall not be located within playgrounds or other areas accessible to children. If a satellite dish is on the premises, it shall be surrounded by a fence or natural barrier (at least 4 feet high) to prevent children from climbing on it.

RATIONALE: Children are at risk for injury if they are allowed to climb on or play near satellite dishes.

TYPE OF FACILITY: *Center; Large Family Child Care Home; Small Family Child Care Home*

STANDARD 5.168
VISIBILITY OF OUTDOOR PLAY AREA

The outdoor play area shall be arranged so all areas are visible to the staff at all times.

RATIONALE: This arrangement promotes the prevention of injury and abuse.

COMMENTS: Compliance can be ascertained by inspection.

TYPE OF FACILITY: *Center; Large Family Child Care Home; Small Family Child Care Home*

STANDARD 5.169
FENCING AND OUTDOOR HAZARDS

The playground site shall be free of hazards and more than 30 feet from hazards such as the following:
a) Electrical transformers;
b) High-voltage power lines;
c) Electrical substations;
d) Air-conditioner units;
e) Railroad tracks;
f) Sources of toxic fumes or gases.

Fencing or another form of barrier such as a hedge or other plants (at least 4 feet high) that restrains the children, and that they cannot climb, must be provided around the play area and around any fixtures within the play area listed above as hazards. Fencing twist wires and bolts shall face away from the playground.

RATIONALE: This measure is essential for preventing access to streets (such as the unsupervised retrieval of a ball from a busy street) and other hazards.

COMMENTS: Children have been known to climb through hedges.

TYPE OF FACILITY: *Center; Large Family Child Care Home; Small Family Child Care Home*

STANDARD 5.170
CLEARANCE REQUIREMENTS OF PLAYGROUND AREAS

Playgrounds shall be laid out to ensure clearance in accordance with the American Society for Testing and Materials (ASTM) *F1487-98 Consumer Safety Performance Specifications for Playground Equipment for Public Use* and the *U.S. Consumer Product Safety Commission (CPSC) Handbook for Public Playground Safety.*

Equipment shall be situated so that clearance space allocated to one piece of equipment does not encroach on that of another piece of equipment.

RATIONALE: This standard ensures ample space to enable movement around and use of equipment and also helps to restrict the number of pieces of equipment within the play area, thus preventing overcrowding and reducing the potential for injury.

COMMENTS: Contact information for the ASTM and the CPSC is located in Appendix BB.

TYPE OF FACILITY: *Center*

STANDARD 5.171
CLEARANCE SPACE FOR SWINGS

Swings shall have a clearance area of 6 feet. The use zone to the front and rear of the swings shall extend a minimum distance of twice the height of the pivot point measured from a point directly beneath the pivot to the protective surface. Swings shall be arranged in accordance with the American Society for Testing and Materials (ASTM) *F1487-98 Consumer Safety Performance Specifications for Playground Equipment for Public Use* and the *U.S. Consumer Product Safety Commission (CPSC) Handbook for Public Playground Safety.*

RATIONALE: A clear space area is necessary to avoid body contact with children in swings (55).

COMMENTS: To calculate zone: [height of the top pivot point of the swing from the ground] x 2 = "use zone" in front of the swing and [height of the top

pivot point of the swing from the ground] x 2 = "use zone" behind the swing. There should be no objects or persons within the "use zone," other than the child on the swing.

Contact information for the ASTM and the CPSC is located in Appendix BB.

TYPE OF FACILITY: *Center; Large Family Child Care Home; Small Family Child Care Home*

STANDARD 5.172
CLEARANCE SPACE FOR FIXED PLAY EQUIPMENT

All fixed play equipment shall have a minimum of 6 feet clearance space from walkways, buildings, and other structures that are not used as part of play activities.

RATIONALE: This standard, based on recommendations from the U.S. Consumer Product Safety Commission (CPSC), is to prevent injuries from falls.

COMMENTS: For further information on playground equipment clearance, contact the CPSC. Contact information is located in Appendix BB.

TYPE OF FACILITY: *Center; Large Family Child Care Home; Small Family Child Care Home*

STANDARD 5.173
SHADING OF METAL OUTDOOR PLAY EQUIPMENT

Metal equipment (especially slides) shall be placed in the shade.

RATIONALE: Placing metal equipment (such as slides) in the shade prevents the buildup of heat on play surfaces. Hot play surfaces can cause burns on children.

TYPE OF FACILITY: *Center; Large Family Child Care Home; Small Family Child Care Home*

STANDARD 5.174
ARRANGEMENT OF PLAY EQUIPMENT

All equipment shall be arranged so that children playing on one piece of equipment will not interfere with children playing on or running to another piece of equipment.

RATIONALE: Equipment should be arranged so collisions between children utilizing different pieces of equipment is prevented (58).

TYPE OF FACILITY: *Center; Large Family Child Care Home; Small Family Child Care Home*

STANDARD 5.175
LOCATION OF MOVING PLAY EQUIPMENT

Moving play equipment, such as swings and merry-go-rounds, shall be located toward the edge or corner of a play area, or shall be designed in such a way as to discourage children from running into the path of the moving equipment.

RATIONALE: Equipment should be arranged so collisions between children utilizing different pieces of equipment is prevented (58). Placing moving equipment around the perimeter of the play area will reduce the numbers of traffic paths around this equipment.

COMMENTS: The play spaces discussed above are assumed to be those at the site and thus are the facility's responsibility. Facilities that do not have on-site play areas but that use playgrounds and equipment in adjacent parks and/or schools may not be able to ensure that children in their facility are playing on equipment or in play space in absolute conformance with the standards presented here. Playgrounds designed for older children might present intrinsic hazards to preschool-age children. Facility managers and parents should seek to ensure that using off-site playgrounds do not pose undue hazards.

TYPE OF FACILITY: *Center; Large Family Child Care Home; Small Family Child Care Home*

STANDARD 5.176
LOCATION OF PLAY AREAS NEAR BODIES OF WATER

Outside play areas shall be free from the following bodies of water:
a) Unprotected swimming and wading pools;
b) Ditches;
c) Quarries;
d) Canals;
e) Excavations;
f) Fish ponds;
g) Other bodies of water.

RATIONALE: Drowning is one of the leading cause of unintentional injury in children under 5 years of age (59). In some parts of the United States, including the South, the Southwest, and California, drowning is the leading cause of death in children under 5 years of age (59).

TYPE OF FACILITY: *Center; Large Family Child Care Home; Small Family Child Care Home*

EQUIPMENT, ENCLOSURES, COVERINGS, AND SURFACING OF PLAYGROUND AND OUTDOOR AREAS

STANDARD 5.177
EXPOSURE TO SUN IN OUTDOOR SPACES

Sunlit areas and shaded areas shall be provided by means of open space and tree plantings or other cover in outdoor spaces.

RATIONALE: Exposure to sun is needed, but children must be protected from excessive exposure. It is estimated that 80 percent of a person's lifetime sun damage occurs before the age of 18 years. (60)

Individuals who suffered severe childhood sunburns are at increased risk for skin cancer. It can take less

than 10 minutes for a child's skin to burn. Practicing sun-safe behavior during childhood is the first step in reducing the chances of getting skin cancer later in life (61).

COMMENTS: A tent, awning, or other simple shelter from the sun should be available.

See STANDARD 2.009 for information on appropriate clothing for playing outdoors. See also STANDARD 3.081 regarding requirements for applying sunscreen.

TYPE OF FACILITY: *Center; Large Family Child Care Home; Small Family Child Care Home*

STANDARD 5.178
ENCLOSURES FOR OUTDOOR PLAY AREAS

The outdoor play area shall be enclosed with a fence or natural barriers. Fences and barriers shall not prevent the observation of children by caregivers. If a fence is used, it shall conform to applicable local building codes. These areas shall have at least two exits, with at least one being remote from the buildings.

Gates shall be equipped with self-closing and positive self-latching closure mechanisms. The latch or securing device shall be high enough or of a type such that small children cannot open it. The openings in the fence shall be no larger than 3½ inches. The fence shall be constructed to discourage climbing. Play areas shall be secured against inappropriate use when the facility is closed.

RATIONALE: This standard helps to ensure proper supervision and protection, prevention of injuries, and control of the area. An effective fence is one that prevents a child from getting over, under, or through it and keeps children from leaving the fenced outdoor play area except when supervising adults are present. Although fences are not childproof, they provide a layer of protection for children who stray from supervision. Small openings in the fence (3½ inches or smaller) prevent entrapment and discourage climbing.

COMMENTS: Fences that prevent the child from obtaining a proper toehold, such as chainlink fences, discourage climbing. Chainlink fences allow for climbing when the links are large enough for a foothold. Children are known to scale fences with diamonds or links that are 2 inches wide. One-inch diamonds are less of a problem. Fence heights must comply with applicable local codes.

The U.S. Consumer Product Safety Commission (CPSC) does not have standards for minimum fence heights around outdoor play areas. However, there is a CPSC standard that requires a 48 inch fence height around swimming pools. The American Society for Testing and Materials (ASTM) is in the process of developing a minimum fence height standard of outdoor playgrounds. Contact information for the CPSC and the ASTM is located in Appendix BB.

TYPE OF FACILITY: *Center; Large Family Child Care Home; Small Family Child Care Home*

STANDARD 5.179
HAZARDOUS CHEMICALS IN THE SOIL OF PLAY AREAS

The soil in play areas shall not contain hazardous levels of any toxic chemical or substance. Where there is reason to believe a problem may exist, the facility shall have soil samples analyzed by an agency responsible for soil testing, or by a soil testing laboratory recommended by the regulatory health agency.

The soil in play areas shall be analyzed for lead content initially and shall be analyzed at least once every 2 years where the exteriors of adjacent buildings and structures are painted with lead-containing paint. Lead in soil shall not exceed 500 ppm (parts per million). Testing and analyses shall be in accordance with procedures specified by the regulating health authority.

RATIONALE: Soil contaminated with toxic materials can poison children. Ensuring that soil in play areas is free of dangerous levels of lead helps prevent lead poisoning (62).

TYPE OF FACILITY: *Center; Large Family Child Care Home; Small Family Child Care Home*

STANDARD 5.180
SANDBOXES

The facility shall adhere to the following requirements for sand play areas:
a) Sandboxes shall be constructed to permit drainage;
b) Sandboxes shall be covered with a lid or other covering when they are not in use.
c) Sandboxes shall be kept free from cat and other animal excrement;
d) Sand play areas shall be distinct from landing areas for slides or other equipment;
e) Sand play area covers shall be adequately secured when they are lifted or moved to allow children to play in the sandbox;
f) Sand used in the box shall be washed, free of organic, toxic, or harmful materials, and fine enough to be shaped easily;
g) Sandboxes shall be regularly cleaned of foreign matter;
h) Sand shall be replaced as often as necessary to keep the sand visibly clean and free of extraneous materials;
i) Sandboxes shall be located away from prevailing winds. If this is not possible, windbreaks using bushes, trees, or fences shall be provided.

RATIONALE: Uncovered sand is subject to contamination and transmission of disease from animal feces (such as toxoplasmosis from cat feces) and insects breeding in sandboxes. No play material should contain toxic or harmful ingredients such as tremolite, an asbestos-like substance. Sand that is used as a building material or is harvested from a site containing toxic substances may contain potentially harmful substances. Sand can come from many sources. Child care providers should be sure they are using sand labeled as a safe play material or sand that is specifically prepared for sandbox use.

COMMENTS: An uncovered sandbox is an invitation for a cat or other animal to defecate or urinate, and therefore is a source for disease transmission (19). See STANDARD 5.070 through STANDARD 5.073, and STANDARD 5.202, for control of insects.

Sand, already installed in play areas, cannot be safely cleaned without leaving residues that could harm children. Replace sand as often as necessary to keep it sufficiently clean to prevent the transmission of disease to children and free of foreign material that could cause injury.

TYPE OF FACILITY: *Center; Large Family Child Care Home; Small Family Child Care Home*

STANDARD 5.181
DESIGN OF PLAY EQUIPMENT

Play equipment shall be of safe design and in good repair. Outdoor climbing equipment and swings shall be set in concrete footings located at least 6 inches below ground surface. Swings shall have soft and flexible seats. Access to play equipment shall be limited to age groups for which the equipment is developmentally appropriate.

RATIONALE: This standard is based on guidelines of the U.S. Consumer Product Safety Commission (CPSC) (58).

COMMENTS: American Society for Testing and Materials (ASTM) references for all playground standards:
* *ASTM F1148-00*
  Standard Consumer Safety Performance Specification for Home Playground Equipment

* *ASTM F1487-98*
  Standard Consumer Safety Performance Specifications for Playground Equipment for Public Use

For more information, contact the ASTM and the CPSC. Contact information is located in Appendix BB.

TYPE OF FACILITY: *Center; Large Family Child Care Home; Small Family Child Care Home*

STANDARD 5.182
INSTALLATION OF PLAY EQUIPMENT

All pieces of play equipment shall be installed as directed by the manufacturer's instructions and specifications. The equipment shall be able to withstand the maximum anticipated forces generated by active use that might cause it to overturn, tip, slide, or move in any way.

RATIONALE: Secure anchoring is a key factor in stable installation, and because the required footing sizes and depths may vary according to type of equipment, the anchoring process should be completed in strict accordance with the manufacturer's specifications.

COMMENTS: If active play equipment is installed indoors, the same requirements for installation and use apply as in the outdoor setting. Bringing playground equipment indoors does not compensate for hard surfaces, inadequate anchoring, or any other hazard that would be prevented by following the manufacturer's instructions.

TYPE OF FACILITY: *Center; Large Family Child Care Home; Small Family Child Care Home*

STANDARD 5.183
PROHIBITED SURFACES FOR PLACING CLIMBING EQUIPMENT

Equipment used for climbing shall not be placed over, or immediately next to, hard surfaces such as asphalt, concrete, dirt, grass, or flooring covered by carpet or gym mats not intended for use as surfacing for climbing equipment.

All pieces of playground equipment shall be surrounded by a shock-absorbing surface. This material may be either the unitary or the loose-fill type, as defined by the guidelines of the U.S. Consumer Product Safety Commission (CPSC) and the standard of the American Society for Testing and Materials (ASTM), extending at least 6 feet beyond the perimeter of the stationary equipment. These shock-absorbing surfaces must conform to the standard stating that the impact of falling from the height of the structure will be less

than or equal to peak deceleration 200G and a Head Injury Criterion (HIC) of 1000 (63). Organic materials that support colonization of molds and bacteria shall not be used. This standard applies whether the equipment is installed outdoors or indoors.

RATIONALE: Head-impact injuries present a significant danger to children. Falls into a shock-absorbing surface are less likely to cause serious injury, because the surface is yielding so peak deceleration and force are reduced (58). The critical issue of surfaces, both under equipment and in general, should receive the most careful attention (58).

COMMENTS: Children should not dig in sand used under swings. It is not necessary to cover sand used in this manner. Sand is not a suitable protective ground covering if pets cannot be kept out of the area.

Two scales are used for measuring the potential severity of falls. One is known as the G-max, and the other is known as the HIC. G-max measures the peak force at the time of impact; HIC measures total force during impact. Levels of 200 G-max or 1000 HIC have been accepted as thresholds for risk of life-threatening injuries. G-max and HIC levels of playground surfaces can be tested in various ways. The easiest one to use is the instrumented hemispherical triaxial headform. Make sure that whoever conducts the test uses a process that conforms to the *ASTM F1292-99 Standard Specification for Impact Attenuation of Surface Systems Under and Around Playground Equipment*. For more information, see *ASTM F355-95 Standard Test Method for Shock-Absorbing Properties of Playing Surface Systems and Materials*.

See Appendix V, for information on depth required for tested shock-absorbing surfacing materials for use under play equipment.

For guidelines on play equipment and surfacing, contact U.S. CPSC. Contact information for the ASTM and the CPSC is located in Appendix BB.

TYPE OF FACILITY: *Center; Large Family Child Care Home; Small Family Child Care Home*

STANDARD 5.184
ENCLOSURE OF MOVING PARTS ON PLAY EQUIPMENT

All pieces of play equipment shall be designed so moving parts (swing components, teeter-totter mechanism, spring-ride springs, and so forth) will be shielded or enclosed.

RATIONALE: This standard is to prevent pinching, catching, or crushing of body parts or clothing.

COMMENTS: For each type of equipment refer to the *Handbook for Public Playground Safety*, published by the U.S. Consumer Product Safety Commission (CPSC) and the *Standard Consumer Safety Performance Specification for Playground Equipment for Public Use* published by the American Society for Testing and Materials (ASTM) for specific standards on dimensions and other characteristics. Contact information for the CPSC and the ASTM is located in Appendix BB.

TYPE OF FACILITY: *Center; Large Family Child Care Home; Small Family Child Care Home*

STANDARD 5.185
MATERIAL DEFECTS AND EDGES ON PLAY EQUIPMENT

All pieces of play equipment shall be free of sharp edges, protruding parts, weaknesses, and flaws in material construction. Sharp edges in wood, metal, or concrete shall be rounded to a minimum of $\frac{1}{2}$-inch radius on all edges. Wood materials shall be sanded smooth and shall be inspected regularly for splintering.

RATIONALE: Any sharp or protruding surface presents a potential for laceration and contusions to the child's body.

TYPE OF FACILITY: *Center; Large Family Child Care Home; Small Family Child Care Home*

STANDARD 5.186
ENTRAPMENT HAZARDS OF PLAY EQUIPMENT

All pieces of play equipment shall be designed to guard against entrapment or situations that may cause strangulation by being too large for a child's head to get stuck or too small for a child's head to fit into. Openings in exercise rings shall be smaller than 3½ inches or larger than 9 inches in diameter. A play structure shall have no openings with a dimension between 3½ inches and 9 inches. In particular, side railings, stairs, and other locations where a child might slip or try to climb through shall be checked for appropriate dimensions.

Protrusions such as pipes or wood ends that may catch a child's clothing are prohibited. Distances between two vertical objects that are positioned near each other shall be 3½ inches or less to prevent entrapment of a child's head. No opening shall have a vertical angle of less than 55 degrees. To prevent entrapment of fingers, no openings shall be larger than 3/8 inch or smaller than 1 inch.

RATIONALE: Any equipment opening between 3½ inches and 9 inches in diameter presents the potential for head entrapment. Similarly, small openings can cause entrapment of the child's fingers (58).

TYPE OF FACILITY: *Center; Large Family Child Care Home; Small Family Child Care Home*

STANDARD 5.187
PLAY EQUIPMENT FOR CHILDREN WITH DISABILITIES.

Play equipment and play surfaces shall be provided for children with disabilities. Play equipment and play surfaces shall conform to recommendations from the Americans with Disabilities Act (ADA).

RATIONALE: Play equipment and play surfaces that are accessible to children with disabilities will encourage all children to play together.

COMMENTS: For additional information regarding playground equipment and play surfaces accessible to children with disabilities, review the Americans with

Disabilities Act Accessibility Guidelines (ADAAG) and the U.S. Access Board's *Guide to ADA Accessibility Guidelines for Play Areas*. Contact information for the ADAAG is located in Appendix BB.

TYPE OF FACILITY: *Center; Large Family Child Care Home; Small Family Child Care Home*

STANDARD 5.188
PLAY EQUIPMENT CONNECTING AND LINKING DEVICES

All bolts, hooks, eyes, shackles, rungs, and other connecting and linking devices of all pieces of playground equipment shall be designed and secured to prevent loosening or unfastening except by authorized individuals with special tools.

RATIONALE: These devices must be securely installed to avoid physical injury to children.

TYPE OF FACILITY: *Center; Large Family Child Care Home; Small Family Child Care Home*

STANDARD 5.189
SIZE AND ANCHORING OF CRAWL SPACES

Crawl spaces in all pieces of playground equipment, such as pipes or tunnels, shall be securely anchored to the ground to prevent movement and shall have a diameter of 23 inches or greater to permit easy access to the space by adults in an emergency or for maintenance.

RATIONALE: Playground equipment components must be secure to prevent sudden falls by children. Adequate access space permits adult assistance and first aid measures.

TYPE OF FACILITY: *Center; Large Family Child Care Home; Small Family Child Care Home*

STANDARD 5.190
DRAINAGE OF PAVED SURFACES

All paved surfaces shall be well-drained to avoid accumulation of water and ice.

RATIONALE: Well-drained paved surfaces help prevent injury and deterioration of the surface by discouraging the accumulation of water and ice.

TYPE OF FACILITY: *Center; Large Family Child Care Home; Small Family Child Care Home*

STANDARD 5.191
WALKING SURFACES

All walking surfaces, such as walkways, ramps, and decks, shall have a non-slip finish.

RATIONALE: Slippery walking surfaces can lead to injury even during activities of children and adults that do not involve play.

COMMENTS: An example of a non-slip finish is asphalt.

TYPE OF FACILITY: *Center; Large Family Child Care Home; Small Family Child Care Home*

STANDARD 5.192
WALKING SURFACE HAZARDS

All walking surfaces and other play surfaces shall be free of holes and abrupt irregularities in the surface.

RATIONALE: This standard prevents injury during play and other activities of children and adults that do not involve play.

TYPE OF FACILITY: *Center; Large Family Child Care Home; Small Family Child Care Home*

STANDARD 5.193
AREAS FOR WHEELED VEHICLES

The area used for wheeled vehicles shall have a flat, smooth, non-slippery surface. A physical barrier shall separate this area from the following:
a)   Traffic;
b)   Streets;
c)   Parking;
d)   Delivery areas;
e)   Driveways;
f)   Stairs;
g)   Hallways used as fire exits;
h)   Balconies;
i)   Pools and other areas containing water.

RATIONALE: Physical separation from environmental obstacles is necessary to prevent potential collision, injuries, falls, and drowning.

TYPE OF FACILITY: *Center*

MAINTENANCE OF ACTIVE PLAY INDOOR AND OUTDOOR AREAS

STANDARD 5.194
REMOVAL OF HAZARDS FROM OUTDOOR AREAS

All outdoor activity areas shall be maintained in a clean and safe condition by removing:
a)   Debris;
b)   Dilapidated structures;
c)   Broken or worn play equipment;
d)   Building supplies and equipment;
e)   Glass;
f)   Sharp rocks;
g)   Stumps and roots;
h)   Twigs;
i)   Toxic plants;
j)   Anthills;
k)   Beehives and wasp nests;
l)   Unprotected ditches;
m)   Wells;
n)   Holes;
o)   Grease traps;
p)   Cisterns;
q)   Cesspools;

r) Unprotected utility equipment;
s) Other injurious material.

Holes or abandoned wells within the site shall be properly filled or sealed. The area shall be well-drained, with no standing water.

A maintenance policy for playgrounds and outdoor areas shall be established and followed.

RATIONALE: Proper maintenance is a key factor when trying to ensure a safe play environment for children. Each playground is unique and requires a routine maintenance check program developed specifically for that setting.

COMMENTS: See STANDARD 8.033, for information regarding the policy for Maintenance of the Facility and Equipment.

TYPE OF FACILITY: *Center; Large Family Child Care; Small Family Child Care Home*

STANDARD 5.195
TOXIC MATERIALS USED ON OUTDOOR PLAY EQUIPMENT

Outdoor play equipment shall not be coated or treated with, nor shall it contain, toxic materials in hazardous amounts that are accessible to children (58).

RATIONALE: Toxic coatings and chemical treatments can transfer to surrounding soil, and directly into children who lick or chew the surface. Examples of such substances are creosote- or arsenic-containing substances that are used to preserve wood exposed to the outdoor weather.

TYPE OF FACILITY: *Center; Large Family Child Care Home; Small Family Child Care Home*

STANDARD 5.196
INSPECTION OF PLAY AREA AND EQUIPMENT

The play area and equipment shall be inspected for safety at regular intervals and the observations documented.

Playground equipment shall be checked according to the manufacturer's instructions for the following:
a) Visible cracks, bending or warping, rusting, or breakage of any equipment;
b) Deformation of open hooks, shackles, rings, links, and so forth;
c) Worn swing hangers and chains;
d) Missing, damaged, or loose swing seats;
e) Broken supports or anchors;
f) Cement support footings that are exposed, cracked, or loose in the ground;
g) Accessible sharp edges or points;
h) Exposed ends of tubing that require covering with plugs or caps;
i) Protruding bolt ends that have lost caps or covers;
j) Loose bolts, nuts, and so forth that require tightening;
k) Splintered, cracked, or otherwise deteriorating wood;
l) Lack of lubrication on moving parts;
m) Worn bearings or other mechanical parts or missing rails, steps, rungs, or seats;
n) Worn or scattered surfacing material;
o) Hard surfaces, especially under swings, slides, and so forth (such as places where resilient material has been shifted away from any surface underneath play equipment);
p) Chipped or peeling paint;
q) Pinch or crush points, exposed mechanisms, juncture, and moving components.

Outdoor play areas shall be checked daily for areas of poor drainage and accumulation of water and ice.

RATIONALE: Regular inspections are critical to prevent deterioration of equipment and accumulation of hazardous materials within the play site, and to ensure that appropriate repairs are made as soon as possible (58). Pools of water may cause children to slip and fall.

COMMENTS: If an off-site play area is used, a safety check for hazardous materials within the play area should be done upon arrival to the off-site playground. Hazardous materials may have been left in the play area by other people before the arrival of children from the child care facility.

See Playground and Equipment Records, STANDARD 8.071 and STANDARD 8.072; and STANDARD 5.070, on keeping play areas free of animal waste. See STANDARD 5.183, for additional information on safe playground equipment. See STANDARD 8.033, for the policy for Maintenance of the Facility and Equipment.

TYPE OF FACILITY: *Center; Large Family Child Care Home; Small Family Child Care Home*

STANDARD 5.197
INSPECTION OF PLAY AREA SURFACING

Any particulate impact absorbing material beneath play equipment shall be checked at least monthly for packing as a result of rain or ice, and if found to be compressed, shall be turned over or raked up to increase resilience capacity. All particulate material, particularly sand, shall be inspected daily for glass and other debris, animal excrement, and other foreign material. Loose fill surfaces shall be hosed down for cleaning and raked or sifted to remove hazardous debris as often as needed to keep the surface free of dangerous, unsanitary materials.

RATIONALE: Surfaces should be impact absorbing. Cold temperatures may cause "packing," which causes the surface material to lose shock-absorbing capacity. Other materials, such as glass, debris, and animal excrement, present potential sources of injury or infection. Maintaining loose fill surfaces provides for proper sanitation.

COMMENTS: Sand is not an appropriate playground covering in areas where pets or animals are a problem.

TYPE OF FACILITY: *Center; Large Family Child Care Home; Small Family Child Care Home*

5.4 SWIMMING, WADING, AND WATER

FENCES, POOL STRUCTURES AND POOL EQUIPMENT

STANDARD 5.198
ENCLOSURE OF BODIES OF WATER

All water hazards, such as pools, swimming pools, stationary wading pools, ditches, and fish ponds, shall be enclosed with a fence that is at least 5 feet high and comes within 3½ inches of the ground. Openings in the fence shall be no greater than 3½ inches. The fence shall be constructed to discourage climbing and kept in good repair.

If the fence is made of horizontal and vertical members (like a typical wooden fence) and the distance between the tops of the horizontal parts of the fence is less than 45 inches, the horizontal parts shall be on the swimming pool side of the fence. The spacing of the vertical members shall not exceed 1¾ inches.

For a chain link fence, the mesh size shall not exceed 1¼ inches square.

Exit and entrance points shall have self-closing, positive latching gates with locking devices a minimum of 55 inches from the ground.

A wall of the child care facility shall not constitute one side of the fence unless the wall has no openings capable of providing direct access to the pool (such as doors, windows, or other openings).

If the facility has a water play area, the following requirements shall be met:
a) Water play areas shall conform to all state and local health regulations;
b) Water play areas shall not include hidden or enclosed spaces;
c) Spray areas and water-collecting areas shall have a non-slip surface, such as asphalt;

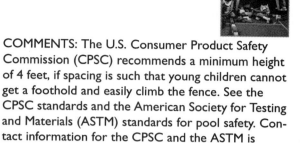

d) Water play areas, particularly those that have standing water, shall not have sudden changes in depth of water;

e) Drains, streams, water spouts, and hydrants shall not create strong suction effects or water-jet forces;

f) All toys and other equipment used in and around the water play area shall be made of sturdy plastic or metal. No glass shall be permitted;

g) Water play areas in which standing water is maintained for more than 24 hours shall be inspected for glass, trash, animal excrement, and other foreign material.

RATIONALE: This standard is meant to prevent injury and drowning (63). Most drownings happen in fresh water, often in home swimming pools (59). Most children drown within a few feet of safety and in the presence of a supervising adult (59). Small fence openings (3½ inches or smaller) prevent children from passing through the fence. All areas must be visible to allow adequate supervision.

An effective fence is one that prevents a child from getting over, under, or through it and keeps the child from gaining access to the pool or body of water except when supervising adults are present. Fences are not childproof, but they provide a layer of protection for a child who strays from supervision.

Fence heights are a matter of local ordinance but it is recommended that it should be at least 5 feet. A house exterior wall can constitute one side of a fence if the wall has no openings providing direct access to the pool.

In fences made up of horizontal and vertical members, children should not be allowed to use the horizontal members as a form of ladder to climb into a swimming pool area. If the distance between horizontal members is less that 45 inches, placing the horizontal members on the pool side of the fence will prevent children using this to climb over and into the pool area. However, if the horizontal members are greater than 45 inches apart, it is more difficult for a child to climb and therefore the horizontal members could be placed on the side of the fence facing away from the pool. (63).

COMMENTS: The U.S. Consumer Product Safety Commission (CPSC) recommends a minimum height of 4 feet, if spacing is such that young children cannot get a foothold and easily climb the fence. See the CPSC standards and the American Society for Testing and Materials (ASTM) standards for pool safety. Contact information for the CPSC and the ASTM is located in Appendix BB.

TYPE OF FACILITY: *Center; Large Family Child Care Home; Small Family Child Care Home*

STANDARD 5.199
ACCESSIBILITY TO ABOVE-GROUND POOLS

Above-ground pools shall have non-climbable sidewalls that are at least 4 feet high or shall be enclosed with an approved fence, as specified in STANDARD 5.198. When the pool is not in use, steps shall be removed from the pool or otherwise protected to ensure that they cannot be accessed.

RATIONALE: This standard is based on best professional experience.

TYPE OF FACILITY: *Center; Large Family Child Care Home; Small Family Child Care Home*

STANDARD 5.200
SENSORS OR REMOTE MONITORS

Sensors or remote monitors shall not be used in lieu of a fence or proper supervision.

RATIONALE: A temporary power outage negates the protection of sensors.

TYPE OF FACILITY: *Center; Large Family Child Care Home; Small Family Child Care Home*

STANDARD 5.201
SAFETY COVERS FOR SWIMMING POOLS

When not in use, in-ground and above-ground swimming pools shall be covered with a safety cover that meets or exceeds the American Society for Testing and Materials (ASTM) standard.

RATIONALE: Fatal injuries have occurred when water has collected on top of a secured pool cover. The depression caused by the water, coupled with the smoothness of the cover material, has proved to be a deadly trap for some children (64). The ASTM standard now defines a safety cover "as a barrier (intended to be completely removed before water use) for swimming pools, spas, hot tubs, or wading pools, attendant appurtenances and/or anchoring mechanisms which reduces--when properly labeled, installed, used and maintained in accordance with the manufacturer's published instructions--the risk of drowning of children under 5 years of age, by inhibiting their access to the contained body of water, and by providing for the removal of any substantially hazardous level of collected surface water" (65).

Safety covers reduce the possibility of contamination by animals, birds, and insects.

COMMENTS: Facilities should check whether the manufacturers warrant their pool covers as meeting ASTM standards. See *ASTM F1346-91 Standard Performance Specification for Safety Covers and Labeling Requirements for All Covers for Swimming Pools, Spas and Hot Tubs.* Contact information for the ASTM is located in Appendix BB.

TYPE OF FACILITY: *Center; Large Family Child Care Home; Small Family Child Care Home*

STANDARD 5.202
INSECT BREEDING HAZARD

No facility shall maintain or permit to be maintained any receptacle or pool, whether natural or artificial, containing water in such condition that insects breeding therein may become a menace to the public health.

RATIONALE: Collection of water in tin cans, flower pots, discarded tires and other refuse, and natural pools of water can provide breeding sites for mosquitoes. Elimination of mosquito breeding sites is one of the basic environmental control methods.

Mosquitoes are responsible for transmitting a variety of diseases. Mosquito-borne viruses such as eastern equine encephalitis, western equine encephalitis, and St. Louis encephalitis have occurred in the United States and Canada (66).

Children can develop allergic reactions to mosquito bites.

TYPE OF FACILITY: *Center; Large Family Child Care Home; Small Family Child Care Home*

DECK AREAS

STANDARD 5.203
DECK SURFACE

A swimming pool shall be surrounded by a 4-foot, nonskid surface and shall be in good repair, free of tears or breaks.

RATIONALE: This standard is to prevent slipping and injury of children and adults and to allow supervising caregivers to walk around all sides of the pool.

COMMENTS: For additional information on toys not allowed on a pool deck, see STANDARD 3.047.

TYPE OF FACILITY: *Center; Large Family Child Care Home; Small Family Child Care Home*

POOL MAINTENANCE AND SAFETY

STANDARD 5.204
POOL PERFORMANCE REQUIREMENTS

Where applicable, swimming pools and built-in wading pool equipment and materials shall meet the health effects and performance standards of the National Sanitation Foundation, or equivalent standards as determined by the regulatory health authority.

RATIONALE: This standard facilitates proper pool operation and maintenance and minimizes injuries.

COMMENTS: To obtain these standards, contact the National Sanitation Foundation. Contact information is located in Appendix BB.

TYPE OF FACILITY: *Center; Large Family Child Care Home; Small Family Child Care Home*

STANDARD 5.205
POOL DRAIN COVERS

All covers for the main drain and other suction ports of swimming and wading pools shall be used under conditions that do not exceed the approved maximum flow rate, be securely anchored using manufacturer-supplied parts installed per manufacturer's specifications, and be in good repair.

RATIONALE: The two types of main drain covers are the grate and the anti-vortex cover. Use of drain covers under conditions that exceed the maximum flow rate can pose a hazard for entrapment. In some instances, children have drowned as a result of their body or hair being entrapped or seriously injured by sitting on drain grates. When drain covers are broken or missing, the body can be entrapped. When a child is playing with an open drain (one with the cover missing), a child can be entrapped by inserting a hand or foot into the pipe and being trapped by the resulting suction. Hair entrapment typically involves females with long, fine hair who are underwater with the head near the suction inlet; they become entrapped when their hair sweeps into and around the cover and not because of the strong suction forces.

COMMENTS: For additional information, see *Guidelines for Addressing Potential Entrapment Hazards Associated with Pools and Spas* from the U.S. Consumer Product Safety Commission (CPSC). Contact information is located in Appendix BB.

TYPE OF FACILITY: *Center; Large Family Child Care Home; Small Family Child Care Home*

STANDARD 5.206
SUPERVISION OF POOL PUMP

When children are in the pool, an adult shall be present. This adult shall be aware of the location of the pump and be able to turn it off in case a child is caught in the drain. Unobstructed access shall be provided to an electrical switch that controls the pump. This adult shall also have immediate access to a working telephone located at the pool.

RATIONALE: The power of suction of a pool drain often requires that the pump be turned off before a child can be removed.

TYPE OF FACILITY: *Center; Large Family Child Care Home; Small Family Child Care Home*

STANDARD 5.207
ELECTRICAL SAFETY FOR POOL AREAS

Electrical safety equipment shall be installed and inspected at and around the pool at intervals as required by the regulatory electrical inspector.

No electrical wires or electrical equipment shall be located over or within 10 feet of the pool area, except as permitted by the National Electrical Code.

RATIONALE: Safety equipment prevents electrical hazards that could be life-threatening. Electrical wires and equipment can produce electrical shock or electrocution.

COMMENTS: The swimming pool manufacturers trade association has a safety code. For electrical safety, a ground-fault circuit-interrupter is mandatory.

The National Electrical Code is available from the Institute of Electrical and Electronics Engineers (IEEE). Contact information for the IEEE is located in Appendix BB.

TYPE OF FACILITY: *Center; Large Family Child Care Home; Small Family Child Care Home*

STANDARD 5.208
LIFESAVING EQUIPMENT

Each swimming pool more than 6 feet in width, length, or diameter shall be provided with a ring buoy and rope, or a rescue tube, or a throwing line and a shepherd's hook. This equipment shall be long enough to reach the center of the pool from the edge of the pool, shall be kept in good repair, and shall be stored safely and conveniently for immediate access.

RATIONALE: This lifesaving equipment is essential. Drowning accounts for a higher rate of death than does illness (67).

TYPE OF FACILITY: *Center; Large Family Child Care Home; Small Family Child Care Home*

STANDARD 5.209
LIFELINE IN POOL

A lifeline shall be provided at the 5-foot break in grade between the shallow and deep portions of the swimming pool.

RATIONALE: This standard is to make the 5-foot depth known to caregivers assisting children in the pool.

TYPE OF FACILITY: *Center; Large Family Child Care Home; Small Family Child Care Home*

STANDARD 5.210
POOL EQUIPMENT AND CHEMICAL STORAGE ROOMS

Pool equipment and chemical storage rooms shall be locked, ventilated, and used only for pool equipment and pool chemicals.

RATIONALE: Pool chemicals are kept in concentrated forms that are hazardous to children. Access to these hazards must be carefully controlled.

TYPE OF FACILITY: *Center; Large Family Child Care Home; Small Family Child Care Home*

STANDARD 5.211
HOT TUBS, SPAS, AND SAUNAS

Children shall not be permitted in hot tubs, spas, or saunas. Areas shall be secured to prevent unsupervised access by children.

RATIONALE: This precaution is to prevent injury and drowning. Toddlers and infants are particularly susceptible to overheating.

Any body of water, including hot tubs, pails, and toilets, presents a drowning risk to young children (59, 67).

TYPE OF FACILITY: *Center; Large Family Child Care Home; Small Family Child Care Home*

STANDARD 5.212
WATER IN CONTAINERS

Bathtubs, buckets, diaper pails, and other pails of water shall be emptied immediately after use.

RATIONALE: In addition to home swimming and wading pools, young children drown in bathtubs and pails. Bathtub drownings are equally distributed in both sexes. Any body of water, including hot tubs, pails, and toilets, presents a drowning risk to young children (59, 67).

An estimated 50 infants and toddlers drown each year in buckets containing liquid used for mopping floors and other household chores. Of all buckets, the 5-gallon size presents the greatest hazard to young children because of its tall straight sides and its weight with even just a small amount of liquid. It is nearly impossible for top-heavy infants and toddlers to free themselves when they fall into a 5-gallon bucket head first (68).

TYPE OF FACILITY: *Center; Large Family Child Care Home; Small Family Child Care Home*

STANDARD 5.213
PORTABLE WADING POOLS

Portable wading pools shall not be permitted.

RATIONALE: Small portable wading pools do not permit adequate control of sanitation and safety, and they promote transmission of infectious diseases (2).

COMMENTS: Sprinklers, hoses, or small individual water buckets are safe alternatives as a cooling or play activity.

TYPE OF FACILITY: *Center; Large Family Child Care Home; Small Family Child Care Home*

STANDARD 5.214
CONSTRUCTION, MAINTENANCE AND INSPECTION OF POOLS

If swimming pools or built in wading pools are on the premises and children use them, the pools shall be constructed, maintained, and used in accordance with applicable state or local regulations and shall be regularly inspected by the health department to ensure compliance.

RATIONALE: This standard is based on state and local regulations and the American Public Health Association (APHA) *Public Swimming Pools Construction and Operation* (69).

COMMENTS: See the U.S. Consumer Product Safety Commission's (CPSC) *Guidelines for Entrapment*

Hazards: Making Pools and Spas Safer. Contact information for the CPSC and the APHA is located in Appendix BB.

TYPE OF FACILITY: *Center*

STANDARD 5.215
POOL SAFETY RULES

Legible safety rules for the use of swimming and built-in wading pools shall be posted in a conspicuous location, and each caregiver responsible for the supervision of children shall read and review them often enough so he/she is able to cite the rules when asked. The facility shall develop and review an emergency plan, as specified in Plan for Urgent Medical Care or Threatening Incidents, STANDARD 8.022.

RATIONALE: This standard is based on state and local regulations and the American Public Health Association (APHA) *Public Swimming Pools Construction and Operation* (76).

COMMENTS: Compliance can be assessed by interviewing caregivers to determine if they know the rules.

For additional information on safety rules for swimming and wading pools, see Water Safety, STANDARD 3.045 throughSTANDARD 3.047. Contact information for the APHA and CPSC is located in Appendix BB.

TYPE OF FACILITY: *Center; Large Family Child Care Home; Small Family Child Care Home*

WATER QUALITY OF SWIMMING/ WADING POOLS

STANDARD 5.216
WATER QUALITY

Water in swimming pools and built-in wading pools that children use shall be maintained between pH 7.2 and pH 7.8. The water shall be

disinfected by available free chlorine between 1.0 ppm and 3.0 ppm, or bromine between 1.0 ppm and 6.0 ppm, or by an equivalent agent approved by the health department. The pool shall be cleaned, and the chlorine level and pH level shall be tested every 2 hours during periods of use.

Equipment shall be available to test for and maintain a measurable residual disinfectant content in the water and to check the pH of the water. Water shall be sampled and a bacteriological analysis conducted to determine absence of *fecal coliform, pseudomonas aeruginosa*, and *Giardia lamblia* at least monthly or at intervals required by the local health authority.

RATIONALE: This practice provides control of bacteria and algae and enhances the participants' comfort and safety. Maintaining pH and disinfectant levels within the prescribed range suppresses bacterial growth to tolerable levels.

This standard is based on state and local regulations and the American Public Health Association (APHA) *Public Swimming Pools Construction and Operation* (65). Bacteriologic water safety must be ensured to prevent the spread of disease via ingestion of pool water.

COMMENTS: If a stabilized chlorine compound is used, the pH shall be maintained between 7.2 and 7.7, and the free available chlorine residual shall be at least 1.50 ppm (parts per million).

For further information, see the American Public Health Association (APHA) *Public Swimming Pools Construction and Operation* (69).

TYPE OF FACILITY: *Center; Large Family Child Care Home; Small Family Child Care Home*

STANDARD 5.217
CHLORINE PUCKS

"Chlorine Pucks" must not be placed in skimmer baskets.

RATIONALE: Although this practice can keep chlorine disinfectant levels high, it can be dangerous

because the "puck" is a concentrated form of chlorine and is very caustic. Curious children may take out a puck and handle it, causing serious skin irritations or burns.

TYPE OF FACILITY: *Center; Large Family Child Care Home; Small Family Child Care Home*

STANDARD 5.218
POOL WATER TEMPERATURE

Water temperatures shall be maintained at no less than 82 degrees F and no more than 88 degrees F while the pool is in use.

RATIONALE: Water temperature for swimming and wading should be warm enough to prevent excess loss of body heat and cool enough to prevent overheating. Because of their relatively larger surface area to body mass, young children can lose or gain body heat more easily than adults.

COMMENTS: Learner pools in public swimming centers are usually at least two degrees warmer than the main pool.

If caregivers are advised on how to recognize when an infant is cold (for instance, the infant becomes unhappy or shows acrocyanosis) and are sensible about the length of time spent in the water, temperature control should not be problem (70).

TYPE OF FACILITY: *Center; Large Family Child Care Home; Small Family Child Care Home*

5.5 INTERIOR AND EXTERIOR WALKWAYS, STEPS, AND STAIRS

STANDARD 5.219
DESIGNATED WALKWAYS, BIKE ROUTES, DROP-OFF AND PICK-UP POINTS

Safe pedestrian crosswalks, drop-off and pick-up points, and bike routes in the vicinity of the facility shall be identified, written in the facility's procedures, and communicated to all children, parents, and staff. Parking for drop-off and pick-up shall not require street side removal of children from a vehicle.

RATIONALE: This procedure reduces the potential of accidents resulting from children's darting into traffic.

COMMENTS: See STANDARD 2.032 for more information on drop-off and pick-up procedures.

TYPE OF FACILITY: *Center; Large Family Child Care Home; Small Family Child Care Home*

STANDARD 5.220
CONSTRUCTION AND MAINTENANCE OF WALKWAYS

Inside and outside stairs, ramps, porches, and other walkways to the structure shall be constructed for safe use as required by the local building code and shall be kept in sound condition, well lighted, and in good repair.

RATIONALE: The purpose of this standard is to prevent injury.

COMMENTS: For additional standards on paved and walking surfaces, see STANDARD 5.190 through STANDARD 5.192.

TYPE OF FACILITY: *Center; Large Family Child Care Home; Small Family Child Care Home*

STANDARD 5.221
GUARDRAILS

For preschoolers and school-age children, bottom guardrails that are no more than 2 feet above the floor shall be provided for all porches, landings, balconies, and similar structures. For infants and toddlers, bottom guardrails shall be no more than 6 inches above the floor, as specified above.

RATIONALE: This standard is to prevent falls from children climbing under the guardrail.

TYPE OF FACILITY: *Center; Large Family Child Care Home; Small Family Child Care Home*

STANDARD 5.222
BALUSTERS

Protective handrails and guardrails shall have balusters at intervals of less than 3½ inches or shall have sufficient protective material to prevent a 3½ inch sphere from passing through.

RATIONALE: This standard is to prevent entrapment of a child's head.

TYPE OF FACILITY: *Center; Large Family Child Care Home; Small Family Child Care Home*

STANDARD 5.223
HANDRAILS

Handrails at a maximum height of 38 inches shall be provided on both sides of stairways and shall be securely attached to the walls or stairs. When railings are installed on the side of stairs open to a stairwell, access to the stairwell shall be prevented by a barrier so a child cannot use the railings as a ladder to jump or fall into the stairwell.

RATIONALE: Model codes, including the National Fire Protection Association *NFPA -101 Life Safety Code*, require handrails to be mounted in the height range of 34 to 38 inches. Such handrails are equally usable by children. The stair researcher, Jake Pauls, has filmed small children effectively using handrails mounted as high as 38 inches. This comes very

naturally to the children because they are used to reaching up to take an adult's hand while walking. There is no justification for forcing the center or home to incur the added expense of installing a second set of handrails closer to the floor.

Although most people are right-handed, some are left-handed. Railings on both sides ensure a readily available handhold in the event of a fall down the stairs. Because right-handed people tend to carry packages in the left hand and keep the right hand free (if either hand is free), a right-hand descending handrail reduces the risk of falling on the stairs. When handrails are installed to allow children a handhold, the stairwell should be designed so the railing does not provide the child with a ladder to climb.

COMMENTS: Open stairwells can be enclosed with rigid vertical materials to prevent falls.

TYPE OF FACILITY: *Center; Large Family Child Care Home; Small Family Child Care Home*

STANDARD 5.224
LANDINGS

Landings shall be provided beyond each interior and exterior door that opens onto a stairway. Dimensions (length and width) of the landing are equal to or greater than the width of the door.

RATIONALE: Landings are necessary to accommodate the swing of the door without pushing the person on the stairway into a precarious position while trying to leave the stairway.

TYPE OF FACILITY: *Center; Large Family Child Care Home; Small Family Child Care Home*

STANDARD 5.225
STAIRWAY GUARDS

Securely installed, effective guards (such as gates) shall be provided at the top and bottom of each open stairway in facilities where infants and toddlers are in care. Gates shall have latching devices that adults (but not children) can open easily in an

emergency. "Pressure gates" or accordion gates shall not be used. Basement stairways shall be shut off from the main floor level by a full door. This door shall be self-closing and shall be kept locked to entry when the basement is not in use. No door shall be locked to prohibit exit at any time.

RATIONALE: Falls down stairs and escape upstairs can injure infants and toddlers. A gate with a difficult opening device can cause entrapment in an emergency.

TYPE OF FACILITY: *Center; Large Family Child Care Home; Small Family Child Care Home*

5.6 MAINTENANCE FOR SAFETY

EXTERIOR MAINTENANCE

STANDARD 5.226
MAINTENANCE OF EXTERIOR SURFACES

Porches, steps, stairs, and walkways shall:
a) Be maintained free from accumulations of water, ice, or snow;
b) Have a non-slip surface;
c) Be kept free of loose objects
d) Be in good repair.

RATIONALE: Trip surfaces lead to injury.

TYPE OF FACILITY: *Center; Large Family Child Care Home; Small Family Child Care Home*

STANDARD 5.227
REMOVAL OF ALLERGEN TRIGGERING MATERIALS FROM OUTDOOR AREAS

Outdoor areas shall be kept free of excessive dust, weeds, brush, high grass, and standing water.

RATIONALE: Dust, weeds, brush, high grass, are potential allergens. Standing water breeds insects.

STANDARD 5.228
CLEANING SCHEDULE

A cleaning schedule for exterior areas shall be developed and assigned to appropriate staff members.

RATIONALE: Developing a cleaning schedule that delegates responsibility to specific staff members helps ensure that the child care facility is appropriately cleaned. Proper cleaning reduces the risk of injury and the transmission of disease.

TYPE OF FACILITY: *Center; Large Family Child Care Home; Small Family Child Care Home*

INTERIOR MAINTENANCE

STANDARD 5.229
FURNACE AND BOILER
MAINTENANCE

Furnace and boiler maintenance shall comply with local building codes, as warranted in writing by the building or fire inspector.

RATIONALE: Building codes are enforced to ensure that buildings are not at significant risk for fire hazards. The facility should keep an emergency manual posted nearby.

TYPE OF FACILITY: *Center; Large Family Child Care Home; Small Family Child Care Home*

STANDARD 5.230
STORAGE AREA MAINTENANCE
AND VENTILATION

Storage areas shall have appropriate lighting and be kept clean. If the area is a storage room, the area shall be mechanically ventilated to the outdoors when chemicals and a janitorial sink are present.

RATIONALE: Spilled items must be removed to promote health and safety. Spilled dry foods could attract rodent and insects. Chemicals and janitorial supplies can build up toxic fumes that can leak into occupied areas if they are not ventilated to the outdoors.

TYPE OF FACILITY: *Center; Large Family Child Care Home; Small Family Child Care Home*

GENERAL MAINTENANCE

STANDARD 5.231
STRUCTURE MAINTENANCE

The structure shall be kept in good repair and safe condition.

Each window, exterior door, and basement or cellar hatchway shall be kept in sound condition and in good repair.

RATIONALE: Older preschool-age and younger school-age children readily engage in play and explore their environments. The physical structure where children spend each day can present caregivers with special safety concerns if the structure is not kept in good repair and maintained in a safe condition. For example, peeling paint in older building may be ingested, floor surfaces in disrepair could cause falls and other injury, and broken glass windows could cause severe cuts or other glass injury.

Children's environments must be protected from exposure to moisture, dust, and excessive temperatures.

TYPE OF FACILITY: *Center; Large Family Child Care Home; Small Family Child Care Home*

STANDARD 5.232
ELECTRICAL FIXTURES AND
OUTLETS MAINTENANCE

Electrical fixtures and outlets shall be maintained in safe condition and good repair.

RATIONALE: Unsafe or broken electrical fixtures and outlets could expose children to serious electrical shock or electrocution. Loose or frayed wires are also unsafe.

COMMENTS: Running an appliance or extension cord underneath a carpet or rug is not recommended because the cord could fray or become worn and cause a fire (5).

TYPE OF FACILITY: *Center; Large Family Child Care Home; Small Family Child Care Home*

STANDARD 5.233
PLUMBING AND GAS MAINTENANCE

Each gas pipe, water pipe, gas-burning fixture, plumbing fixture and apparatus, or any other similar fixture, and all connections to water, sewer, or gas lines shall be maintained in good, sanitary working condition.

RATIONALE: Pipe maintenance prevents injuries from hazardous and unsanitary conditions.

COMMENTS: See also STANDARD 5.058, for information on the proper installation of gas pipes, water pipes, gas-burning fixtures, and plumbing fixtures and apparatus.

TYPE OF FACILITY: *Center; Large Family Child Care Home; Small Family Child Care Home*

STANDARD 5.234
CLEANING OF HUMIDIFIERS AND RELATED EQUIPMENT

Humidifiers, dehumidifiers, and air-handling equipment that involves water shall be cleaned and sanitized according to manufacturers' instructions.

RATIONALE: These appliances provide comfort by controlling the amount of moisture in the indoor air. To get the most benefit, the facility should follow all instructions. If the facility does not follow recommended care and maintenance guidelines, microor-

ganisms may be able to grow in the water and become airborne, which may lead to respiratory problems.

COMMENTS: For additional information, contact the U.S. Consumer Product Safety Commission (CPSC) and the Association of Home Appliance Manufacturers. Contact information is located in Appendix BB.

TYPE OF FACILITY: *Center; Large Family Child Care Home; Small Family Child Care Home*

5.7 TRANSPORTATION

VEHICLES

STANDARD 5.235
VEHICLE LICENSE

A caregiver who provides transportation for children or contracts to provide transportation, shall license the vehicle according to the laws of the state.

RATIONALE: For the children's safety, caregivers must comply with minimum requirements governing the transportation of children in their care, in the absence of a parent.

TYPE OF FACILITY: *Center; Large Family Child Care Home; Small Family Child Care Home*

STANDARD 5.236
VEHICLE CHILD RESTRAINT SYSTEMS

Age and size appropriate vehicle child restraint systems shall be used for children under 80 pounds and 4 feet 9 inches. Vehicle child restraint systems shall be secured in back seats only. Infants shall ride facing the back of the car until they have reached one year of age and weigh at least 20 pounds. A booster child safety seat shall be used when the child has outgrown a convertible child safety seat but is too small to fit properly in a vehicle safety belt.

All children, who weigh at least 80 pounds are at least 4 feet 9 inches in height, shall wear seatbelts.

RATIONALE: Motor vehicle crashes are the leading cause of death of children in the United States (71). Children who are not buckled are 11 times more likely to die in a motor vehicle crash than children who are buckled (72).

The safest place for all infants and children under 12 years of age to ride is in the back seat. Head-on crashes cause the greatest number of serious injuries. A child sitting in the back seat is farthest away from the impact and less likely to be injured or killed. Additionally, many newer cars have air bags in the front seats. Air bags inflate at speeds up to 200 mph and can injure small children who may be sitting too close to the air bag or who are positioned incorrectly in the seat. A rapidly inflating air bag can hit the back of an infant seat behind a baby's head and cause severe injury or death.

Infants under 1 year of age have less rigid bones in the neck. If placed in a child safety seat facing forward, a collision could snap the infant's head forward, causing neck and spinal cord injuries. If placed in a child safety seat facing to the rear of the car, the force of a collision is spread across the infant's entire body. The rigidity of the bones in the neck, in combination with the connecting ligaments determine whether the spinal cord will remain intact in the vertebral column. Based on physiologic measures, immature and incompletely ossified bones will separate more easily than more mature vertebrae, leaving the spinal cord as the last link between the head and the torso (77). At 12 months of age, more moderate consequences seem to occur than before 12 months of age (78). Rearward positioning that spreads deceleration forces over the largest possible area is an advantage at any age.

The National Highway and Transportation Safety Administation (NHTSA) recommends that children should be in booster child safety seats until they weigh at least 80 pounds and have reached the height of 4 feet 9 inches (75). When the vehicle safety belt

fits properly, the lap belt lies low and tight across the child's hips (not the abdomen) and the shoulder belt lies flat across the shoulder, away from the neck and face.

COMMENTS: Seat restraint systems are often installed in cars incorrectly (73). Some police departments and car dealerships offer free inspections to ensure that child safety seats are installed correctly. For more information on vehicle child restraint systems, see STANDARD 2.033.

TYPE OF FACILITY: *Center; Large Family Child Care Home; Small Family Child Care Home*

STANDARD 5.237
EMERGENCY EQUIPMENT AND INFORMATION DURING TRANSPORT

Each vehicle shall be equipped with a first aid kit, emergency identification and contact information for all children being transported, and a means of immediate communication to summon help (such as a cell phone).

When transporting children with chronic medical conditions (such as asthma, diabetes, or seizures), their emergency care plans and supplies or medications shall be available. The responsible adult shall be trained to recognize and respond appropriately to the emergency.

RATIONALE: Caregivers must be able to respond to the needs of children in case of injury or emergency. Because no environment is totally injury-proof, adequate supplies and emergency information must be available. The staff must be knowledgeable in their use.

COMMENTS: For information on contents of first aid kits, see STANDARD 5.093.

TYPE OF FACILITY: *Center; Large Family Child Care Home; Small Family Child Care Home*

STANDARD 5.238
INTERIOR TEMPERATURE OF VEHICLES

The interior of vehicles used to transport children shall be maintained at a comfortable temperature to children. When the vehicle's interior temperature exceeds 82 degrees F and providing fresh air through open windows cannot reduce the temperature, the vehicle shall be air-conditioned. When the interior temperature drops below 65 degrees F and when children are feeling uncomfortably cold, the interior shall be heated.

RATIONALE: Some children have problems with temperature variations. Whenever possible, open windows to provide fresh air to cool a hot interior is preferable before using air conditioning. Over-use of air conditioning can increase problems with respiratory infections and allergies. Excessively high temperatures in vehicles can cause neurological damage in children (74).

COMMENTS: In geographical areas that are prone to very cold or very hot weather, a small thermometer should be kept inside the vehicle. In areas that are very cold, adults tend to wear very warm clothing and children tend to wear less clothing than might actually be required. Adults in a vehicle, then, may be comfortable while the children are not. When air conditioning is used, adults might find the cool air comfortable, but the children may find that the cool air is uncomfortably cold. To determine whether the interior of the vehicle is providing a comfortable temperature to children, a thermometer should be used and children in the vehicle should be asked if they are comfortable.

TYPE OF FACILITY: *Center; Large Family Child Care Home; Small Family Child Care Home*

STANDARD 5.239
BACKUP VEHICLES

When vehicles are transporting children, a backup vehicle shall always be available and shall be dispatched immediately in case of emergency.

Documentation of these arrangements shall be included in the facility's written transportation plan.

RATIONALE: Children cannot be left sitting in a disabled vehicle. A backup vehicle must be dispatched and the children transferred immediately.

COMMENTS: Transportation contracts are best arranged with this provision. See also STANDARD 8.031, for information on a written plan. See STANDARD 2.029, for procedures to assure that children are counted when transported.

TYPE OF FACILITY: *Center; Large Family Child Care Home; Small Family Child Care Home*

STANDARD 5.240
PREVENTIVE MAINTENANCE OF VEHICLES

A caregiver shall assure that preventive maintenance of the vehicle is carried out according to the manufacturer's specifications. Vehicles the facility operates shall be cleaned and inspected inside and out at least weekly.

RATIONALE: Weekly cleaning and inspection help to ensure that the vehicle will be kept free of visible accumulation of soil and litter inside and that signs, lights, tires, and other safety features of the vehicle, such as coolant, brake fluid, oil are checked and operating effectively.

TYPE OF FACILITY: *Center; Large Family Child Care Home; Small Family Child Care Home*

BICYCLES AND BIKE ROUTES

STANDARD 5.241
BIKE ROUTES

For facilities providing care for school-age children and permitting bicycling as an activity, the bike routes allowed shall be reviewed and approved in writing by the local police and taught to the children in the facility.

RATIONALE: School-age children who use bicycles for transportation should use bike routes that present the lowest potential for injury. Review and approval of bike routes by the local police minimizes the potential danger.

TYPE OF FACILITY: *Center; Large Family Child Care Home; Small Family Child Care Home*

STANDARD 5.242
SAFETY HELMETS

All children shall wear approved safety helmets while riding toys with a wheel-base of more than 20 inches in diameter. Approved helmets shall meet the standards of either the U.S. Consumer Product Safety Commission (CPSC), American Society for Testing and Materials (ASTM), or the Snell Memorial Foundation.

RATIONALE: Bicycle injuries represent a leading cause of death and injury in children (71). Every year over 200 children are killed by bicycle related injuries (71). Many children and adults are not using safety helmets. Use of safety helmets has shown reduction in serious head and brain injury.

COMMENTS: The U.S. Consumer Product Safety Commission standard became effective in March 1999. Bike helmets manufactured or imported for sale in the U.S. after March 1999 must meet the CPSC standard. Helmets made before this date will not have a CPSC approval label. However, helmets made before this date should have an ASTM approval label. The American National Standard Institute (ANSI) standard for helmet approval has been withdrawn and ANSI approval labels will no longer appear on helmets.

For more information, contact the CPSC, the ASTM, and the Snell Memorial Foundation. Contact information is located in Appendix BB.

TYPE OF FACILITY: *Center; Large Family Child Care Home; Small Family Child Care Home*

REFERENCES

1. Committee on Environment Health. Ambient air pollution: respiratory hazards to children. *Pediatrics.* 1993;91(6):1210-1213.

2. American Academy of Pediatrics. *Handbook of Pediatric Environmental Health.* Elk Grove Village, Ill: American Academy of Pediatrics; 1999.

3. National Association for the Education of Young Children. *Planning Environments for Young Children.* Washington, DC: National Association for the Education of Young Children; 1977.

4. Deitch S, ed. *Health in Day Care: A Manual for Health Professionals.* Elk Grove Village, Ill: American Academy of Pediatrics; 1987.

5. *Well Beings: A Guide to Promote the Physical Health, Safety and Emotional Well-Being of Children in Child Care Centres and Family Day Care Homes.* 2nd ed. Ottawa, ON: Canadian Paediatric Society; 1996.

6. Greenman J. *Caring Spaces, Learning Places: Children's Environments that Work.* Redmond, Wash: Exchange Press Inc.; 1988.

7. Daneault S, Beusoleil M, Messing K. Air quality during the winter in Quebec day-care centers. *Am J Public Health.* 1992;82:432-434.

8. *National Fire Protection Association (NFPA) 101®: Life Safety® Code, 2000 Edition.* Quincy, Mass: NFPA; 2000.

9. American Society of Heating, Refrigeration and Air-conditioning Engineers Inc. (ASHRAE) Ventilation for acceptable indoor air quality. Atlanta, Ga: ASHRAE; 1989:Standard 62-1989R.

10. Environmental Protection Agency (EPA).*The Inside Story: A Guide to Indoor Air Quality.* Washington, DC: EPA; 1995:EPA 402-K-93-007.

11. Environmental Protection Agency (EPA). *Indoor Air Pollution: An Introduction for Health Professionals.* Washington, DC: EPA; 1994.

12. US Consumer Product Safety Commission (CPSC). *What You Should Know About Combustion Appliances and Indoor Air Pollution.* Washington, DC: CPSC; 1991:452.

13. US Consumer Product Safety Commission (CPSC). *What You Should Know About Space Heaters.* Washington, DC: CPSC; 1988:463.

14. US Consumer Product Safety Commission (CPSC). Mah, J. et al. *1997 Residential Fire Loss Estimates.* Washington, DC: CPSC; 1999.

15. Ytterstad B, Smith GS, Coggan CA Harstad. Injury prevention study: prevention of burns in young children by community based interventions. *Inj Prev.* 1998; 4:176-180.

16. McLoughlin E, Vince CJ, Lee AM, et al. Project burn prevention: outcomes and implications. *Am J Public Health.* 1982;82:241-247.

17. *American National Standard: Guide to Educational Facilities Lighting.* New York, NY: Illuminating Engineering Society of North America; 1998:ANSI /IES RP3-1988.

18. Safe Drinking Water Act Amendments, 110 USC § 613 (1996).

19. Villar RG, et al. Parent and pediatrician knowledge, attitudes, and practices regarding pet-associated hazards. *Arch Pediatr Adolesc Med.* 1998:152(10):1035-7.

20. Brown MZ, Gerberich, SG. Disabling injuries to childcare workers in Minnesota, 1985 to 1990. An analysis of potential risk factors. *J Occup Med.* 1993;35(12):1236-43.

21. Grantz RR, Claffey A. Adult health in child care: health status, behaviors, and concerns of teachers, directors, and family child care providers. *Early Child Res Q.* 1996;22(2):243-67.

22.   McIntire MS, ed. *Injury Control for Children and Youth.* Elk Grove Village, Ill: American Academy of Pediatrics Committee on Accident and Poison Prevention; 1987.

23.   US Consumer Product Safety Commission (CPSC). *Stair Steps and Baby Walkers Don't Mix.* Washington, DC: (CPSC); 2000. Available at: http://www.cpsc.gov/cpscpub/pubs/pub_idx.html. Accessed November 26, 2000.

24.   American Academy of Pediatrics Committee on Injury and Poison Prevention. Injuries associated with infant walkers. *Pediatrics.* 1995;95(5):778-780.

25.   US Consumer Product Safety Commission (CPSC). *The Consumer Product Safety Commission Gets New, Safer Baby Walkers on the Market.* Washington, DC: CPSC; 1998:5086.

26.   Aronson, SA. Updates on healthy eating and walkers. *Child Care Info Exch.* 2000;134:30.

27.   US Consumer Product Safety Commission (CPSC). McDonald, J. *Toy-Related Deaths and Injuries, Calendar Year 1998.* Washington, DC: CPSC; 1999. Available at: http://www.cpsc.gov/cpscpub/pubs/pub_idx.html. Accessed November 26, 2000.

28.   Churchill RB, Pickering LK. Infection control challenges in child-care centers. *Infect Dis Clin North Am.* 1997;11(2):347-65.

29.   Van R, Morrow AL, Reves RR, Pickering LK. Environmental contamination in child day-care centers. *Am J Epidemiol.* 1991;133(5):460-70.

30.   Chang A, Lugg MM, Nebedum A. Injuries in preschool children enrolled in day care centers. *Pediatrics.* 1989;83:272-277.

31.   Centers for Disease Control and Prevention (CDC). *The ABCs of Safe and Healthy Child Care.* Atlanta, Ga: CDC; 1997. Available at: http://www.cdc.gov/ncidod/hip/abc/polici5a.htm. Accessed November 29, 2000.

32.   Youniss J, Litovitz T, Villanueva P. Characterization of US poison centers: a 1998 survey conducted by the American Association of Poison Control Centers. *Vet Hum Toxicol.* 2000;42(1):43-53.

33.   Kynaston JA, Patrick MK, Shepard RW, Raivadera BV, Cleghorn GI. The hazards of automatic-dishwasher detergent. *Med J Aust.* 1989;151(1):5-7.

34.   Cornish LS, Parsons BJ, Dobbin MD. Automatic dishwasher detergent poisoning: opportunities for prevention. *Aust N Z J Public Health.* 1996;20(3):278-83.

35.   *What You Need to Know About the Safety of Art and Craft Materials.* Hanson, Mass: Art and Creative Materials Institute; 2000.

36.   *Handbook of Common Poisonings in Children.* 3rd ed. Elk Grove Village, Ill: American Academy of Pediatrics; 1995.

37.   Blumenthal DS, ed. *Introduction to Environmental Health.* New York, NY: Springer Publishing Company, Inc.; 1985.

38.   American Academy of Pediatrics Committee on Environmental Health. Screening for elevated blood lead levels. *Pediatrics.* 1998;101(6):1072-1078.

39.   US Consumer Product Safety Commission (CPSC); *CPSC Finds Lead Poisoning Hazard for Young Children in Imported Vinyl Miniblinds.* Washington, DC: CPSC; 1996:96-150. Available at: http://www.cpsc.gov/cpscpub/prerel/prhtml96/96150.html. Accessed November 29, 2000.

40.   Olds, AR. *Child Care Design Guide.* New York, NY: McGraw-Hill; 2001.

41.   Fleming DW, Cochi SL, Hightower AW, et al. Childhood upper respiratory tract infections: to what degree is incidence affected by day-care attendance? *Pediatrics.* 1987;79:55-60.

42.   Shelov, SP, Hannemann, RE, eds. *Caring for Your Baby and Young Child: Birth to Age 5.* 2nd ed. Elk Grove Village, Ill: American Academy of Pediatrics; 1998.

43. Aronson, SS. The ideal diaper changing station. *Child Care Information Exchange*. 1999;130:92.

44. US Consumer Product Safety Commission (CPSC). *The Safe Nursery*. Washington, DC: CPSC; 1997:202. Available at: http://www.cpsc.gov/cpscpub/pubs/202.pdf. Accessed November 29, 2000.

45. O'Connor MS, et al. Self-reported safety practices in child care facilities. *Am J Prev Med*. 1992;8(1):14-18.

46. Erdmann TC, et al. Tap water burn prevention: the effect of legislation. *Pediatrics*. 1992;88(3):572-577.

47. Witt CS, Warden J. Can home laundries stop the spread of bacteria in clothing? *Textile Chemist Colorist*. 1971;3(7):55-57.

48. Wannamaker LW. The epidemiology of streptococcal infections. In: McCarty M, ed. *Streptococcal Infections*. New York, NY: Columbia University Press; 1954.

49. *Safe & Sound for Baby: A Guide to Juvenile Product Safety, Use and Selection*. 2nd ed. Moorestown, NJ: Juvenile Products Manufacturers Association; 2000.

50. US Consumer Product Safety Commission (CPSC). *CPSC Warns Parents About Infant Strangulations Caused by Failure of Crib Hardware*. Document #5025. Washington, DC: CPSC; 1996:5025. Available at: http://www.cpsc.gov/cpscpub/pubs/5025.html. Accessed November 29, 2000.

51. American Academy of Pediatrics, Task Force on Infant Sleep Position and Sudden Infant Death Syndrome. Changing concepts of sudden infant death syndrome: implications for infant sleeping environment and sleep position (RE9946). *Pediatrics*. 2000;105(3):650-656.

52. McLoughlin E, Crawford JD. Burns. *Pediatr Clin North Am*. 1985;32:61-75.

53. Baker SP, Fisher RS. Childhood asphyxiation by choking and suffocation. *JAMA*. 1980;244:1343-1346.

54. US Consumer Product Safety Commission (CPSC). *Children Can Strangle in Window Covering Cords*. Washington, DC: CPSC; 1996:5114. Available at: http://www.cpsc.gov/cpscpub/pubs/5114.pdf. Accessed November 29, 2000.

55. US Consumer Product Safety Commission (CPSC). *Guidelines for Drawstrings on Children's Outerwear*. Washington, DC: CPSC; 1999:208. Available at: http://www.cpsc.gov/cpscpub/pubs/208.pdf. Accessed November 29, 2000.

56. Kraus JE. Effectiveness of measures to prevent unintentional deaths of infants and children from suffocation and strangulation. *Public Health Rep*. 1985;100:231-240.

57. American Academy of Pediatrics. Committee on Injury and Poison Prevention. Firearm-related injuries affecting the pediatric population (RE9926). *Pediatrics*. 2000;105(4):888-895.

58. US Consumer Product Safety Commission (CPSC). *Handbook for Public Playground Safety*. Washington, DC: CPSC; 1997: 325. Available at: http://www.cpsc.gov/cpscpub/pubs/325.pdf. Accessed November 30, 2000.

59. US Consumer Product Safety Commission (CPSC). *How to Plan For the Unexpected: Preventing Child Drownings*. Washington, DC: U.S. Consumer Product Safety Commission; 1994:359. Available at: http://www.cpsc.gov/cpscpub/pubs/359.html. Accessed November 30, 2000.

60. American Academy of Dermatology. Press Release Children at risk: protecting our children from skin cancer. [press release]. Schaumburg, Ill: American Academy of Dermatology; April 26, 2000. Available at: http://www.aad.org/PressReleases/protectchild.html. Accessed November 30, 2000.

61. National Coalition for Skin Cancer Prevention. *The Radiating Facts*. Available at http://www.sunsafety.org/radiate.htm. Accessed November 30, 2000.

62. *Preventing Lead Poisoning in Young Children*. Atlanta Ga: Centers for Disease Control; 1991.

63. US Consumer Product Safety Commission (CPSC). *Safety Barrier Guidelines for Home Pools*. Washington, DC: CPSC; 1994.

64. US Consumer Product Safety Commission (CPSC). *Guidelines for Addressing Potential Entrapment Hazards Associated with Pools and Spas*. Washington, DC: CPSC; 1998: 363. Available at: http://www.cpsc.gov/cpscpub/pubs/363.pdf. Accessed November 30, 2000.

65. *Standard performance specification for safety covers and labeling requirements for all covers for swimming pools, spas, and hot tubs, F 1346-91*. West Conshohocken, Pa: American Society for Testing and Materials; 1991.

66. American Public Health Association (APHA). Beneson, AS. *Control of Communicable Diseases Manual*. 16th ed. Washington, DC: APHA; 1995.

67. Rivera, FP. Pediatric injury control in 1999: where do we go from here? *Pediatrics*. 1999;103(4):883-888.

68. US Consumer Product Safety Commission (CPSC). *Infants & Toddlers Can Drown in 5-Gallon Buckets*. Washington, DC: CPSC; 1996:5006.

69. American Public Health Association (APHA). *Public Swimming Pools. Recommended Regulations for Design, Construction, Operation and Maintenance*. Washington, DC: APHA; 1981.

70. Coleman H, Finlay FD. When is it safe for babies to swim? *Profess Care Mother Child*. 1995;5(3):85-86.

71. National SAFE KIDS Campaign. *Bicycle Injurys, 1999*. Available at: http://www.safekids.org/fact99/bike99.html. Accessed November 30, 2000.

72. US Dept of Transportation. *Children: Traffic Safety Facts 1997*. Washington, DC: US Dept of Transportation, National Highway and Transportation Safety Administration; 1998.

73. Decina LE, Knoebel KY. Child safety seat misuse patterns in four states. *Accid Anal Prev*. 1997;29:125-32.

74. Gibbs LI, Lawrence DW, Kohn MA. Heat exposure in an enclosed automobile. *J La State Med Soc*. 1995;147(12):545-6.

75. Klinich, KD, et al. *Study of older child restraint/booster seat fit and NASS injury analysis*. East Liberty, OH: US Dept of Transportation, National Highway and Transportation Safety Administration, Vehicle Research and Test Center; 1994.

76. *Daylighting in Schools: An Investigation Into the Relationship Between Daylighting and Human Performance*. Fair Oaks, Calif: Heschong Mahone Group; 1999. Available at: http://www.h-m-g.com . Accessed November 30, 2000.

77. Huelke, DF, et al. *Car crashes and non-head impact cervical spine injuries in infants and children*. Warrendale, PA: Society of Automotive Engineers; 1993.

78. Weber, K, et al. *Investigation of dummy response and restraint configuration factors associated with upper spinal cord injury in a forward-facing child restraint*. Warrendale, PA: Society of Automotive Engineers; 1993.

79. Unpowered scooter-related injuries -- United States, 1998-2000. *CDC MMWR Weekly*. 2000; 49:1108-1110.

Infectious Diseases

6.1 RESPIRATORY TRACT INFECTIONS

Please note that if a staff member has no contact with the children, or with anything with which the children come in contact, the staff requirements in these standards do not apply to that staff member.

HAEMOPHILUS INFLUENZAE TYPE B (Hib)

STANDARD 6.001
IMMUNIZATION FOR *HAEMOPHILUS INFLUENZAE* TYPE B

All children in child care shall have received age-appropriate immunizations with an *H. influenzae* type b (Hib) conjugate vaccine (1).

Children in child care, who are not immunized or not age-appropriately immunized, shall be excluded from care immediately if the child care facility has been notified of a documented case of an invasive Hib infection. These children shall be allowed to return when the risk of infection is no longer present, as determined by the health department.

RATIONALE: Appropriate immunization of children with an *H. influenzae* type b conjugate vaccine prevents the occurrence of disease and decreases the rate of carriage of this organism, thereby decreasing the risk of transmission to others (2, 3).

COMMENTS: Transmission of *H. influenzae* type b may occur among unimmunized young children in group child care, especially children younger than 24 months of age.

For additional regarding Hib disease, consult the *Red Book* from the American Academy of Pediatrics (AAP). Contact information for the AAP is located in Appendix BB.

TYPE OF FACILITY: *Center; Large Family Child Care Home; Small Family Child Care Home*

STANDARD 6.002
INFORMING PARENTS OF HIB EXPOSURE

If a child with invasive *H. influenzae* type b (Hib) infection has been in care, the facility shall inform parents of other children who attend the facility, after consultation with the health department, that their children may have been exposed to the Hib bacteria and may have greater risk of developing serious Hib disease if their child is unimmunized or incompletely immunized. The facility shall recommend that parents contact their child's health care provider.

RATIONALE: The risk of secondary cases of Hib disease occurring among child care contacts does not seem to be uniform. Studies of child care contacts of children with Hib disease have varied in identification of an increased risk of Hib disease in this setting (4, 5, 6, 7).

In general, the risk of secondary Hib disease is probably lower for child care contacts than it is for household contacts. The risk of secondary cases of Hib disease occurring among child care attendees is greatest among, and may be limited to, children younger than 2 years of age who are not immunized (6). In settings with more than one classroom, increased risk has been shown only for children in the classroom of the infected child (6, 7).

COMMENTS: Sample letters of notification to parents that their child may have been exposed to an infectious disease are contained in the (National Academy for the Education of Young Children (NAEYC) publication, *Healthy Young Children*. Contact information is located in Appendix BB.

For information about health education for children, staff, and parents, see STANDARD 2.060 through STANDARD 2.067.

For additional information regarding Hib disease, consult the *Red Book* from the American Academy of Pediatrics (AAP). Contact information for the AAP is located in Appendix BB.

TYPE OF FACILITY: *Center; Large Family Child Care Home; Small Family Child Care Home*

STANDARD 6.003
INFORMING PUBLIC HEALTH
AUTHORITIES OF HIB CASES

Local and/or state public health authorities shall be notified immediately about cases of *H. influenzae* type b (Hib) infections involving children or child care providers in the child care setting. Facilities shall cooperate with their health department in notifying parents of children who attend the facility about exposure to children with Hib disease. This may include providing local health officials with the names and telephone numbers of parents of children in classrooms or facilities involved.

The health department may recommend rifampin, an antibiotic taken to prevent infection, for children in care and staff members, to prevent secondary spread of Hib disease in the facility. Antibiotic prophylaxis is not recommended for pregnant women because the effect of rifampin on the fetus has not been established.

RATIONALE: Because the risk of secondary cases of Hib disease seems to be variable among child care contacts of children with Hib disease, opinions differ as to the most appropriate guidelines for the use of rifampin to prevent infection in the child care setting. Rifampin treatment of children exposed to a child with Hib disease can reduce the prevalence of Hib respiratory tract colonization in treated children and reduce the subsequent risk of invasive Hib infection, particularly in children under 2 years of age (6). Prophylaxis should be initiated as soon as possible, when 2 or more cases of invasive disease have occurred within 60 days and when unimmunized or incompletely immunized children attend the child care facility.

In addition, children who are not immunized or are not age-appropriately immunized should receive a dose of vaccine and should be scheduled for completion of the *Recommended Childhood Immunization Schedule* from the American Academy of Pediatrics (AAP) (1, 8). See Appendix G.

COMMENTS: For additional information regarding Hib disease, consult the *Red Book* from the American Academy of Pediatrics (AAP). Contact information for the AAP is located in Appendix BB.

TYPE OF FACILITY: *Center; Large Family Child Care Home; Small Family Child Care Home*

STREPTOCOCCUS PNEUMONIAE

STANDARD 6.004
IMMUNIZATION WITH *S. PNEUMONIAE* CONJUGATE VACCINE

All children less than 23 months of age in child care shall have received age-appropriate immunizations with *S. pneumoniae* conjugate vaccine. Children age 24 to 59 months of age at high risk of invasive disease caused by *S. pneumoniae* (including sickle cell disease, asplenia, HIV, chronic illness or immunocompromised) shall be recommended to receive *S. pneumoniae* conjugate vaccine. All other children 24-59 months of age shall be encouraged to be protected against invasive *S. pneumoniae* disease through immunization, especially children who attend out-of-home child care and children of American Indian, Alaska Native, and African-American descent (9, 10, 11).

RATIONALE: Pneumococcal disease among children in out-of-home child care has been reported more frequently over the last decade in the U.S. and other developed countries. In the U.S., the risk for contracting an invasive pneumococcal infection in out-of-home child care (as defined as child care greater than 4 hours/week outside the home) increases by 2 to 3 times in children less than 60 months of age. Appropriate immunization of children with *S. pneumoniae* conjugate vaccine prevents the occurrence of disease and decreases transmission to others.

The risk for invasive disease is greatest in children who attend out-of-home child care and children of American Indian, Alaska Native, and African-American descent (10, 11).

COMMENTS: For additional information regarding *S. pneumoniae* disease, consult the *Red Book* from the American Academy of Pediatrics (AAP). See also Appendix G. Contact information for the AAP is located in Appendix BB.

TYPE OF FACILITY: *Center; Large Family Child Care Home; Small Family Child Care Home*

STANDARD 6.005
INFORMING PUBLIC HEALTH AUTHORITIES OF INVASIVE S. PNEUMONIAE

Local and/or state public health authorities shall be notified immediately about cases of invasive *S. pneumoniae* infections involving children or child care providers in the child care setting. Facilities shall cooperate with their health department in notifying parents of children who attend the facility about exposure to children with invasive *S. pneumoniae* disease. This may include providing local health officials with the names and telephone numbers of parents of children in classrooms or facilities involved.

RATIONALE: Secondary spread of *S. pneumoniae* in child care has been reported, but the degree of risk of secondary spread in child care facilities is unknown (12). Prophylaxis of contacts after the occurrence of a single case of invasive *S. pneumoniae* disease is not recommended.

In addition, children who are not immunized or are not age-appropriately immunized should receive a dose of vaccine and should be scheduled for completion of the *Recommended Childhood Immunization Schedule* from the American Academy of Pediatrics (AAP) (9). See Appendix G.

COMMENTS: For additional information regarding *S. pneumoniae* disease, consult the *Red Book* from the American Academy of Pediatrics (AAP). Contact information for the AAP is located in Appendix BB.

TYPE OF FACILITY: *Center; Large Family Child Care Home; Small Family Child Care Home*

NEISSERIA MENINGITIDIS (MENINGOCOCCUS)

STANDARD 6.006
INFORMING PUBLIC HEALTH AUTHORITIES OF MENINGOCOCCAL INFECTIONS

Local and/or state public health authorities shall be notified immediately about cases of meningococcal infections involving children or child care providers in the child care setting. Facilities shall cooperate with their local health department officials in notifying parents of children who attend the facility about exposures to children with meningococcal infections. This may include providing local health officials with the names and telephone numbers of parents of children in involved classrooms or facilities.

RATIONALE: *Neisseria meningitidis* is an important cause of bacterial meningitis in childhood. The infection is spread from person to person by direct contact with respiratory tract secretions (including large droplets) that contain *N. meningitidis* organisms.

COMMENTS: Sample letters of notification to parents that their child may have been exposed to an infectious disease are contained in the National Academy for the Education of Young Children (NAEYC) publication, *Healthy Young Children*. Contact information is located in Appendix BB.

For information about health education for children, staff, and parents, see STANDARD 2.060 through STANDARD 2.067.

For additional information regarding meningococcal disease, consult the *Red Book* from the American Academy of Pediatrics (AAP). Contact information for the AAP is located in Appendix BB.

TYPE OF FACILITY: *Center; Large Family Child Care Home; Small Family Child Care Home*

STANDARD 6.007
HEALTH DEPARTMENT RECOMMENDATIONS ON ANTIBIOTICS

When the health department recommends administering an antibiotic to prevent secondary infection of meningococcal disease within the facility, an antibiotic to prevent an infection shall be administered to staff members and children, with parental permission (13, 14, 15).

RATIONALE: Children and staff exposed, by close contact for an extended period to the child first infected with meningococcal disease, are at risk for contracting invasive meningococcal disease (13). The attack rate of meningococcal disease for this population is more than 300 times higher than rates in the general population (14).

Because outbreaks may occur in child care settings, chemoprophylaxis with rifampin or ceftriaxone is indicated for exposed child care contacts. Children in child care who are exposed to a child or an adult with meningococcal infection should receive rifampin or ceftriaxone as soon as possible to prevent an infection, preferably within 24 hours of diagnosis of the primary case (14, 15). In contacts over 18 years of age, ciprofloxacin is effective. Rifampin and ciprofloxacin are not recommended for pregnant women.

COMMENTS: For additional information regarding meningococcal disease, consult the *Red Book* from the American Academy of Pediatrics (AAP). Contact information for the AAP is located in Appendix BB.

TYPE OF FACILITY: *Center; Large Family Child Care Home; Small Family Child Care Home*

STANDARD 6.008
PROTECTIVE MEASURES FOR
MENINGOCOCCAL INFECTION

When an antibiotic to prevent an infection with *Neisseria meningitidis* (meningococcal infection) is indicated for child care contacts, all children and staff members, for whom prophylaxis has been recommended, shall be excluded from attending the facility until these measures have begun. Any exposed individual who develops a febrile illness (one accompanied by a fever) shall receive prompt medical evaluation.

New entry children shall not be enrolled in a child care facility in which a case of invasive *N. meningitidis* has been documented until 2 months has elapsed since the diagnosis was made.

RATIONALE: Children and staff exposed, by close contact for an extended period to the child first infected with meningococcal disease, are at risk for contracting invasive meningococcal disease (13). The attack rate of meningococcal disease for this population is more than 300 times higher than rates in the general population (14).

Because outbreaks may occur in child care settings, chemoprophylaxis with rifampin or ceftriaxone is indicated for exposed child care contacts. Children in child care who are exposed to a child or an adult with meningococcal infection should receive rifampin or ceftriaxone as soon as possible to prevent an infection, preferably within 24 hours of diagnosis of the primary case (14, 15). In contacts over 18 years of age, ciprofloxacin is effective. Rifampin and ciprofloxacin are not recommended for pregnant women.

COMMENTS: For additional information regarding meningococcal disease, consult the *Red Book* from the American Academy of Pediatrics (AAP). Contact information for the AAP is located in Appendix BB.

TYPE OF FACILITY: *Center; Large Family Child Care Home; Small Family Child Care Home*

PERTUSSIS

STANDARD 6.009
INFORMING PUBLIC HEALTH
AUTHORITIES OF PERTUSSIS CASES

Local and/or state public health authorities shall be notified immediately about cases of pertussis involving children or child care providers in the child care setting. Facilities shall cooperate with their local health department officials in notifying parents of children who attend the facility about exposures to children with pertussis. This may include providing the health department officials with the names and telephone numbers of parents of children in the classrooms or facilities involved.

Guidelines for use of antibiotics and immunization for prevention of pertussis in individuals who have been in contact with children who have pertussis shall be implemented in cooperation with officials of the health department. Children and staff who have been exposed to pertussis, especially those who are incompletely immunized, shall be observed for respiratory tract symptoms for 20 days after the last contact with the infected person.

RATIONALE: Notification of health department officials when pertussis occurs in a child or staff member

in a child care center will help ensure the following (16, 17):
a) All children have received age-appropriate immunization;
b) Erythromycin prophylaxis (or other recommended antibiotic therapy, if erythromycin is not tolerated) is provided to those exposed to the child first infected with pertussis;
c) Children and adults are observed for respiratory tract symptoms.

COMMENTS: Sample letters of notification to parents that their child may have been exposed to an infectious disease are contained in the National Academy for the Education of Young Children (NAEYC) publication, *Healthy Young Children*. Contact information for the NAEYC is located in Appendix BB.

For information about health education for children, staff, and parents, see STANDARD 2.060 through STANDARD 2.067.

For additional information regarding pertussis, consult the *Red Book* from the American Academy of Pediatrics (AAP). Contact information for the AAP is located in Appendix BB.

TYPE OF FACILITY: *Center; Large Family Child Care Home; Small Family Child Care Home*

STANDARD 6.010
PROPHYLACTIC TREATMENT FOR PERTUSSIS

When there is a known or suspected occurrence of pertussis in a child care facility, all staff members and children in care shall initiate the appropriate prophylactic treatment (usually administration of erythromycin or another appropriate antibiotic) and any additional treatment deemed medically necessary by a health care provider before they are allowed to return to the facility.

Adults and children who have been in contact with a person infected with pertussis shall be monitored closely for respiratory tract symptoms for 20 days after the last contact with the infected person.

RATIONALE: Even if outbreaks of pertussis in child care facilities have not been reported, children and staff who attend out-of-home child care occasionally contract pertussis. The spread of infection to contacts who are incompletely immunized can be reduced by treating the primary case and susceptible contacts with prophylactic antibiotics, usually erythromycin (16, 17).

COMMENTS: For additional information regarding pertussis, consult the *Red Book* from the American Academy of Pediatrics (AAP). Contact information for the AAP is located in Appendix BB.

TYPE OF FACILITY: *Center; Large Family Child Care Home; Small Family Child Care Home*

STANDARD 6.011
EXCLUSION FOR PERTUSSIS

Children and staff members with characteristic symptoms (primarily cough) of pertussis shall be excluded from child care pending evaluation by a health care provider. The child or staff member may not return to the facility until:
a) Five days after initiation of a 10-14 day course of erythromycin or other recommended antibiotic therapy;
b) Three to four weeks after the onset of the cough;
c) The medical condition allows.

RATIONALE: Even if outbreaks of pertussis in child care facilities have not been reported, children and staff who attend out-of-home child care occasionally contract pertussis. The spread of infection to contacts who are incompletely immunized can be reduced by treating the primary case and susceptible contacts with prophylactic antibiotics, usually erythromycin (16, 17).

COMMENTS: For additional information regarding pertussis, consult the *Red Book* from the American Academy of Pediatrics (AAP). Contact information for the AAP is located in Appendix BB.

TYPE OF FACILITY: *Center; Large Family Child Care Home; Small Family Child Care Home*

GROUP A STREPTOCOCCAL (GAS) INFECTION

STANDARD 6.012
EXCLUSION FOR GROUP A STREPTOCOCCAL INFECTIONS

Children with group A streptococcal (GAS) respiratory tract, skin, or ear infections shall be excluded from child care until 24 hours after antibiotic treatment has been initiated and until the child has no fever for 24 hours.

RATIONALE: Streptococcal respiratory tract infections and scarlet fever resulting from GAS have been reported in children in child care, but are not a major problem (18, 19). Group A streptococcal respiratory tract infections may resolve without treatment; however, GAS respiratory tract infections can be complicated by pneumonia, arthritis, rheumatic fever, and glomerulonephritis (20).

Early identification and treatment of GAS infection in children and adults are important in reducing transmission and subsequent occurrence of disease. Consultation with the health department is advised when high rates of streptococcal infection occur in child care facilities. Parents of children exposed to a child with documented GAS infection should be notified of the exposure.

COMMENTS: For additional information regarding group A streptococcal respiratory tract infection, consult the *Red Book* from the American Academy of Pediatrics (AAP). Contact information for the AAP is located in Appendix BB.

TYPE OF FACILITY: *Center; Large Family Child Care Home; Small Family Child Care Home*

STANDARD 6.013
INFORMING CAREGIVERS OF GROUP A STREPTOCOCCAL INFECTION

Parents who become aware that their child is infected with group A streptocci (GAS), has strep throat, or has scarlet fever, shall inform caregivers within 24 hours.

When exposure to GAS infection occurs, caregivers, in cooperation with health department officials, shall inform the parents of other children who attend the facility, that their children may have been exposed.

RATIONALE: Periodically, the incidence of rheumatic fever seems to increase (20). Identification and treatment of streptococcal infections of the respiratory tract are central to preventing rheumatic fever. Therefore, awareness of the occurrence of streptococcal infection in child care is important. Adult child care staff members are not immune to streptococcal infections and may be carriers of organisms that cause disease in children. When outbreaks of streptococcal disease occur, interventions are available to limit transmission of streptococcal infection. Consultation with the health department is advised when high rates of streptococcal infection occur in child care facilities.

This information could be useful to the exposed child's health care provider if the exposed child develops illness.

COMMENTS: Sample letters of notification to parents that their child may have been exposed to an infectious disease are contained in the (National Academy for the Education of Young Children (NAEYC) publication, *Healthy Young Children*. Contact information is located in Appendix BB.

For information about health education for children, staff, and parents, see STANDARD 2.060 through STANDARD 2.067.

For additional information regarding group A streptococcal infections, consult the *Red Book* from the American Academy of Pediatrics (AAP). Contact information for the AAP is located in Appendix BB.

TYPE OF FACILITY: *Center; Large Family Child Care Home; Small Family Child Care Home*

TUBERCULOSIS

STANDARD 6.014
MEASURES FOR DETECTION AND CONTROL OF TUBERCULOSIS

Local and/or state public health authorities shall be notified immediately about suspected cases of tuberculosis disease involving children or child care providers in the child care setting. Facilities shall cooperate with their local health department officials in notifying parents of children who attend the facility about exposures to children or staff with tuberculosis disease. This may include providing the health department officials with the names and telephone numbers of parents of children in the classrooms or facilities involved.

Tuberculosis transmission shall be controlled by requiring regular and substitute staff members and volunteers to have their tuberculosis status assessed with a one-step or two-step Mantoux intradermal skin test prior to beginning employment unless they produce documentation of the following:
a) A positive Mantoux intradermal skin test result in the past, or
b) Tuberculosis disease that has been treated appropriately in the past.

The one-step Mantoux intradermal tuberculin test shall suffice except that for individuals over 60 years of age or those who have a medical condition that reduces their immune response, the use of the two-step method is required. Individuals with a positive Mantoux intradermal skin test or tuberculosis disease in the past shall be evaluated with chest radiographs and shall be cleared for work by their physician or a health department official. Review of the health status of any staff member with a positive Mantoux intradermal skin test or tuberculosis disease in the past shall be part of the routine annual staff health appraisal (21).

In large and small family child care homes, this requirement applies to all adolescents and adults who are present while the children are in care.

Tuberculosis screening by Mantoux intradermal skin testing, using the one-step procedure, of staff members with previously negative skin tests shall not be repeated on a regular basis unless required by the local or state health department. Anyone who develops an illness consistent with tuberculosis shall be evaluated promptly by a physician. Staff members with previously positive skin tests shall be under the care of a physician who, annually, will document the risk of contagion related to the person's tuberculosis status by performing a symptom review including asking about chronic cough, unintentional weight, unexplained fever and other potential risk factors.

RATIONALE: Young children acquire tuberculosis infection from infected adults or occasionally, infected adolescents (21). Tuberculosis organisms are spread by inhalation of a small particle aerosol produced by coughing or sneezing by an adult or adolescent with contagious (active) pulmonary tuberculosis. Transmission usually occurs in an indoor environment. Tuberculosis is not spread through objects such as clothes, dishes, floors, and furniture.

The one-step Mantoux method of intradermal PPD skin testing involves injecting the material known as PPD into the skin so that a bleb is raised as the material is injected. For most healthy individuals, the one-step test is sufficient to detect latent TB or active TB disease. TB testing depends on cell-mediated immunity and the anemnestic or memory response where the body recalls a previous encounter with the antigen and reacts to it. In older individuals and those who have one of a group of specific conditions that reduce immune response, the first Mantoux test can produce a false negative response to a first test. In these individuals, the two-step method is recommended, involving repeating the Mantoux test procedure with an interval of at least one week to get an accurate result. Anamestic memory for most antigens occurs within one week after stimulation with the substance -thus a second test may be positive when a first is negative and indicate that an individual has latent TB or TB disease.   The need for a two-step test for individuals under 60 years of age should be determined by the clinician performing the test or by the local department of health.

COMMENTS: The two stages of tuberculosis are:
a) Latent tuberculosis infection, when the tuberculosis germ is in the body and causes a positive Mantoux intradermal skin test but does not cause sickness;
b) Active tuberculosis (tuberculosis disease), when the tuberculosis germ is in the body and causes sickness.

Virtually all tuberculosis is transmitted from adults and adolescents with tuberculosis disease. Infants and young children with tuberculosis are not likely to transmit the infection to other children or adults because they generally do not produce sputum and are unable to forcefully cough out large numbers of organisms into the air.

Only Mantoux intradermal skin test, containing 5 tuberculin units of purified protein derivative administered intradermally, should be used for skin testing. Multiple puncture tests should no longer be used because several problems severely limit their use. Problems include a lack of antigen standardization, false-positive and false negative results, and variable sensitivity and specificity.

For additional information regarding tuberculosis, consult the *Red Book* from the American Academy of Pediatrics (AAP). Contact information for the AAP is located in Appendix BB.

TYPE OF FACILITY: *Center; Large Family Child Care Home; Small Family Child Care Home*

STANDARD 6.015
ATTENDANCE OF CHILDREN WITH TUBERCULOSIS INFECTION

Children with tuberculosis infection or disease can attend child care if they are receiving appropriate therapy.

RATIONALE: Children can return to regular activities as soon as effective therapy has been instituted, adherence to therapy has been documented, and clinical symptoms have disappeared. If approved by local health officials, children may attend out-of-home child care once they are considered non-infectious to others.

COMMENTS: For additional information regarding tuberculosis, consult the *Red Book* from the American Academy of Pediatrics (AAP). Contact information for the AAP is located in Appendix BB.

TYPE OF FACILITY: *Center; Large Family Child Care Home; Small Family Child Care Home*

PARVOVIRUS B19

STANDARD 6.016
ATTENDANCE OF CHILDREN WITH ERYTHEMA INFECTIOSUM (EI)

Children who develop erythema infectiosum (EI), also known as fifth disease, following infection with parvovirus B19, shall be allowed to attend child care because they are no longer contagious when signs and symptoms appear.

RATIONALE: EI is caused by parvovirus B19. EI begins with a fever, headache, and muscle aches, and is followed by a rash, which is intensely red with a "slapped cheek" appearance. A lace-like rash appears on the rest of the body. Isolation or exclusion of an immunocompetent person with parvovirus B19 infection in the child care setting is not necessary because little to no virus is present in the respiratory tract secretions at the time of occurrence of the rash (22).

COMMENTS: For additional information regarding parvovirus B19, consult the *Red Book* from the American Academy of Pediatrics (AAP). Contact information for the AAP is located in Appendix BB.

TYPE OF FACILITY: *Center; Large Family Child Care Home; Small Family Child Care Home*

UNSPECIFIED RESPIRATORY TRACT INFECTION

STANDARD 6.017
ATTENDANCE OF CHILDREN WITH UNSPECIFIED RESPIRATORY TRACT INFECTION

Children without fever who have mild symptoms associated with the common cold, sore throat, croup, bronchitis, rhinitis (runny nose), or otitis media (ear infection) shall not be denied admission to child care, sent home from child care, or separated from other children in the facility unless their illness is characterized by one or more of the following conditions:

a) The illness has a specified cause that requires exclusion, as determined by other specific performance standards in Child Inclusion/Exclusion/Dismissal, STANDARD 3.065 through STANDARD 3.068;

b) The illness limits the child's comfortable participation in child care activities;

c) The illness results in a need for more care than the staff can provide without compromising the health and safety of other children.

Treatment with antibiotics shall not be required or otherwise encouraged as a condition for attendance of children with mild respiratory tract infections unless directed by local health authorities.

RATIONALE: The incidence of acute diseases of the respiratory tract, including the common cold, croup, bronchitis, pneumonia, and otitis media, is high in infants and young children, whether they are cared for at home or attend out-of-home facilities (23). Studies suggest that children who attend child care facilities have a significantly higher risk of upper and lower respiratory tract infections compared to children who are cared for at home and that infants and young children in child care have a higher incidence of these infections when they first begin to attend child care (24, 25, 26).

Children, 3 years of age and younger, experience an average of 5 to 10 respiratory tract infections each year, most of which are not severe and are caused by viruses that infect the respiratory tract (27). There is no evidence that the incidence of most acute diseases of the respiratory tract can be reduced among children in child care by any specific intervention other than routine sanitation and personal hygiene.

Exclusion of ill children from the facility has not been found of value in preventing common respiratory infections.

When compliance with environmental infection control practices is high in child care settings, a reduction in episodes of colds is possible (28). Most children with viral respiratory tract infections remain infectious for at least 5 to 8 days. Frequently, infected children are shedding viruses before they are obviously ill, and some infected children never become overtly ill. Therefore, excluding children with respiratory tract disease from child care is not likely to limit transmission of respiratory tract infections in the child care setting.

The inappropriate use of antibiotics is a serious public health problem leading to development of antibiotic resistance (29, 30). Inappropriate antibiotic use in child care for mild respiratory tract infections is common even though these infections are often caused by viruses. Parents may attempt to pressure physicians into prescribing antibiotics for infections because they falsely believe that antibiotics will shorten the time when their children are excluded from child care.

COMMENTS: Uncontrolled coughing, difficult or rapid breathing, and wheezing (if associated with difficult breathing or if the child has no history of asthma) may represent severe illness or even a life-threatening condition. Exclusion in these cases is for the child's safety. The child should receive medical care before being allowed to return to the facility.

For additional information regarding unspecified respiratory tract infections, consult the *Red Book* from the American Academy of Pediatrics (AAP). Contact information for the AAP is located in Appendix BB.

TYPE OF FACILITY: *Center; Large Family Child Care Home; Small Family Child Care Home*

6.2 HERPES VIRUSES

Please note that if a staff member has no contact with the children, or with anything with which the children come in contact, the staff requirements in these standards do not apply to that staff member.

HERPES SIMPLEX

STANDARD 6.018
DISEASE RECOGNITION AND CONTROL OF HERPES SIMPLEX VIRUS

Children with herpetic gingivostomatitis, an infection of the mouth caused by the herpes simplex virus, who do not have control of oral secretions shall be excluded from child care. In selected situations, children with mild disease who are in control of their mouth secretions may not have to be excluded. The facility's health consultant or health department officials shall be consulted.

Child care providers with herpetic gingivostomatitis, cold sores, or herpes labialis shall do the following:
a) Refrain from kissing and nuzzling children;
b) Refrain from sharing food and drinks with children and other caregivers;
c) Avoid touching the lesions;
d) Wash their hands frequently;
e) Cover any skin lesion with a bandage, clothing, or an appropriate dressing.

Child care providers shall be instructed in the importance of and technique for handwashing and other measures aimed at limiting the transfer of infected material, such as saliva, tissue fluid, or fluid from a skin sore.

RATIONALE: Initial herpes simplex virus disease in children often produces a sudden illness of short duration characterized by fever and sores around and within the mouth. Illness and viral excretion may persist for a week or more; severe open skin sores may prevent oral intake and necessitate hospitalization (31). Recurrent oral herpes is manifested as small, fluid-filled blisters on the lips and entails a much shorter period of virus shedding from sores. Adults and children also can shed the virus in oral secretions in the absence of identifiable sores.

Although the risk of transmission of herpes simplex virus in the child care setting has not been documented, spread of infection within families has been reported and is thought to require direct contact with infected secretions (31). Transmission of herpes simplex in child care is uncommon (32).

COMMENTS: For additional information on policies, staff education, on recognizing and controlling herpes simplex and varicella-zoster (chickenpox) viruses, see Training STANDARD 1.023 through STANDARD 1.033; Hygiene STANDARD 3.012 through STANDARD 3.027, Child Inclusion/Exclusion/Dismissal, STANDARD 3.065 through STANDARD 3.068; and Notification of Parents, STANDARD 3.084 and STANDARD 3.085.

For additional information regarding herpes simplex, consult the *Red Book* from the American Academy of Pediatrics (AAP). Contact information for the AAP is located in Appendix BB.

TYPE OF FACILITY: *Center; Large Family Child Care Home; Small Family Child Care Home*

VARICELLA-ZOSTER (CHICKENPOX) VIRUS

STANDARD 6.019
STAFF AND PARENT NOTIFICATION ABOUT VARICELLA-ZOSTER (CHICKENPOX) VIRUS

The child care facility shall notify all staff members and parents when a case of chickenpox occurs, informing them of the greater likelihood of serious infection in susceptible adults, the potential for fetal damage if infection occurs during pregnancy, and the risk of severe varicella in children or adults whose immune systems are impaired for any reason including HIV infection, steroid use, cancer chemotherapy, or organ transplantation (33).

RATIONALE: About 5 to 10 percent of adults will be susceptible to varicella-zoster virus. Susceptible child care staff members who are pregnant and are exposed to children with chickenpox should be referred to physicians or other health professionals who are knowledgeable in the area of varicella infection during pregnancy within 24 hours after the exposure is recognized. The Centers for Disease Control and Prevention (CDC) and the American Academy of Pediatrics (AAP) recommend the use of varicella vaccine in non-pregnant susceptible persons 12 months of age and older within 72 hours after exposure to varicella (33, 34).

COMMENTS: Sample letters of notification to parents that their child may have been exposed to an infectious disease are contained in the National Academy for the Education of Young Children (NAEYC) publication, *Healthy Young Children*. Contact information is located in Appendix BB.

For information about health education for children, staff, and parents, see STANDARD 2.060 through STANDARD 2.067.

For additional information regarding varicella, consult the *Red Book* from the American Academy of Pediatrics (AAP). Contact information for the AAP is located in Appendix BB.

TYPE OF FACILITY: *Center; Large Family Child Care Home; Small Family Child Care Home*

STANDARD 6.020
EXCLUSION OF CHILDREN WITH VARICELLA-ZOSTER (CHICKENPOX) VIRUS

Children who develop chickenpox shall be excluded until all sores have dried and crusted (usually 6 days).

Staff members or children with shingles (herpes zoster) shall keep sores covered by clothing or a dressing until sores have crusted. The need for excluding an infected person shall be decided based on the recommendations of the person's health care provider. If a conflict or question about return to the child care facility arises, the facility shall consult personnel at the health department. Until the conflict is resolved, readmission shall be delayed.

RATIONALE: Exclusion of children infected with varicella-zoster virus may not control illness in child care, but exclusion may help control disease caused by this virus in some individuals (such as adults, children and adults who have a compromised immune system, and newborn infants).

The chickenpox virus seems to be present in respiratory tract secretions and to be shed from the mouth and throat as well as from skin lesions. Spread from oral or respiratory tract secretions to susceptible contacts is likely.

With shingles, the virus is present in small, fluid-filled blisters, and is spread by direct contact. Sores that are covered seem to pose little risk to susceptible persons. Older children and staff members with herpes zoster should be instructed to wash their hands if they touch potentially infectious lesions.

About 5 to 10 percent of adults will be susceptible to varicella-zoster virus. Susceptible child care staff members who are pregnant and are exposed to children with chickenpox should be referred to physicians or other health care professionals who are knowledgeable in the area of varicella infection during pregnancy within 24 hours after the exposure is recognized.

COMMENTS: Initial viral infection with varicella-zoster virus produces an acute fever and the appearance of chickenpox blisters; reactivation of the virus results in shingles (herpes zoster). See STANDARD 6.023, for more information on shingles.

Routine use of varicella vaccine as recommended by the American Academy of Pediatrics (AAP) and the Centers for Disease Control and Prevention (CDC) will reduce the likelihood of transmission of wild type strains of varicella virus (33, 34, 35).

In mild cases with only a few sores and rapid recovery, an otherwise healthy child may be able to return to child care sooner once the lesions are crusted. Children whose immune system does not function properly and children with more severe cases of chickenpox shall be excluded from child care until lesions are crusted.

For additional information regarding varicella, consult the *Red Book* from the AAP. Contact information for the AAP is located in Appendix BB. For information about health education for children, staff, and parents, see STANDARD 2.060 through STANDARD 2.067.

TYPE OF FACILITY: *Center; Large Family Child Care Home; Small Family Child Care Home*

CYTOMEGALOVIRUS (CMV)

STANDARD 6.021
STAFF EDUCATION AND POLICIES ON CYTOMEGALOVIRUS (CMV)

Facilities that employ women of childbearing age shall educate these workers with regard to the following:
a) The increased probability of exposure to cytomegalovirus (CMV) in the child care setting;
b) The potential for fetal damage when CMV is acquired during pregnancy;
c) Hygiene measures (especially handwashing and avoiding contact with urine, saliva, and nasal secretions) aimed at reducing the acquisition of CMV;
d) The availability of counseling and testing for serum antibody to CMV to determine the child care provider's immune status.

Female employees of childbearing age shall be referred to their personal health care providers or to the health department authority for counseling about their risk of cytomegalovirus (CMV) infection. This counseling may include testing for serum antibodies to CMV to determine the employee's immunity against CMV infection.

RATIONALE: CMV is the leading cause of congenital infection in the United States, with approximately 1% of live born infants infected prenatally (36). While most infected fetuses escape resulting illness or disability, 10 to 20 percent will have hearing loss, mental retardation, cerebral palsy, or vision disturbances. Although maternal immunity does not prevent congenital CMV infection, evidence indicates that initial acquisition of CMV during pregnancy (primary maternal infection) carries the greatest risk for resulting illness or disability of the fetus (36).

Children enrolled in child care facilities are more likely to acquire CMV than are children cared for at home. Epidemiologic data, as well as laboratory testing of viral strains, has provided evidence for child-to-child transmission of CMV in the child care setting (36). Rates of CMV excretion have varied among facilities and even between class groups within a facility. Children between 1 and 3 years of age have the highest rates of excretion; published studies report rates between 20 to 80 percent in this age group. Children who acquire CMV from a maternal source or in a facility may continue to excrete the virus for years (37). Thus, it is reasonable to conclude that child care staff members are more likely to come into contact with CMV-excreting children than are individuals in any other known situation or occupation.

Epidemiologic data and study of CMV strains have shown that premature newborn infants who acquire CMV in the nursery can transmit the virus to their parents (38). Moreover, parents of children attending centers have a higher rate of development of antibodies to CMV than parents of children kept at home (39). Parental infection with CMV is related to the child's CMV excretion (38, 39, 40).

With regard to child-to-staff transmission, studies have shown a high rate of infection with CMV among child care workers with annual rates ranging from 14 to 20 percent (41, 42, 43). Therefore, exposure to CMV with the higher rate of acquisition that occurs in child care staff will most likely lead to a higher rate of gestational CMV infection in staff members without antibodies to CMV and an increased rate of congenital CMV infection in their offspring (36). Women who have antibodies to CMV can be reassured that their risk of having an infant damaged by congenital CMV infection is low.

With current knowledge on the risk of CMV infection in child care staff members and the potential conse-quences of gestational CMV infection, child care staff members should receive counseling in regard to the risks.

COMMENTS: Assays for measuring antibody to CMV are available commercially and seem to perform well when used by qualified laboratories. They are accepted for screening blood products, transfusion recipients, and organ donors and recipients.

For additional information regarding CMV, consult the *Red Book* from the American Academy of Pediatrics (AAP). Contact information for the AAP is located in Appendix BB.

TYPE OF FACILITY: *Center; Large Family Child Care Home; Small Family Child Care Home*

STANDARD 6.022
ATTENDANCE AND TESTING OF CHILDREN WITH CMV

Testing children to detect CMV excretion or excluding children known to be CMV infected is not recommended. All infants and toddlers shall be assumed to be infected with CMV.

RATIONALE: Testing of urine and saliva for CMV excretion in children is expensive and is likely to be misleading, since excretion of CMV by children in child care is intermittent and common (39, 40).

COMMENTS: For additional information regarding CMV, consult the *Red Book* from the American Academy of Pediatrics (AAP). Contact information for the AAP is located in Appendix BB.

TYPE OF FACILITY: *Center; Large Family Child Care Home; Small Family Child Care Home*

6.3 ENTERIC (DIARRHEAL) AND HEPATITIS A VIRUS (HAV) INFECTIONS

Please note that if a staff member has no contact with the children, or with anything with which the children come in contact, the staff requirements in these standards do not apply to that staff member.

STANDARD 6.023
CONTROL OF ENTERIC (DIARRHEAL) AND HEPATITIS A VIRUS INFECTIONS

Facilities shall employ the following procedures, in addition to those stated in Inclusion/Exclusion/Dismissal, STANDARD 3.065 through STANDARD 3.068, to prevent and control infections of the gastrointestinal tract (including diarrhea) or liver:

a) Children who cannot use a toilet for all bowel movements while attending the facility and who develop diarrhea shall be removed from the facility by their parent or legal guardian. Pending arrival of the parent or legal guardian, the child shall not be permitted to have contact with other children or be placed in areas used by adults who have contact with children in the facility. This shall be accomplished by removing the ill child to a separate area of the child care center or, if not possible, to a separate area of the child's room. The area shall be one where the child is supervised by an adult known to the child, and where the toys, equipment, and surfaces will not be used by other children or adults until after the ill child leaves and after the surfaces have been disinfected. When moving a child to a separate area of the facility creates problems with supervision of the other children, as in small family child care homes, the ill child shall be kept as comfortable as possible, with minimal contact between ill and well children, until the parent or legal guardian arrives. The child who requires separation because of diarrhea shall be separated from the group upon the onset of the diarrhea. Caregivers with diarrhea as defined in STANDARD 3.069 shall be excluded. Separation and exclusion of children or caregivers shall not be deferred pending health assessment or laboratory testing to identify an enteric pathogen.

b) A child who develops jaundice (when skin and white parts of the eye are yellow) while attending child care shall be separated from other children and the child's parent or legal guardian shall be called to remove the child. The child shall remain separated from the other children as described above until the parent or legal guardian arrives and removes the child from the facility.

c) Exclusion for acute diarrhea shall continue until either the diarrhea stops or the continued loose stools are deemed not to be infectious by a licensed health care professional. Exclusion for hepatitis A virus (HAV) as specified in item b) above shall continue for one week after onset of illness or until immune globulin has been administered to appropriate children and staff at the facility. See also STANDARD 3.065, on inclusion/exclusion/dismissal of children with diarrhea.

d) Alternate care for children with diarrhea or hepatitis A in special facilities for ill children shall be provided only in facilities that can provide separate care for children with infections of the gastrointestinal tract (including diarrhea) or liver. See also STANDARD 3.070 through STANDARD 3.080, on caring for ill children.

e) Children and caregivers who excrete intestinal pathogens but no longer have diarrhea generally may be allowed to return to child care once the diarrhea resolves, except for the case of infections with *Shigella, E. coli 0157:H7* or *Salmonella typhi.* For *Shigella* and *E.coli 0157:H7* two negative stool cultures are required for readmission, unless state requirements differ. For *Salmonella typhi*, three negative cultures are required. For Salmonella species other that *S.typhi* stool cultures are not required from asymptomatic individuals.

f) The local health department shall be informed within 24 hours of the occurrence of hepatitis A virus infection or an increased frequency of diarrheal illness in children or staff in a child care facility.

g) In addition to the recommended postexposure prophylaxis, hepatitis A immunization shall be considered in child care settings with ongoing or recurrent outbreaks, especially in communities where routine immunization of children for hepatitis A is recommended (44). In the absence of ongoing outbreaks, immunization in child care centers shall be used to implement routine hepatitis A immunization, particularly in communities where cases in the child care facility contribute substantially to the total number of hepatitis A cases and seem play a role in sustaining community-wide outbreaks.

h) If there has been an exposure to a case of hepatitis A or diarrhea in the child care facility, caregivers shall inform parents of other children in the facility, in cooperation with the health department, that their children may have been exposed to children with hepatitis A virus (HAV) infection or diarrheal illness.

i) These procedures shall be implemented in addition to those stated in STANDARD 3.065 through STANDARD 3.068.

RATIONALE: Intestinal organisms, including hepatitis A virus, cause disease in children, child care providers, and close family members (45, 46, 47, 48). The primary age groups involved are children younger than 3 years of age who wear diapers. Disease has occurred in outbreaks within centers and as sporadic episodes. Although many intestinal agents can cause diarrhea in children in child care, rotavirus, other enteric viruses, *Giardia lamblia*, *Shigella*, and *Cryptosporidium* have been the main organisms implicated in outbreaks. In addition, excretion of intestinal agents, particularly *Giardia lamblia* and rotavirus, has been shown to occur in children who show no symptoms (49, 50). The significance of this phenomenon in transmission is unknown. Child care providers should observe children for signs of disease to permit early detection and implementation of control measures. Facilities should consult the local health department to determine whether the increased frequency of diarrheal illness requires public health intervention.

The most important characteristic of child care facilities associated with increased frequencies of diarrhea or hepatitis A is the presence of young children who are not toilet-trained (47, 51). Contamination of hands, communal toys, and other classroom objects is common and plays a role in the transmission of enteric pathogens in child care facilities.

Studies commonly find that fecal contamination of the environment is frequent in centers and is highest in infant and toddler areas where diarrhea or hepatitis A are known to occur most often (52, 53). Studies indicate that the risk of diarrhea is significantly higher for children in centers than in age-matched children cared for at home or in small family child care homes (8). The spread of infection from children who are not toilet-trained to other children in child care facilities or to their families is common, particularly when *Shigella*, rotavirus and other enteric viruses, *Giardia lamblia*, *Cryptosporidium*, or hepatitis A virus (HAV) is the causal agent (45).

To decrease diarrheal disease in child care, the staff and parents must be educated about modes of transmission as well as practical methods of prevention and control. Staff training in handwashing and hygiene, combined with close monitoring of staff compliance, is associated with a significant decrease in infant and toddler diarrhea (54, 55). Staff training on a single occasion, without close staff monitoring, however, does not result in a decrease in diarrhea rates; this finding emphasizes the importance of monitoring as well as education (54,55). Therefore, appropriate hygienic practices, hygiene monitoring, and education are important in limiting infections of the intestines or liver in child care.

The Centers for Disease Control and Prevention (CDC) recommends excluding children with diarrhea (for any reason) from child care until diarrhea has resolved. This standard is more lenient than the CDC recommendation by allowing children whose feces are contained by use of a toilet to remain in care. Because outbreaks are rare in groups of toilet-trained children, a more lenient approach may be taken in this age group.

COMMENTS: See also the environmental and personal hygiene standards given in the following standards to prevent and control infections of the gastrointestinal tract (including diarrhea) or liver:
1) STANDARD 3.070 through STANDARD 3.080, on caring for ill children;
2) STANDARD 3.012 through STANDARD 3.019, on toileting and diapering;
3) STANDARD 3.020 throughSTANDARD 3.024, on handwashing;
4) STANDARD 3.028 through STANDARD 3.040, on sanitation, disinfection, and maintenance;
5) STANDARD 4.050 through STANDARD 4.060, on food safety;
6) STANDARD 3.042 through STANDARD 3.044, on animals;
7) STANDARD 8.046 through STANDARD 8.052, on child records;
8) STANDARD 5.219 through STANDARD 5.225, on interior maintenance;
9) STANDARD 8.035 and STANDARD 8.036, on food handling, feeding, and nutrition policies.

Sample letters of notification to parents that their child may have been exposed to an infectious disease are contained in the (National Academy for the Education of Young Children (NAEYC) publication, *Healthy Young Children*. Contact information is located in Appendix BB.

For information about health education for children, staff, and parents, see STANDARD 2.060 through STANDARD 2.067.

For additional information regarding enteric (diarrheal) and hepatitis A virus (HAV) infections, consult the *Red Book* from the American Academy of Pediatrics (AAP). Contact information for the AAP is located in Appendix BB.

TYPE OF FACILITY: *Center; Large Family Child Care Home; Small Family Child Care Home*

STANDARD 6.024
STAFF EDUCATION AND POLICIES ON ENTERIC (DIARRHEAL) AND HAV INFECTIONS

Facilities shall adhere to the following staff educational policies to prevent and control infections of the gastrointestinal tract (mainly diarrhea) or liver:
a) The facility shall conduct ongoing continuing education for staff members, to include the following:
 1) Methods of transmission of pathogens that cause diarrhea and hepatitis A virus;
 2) Recognition and prevention of diarrhea and disease associated with hepatitis A virus infection;
b) All caregivers, food handlers, and maintenance staff shall receive ongoing education and monitoring concerning handwashing and cleaning of environmental surfaces as specified in the facility's plan. See STANDARD 3.020 through STANDARD 3.023, on handwashing; and STANDARD 3.028 through STANDARD 3.040, on sanitation, disinfection, and maintenance;
c) At least annually, the director shall review all procedures related to preventing diarrhea and hepatitis A virus infections. Each caregiver, food handler, and maintenance person shall review a written copy of these procedures or view a video, which shall include age-specific criteria for inclusion and exclusion of children who have a diarrheal illness or hepatitis A virus infection and infection control procedures. See Child Inclusion/Exclusion/Dismissal, STANDARD 3.065 through STANDARD 3.068;

d) Guidelines for administration of immune globulin and immunization against hepatitis A virus shall be enforced to prevent infection in contacts of children with hepatitis A disease (44, 56).

RATIONALE: Staff training in hygiene and monitoring of staff compliance have been shown to reduce the spread of diarrhea (51, 54, 55, 57). These studies suggest that training combined with outside monitoring of child care practices can modify staff behavior as well as the occurrence of disease.

Child care providers should observe children for signs of disease to permit early detection and implementation of control measures. Facilities should consult the local health department to determine whether the increased frequency of diarrheal illness requires public health intervention.

COMMENTS: For additional information regarding enteric (diarrheal) and hepatitis A virus (HAV) infections, consult the *Red Book* from the American Academy of Pediatrics (AAP). Contact information for the AAP is located in Appendix BB.

TYPE OF FACILITY: *Center; Large Family Child Care Home; Small Family Child Care Home*

STANDARD 6.025
DISEASE SURVEILLANCE OF ENTERIC (DIARRHEAL) AND HAV INFECTIONS

The child care facility shall cooperate with local health authorities in notifying all staff and parents of other children who attend the facility of possible exposure to hepatitis A, and diarrheal agents such as *E. coli: 0157:H7, Shigella,* rotavirus and other enteric viruses, *Salmonella, Campylobacter, Giardia lamblia,* and *Cryptosporidium.*

RATIONALE: Intestinal organisms, including hepatitis A virus, cause disease in children, child care providers, and close family members (45, 46, 47, 48). Disease has occurred in outbreaks within centers and as sporadic episodes (45, 49, 58). Although many intestinal agents can cause diarrhea in children in child care, rotavirus, other enteric viruses, *Giardia lamblia, Shigella,* and *Cryptosporidium* have been the main organisms implicated in outbreaks.

Child care providers should observe children for signs of disease to permit early detection and implementation of control measures. Facilities should consult the local health department to determine whether the increased frequency of diarrheal illness requires public health intervention.

COMMENTS: Sample letters of notification to parents that their child may have been exposed to an infectious disease are contained in the (National Academy for the Education of Young Children (NAEYC) publication, *Healthy Young Children*. Contact information is located in Appendix BB.

For information about health education for children, staff, and parents, see STANDARD 2.060 through STANDARD 2.067.

For additional information on enteric (diarrheal) and hepatitis A virus infections, see Training, STANDARD 1.023 through STANDARD 1.033; and Notification of Parents, STANDARD 3.084 and STANDARD 3.085. Also, consult the *Red Book* from the American Academy of Pediatrics (AAP). Contact information for the AAP is located in Appendix BB.

TYPE OF FACILITY: *Center; Large Family Child Care Home; Small Family Child Care Home*

STANDARD 6.026
MAINTENANCE OF RECORDS ON INCIDENTS OF DIARRHEA

The facility shall maintain a record of children and caregivers who have diarrhea while at home or at the facility. This record shall include:
a) The child or caregiver's name;
b) Dates the child or caregiver is ill;
c) Reason for diarrhea, if known;
d) Whether the child or caregiver was in attendance at the child care facility during the diarrhea episode;
e) Any leakage of feces from the diaper while the child was in attendance at the child care facility.

The facility shall notify the local health department authorities whenever there have been two or more children with diarrhea in a given classroom or three or more unrelated children (not siblings) within the facility within a 2-week period.

RATIONALE: Disease surveillance and reporting to the local health department authorities are critical in preventing and controlling diseases in the child care setting. A major purpose of surveillance is to allow early detection of disease and prompt implementation of control measures. Ascertaining whether a child who attends a facility is ill is important when evaluating childhood illnesses; ascertaining whether an adult who works in a facility or is a parent of a child attending a facility is ill is important when considering a diagnosis of hepatitis A and other diseases transmitted by the fecal-oral route. Causes of these infections in household contacts may require questioning about illness in the child attending child care and testing the child for infection. Information concerning communicable disease in a child care attendee, staff member, or household contact should be communicated to public health authorities, to the child care director, to all staff and to all parents with children in the facility.

COMMENTS: For more information on reporting requirements for communicable disease, see STANDARD 3.086 and STANDARD 3.087.

TYPE OF FACILITY: *Center; Large Family Child Care Home; Small Family Child Care Home*

6.4 BLOODBORNE INFECTIONS

Hepatitis B virus, HIV, and hepatitis C virus are bloodborne pathogens. Although the risk of contact with blood containing one of these viruses is low in the child care setting, appropriate infection control practices will prevent transmission of bloodborne pathogens if exposure occurs (59, 60, 61, 62).

Please note that if a staff member has no contact with the children, or with anything with which the children come in contact, these standards do not apply to that staff member.

HEPATITIS B VIRUS (HBV)

STANDARD 6.027
DISEASE RECOGNITION AND
CONTROL OF HBV INFECTION

Facilities shall have written policies for inclusion and exclusion of children known to be infected with hepatitis B virus (HBV) and immunization of children with hepatitis B vaccine as part of their routine immunization schedule. When a child who is an HBV carrier is admitted to a facility, the facility director or the caregiver usually responsible for the child shall be informed.

Children who carry HBV chronically and who have no behavioral or medical risk factors, such as aggressive behavior (biting and frequent scratching), generalized dermatitis (weeping skin lesions), or bleeding problems shall be admitted to the facility without restrictions.

Testing of children for HBV shall not be a prerequisite for admission to facilities.

With regard to infection control measures, every person shall be assumed to be an HBV carrier. Child care personnel shall adopt standard precautions, as outlined in Prevention of Exposure to Blood, STANDARD 3.026 and STANDARD 3.027.

Toys and objects that young children (infants and toddlers) mouth shall be cleaned and sanitized, as stated in STANDARD 3.036 through STANDARD 3.038.

Toothbrushes shall be individually labeled so that the children do not share toothbrushes, as specified in STANDARD 5.095.

RATIONALE: Transmission of HBV in the child care setting is of concern to public health authorities. Children who are HBV carriers (particularly children born in countries highly endemic for HBV) can be expected to require child care (62, 63, 64, 65, 66). The risk of transmitting the disease in child care is theoretically small, though, because blood or infected body fluid must get inside another body for it to transmit HBV infection and because immunization of infants as part of the routine childhood immunization schedule has decreased the number of susceptible children. Immunization not only will reduce the potential for transmission but also will allay anxiety about transmission from children and staff in the child care setting who may be carriers of hepatitis B.

The risk of disease transmission from an HBV-carrier child or staff member with no behavioral risk factors and without generalized dermatitis or bleeding problems is considered very low. This extremely low risk does not justify exclusion of an HBV-carrier child from out-of-home care, nor does it justify the routine screening of children as possible HBV carriers prior to admission to child care.

HBV transmission in a child care setting is most likely to occur through direct exposure via bites or scratches that break the skin and introduce blood or body secretions from the HBV carrier into the victim. Indirect transmission via blood or saliva through environmental contamination may be possible but has not been documented. Saliva contains much less virus (1/ 1000) than blood; therefore, the potential infection from saliva is lower. In gibbons and chimpanzees, saliva has been shown to be infectious only when inoculated through the skin; it has not caused infection when administered by aerosol through the nose or mouth, by ingestion through the mouth, or by toothbrush on the gums (62).

No data are available to indicate the risk of transmission if a susceptible person bites an HBV carrier. When the HBV statuses of both the biting child and the victim are unknown, the risk of HBV transmission would be extremely low because of the expected low incidence of HBV carriage by children of preschool-age and the low efficiency of disease transmission by bite exposure. Because a bite in this situation is extremely unlikely to involve an HBV-carrier child, screening is not warranted, particularly in children who are immunized appropriately against HBV (62).

COMMENTS: Parents are not required to share information about their child's HBV status, but they should be encouraged to do so.

For additional information regarding HBV, consult the *Red Book* from the American Academy of Pediatrics (AAP). Contact information for the AAP is located in Appendix BB.

TYPE OF FACILITY: *Center; Large Family Child Care Home; Small Family Child Care Home*

STANDARD 6.028
OBSERVATION AND FOLLOW-UP OF A CHILD WHO IS AN HBV CARRIER

The primary caregiver shall observe a child who is a known hepatitis B virus (HBV) carrier and the other children in the group for development of aggressive behavior (such as biting or frequent scratching) that might facilitate transmission of HBV. When this type of behavior occurs, the child's health care provider or the health department shall evaluate the need for immediate disease prevention measures with hepatitis B immune globulin and shall reevaluate the child's continuing attendance in the facility.

RATIONALE: Regular assessment of behavioral risk factors and medical conditions of enrolled children who are HBV carriers is important. It is helpful if the center director and primary caregivers are informed that a known HBV-carrier child is in care. However, parents are not required to share this information. Most children in child care facilities have been immunized against hepatitis B as part of their routine immunization schedule, minimizing the risk of transmission (62).

COMMENTS: For additional information regarding HBV infections, consult the *Red Book* from the American Academy of Pediatrics (AAP). Contact information for the AAP is located in Appendix BB.

TYPE OF FACILITY: *Center; Large Family Child Care Home; Small Family Child Care Home*

STANDARD 6.029
STAFF EDUCATION ON PREVENTION OF BLOODBORNE DISEASES

All caregivers shall receive regular training on how to prevent transmission of bloodborne diseases, including hepatitis B virus (HBV).

RATIONALE: Efforts to reduce the risk of transmitting diseases in child care through hygienic and environmental standards in general should focus primarily on blood precautions and ensuring that children are appropriately immunized against hepatitis B virus.

COMMENTS: For additional information regarding HBV infections, consult the *Red Book* from the American Academy of Pediatrics (AAP). Contact information for the AAP is located in Appendix BB. also Continuing Education, STANDARD 1.029 through STANDARD 1.033.

TYPE OF FACILITY: *Center; Large Family Child Care Home; Small Family Child Care Home*

STANDARD 6.030
INFORMING PUBLIC HEALTH AUTHORITIES OF HBV CASES

Staff members known to have acute or chronic hepatitis B virus (HBV) shall not be restricted from work but shall receive training on how to prevent transmission of bloodborne diseases. Cases of acute HBV in any child or employee of a facility shall be reported to the health department for a determination of the need for further investigation or preventive measures.

RATIONALE: The risk of disease transmission from a HBV carrier child or staff member with normal behavior and without generalized dermatitis or bleeding problems is considered very low. This extremely low risk does not justify exclusion of an HBV-carrier staff member from providing child care, nor does it justify the routine screening of staff as possible HBV carriers prior to admission to child care.

COMMENTS: For additional information regarding HBV infections, consult the *Red Book* from the American Academy of Pediatrics (AAP). Contact information for the AAP is located in Appendix BB.

See also Continuing Education, STANDARD 1.029 through STANDARD 1.033; Prevention of Exposure to Blood, STANDARD 3.026 and STANDARD 3.027; Reporting Illness, STANDARD 3.086 and STANDARD 3.087.

TYPE OF FACILITY: *Center; Large Family Child Care Home; Small Family Child Care Home*

HYGIENE FOR HEPATITIS B VIRUS (HBV) INFECTION

STANDARD 6.031
HANDLING OF INJURIES TO A HBV CARRIER

Injuries that lead to bleeding by a hepatitis B virus (HBV) carrier child or adult shall be handled promptly in the manner recommended for any such injury in any child or adult using standard precautions.

RATIONALE: Efforts to reduce the risk of transmitting diseases in child care through hygienic and environmental standards in general should focus primarily on blood precautions and ensuring appropriate immunization against hepatitis B virus.

COMMENTS: For additional information regarding HBV infections, consult the *Red Book* from the American Academy of Pediatrics (AAP). Contact information for the AAP is located in Appendix BB. See STANDARD 3.026 and STANDARD 3.027, on the prevention of exposure to blood.

TYPE OF FACILITY: *Center; Large Family Child Care Home; Small Family Child Care Home*

HEPATITIS C VIRUS (HCV)

STANDARD 6.032
INFECTION CONTROL MEASURES WITH HCV

Standard precautions, as outlined in STANDARD 3.026, shall be followed to prevent infection with hepatitis C virus (HCV) infection. Children with HCV infection shall not be excluded from out-of-home child care.

RATIONALE: Transmission risks of HCV infection in a child care setting are unknown. The general risk of HCV infection from percutaneous exposure to infected blood is estimated to be 10 times greater than that of HIV but lower than that of hepatitis B virus (HBV) (61). Transmission of HCV via contamination of mucous membranes or broken skin probably

has an intermediate risk between that for blood infected with HIV and HBV.

COMMENTS: For additional information regarding HCV infections, consult the *Red Book* from the American Academy of Pediatrics (AAP). Contact information for the AAP is located in Appendix BB.

TYPE OF FACILITY: *Center; Large Family Child Care Home; Small Family Child Care Home*

HUMAN IMMUNODEFICIENCY VIRUS (HIV)

ADMINISTRATIVE POLICIES ON HIV INFECTIONS

STANDARD 6.033
ATTENDANCE OF CHILDREN WITH HIV

Children infected with human immunodeficiency virus (HIV) shall be admitted to child care provided that their health, neurological development, behavior, and immune status are acceptable, as determined on a case-by-case basis by persons knowledgeable in the area of HIV infection, including the child's health care provider. These individuals must be able to evaluate whether the child will receive optimal care in the specific facility being considered and whether an HIV-infected child poses a potential threat to others.

RATIONALE: No reported cases of HIV infection are known to have resulted from transmission in out-of-home child care. Although the risk of transmission of HIV infection to children in the child care setting seems to be extremely low, data does not exist that directly addresses this issue. Guidelines can most reasonably provide methods to reduce the risk of transmission of HIV infection to caregivers in out-of-home child care (59).

COMMENTS: For additional information regarding HIV, consult the *Red Book* from the American Academy of Pediatrics (AAP). Contact information for the AAP is located in Appendix BB.

TYPE OF FACILITY: *Center; Large Family Child Care Home; Small Family Child Care Home*

STANDARD 6.034
PROTECTING HIV-INFECTED CHILDREN AND ADULTS IN CHILD CARE

Parents of all children, including human immuno-deficiency virus (HIV) infected children, shall be notified immediately if the child has been exposed to chickenpox, tuberculosis, fifth disease (parvovirus B19), diarrheal disease, measles, or other infectious diseases through other children in the facility.

Children whose immune systems do not function properly to prevent infection and who are exposed to measles or chickenpox shall be referred immediately to their health care provider to receive the appropriate preventive measure (immune globulin or immunization) following exposure and decision about readmission to the child care facility (33, 67).

Caregivers known to be HIV-infected shall be notified immediately if they have been exposed to chickenpox, fifth disease, tuberculosis, diarrheal disease, or measles through children in the facility. If they have been exposed to measles or chickenpox, they shall receive an appropriate preventive measure (immune globulin or immunization) after exposure (33, 67). Their return to work after exposure shall be determined jointly by the director of the center (or, in the cases of large family child care homes and small family child care homes, the primary caregiver) and the health care provider for the HIV-infected caregiver.

Information regarding a child whose immune system does not function properly to prevent infection, whatever the cause, shall be available to caregivers who need to know so they can reduce the likelihood of transmission of infection to the child. Accordingly, infections in other children and staff members in the facility shall be brought to the prompt attention of the parent of the child whose immune system does not function properly. The parent may elect to seek medical advice regarding the child's continued participation in the facility. Injuries that lead to bleeding by a child with human

immunodeficiency virus (HIV) shall be handled promptly in the manner recommended for any such injury in any child using standard precautions.

RATIONALE: The immune system of children and adults who are infected with HIV often does not function properly to prevent infections. Children and adults with immunosuppression for multiple other reasons are at greater risk for severe complications from several infections including chickenpox, CMV, tuberculosis, *Cryptosporidium, Salmonella,* and measles virus (68). Available data indicate that infection with measles is a more serious illness in HIV-infected children than in children who are not HIV-infected. The first deaths from measles in the United States reported to the Centers for Disease Control and Prevention (CDC) after 1985 were in HIV-infected children (67).

Caregivers should know about a child's special health needs so they can offer protection for that child. Care-givers' need to know does not require knowledge of a child's HIV status, because children whose immune system does not function properly because of other acquired and congenital causes may be in the facility. Standard precautions should be adopted in caring for all adults and all children in out-of-home child care when blood or blood-containing body fluids are handled to minimize the possibility of transmission of any bloodborne disease (59).

COMMENTS: Staff should have training on standard precautions for bloodborne pathogens, HIV and other causes of immune deficiency, confidentiality and implications of suspicions about HIV status.

All caregivers should be taught the basic principles of individuals' rights to confidentiality. See STANDARD 8.054 and STANDARD 8.055.

For additional information on administrative policies on HIV infection, see Confidentiality and Access to Records, STANDARD 8.053 through STANDARD 8.057. See STANDARD 3.026 and STANDARD 3.027, on prevention of exposure to blood. Also consult the *Red Book* from the American Academy of Pediatrics (AAP). Contact information for the AAP is located in Appendix BB.

TYPE OF FACILITY: *Center; Large Family Child Care Home; Small Family Child Care Home*

PREVENTING TRANSMISSION OF HIV INFECTION

STANDARD 6.035
STAFF EDUCATION ABOUT PREVENTING TRANSMISSION OF HIV INFECTION

Caregivers shall be knowledgeable about routes of transmission and about prevention of transmission of bloodborne pathogens, including human immunodeficiency virus (HIV) and shall practice measures recommended by the U.S. Public Health Service for prevention of transmission of these infections.

RATIONALE: Unwarranted fear about HIV transmission in child care should be dispelled. Studies examining transmission of HIV support the concept that HIV is not a highly infectious agent (64). The major routes of transmission are through sexual contact, through contact with blood or body fluids containing blood, and from mother to child during the birth process. Several studies have shown that HIV-infected persons do not spread the HIV virus to other members of their households except through sexual contact.

HIV has been isolated in low volumes in saliva, urine, and human milk. Transmission of HIV through saliva seems to be uncommon. Cases suggest that contact with blood from an HIV-infected individual is a possible mode of transmission through contact between broken skin and blood or blood-containing fluids. Theoretically, biting is a possible mode of transmission of bloodborne illness, such as HIV infection. However, the risk of such transmission is believed to be rare. If a bite results in blood exposure to either person involved, the U.S. Public Health Service recommends postexposure follow-up, including consideration of postexposure prophylaxis (69).

COMMENTS: For additional information regarding HIV, consult the *Red Book* from the American Academy of Pediatrics (AAP). Contact information for the AAP is located in Appendix BB. See STANDARD 1.029 through STANDARD 1.033, on Continuing Education and STANDARD 3.026 and STANDARD 3.027, on the prevention of exposure to blood.

TYPE OF FACILITY: *Center; Large Family Child Care Home; Small Family Child Care Home*

STANDARD 6.036
ABILITY OF CAREGIVERS WITH HIV INFECTION TO CARE FOR CHILDREN

Human immunodeficiency virus (HIV) infected adults with no symptoms of illness may care for children in facilities provided they do not have open skin sores or other conditions that would allow contact of their body fluids with children or other adults.

RATIONALE: Based on available data, there is no reason to believe that HIV-infected adults will transmit HIV in the course of their normal child care duties. Therefore, HIV-infected adults who do not have open skin sores that cannot be covered or other conditions that would allow contact with their body fluids may care for children in facilities. Immunosuppressed adults with acquired immunodeficiency syndrome (AIDS) may be more likely to acquire infectious agents from children and should consult with their own health care providers regarding the advisability of their continuing to work in a facility (68).

COMMENTS: For additional information regarding HIV, consult the *Red Book* from the American Academy of Pediatrics (AAP). Contact information for the AAP is located in Appendix BB.

TYPE OF FACILITY: *Center; Large Family Child Care Home; Small Family Child Care Home*

6.5 SKIN INFECTIONS

SCABIES

STANDARD 6.037
ATTENDANCE OF CHILDREN WITH SCABIES

Children with scabies shall be removed from the child care facility until appropriate treatment has been administered. Children shall be allowed to return to child care after treatment has been completed.

RATIONALE: Scabies is caused by a mite which is associated with an intensely itchy, red rash. Transmission usually occurs through prolonged close personal contact. Epidemics and localized outbreaks may require stringent and consistent measures to treat contacts. Caregivers who have had prolonged skin-to-skin contact with infested persons may benefit from prophylactic treatment. Environmental disinfestation is unnecessary and unwarranted. Bedding and clothing that is worn next to the skin before treatment should be washed.

COMMENTS: For additional information regarding scabies, consult the *Red Book* from the American Academy of Pediatrics (AAP). Contact information for the AAP is located in Appendix BB.

TYPE OF FACILITY: *Center; Large Family Child Care Home; Small Family Child Care Home*

PEDICULOSIS CAPITIS (HEAD LICE)

STANDARD 6.038
ATTENDANCE OF CHILDREN WITH HEAD LICE

Children shall not be excluded immediately or sent home early from child care because of head lice. Parents of affected children shall be notified and informed that their child must be treated properly before returning to the child care facility the next day.

Children and staff who have been in close contact with an affected child shall be examined and treated if infested. Infestation shall be identified by the presence of adult lice or nits (eggs) on a hair shaft 3 to 4 mm from the scalp (69).

RATIONALE: Head lice infestation in children attending child care is common in the U.S. and is not a sign of poor hygiene. Head lice are not a health hazard because they are not responsible for spread of any disease. After proper application of an appropriate pediculicide, reinfestation of children from an untreated infested person is more common than treatment failure.

COMMENTS: Differentiation of nits from benign hair casts (a layer of cells that easily slides off the hair shaft), plugs of skin cells, and debris can be difficult (69).

For additional information regarding head lice, consult the *Red Book* from the American Academy of Pediatrics (AAP). Contact information for the AAP is located in Appendix BB.

TYPE OF FACILITY: *Center; Large Family Child Care Home; Small Family Child Care Home*

RINGWORM

STANDARD 6.039
ATTENDANCE OF CHILDREN WITH RINGWORM

Children with ringworm of the scalp or body shall receive appropriate treatment. Children receiving treatment shall not be excluded from child care.

Children and staff in close contact with an affected child shall receive periodic inspections for early lesions and receive prompt therapy.

RATIONALE: Ringworm infection results from a fungus that is transmitted by contact with an infected person (scalp and body) and by contact with infected animals (body). Treatment of ringworm of the scalp with oral medicine for 4 to 6 weeks and of ringworm of the body with topical medicine for 4 weeks is effective.

COMMENTS: Ribbons, combs, and hairbrushes should not be shared among children and staff.

For additional information regarding ringworm, consult the *Red Book* from the American Academy of Pediatrics (AAP). Contact information for the AAP is located in Appendix BB.

TYPE OF FACILITY: *Center; Large Family Child Care Home; Small Family Child Care Home*

READER'S NOTE ON JUDICIOUS USE OF ANTIBIOTICS

The spread of antimicrobial resistance is an issue of concern to patients and parents as well as to health care professionals. Children treated with antibiotics are at increased risk of becoming carriers of resistant bacteria and if they develop an illness from resistant bacteria, they are more likely to fail antimicrobial therapy. For several conditions, such as acute otitis media, sinusitis, and pharyngitis due to group A streptococcal organisms, antibiotic therapy is indicated, but for other conditions such as the common cold and nonspecific cough illness/bronchitis, therapy is not indicated. Principles of judicious use of antimicrobial agents with detailed supporting evidence were published by the American Academy of Pediatrics (AAP), the American Academy of Family Practice (AAFP), and the Centers for Disease Control and Prevention (CDC) to identify areas where antimicrobial therapy might be curtailed without compromising patient care (30).

REFERENCES

1. American Academy of Pediatrics, Committee on Infectious Disease. Recommended childhood immunization schedule - United States, January - December 2001. *Pediatrics.* 2001;107:202-204.

2. Adams WG, Deaver KA, Cochi SL, et al. Decline of childhood *Haemophilus influenzae* type b (Hib) disease in the Hib vaccine era. *JAMA.* 1993;269:246.

3. Murphy TV, White KE, Pastor P, et al. Declining incidence of *Haemophilus influenzae* type b disease since introduction of vaccination. *JAMA.* 1993;269:246.

4. Osterholm MT, Pierson LM, White KE, et al. The risk of a subsequent transmission of *Haemophilus influenzae* type b disease among children in day care. *N Engl J Med.* 1987;316:1-5.

5. Murphy TV, Clements JF, Breedlove JA, et al. Risk of subsequent disease among day-care contacts of patients with systemic *Haemophilus influenzae* type b disease. *N Engl J Med.* 1987; 316:5 - 10.

6. Makintubee S, Istre GR, Ward JI. Transmission of invasive *Haemophilus influenzae* type b disease in day care settings. *J Pediatr.* 1987;111:180-186.

7. Fleming DW, Leibenhaut MH, Albanes D, et al. Secondary *Haemophilus influenzae* type b in day care facilities: risk factors and prevention. *JAMA.* 1985;254:509-514.

8. Pickering LK, Osterholm M. Infectious diseases associated with out-of-home child care. In: Long SS, Pickering LK, Prober CG, eds. *Principles and Practice of Pediatric Infectious Diseases.* Kent, United Kingdom: Churchill-Livingstone; 1997:31-39.

9. American Academy of Pediatrics, Committee on Infectious Diseases. Prevention of pneumococcal infections including the use of pneumococcal conjugate and polysaccharide vaccines and antibiotic prophylaxis. *Pediatrics.* In press.

10. Centers for Disease Control and Prevention (CDC). Prevention of Pneumococcal Disease Among Infants and Young Children Using the Pneumococcal Conjugate Vaccine: Report to the Advisory Committee on Immunization Practice. Atlanta, Ga: CDC; In press.

11. Levine OS, Farley M, Harrison LK, et al. Risk factors for invasive pneumococcal disease in children: a population-based case control study in North America. *Pediatrics.* 1999;103.

12. Rauch AM, O'Ryan M, Van R, et al. Invasive disease due to multiply resistant *Streptococcus pneumoniae* in Houston, Texas day-care centers. *Am J Dis Child.* 1990;144:933-27.

13. Van Deuren M, Brandtzaeg P, van der Meer JWM. Update on meningococcal disease with emphasis on pathogenesis and clinical management. *Clin Microbiol Rev.* 2000;13:144-66.

14. American Academy of Pediatrics, Committee on Infectious Diseases. Meningococcal disease prevention and control strategies for practice-based physicians. *Pediatrics.* 1996;97:404-11.

15. Centers for Disease Control and Prevention. Prevention and control of meningococcal disease: recommendations of the Advisory Committee on Immunization Practices (ACIP). *Mor Mortal Wkly Rev CDC Surveill Summ.* 2000;49(RR-07):1-10.

16. American Academy of Pediatrics, Committee on Infectious Diseases. Acellular pertussis vaccine: recommendations for use as the initial series in infants and children. *Pediatrics.* 1997;99:282-8..

17. Centers for Disease Control and Prevention. Pertussis vaccination: use of acellular pertussis vaccines among infants and young children: recommendations of the Advisory Committee on Immunization Practices(ACIP). *Mor Mortal Wkly Rev CDC Surveill Summ.* 1997;46:1-25.

18. Smith TD, Wilkinson V, Kaplan EL. Group A streptococcus-associated upper respiratory tract infections in a day-care center. *Pediatrics.* 1989;83:380-384.

19. Falck G, Kjellander J. Outbreak of group A streptococcal infection in a day-care center. *Pediatr Infect Dis J.* 1992;11:914-9.

20. American Academy of Pediatrics, Committee on Infectious Diseases. Severe invasive group A streptococcal infections: subject review. *Pediatrics*. 1998;101-136-40.

21. Leggiadro RT, Callery B, Dowdy S, et al. An outbreak of tuberculosis in a family day care home. *Pediatr Infect Dis J*. 1989;8:52-4.

22. Torok TJ. Parovirus B19 and human disease. *Adv Intern Med*. 1992;37:431-55.

23. Churchill RB, Pickering LK. Infection control challenges in child care centers. *Infect Dis Clin N Am*. 1997;11:347-65.

24. Louhiala PJ, Jaakola N, Ruotsalainen R, et al. Form of day care and respiratory infections among Finnish children. *Am J Public Health*. 1995;85:1109-12.

25. Nafstad P, Hagen JA, Oie L, et al. Day care centers and respiratory health. *Pediatrics*. 1999;103:753-58.

26. Alho OP, Laara E, Oja H. Public health impact of various risk factors for acute otitis media in Northern Finland. *Am J Epidemiol*. 1996;143:1149-56.

27. Fleming DW, Cochi SL, Hightower AW, Broome CV. Childhood upper respiratory tract infections: to what degree is incidence affected by day-care attendance? *Pediatrics*. 1987;79:55-60.

28. Roberts L, Smith W, Jorm L, et al. Effect of infection control measures on the frequency of upper respiratory infection in child care: a randomized controlled trial. *Pediatrics*. 2000;105:738-42.

29. Homes SJ, Morrow AL, Pickering LK. Child care practices: effects of social changes on epidemiology of infectious diseases and antibiotic resistance. *Epidemiol Rev*. 1996;18:10-28.

30. Dowell SF, Schwartz B, Phillips WR, et al. Principles of judicious use of antimicrobial agents for pediatric upper respiratory tract infections. *Pediatrics*. 1998;101(S):163.

31. Prober CG. Herpes simplex virus. In: SS Long, LK Pickering, CG Prober, eds. *Principles and Practice of Pediatric Infectious Diseases*. Kent, United Kingdom: Churchill Livingston; 1997:1134-44.

32. Schmitt DL, Johnson DW, Henderson FW. Herpes simplex type I infections in group care. *Pediatr Infect Dis J*. 1991;10:729-34.

33. Centers for Disease Control and Prevention. Prevention of varicella: update recommendations of the Advisory Committee on Immunization Practices (ACIP). *Mor Mortal Wkly Rep CDC Surveill Summ*. 1999;48(RR-6):1-5.

34. American Academy of Pediatrics, Committee on Infectious Diseases. Varicella vaccine update. *Pediatrics*. 2000; 105:136-41.

35. American Academy of Pediatrics, Committee on Infectious Diseases. Recommendations for the use of live attenuated varicella vaccine. *Pediatrics*. 1995;95:791-96.

36. Pass RF. Cytomegalovirus. In: Long SS, Pickering LK, Prober CG, eds. *Principles and Practices of Pediatric Infectious Diseases*. Kent, United Kingdom: Churchill Livingstone; 1997:1154-65.

37. Pass RF, Hutto C. Group day care and cytomegaloviral infections of mothers and children. *Rev Infect Dis*. 1986;8:599-605.

38. Yeager AS. Transmission of cytomegalovirus to mothers by infected infants: another reason to prevent transfusion-acquired infections. *Pediatr Infect Dis*. 1983;2:295-297.

39. Pass RF, Hutto C, Ricks R, Cloud GA. Increased rate of cytomegalovirus infection among parents of children attending day care centers. *N Engl J Med*. 1986;314:1414-1418.

40. Adler SP. Molecular epidemiology of cytomegalovirus: evidence for viral transmission to parents from children infected at a day care center. *Pediatr Infect Dis*. 1986;5:315-318.

41. Pass RF, Hutto C, Cloud G. Day care workers and cytomegalovirus infection. *Clin Res*. 1988;36:65A.

42. Adler SP. Cytomegalovirus and child day care: evidence for increased infection rate among day care workers. *N Engl J Med.* 1989;321:1290-96.

43. Murph J, Baron JC, Brown K, et al. The occupational risk of cytomegalovirus infection among day-care providers. *JAMA.* 1991;265:603-608.

44. Centers for Disease Control and Prevention. Prevention of hepatitis A through active or passive immunization: recommendations of the Advisory Committee on Immunization Practices (ACIP). *Mor Moral Wkly Rep CDC Surveill Summ.* 1999;48(RR-12):1-37.

45. Pickering LK, Evans DG, Dupont HL, et al. Diarrhea caused by *Shigella*, rotavirus and *Giardia* in day care centers: prospective study. *J Pediatr.* 1981;99:51-56.

46. Barlett AV, Moore M, Gary GW, et al. Diarrheal illness among infants and toddlers in child day care centers. *J Pediatr.* 1985;107:495-502.

47. Hadler SC, Erben JJ, Francis DP, et al. Risk factors for hepatitis A in day care centers. *J Infect Dis.* 1982;145:255-261.

48. Hadler SC, Webster HM, Erben JJ, et al. Hepatitis A in day care centers: a community-wide assessment. *N Engl J Med.* 1980;302:1222-1227.

49. Pickering LK, Woodward WE, Dupont HL, et al. Occurrence of *Giardia lamblia* in children in day care centers. *J Pediatr.* 1984;104:522-526.

50. Pickering LK, Barlett AVE, Reves RR, Morrow A. Asymptomatic rotavirus before and after rotavirus diarrhea in children in day care centers. *J Pediatr.* 1988;112:361-365.

51. Sullivan P, Woodward WE, Pickering LK, et al. A longitudinal study of the occurrence of diarrheal disease in day care centers. *Am J Public Health.* 1984; 74:987-991.

52. Keswick BH, Pickering LK, Dupont HL, et al. Survival and detection of rotavirus on environmental surfaces in day care centers. *Appl Environ Microbiol.* 1983;46:813-816.

53. Weniger BG, Puttenber J, Goodman RA. Fecal coliforms on environmental surfaces in two day care centers. *Appl Environ Microbiol.* 1983;45:733-735.

54. Bartlett AV, Jarvis BA, Ross V, et al. Diarrheal illness among infants and toddlers in day care centers: effects of active surveillance and staff training without subsequent monitoring. *Am J Epidemiol.* 1988;127:808-817.

55. Roberts L, Jorm L, Patel M, et al. Effect of infection control measures on the frequency of diarrheal episodes in child care: a randomized, controlled trial. *Pediatrics.* 2000;105:743-46.

56. American Academy of Pediatrics, Committee on Infectious Diseases. Prevention of hepatitis A infections: guidelines for use of hepatitis A vaccine and immune globulin. *Pediatrics.* 1996;98:1207-15.

57. Aronson SS, Aiken LS. Compliance of child care programs with health and safety standards: impact of program evaluation and advocate training. *Pediatrics.* 1980;65:318-325.

58. Mitchell DK, Van R, Morrow AL, et al. Outbreaks of astrovirus gastroenteritis in day care centers. *J Pediatr.* 1993;123:725-32.

59. American Academy of Pediatrics, Committee on Pediatric AIDS and Committee on Infectious Disease. Issues related to human immunodeficiency virus transmission in schools, child care, medical settings, the home, and community. *Pediatrics.* 1999;104:318-24.

60. American Academy of Pediatrics, Committee on Infectious Diseases. Hepatitis C viral infection. *Pediatrics.* 1998;101:481

61. Centers for Disease Control and Prevention. Recommendations for prevention and control of hepatitis C virus (HCV) infection and HCV-related chronic disease. *Mor Mortal Wkly Rev CDC Surveill Summ.* 1998;47(RR-19):1-38.

62. Centers for Disease Control and Prevention. Hepatitis B virus infection: a comprehensive immunization strategy to eliminate transmission in the United States: recommendations of the Advisory Committee on

Immunization Practices. *Mor Mortal Wkly Rev CDC Surveill Summ*. In press.

63. Deseda DD, Shapiro CN, Carroll K. Hepatitis B virus transmission between a child and staff member at a day-care center. *Pediatr Infect Dis J*. 1994;13:828.

64. Tokars JL, Marcus R, Culver DH, et al. Surveillance of HIV infection and zidovudine use among healthcare workers after occupational exposure to HIV-infected blood: the Centers for Disease Control cooperative needle stick surveillance group. *Ann Intern Med*. 1993;118:913-9.

65. Shapiro CN, McCaig LF, Genesheimer KF, et al. Hepatitis B virus transmission between children in day care. *Pediatr Infect Dis J*. 1989;8(87)0-75.

66. Reves RR, Pickering LK. Impact of child day care on infectious diseases in adults. *Infect Dis Clin North Am*. 1992;6:239-50.

67. American Academy of Pediatrics, Committee on Infectious Diseases. Measles immunization in HIV infected children, 1999. *Pediatrics*. 1999;103:1057-60.

68. Centers for Disease Control and Prevention. 1999 USPHS/IDSA guidelines for the prevention of opportunistic infections in persons infected with human immunodeficiency virus. *Mor Mortal Wkly Rep CDC Surveill Summ*. 1999;48(RR-10):1-6.

69. American Academy of Pediatrics, Committee on Infectious Diseases. *Red book 2000: Report of the committee on infectious diseases*. Elk Grove Village, Ill: American Academy of Pediatrics; 2000.

CHAPTER 7

Children Who are Eligible for Services Under IDEA

CHILDREN WHO ARE ELIGIBLE FOR SERVICES UNDER IDEA (Individuals with Disabilities Education Act)

7.1 GUIDING PRINCIPLES FOR THIS CHAPTER AND INTRODUCTION

The information in Chapter 7 is provided to acquaint child care providers with programs available for children who are eligible for services under IDEA. It also identifies roles the child care provider might have in achieving optimum developmental opportunities for children who are receiving services under IDEA. Because Chapter 7 focuses on children eligible for services under IDEA, a federal law, the reader is encouraged to review relevant state statutes, regulations, state and county agency policies concerning specific situations or diseases. This publication focuses on national standards and does not address specific state and county requirements or variances from federal education law.

THE CONTENT OF THIS CHAPTER WAS PREPARED WITH THE GUIDANCE OF FOUR PRINCIPLES:

1) Standards that are relevant to children with special needs, as well as to all children, are integrated into other chapters within this document. This does not diminish the importance of making sure that children with disabilities or chronic illnesses receive the special care that typically developing children would not require to participate fully in the child care service.

2) Standards for children with special needs have been integrated throughout this book with those for all other children to promote an inclusionary approach. Standards in this chapter are primarily those that apply solely to the general special service needs and planning mechanisms, as addressed in IDEA, for a child whose needs differ from those of a typically developing child. See page 324 for a list of standards, now found in other chapters, that address health, safety, nutritional, and transportation issues for care of children with special needs.

3) This chapter includes standards that enable accommodation and inclusion of children with disabilities and special health care needs in child care facilities to achieve a level of participation as close as possible to that of typically developing children. The content of these standards will not segregate or discriminate against participation of children with special needs, but specify the practices needed to compensate for the child's disability or chronic illness so that full, safe inclusion in child care can occur.

4) While parental consent is required to obtain information about a child's special needs, the child care provider should be able to obtain parental consent to seek information that is relevant to meeting the health and safety needs of the child in the child care setting.

SERVING CHILDREN WITH SPECIAL NEEDS UNDER IDEA

The Individuals with Disabilities Education Act (IDEA), a federal law most recently amended in 2000(1), affords caregivers a unique opportunity to support children whose special needs might affect their educational success as well as impact upon both the children and families in other ways in the child care setting. The purpose of the law is to provide "free appropriate public education" regardless of disability or chronic illness to all "eligible" children, ages birth through 21 years, in a natural and/or least restrictive environment. Eligible children under IDEA include those with mental, physical or emotional disabilities, who, because of their disability or chronic illness, require special instruction in order to learn. Part B of this statute supports the needs of eligible preschool-age children through the local school district. Part C provides for a collaborative system to serve the needs of eligible infants and toddlers between the ages of birth and three years through early intervention. Child care programs can play a significant role in offering services required by children with special needs in the child care setting.

HISTORICAL INFORMATION

The original statute of IDEA, titled The Education of All Handicapped Children Act(2), was passed in

1975. It initially covered only children aged five through 21 years old in what is today identified as Part B of the act. This law was amended in 1986 (3) to include preschool education services to children aged three to five and early childhood services to children from birth through age two. The infant and toddler portion of the act, which was Part H when initially passed, is now Part C under the 1997 reauthorized version of the act. The law is now identified as the Individuals with Disabilities Education Act. Information about IDEA can be obtained from the Office of Special Education and Rehabilitative Services (OSERS), U.S. Department of Education. Contact information for OSERS is located in Appendix BB.

PART C SUPPORTS COLLABORATIVE EFFORTS

Part C of IDEA makes federal funds available for states to implement a system of early intervention services for eligible infants and toddlers and their families. The state department of education may be the lead agency or may designate another agency to provide the assessment, coordination of services, and administrative functions required under Part C. The intent of Part C is to enhance the development of, and to provide other needed services for, infants and toddlers who have developmental delays or are at risk of developing such delays and to support the capacity of families to enhance the development of their children in the home and community. A further intent is to transition children to effective and inclusionary school-age services.

Although each state must designate a lead agency for implementing this federally funded program, the program is designed to be a coordinated, collaborative effort among a variety of state agencies for screening of children, assessment, service coordination and development of an Individualized Family Service Plan (IFSP) for every eligible infant or toddler and his or her family. The IFSP describes early intervention services for an infant or toddler and the child's family, including family support and the child's educational, therapeutic, and health needs.

Among the more important aspects of this inter-agency model is the belief that children and their families should be viewed from the perspective of an ability model rather than a deficit model, i.e., emphasizing the strengths and capabilities of the

family and child rather than the family's or child's perceived weaknesses. This means that the approach of the providers of services and supports identified in the Individualized Family Service Plan should be that of enhancing and supporting already-existing resources, priorities, and concerns of the child and family rather than assuming that services can correct "deficiencies" of the child or family.

The focus of services and supports to the child and family under Part C is the achievement of two related goals:

1) To enhance and support the development of young children with disabilities and chronic illness and minimize their need for special education and related services when they enter the public school system.

2) To maximize the potential for infants and toddlers with disabilities and chronic illness to enjoy the benefits of their communities and grow into adults capable of living independently, pursuing vocations, and participating in the benefits their communities offer all citizens.

SERVING CHILDREN IN NATURAL ENVIRONMENTS

Part C of the IDEA emphasizes delivery of services in natural environments. These are defined generally as settings that are "natural or normal for the child's same-age peers who have no disabilities." Natural environments reflect those places that are routinely used by families and typically developing children and represent a wide variety of options such as the child's home, the neighborhood, community programs and services such as child care centers, parks, recreation centers, stores, malls, museums, etc. By incorporating elements of the child's regular environment—furniture, toys, schedule, siblings, care providers, extended family, etc.—in the planning and delivery of services and supports, the family and providers can best discover the child's talents and gifts and enhance these in the normal course of play, relationships, and caregiving.

Learning about and understanding the child's routines and using real life opportunities and activities, such as eating, playing, interacting with others, and working on developmental skills, greatly enhances a child's ability to achieve the functional outcomes

identified in the IFSP. For these reasons, it is critical to have a representative from the child care setting that the child attends or may attend at the table when the IFSP is developed or revised. It is also imperative that written informed consent is obtained from parents before confidential information (written or verbal) is shared among providers. For these same reasons, it is essential that a child care provider become familiar with a child's IFSP and understand both the role the provider is to play and the resources available through the IFSP to support the family and child care provider.

Other federal legislation, such as the Americans with Disabilities Act (ADA) (4) and Section 504 of the Rehabilitation Act of 1973 (5), prohibit discrimination against children and adults with disabilities by requiring equal access to offered programs and services. The IDEA promotes inclusion of infants, toddlers, and preschoolers in the same activities as their peers by providing support in the form of services and funds, some of which may be available to support eligible children in the child care setting.

PART B AND THE INDIVIDUALIZED EDUCATION PROGRAM

Three-and four-year olds eligible for services under Part B of the IDEA are served through a written Individualized Education Program (IEP). This document is similarly developed by a team with the local education agency assuming responsibility for its implementation in either a public preschool program or a private preschool setting. Although federal funds are not specifically designated to support services provided by agencies outside of the public school system, local education agencies may contract with private providers for preschool services and cover educationally related services identified in the IEP, such as speech and language therapy, in the preschool setting.

Child care providers should become as familiar with a preschooler's special needs as identified in the IEP as they are with the services for an infant or toddler set forth in an IFSP. The provider may wish to send a representative, with prior informed written parental consent, to the child's IEP review meetings to share valuable insight and information regarding the child's special needs in both the educational and child care settings.

The standards in this chapter articulate those opportunities and responsibilities that child care agencies share with other agencies in serving a child with special needs, whether the child is served through an Individualized Family Service Plan or an Individualized Education Program.

7.2 INCLUSION OF CHILDREN WITH SPECIAL NEEDS IN THE CHILD CARE SETTING

STANDARD 7.001
INCLUSION IN ALL ACTIVITIES

Facilities shall include children with disabilities and other special needs (such as chronic illnesses) and children without disabilities in all activities possible.

RATIONALE: The goal is to provide fully integrated care to the extent feasible given each child's limitations. Federal laws and some state laws do not permit discrimination on the basis of the disability (Americans with Disabilities Act (ADA) and Section 504 of the Rehabilitation Act) (4, 5).

Studies have found the following benefits of inclusive child care: Children with special needs develop increased social skills and self-esteem; families of children with special needs gain social support and develop more positive attitudes about their child; children and families without special needs become more understanding and accepting of differences and disabilities; caregivers learn from working with children, families, and service providers and develop skills in individualizing care for all children (6, 7).

COMMENTS: Child care providers may need to seek professional guidance and obtain appropriate training in order to include children with special needs, such as children with severe disabilities and other special needs such as chronic illnesses, into child care settings. These may include technology-dependent children and children with serious and severe chronic medical problems. Every attempt should be made, however, to achieve inclusion.

The facility should pursue the many funding mechanisms available to supplement funding for services in the facility. These resources usually require the parents' consent and may require that the parents actively pursue their rights and the provider's rights. Even so, child care providers can and should discuss options with the parents as potential sources of financial assistance for the needed services. These sources might include:

a) Medicaid, including waiver funding (Title XIX);
b) Private health insurance;
c) State or federal funds for child care, education, or for Children with Special Health Care Needs (Title V);
d) IDEA (particularly Part C funding);
e) Community resources (such as volunteers, lending libraries, free equipment available from community-based organizations);
f) Tax incentives (credits and deductions available under federal law to most for-profit child care programs);
g) Local Community Development Block Grants (CDBG) and other community development funding.

TYPE OF FACILITY: *Center; Large Family Child Care Home; Small Family Child Care Home*

STANDARD 7.002
PLANNING FOR INCLUSION

Planning for needed resources, support, and education for staff and administrators to increase understanding and knowledge by staff, parents, and children without disabilities shall facilitate the inclusion and participation of children with special needs at the facility.

RATIONALE: Inclusion without adequate preparation, understanding, training, mobilization of resources, and development of skills among all those involved, may lead to failure.

COMMENTS: The utilization of age-appropriate resources (including, but not limited to, brochures, books, guest speakers, and advice from parents of children with special needs) should be a component of any education program. Methods may vary according to need and availability. The facility should provide opportunities to discuss the similarities as well as the differences among all the children enrolled. These discussions are useful preparatory exercises that can be

assisted by including parents in the group discussions. Professionals or knowledgeable parents who are effective teachers should assure that, to the extent permitted by the parents of a child with special needs, caregivers and typically developing children in the facility receive presentations and discussions about the special equipment that the children with special needs may require and use. Children without disabilities should be given the opportunity to explore and learn about these items. Providers should take special care to apply the principles of cultural competency and general sensitivity in all communications with parents and when discussing the child and the family, particularly in discussion of an inherited condition.

TYPE OF FACILITY: *Center; Large Family Child Care Home; Small Family Child Care Home*

7.3 PROCESS PRIOR TO ENROLLING AT A FACILITY

STANDARD 7.003
INITIAL ASSESSMENT

Children with special needs and their families shall have access to and be encouraged to receive a multidisciplinary assessment by qualified individuals, using reliable and valid age and culturally appropriate instruments and methodologies, before the child starts in the facility. If the parent consents to disclose the information and if the information is relevant to health and safety concerns in the child care setting, this evaluation shall consist of the following:

a) Results of medical and developmental examinations;
b) Assessments of the child's cognitive functioning or current overall functioning;
c) Evaluations of the family's needs, concerns, and priorities;
d) Other evaluations as needed.

The multidisciplinary assessment shall be voluntary and focus on the family's priorities, concerns, and resources that are relevant to providing services to the child and that optimize the child's development.

RATIONALE: The definitive characteristic of services for children is the necessity of individualizing their care to meet their needs. Therefore, individual assessments must precede services.

The family's needs, values, and childrearing practices are highly relevant and respected in the provision of care to the child; however, the child's special needs continue to be the central focus of intervention.

COMMENTS: This comprehensive assessment need not be carried out by the facility itself but instead, could be done largely by an outside center, clinic, school district Child Find team, or professionals who conduct evaluations of this nature. The multi-disciplinary assessment must be administered by qualified individuals using reliable and valid age and culturally appropriate instruments and methodologies. The designated lead agency for Part C may be responsible or may delegate the responsibility to another agency. This evaluation forms the basis of planning for the child's needs in the child care setting and for the pertinent information available to the staff. The comprehensive assessment should include the development of a written plan for the child's caregivers that they believe they can implement.

The facility should pursue the many funding mechanisms available to supplement funding for services in the facility. Even so, child care providers can and should discuss these options with the parents as potential sources of financial assistance for the needed services. These sources might include:
a) Medicaid, including waiver funding (Title XIX);
b) Private health insurance;
c) State or federal funds for child care, education, or for Children with Special Health Care Needs (Title V);
d) IDEA (particularly Part C funding);
e) Tax incentives (credits and deductions available under federal law to most for profit child care programs);
f) Local Community Development Block Grants (CDBG) and other community development funding.

TYPE OF FACILITY: *Center; Large Family Child Care Home; Small Family Child Care Home*

7.4 DEVELOPING A SERVICE PLAN FOR A CHILD WITH SPECIAL NEEDS

STANDARD 7.004
DETERMINING THE TYPE AND FREQUENCY OF SERVICES

The parents of a child with special needs, the child's primary health care provider, any authorized service coordinator, and the child care provider shall discuss and determine the type and frequency of the services to be provided by the child care facility.

RATIONALE: To serve children with varying forms and severities of disability, child care providers should take a flexible approach to combine and deliver services. Parents must be involved to assure that the plan is compatible with their care and expectations for the child.

COMMENTS: In facilities that are not designed primarily to serve a population with special needs, the additional therapeutic services may be obtained through consultants or arrangements with outside programs serving children with special needs. These services may be available, as arranged, through the Individualized Family Service Plan (IFSP) or the Individualized Education Program (IEP). The child care provider may become a member of the IEP team if the parent of a child with special needs so requests.

When there is an IFSP, IDEA requires the appointment of an authorized service coordinator. For more information on authorized service coordinators, see STANDARD 7.007.

TYPE OF FACILITY: *Center; Large Family Child Care Home; Small Family Child Care Home*

STANDARD 7.005
FORMULATION OF AN ACTION PLAN

The formulation of an action plan, as determined by the child's needs, shall be based on the assessment process specified in STANDARD 7.003 and STANDARD 7.004. Such a plan shall be written and shall be maintained as part of each child's confidential record.

RATIONALE: The plan may be developed and implemented after the parents have discussed and approved it. The facility shall keep the plan as a permanent part of the child's confidential record.

COMMENTS: All issues and questions should be dealt with during the discussion with families; consensus should be obtained and the plan written accordingly. Parents should provide written consent for the agreement to any plan before implementation for the child. Parents may revoke their consent at any time by written notice. This is standard procedure in the implementation of the Individuals with Disabilities Education Act (IDEA) for those child care programs involved with the Individualized Education Program (IEP) and the Individualized Family Service Plan (IFSP). All release of information must be in accordance with IDEA.

For additional information on the discussion process, see Parental Involvement, STANDARD 2.050 through STANDARD 2.053.

TYPE OF FACILITY: *Center; Large Family Child Care Home; Small Family Child Care Home*

STANDARD 7.006
DETERMINATION OF ELIGIBILITY FOR SPECIAL SERVICES

The Individualized Family Service Plan (IFSP) or Individualized Education Program (IEP) and any other plans for special services shall be developed for children identified as eligible in collaboration with the family, representatives from disciplines and organizations involved with the child and family, the child's health care provider, and the staff of the facility, depending on the family's wishes, the agency's resources, and state laws and regulations.

RATIONALE: For the IFSP, IEP, or any other needed or required special service plan to provide systematic guidance of the child's developmental achievement and to promote efficient service delivery, service providers from all of the involved disciplines/settings must be familiar with the overall multidisciplinary or interdisciplinary plans and work toward the same goals for the child. To be optimally effective, one comprehensive IFSP or IEP is developed and one care coordinator is designated to oversee implementation of the plan. If the parents choose to involve them, the child care providers should be partners in developing and implementing the IFSP or IEP to obtain the best possible evaluation and plan for the child within the child care facility

COMMENTS: Development and implementation of the IFSP or IEP is a team effort. The various aspects of planning include the input of the child care program in which the child is enrolled in the evaluation for eligibility for Part B or C, the development of IFSP/IEP, and the child care program's role in implementation. Components of the IFSP or IEP may include elements developed to meet service needs developed elsewhere, when applicable in the child care setting.

See Coordination and Documentation, STANDARD 7.010.

TYPE OF FACILITY: *Center; Large Family Child Care Home; Small Family Child Care Home*

STANDARD 7.007
DESIGNATION AND ROLE OF STAFF PERSON RESPONSIBLE FOR COORDINATING CARE

If a child has an Individualized Education Program (IEP) or Individualized Family Service Plan (IFSP), the child care facility shall designate one person in the child care setting to be responsible for coordinating care within the facility and with any caregiver or coordinator in other service settings, in accordance with the written plan. Although this person may have other duties, the role of the designated person shall include:
a) Documentation of coordination;
b) Written communication with other care or service providers for the child, to ensure a coordinated, coherent service plan;
c) Sharing information about the plan, staff conferences, written reports, consultations,

and other services provided to the child and family. Informed, written parental consent shall be sought before sharing this confidential information;

d) Ensuring implementation of the components of the plan that is relevant to the facility.

When the evaluators are not part of the child care staff, the lead agency shall develop a formal mechanism for coordinating reevaluations and program revisions. The designated staff member from the facility shall routinely be included in the evaluation process and team conferences.

RATIONALE: One person being responsible for coordinating all elements of services avoids confusion and allows easier and more consistent communication with the family. When carrying out coordination duties, this person is called a care coordinator or a service coordinator. Each child should have a care coordinator or service coordinator assigned at the time the service plan is developed.

With more than half of all mothers in the workforce, caregivers other than the parents (such as teachers, grandparents, or neighbors) frequently spend considerable time with the children. These child care providers need to know and understand the aims and goals of the service plan; otherwise, program approaches will not carry over into the home environment.

This requirement does not preclude outside agencies or child care providers from having their own care coordinator, service coordinator, or case manager. The intent is to ensure communication and coordination among all the child's sources of care, both in the facility and elsewhere in the community. The care coordinator or service coordinator does not have responsibility for directly implementing all program components but, rather, is accountable for checking to make sure the plans in the facility are being carried out, encouraging implementation of the service plan, and helping obtain or gain access to services.

A facility assuming responsibility for serving children with developmental disabilities, mental illness, or chronic health impairments must develop mechanisms for identifying the needs of the children and families and obtaining appropriate services, whether or not those children have an IEP/IFSP.

COMMENTS: Usually, the person who coordinates care or services within the child care facility will not be the person assigned to coordinate care or provide overall case management for the child and family.

Nevertheless, the facility may assume both roles if the parents so request and state law permits. The components and the role may vary, and each facility will determine these components and roles, which may depend on the roles and responsibilities of the staff in the facility and the responsibilities assumed by the family and care providers in the community.

For additional information on coordination with outside agencies, see also Consultants and Technical Assistance for Children with Special Needs, RECOMMENDATION 9.035 and RECOMMENDATION 9.036.

TYPE OF FACILITY: *Center; Large Family Child Care Home; Small Family Child Care Home*

STANDARD 7.008
DEVELOPMENT OF MEASURABLE OBJECTIVES

The service plan for a child with special needs shall include long-range services aimed at enhancing and improving the child's health and developmental achievement, based on measurable, functional outcomes agreed to by the parent. Each functional outcome objective shall delineate the services, along with the designated responsibility for provision and financing.

With the assistance of the child's service coordinator, the child care provider shall contribute to the assessment of measurable outcome objectives (service plan) within the child care setting at least every three months, or more often if the child's or family's circumstances change, and shall contribute to a full, documented case review each year. Re-evaluations shall consider a self-assessment by the caregiver of the caregiver's competence to provide services that the child requires.

Service reviews shall involve the child care staff or persons providing the intervention and supervision, the parents, and any independent observers. The results of such evaluations shall be documented in a written plan given to each of the child's caregivers and the child's family. Such conferences and lists of participants shall be documented in the child's health record at the facility.

Each objective shall include persons responsible for its monitoring.

RATIONALE: When measurable-outcome objectives form the basis for the service plan, the family and service providers jointly formulate the expected and desired outcomes for the child and family. By using measurable-outcome objectives rather than service units, all interested parties can concentrate on how well the child is achieving the outcome objectives. Thus, for example, progress toward speech development assumes more importance than the number of hours of speech therapy provided.

Further, measurable outcome objectives constitute an individualized approach to meeting the needs of the child and family and, as such, can be integrated into, but are not solely dependent upon, the array of services available in a specific geographic area. The measurable-outcome objectives will provide the facility with a meaningful framework for enhancing the child's health and developmental status on an ongoing basis.

Regularly scheduled reassessments of the outcome objectives provide the family and service providers with a framework for anticipating changes in the kind of services that may be needed, the financial requirements for providing the services, and identification of the appropriate service provider. The changing needs of children with disabilities do not always follow a predictable course. Ad hoc reevaluations may be necessitated by changes in circumstances.

COMMENTS: The defining of measurable objectives provides a useful structure for the caregiver and aids in assessing the child's progress and the appropriateness of components of the service plan. Though this principle should apply to all children in all settings, implementation, especially in small and large family child-care homes, will require ongoing assistance from, and participation of, specialists, including those connected with programs outside of the child care setting, to provide the needed services.

Many facilities that provide intervention services review the child's progress at least every 3 months. This is not a comprehensive review, but an interim analysis of the progress toward meeting objectives and to decide if any modifications are needed in the service plan and its implementation. Generally, the entire plan and the child's progress receive a comprehensive review annually. It is likely that caregivers will need training on development of goals and the means of assessing progress.

It is assumed that staff members who interact with the child will have the training described in Preservice Qualifications and Special Training, STANDARD 1.007 through STANDARD 1.022, and Training, STANDARD 1.023 through STANDARD 1.033, including child growth and development, and that these topics will extend their basic knowledge and skills to help them work more effectively with children who have special needs and their families. Caregivers should have a basic knowledge of what constitutes special needs, supplemented by specialized training for children with special needs. The number of hours offered in any inservice training program should be determined by the experience and professional background of the staff.

Training and other technical assistance can be obtained from the following sources:
a) American Academy of Pediatrics (AAP);
b) American Nurses' Association (ANA);
c) National Association for the Education of Young Children (NAEYC) and its local chapters;
d) State and community nursing associations;
e) National therapy associations;
f) National Association of Child Care Resource and Referral Agencies (NACCRRA) and its local resource and referral agencies;
g) Federally funded University Centers for Excellence in Developmental Disabilities Education, Research, and Service for individuals with developmental disabilities;
h) Other colleges and universities with expertise in training people to work with children who have special needs;
i) Community-based organizations serving people with disabilities (United Cerebral Palsy Associations, The ARC, Easter Seals, American Diabetes Association, American Lung Association, etc.)

The State-designated lead agency responsible for implementing IDEA may provide additional help. If the child has an IFSP, the lead agency will be responsible for coordinating the review process. If the child has an IEP, the local education agency will be responsible for seeing that the review occurs. If not, a less formal evaluation process may need to be conducted.

Assessments may be the financial responsibility of the IDEA Part C State-designated lead agency. Funding available through implementation of IDEA Part C should provide resources to assist in implementing the IFSP.

See STANDARD 8.052, for additional information on the documentation of child health records.

TYPE OF FACILITY: *Center; Large Family Child Care Home; Small Family Child Care Home*

STANDARD 7.009
CONTRACTS AND
REIMBURSEMENT

If a child with special needs has an Individualized Family Service Plan (IFSP), the lead agency shall arrange and contract for specialized services to be conducted in the child care facility. If a child with special needs has an Individualized Education Program (IEP), the local education agency shall arrange and contract for specialized services to be conducted in the child care facility.

If the child or the specialized service is not covered by IEP/IFSP:
• The child care provider shall cover the cost when the service is reasonable and necessary for the child to participate in the program;
• The parent or source arranged by the parent shall cover the cost when the service is not a reasonable expectation of the child care provider or if it is provided while the child is in child care only for convenience and is separately billable (such as speech therapy).

RATIONALE: Child care facilities may have to collaborate with other service providers to meet the needs of a child and family, particularly if the number of children who require these services is too few to maintain the service onsite. To achieve maximum benefit from services, those services should be provided in the setting that is the most natural and convenient for the child and family. Whenever possible, treatment specialists (therapists) should provide these services in the facility where the child receives daytime care.
"Reasonableness" is a legal standard that looks at the impact of cost and other factors.

COMMENTS: The agency that has evaluated the child and/or is planning the entire service plan, or the facility, should make the arrangements. The specific

methods by which these services will be coordinated with the child care facility is determined locally.

The facility should pursue the many funding mechanisms available to supplement funding for services in the facility. Even so, child care providers can and should discuss these options with the parents as potential sources of financial assistance for the needed accommodations. These sources might include:
a) Medicaid, including waiver funding (Title XIX);
b) Private health insurance;
c) State or federal funds for child care, education, or for Children with Special Health Care Needs (Title V);
d) IDEA (particularly Part C funding);
e) Community resources (such as volunteers, lending libraries, free equipment available from community-based organizations);
f) Tax incentives (credit and deductions available under federal law to most for profit child care programs);
g) Local Community Development Block Grants (CDBG) and other community development funding.

TYPE OF FACILITY: *Center*

7.5 COORDINATION AND
DOCUMENTATION

STANDARD 7.010
COORDINATING AND
DOCUMENTING SERVICES

Services for all children shall be coordinated in a systematic manner so the facility can document all of the services the child is receiving inside of the facility and is aware of the services the child is receiving outside of the facility. If the parents of a child with special needs so choose, the facility shall be an integral component of the child's overall service plan.

RATIONALE: Coordination of services is a fundamental component in implementing a plan for care of a child with special needs. This is particularly true of the need to coordinate the medical care with

specialized developmental services, therapies, and child care procedures in the facility.

COMMENTS: Children with Individualized Family Service Plans (IFSP) have a service coordinator; children with Individualized Education Programs (IEP) have a primary provider or other identified service coordinator. These are the contact persons within the local education agency or lead agency. This method of service coordination is consistent throughout all of the states under the IDEA. Child care providers need to become informed of how this system works and what their responsibilities are.

TYPE OF FACILITY: *Center; Large Family Child Care Home; Small Family Child Care Home*

STANDARD 7.011
WRITTEN REPORTS TO
CHILD CARE PROVIDERS

With the prior written, informed consent of the parent in the parent's native language, child care facilities may obtain written reports on Individualized Family Service Plans (IFSPs) or Individualized Education Programs (IEPs), conferences, and treatments provided.

RATIONALE: This information is confidential and parental consent for release is required if the child care facility is to gain access to it. Written documentation ensures better accountability.

TYPE OF FACILITY: *Center; Large Family Child Care Home; Small Family Child Care Home*

7.6 PERIODIC REEVALUATION

STANDARD 7.012
REEVALUATION PROCESS

The care coordinator shall ensure that formal reevaluations of the child's functioning and health care needs in the child care setting and the family's needs are conducted at least yearly, or as often as is necessary to deal with changes in the child's or family's circumstances. This reevaluation shall include the parent and child care provider. Such conferences and lists of participants shall be documented in the child's health record at the facility.

RATIONALE: The changing needs of children with developmental disabilities do not follow a predictable course. A periodic, thorough process of reevaluation is essential to identify appropriate goals and services for the child. The child's primary health care provider and the program's health consultant should be involved in the development and reevaluation of the plan. A child's health is such an integral part of his or her availability to learn and to retain learned information that health/development-related information is critical for a complete review/reevaluation process to occur.

COMMENTS: Though regular intervention services are recommended for review at 3-month intervals, ad hoc reevaluations may be necessitated by changes in circumstances. See STANDARD 7.008.

TYPE OF FACILITY: *Center; Large Family Child Care Home; Small Family Child Care Home*

STANDARD 7.013
STATEMENT OF PROGRAM NEEDS AND PLANS

Each reevaluation conference shall result in a new statement of program needs and plans which parents have agreed to and support.

RATIONALE: Continued collaboration, participation, and coordination among all involved parties are essential.

TYPE OF FACILITY: *Center; Large Family Child Care Home; Small Family Child Care Home*

7.7 ASSESSMENT OF FACILITIES FOR CHILDREN WITH SPECIAL NEEDS

STANDARD 7.014
FACILITY SELF-ASSESSMENT

Facilities that serve children eligible for services under IDEA, shall have a written self-assessment developed in consultation with an expert multi-disciplinary team of professionals experienced in the care and education of children with special needs. These self-assessments shall be used to create a plan for the facility to determine how it may become more accessible and ready to care for children with disabilities. The facility shall review and update the plan at least every 2 years, unless a caregiver requests a revision at an earlier date.

RATIONALE: A self-assessment stimulates thought about the caregiver's present capabilities and attitudes and the medical and educational particulars of a range of special needs, from mild to severe disabilities. Also, parents will have the opportunity to review the records of the written self-assessment and decide whether a facility is well-prepared to handle children with, for example, mental retardation or hearing impairment but is not able to offer proper care to a child with more complex medical needs.

COMMENTS: All programs must be willing to care for children with special needs. Under both the Americans with Disabilities Act (ADA) and Section 504 of the Rehabilitation Act of 1973, a program must make reasonable accommodations in order to properly serve a child with special needs. An important source of information for self-assessment is interviewing the parents of children with special needs to see how well the program is working for their family and what could be improved. "Reasonableness" is a legal standard that looks at cost and other factors. Section 504 applies to recipients of federal funds. The ADA extends coverage to private entities that do not receive federal funds.

Additionally, the parent has the right to choose which child care program will care for her/his child. Self-assessment should be done to evaluate what the program needs to do to be more inclusive by developing staff capability and program activities to accommodate the child's needs.

The Child Care Law Center (CCLC) offers materials that can be used to assess a child care facility to determine its readiness to care for children with special needs. Contact information for CCLC is located in Appendix BB.

TYPE OF FACILITY: *Center; Large Family Child Care Home; Small Family Child Care Home*

STANDARD 7.015
TECHNICAL ASSISTANCE IN DEVELOPING PLAN

The caregiver shall seek technical assistance in developing and formulating the plan for future services for children with special needs.

RATIONALE: Assistance is needed where caregivers lack specific capabilities.

COMMENTS: Documentation of the caregiver's request and of the regulating agencies' responses in offering or providing assistance furnishes evidence of compliance. State regulatory agencies should be in a position to provide such assistance to facilities. See Consultants and Technical Assistance for Children with Special Needs, RECOMMENDATION 9.035 and RECOMMENDATION 9.036.

Training and other technical assistance can be obtained from the following:
a) Child's primary health care provider;

b) Program's health consultant;

c) American Academy of Pediatrics (AAP);

d) American Nurses' Association (ANA);

e) State and community nursing associations;

f) National therapy associations;

g) Local resource and referral agencies;

h) Federally funded University Centers for Excellence in Developmental Disabilities Education, Research, and Service for individuals with developmental disabilities;

i) Other colleges and universities with expertise in training others to work with children who have special needs;

j) Community-based organizations serving people with disabilities (Easter Seals, American Diabetes Association, American Lung Association, etc.);

k) ADA regional technical assistance offices.

See RECOMMENDATION 9.030 through RECOMMENDATION 9.036, on state technical assistance.

TYPE OF FACILITY: *Center; Large Family Child Care Home; Small Family Child Care Home*

STANDARD 7.016
REVIEW OF PLAN FOR SERVING CHILDREN WITH SPECIAL NEEDS

The facility's plan for serving children with special needs shall be reviewed at least annually to see if it is in compliance with the legal requirements of the Americans with Disabilities Act (ADA) and Section 504 of the Rehabilitation Act of 1973 and is achieving the overall objectives for the agency or facility.

RATIONALE: An annual review by caregivers is a cornerstone of any quality assurance procedure.

COMMENTS: See Consultants and Technical Assistance for Children with Special Needs, RECOMMENDATION 9.035 and RECOMMENDATION 9.036. See also Parental Participation, STANDARD 2.053.

TYPE OF FACILITY: *Center; Large Family Child Care Home; Small Family Child Care Home*

ADDITIONAL STANDARDS FOR PROVIDERS CARING FOR CHILDREN WITH SPECIAL NEEDS

Procedures for Obtaining Medical Information	8.013
Therapy and Treatment Services	8.016
Health History and Immunizations	8.046
Parental Participation	2.050, 2.051, 2.053, 2.057
Parent/Caregiver Collaboration	2.044
Program Activities	2.002
Contact with Outside Agencies	2.058, 2.059
Information Exchange	8.015, 8.053
Qualifications for Directors	1.014
Qualifications for Caregiving Staff	1.017, 1.019, 1.020
Child:Staff Ratio	1.001 through 1.003
Health Consultants	1.040 through 1.044,
Orientation Training	1.023 through 1.025
Continuing Education	1.029, 1.030
CPR/First Aid Certification	1.026
Emergency Plan	3.049
Transportation	2.029, 2.033, 2.038
Exit Accessibility	5.021
Facility Accessibility	5.004
Playroom Floor Space	5.112
Areas for Therapeutic Intervention	5.150
Storage for Adaptive Equipment	5.152
Therapeutic and Recreational Equipment	5.097
Nutritional Planning	4.008, 4.009,
Food Allergies	4.010
Toilet learning/training	2.005
Seizures (Including Epilepsy)	3.060, 3.061

Asthma	3.062
Special Procedures/ Adaptations	3.063
Special Adaptive Equipment	1.024, 5.098, 5.099
Review of Child's Records, Progress, and Future Planning	8.018

REFERENCES

1. The Individuals with Disabilities Education Act Amendments of 1997, 20 USC § 1400 (1997).

2. The Education for All Handicapped Children Act, 20 USC § 1400 (1975).

3. Education of the Handicapped Act Amendments of 1986, 20 USC § (1986).

4. The Americans with Disabilities Act, 3 USC § 421 (1990).

5. The Rehabilitation Act, 29 USC § 701 (1973).

6. Buyesse V, Bailey DB. Behavioral and developmental outcomes in young children with disabilities in integrated and segregated settings: a review of comparative studies. *J Spec Educ.* 1993;26(4):434-461.

7. Diamond KE, Hestenes LL, O'Connor CE. Integrating young children with disabilities in preschool: problems and promise. *Young Child.* 1994;49(2):68-75.

ADDITIONAL RESOURCES

The following resources are provided for individuals who want to read further on issues presented here or who need further guidance on caring for children with special needs.

Beckman PJ, ed. Strategies for Working With Families of Young Children With Disabilities. Baltimore, Md: Paul H. Brookes; 1996.

Bricker D. *Early Education of At-Risk and Handicapped Infants, Toddlers and Preschool Children.* Glenview, Ill: Scott Foresman and Co; 1986.

Bricker D, Cripe JJ. *An Activity-Based Approach to Early Intervention.* Baltimore, Md: Paul H. Brookes; 1998.

Bourland B, Lillie D. *Special Things for Special Kids.* Chapel Hill, NC: Frank Porter Graham Child Development Center; 1985.

Cook R, Armbruster V. *Adapting Early Childhood Curricula: Suggestions for Meeting Special Needs.* St. Louis, Mo: Mosby; 1983.

Cook R, Tessier, Armbruster V. *Adapting Early Childhood Curricula for Children With Special Needs.* Columbus, OH: Merrill Publishing Company; 1987.

Deinier PD. *Resources for Teaching Young Children With Special Needs.* New York, NY: Harcourt Brace Jovanovich, Inc; 1983.

Devinsky O. Current concepts: patients with refractory seizures. *New Eng J Med.* 1999;340:1565-1570.

Finnie N. *Handling the Young Cerebral Palsied Child at Home.* New York, NY: EP Dutton; 1974.

Guralnick MJ, ed. *The Effectiveness of Early Intervention.* Baltimore, Md: Paul H. Brookes; 1997.

Hanson M. *Teaching the Infant with Down Syndrome.* Austin, Tex: Pro-Ed; 1987.

Hanson M, Lynch E. *Early Intervention. Implementing Child and Family Services for Infants and Toddlers Who Are At Risk or Disabled.* Austin, Tex: Pro-Ed; 1989.

Johnson-Martin NM, Jens KG, Attermeier SM, Hacker BJ. *The Carolina Curriculum for Preschoolers With Special Needs.* Baltimore, Md: Paul H. Brookes; 1991.

Linder TW. Transdisciplinary Play-Based Intervention. Baltimore, Md: Paul H Brookes; 1993.

The More We Get Together: Adapting the Environment for Children with Disabilities. New York, NY: The Nordic Committee on Disability in cooperation with the World Rehabilitation Fund Inc; 1985.

Newacheck PW, Strickland B, Shonkoff JP, et al. An epidemiologic profile of children with special health care needs. *Pediatrics.* 1998;102:117-123.

Odom SL, McLean ME, eds. *Early Intervention/Early Childhood Special Education: Recommended Practices.* Austin, Tex: Pro-Ed Inc.; 1996.

Peterson N. *Early Intervention for Handicapped and At-Risk Children.* Denver, Colo: Love Publishing Co; 1987.

Topics in Early Childhood Special Education. Austin, Tex: Pro Ed; 1991;10:4.

Rosin P, Whitehead AD, Tuchman LI, Jesien GS, Bugun AL, Irwin L. *Partnerships in Family-Centered Care.* Baltimore, Md: Paul H. Brookes; 1996.

Rosenkoetter SE, Hains AH, Fowler SA. *Bridging Early Services for Children With Special Needs and Their Families.* Baltimore, Md: Paul H Brookes; 1994.

Safford P. *Integrating Teaching in Early Childhood.* White Plains, NY. Longman Inc; 1989.

Segal M. *In Time of Love. Caring for the Special Needs Baby.* New York, NY: Newmarket Press; 1988.

Souweize J, Crimmins S, Mazel C. *Mainstreaming: Ideas for Teaching Young Children.* Washington, DC: National Association for the Education of Young Children; 1981.

Stray-Gundersen K. *Babies With Down Syndrome.* Kensington, Md: Woodbine House; 1986.

Westbrook LE, Silver EJ, Stein REK. Implications for estimates of disability in children: a comparison of definitional components. *Pediatrics.* 1998;101:1025-1030.

Widerstrom AH, Mowder BA, Sandall SR. *At-risk and Handicapped Newborns and Infants: Development, Assessment, and Intervention.* Englewood Cliffs, NJ: Prentice Hall; 1991.

Widerstrom AH, Mowder BA, Sandall SR. *Infant Development and Risk.* 2nd ed. Baltimore, Md: Paul H. Brookes; 1997.

CHAPTER 8

Administration

8.1 IDENTIFIABLE GOVERNING BODY/ACCOUNTABLE INDIVIDUAL

STANDARD 8.001
GOVERNING BODY OF THE FACILITY

The facility shall have an identifiable governing body or person with the responsibility for and authority over the operation of the center or program. The governing body shall appoint one person at the facility, or two in the case of co-directors, who is responsible for day-to-day management. The administrator for facilities licensed for more than 100 children shall have no other assigned duties. Responsibilities of the person responsible for the operation of the facility shall include, but shall not be limited to, the following:

a) Ensuring stable and continuing compliance with all applicable rules, regulations, and facility policies and procedures;
b) Developing and implementing policies that promote the achievement of quality child care;
c) Ensuring that all written policies are updated and used, as described in this chapter;
d) Hiring, firing, assigning roles, duties, and responsibility to, supervising, and evaluating personnel;
e) Providing orientation of all new parents, employees, and volunteers to the physical structure, policies, and procedures of the facility. See Orientation Training, STANDARD 1.023 through STANDARD 1.025
f) Notifying all staff, volunteers, and parents of any changes in the facility's policies and procedures;
g) Providing for continuous supervision of visitors and all non-facility personnel;
h) When problems are identified, planning for corrective action, assigning and verifying that a specific person corrects the problem by a specified date;
i) Arranging or providing repair, maintenance, supplemental education, or other services at the facility;
j) Providing or arranging for inservice training for staff and volunteers, based on the needs of the facility and qualifications and skills of staff and volunteers. See Continuing Education, STANDARD 1.029 through

STANDARD 1.036;
k) Recommending an annual budget and managing the finances of the facility;
l) Maintaining required records for staff, volunteers, and children at the facility;
m) Providing for parent involvement, including parent education. See Parent Relationships, STANDARD 2.044 through STANDARD 2.057;
n) Reporting to the governing or advisory board on a regular basis as to the status of the facility's operation;
o) Providing oversight of research studies conducted at the facility and joint supervision of students using the facility for clinical practice.

RATIONALE: Management principles of quality improvement in any human service require identification of goals and leadership to ensure that all those involved (those with authority and experience, and those affected) participate in working toward those goals. Problem-solving approaches that are effective in other settings also work in early childhood programs. This standard describes accepted personnel management practices. General administrative management starts with the principle of "unity of command" with role definitions clearly defined and communicated along with performance expectations, and implementation of routinely scheduled evaluation of staff performance. For any organization to function effectively, lines of responsibility must be clearly delineated, with an individual who is designated to have ultimate responsibility.

COMMENTS: Management to ensure that policy is carried out includes providing staff and parents with written handbooks, training, supervising with frequent feedback, and monitoring with checklists. A national survey of model health and safety practices in facilities, a project through the American Public Health Association (APHA) and the American Academy of Pediatrics (AAP), found exemplary facilities that had effective surveillance procedures. For example, in one of these facilities, an observation checklist was developed covering every area of the facility from parking lot to classrooms. Two individuals were assigned to walk around the center noting whether all items on the checklist were in good order. The two individuals were a parent and a staff member, or the director and a staff member. When any deficiencies were found, the process included identifying a person responsible for correcting the problem and a date by which correction should occur.

A comprehensive site observation checklist is available in the print version of *Model Child Care Health Policies*. Copies of this publication can be purchased from the National Association for the Education of Young Children (NAEYC) or from the American Academy of Pediatrics (AAP). Contact information for the NAEYC and the AAP can be found in Appendix BB.

TYPE OF FACILITY: *Center*

STANDARD 8.002
WRITTEN DELEGATION OF ADMINISTRATIVE AUTHORITY

There shall be written delegation of administrative authority, designating the person in charge of the facility and the person(s) in charge of individual children, for all hours of operation.

RATIONALE: Caregivers are responsible for the protection of the children in care at all times. In group care, each child must be assigned to an adult to ensure individual children are supervised and individual needs are addressed. Children should not be placed in the care of unauthorized family members or other individuals.

TYPE OF FACILITY: *Center*

STANDARD 8.003
ACCESS TO FACILITY RECORDS

The designated person in charge shall have access to the records necessary to manage the facility and shall allow regulatory staff access to the facility and records.

RATIONALE: Those with responsibility must have access to the information required to carry out their duties and make reasonable decisions.

TYPE OF FACILITY: *Center*

8.2 MANAGEMENT AND HEALTH POLICIES AND STATEMENT OF SERVICES

STANDARD 8.004
CONTENT OF POLICIES

The facility shall have policies to specify how the caregiver addresses the developmental functioning and individual or special needs of children of different ages and abilities who can be served by the facility. These policies shall include, but not be limited to, the items described in STANDARD 8.005 and below:
a) Admission and Enrollment;
b) Supervision;
c) Discipline;
d) Care of Acutely Ill Children;
e) Child Health Services;
f) Use of Health Consultants
g) Health Education
h) Medications;
i) Emergency Plan;
j) Evacuation Plan, Drills, and Closings;
k) Authorized Caregivers;
l) Safety Surveillance;
m) Transportation and Field Trips;
n) Sanitation and Hygiene;
o) Food Handling, Feeding, and Nutrition;
p) Sleeping
q) Evening and Night Care Plan;
r) Smoking, Prohibited Substances, and Firearms;
s) Staff Health, Training, Benefits, and Evaluation;
t) Maintenance of the Facility and Equipment;
u) Review and Revision of Policies, Plans, and Procedures, STANDARD 8.040 and STANDARD 8.041.

The facility shall have specific strategies for implementing each policy. For centers, all of these items shall be written.

RATIONALE: Facility policies should vary according to the ages and abilities of the children enrolled to accommodate individual or special needs. Program planning should precede, not follow, the enrollment and care of children at different developmental levels and with different abilities. Neither plans nor policies affect quality unless the program has devised a way to implement the plan or policy.

TYPE OF FACILITY: *Center; Large Family Child Care Home; Small Family Child Care Home*

STANDARD 8.005
INITIAL PROVISION OF WRITTEN INFORMATION TO PARENTS AND CAREGIVERS

At enrollment, and before assumption of supervision of children by caregivers at the facility, the facility shall provide parents and caregivers with a statement of services, policies, and procedures that shall include at least the following information along with the policies listed in STANDARD 8.004:

a) The licensed capacity, child:staff ratios, ages and number of children in care. If names of children and parents are made available, parental permission for any release to others shall be obtained;

b) Services offered to children including daily activities, sleep positioning policies and arrangements, napping routines, guidance and discipline policies, diaper changing and toilet learning/training methods, child handwashing, oral health, and health education. Any special requirements for a child shall be clearly defined in writing before enrollment;

c) Hours and days of operation;

d) Admissions criteria, enrollment procedures, and daily sign-in/out policies, including forms that must be completed;

e) Policies for termination and notice by the parent or the facility;

f) Policies regarding payments of fees, deposits, and refunds;

g) Planned methods and schedules for conferences or other methods of communication between parents and staff;

h) Plan for Urgent and Emergency Medical Care or Threatening Incidents. See Emergency Procedures, STANDARD 3.048 through STANDARD 3.052; and Plan for Urgent Medical Care or Threatening Incidents, STANDARD 8.022 and STANDARD 8.023.

i) Evacuation procedures and alternate shelter arrangements for fire, natural disasters, and building emergencies. See Evacuation Plan, Drills, and Closings, STANDARD 8.024 through STANDARD 8.027;

j) Nutrition. Schedule of meals and snacks. See General Requirements, STANDARD 4.001 through STANDARD 4.010; Requirements for Special Groups or Ages of Children, STANDARD 4.011 through STANDARD 4.025 and Plans and Policies for Food Handling, Feeding, and Nutrition, STANDARD 8.035 and STANDARD 8.036;

k) Policy for food brought from home. See Food Brought from Home, STANDARD 4.040 and STANDARD 4.041;

l) Policy on infant feeding. See Nutrition for Infants, STANDARD 4.011 through STANDARD 4.021 and Plans and Policies for Food Handling, Feeding, and Nutrition, STANDARD 8.035 and STANDARD 8.036;

m) Policies for staffing including the use of volunteers, helpers, or substitute caregivers, child:staff ratios, deployment of staff for different activities, authorized caregivers, methods used to ensure continuous supervision of children. See Child:Staff Ratio and Group Size, STANDARD 1.001 through STANDARD 1.005;

n) Policies for sanitation and hygiene. See Hygiene and Sanitation, Disinfection, and Maintenance, STANDARD 3.012 through STANDARD 3.040;

o) Non-emergency transportation policies. See Transportation, STANDARD 2.029 through STANDARD 2.038;

p) Presence and care of any pets or any other animals on the premises. See Animals, STANDARD 3.042 through STANDARD 3.044;

q) Policy on health assessments and immunizations. See Daily Health Assessment, STANDARD 3.001 and STANDARD 3.002; Preventive Health Services, STANDARD 3.003 through STANDARD 3.004; and Immunizations, STANDARD 3.005 through STANDARD 3.007;

r) Policy regarding care of acutely ill children, including exclusion or dismissal from the facility. See Child Inclusion/Exclusion/Dismissal, STANDARD 3.065 through STANDARD 3.068; Caring for Ill Children, STANDARD 3.070 through STANDARD 3.080; and Plan for the Care of Acutely Ill Children, STANDARD 8.011 and STANDARD 8.012;

s) Policy on administration of medications. See Medications, STANDARD 3.081 through STANDARD 3.083; and Medication Policy, STANDARD 8.021;

t) Policy on use of child care health consultants. See STANDARD 1.040 through

STANDARD 1.044;
u) Policy on health education. See STANDARD 2.060 through STANDARD 2.067.
v) Policy on smoking, tobacco use, and prohibited substances. See Smoking and Prohibited Substances, STANDARD 3.041 and Policy on Smoking, Tobacco Use, Prohibited Substances, and Firearms, STANDARD 8.038 and STANDARD 8.039;
w) Policy on confidentiality of records. See STANDARD 8.054.

Parents and caregivers shall sign that they have reviewed and accepted this statement of services, policies and procedures.

RATIONALE: The *Model Child Care Health Policies* has all of the necessary text to comply with this standard organized into a single document. Each policy has a place for the facility to fill in blanks to customize the policies for a specific site. The text of the policies can be edited to match individual program operations. Since the task of assembling all the items listed in this standard is formidable, starting with a template such as *Model Child Care Health Policies* can be helpful.

COMMENTS: Parents are encouraged to interact with their own children and other children at drop-off and pick-up times and during visits at the center. Parents and caregivers, including volunteers, may have different approaches to routines than those followed by the facility. Review of written policies and procedures by all adults prior to contact with the children in care helps ensure consistent implementation of carefully considered decisions about how care should be provided at the facility.

For large and small family child care homes, a written statement of services, policies and procedures is recommended but not required. If the statement is provided orally, parents should sign a statement attesting to their acceptance of the statement of services, policies and procedures presented orally to them. *Model Child Care Health Policies* can be adapted to these smaller settings.

Copies of the current edition of *Model Child Care Health Policies* can be purchased from the National Association for the Education of Young Children

(NAEYC) or from the American Academy of Pediatrics (AAP). Contact information for the NAEYC and the AAP is located in Appendix BB.

TYPE OF FACILITY: *Center; Large Family Child Care Home; Small Family Child Care Home*

ADMISSION AND ENROLLMENT POLICY

STANDARD 8.006
NONDISCRIMINATION POLICY

The facility's written admission policy shall be nondiscriminatory in regard to race, culture, sex, religion, national origin, ancestry, or disability. A copy of the policy and definitions of eligibility shall be available for review on demand.

RATIONALE: Nondiscriminatory policies advocate for quality child care services for all children regardless of the child's citizenship, residency status, financial resources, and language differences.

COMMENTS: Facilities should be able to accommodate all children except those whose needs require extreme modifications beyond the capability of the facility's resources. However, facilities should not have blanket policies against admitting children with disabilities. Instead, a facility should make an individual assessment of a child's needs and the facility's ability to meet those needs. Federal laws do not permit discrimination based on disability (Americans with Disabilities Act). Inclusion of children with disabilities in all child care and early childhood educational programs is strongly encouraged. See Chapter 7, Children Who Are Eligible for Services Under the Individuals with Disabilities Education Act (IDEA), for more information on the Americans with Disabilities Act (ADA).

TYPE OF FACILITY: *Center; Large Family Child Care Home; Small Family Child Care Home*

STANDARD 8.007
EXCHANGE OF INFORMATION
UPON ENROLLMENT

Arrangements for enrollment of children shall be made in person by the parents or legal guardians. The facility shall advise the parents/legal guardians of their responsibility to provide information to the facility regarding their children.

RATIONALE: Parents or legal guardians must be fully informed about the facility's services before delegating responsibility for care of the child. The facility and parents must exchange information necessary for the safety and health of the child.

TYPE OF FACILITY: *Center; Large Family Child Care Home; Small Family Child Care Home*

DISCIPLINE POLICY

STANDARD 8.008
CONTENT OF WRITTEN
DISCIPLINE POLICY

Each facility shall have and implement a written discipline policy that outlines positive methods of guidance (described in Discipline, STANDARD 2.039 through STANDARD 2.043) appropriate to the ages of the children enrolled. It shall explicitly describe positive, nonviolent, non-abusive methods for achieving discipline. These shall include the following:
a) Redirection;
b) Planning ahead to prevent problems;
c) Encouragement of appropriate behavior;
d) Consistent, clear rules;
e) Children involved in solving problems.

All caregivers shall sign an agreement to implement the facility's discipline policy.

All facilities shall have written discipline policies.

RATIONALE: Caregivers are more likely to avoid abusive practices if they are well-informed about effective, non-abusive methods for managing children's behaviors. Positive methods of discipline

create a constructive and supportive social group and reduce incidents of aggression.

COMMENTS: Examples of appropriate alternatives to corporal punishment for infants and toddlers include brief, verbal expressions of disapproval; for pre-schoolers, "time out" (such as an out-of-group activity) under adult supervision; for school-age children, denial of privileges. A helpful resource for discussion of staff-child interactions is the National Association for the Education of Young Children's (NAEYC) Guide to Accreditation. Contact information for the NAEYC is located in Appendix BB.

TYPE OF FACILITY: *Center; Large Family Child Care Home, Small Family Child Care Home*

STANDARD 8.009
IMPLEMENTATION OF DISCIPLINE
POLICY

The caregiver shall implement a policy that promotes positive guidance and discipline techniques and prohibits corporal punishment, psychological abuse, humiliation, abusive language, binding or tying to restrict movement, and the withdrawal or forcing of food and other basic needs, as outlined in STANDARD 2.043. A policy explicitly stating the consequence for staff who exhibit these behaviors shall be determined and reviewed and signed by each staff member prior to hiring.

RATIONALE: Corporal punishment may be physical abuse or may become abusive very easily. Emotional abuse can be extremely harmful to children, but, unlike physical or sexual abuse, it is not adequately defined in most state child abuse reporting laws. Corporal punishment is clearly prohibited in small family child care homes in 47 states, and is prohibited in centers in 50 states (1, 2). Research links corporal punishment with negative effects such as later criminal behavior and impairment of learning (3-5). Primary factors supporting the prohibition of certain methods of punishment include current child development theory and practice, legal aspects (namely that a caregiver is not acting in place of parents with regard to the child), and increasing liability suits.

TYPE OF FACILITY: *Center; Large Family Child Care Home; Small Family Child Care Home*

STANDARD 8.010
POLICY ON CHILDRENS' ACTS OF AGGRESSION

The facility shall have policies for dealing with acts of aggression and fighting (such as biting and hitting) by children. These policies shall include:
a) Separation of the children involved;
b) Immediate attention to the individual child or caregiver who was bitten;
c) Notification to parents of children involved in the incident, if an injury requires first aid or medical attention, as specified in Incidence Logs of Illness, Injury, and Other Situations That Require Documentation, STANDARD 8.061 through STANDARD 8.064;
d) Review of the adequacy of the caregiver supervision and appropriateness of facility activities;
e) Administrative policy for dealing with recurrences.

RATIONALE: Aggressive acts, both intentional and unintentional, occur in out-of-home care settings (6, 7). Administrative guidelines are necessary for the management of recurrent acts of aggression and should be developed within the facility based on the resources and structure of the facility. Potential injuries and infections that may be incurred when caring for young children are health and safety hazards for caregivers. Training and educational materials should be provided to caregivers to help them understand how best to prevent and respond to these situations.

COMMENTS: In general, reducing child:staff ratios and child group sizes, having training for caregivers, and using positive guidance and discipline techniques that care for the victim and avoid rewarding the aggressor with attention, will help to decrease acts of aggression (such as biting and hitting). For additional information on discipline policy, see also Discipline, STANDARD 2.039 through STANDARD 2.043.

Biting and hitting are manifestations of different emotional feelings at different ages. Biting is a common behavior in the infant or toddler who is expressing a feeling. Hitting may be an immature behavior with no malicious intent.

TYPE OF FACILITY: *Center; Large Family Child Care Home; Small Family Child Care Home*

PLAN FOR THE CARE OF ACUTELY ILL CHILDREN AND CAREGIVERS

STANDARD 8.011
CONTENT AND DEVELOPMENT OF THE PLAN FOR CARE OF ILL CHILDREN AND CAREGIVERS

The facility's plan for the care of ill children and caregivers shall be developed in consultation with the facility's health consultant. See STANDARD 1.040 through STANDARD 1.044. This plan shall include:
a) Policies and procedures for urgent and emergency care;
b) Admission and inclusion/exclusion policies. Conditions that require that a child be excluded and sent home are specified in Child Inclusion/Exclusion/Dismissal, STANDARD 3.065 through STANDARD 3.068;
c) A description of illnesses common to children in child care, their management, and precautions to address the needs and behavior of the ill child as well as to protect the health of other children and caregivers. See Infectious Diseases, STANDARD 6.001 through STANDARD 6.039;
d) A procedure to obtain and maintain updated individual emergency care plans for children with special health care needs;
e) A procedure for documenting the name of person affected, date and time of illness, a description of symptoms, the response of the caregiver to these symptoms, who was notified (such as a parent, legal guardian, nurse, physician, health department), and the response;
f) The standards described in Reporting Illness, STANDARD 3.087 and STANDARD 3.088; and Notification of Parents, STANDARD 3.084 and STANDARD 3.085.
g) Medication Policy. See STANDARD 8.021.

All child care facilities shall have written policies for the care of ill children and caregivers.

RATIONALE: The policy for the management of ill children should be developed in consultation with health care providers to address current understanding of the technical issues of contagion and other health risks. In group care, the facility must address

the well-being of all those affected by illness: the ill child, the staff, parents of the ill child, other children in the facility and their parents, and the community. Where compromises must be made, the priority of the policy should be to meet the needs of the ill child. The policy should address the circumstances under which separation of the ill child from the group is required; the circumstances under which the caregiver, parents, legal guardian, or other designated persons need to be informed; and the procedures to be followed in these cases. The policy should take into consideration:
a) The physical facility;
b) The number and the qualifications of the facility's personnel;
c) The fact that children do become ill frequently and at unpredictable times;
d) The fact that working parents often are not given leave for their children's illnesses (8).

Infectious diseases are a major concern of parents and caregivers. Since children, especially those in group settings, can be a reservoir for many infectious agents, and since caregivers come into close and frequent contact with children, caregivers are at risk for developing a wide variety of infectious diseases. Following the infection control standards will help protect both children and caregivers from communicable disease. Recording the occurrence of illness in a facility and the response to the illness characterizes and defines the frequency of the illness, suggests whether an outbreak has occurred, may suggest an effective intervention, and provides documentation for administrative purposes.

COMMENTS: Facilities may comply by adopting a model policy and using reference materials as authoritative resources. The *Model Child Care Health Policies*, the print or internet version available from NAEYC and the AAP, may be helpful; or see the *Red Book* or *Preparing for Illness*, a booklet which translates the recommendations of the *Red Book* for child care providers, available from the AAP. Check for other materials provided by the licensing agency, resource and referral agency, or health department. Training for staff on management of illness can be facilitated by using *Part 6: Illness in Child Care*, of the video series developed to illustrate how to comply with the standards in *Caring for Children*. The video series is available from the AAP and NAEYC. See the sample symptom record in Appendix F. The sample symptom record is also provided in *Healthy Young Children* produced by the NAEYC. See also a sample document for permission for medical condition treatment in Appendix W. Contact information for

the National Association for the Education of Young Children (NAEYC) and the American Academy of Pediatrics (AAP) can be found in Appendix BB.

TYPE OF FACILITY: *Center; Large Family Child Care Home; Small Family Child Care Home*

STANDARD 8.012
EXCLUSION AND ALTERNATIVE CARE FOR CHILDREN

At the discretion of the person authorized by the child care provider to make such decisions, children who are ill shall be excluded from the child care facility for the conditions defined in STANDARD 3.065 through STANDARD 3.068.

When children are not permitted to receive care in their usual child care setting and cannot receive care from a parent or relative, they shall be permitted to receive care in one of the following arrangements, if the arrangement meets the applicable standards:
a) Care in the child's usual facility in a special area for care of ill children;
b) Care in a separate small family child care home or center that serves only children with illness or temporary disabilities;
c) Care by a child care worker in the child's own home.

RATIONALE: Young children who are developing trust, autonomy, and initiative require the support of familiar caregivers and environments during times of illness to recover physically and avoid emotional distress (9). Young children enrolled in group care experience a higher incidence of mild illness (such as upper respiratory infections or otitis media) and other temporary disabilities (such as exacerbation of asthma or eczema) than those who have less interaction with other children. Sometimes, these illnesses preclude their participation in the usual child care activities. Most state regulations require that children with certain conditions be excluded from their usual care arrangement (10). To accommodate situations where parents cannot provide care for their own ill children, several types of alternative care arrangements have been established.

When children with possible communicable diseases are present in the alternative care arrangements, preventing the further spread of disease is a priority. Although most facilities claim to adhere to general

principles of prevention and control of communicable disease, in a study of such practices, only one facility followed strict isolation procedures (11). In another study, a facility providing care for ill children demonstrated no additional transmission of communicable disease from the children served to the rest of the well children attending the usual child care facilities (12).

COMMENTS: Working parents should be entitled to family sick leave days to care for their ill children. Professionals and the public generally agree that when a child is seriously ill, or when it is not yet clear that the illness is a mild one, the parent should be able to stay home with the child. When a child is recuperating from a mild illness that precludes participation in the child's usual child care setting, parents may need alternative arrangements. At a minimum, working parents should be able to use their own sick or personal days to care for their ill children. However, children are ill frequently; some parents need help in making alternative arrangements for the days when the child is not very ill and the parents need to be at work. Facilities unable to care for ill children should be supportive and helpful to parents, giving them ideas for alternative arrangements. However, the responsibility for care cannot be transferred from the parent to the child care provider unless the caregiver is willing to accept this responsibility. The decision to accept responsibility for the care of ill children should rest with a designated person at the child care facility, who must weigh staffing and programmatic considerations that affect this decision. Though considerations may vary from one instance to another, parents must know who will make the decision.

Sometimes a child can be included in the facility's regular group of children, with modified activities. Sometimes a center can set up a "get well room" where ill children not able to participate with the regular group can receive care. Some centers have set up satellite small family child care homes for their enrolled children. Ideally, the children know the caregiver because the caregiver works at the center when no child is ill. Similarly, a child's regular small or large family child care home provider could include the child in the regular group if appropriate, or might have a "get well room," if adequate supervision can be provided. Other alternative care arrangements include a worker sent by a home health agency or

from a pool of caregivers to the child's home, arrangements in a pediatric unit of a hospital, pediatric office, or other similar setting. Special facilities caring only for ill children should meet more specialized requirements.

For more information regarding caring for ill children, see STANDARD 3.070 through STANDARD 3.080.

TYPE OF FACILITY: *Center; Large Family Child Care Home; Small Family Child Care Home*

HEALTH PLAN FOR CHILD HEALTH SERVICES

STANDARD 8.013
WRITTEN PROCEDURE FOR OBTAINING PREVENTIVE HEALTH SERVICE INFORMATION

Each facility shall develop and follow a written procedure for obtaining necessary medical information including immunizations (see *Recommended Childhood Immunization Schedule* in Appendix G) and periodic preventive health assessments (see *Recommendations for Preventive Pediatric Health Care* in Appendix H) as recommended by the American Academy of Pediatrics (AAP) and the Health Care Financing Administration of the U.S. Department of Health and Human Services (13, 14). Facility staff shall encourage parents/legal guardians to schedule these preventive health services in a timely fashion.

Documentation of an age-appropriate health assessment that includes an update of immunizations and screenings shall be filed in the child's record at the facility within 6 weeks of admission and following each subsequent routinely scheduled preventive health care visit. The staff of the facility shall review the admission and all subsequent reports of the child's health assessment visits that occur while the child is enrolled and shall offer a list of concerns for the parents to bring to upcoming check-up visits. Medical information shall include any information needed for the special medical care of the child. Questions raised by child care staff shall be directed to the family or, with parental permission, to the child's health care clinician for explanation and discussion of the implications for care.

Centers shall have written procedures for the verification of compliance with recommended immunizations and periodic health assessments of children. Centers shall maintain confidential records of immunizations, periodic health assessments and any special medical considerations.

RATIONALE: Health assessments are important to ensure prevention, early detection of remediable problems, and planning for adaptations needed so that all children can reach their potential. When age-appropriate health assessments and use of health insurance benefits are promoted by child care providers, children enrolled in child care will have increased access to immunizations and other preventive services (15). With the expansion of eligibility for medical assistance and the new federal subsidy of state child health insurance plans (Title XIX and Title XXI of the Social Security Act), the numbers of children who lack insurance for routine preventive health care should be limited to those in middle income families whose parents' employers do not provide coverage.

Requirements for the documentation of preventive health care provides an important safety net for children of busy parents who may be unfamiliar with or lose track of the schedule their children should follow for routine care. At least one state audits a sample of child health records in every child care center and large family child care home for compliance with a licensing requirement for documentation that enrolled children are up-to-date with the AAP schedule. Over several years of audit, the aggregated data have been used to target pockets of need, leading to a steady improvement in services. In conversation with S.S. Aronson, MD (September 2000), compliance with immunization requirements was documented for over 90% of the children in 1999; screening tests were documented for up to two-thirds of the children, depending on the test.

The facility must have accurate, current information regarding the medical status and treatment of each child so it will be able to determine and adjust its capability to provide needed services.

COMMENTS: The facility should expect and encourage regular health assessments. Assistance for caregivers and low income parents can be obtained through the Medicaid Early Periodic Screening and Diagnostic Treatment (EPSDT) program (Title XIX) and the state's version of the federal Child Health Insurance Program (S-CHIP or Title XXI) (17).

Most states require that child care providers document that the child's health records are up-to-date to protect the child and other children whom the under-immunized child would expose to increased risk of vaccine-preventable disease. State regulations regarding immunization requirements for children may differ, but the child care facility should strive to comply with the national, annually published, *Recommended Childhood Immunization Schedule*, from the American Academy of Pediatrics' (AAP), Centers for Disease Control and Prevention (CDC), and the Academy of Family Practice (AFP). See Appendix G. Contact information for the AAP, CDC, and AFP is located in Appendix BB.

A child's entrance into the facility need not be delayed if an appointment for health supervision is scheduled. Often appointments for well-child care must be scheduled several weeks in advance. In such cases, the child care facility must obtain a medical history report from the parents and documentation of an appointment for routine health supervision, as a minimum requirement for the child to attend the facility on a routine basis. The child should receive immunizations as soon as practical to prevent an increased exposure to vaccine-preventable diseases.

Local public health staff (such as the staff of immunization units, EPSDT programs) should provide assistance to caregivers in the form of record-keeping materials, educational materials, and on-site visits for education and help with surveillance activities. A copy of a form to use for documentation of routine health supervision services is available from the National Association for the Education of Young Children (NAEYC) or the AAP in the *Model Child Care Health Policies*. Contact information for the NAEYC and the AAP is located in Appendix BB.

As more child care providers begin to use computers to reduce the complexity of record-keeping, they may want to use software for checking immunization status for age and documentation of the child's status for other services of routine preventive care. Such software for immunization checks is in common use nationally (18). Clinic Assessment Software Application (CASA) is a menu-driven relational database developed by the National Immunization Program of the Centers for Disease Control and Prevention

(CDC) as an assessment tool for immunization clinics and health care providers. This application is used for the data entry and analysis of immunization status. It includes reminder and recall tracking capabilities as well as other special features. CASA produces reports from a menu and provides programmatic feedback on the up-to-date status of individual children and for a group of children in an age range set by the user. In conversation with S.S. Aronson (July 2001), customized, non-commercial software (called ECELSTRAK) that checks children's status for all routine health supervision services (screenings and immunizations) is being used for a statewide audit of child care health records in Pennsylvania's licensing of child care facilities. Commercial software that incorporates the decision rules for routine health supervision services is being developed and may be commercially available soon.

Health professionals can photocopy, then update old reports with strike-outs, added dates, and initials over the course of several visits. Having to fill out the form brings up the issue of the child's use of child care as part of the check-up visit and fosters discussions related to the child's adjustment and the parent's satisfaction with the arrangements.

For a sample *Child Health Assessment* that includes immunization and preventive health records, see Appendix Z. See STANDARD 8.053 for information on confidentiality and access to records.

TYPE OF FACILITY: *Center; Large Family Child Care Home; Small Family Child Care Home*

STANDARD 8.014
DOCUMENTATION OF EXEMPTIONS AND EXCLUSION OF CHILDREN WHO LACK IMMUNIZATIONS

Exemptions from the requirement for up-to-date immunization made for religious or medical reasons shall be documented in the child's record. A child whose immunizations are not kept up-to-date shall be excluded after three written reminders to parents over a 3-month period. If more than one immunization is needed in a series, time shall be allowed for the immunizations to be obtained at the appropriate intervals.

RATIONALE: National surveys document that child care has a positive influence on protection from vaccine-preventable illness (20). Immunizations should be required for all children in child care settings. Facilities must consider the consequences if they accept responsibility for exposing a child who cannot be fully immunized because of immaturity to a child who may bring disease to the facility because of refusal to be immunized. Although up to 6 weeks after the child starts to participate in child care may be allowed for the acquisition of immunizations for which the child is eligible, parents should maintain their child's immunization status according to the nationally recommended schedule to avoid potential exposure of other children in the facility to vaccine-preventable disease.

COMMENTS: See Appendix G, for the *Recommended Childhood Immunization Schedule* from the American Academy of Pediatrics (AAP). Check for the new schedule that is posted each January on the AAP (www.aap.org) and CDC (www.cdc.gov) websites. When a child who has a medical exemption from immunization is included in child care, reasonable accommodation of that child requires planning to exclude such a child in the event of an outbreak. For children who are incompletely immunized because of the parents' religious reasons, the facility may be at legal risk for allowing exposure of the child and other children in the facility to increased risk of vaccine-preventable infections. Prudent child care providers should discuss with an attorney, the liability risk for enrolling a child whose parents refuse to accept immunization of their child for non-medical reasons.

TYPE OF FACILITY: *Center; Large Family Child Care Home; Small Family Child Care Home*

STANDARD 8.015
IDENTIFICATION OF CHILD'S MEDICAL HOME AND PARENTAL CONSENT FOR INFORMATION EXCHANGE

As part of the enrollment of a child, the child care provider shall ask the family to identify the child's health care providers (medical home) and to provide written consent to enable the caregiver to establish communication with those providers. The family will always be informed prior to the use of the permission unless it is an emergency or a suspected abusive situation. The providers with whom the facility shall exchange information with parental consent shall include:

a) Sources of regular medical and dental care (such as the child's health care provider, dentist, and medical facility);
b) Source of emergency services, when required;
c) Special clinics the child may attend, including sessions with medical specialists and registered dietitians;
d) Special therapists for the child (such as occupational, physical, speech, nutrition). These special therapists shall provide written documentation of the services rendered;
e) Counselors, therapists, or mental health service providers for parents (such as social workers, psychologists, or psychiatrists).

RATIONALE: Primary health care providers are involved not only in the medical care of the child but in the ecological system in which the child exists. A major barrier to productive working relationships between child care and health care providers is inadequacy of communication channels (21, 22).

Knowing who is treating the child and coordinating services with these sources of service is vital to the ability of the caregivers to offer appropriate care of the child. Every child should have a health care provider for primary care, and those with special needs will have therapists and consultants.

COMMENTS: A source of health care may be a community clinic, a public health department, or a primary health care provider. Families should also know the location of the hospital emergency room nearest to their home. The emergency room is not an appropriate place for routine care, but may properly be used in an emergency. Education and information for caregivers about community resources is a good topic for staff training.

For more information regarding communication between a child's care facility and that child's health care providers, see STANDARD 2.054. See STANDARD 8.053 through STANDARD 8.057, regarding confidentiality and access to records. For a sample *Child Health Assessment* that includes important health information, see Appendix Z See

also a sample document for permission for medical condition treatment in Appendix W.

TYPE OF FACILITY: *Center; Large Family Child Care Home; Small Family Child Care Home*

STANDARD 8.016
INFORMATION SHARING ON THERAPIES AND TREATMENTS NEEDED

The person at the child care facility who is responsible for planning care for the child shall seek information on therapies and treatments being provided to the child that are directly relevant to the health and safety of the child in the child care facility. The consent of the child's parents shall be obtained before this confidential information is sought.

RATIONALE: The facility must have accurate, current information regarding the medical status and treatment of the child so it will be able to determine the facility's capability to provide needed services or to obtain them elsewhere.

TYPE OF FACILITY: *Center; Large Family Child Care Home; Small Family Child Care Home*

STANDARD 8.017
INFORMATION SHARING ON FAMILY HEALTH

Families shall be asked to share information about family health (such as chronic diseases) that might affect the child's health.

RATIONALE: A family history of chronic disease helps child care providers understand family stress and experiences of the child within the family.

COMMENTS: Information on family health can be gathered by simply asking parents to tell the caregiver about any chronic health problems that the child's parents, siblings, or household members have or by requesting that this information be supplied by the child's primary health care provider.

Family management of chronic illness may require additional support services.

TYPE OF FACILITY: *Center; Large Family Child Care Home; Small Family Child Care Home*

DEPARTURE AND TRANSITION PROCESS

STANDARD 8.018
PLANNING FOR CHILD'S
TRANSITION TO NEW SERVICES

If a parent requests assistance with the transition process from the facility to a public school or another program, the designated care or service coordinator at the facility shall review the child's records, including needs, learning style, supports, progress, and recommendations and shall obtain written informed consent from the parent prior to sharing information at a transition meeting, in a written summary, or in some other verbal or written format.

The process for the child's departure shall also involve sharing and exchange of progress reports with other care providers for the child and the parents or legal guardian of the child within the realm of confidentiality guidelines.

The facility shall determine in what form and for how long archival records of transitioned children shall be maintained by the facility.

RATIONALE: Families in transition benefit when support and advocacy are available from a facility representative who is aware of their needs and of the community's resources. This process is essential in planning the child's departure or transition to another program. Information regarding successful behavior strategies, motivational strategies, and similar information may be helpful to staff in the setting to which the child is transitioning.

COMMENTS: Some families are capable of advocating effectively for themselves and their children; others require help negotiating the system outside of the facility. An interdisciplinary process is encouraged. Though coordinating and evaluating health and therapeutic services for children with special needs is

primarily the responsibility of the school district or regional center, staff from the child care facility (one of many service providers) should participate, as staff members have had a unique opportunity to observe the child. In small and large family child care homes where an interdisciplinary team is not present, the caregivers should participate in the planning and preparation along with other care or treatment providers, with the parents written consent.

It is important for all providers of care to coordinate their activities and referrals; otherwise the family may not be well informed. If records are shared electronically, providers should ensure that the records are encrypted for security and confidentiality.

For more information on confidentiality, see Confidentiality and Access to Records, STANDARD 8.053 through STANDARD 8.057.

TYPE OF FACILITY: *Center; Large Family Child Care Home; Small Family Child Care Home*

STANDARD 8.019
FORMAT FOR THE TRANSITION
PLAN

Each service agency or caregiver shall have a format and timeline for the process of developing a transition plan to be followed when each child leaves the facility. The plan shall include the following components:
a) Review and final preparation of the child's records;
b) A child and family needs assessment;
c) Identification of potential child care, educational, or programmatic arrangements.

RATIONALE: Many factors contribute to the success or failure of a transition. These concerns can be monitored effectively when a written plan is developed and followed to ensure that all steps in a transition are included and are undertaken in a timely, responsive manner.

COMMENTS: Though the child care provider can and should offer support in this process, child care is a free-market system where the parent is the consumer and decision-maker.

It is best if the process of planning begins at least 3 months prior to the anticipated transition since finding the proper facility for a child can be a complex and time consuming process in some communities. Each agency can adapt the format to its own needs. However, consistent formats for planning and information exchange, requiring written parental consent, would be useful to both caregivers and families in both localities when children with special needs are involved. The use of outside consultants for small and large family child care homes is especially important in meeting this type of standard.

TYPE OF FACILITY: *Center; Large Family Child Care Home; Small Family Child Care Home*

HEALTH CONSULTATION

STANDARD 8.020
ARRANGEMENTS FOR USE OF
HEALTH CONSULTANTS

Every facility shall seek the services of a health consultant. This health consultant will provide the facility with ongoing consultation to assist in the development of written policies relating to health and safety, as specified in Health Consultants, STANDARD 1.040 through STANDARD 1.044.

RATIONALE: Caregivers rarely are trained health care professionals. Health consultants can help develop and implement written policies for prevention and management of injury and disease. Advance planning in this area can reduce stress for caregivers, parents, and health professionals.

Use of health consultants for child care is becoming a reality. In 1998, 24 states and one city required regulated facilities to have a health consultant (23). Many states have been developing health consultation services due in part to a national program funded by the Maternal and Child Health Bureau, Health Resources and Services Administration (HRSA) to help every state implement the Healthy Child Care America Campaign. Training programs for health consultants have been developed by Early Childhood Education Linkage System (ECELS), American Public Health Association (APHA), and the National Training Institute for Child Care Health Consultants (NTI) at the University of North Carolina (UNC-CH).

COMMENTS: Unless provided through a public health system, the health consultant's services are difficult to obtain particularly for small family child care homes. Caregivers should seek services from the public health resources, pay for consultation from community nursing services, seek the services of a health consultant through state and local professional organizations, such as the following resources:

a) Local chapters of the American Academy of Pediatrics;
b) American Nurses' Association;
c) Visiting Nurse Association;
d) American Academy of Family Physicians;
e) National Association of Pediatric Nurse Practitioners;
f) National Association for the Education of Young Children;
g) National Association for Family Child Care;
h) National Resource Center for Health and Safety in Child Care;
i) National Training Institute for Child Care Health Consultants;
j) State and local health departments (especially the public health nursing departments, the environmental health departments, and the state communicable disease specialist's or epidemiologist's office);
k) State Injury Prevention Director.

Caregivers should not overlook parents of children enrolled in their facilities who are health professionals capable of performing as child care health consultants. The specific policies for an individual facility depend on the resources available to that facility (23). To be effective, a health consultant should know what resources are available in the community and should involve caregivers and parents in setting policies. Setting policies in cooperation with both caregivers and parents will better ensure successful implementation (23). Licensing requirements for facilities increasingly require that facilities make specific arrangements with a health consultant to assist in the development of written policies for the prevention and control of disease.

Child care facilities should offer health consultants some form of compensation for services to foster access and accountability.

TYPE OF FACILITY: *Center; Large Family Child Care Home; Small Family Child Care Home*

MEDICATION POLICY

STANDARD 8.021
WRITTEN POLICY ON USE OF MEDICATIONS

The facility shall have a written policy for the use of any prescription medication that has been prescribed to a particular child by that child's primary health care provider. The facility shall also have a written policy for the use of any nonprescription oral or topical medication that the facility keeps on hand to use with parental consent when the medication may be indicated.

A medication record maintained on an ongoing basis by designated staff shall include the following:
a) Specific, signed parental consent for the caregiver to administer medication;
b) Prescription by a health care provider, if required;
c) Administration log;
d) Checklist information on medication, including possible side effects, brought to the facility by the parents.

The facility shall consult with the State Board of Nursing or their health consultant about required training and documentation for medication administration and develop a plan regarding medication administration training.

> RATIONALE: Caregivers need to be aware of what medication the child is receiving and when, who prescribed the medicine, and what the known reactions or side effects may be in the event that a child has a negative reaction to the medicine (24). A child's reaction to medication may occasionally be extreme enough to initiate the protocol developed for emergencies. This medication record is especially important if medications are frequently prescribed or if long-term medications are being used.

> COMMENTS: A sample medication administration policy is provided in *Model Child Care Health Policies*, from the National Association the Education of Young Children (NAEYC) and the American Academy of

Pediatrics (AAP). The medication record contents and format, as well as policies on handling medications, are provided in the AAP publication *Health in Day Care: A Manual for Health Professionals*. A sample medication administration log is provided in *Healthy Young Children* from the NAEYC. Contact information for the AAP and the NAEYC is located in Appendix BB

For additional information on medications, see STANDARD 3.081 through STANDARD 3.083. See also a sample document for permission for medical condition treatment in Appendix W.

TYPE OF FACILITY: *Center; Large Family Child Care Home; Small Family Child Care Home*

PLAN FOR URGENT MEDICAL CARE OR THREATENING INCIDENTS

STANDARD 8.022
WRITTEN PLAN AND TRAINING FOR HANDLING URGENT MEDICAL CARE OR THREATENING INCIDENTS

The facility shall have a written plan for reporting and managing any incident or unusual occurrence that is threatening to the health, safety, or welfare of the children, staff, or volunteers. The facility shall also include procedures of staff training on this plan.

The following incidents, at a minimum, shall be addressed in the plan:
a) Lost or missing child;
b) Suspected sexual, physical, or emotional abuse or neglect of a child (as mandated by state law);
c) Injuries requiring medical or dental care;
d) Serious illness requiring hospitalization, or the death of a child or caregiver, including deaths that occur outside of child care hours.

The following procedures, at a minimum, shall be addressed in the plan:
a) Provision for a caregiver to accompany a child to the source of urgent care and remain with

the child until the parent or legal guardian assumes responsibility for the child;

b) Provision for a backup caregiver or substitute (see Substitutes, STANDARD 1.037 through STANDARD 1.039) for large and small family child care homes to make this feasible. Child:staff ratios must be maintained at the facility during the emergency;

c) The source of urgent medical and dental care (such as a hospital emergency room, medical or dental clinic, or other constantly staffed facility known to caregivers and acceptable to parents);

d) Assurance that the first aid kits are resupplied following each first aid incident, and that required contents are maintained in a serviceable condition, by a periodic review of the contents;

e) Policy for scheduled reviews of staff members' ability to perform first aid for averting the need for emergency medical services.

RATIONALE: Emergency situations are not conducive to calm and composed thinking. Drafting a written plan provides the opportunity to prepare and to prevent poor judgements made under the stress of an emergency.

An organized, comprehensive approach to injury prevention and control is necessary to ensure that a safe environment is provided to children in child care. Such an approach requires written plans, policies, procedures, and record-keeping so that there is consistency over time and across staff and an understanding between parents and caregivers about concerns for, and attention to, the safety of children.

Routine restocking of first aid kits is necessary to ensure supplies are available at the time of an emergency.

Management within the first hour or so following a dental injury may save a tooth.

COMMENTS: Parents may also have on file their preferred dentists in case of emergency. Parents should be notified, if at all possible, before dental services are rendered, but emergency care should not be delayed because the child's own dentist is not immediately available.

TYPE OF FACILITY: *Center; Large Family Child Care Home; Small Family Child Care Home*

STANDARD 8.023
REVIEW OF WRITTEN PLAN FOR URGENT CARE

The facility's written plan for urgent medical care and threatening incidents shall be reviewed with each employee upon employment and yearly thereafter in the facility to ensure that policies and procedures are understood and followed in the event of such an occurrence.

RATIONALE: Emergency situations are not conducive to calm and composed thinking. Drafting a written plan and reviewing it in preservice meetings with new employees and annually thereafter, provides the opportunity to prepare and to prevent poor judgements made under the stress of an emergency.

An organized, comprehensive approach to injury prevention and control is necessary to ensure that a safe environment is provided to children in child care. Such an approach requires written plans, policies, procedures, and record-keeping so that there is consistency over time and across staff and an understanding between parents and caregivers about concerns for, and attention to, the safety of children.

For additional information on emergency plans, see also Evacuation Plan, Drills, and Closings, STANDARD 8.024 through STANDARD 8.027; and Emergency Procedures, STANDARD 3.048 through STANDARD 3.052. See Appendix Y, for a sample *Incident Report Form.*

TYPE OF FACILITY: *Center; Large Family Child Care Home; Small Family Child Care Home*

EVACUATION PLAN, DRILLS, AND CLOSINGS

STANDARD 8.024
WRITTEN EVACUATION PLAN

The facility shall have a written plan for reporting and evacuating in case of fire, flood, tornado, earthquake, hurricane, blizzard, power failure, bomb threat, or other disaster that could create structural damages to the facility or pose health and safety hazards to the children and staff. The facility shall also include procedures for staff training on this emergency plan.

RATIONALE: Emergency situations are not conducive to calm and composed thinking. Drafting a written plan provides the opportunity to prepare and to prevent poor judgments made under the stress of an emergency. An organized, comprehensive approach to injury prevention and control is necessary to ensure that a safe environment is provided children in child care. Such an approach requires written plans, policies, procedures, rehearsals, and record-keeping so that there is consistency over time and across staff and an understanding between parents and caregivers about concerns for, and attention to, the safety of the children and staff.

COMMENTS: Diagrammed evacuation procedures are easiest to follow in an emergency. Floor plan layouts that show two alternate exit routes are best. Plans should be clear enough that a visitor to the facility could easily follow the instructions. A sample emergency evacuation plan is provided in *Healthy Young Children* from the National Association for the Education of Young Children (NAEYC). Contact information for the NAEYC is located in Appendix BB. See Appendix Y, for a sample *Incident Report Form*.

TYPE OF FACILITY: *Center; Large Family Child Care Home; Small Family Child Care Home*

STANDARD 8.025
IMPLEMENTING EVACUATION DRILLS

Evacuation drills for natural disasters shall be practiced in areas where they occur:
a) Tornadoes, on a monthly basis in tornado season;
b) Floods, before the flood season;
c) Earthquakes, every 6 months;
d) Hurricanes, annually.

RATIONALE: Regular evacuation drills constitute an important safety practice in areas where these natural disasters occur.

TYPE OF FACILITY: *Center; Large Family Child Care Home; Small Family Child Care Home*

STANDARD 8.026
USE OF DAILY ROSTER DURING DRILLS

The center director or his/her designee shall use a daily class roster in checking the evacuation and return to a safe space for ongoing care of all children and staff members in attendance during an evacuation drill. Small and large family home child caregivers shall count to be sure that all children are safely evacuated and returned to a safe space for ongoing care during an evacuation drill.

RATIONALE: Use of a roster ensures that all children are accounted for. Evacuation of the usual child care facility is only the first step. Children and staff must have a safe and appropriately supplied place of refuge where children can receive care until parents can arrive to provide care for their children. Parents should be informed in advance of the location of this alternate site so that in an emergency, they can go directly there instead of needing to search for their children during a crisis.

TYPE OF FACILITY: *Center; Large Family Child Care Home; Small Family Child Care Home*

STANDARD 8.027
APPROVAL AND IMPLEMENTATION OF FIRE EVACUATION PROCEDURE

A fire evacuation procedure shall be approved by a fire inspector for centers and by a local fire department representative for large and small family child care homes during an annual on-site visit when an evacuation drill is observed and the facility is inspected for fire safety hazards. The procedure shall be practiced at least monthly from all exit locations at varied times of the day and during varied activities, including nap time.

RATIONALE: The extensive turnover of both staff and children, in addition to the changing developmental ability of children to participate in evacuation procedures in child care, necessitates frequent practice of the evacuation drill. Practicing fire evacuation procedures on a monthly basis helps make these procedures routine for everyone.

Fires are responsible for the great majority of burn deaths (25). The routine practice of emergency evacuation plans fosters calm, competent use of the plans in an emergency.

COMMENTS: Fire prevention programs for planning exit routes in the home are readily available. One such program is called "EDITH" ("Exit Drill In The Home"), which applies to one's own family. This, or a similar program, is available from some local fire departments.

The facility should time the procedure and aim to evacuate all persons in a specific number of minutes recommended by the local fire department for that facility. See STANDARD 8.069, for information on evacuation drill records. See also Posting Documents, STANDARD 8.077.

TYPE OF FACILITY: *Center; Large Family Child Care Home; Small Family Child Care Home*

AUTHORIZED CAREGIVERS

STANDARD 8.028
AUTHORIZED PERSONS TO PICK UP CHILD

Names, addresses, and telephone numbers of persons authorized to take a child under care out of the facility shall be maintained. The facility shall establish a mechanism for identifying a person for whom the parents have given the facility prior written authorization to pick up their child. Also, policies shall address how the facility will handle the situation if a parent arrives who is intoxicated or otherwise incapable of bringing the child home safely, or if a non-custodial parent attempts to claim the child without the consent of the custodial parent.

RATIONALE: Caregivers must not be unwitting accomplices in schemes to gain custody of children by accepting a telephone authorization provided falsely by a person claiming to be the child's custodial parent or claiming to be authorized by the parent to pick up the child.

COMMENTS: When a parent wants to authorize additional persons to pick up their child, documentation of this request should be kept in the child's file.

The facility can use photo identification, photographs supplied by the parents or taken with a camera by the facility, as a mechanism for verifying the identification of a new person to whom the parents have given written authorization to pick up their child.

Child care providers should not attempt to handle on their own an unstable (for example, intoxicated) parent who wants to be admitted but whose behavior poses a risk to the children. Child care providers should consult local police or the local child protection agency about their recommendations for how staff can obtain support from law enforcement authorities to avoid incurring increased liability by releasing a child into an unsafe situation or by improperly refusing to release a child.

TYPE OF FACILITY: *Center; Large Family Child Care Home; Small Family Child Care Home*

STANDARD 8.029
POLICY ON ACTIONS TO BE FOLLOWED WHEN NO AUTHORIZED PERSON ARRIVES TO PICK UP A CHILD

Child care facilities shall have a written policy identifying actions to be taken when no authorized person arrives to pick up a child. The plan shall be developed in consultation with the child care health consultant and child protective services.

In the event of emergency situations arising that may make it impossible for a parent to pick up a child as scheduled or to notify the authorized contact to do so, the facility shall attempt to reach each authorized contact, as listed in the facility's records. If these efforts fail, the facility shall immediately implement the written policy on actions to be followed when no authorized person arrives to pick up a child.

RATIONALE: A natural disaster or tragic event such as a car crash or terrorist attack may lead to the parent being hurt or delayed due to transportation problems related to the event.

TYPE OF FACILITY: *Center; Large Family Child Care Home; Small Family Child Care Home*

STANDARD 8.030
DOCUMENTATION OF DROP OFF AND PICK UP OF CHILD

Caregiving adults (parents and staff) who bring the child to or remove the child from the facility shall sign a roster with the names of the children noting the time of arrival and departure, and use an established mechanism to ensure that the caregiver accepting or relinquishing the care of the child is aware that the child is being dropped off or picked up.

RATIONALE: The keeping of accurate records of admission and release is of utmost importance to the caregiver in relation to establishing who is in the care of the facility at any one time. Accurate record keeping also aids in tracking the amount (and date) of service for reimbursement and for allows for documentation in the event of legal action involving the facility.

COMMENTS: Time clocks and cards can serve as verification, but they should be signed by the adult who drops off and picks up the child each day. Some notification system must be used to alert the caregiver whenever the responsibility for the care of the child is being transferred to or from the caregiver to another person.

TYPE OF FACILITY: *Center; Large Family Child Care Home*

TRANSPORTATION AND FIELD TRIPS

STANDARD 8.031
TRANSPORTATION POLICY FOR CENTERS

Written policies shall address the safe transport of children by vehicle to or from the facility, including on field trips, home pick-ups and deliveries, and special outings. The transportation policy shall include:
a) Licensing of vehicles and drivers
b) Operation and maintenance of vehicles. See Vehicles, STANDARD 5.235 through STANDARD 5.240;

c) Driver selection, training, and supervision. See Qualifications of Drivers, STANDARD 2.030;
d) Child:staff ratio during transport. See STANDARD 1.004;
e) Permitted and prohibited activities during transport;
f) Backup arrangements for emergencies;
g) Seat belt and car seat use. STANDARD 2.033;
h) Drop-off and pick-up plans. See STANDARD 2.032.

RATIONALE: Motor vehicle crashes are the leading cause of death in the United States (26). Therefore, it is necessary for the safety of children to require that the caregiver comply with requirements governing the transportation of children in care, in the absence of the parent.

COMMENTS: Maintenance should include an inspection checklist for every trip. Vehicle maintenance service should be performed according to the manufacturer's recommendations or at least every 3 months.

TYPE OF FACILITY: *Center*

STANDARD 8.032
TRANSPORTATION POLICY FOR HOMES

Written policies shall address the safe transport of children by vehicle to and from the small or large family child care home for any reason, including field trips or special outings. The following shall be provided for:
a) Child:staff ratio during transport;
b) Backup arrangements for emergencies;
c) Seat belt and car seat use;
d) Licensing of vehicles and drivers;
e) Maintenance of the vehicles;
f) Safe use of air bags.

RATIONALE: Motor vehicle crashes are the leading cause of death in the United States (26). Therefore, it is necessary for the safety of children to require that the caregiver comply with minimum requirements governing the transportation of children in care, in the absence of the parent.

COMMENTS: For information on child:staff ratio during transport, see STANDARD 1.004. For information on seat belt and car seat use, see STANDARD 2.033.

TYPE OF FACILITY: *Large Family Child Care Home; Small Family Child Care Home*

MAINTENANCE AND USE OF THE FACILITY AND EQUIPMENT

STANDARD 8.033
POLICY ON USE AND MAINTENANCE OF PLAY AREAS

Child care facilities shall have policies related to:
a) Safety, purpose, and use of indoor and outdoor equipment for gross motor play;
b) Supervision of indoor and outdoor play spaces;
c) Staff training (to be addressed as employees receive training for other safety measures);
d) Recommended inspections of the facility and equipment, as follows:
　1) Inventory, once (at the time of purchase). Updated when changes to equipment are made in the playground;
　2) Audits of the active (gross motor) play areas (indoors and outdoors) by an individual with specialized training in playground inspection, once a year;
　3) Inspections, once a month;
　4) Whenever injuries occur.

For centers, the policies shall be written.

RATIONALE: Properly laid out play spaces, properly designed and maintained equipment, installation of energy-absorbing surfaces, and adequate supervision of the play space by caregivers/parents help to reduce both the potential and the severity of injury (27). Written policies and procedures are essential for education of staff and may be useful in situations where liability is an issue. The technical issues associated with the selection, maintenance, and use of playground equipment and surfacing are so complex that specialized training is required to conduct annual inspections. Active play areas are associated with the most frequent and the most severe injuries in child care (19).

COMMENTS: The increasing number of children in out-of-home care, as well as an increasing awareness and understanding of issues in child safety, combine to highlight the importance of developing and maintaining safe play spaces for children in child care settings. Parents expect that their child will be adequately supervised and will not be exposed to hazardous play environments, yet will have the opportunity for free, creative play.

To obtain information on identifying a Certified Playground Safety Inspector (CPSI) to inspect a playground, contact the National Parks and Recreation Association (NPRA) on official company letterhead requesting a list of CPSI's in the appropriate state. They will fax a list within 2 weeks. Contact information for NPRA is located in Appendix BB.

For additional information, see Playground and Equipment Records, STANDARD 8.071 and STANDARD 8.072.

TYPE OF FACILITY: *Center; Large Family Child Care Home; Small Family Child Care Home*

PLAN FOR SANITATION AND HYGIENE

STANDARD 8.034
SANITATION POLICIES AND PROCEDURES

The child care facility shall have written sanitation policies and procedures for the following items:
a) Maintaining equipment used for handwashing, toilet use, and toilet learning/training in a sanitary condition, as specified in Toilet, Diapering, and Bath Areas, STANDARD 5.116 through STANDARD 5.135; Toileting and Diapering, STANDARD 3.012 through STANDARD 3.019; and Sanitation, Disinfection, and Maintenance of Toilet Learning/Training Equipment, Toilets, and Bathrooms, STANDARD 3.029 through STANDARD 3.033;
b) Maintaining diaper changing areas and equipment in a sanitized condition, as specified in Diaper Changing Areas, STANDARD 5.132;
c) Maintaining toys in a sanitized condition in facilities, as specified in Selection, Sanitation, Disinfection, and Maintenance of Toys and

Objects, STANDARD 3.036 through STANDARD 3.038;

d) Managing pets or other animals in a safe and sanitary manner, as specified in Animals, STANDARD 3.042 through STANDARD 3.044;

e) Proper handwashing procedures consistent with the method described in STANDARD 3.021 and STANDARD 3.022. The facility shall display handwashing instruction signs conspicuously;

f) Personal hygiene of caregivers and children as specified in Handwashing, STANDARD 3.020 through STANDARD 3.023;

g) Practicing environmental sanitation policies and procedures, as specified in Interior Maintenance, STANDARD 5.229 through STANDARD 5.234;

h) Maintaining sanitation for food preparation and food service as specified in Kitchen Maintenance, STANDARD 4.055; Food Brought From Home, STANDARD 4.061 through STANDARD 4.065; Kitchen and Equipment, STANDARD 4.042 through STANDARD 4.049; Food Safety, STANDARD 4.050 through STANDARD 4.060; and Maintenance, STANDARD 4.061 through STANDARD 4.065.

RATIONALE: Many communicable diseases can be prevented through appropriate hygiene and sanitation practices. Bacterial cultures of environmental surfaces in facilities, which are used to gauge the adequacy of sanitation and hygiene practices, have demonstrated evidence of fecal contamination. Contamination of hands, toys, and other equipment in the room has appeared to play a role in the transmission of diseases in child care settings (28). Regular and thorough cleaning of toys, equipment, and rooms helps to prevent transmission of illness (29).

Animals, including pets, can be a source of illness for people, and people may be a source of illness for animals (29).

The steps involved in effective handwashing (to reduce the amount of bacterial contamination) are easily forgotten. Posted signs provide frequent reminders to staff and orientation for new staff. Education of caregivers regarding handwashing, cleaning, and other sanitation procedures can reduce the occurrence of illness in the group of children with whom they work (30).

Illnesses may be spread by way of:
a) Human waste (such as urine and feces);
b) Body fluids (such as saliva, nasal discharge, eye discharge, open skin sores, and blood);
c) Direct skin-to-skin contact;
d) Touching a contaminated object;
e) The air, in droplets that result from sneezes and coughs.

Since many infected people carry communicable diseases without symptoms, and many are contagious before they experience a symptom, caregivers need to protect themselves and the children they serve by carrying out, on a routine basis, universal precautions and sanitation procedures that approach every potential illness-spreading condition in the same way.

Handling food in a safe and careful manner prevents the growth of bacteria and fungi. Outbreaks of foodborne illness have occurred in many settings, including child care facilities.

COMMENTS: *The ABC's of Safe and Healthy Child Care* developed by the Centers for Disease Control (CDC) and distributed by the National Technical Information Service (NTIS) is a handbook that provides guidance for maintaining safe and healthy child care practices in all settings. Contact information for the NTIS is located in Appendix BB.

Making Food Healthy and Safe for Children from the National Center for Education in Maternal and Child Health (NCEMCH) is a guide for meeting nutrition standards in child care settings. Contact information for the NCEMCH is located in Appendix BB.

TYPE OF FACILITY: *Center; Large Family Child Care Home; Small Family Child Care Home*

PLANS AND POLICIES FOR FOOD HANDLING, FEEDING, AND NUTRITION

STANDARD 8.035
FOOD AND NUTRITION SERVICE POLICIES AND PLANS

The facility shall have a food handling, feeding, and nutrition plan under the direction of the

administration that addresses the following items and delegates responsibility for each:
a) Kitchen layout;
b) Food procurement, preparation, and service;
c) Staffing;
d) Nutrition education.

A Child Care Nutrition Specialist and a food service expert shall provide input for and facilitate the development and implementation of a written nutrition plan for the child care center or programs.

RATIONALE: Having a plan that clearly delegates responsibility and that encompasses the pertinent nutrition elements will promote the optimal health of children and staff in child care settings.

COMMENTS: For more information on Child Care Nutrition Specialists, see STANDARD 4.026 and STANDARD 4.027 and Appendix C. For information on nutrition education, see STANDARD 4.069 and STANDARD 4.070.

TYPE OF FACILITY: *Center; Large Family Child Care Home; Small Family Child Care Home*

STANDARD 8.036
INFANT FEEDING POLICIES

Policies about infant feeding shall be developed with the input and approval of the child's health care provider and the Child Care Nutrition Specialist and shall include the following:
a) Storage and handling of expressed human milk;
b) Determination of the kind and amount of commercially prepared formula to be prepared for infants as appropriate;
c) Preparation, storage, and handling of formula;
d) Proper handwashing of the caregiver;
e) Use and proper disinfection of feeding chairs and of mechanical food preparation and feeding devices, including blenders, feeding bottles, and food warmers;
f) Whether formula or baby food shall be provided from home, and if so, how much food preparation and use of feeding devices, including blenders, feeding bottles, and food warmers, shall be the responsibility of the caregiver;
g) A prohibition against bottle propping or prolonged feeding;

h) Caregivers shall hold infants during bottle-feeding;
i) Specification of the number of children who can be fed by one adult at one time;
j) Handling of food intolerance or allergies (such as to cow's milk, peanuts, orange juice, eggs, or wheat);
k) Responding to infants' need for food in a flexible fashion to allow demand feedings in a manner that is consistent with the developmental abilities of the child.

Written policies for each infant about infant feeding shall be developed with each individual infant's parents.

RATIONALE: Growth and development during infancy require that nourishing, wholesome, and developmentally appropriate food be provided, using safe approaches to feeding. Because individual needs must be accommodated and improper practices can have dire consequences for the child's health and safety, the policies for infant feeding should be developed with professional nutritionists and the child's parents.

COMMENTS: For information on nutrition requirements for infants, see STANDARD 4.011 through STANDARD 4.021. For information on meal service, seating, and supervision, see STANDARD 4.028 through STANDARD 4.039. For information on food allergies, see STANDARD 4.007, STANDARD 4.009, and STANDARD 4.010.

TYPE OF FACILITY: *Center; Large Family Child Care Home; Small Family Child Care Home*

EVENING AND NIGHT CARE PLAN

STANDARD 8.037
PLANS FOR EVENING AND NIGHTTIME CARE

Facilities that provide evening and nighttime care shall have plans for such care that include the supervision of sleeping children as specified in Supervision, STANDARD 2.028; the management and maintenance of sleep equipment as specified in Sleeping, STANDARD 5.142 through STANDARD 5.148; and Selection, Sanitation, Disinfection, and

Maintenance of Bedding, as specified in
STANDARD 3.039 and
STANDARD 3.040.

Centers shall have written plans for evening and
nighttime care, including emergency plans.

RATIONALE: Evening and nighttime child care routines are significantly different from those required for
daytime and should be addressed in a comprehensive
and predetermined manner.

TYPE OF FACILITY: *Center; Large Family Child Care
Home; Small Family Child Care Home*

POLICY ON SMOKING, TOBACCO USE, PROHIBITED SUBSTANCES, AND FIREARMS

STANDARD 8.038
POLICIES PROHIBITING SMOKING, TOBACCO, ALCOHOL, ILLEGAL DRUGS, AND TOXIC SUBSTANCES

Facilities shall have written policies specifying that
smoking, use of chewing tobacco, use of alcohol,
use or possession of illegal drugs, over-use or
inappropriate use of prescribed drugs, or unauthorized potentially toxic substances are prohibited in
the facility at all times (including outdoor play
areas) and during all times when caregivers are
responsible for the supervision of children, including times when children are transported and during field trips. The facility shall provide information
to employees about available drug, alcohol, and
tobacco counseling and rehabilitation and
employee assistance programs.

RATIONALE: The age, defenselessness, and lack of
discretion of the child under care make this prohibition an absolute requirement. The hazards of secondhand smoke warrant the prohibition of smoking in
proximity of child care areas at any time. Residual
toxins from smoking at times when the children are

not using the space can trigger asthma and allergies
when the children do use the space.

Smoking in outdoor areas when children are not
present is acceptable. The use of alcoholic beverages
in family homes while children are not in care is also
permissible.

COMMENTS: The policies related to smoking and
use of prohibited substances should be discussed via
handouts or pamphlets that are given to parents,
especially those who have children in small family child
care homes or school-age child care facilities, and
staff, to inform them of the dangers of these prohibited substances and of services to prevent their use.
For family child care home providers who smoke,
provisions will need to be made to assure that children are not left unsupervised while the caregiver
smokes. In addition, it is strongly urged that, whenever possible, the caregivers be non-tobacco users
because of the role model effect of tobacco users on
children.

TYPE OF FACILITY: *Center; Large Family Child Care
Home; Small Family Child Care Home*

STANDARD 8.039
POLICY PROHIBITING FIREARMS

Firearms shall be prohibited in centers. If firearms
are present in large or small family homes, they
shall have child protective devices and be
unloaded. They shall be kept under lock and key
and be inaccessible to children. Ammunition shall
be stored in locked storage, separate from firearms and inaccessible to children. Parents shall be
notified that firearms are on the premises.

RATIONALE: Children have a natural curiosity about
firearms and have often seen their use glamorized on
television. The potential for a tragic accident is great.

TYPE OF FACILITY: *Center; Large Family Child Care
Home; Small Family Child Care Home*

REVIEW AND REVISION OF POLICIES, PLANS, AND PROCEDURES

STANDARD 8.040
AVAILABILITY OF POLICIES, PLANS, PROCEDURES

At least annually or when changes are made, the facility shall make policies, plans, and procedures available to all persons affected (including parents and staff). When a child enters a facility, parents shall sign a statement that they have read and/or understand the content of the policies.

Parents who are not able to read shall have the policies presented orally to them. Parents who are not able to understand the policies because of a language barrier shall have the policies presented to them in a language with which they are familiar.

RATIONALE: State of the art information changes. A yearly review encourages child care administrators to keep information and policies current. Current information on health and safety practices that is shared and developed cooperatively among caregivers and parents invites more participation and compliance with health and safety practices.

COMMENTS: This standard assumes that all disciplines that support and inform child care services such as health, public safety, emergency preparedness, and regulatory agencies have systems for disseminating current and accurate information that affects the health of all people in child care settings.

TYPE OF FACILITY: *Center; Large Family Child Care Home*

STANDARD 8.041
HEALTH CONSULTANT'S REVIEW OF HEALTH POLICIES

At least annually or when changes are made in the health policies, the facility shall obtain a review of the policies from a health consultant.

RATIONALE: Changes in health information may require changes in the health policies of a child care

facility. These changes are best known to health professionals who stay in touch with sources of updated information and can suggest how the new information applies to the operation of the child care program. For example, when the information on the importance of back-positioning for putting infants down to sleep became available, it needed to be added to child care policies. Frequent changes in recommended immunization schedules offer another example of the need for review and modification of health policies.

COMMENTS: For information on Health Consultants, see STANDARD 1.040 through STANDARD 1.044.

TYPE OF FACILITY: *Center*

8.3 PROGRAM OF ACTIVITIES

STANDARD 8.042
PLAN FOR PROGRAM ACTIVITIES

The facility shall have a written comprehensive and coordinated planned program of daily activities based on a statement of principles for the facility that sets out the elements from which the daily plan is to be built. The program of activities shall:
a) Address each developmental age group served, that is, infants, toddlers, preschoolers, school-age children, and children with special needs;
b) Cover the elements of developmental activities specified in STANDARD 2.001 through STANDARD 2.028;
c) Maintain the child:staff ratios described in Child:Staff Ratio and Group Size, STANDARD 1.001 through STANDARD 1.005;
d) Provide for incorporation of specific health, development, and safety education activities into the curriculum on a daily basis throughout the year. Topics of health education shall include health promotion and disease prevention strategies, physical, oral/dental, mental, and social health, and nutrition;
e) Offer a parent education plan about child health. Such a plan shall have been reviewed and approved by a licensed health professional, who may also serve as the facility's health consultant (see Health Consultants, STANDARD 1.040 through STANDARD 1.044). This plan shall primarily

involve personal contacts with parents by knowledgeable caregivers. The parent education plan shall include topics identified in Health Education for Parents, STANDARD 2.065 through STANDARD 2.067, and cover the importance of developmentally appropriate activities.

RATIONALE: Those who provide child care and early childhood education must themselves be clear about the components of their program. Child care is a "delivery of service" involving a contractual relationship between provider and consumer. A written plan helps to specify the components of the service and contributes to responsible operations that are conducive to sound child development and safety practices, and to positive consumer relations. The process of preparing plans promotes thinking about programming for children. Plans also allow for monitoring and for accountability. An increasing number of centers and homes are serving children with special needs.

Early childhood specialists and pediatricians agree that cognitive, emotional/social, and physical development are inseparable. The child's health influences all areas of development. Continuity of responsive, affectionate care must be coupled with recognition by the caregiver of the child's developmental phase or stage to provide opportunities for the child to learn and mature through play (31, 32). Young children learn better by experiencing an activity and observing behavior than through didactic training (32). There is a "reciprocal relationship" between learning and play. Play experiences are closely related to learning (33).

Parental behavior can be modified by education (33). Parents should be involved with the facility as much as possible. The concept of parent control and empowerment is key to successful parent education in the child care setting (33). Although research has not shown whether a child's eventual success in education or in society is related to parent education, support and education for parents lead to better parenting abilities (33).

COMMENTS: Examples of parental health education activities include the following topics:
a) Importance of having a primary health care provider (medical home) for each child;
b) Verbal explanation of principles of personal hygiene;
c) Discussions about the nutritional value of snacks;
d) The importance of implementing effective child passenger and other safety practices;
e) The value of exercise.

Examples of child development activities include:
a) Importance of talking and reading to children;
b) Importance of creative play activities;
c) Encouraging children to experience their natural environments.

Parents and staff can experience mutual learning in an open, supportive setting. Suggestions for topics and methods of presentation are widely available. For example, the publication catalogs of the National Association for the Education of Young Children (NAEYC) and of the American Academy of Pediatrics (AAP) contain many materials for child, parent and staff education on child development, the importance of attachment and temperament, and other health issues. A certified health education specialist can also be a source of assistance. The American Association for Health Education (AAHE) and the National Commission for Health Education Credential ling, Inc. (NCHEC) provide information on this speciality. Contact information for the NAEYC, AAP, AAHE, and NCHEC is located in Appendix BB.

TYPE OF FACILITY: *Center; Large Family Child Care Home; Small Family Child Care Home*

STANDARD 8.043
EXCHANGE OF INFORMATION AT TRANSITIONS

Communication to facilitate transitions that occurs at times when children are being dropped off or picked up and other interactions with parents shall be the responsibility of the large or small family home child caregiver or the designated center or school-age child care provider on each shift. These caregivers shall be trained in health and development and shall observe each assigned child's physical condition, behavior, and personality factors on arrival and throughout the time when the child is in care. When several staff shifts are involved, information about the child shall be exchanged between caregivers assigned to each shift.

RATIONALE: Personal contact on a daily basis between the child care staff and parents is essential to ensure the transfer of information required to provide for the child's needs. Information about the child's experiences and health during the interval when an adult other than the parent is in charge should be provided to parents because they may need such information to understand the child's later behavior.

COMMENTS: This designated caregiver could be the health advocate. See Qualifications for Health Advocates, STANDARD 1.021.

TYPE OF FACILITY: *Center; Large Family Child Care Home; Small Family Child Care Home*

8.4 PERSONNEL POLICIES

STANDARD 8.044
WRITTEN PERSONNEL POLICIES

The facility shall have and implement written personnel policies. All written policies shall be reviewed and signed by the employee affected by them upon hiring and annually thereafter. Small family child care home providers shall develop policies for themselves, which are reviewed and revised annually. These policies shall address the following items:

a) A wage scale with merit increases;
b) Scheduled increases of small family child care home fees;
c) Sick leave;
d) Vacation leave;
e) Family, parental, medical leave;
f) Personal leave;
g) Educational benefits;
h) Health insurance and coverage for occupational health services;
i) Social security or other retirement plan;
j) Holidays;
k) Workers' compensation or a disability plan as required by the number of staff;
l) Minimally, breaks totaling 30 minutes within an 8-hour period of work, or as required by state labor laws;
m) Maternity benefits;
n) Overtime/compensatory time policy;
o) Grievance procedures;
p) Probation period;
q) Grounds for termination;
r) Training of new caregivers and substitute staff. See Training, STANDARD 1.023 through

STANDARD 1.034; and Substitutes, STANDARD 1.037 through STANDARD 1.039;
s) Personal/bereavement leave;
t) Disciplinary action;
u) Periodic review of performance. See Performance Evaluation, STANDARD 1.051 through STANDARD 1.057;
v) Exclusion policies pertaining to staff illness. See Staff Exclusion, STANDARD 3.069;
w) Staff health appraisal. See STANDARD 1.045 and STANDARD 1.046;
x) Professional development leave.

Centers and large family child care homes shall have written policies that address all of these items. Small family child care homes shall have written policies that address items f, j, l, m, o, p, s, v.

RATIONALE: Written personnel policies provide a means of staff orientation and evaluation essential to the operation of any organization. Caregivers who are responsible for compliance with policies must have reviewed them.

The quality and continuity of the caregiving workforce is the main determiner of the quality of care. Nurturing the nurturers is essential to prevent burnout and promote retention. Fair labor practices should apply to child care as well as other work settings. Child care workers should be considered as worthy of benefits as workers in other career areas.

Medical coverage should include the cost of the health appraisals and immunizations required of child care workers, and care for the increased incidence of communicable disease and stress-related conditions in this work setting.

Sick leave is important to minimize the spread of communicable diseases and maintain the health of staff members. Sick leave may promote recovery from illness and thereby decreases the further spread or recurrence of illness.

Other benefits contribute to higher morale and less staff turnover, thus promoting quality child care. Lack of benefits is a major reason reported for high turnover of child care staff (34).

The potential for acquiring injuries and infections when caring for young children is a health and safety risk for child care workers. Information abounds about the incidence of infectious disease for children in child care settings. Staff members come into close and frequent contact with children and their excretions and secretions and are vulnerable to these illnesses as well, as children are reservoirs for many infectious agents. In addition, many child care workers are women who are planning a pregnancy or who are pregnant, and they may be vulnerable to the potentially serious effects of infection on the outcome of pregnancy.

COMMENTS: Staff benefits may be appropriately addressed in center personnel policies and in state and federal labor standards. Not all the material in such policies is necessarily appropriate for state child care licensing requirements.

Although the business plan of the caregiver will determine the scope of benefits the caregiver can offer, this standard outlines the types of benefits that must be considered to control staff turnover and reduce stress, which decreases caregiver performance. Some benefits may be beyond the reach of a small family child care home provider's capability.

The Center for the Child Care Workforce (CCW) has developed model work standards for both center-based staff and family child care home providers with specific recommendations for these elements of personnel policies. Model Work Standards serve as a tool to help programs assess the quality of the work environment and set goals to make improvements. For more information, contact the CCW. Contact information is located in Appendix BB.

A policy of encouraging sick leave, even without pay, or of permitting a flexible schedule will allow the caregiver to take time off when needed for illness. An acknowledgment that the facility does not provide paid leave but does give time off will begin to address workers' rights to these benefits and improve quality of care. There may be other nontraditional ways to achieve these benefits.

The subsidy costs of staff benefits will need to be addressed for child care to be affordable to parents.

Staff benefits may be appropriately addressed in center personnel policies and in state and federal labor standards. Not all the material that has to be addressed in these policies is appropriate for state child care licensing requirements. Having facilities

acknowledge which benefits they do provide will help to enhance the general awareness of staff benefits among child care workers and other concerned parties. Currently, this standard is difficult for many facilities to achieve, but new federal programs and shared access to small business benefit packages will help. Many options are available for providing leave benefits and education reimbursements, ranging from partial to full employer contribution, based on time employed with the facility.

Providers should be encouraged to have health insurance. Health benefits can include full coverage, partial coverage (at least 75% employer paid), or merely access to group rates. Some local or state child care associations offer reduced group rates for health insurance for child care facilities and individual providers.

For more information, see *Creating Better Child Care Jobs: Model Work Standards for Teaching Staff of Center-Based Child Care* and *Creating Better Family Child Care Jobs: Model Work Standards* from the Center for the Child Care Workforce (CCW). Contact information for the CCW is located in Appendix BB.

TYPE OF FACILITY: *Centers; Large Family Child Care Home; Small Family Child Care Home*

8.5 WRITTEN STATEMENT OF SERVICES

STANDARD 8.045
WRITTEN STATEMENT OF SERVICES

The facility shall provide parents with a written statement of services that contains the items specified in Management and Health Policy and Statement of Services, STANDARD 8.004 through STANDARD 8.041. Parents shall sign this statement of services.

RATIONALE: Parents will need a written statement of services to refer to from time to time. Having the parent sign the statement of services helps to emphasize the contractual relationship between the parent and the child care facility and prevent later, stressful

disputes about whether the parent was informed about the content of the statement.

TYPE OF FACILITY: *Center; Large Family Child Care Home; Small Family Child Care Home*

8.6 SPECIAL NEEDS PLAN

For information on planning for the care of children with special needs who have an IFSP/IEP, see Chapter 7, Children Receiving Services Under IDEA.

8.7 RECORDS

CHILD RECORDS

STANDARD 8.046
CONTENTS OF CHILD RECORDS

The facility shall maintain a file for each child in one central location within the facility. This file shall be kept in a confidential manner (see Confidentiality and Access to Records, STANDARD 8.053 through STANDARD 8.057) but shall be immediately available to the child's caregivers (who shall have parental consent for access to records), parents or legal guardian, and the licensing authority upon request.

The file for each child shall include the following:
a) Pre-admission enrollment information;
b) Health report and immunization record, completed and signed by the child's health care provider, preferably prior to enrollment or no later than 6 weeks after admission. This record shall document the most recent assessment based on the standard age-related schedule of the American Academy of Pediatrics (AAP);
c) Admission agreement signed by the parent at enrollment;
d) Health history, completed by the parent at admission, preferably with staff involvement;
e) Medication record, maintained on an ongoing basis by designated staff.

RATIONALE: The health and safety of individual children requires that information regarding each child in care be kept and made available on a need-to-know basis. Prior informed, written consent of the parent/guardian is required for the release of records/information (verbal and written) to other service providers, including process for secondary release of records. Consent forms should be in the native language of the parents, whenever possible, and communicated to them in their normal mode of communication. Foreign language interpreters should be used whenever possible to inform parents about their confidentiality rights.

COMMENTS: See STANDARD 8.053 for information on confidentiality and access to records.

TYPE OF FACILITY: *Center; Large Family Child Care Home; Small Family Child Care Home*

STANDARD 8.047
PRE-ADMISSION ENROLLMENT
INFORMATION FOR EACH CHILD

The file for each child shall include the following pre-admission enrollment information:
a) The child's name, address, sex, and date of birth;
b) The full names of the child's parents or legal guardians, and their home and work addresses and telephone numbers. Telephone contact numbers shall be confirmed by a call placed to the contact number during the facility 's hours of operation. Names, addresses, and telephone numbers shall be updated at least quarterly;
c) The names, addresses, and telephone numbers of at least two additional persons to be notified in the event that the parents or legal guardians cannot be located. Telephone information shall be confirmed and updated as specified in item b above;
d) The names and telephone numbers of the child's primary sources of medical care, emergency medical care, and dental care;
e) The child's health payment resource;
f) Written instructions of the parent, legal guardian, and the child's health care provider for any special dietary needs or special needs due to a health condition; or any other special instructions from the parent;
g) Scheduled days and hours of attendance;

h) In the event that one parent is the sole legal guardian of the child, legal documentation evidencing his/her authority;

i) Enrollment date, reason for entry in child care, and fee arrangements;

j) Signed permission to act on parent's behalf for emergency treatment and for use of syrup of ipecac, if medically indicated. See STANDARD 3.050;

k) Authorization to release child to anyone other than the custodial parent. See Authorized Caregivers, STANDARD 8.028 through STANDARD 8.030.

The emergency information in items a through e above shall be obtained in duplicate with original parent/legal guardian signatures on both copies. One copy shall be in the child's confidential record and one copy shall be easily accessible at all times. This information shall be updated quarterly and as necessary. A copy of the emergency information must accompany the child to all offsite excursions.

RATIONALE: These records and reports are necessary to protect the health and safety of children in care. An organized, comprehensive approach to injury prevention and control is necessary to ensure that a safe environment is provided for children in child care. Such an approach requires written plans, policies, procedures, and record-keeping so that there is consistency over time and across staff and an understanding between parents and caregivers about concerns for, and attention to, the safety of children.

Emergency information is the key to obtaining needed care in emergency situations (35). Caregivers must have written parental permission to allow them access to information they and Emergency Medical Services personnel may need to care for the child in an emergency (35). Contact information must be verified for accuracy. See Appendix X, for the *Emergency Information Form for Children with Special Needs*, developed by the American Academy of Pediatrics (AAP), the American College of Emergency Physicians (ACEP) and the Emergency Medical Services for Children National Resource Center (EMSC). Contact information for the AAP, ACEP and EMSC is located in Appendix BB.

Health payment resource information is usually required before any non-life-threatening emergency care is provided.

COMMENTS: Duplicate records are easily made using multiple-copy forms, carbon paper, or photocopying.

TYPE OF FACILITY: *Center; Large Family Child Care Home; Small Family Child Care Home*

STANDARD 8.048
CONTENTS OF CHILD'S HEALTH REPORT

The file for each child shall include a health report of an age-appropriate health assessment completed and signed by the child's health care provider. Preferably, this report shall be submitted prior to enrollment, but it shall be submitted no later than 6 weeks after admission. The health report shall include the following medical and developmental information:

a) Records of the child's immunizations;

b) A description of any disability, sensory impairment, developmental variation, seizure disorder, or emotional or behavioral disturbance that may affect adaptation to child care (including previous surgery, serious illness, history of prematurity, if relevant);

c) An assessment of the child's growth based on the percentile for height, weight, and, if the child is younger than 24 months, head circumference;

d) A description of health problems or findings from an examination or screening that needs follow-up;

e) Results of screenings—vision, hearing, dental, nutrition, developmental, tuberculosis, hematocrit or hemoglobin, urine, lead, blood pressure and so forth;

f) Dates of significant communicable diseases (such as chickenpox);

g) Prescribed medication(s), including information on recognizing, documenting, reporting, and responding to potential side effects;

h) A description of current acute or chronic health problems and a special care plan that defines routine and emergency management that might be required by the child while in child care. The care plan for the child with acute or chronic health problems shall include specific instructions for caregiver observations, program activities or services that differ from those required by typically developing children. Such instructions shall include specific teaching and return demonstration of the ability of caregivers to provide medications, procedures, or implement modifications required by children with asthma, severe allergic reactions, diabetes, medically-indicated special feedings, seizures, hearing impairments, vision problems or any other condition that requires accommodation in child care;

i) A description of serious injuries sustained by the child in the past that required medical attention or hospitalization;

j) Other special instructions for the caregiver.

The health report shall include space for additional comments about the management of health problems and for additional health-related data offered by the health care provider or required from the facility.

The health report shall be updated at each age-appropriate health assessment by supplemental notes dated and signed by the child's health provider on a copy of the previous health report or by submission of a new report and whenever the child's health status changes.

RATIONALE: The requirement of a health report for each child reflecting completion of health assessments and immunizations is a valid way to ensure timely preventive care for children who might not otherwise receive it and can be used in decision-making at the time of admission and during ongoing care (35). This requirement encourages families to have a primary health care provider (medical home) for each child where timely and periodic well-child evaluations are done. The objective of timely and periodic evaluations is to permit detection and counseling for improved oral, physical, mental, and emotional/social health (14). The reports of such evaluations provide a conduit for communication of information that helps the health professional and the child care provider determine appropriate services for the child. When the parent carries the request for the report to the health professional, concerns of the child care provider can be delivered by the parent to the child's health professional and consent for communication is thereby given. The parent can give written consent for direct communication between the health care provider and the caregiver so that the forms can be faxed or mailed.

Quality child care requires information about the child's health status and need for accommodations in child care (35).

COMMENTS: The purpose of a health report is to:

a) Give information about a child's health history, special needs, and current health status to allow the caregiver to provide a safe setting and healthful experience for each child;

b) Promote individual and collective health by fostering compliance with approved standards for health care assessments and immunizations;

c) Document compliance with licensing standards;

d) Serve as a means to ensure early detection of health problems and a guide to steps for remediation;

e) Serve as a means to facilitate and encourage communication and learning about the child's needs among caregivers, health care providers, and parents.

If the child's medical record is not available at the time the child is enrolled in a program, child care providers can offer a 6-week grace period when the parent can arrange to obtain the medical record, but written permission should be obtained from the child's parent or guardian to contact the child's primary health care provider in case of an emergency. The child care provider should also ask whether or not there are any health problems (such as allergies, asthma, or developmental irregularities) that might affect the child's participation in the program.

The requirement for updated health reports does not mean that the child should have a special examination for entry into child care or at intervals related to duration of participation in child care. The evaluations by the child's health professional should occur according to the national schedule for routine preventive care. The medical reports should confirm that the child has received all the age appropriate services outlined in the guidelines for assessments of the American Academy of Pediatrics (AAP), Bright Futures, or Medicaid's Early Periodic Screening and Diagnostic Treatment (EPSDT) program (14, 37, 41).

The report submitted upon enrollment can document a previous age-appropriate examination if the child is not due for the next check-up visit. Updates of the report should address new immunizations, contagious diseases, new or changed medications, and new or changed special concerns. Busy clinicians appreciate having the parent and child care provider complete as much information on the medical report as possible, so that they know what information the child care provider already has on hand and what information needs to be added. Filling in the child's and child care provider's identifying information, and previously provided immunization dates are evidence to the clinician of an interest in sharing information and the paperwork burden.

Health data should be presented in a form usable by caregivers to identify any special needs for care. Local Early Periodic Screening and Diagnostic Treatment (EPSDT) program contractor, if available, should be called upon to help with liaison and education activities. In some situations, screenings may be performed at the facilities. When clinicians do not fill out forms completely enough to assist the caregiver in understanding the significance of health assessment findings or the unique characteristics of a child, the caregiver should obtain parental consent to contact the child's clinician to explain why the information is needed and to request clarification.

Samples of a health care provider's exam form and special care plans for children with chronic illness are provided in *Model Child Care Health Policies* from the National Association for the Education of Young Children (NAEYC) or the American Academy of Pediatrics (AAP). Contact information for the NAEYC and the AAP is located in Appendix BB.

The AAP recommends vision and hearing screenings at every health supervision visit, with objective vision screening and measurement of visual acuity by 4 years of age, and objective hearing screening (audiometry) by 5 years of age. The AAP recommends that all children have their first dental exam, by an oral health professional, at 3 years of age. A primary health care provider could examine the mouth of a child up to 3 years of age. After 3 years, the child should visit a dentist for examinations at intervals prescribed by the dentist. Children with suspected oral problems should see a dentist immediately, regardless of age or interval. These guidelines are described in "A Guide to Children's Dental Health," a brochure published by the AAP. Bright Futures recommends the first dental exam, by an oral health professional, at 12 months of age. Contact information for the AAP is located in Appendix BB.

See Appendix H, for *Recommendations for Preventive Pediatric Health Care.*

TYPE OF FACILITY: *Center; Large Family Child Care Home; Small Family Child Care Home*

STANDARD 8.049
CONTENTS OF ADMISSION AGREEMENT

The file for each child shall include an admission agreement signed by the parent at enrollment. The agreement shall include the following:
a) Admission agreement or contract stating the rule prohibiting corporal punishment and verbal abuse. See Discipline Policy, STANDARD 8.008 through STANDARD 8.010;
b) Admission agreement or contract stating that all parents may visit the site at any time when their child is there, and that they will be admitted immediately. See STANDARD 2.046;
c) Documentation of written consent signed and dated by the parent or legal guardian for:
   1) Emergency transportation;
   2) All other transportation provided by the facility. See STANDARD 1.004; and Transportation, STANDARD 2.029 through STANDARD 2.038;
   3) Planned or unplanned activities off-premises. Such consent shall give specific information about where, when, and how such activities shall take place, including specific information about walking to and from activities away from the facility;
   4) Telephone authorizations for release of the child. See Authorized Caregivers, STANDARD 8.028 through STANDARD 8.030;
   5) Swimming/wading, if the child will be participating. See STANDARD 1.005, on child:staff ratio; Water Safety, STANDARD 3.045 through STANDARD 3.047; and Swimming, Wading, and Water, STANDARD 5.198 through STANDARD 5.218;
   6) Any health service obtained for the child by the facility on behalf of the parent. Such consent shall be specific for the type of care provided to meet the tests for "informed consent" to cover on-site screenings or other services provided;

7) Release of any information to agencies, schools, or providers of services. See Confidentiality and Access to Records, STANDARD 8.053 through STANDARD 8.057;

8) Authorization to release the child to any-one other than the custodial parent;

9) Emergency treatment;

10) Administration of medications (standing orders and short-term). See Medication Policy, STANDARD 8.021;

k) Statement that parent has received and dis-cussed a copy of the state child abuse report-ing requirements.

RATIONALE: Positive guidance and discipline is more effective than corporal punishment, which may become abusive very easily.

The open-door policy may be the single most impor-tant method of preventing the abuse of children in child care (35). When access is restricted, areas observable by the parent may not reflect the care the children actually receive.

These records and reports are necessary to protect the health and safety of children in care.

These consents are needed by the person delivering the medical care. Advance consent for emergency medical or surgical service is not legally valid, since the nature and extent of injury, proposed medical treatment, risks, and benefits cannot be known until after the injury occurs.

The parent/child care partnership is vital. Participa-tion of parents in decisions concerning children is a primary goal of Head Start (31).

COMMENTS: See also a sample document for permission for medical condition treatment in Appendix W.

TYPE OF FACILITY: *Center; Large Family Child Care Home; Small Family Child Care Home*

STANDARD 8.050
CONTENTS OF CHILD CARE PROGRAM'S HEALTH HISTORY

The file for each child shall include a health history completed by the parent at admission, preferably with staff involvement. This history shall include the following:

a) Identification of the child's pediatric primary care clinician or designated "medical home";

b) Developmental variations, sensory impairment, or disabilities that may need consideration in the child care setting;

c) Description of current physical, social, and lan-guage developmental levels;

d) Current medications. See Medication Policy, STANDARD 8.021; and Medications, STANDARD 3.081 through STANDARD 3.083;

e) Special concerns (such as allergies, chronic ill-ness, pediatric first aid information needs);

f) Specific diet restrictions, if the child is on a special diet;

g) Individual characteristics or personality factors relevant to child care;

h) Special family considerations;

i) Dates of communicable diseases.

RATIONALE: A health history is the basis for meeting the child's needs in health, mental and social areas in the child care setting and should be thoroughly under-stood by the significant child care provider at the time of registration or upon its receipt.

COMMENTS: A sample developmental health history is provided in *Healthy Young Children* from the National Association for the Education of Young Chil-dren (NAEYC). Contact information for the NAEYC is located in Appendix BB.

For a sample *Child Health Assessment*, see Appendix Z.

TYPE OF FACILITY: *Center; Large Family Child Care Home; Small Family Child Care Home*

STANDARD 8.051
CONTENTS OF MEDICATION RECORD

The file for each child shall include a medication record maintained on an ongoing basis by desig-nated staff. The medication record shall include the following:

a) Specific signed parent consent for the care-giver to administer medication;

b) Prescription by a health care provider, if required;

c) Administration log;
d) Checklist information on medication brought to the facility by the parents.

RATIONALE: Caregivers should not administer medication based solely on a parent's request. Before assuming responsibility for administration of medicine, facilities must have written confirmation of a physician or nurse practitioner's orders to include clear, accurate instruction and medical confirmation of the child's need for medication while in the facility.

COMMENTS: The medication record contents and format, as well as policies on handling of medications, are provided in *Model Child Care Health Policies,* 3rd edition, from the American Academy of Pediatrics (AAP). Contact information for the AAP is located in Appendix BB.

A sample medication administration log is provided in *Healthy Young Children* from the National Association for the Education of Young Children (NAEYC). Contact information for the NAEYC is located in Appendix BB.

For additional information, see Medications, STANDARD 3.081 through STANDARD 3.083; and Medication Policy, STANDARD 8.021. See also a sample document for permission for medical condition treatment in Appendix W.

TYPE OF FACILITY: *Center; Large Family Child Care Home; Small Family Child Care Home*

STANDARD 8.052
CONTENTS OF FACILITY HEALTH RECORD FOR EACH CHILD

The file for each child shall include a facility health record maintained on an ongoing basis by designated staff. The facility health record shall include:
a) Staff and parent observations of the child's health status and physical condition;
b) Response to any treatment provided while the child is in child care, and any observable side effects;
c) Notations of health-related referrals and follow-up action;

d) Notations of health-related communications with parents or the child's health care providers;
e) Staff observations of the child's learning and social activity;
f) Documentation of planned communication with parents and a list of participants involved. See Regular Communication, STANDARD 2.047 and STANDARD 2.048;
g) Documentation of parent participation in health education. See Health Education for Parents, STANDARD 2.065 through STANDARD 2.067.

RATIONALE: A facility health record maintained by caregivers can document caregivers' observations and concerns that may lead to intervention decisions.

COMMENTS: The facility health record is a confidential, chronologically-oriented location for the recording of staff observations, patterns of illness, and parent concerns, can be followed and can become guidelines for intervention, if needed.

Facility observation records provide useful information over time on each child's unique characteristics. Parents and caregivers can use these records in planning for the child's needs. On occasion, the child's health care provider can use them as an aid in diagnosing health conditions.

"Hands-on" opportunities for parents to work with their own child or others in the company of caregivers should be encouraged and documented.

Staff notations on communication with parents can be in a "parent log" separate from the child's health record.

See a sample symptom record, Appendix F. See also a sample document for permission for medical condition treatment in Appendix W.

TYPE OF FACILITY: *Center; Large Family Child Care Home; Small Family Child Care Home*

CONFIDENTIALITY AND ACCESS TO RECORDS

STANDARD 8.053
PARENTAL INFORMED CONSENT BEFORE SHARING CHILD'S HEALTH RECORDS

With prior written informed consent of the parent, child care facilities may share the child's health records including conference reports, service plans, and follow-up reports, as needed, with other service providers, including child care health consultants and specialized agencies providing services, as confidentiality guidelines or state laws permit. Effort shall be made to inform parents prior to any such communication.

The facility shall have policies and procedures that cover the exchange of information among parents, the facility, and other professionals or agencies that are involved with the child and family before the child enters the facility, during the time the child is cared for in the facility, and after the child leaves the facility. For centers, these shall be written policies and procedures.

If other children are mentioned in a child's record that is authorized for release, the confidentiality of those children shall be maintained. The record shall be edited to remove any information that could identify another child.

RATIONALE: The exchange of information about the child and family among providers of service can greatly enhance the effectiveness of child and family support and should be accomplished with sensitivity to issues of confidentiality and the need to know. This information is confidential, and parental consent for release is required if the child care facility is to gain access to it. Prior informed, written consent of the parent/guardian is required for the release of records/information (verbal and written) to other service providers, including process for secondary release of records. Consent forms should be in the native language of the parents, whenever possible, and communicated to them in their normal mode of communication. Foreign language interpreters should be used whenever possible to inform parents about their confidentiality rights. At the time when facilities obtain prior, informed consent from parents for release of records, caregivers should inform parents

who may be looking at the records, e.g., child care health consultants, licensing agencies.

Procedures should be developed and a method established to ensure accountability and to ensure that the exchange is being carried out. The child's record shall be available to the parents for inspection at all times.

COMMENTS: The responsibility for a child's health is shared by all those responsible for the child: parents, health professionals, and caregivers. Three-way alliances among the pediatric primary care clinician, the child care provider, and the parents should be encouraged to promote the optimal health and safety of the child. Caregivers should expect parents to transfer to them health information about the child given to and by health professionals. Such transfer of information is often facilitated by the use of forms, but telephone communication, with parental consent, is also appropriate to clarify concerns about a specific child. If a parent does not give permission, caregivers can use state override procedures when it is in the child's best interest to do so. Caregivers should also expect health professionals to provide their expertise for the formulation and implementation of facility policies and procedures.

If records are shared electronically, providers should ensure that the records are encrypted for security and confidentiality.

TYPE OF FACILITY: *Center; Large Family Child Care Home; Small Family Child Care Home*

STANDARD 8.054
WRITTEN POLICY ON CONFIDENTIALITY OF RECORDS

The facility shall establish and follow a written policy on confidentiality of the records of staff and children that ensures that the facility will not disclose material in the records without the written consent of parents (with legal custody) or legal guardian for children, or of staff for themselves.

The director of the facility shall decide who among the staff may have confidential information shared with them. Clearly, this decision must be made selectively, and all caregivers shall be taught the basic principles of all individuals' rights to confidentiality.

Written releases shall be obtained from the child's parent or legal guardian prior to forwarding information and/or the child's records to other service providers. The content of the written procedures for protecting the confidentiality of medical and social information shall be consistent with federal, state, and local guidelines and regulations and shall be taught to caregivers. Confidential medical information pertinent to safe care of the child shall be provided to facilities within the guidelines of state or local public health regulations. However, under all circumstances, confidentiality about the child's medical condition and the family's status shall be preserved unless such information is released at the written request of the family, except in cases where abuse or neglect is a concern. In such cases, state laws and regulations apply.

RATIONALE: Confidentiality must be maintained to protect the child and family and is defined by law (38). Serving children and families involves significant facility responsibilities in obtaining, maintaining, and sharing confidential information. Each caregiver must respect the confidentiality of information pertaining to all families, staff, and volunteers served.

Someone in each facility must be authorized to make decisions about the sharing of confidential information, and the director is the logical choice. However, the decision about sharing information must also involve the parent(s) or family. Sharing of confidential information shall be selective and shall be based on a need to know and on the parent's authorization for disclosure of such information.

Requiring written releases ensures confidentiality. Continuity of care and information is invaluable during childhood when growth and development are rapidly changing.

COMMENTS: Parental trust in the caregiver is the key to the caregiver's ability to work toward health promotion and to obtain needed information to use in decision making and planning for the child's best interest. Assurance of confidentiality fosters this trust. When custody has been awarded to only one parent, access to records must be limited to the custodial parent. In cases of disputed access, the facility may need to request that the parents supply a copy of the court document that defines parental rights. Operational control to accommodate the health and

safety of individual children requires basic information regarding each child in care.

Release formats may vary from state to state and within facilities. User friendly forms furnished for all caregivers may facilitate the exchange of information.

This standard applies to the sharing of any personal information.

TYPE OF FACILITY: *Center*

STANDARD 8.055
DISCLOSURE POLICY REGARDING PERSONAL INFORMATION

Caregivers shall not disclose or discuss personal information regarding children and their relatives with any unauthorized person. Confidential information shall be seen by and discussed only with staff members who need the information in order to provide services. Caregivers shall not discuss confidential information about families in the presence of others in the facility.

RATIONALE: Confidentiality must be maintained to protect the child and family and is defined by law (38). Serving children and families involves significant facility responsibilities in obtaining, maintaining, and sharing confidential information. Each caregiver must respect the confidentiality of information pertaining to all families served.

Someone in each facility must be authorized to make decisions about the sharing of confidential information, and the director is the logical choice. However, the decision about sharing information must also involve the parent(s) or family. Sharing of confidential information shall be selective and shall be based on a need-to-know basis and on the parent's authorization for disclosure of such information.

Requiring written releases ensures confidentiality. Continuity of care and information is invaluable during childhood when growth and development are rapidly changing.

Child care programs should make sure that their confidentiality policy allows sharing of necessary health information with their Health Consultant.

TYPE OF FACILITY: *Center; Large Family Child Care Home; Small Family Child Care Home*

STANDARD 8.056
RELEASE OF CHILD'S RECORDS

Upon parent request, designated portions or all of the child's records shall be copied and released to specific individuals named and authorized in writing by the parents to receive this information. The originals shall be retained by the facility.

RATIONALE: The facility must retain the original records in case legal defense is required, but parents have the right to know and have the full contents of the records. Sending the record to another source of service for the child may enhance the ability of other service providers to provide appropriate care for the child and family. The parents' written requests must be specific about to whom the record is being released, for what purpose, and what parts of the record are being copied and sent.

COMMENTS: Parents may want a copy of the record themselves or may want the record sent to another source of care for the child. An effective way to educate parents on the value of maintaining the child's developmental and health information is to have them focus on their own child's records. Such records should be used as a mutual education tool by parents and caregivers. Facilities may charge a reasonable fee for making a copy.

TYPE OF FACILITY: *Center*

STANDARD 8.057
AVAILABILITY OF RECORDS TO LICENSING AGENCY

Where these standards require the facility to have written policies, reports, and records, these records shall be available to the licensing agency for inspection. In addition, the facility shall make available any other policies, reports, or records that are required by the licensing agency that are not specified in these standards.

RATIONALE: The licensing agency monitors policies, reports, and records required to determine the facility's compliance with licensing regulations. Inspection of the policies, reports, and records required by licensing regulations may also include inspection of those addressed by the standards.

TYPE OF FACILITY: *Center; Large Family Child Care Home; Small Family Child Care Home*

PERSONNEL RECORDS

STANDARD 8.058
MAINTENANCE AND CONTENT OF STAFF RECORDS

Individual files for all staff members and volunteers, shall be maintained in a central location within the facility and shall contain the following:
a) The individual's name, birth date, address, and telephone number;
b) The position application, which includes a record of work experience and work references; verification of reference information, education, and training; and records of any checking for driving records, criminal records and/or listing in child abuse registry. See Individual Licensure/Certification, STANDARD 1.006, and Training, STANDARD 1.023 through STANDARD 1.039;
c) The health assessment record, a copy of which, having been dated and signed by the employee's health care provider, shall be kept in a confidential file in the facility. This record shall be updated by another health appraisal when recommended by the staff member's health care provider or supervisory or regulatory/certifying personnel (32). See Staff Health Appraisals, STANDARD 1.045 and STANDARD 1.046;
d) The name and telephone number of the person, physician, or health facility to be notified in case of emergency;
e) The job description or the job expectations for staff and substitutes. See General Qualifications for All Caregivers, STANDARD 1.007 through STANDARD 1.013;
f) Required licenses, certificates, and transcripts. See Individual Licensure/Certification, STANDARD 1.006;
g) The date of employment or volunteer assignment;
h) A signed statement of agreement that the employee understands and will abide by the following:
   1)Regulations and statutes governing child care;

2) Personnel policies and procedures. See Personnel Policies, STANDARD 8.044;

3) Health Policies and Procedures. See Management and Health Policies and Statement of Services, STANDARD 8.004 and STANDARD 8.005;

4) Discipline policy. See Discipline Policy, STANDARD 8.008 through STANDARD 8.010; and Discipline, STANDARD 2.039 through STANDARD 2.043;

5) Guidelines for reporting suspected child abuse, neglect, and sexual abuse;

6) Confidentiality policy. See STANDARD 8.054.

i) The date and content of staff and volunteer orientation(s);

j) A daily record of hours worked, including paid planning time and parent conference time;

k) A record of continuing education for each staff member and volunteer. See Continuing Education, STANDARD 1.029 through STANDARD 1.033;

l) Written performance evaluations. See Performance Evaluation, STANDARD 1.051 through STANDARD 1.057.

RATIONALE: Complete identification of staff, paid or volunteer, is an essential step in safeguarding children in child care. Maintaining complete records on each staff person employed at the facility is a sound administrative practice. Employment history, a daily record of days worked, performance evaluations, a record of benefits, and whom to notify in case of emergency provide important information for the employer. Licensors will check the records to assure that applicable licensing requirements are met (such as identifying information, educational qualifications, health assessment on file, record of continuing education, signed statement of agreement to observe the discipline policy, and guidelines for reporting suspected child abuse, neglect, and sexual abuse).

Emergency contact information for staff, paid or volunteer, is needed in child care in the event that an adult becomes ill or injured at the facility.

The signature of the employee confirms the employee's notification of responsibilities that might otherwise by overlooked by the employee.

TYPE OF FACILITY: *Center; Large Family Child Care Home*

ATTENDANCE RECORDS

STANDARD 8.059
MAINTENANCE OF DAILY ATTENDANCE RECORDS

The facility shall keep daily attendance records and shall require parents to sign the child in and out, listing the times of arrival and departure of the child. The sign-in and out records shall be kept on file with the daily attendance records.

RATIONALE: Operational control to accommodate the health and safety of individual children requires basic information regarding each child in care. This standard ensures that the facility knows which children are receiving care at any given time. It aids in the surveillance of child:staff ratios and provides data for program planning. Past attendance records are essential in conducting complaint investigations including child abuse.

COMMENTS: See a sample enrollment, attendance, and symptom record in Appendix F.

TYPE OF FACILITY: *Center; Large Family Child Care Home; Small Family Child Care Home*

STANDARD 8.060
MAINTENANCE OF STAFF ATTENDANCE RECORDS

Centers shall keep daily attendance records listing the names of each caregiver and/or substitute in attendance, the hours each individual worked, and the names of the children in their care.

RATIONALE: Promoting the health and safety of individual children requires keeping records regarding each child in care. This standard ensures that the facility knows which children are receiving care at any given time and who is responsible for directly supervising each child. It also aids in the surveillance of child:staff ratios and provides data for program planning. Past attendance records are essential in conducting complaint investigations including child abuse.

TYPE OF FACILITY: *Center*

INCIDENCE REPORTS OF ILLNESS, INJURY, AND OTHER SITUATIONS THAT REQUIRE DOCUMENTATION

TYPE OF FACILITY: *Center; Large Family Child Care Home; Small Family Child Care Home*

STANDARD 8.061
RECORDS OF ILLNESS

In situations where illnesses are reported by a parent or become evident while a child or staff member is at the facility and may potentially require exclusion, the facility shall record the following:
a)   Date and time of the illness;
b)   Person affected;
c)   Description of the symptoms;
d)   Response of the staff to these symptoms;
e)   Persons notified (such as a parent, legal guardian, nurse, physician, or the local health department representative, if applicable), and their response;
f)   Name of person completing the form.

RATIONALE: Recording the occurrence of illness in a facility and the response to the illness characterizes and defines the frequency of the illness, suggests whether an outbreak has occurred, may suggest an effective intervention, and provides documentation for administrative purposes.

COMMENTS: Surveillance for symptoms can be accomplished easily by using a combined attendance and symptom record. Any symptoms can be noted when the child is signed in, with added notations made during the day when additional symptoms appear. Simple forms, for a weekly or monthly period, that record data for the entire group help caregivers spot patterns of illness for an individual child or among the children in the group or center.

For a sample enrollment/attendance/symptom record, see Appendix F. For a sample *Incident Report Form*, see Appendix Y. Multicopy forms can be used to make copies of an injury report simultaneously for the child's record, for the parent, for the folder that logs all injuries at the facility, and for the regulatory agency. Facilities should secure the parent's signature on the form at the time it is presented to the parent. For information on the inclusion/exclusion/dismissal of children from child care, see STANDARD 3.065 through STANDARD 3.068.

STANDARD 8.062
RECORDS OF INJURY

When an injury occurs in the facility that requires first aid or medical attention for a child or adult, the facility shall complete a report form that provides the following information:
a)   Name, sex, and age of the injured person;
b)   Date and time of injury;
c)   Location where injury took place;
d)   Description of how the injury occurred, including who (name, address and phone number) saw the incident and what they reported, as well as what was reported by the child;
e)   Body part(s) involved;
f)   Description of any consumer product involved;
g)   Name and location of the staff member responsible for supervising the child at the time of the injury;
h)   Actions taken on behalf of the injured following the injury;
i)   Recommendations of preventive strategies that could be taken to avoid future occurrences of this type of injury;
j)   Name of person who completed the report;
k)   Name and address of the facility.

Three copies of the injury report form shall be completed. One copy shall be given to the child's parent or legal guardian (or to the injured adult). The second copy shall be kept in the child's (or adult's) folder at the facility, and the third copy shall be kept in a chronologically filed injury log that is periodically reviewed for patterns of injury. This last copy shall be kept in the facility for the period required by the state's statute of limitations.

RATIONALE: Injury patterns and child abuse can be discerned from such records and can be used to prevent future problems (35). A report form is also necessary for providing information to the child's parents and health care provider and other appropriate health agencies.

COMMENTS: For a sample *Incident Report Form*, see Appendix Y. Multicopy forms can be used to make copies of an injury report simultaneously for the child's record, for the parent, for the folder that logs all injuries at the facility, and for the regulatory agency. Facilities should secure the parent's signature on the form at the time it is presented to the parent. For additional information on the review of injury and illness logs, see STANDARD 8.064. For a sample *Incident Report Form*, see Appendix Y.

TYPE OF FACILITY: *Center; Large Family Child Care Home; Small Family Child Care Home*

STANDARD 8.063
DOCUMENTATION OF DEATH, INJURY OR ILLNESS

The facility shall document that a child's parent or legal guardian was notified immediately in the event of a death of their child or of an injury or illness of their child that required professional medical attention.

The licensing agency and/or health department shall be notified by the next working day of each of the following events:
a) Injury or illness that required medical attention;
b) Reportable communicable disease;
c) Death;
d) Any other significant event relating to health and safety (such as a lost child, a fire or other structural damage, work stoppage, or closure).

RATIONALE: The licensing agency should be notified by the next working day of any of the events listed above because each involves special action by the agency to protect children, their families, and/or the community. If an injury, death or any of the events in item d occur due to negligence by the provider, immediate suspension of the license may be necessary. Public health staff can assist in stopping the spread of the communicable disease if they are notified quickly by the licensing agency. The action by the facility in response to an illness requiring medical attention is subject to licensing review.

A report form that records injury, child abuse, illness, or death is also necessary for providing information to the child's parents and health care provider, other appropriate health agencies, and the insurance companies covering the parents and the center.

COMMENTS: Surveillance for symptoms can be accomplished easily by using a combined attendance and symptom record. Any symptoms can be noted when the child is signed in, with added notations made during the day when additional symptoms appear. Simple forms, for a weekly or monthly period, that record data for the entire group help caregivers spot patterns of illness for an individual child or among the children in the group or center.

For a sample enrollment/attendance/symptom record, see Appendix F. For a sample *Incident Report Form*, see Appendix Y. Multicopy forms can be used to make copies of an injury report simultaneously for the child's record, for the parent, for the folder that logs all injuries at the facility, and for the regulatory agency. Facilities should secure the parent's signature on the form at the time it is presented to the parent.

TYPE OF FACILITY: *Center; Large Family Child Care Home; Small Family Child Care Home*

STANDARD 8.064
ACCESSIBILITY OF INJURY AND ILLNESS REPORTS

The completed injury and illness report forms shall be made available to health consultants and other appropriate health agencies for review and analysis. In addition to maintaining a record for documentation of liability, forms shall be used to identify patterns of injury and illness occurring in child care that are amenable to prevention. The injury and illness log shall be reviewed by caregivers at least semi-annually and inspected by licensing staff and health consultants at least annually.

RATIONALE: Injury patterns and child abuse can be detected from such records and can be used to prevent future problems (35). A report form is also necessary for providing information to the child's parents and health care provider and other appropriate health agencies.

COMMENTS: Surveillance for symptoms can be accomplished easily by using a combined attendance and symptom record. Any symptoms can be noted when the child is signed in, with added notations made during the day when additional symptoms appear. Simple forms, for a weekly or monthly period, that record data for the entire group help caregivers spot patterns of illness for an individual child or among the children in the group or center.

For a sample enrollment/attendance/symptom record, see Appendix F. For a sample *Incident Report Form*, see Appendix Y. Multicopy forms can be used to make copies of an injury report simultaneously for the child's record, for the parent, for the folder that logs all injuries at the facility, and for the regulatory agency. Facilities should secure the parent's signature on the form at the time it is presented to the parent. For additional information, see *Model Child Care Health Policies,* 3rd edition, from the American Academy of Pediatrics (AAP). Contact information for the AAP is located in Appendix BB.

See Inspections, RECOMMENDATION 9.017 through RECOMMENDATION 9.019. See also Health Consultants, STANDARD 1.040 through STANDARD 1.044.

TYPE OF FACILITY: *Center; Large Family Child Care Home; Small Family Child Care Home*

LICENSING AND LEGAL RECORDS

STANDARD 8.065
RECORD OF VALID LICENSE, CERTIFICATE OR REGISTRATION OF FACILITY

Every facility shall hold a valid license or certificate of, or documentation of, registration prior to operation as required by the local and/or state statute.

RATIONALE: Licensing/registration provides recognition that the facility meets regulatory requirements.

TYPE OF FACILITY: *Center; Large Family Child Care Home; Small Family Child Care Home*

STANDARD 8.066
MAINTENANCE AND DISPLAY OF INSPECTION REPORTS

The facility shall maintain and display, in one central area within the facility, current copies of inspection reports required by the state licensing office. These reports and documentation include the following:
a) Licensing/registration reports;
b) Fire inspection reports;
c) Sanitation inspection reports;
d) Building code inspection reports;
e) Plumbing, gas, and electrical inspection reports;
f) Zoning approval;
g) Results of all water tests. See Water Testing, STANDARD 5.059 through STANDARD 5.063;
h) Evacuation drill records. See Evacuation Plan, Drills, and Closings, STANDARD 8.024 through STANDARD 8.027;
i) Any accreditation certificates;
j) Reports of legal actions against the facility and documentation that all required corrections have been completed;
k) Results of lead paint tests. See STANDARD 5.110;
l) Insurance records. See Insurance Records, STANDARD 8.070.

RATIONALE: Facility safeguarding is not achieved by one agency carrying out a single regulatory program. Total safeguarding is achieved through a multiplicity of regulatory programs and agencies. Licensing staff, consumers, and concerned individuals benefit from having documents of regulatory approval and legal action in one central location. Parents, staff, consultants, and visitors should be able to assess the extent of evaluation and compliance of the facility with regulatory and voluntary requirements. Accreditation documentation provides additional information about surveillance and quality improvement efforts of the facility.

TYPE OF FACILITY: *Center; Large Family Child Care Home; Small Family Child Care Home*

STANDARD 8.067
WRITTEN PLAN TO RESOLVE DEFICIENCIES

When deficiencies are identified during annual policy and performance reviews by the licensing department, funding agency, or accreditation organization, the director or small or large family child care home provider shall follow a written plan for resolution, developed with the regulatory agency.

This plan shall include the following:
a) Description of the problem;
b) Proposed timeline for resolution;
c) Designation of responsibility for correcting the deficiency;
d) Description of the successful resolution of the problem.

For centers, this shall be a written plan.

RATIONALE: A written plan or contract for change is more likely to achieve the desired change.

COMMENTS: Simple problems amenable to immediate correction do not require extensive documentation. For these, a simple notation of the problem and that the problem was immediately corrected will suffice. However, a notation of the problem is necessary so that recurring problems of the same type can be addressed by a more lasting solution.

TYPE OF FACILITY: *Center; Large Family Child Care Home; Small Family Child Care Home*

FIRE PROTECTION EQUIPMENT RECORDS

STANDARD 8.068
AVAILABILITY OF REPORTS ON INSPECTIONS OF FIRE PROTECTION DEVICES

A report of the inspection and maintenance of fire extinguishers and smoke detectors or other fire prevention mechanisms shall be available for

review. The report shall include the following information:
a) Location of the fire extinguishers, smoke detectors, or other equipment;
b) Date the inspection was performed and by whom;
c) Condition of the equipment;
d) Description of any service provided for the equipment.

Fire extinguishers shall be inspected semi-annually. Smoke detectors shall be inspected monthly.

Inspections shall be performed in compliance with local and/or state regulations.

RATIONALE: A fire extinguisher may lose its effectiveness over time. It should work properly at any time in case it is needed to put out a small fire or to clear an escape path (39). Since chemicals tend to separate within the canister, maintenance instructions (such as "Invert containers at least semi-annually") should be followed.

Smoke detectors are often powered by batteries and will need to be checked monthly to ensure they are in operating condition.

COMMENTS: Caregivers can do the inspection themselves, since many fire extinguishers are equipped with gauges that can be read easily.

TYPE OF FACILITY: *Center; Large Family Child Care Home; Small Family Child Care Home*

EVACUATION DRILL RECORDS

STANDARD 8.069
EVACUATION DRILL RECORD

A record of evacuation drills shall be kept on file. Each date and time shall be recorded.

RATIONALE: Routine practice of emergency evacuation plans fosters calm, competent use of the plans in an emergency.

COMMENTS: For information on evacuation plans, drills, and closings, see STANDARD 8.024 through STANDARD 8.027. For additional information on evacuation drill records, see also STANDARD 8.077, on posting fire evacuation procedures.

TYPE OF FACILITY: *Center; Large Family Child Care Home; Small Family Child Care Home*

INSURANCE RECORDS

STANDARD 8.070
INSURANCE COVERAGE

Facilities shall carry the following insurance:
a) Accident insurance on children;
b) Liability insurance;
c) Vehicle insurance on any vehicle owned or leased by the facility and used to transport children.

Small and large family child care home providers shall carry this insurance if available.

RATIONALE: With the current increase in litigation, reasonable protection against liability action through proper insurance is essential for reasons of economic security, peace of mind, and public relations. Requiring insurance reduces risks because insurance companies stipulate compliance with health and safety regulations before issuing or continuing a policy. Property insurance would also be desirable since the costs of adverse events occurring at a facility can easily cause a financial disaster that can disrupt children's care. Protection, via insurance, must be secured to provide stability and protection for both the individuals and the facility. Liability insurance carried by the facility provides recourse for parents of children enrolled in the event of negligence.

COMMENTS: The liability insurance should include coverage for administration of medications, as well as for unintentional injuries and illnesses. Individual health injury coverage may be documented by evidence of personal health insurance coverage as a dependent. Workers' compensation covers adult injuries in the case of an accident.

TYPE OF FACILITY: *Center; Large Family Child Care Home; Small Family Child Care Home*

PLAY AREA AND EQUIPMENT RECORDS

STANDARD 8.071
RECORDS OF PROPER INSTALLATION AND MAINTENANCE OF FACILITY EQUIPMENT

The facility shall maintain all information and records pertaining to the manufacture, installation, and regular inspection of facility equipment. No second-hand equipment shall be used in areas occupied by children, unless all pertinent data, including the manufacturer's instructions, can be obtained from the previous owner or from the manufacturer.

RATIONALE: Information regarding manufacture, installation, and maintenance of equipment is essential so that the staff can follow appropriate instructions regarding installation, repair, and maintenance procedures. Also, in the event of recalls, the information provided by the manufacturer allows the owner to identify the applicability of the recall to the equipment on hand. While second-hand office furnishings might be safe to use without having manufacturer's instructions; products used in areas occupied by children must have these instructions for identification, maintenance, repair and reference in case of recall.

COMMENTS: Notwithstanding these guidelines, individual jurisdictions may have specific regulations regarding information, records, equipment, policies, and procedures.

For more information regarding facility equipment, contact the U.S. Consumer Product Safety Commission (CPSC) and the National Program for Playground Safety. Also see the *Safe and Active Play* video from the American Academy of Pediatrics (AAP). Contact information is located in Appendix BB.

TYPE OF FACILITY: *Center; Large Family Child Care Home; Small Family Child Care Home*

STANDARD 8.072
REPORTS OF MONTHLY
MAINTENANCE CHECKS

Report forms shall be used to record the results of monthly maintenance checks of play equipment and surfaces. These forms shall be reviewed by the facility annually and shall be retained for the number of years required by the state's statute of limitations.

RATIONALE: Written records of monthly maintenance checks and appropriate corrective action are necessary to reduce the risk of potential injury. Annual review of such records provides a mechanism for periodic monitoring and improvement.

COMMENTS: A sample site checklist is provided in *Model Child Care Health Policies*, from the National Association for the Education of Young Children (NAEYC). Contact information for the NAEYC is located in Appendix BB.

For additional information on playground and equipment records, see also Maintenance of Playground and Outdoor Areas, STANDARD 5.194 through STANDARD 5.231; and Maintenance of the Facility and Equipment, STANDARD 8.033.

TYPE OF FACILITY: *Center; Large Family Child Care Home*

CONSULTATION RECORDS

STANDARD 8.073
DOCUMENTATION OF HEALTH
CONSULTATION/TRAINING VISITS

Documentation of health consultation/training visits shall be maintained in the facility's files. Documentation of the health consultation/training experiences shall also be provided to caregivers.

RATIONALE: Health consultants, licensing agents, health departments, and fellow caregivers should reinforce the importance of appropriate health behavior. Documentation of consultation by a health consultant or other health professional provides the opportunity

to evaluate the use of recommendations and training provided by the consultant.

COMMENTS: Documentation can take the form of a list of recommendations and training topics addressed. Documentation can include:
a) Who the consultant was;
b) The topic discussed;
c) Availability of certification for caregivers' training;
d) When, where, and how the consultation took place;
e) Any recommended follow-up.

See Health Consultants, STANDARD 1.040 through STANDARD 1.044, on health consultant responsibilities and qualifications.

TYPE OF FACILITY: *Center; Large Family Child Care Home; Small Family Child Care Home*

FOOD SERVICE RECORDS

STANDARD 8.074
RECORDS OF NUTRITION
SERVICES

The facility shall maintain records covering the nutrition services budget, expenditures for food, menus, numbers and types of meals served daily with separate recordings for children and adults, inspection reports made by health authorities, and recipes. Copies shall be maintained in the facility files for at least one year.

RATIONALE: Food service records permit efficient and effective management of the facility's nutrition component and provide data from which a Child Care Nutrition Specialist can develop recommendations for program improvement. If a facility is large enough to employ a supervisor for food service who holds certification equivalent to the Food Service Manager's Protection (Sanitation) certificate, records of this certification should be maintained.

COMMENTS: See Appendix C, for additional information on Child Care Nutrition Specialists.

TYPE OF FACILITY: *Center; Large Family Child Care Home*

COMMUNITY RESOURCE FILE

STANDARD 8.075
COMMUNITY RESOURCE INFORMATION

The facility shall obtain or have access to a community resource file that is updated at least annually. This resource file shall be made available to parents as needed. For families who do not speak English, community resource information shall be provided in the parents' native language or through the use of interpreters.

RATIONALE: Caregivers should have access to available resources in a variety of fields (such as physical and mental health care, nutrition, safety, oral health care, and developmental disabilities) (21). When physical, mental, or social health concerns are raised for the child or for the family, they should be addressed appropriately, often by referring the family to resources available in the community. Facilities with a significant number of families who do not speak English should provide materials in the parents' native language or make this information available through the use of an interpreter (40).

COMMENTS: In many communities, community agencies (such as resource and referral agencies) offer community resource files and may be able to supply updated information or service directories to local caregivers. Even small family child care home providers will be able to maintain a simple list of telephone numbers of human services, such as that published in the telephone directory. If a resource file is maintained, it must be updated regularly and should be used by a caregiver knowledgeable about health and the community.

Pediatricians and other pediatric primary care clinicians should be identified as professionals who can help families work with child care providers to promote the health and safety of children in child care programs (21).

TYPE OF FACILITY: *Center*

LARGE AND SMALL FAMILY CHILD CARE HOME RECORDS

STANDARD 8.076
MAINTENANCE OF RECORDS

Large and small family child care home providers shall maintain the following records:
a) A copy of the facility's license or registration, all inspection reports, correction plans for deficiencies, and any legal actions. See Licensing and Legal Records, STANDARD 8.065 through STANDARD 8.067; and Posting Documents, STANDARD 8.077;
b) Physical health records for any adult who has direct contact with children, and for family members who are present when the children are in care. See Pre-employment Staff Health Appraisal, Including Immunizations, STANDARD 1.045; and Ongoing Staff Health Appraisals, STANDARD 1.046;
c) Training records of the caregiver and any assistants. See Training, STANDARD 1.023 through STANDARD 1.036;
d) Criminal history records and child abuse records, as required by state licensing regulations. See Licensure/Certification of Qualified Individuals, STANDARD 1.006; and General Qualifications for All Caregivers, STANDARD 1.007;
e) Results of well-water tests where applicable. See Licensing and Legal Records, STANDARD 8.066; and Water Testing, STANDARD 5.059 through STANDARD 5.063;
f) Results of lead paint tests. See STANDARD 5.110;
g) Insurance records. See Insurance Records, STANDARD 8.070;
h) Child records. See Child Records, STANDARD 8.046 through STANDARD 8.052;
i) Attendance records. See Attendance Records, STANDARD 8.059 and STANDARD 8.060;
j) List of reportable diseases. See Reporting Illness, STANDARD 3.086 through STANDARD 3.088;
k) Injury report form. See Incidence Logs of Illness, Injury, and Other Situations That Require Documentation, STANDARD 8.061 through STANDARD 8.064;

l) Fire extinguisher records and smoke detector battery checks. See Fire Protection Equipment Records, STANDARD 8.068;

m) Evacuation drill records. See Evacuation Drill Records, STANDARD 8.069;

n) Play area and equipment records. See STANDARD 8.071 and STANDARD 8.072;

o) Consultation records. See STANDARD 8.073.

RATIONALE: Operational control to accommodate the health and safety of individual children requires that information regarding each child in care be kept and made available on a need-to-know basis. These records and reports are necessary to protect the health and safety of children in care.

An organized, comprehensive approach to injury prevention and control is necessary to ensure that a safe environment is provided for children in child care. Such an approach requires written plans, policies, and procedures, and record keeping so that there is consistency over time and across staff and an understanding between parents and caregivers about concerns for, and attention to, the safety of children.

TYPE OF FACILITY: *Large Family Child Care Home; Small Family Child Care Home*

8.8 POSTING DOCUMENTS

STANDARD 8.077
PUBLIC POSTING OF DOCUMENTS

In a conspicuous place, centers and large family child care homes shall post the following items:

a) The faculty's license or registration (which also includes the telephone number for filing complaints with the regulatory agency), as specified in Licensing and Legal Records, STANDARD 8.065 through STANDARD 8.067;

b) A statement informing parents/legal guardians about how they may obtain a copy of the licensing or registration requirements from the regulatory agency;

c) Information on procedures for filing complaints with the regulatory authority. See Procedures for Complaints and Reporting, RECOMMENDATION 9.020 through RECOMMENDATION 9.022;

d) Inspection and any accreditation certificates, as specified in Licensing and Legal Records, STANDARD 8.065 and STANDARD 8.066;

e) Reports of any legal sanctions, as specified in Licensing and Legal Records, STANDARD 8.067;

f) A notice that inspection reports, legal actions, and compliance letters are available for inspection in the facility;

g) Evacuation plan, as specified in STANDARD 8.024 through STANDARD 8.027

h) Fire evacuation procedures, to be posted in each room of the center;

i) Procedures for the reporting of child abuse consistent with state law and local law enforcement and child protective service contacts;

j) Notice announcing the "open-door policy" (that parents may visit at any time and will be admitted without delay) and the action the facility will take to handle a visitor's request for access if the caregiver is concerned about the safety of the children. See Written Statement of Services, STANDARD 8.045;

k) A roster of the children in each facility room in child care centers, or a list of children in the facility in family child care homes that lists the names of all children who receive care in that room in the center or in the family child care home, the name of the caregiver primarily responsible for each child, and the names of children presently in attendance;

l) A current weekly menu of any food or beverage served in the facility for parents and caregivers. The facility shall provide copies to parents, if requested. Copies of menus served shall be kept on file for 1 year. See also Food Service Records, STANDARD 8.074;

m) A statement of nondiscrimination for programs participating in the United States Department of Agriculture (USDA) Child and Adult Care Food Program;

n) A copy of the policy and procedures for discipline, including the prohibition of corporal punishment. This requirement also applies to school-age child care facilities. See also Discipline Policy, STANDARD 8.008 through STANDARD 8.010;

o) Legible safety rules for the use of swimming and built-in wading pools if the facility has such pools. Safety rules shall be posted conspicuously on the pool enclosure. See also Safety

Rules, STANDARD 5.215, and Water Safety, STANDARD 3.045 through STANDARD 3.047;

p) Phone numbers and instructions for contacting the fire department, police, emergency medical services, physicians, dentists, rescue and ambulance services, and the poison control center; the address of the facility; and directions to the facility from major routes north, south, east, and west. This information shall be conspicuously posted adjacent to the telephone;

q) A list of reportable communicable diseases as required by the state and local health authorities. See Reporting Illness, STANDARD 3.086 and STANDARD 3.087;

r) Employee rights and safety standards as required by the Occupational Safety and Health Administration (OSHA) and/or state agencies.

RATIONALE: Each local and/or state regulatory agency gives official permission to certain persons to operate child care programs by virtue of their compliance with standards. Therefore, documents relating to investigations, inspections, and approval to operate should be made available to consumers, caregivers, concerned persons, and the community. Posting other documents listed in this standard increases access to parents over having the policies filed in a less accessible location.

Awareness of the child abuse reporting requirements and procedures is essential to the prevention of child abuse. State requirements may differ, but those for whom the reporting of child abuse is mandatory usually include child care personnel. Information on how to call and how to report should be readily available to parents and caregivers. Therefore, posting these instructions is necessary.

The open-door policy may be the single most important method for preventing the abuse of children in child care(35). When access is restricted, areas observable by the parents may not reflect the care the children actually receive.

Identification of primary caregiver responsibility helps identify responsibility for supervision and monitoring of developmental progress of the child over time. In addition, primary caregiver assignments foster and channel meaningful communication between parents and caregivers. A posted roster also helps parents see how facility responsibility is assigned and know which children receive care in their child's group.

To ensure that children receive the minimum daily requirements of nutrients, parents need to know the daily menu provided by the facility.

Parents and caregivers must have a common basis of understanding about what disciplinary measures are to be used to avoid conflict and promote consistency in approach between caregivers and parents. Corporal punishment may be physical abuse or become very abusive easily.

Parents have a right to see any reports and notices of any legal actions taken against the facility that have been sustained by the court. Since unfounded suits may be filed, knowledge of which could undermine parent confidence, only actions that result in corrections or judgment needs to be made accessible.

The caregiver and parents need to know how an unstable (such as intoxicated) parent who wants admittance but whose behavior presents a risk to children will be handled.

Parents need to know what food and beverages their children receive while in child care. Menus filed should reflect last-minute changes so that parents and any nutrition consultant who reviews these documents can get an accurate picture of what was actually served.

Pool safety requires reminders to users of pool rules (16).

In an emergency, phone numbers must be immediately accessible.

COMMENTS: Compliance can be measured by looking for posted documents.

A sample telephone emergency list is provided in *Healthy Young Children* from the National Association for the Education of Young Children (NAEYC). Contact information for the NAEYC is located in Appendix BB.

When it is possible to translate documents into the native language of the parents of children in care, it increases the level of communication between facility and parents.

TYPE OF FACILITY: *Center; Large Family Child Care Home*

8.9 CONTRACTS

STANDARD 8.078
REQUIREMENTS FOR COMPLIANCE OF CONTRACT SERVICES

The facility shall assure that any contracted services will comply with all applicable standards.

RATIONALE: Whether the caregiver performs the services directly or arranges for them to be performed, children's interests must be equally well protected.

COMMENTS: The contract language should not only specify the requirement for compliance, but should also define methods for monitoring and for redress. An example of such a contract is a food service contract.

TYPE OF FACILITY: *Center; Large Family Child Care Home; Small Family Child Care Home*

8.10 DROP-IN CARE

STANDARD 8.079
REQUIREMENTS FOR COMPLIANCE OF DROP-IN CARE FACILITIES

Facilities that provide drop-in care (any individual child receives fewer than 30 days of care per year) shall comply with all of the standards except for those in Health Plan for Child Health Services, STANDARD 8.013 through STANDARD 8.017; and Child Records, STANDARD 8.046 through STANDARD 8.052.

Before leaving their child at the child care facility, parents shall provide evidence that the child is up-to-date with recommended immunizations, as specified in Immunizations, STANDARD 3.005 through STANDARD 3.007.

Drop-in care shall not result in licensed capacity being exceeded.

RATIONALE: Except for the time of participation at the facility, the needs for staff, equipment, and policies and procedures to protect children are the same for children receiving brief child care as for children in continuous care.

COMMENTS: See RECOMMENDATION 9.004, for additional information on drop-in facilities.

TYPE OF FACILITY: *Center; Large Family Child Care Home; Small Family Child Care Home*

REFERENCES

1. *1999 Family Child Care Licensing Study.* Washington, DC: The Children's Foundation; 1999.

2. *1999 Child Care Center Licensing Study.* Washington, DC: The Children's Foundation; 1999.

3. Paintal, S. Banning corporal punishment of children: a position paper. *Child Educ.* 1999;76(1):36-39.

4. *Collection of "Clearinghouse Notes."* Denver, Colo: Education Commission of the States; 1997.

5. Committee on School Health, American Academy of Pediatrics. Corporal punishment in the schools. *Pediatrics.* 2000;106(2):343.

6. Strauman-Raymond K, Lie L, Kempf-Berkseth J. Creating a safe environment for children in daycare. *J Sch Health.* 1993;63(6):254-257.

7. Solomons HC, Elardo R. Biting in day care centers: incidence, prevention, and intervention. *J Pediatr Health Care.* 1991;5:191-196.

8. Pennsylvania Chapter, American Academy of Pediatrics. *Preparing for Illness: A Joint Responsibility for Parents and Caregivers.* 4th ed. [Brochure]. Washington, DC: National Association for the Education of Young Children, 1999.

9. Crowley, A. Sick child care: a developmental perspective. *J Pediatr Health Care.* 1994;8:261-267.

10. National Resource Center for Health and Safety in Child Care. *Individual states child care licensure regulations.* Available at: http://nrc.uchsc.edu/index.html. Accessed November 26, 2000.

11. Tauxe RV, Johnson KE, Boase JC, et al. Control of day care shigellosis: a trial of convalescent day care in isolation. *Am J Public Health.* 1987;76:627-630.

12. MacDonald KL, White KE, Heiser JL, Gabriel L, Osterholm MT. Evaluation of a sick child day care program: lack of detected increased risk of subsequent illness. *J Pediatr InfectDis.* 1990;9(1):15-20.

13. American Academy of Pediatrics, Committee on Infectious Disease. Recommended childhood immunization schedule - United States, January - December 2001. *Pediatrics.* 2001;107:202-204.

14. Green M, ed. *Bright Futures: Guidelines for Health Supervision of Infants, Children, and Adolescents.* Arlington, Va: National Center of Education in Maternal and Child Health; 1994.

15. Haskins R, Kotch J. Day care and illness: evidence, costs and public policy. *Pediatrics.* 1986;77(suppl 6, pt 2):951-982.

16. American Public Health Association (APHA). *Public Swimming Pools. Recommended Regulations for Design and Construction, Operation and Maintenance.* Washington, DC: APHA; 1981.

17. Health Care Financing Administration, Children's Health Insurance Program (CHIP). CHIP Homepage. Available at: www.hcfa.gov/init/children.htm. Accessed August 31, 2000.

18. Centers for Disease Control and Prevention (CDC). CDC Clinic Assessment Software Application (CASA). Atlanta, Ga: CDC; 1996. Available at: www.cdc.gov/nip/casa. Accessed on November 26, 2000.

19. Rivara FP, Sacks, JJ. Injuries in child day care: an overview. *Pediatrics.* 1994;94(suppl 6, pt 2):1031-1033.

20. Aronson SS. Maintaining health in child care settings. In: Gunzenhauser, N, Caldwell, BM, eds. *Group Care for Young Children.* New Brunswick, NJ: Johnson & Johnson Baby Products Company, 1986

21. American Academy of Pediatrics, Committee on Early Childhood, Adoption, and Dependent Care. Policy statement: the pediatrician's role in promoting the health of a patient in day care. *Pediatrics.* 1993;92(3):489-492.

22. Goodman RA, Lie LA, Deitch SR, et al. Relationship between day care and health providers. *Rev Infect Dis.* 1986;8(4).

23. Crowley AA. Child care health consultation: the Connecticut experience. *Matern Child Health J.* 2000;4:67-75.

24. American Academy of Pediatrics. Medication administration in child care. *Healthy Child Care Am Newsletter.* 1999;Summer:1,4-5.

25. Baker SP, O'Neill B, Ginsburg MJ, Li G. *The Injury Fact Book.* 2nd ed. New York, NY: Oxford University Press; 1991.

26. *Injury Facts.* Chicago, IL: National Safety Council, 1999.

27. Consumer Product Safety Commission (CPSP). *Handbook for Public Playground Safety.* Washington, DC: CPSC; 1997. Available at: http: www.cpsc.gov/cpscpub/pubs/pub_idx.html. Accessed on November 26, 2000.

28. Churchill RB, Pickering LK. Infection control challenges in child-care centers. *Infect Dis Clin North Am.* 1997;11(2):347-365.

29. Chin J, ed. *Control of Communicable Diseases Manual.* Washington, DC: American Public Health Association; 2000.

30. Niffenegger JP. Proper hand-washing promotes wellness in child care. *J Pediatr Health Care.* 1997;11:26.

31. US Dept of Health and Human Services. *Head Start Program Performance Standards.* Washington, DC: US Dept of Health & Human Services, Head Start Bureau; 2000.

32. Kendrick AS, Kaufman R, Messenger KP, eds. *Healthy Young Children: A Manual for Programs.* Washington, DC: National Association for the Education of Young Children; 1995.

33. Shore R. *Rethinking the Brain: New Insights into Early Development.* New York, NY: Families and Work Institute; 1997.

34. Whitebook M, Bellm D. *Taking on Turnover: An Action Guide for Child Care Center Teachers and Directors.* Washington, DC: Center for the Child Care Work Force; 1999.

35. Deitch S, ed. *Health in Day Care: A Manual for Health Care Professionals.* Elk Grove Village, Ill: American Academy of Pediatrics; 1987.

36. American Academy of Pediatric Dentistry. *1999-00 American Academy of Pediatric Dentistry Reference Manual.* Available at: www.aapd.org. Accessed on September 6, 2000.

37. Rhodes AM. EPSDT: the law. *Am J Matern Child Nurs.* 1992;17:261.

38. Family Educational Rights & Privacy Act (FERPA), 20 USC § 1232 (1974).

39. US Fire Administration. *US Fire Administration, Fire Safety & Education Website.* Available at: www.usfa.fema.gov. Accessed August 31, 2000.

40. National Association for the Education of Young Children (NAEYC). *Accreditation Criteria & Procedures of the National Association for the Education of Young Children:* 1998 ed. Washington, DC: NAEYC; 1998.

41. American Academy of Pediatrics (AAP), Committee on Practice and Ambulatory Medicine. *Recommendations for Preventive Pediatric Health Care.* Elk Grove Village, Ill: AAP; 1999:RE9939.

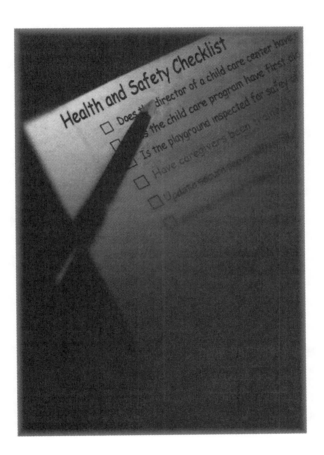

CHAPTER 9

Licensing and Community Action

This chapter contains recommendations for the responsibilities of agencies, organizations, and society, not for the individual caregiver or child care facility. These recommendations provide the support systems for implementation of the standards in the preceding chapters. Although many of these recommendations are directed to state administrative activity, they define necessary actions to assure the health and safety of children in out-of-home settings

9.1 THE REGULATORY AGENCY

THE REGULATORY POLICY

RECOMMENDATION 9.001 REGULATION OF ALL OUT-OF-HOME CHILD CARE

Every state should have a statute that identifies the regulatory agency and mandates the licensing and regulation of all full-time and part-time out-of-home care of children, regardless of setting, except care provided by parents or legal guardians, grandparents, siblings, aunts, or uncles or when a family engages an individual to care solely for their children (1).

DISCUSSION: A state statute gives government the authority to protect children as vulnerable and dependent citizens and to protect families as consumers of child care service. Licensing must have a statutory basis, because it is unknown to the common law. The statute must address the administration and location of the responsibility. Fifty states have child care regulatory statutes. The laws of some states exempt part day centers, school-age child care, care provided by religious organizations, lessons, summer camps or care provided in small or large family child care homes. These exclusions and gaps in coverage expose children to unacceptable risks.

RECOMMENDATION 9.002 ROLE OF LICENSING AGENCY

The licensing agency should issue permits of operation to all facilities that comply with standards.

DISCUSSION: Every child has a right to protective care that meets the standards, regardless of the child

care setting in which the child is enrolled. Public and private schools, nurseries, preschools, centers, child development programs, babysitting centers, early childhood observation centers, small and large family child care homes, and all other settings where young children receive care by individuals who are not close relatives should be regulated. Facilities have been able to circumvent rules and regulations in some states by claiming to be specialized facilities. Nothing in the educational philosophy, religious orientation, or setting of an early childhood program inherently protects children from health and safety risks or provides assurance of quality of child care.

Any exemptions for care provided outside the family may place children at risk. In addition to the basic protection afforded by stipulating requirements and inspecting for licensing, facilities should be required to be authorized for operation. Authorization for operation gives states a mechanism to identify facilities and individuals that are providing child care and authority to monitor compliance. These facilities and individuals may be identified as potential targets for training, technical assistance, and consultation services. Currently, many church run nurseries, nursery schools, group play centers, and home based programs operate incognito in the community because they are not required to notify any centralized agency that they care for children.

The lead agency for licensing of child care in most states is the human services agency. However, the state public health agency can be an appropriate licensing authority for safeguarding children in some states. The education system is increasingly involved in providing services to children in early childhood. The standards should be equally stringent no matter what agency assumes the responsibility for regulating child care.

Home care, which is the care of a child in his/her own home by someone whom the parent has employed, is not care within the family. This type of care should not be licensed as a facility. The relationship between the parent and caregiver is that of employer and employee rather than that of purchaser and provider of care, thus licensing or certification of the individual who provides such care, rather than of the service itself, is desirable and recommended.

A good resource on licensing, regulatory, and enforcement issues is the National Association for Regulatory Administration (NARA), an international professional organization for licensors, dedicated to promoting excellence in human care regulation and licensing through leadership, education, collaboration, and services. Contact information for NARA is located in Appendix BB. In addition, the Position

Statement on Licensing and Public Regulation of Early Childhood Programs published by the National Association for the Education of Young Children (NAEYC) includes rationale for policy decisions related to licensing and regulation (1). See Appendix AA, for the NAEYC position statement on licensing.

RECOMMENDATION 9.003
CRIMINAL RECORD AND CHILD ABUSE CHECKS

Every state should have a statute which mandates the licensing agency or other authority to obtain a criminal records check and a child abuse registry check on every prospective child care staff person, volunteer, or on a family child care home provider's family member who is over 10 years of age and who comes in contact with children. The expense of criminal records check and child abuse registry checks should be a public responsibility. No staff should be unsupervised with the children until a negative report has been received by the agency. Volunteers should not be unsupervised with the children at any time.

DISCUSSION: The cost of criminal records checks, where they have been implemented, has become an additional financial burden on programs, which are forced to pass on the expense to parents or staff. Placing the burden on potential new staff, volunteers, and substitute caregivers themselves proves to be another disincentive to enter this field of work. In many cases juvenile records are sealed and can not be used for the purposes of background checks. Juvenile offender records begin at age 10.

Some states have established definitions for regular volunteers (for whom criminal record and child abuse registry checks should be required) and for short-term visitors, such as entertainers and others, who will not be unsupervised with the children.

FACILITY LICENSING

RECOMMENDATION 9.004
UNIFORM CATEGORIES AND DEFINITIONS

Each state should adopt uniform categories and definitions for its own licensing requirements. While states may use different terms, every state should have individual standards that are applied to the following types of facilities:

a) *Small family child care home*: A facility providing care and education of one to six children, including preschool children of the caregiver, in the home of the caregiver;

b) *Large family child care home*: A facility providing care and education of 7 to 12 children, including preschool children of the caregiver, in the home of the caregiver, with one or more qualified adult assistants to meet child:staff ratio requirements;

c) *Center*: A facility providing care and education of any number of children in a nonresidential setting, or 13 or more children in any setting if the facility is open on a regular basis (for instance, if it is not a drop-in facility);

d) *Drop-in facility*: A facility providing care that occurs for fewer than 30 days per year per child, either on a consecutive or intermittent basis, or on a regular basis but for a series of different children;

e) *School-age child care facility*: A facility offering activities to school-age children before and after school, during vacations, and non-school days set aside for such activities as teachers' in-service programs;

f) *Facility for children with special needs*: A facility providing specialized care and education in a setting of one or more children who cannot be accommodated in a setting with typically developing children (2). See Children Who are Eligible for Services Under the Individuals with Disabilities Education Act (IDEA), STANDARD 7.001 through STANDARD 7.016;

g) *Facility for ill children*: A facility providing care of one or more ill children who are temporarily excluded from care in their regular child care setting. See Caring for Ill Children, STANDARD 3.070 through STANDARD 3.080;

   1) *Integrated or small group care for ill children*: A facility that has been approved by the licensing agency to care for well children and to include up to six ill children;

   2) *Special facility for ill children*: A facility that cares only for ill children, or a facility that cares for more than six ill children at a time;

DISCUSSION: Lack of standard terminology hampers the ability of citizens and professionals to compare

rules from state to state or to apply national guidance material to upgrade the quality of care (1). For example, child care for 7 to 12 children in the residence of the caregiver may be referred to as family day care, a group day care home, or a mini-center in different states. While it is not essential that each state use the same terms and some variability in definitions of types of care may occur, terminology should be consistent within the state and as consistent as possible from state to state in the way different types of settings are classified. Child care facilities should be differentiated from community facilities that primarily care for the mentally retarded, the elderly, and other adults and teenagers who need supervised care.

RECOMMENDATION 9.005 CARE OF ILL CHILDREN NOT REQUIRING EXCLUSION

Any facility should be encouraged to care for ill children who do not need to be excluded, as defined in STANDARD 3.068, provided that the licensing authority has approved the facility's written plan describing the symptoms or conditions that the facility is prepared to accommodate and procedures for daily care for such children. Facility types should be specific to the child's developmental level.

DISCUSSION: Children enrolled in child care are of an age that places them at increased risk for acquiring infectious diseases. Many children with illness (particularly mild respiratory tract illness without fever) can continue to attend and participate in activities in their usual facility. This perspective is reflected in the standards for excluding children from child care attendance. See Inclusion/Exclusion/ Dismissal of Ill Children, STANDARD 3.065 through STANDARD 3.068.

Clearly, when children with possible communicable diseases are present in the alternative care arrangements, emphasis on preventing further spread of disease is as important as in the usual facilities. Prevention of additional cases of communicable disease should be a key objective in these alternative care arrangements for children with minor illness and temporary disability.

Current state regulations concerning exclusion of children from facilities because of illness may be more restrictive than these standards. Some states currently require isolation of a child who becomes ill during the day while attending the facility, and for an ill child who is not expected to return to the facility the

following day (5). The most common alternative care arrangement is for a parent of the ill child to stay home from work and care for the child. Some states have established regulations governing child care for sick children (5).

Data are inadequate by which to judge the impact of group care of ill children on their subsequent health and on the health of their families and community. The principles and standards proposed in this manual represent the most current views of pediatric and infectious disease experts on providing this special form of child care. These standards will require revision as new information on disease transmission in these facilities becomes available. The National Association for Sick Child Daycare (NASCD) conducts and sponsors original research on issues related to sick child care and helps establish sick care facilities across the nation. Contact information for the NASCD is located in Appendix BB.

INDIVIDUAL CREDENTIALING/ CERTIFICATION

RECOMMENDATION 9.006 CREDENTIALLING OF INDIVIDUAL CHILD CARE PROVIDERS

All persons who provide child care or who may be responsible for children or alone with children in a facility should be individually credentialed by a state licensing agency or credentialing body recognized by the state child care regulatory agency. The credential should be granted to individuals who meet age, education, and experience qualifications, whose health status facilitates providing safe and nurturing care, and who have no record of conviction for criminal offenses against persons, especially children, or confirmed act of child abuse. The state should establish qualifications for differentiated roles in child care and a procedure for verifying that the individual who is authorized to perform a specified role meets the qualifications for that role.

DISCUSSION: Individual credentialing will enhance child health and development and protect children by ensuring that the staff who care for children are healthy and are qualified for their roles. The current system, in which the details of staff qualifications and ongoing training are checked as part of facility inspection, is cumbersome for child care administrators and

licensing inspectors alike. If staff qualifications were established as part of a separate, more central process, the licensing agency staff could check center records of character references and whether staff members have licenses for the roles for which they are employed.

In a centralized individual credentialing system, successful completion of education should be verified by requiring the individual to submit evidence of completion of credit-bearing courses that have been previously approved as meeting the state's requirements to a central verification office where this transcript should be continually updated. Criminal records and child abuse registries should be checked by state licensing agency staff for evidence of behavior that would disqualify an individual for work in specified child care roles. Evidence of a recent health examination indicating ability to care for children can be submitted at the same time. The center director then knows whether job applicants who have been working in the field previously are qualified at the time they apply for the job, without lengthy waiting for background checks of a prospective employee and without having to hire before background checks have been completed. By this means, children are not exposed to health and safety risks from understaffing, or to care by unqualified or even dangerous individuals employed provisionally because the results of a check are not yet available to the director.

Centralizing individual credentialing, qualifying, or licensing (whichever term is consistent with the state's approach to authorizing legal professional activity) will improve control over quality, encourage a career ladder with increasing qualifications, and reduce the risk of abuse. It will help consumers know that individuals who are caring for their children have met basic requirements for consumer protection. Such a process is analogous to that provided for other education professionals (teachers), and even those service providers with less potential for harm than is involved in caring for children (such as beauticians, barbers, taxi drivers).

The cost of individual certification, credentialing, or licensure will be offset by the benefits to consumers of reliable and consistent qualifications of child care personnel. Program administrators, licensors, and child care personnel, who do not have to undertake the tedious process of verification of each portion of an individual's credentials during all site visits, when sites are licensed, or when individuals change jobs, will experience cost savings and assurance of compliance. Public and private policymakers should use financial and other incentives to help caregivers meet credentialing requirements. They should encourage community colleges to offer courses

appropriate for provider training at times convenient for child care workers to attend.

Periodic renewal of the credential should be required, and should be related to requirements for continuing education and the absence of founded claims of child abuse or criminal convictions. The requirement for renewable certification is likely to deter people from applying for work in child care as a way of gaining access to children for sexual purposes since the process would include a check of the child abuse registry (3).

While there is value in checking criminal records, not all criminal records represent hazards for children so serious as to prohibit the individual from working in a child care setting. States should specify which crimes defined in the state's criminal code will prohibit certification and whether any other crimes should limit the ability of the individual to be certified for certain roles. Individuals who have been convicted of violent and/or sexual crimes should not work in child care settings. States should be careful not to rely entirely on criminal record checks to prevent abuse. This method is expensive and does not result in a high number of "hits" as records are checked, because many abusers have not yet been convicted of a crime. In addition, states should rely on other, less costly measures to protect children. The Federal Bureau of Investigation (FBI) maintains a central criminal file. Contact information for the FBI is located in Appendix BB. If all caregivers are certified, and are required to present or post their certificates where they work, their identity, background, and competence can be documented. Checking compliance requires simple inspection of the certificate and verification by contacting the state agency that maintains the computerized registry of qualified individuals. Precautions against forgery should be built into the system.

For information on individual staff qualifications, see Preservice Qualification and Special Training, STANDARD 1.007 through STANDARD 1.022.

RECOMMENDATION 9.007 LICENSING AGENCY PRE-LICENSING PROCEDURES

Before granting a license to a facility, the licensing agency should check as specified below for a record of a physical examination and for educational qualifications, and should check criminal records, juvenile records and the child abuse registry for all adults who are permitted to be alone with children in a facility. The licensing agency should also check the criminal record files and child abuse registry, as specified below, for all persons over 10 years of age who live in a small or large family child care home where child care is provided.

a) Staff health appraisals, as specified in Pre-employment Staff Health Appraisal, STANDARD 1.045;
b) Educational requirements, as specified in STANDARD 1.009, STANDARD 1.014, STANDARD 1.017 through STANDARD 1.019;
c) Criminal record files, for crimes of violence against persons, especially children, within the state of residence, and for personnel who have moved into the state within the past 5 years, federal or out of state criminal records of the other state(s) where the individual has resided in the past 5 years;
d) The child abuse registry, for a known history of child abuse or neglect in the state of residence and for personnel who have moved into the state within the past 5 years, the other state(s) where the individual has resided in the past 5 years.

DISCUSSION: In many cases juvenile records are sealed and cannot be used for the purposes of background checks. Ten years is the minimum age to be adjudicated a juvenile offender.

ALTERNATIVE MEANS OF COMPLIANCE

RECOMMENDATION 9.008 ALTERNATIVE MEANS OF COMPLIANCE

Alternative means of compliance should be granted from state licensing requirements when the intent of the requirement is being met by equivalent means and does not compromise the health, safety or protection of children.

DISCUSSION: The ability to grant alternative means of compliance recognizes the variety of settings and services that can effectively and safely meet children's needs. Flexibility in applying licensing regulations should be permitted to the extent that children's need for protection is met.

THE REGULATION SETTING PROCESS

RECOMMENDATION 9.009 RATIONAL BASIS OF REGULATIONS

The state child care regulatory agency should formulate, implement, and enforce regulations that reduce risks to children in out-of-home child care.

DISCUSSION: Regulations describe the minimum performance required of a facility. Regulations must be:
* Understandable to any reasonable citizen;
* Specific enough that any person knows what is to be done and what is not to be done;
* Enforceable, in that they are capable of measurement;
* Consistent with new technical knowledge and changes in public views to offer necessary protection.

RECOMMENDATION 9.010 COMMUNITY PARTICIPATION IN DEVELOPMENT OF LICENSING RULES

State licensing rules should be developed with active community participation by all interested parties including parents, service providers, advocates, professionals in medical and child development fields, funding and training sources.

Regulations formulated through a representative citizen process should come before the public at well-publicized public hearings held at convenient times and places in different parts of the state. The licensing rules should be re-examined and revised at least every 5 years. The regulatory development process should include many opportunities for public debate and discussion as well as the ability to provide written input.

DISCUSSION: The legal principle of broad interest representation has long been applied to the formulation of regulations for child care. Changes in regulation can be implemented only with broad support from the different interests affected. State administrative laws and constitutional principles require public review. The interests of the child must take precedence over all other interests.

RECOMMENDATION 9.011
COLLABORATIVE DEVELOPMENT OF CHILD CARE REQUIREMENTS AND GUIDELINES

Local and state health departments, child care licensing agencies, health professionals, attorneys, caregivers, parents, and representatives of the business community, including employers, should work together to develop child care licensing requirements and guidelines for ill children.

DISCUSSION: Local and state health departments have the legal responsibility to control communicable diseases in their jurisdictions (4). To meet this responsibility, health departments generally have the expertise to provide leadership and technical assistance to licensing authorities, caregivers, parents, and health professionals in the development of licensing requirements and guidelines for the management of ill children. The heavy reliance on the expertise of local and state health departments in the establishment of facilities to care for ill children has fostered a partnership in many states among health departments, licensing authorities, caregivers, and parents for the adequate care of ill children in child care settings. In addition, the business community has a vested interest in assuring that parents have facilities that provide quality care for ill children so parents can be productive in the workplace. This vested interest is likely to produce meaningful contributions from the business community to creative solutions and innovative ideas about how to approach the regulation of facilities for ill children. All stakeholders in the care of ill children should be involved for the solutions that are developed in regulations to be most successful.

See also Caring for Ill Children, STANDARD 3.070 through STANDARD 3.080.

ADMINISTRATION OF THE LICENSING AGENCY

GENERAL

RECOMMENDATION 9.012
ADEQUACY OF STAFF AND FUNDING FOR REGULATORY ENFORCEMENT

All phases of regulatory administration should have authorization, funding, and enough qualified staff to monitor and enforce the law and regulations of the state.

DISCUSSION: For regulations to be effective, the regulatory body must formulate, implement, and enforce licensing requirements and assure that licensing inspectors are both sufficient in numbers and capable of fairly and effectively developing and applying the regulations. Funds for all phases of the licensing process should be provided or faulty administrative operations may result, such as inadequate protection of children, formulation of irresponsible standards, inadequate investigations, and insufficient and unfair enforcement.

STAFF TRAINING

RECOMMENDATION 9.013
TRAINING AND PERFORMANCE MONITORING OF LICENSING INSPECTORS

Licensing inspectors should receive initial and periodic competency-based training to monitor compliance with licensing standards. Competency should be initially and periodically assessed by simultaneous, independent monitoring by a skilled licensing inspector until the trainee attains the necessary skills.

DISCUSSION: Objective assessment of compliance is a learned skill that can be fostered by classroom and self teaching methods but should be mastered through direct practice and apprenticeship. To ensure consistent protection of children, licensing inspectors should undergo periodic retraining and reevaluation to assess their ability to recognize sound and unsound practices. In addition, all staff involved in licensing such as agency directors, attorneys, policy staff, managers, clerical/support personnel and information system staff need periodic training updates. Training for licensors should include best practice and programming, child development theory, and law enforcement.

STAFFING CAPABILITY

RECOMMENDATION 9.014
FREQUENCY OF INSPECTIONS OF FACILITIES

Sufficient numbers of licensing inspectors should be hired to provide sufficient time visiting and inspecting facilities to insure compliance with regulations.

DISCUSSION: Licensing centers and large family child care homes should require at least one pre-licensing visit, and at least one more visit after granting of the provisional license, and after children are in attendance, to determine that all requirements are being met and that a full license can be granted. In addition, licensing inspectors should follow up promptly, based on priority of severity and on complaints of noncompliance made by parents and the general public. They should make routine unannounced inspections at least annually to determine continued compliance, and they should study compliance at length at the time of re-licensing. The most effective way of ensuring compliance with standards is through the licensors' presence in facilities, identifying deficiencies and giving technical assistance/consultation to bring about compliance. Workloads should be designed so that the licensing inspectors' time is not consumed by in-office tasks.

RECOMMENDATION 9.015
EDUCATION AND EXPERIENCE OF LICENSING INSPECTORS

Licensing inspectors, and others in licensing positions, should be pre-qualified by education and experience to be knowledgeable about the form of child care they are assigned to inspect. They should receive no less than 40 clock hours of orientation training upon employment. In addition, they should receive no less than 24 clock hours of continuing education each year, covering the following topics and other such topics as necessary based on competency needs:
a) The licensing statutes and rules for child care;
b) Other applicable state and federal statutes and regulations;
c) The historical, conceptual and theoretical basis for licensing, investigation, and enforcement;
d) Technical skills related to the person's duties and responsibilities, such as investigative techniques, interviewing, rule-writing, due process, and data management;
e) Child development, early childhood education principles, child care programming, scheduling, and design of space;
f) Law enforcement and the rights of licensees;
g) Center and large or small family child care home management;
h) Child and staff health in child care;
i) Detection, prevention, and management of child abuse;
j) Practical techniques for inclusion of children with special needs;
k) Exclusion/inclusion of ill children;
l) Health, safety, and nutrition;
m) Recognition of hazards.

DISCUSSION: Licensing inspectors are a point of contact and linkage for caregivers and sources of technical information needed to improve the quality of child care. This is particularly true for areas not usually within the network of early childhood professionals, such as health and safety expertise. Unless the licensing inspector is competent and able to recognize areas where facilities need to improve their health and safety provisions, the opportunity for such linkages will be lost.

RECOMMENDATION 9.016
TRAINING OF LICENSING AGENCY PERSONNEL ABOUT CHILD ABUSE

Staff and administrators in licensing agencies and state supported resource and referral agencies should receive 16 hours of training about child abuse with an emphasis on how child abuse occurs in child care.

DISCUSSION: Licensing and resource and referral persons should be as well informed about child abuse issues as caregivers, or better. States should establish inspection procedures to ensure compliance of their agency personnel.

INSPECTIONS

RECOMMENDATION 9.017
STATUTORY AUTHORIZATION OF ON-SITE INSPECTIONS

The state statute should authorize the state regulatory agency to conduct on-site inspections.

DISCUSSION: The National Association for the Education of Young Children (NAEYC) Position Statement says, "Effective enforcement requires periodic on-site inspections on both an announced and unannounced basis with meaningful sanctions for noncompliance" (1). When unannounced inspections are used, they should be conducted at any hour the facility is in operation, i.e., evenings and nights included if the facility operates at those times. NAEYC recommends that all centers and large and small family child care homes receive at least one site visit per year. Unannounced inspections have been shown to be especially effective when targeted to providers with a history of low compliance. (1)

RECOMMENDATION 9.018
INITIAL INSPECTION AND AT LEAST ONE ANNUAL INSPECTION

The licensing inspector should make an initial inspection upon receipt of the application for license (either announced or unannounced within a specified time frame), and at least one annual inspection to each center and large and small family child care home thereafter. These inspections may be announced or unannounced.

The schedule of inspections depends upon the quality of the facility as measured by:
a) The results of an annual inspection by a regulatory inspector;
b) Concerns raised about compliance with rules by visitors who provide technical assistance and training for the child care providers;
c) Inspections initiated because of complaints.

The number of inspections should not include those inspections conducted for the purpose of investigating complaints. Parents should be given a summary list of rules and a telephone number for reporting violations and should be encouraged to observe the facility for compliance.

DISCUSSION: The initial inspection and consultation often lead to full compliance with health, safety, and program standards, but over time, compliance may slip. Supervision and monitoring of child care facilities are critical to facilitate compliance with the rules in order to prevent or correct problems before they become serious. Technical assistance and consultation on an on-going basis can be very successful in helping programs to achieve compliance with the rules and even to go beyond the basic level of quality. These positive strategies are most effective when they are coupled with the non-regulatory methods used by other parts of the early care and education community to promote quality (such as accreditation, training/education, peer support, and consumer education). All of these methods are most effective when they work together within a coordinated child care system.

Family child care home providers need the same level of support as do larger child care programs. When the licensing agency is not able to make annual inspections, additional contact and support can be provided by other sources, such as the Child and Adult Food Program, a mentor caregiver, or a designated child care health consultant. In these situations, the on-site monitors are encouraged to inspect the facility for basic health and safety hazards and to report to the licensing agency observations of any substantial non-compliance with rules. State statutes and policy differ on the frequency of on-site inspections. Since the average duration of a small family child care home is often less than two years, more frequent visits of licensing inspectors or consultants to these facilities might help keep them in the system and improve the quality of care.

Recent changes in welfare policies have, in some states, supported the growth of "informal" family child care, which is "legally exempt" from regulation. As a consequence, some children who may benefit most from a high quality child care program are in programs that are never visited by a regulator of any kind.

RECOMMENDATION 9.019
MONITORING STRATEGIES

The licensing agency should adopt monitoring strategies that ensure compliance with licensing requirements. When these strategies do not include a total annual review of all licensing requirements, the agency should review selected policies and performance indicators and/or conduct a random sampling of licensing requirements at least annually. The licensing agency should have procedures and staffing in place to increase the level of compliance monitoring for any facility found in significant noncompliance.

DISCUSSION: Due to an insufficient number of inspectors in licensing agencies across the country, it is important to use various methods in the licensing process to insure quality.

PROCEDURES FOR COMPLAINTS AND REPORTING

RECOMMENDATION 9.020
PROCEDURE FOR RECEIVING COMPLAINTS

Each licensing agency should have a procedure for receiving complaints regarding violation of the regulations. Such complaints should be recorded, investigated, and appropriate action, if indicated, should be taken.

DISCUSSION: The telephone number for filing complaints should be listed on material about licensing that is given to parents by the state licensing agency or the resource and referral agency. At a minimum, the licensing agency has responsibility for consumer protection. Complaints serve as an early warning before more serious adverse events occur. A fair and equitable process for handling complaints is essential to protect both the person complaining and the target of the complaint from harassment.

RECOMMENDATION 9.021
WHISTLE-BLOWER PROTECTION UNDER STATE LAW

State law should ensure that caregivers and child care staff who report violation of licensing requirements in the settings where they work are immune from discharge, retaliation, or other disciplinary action for that reason alone, unless it is proven that the report was malicious.

DISCUSSION: Staff in child care facilities are in an excellent position to note areas of noncompliance with licensing requirements in the setting where they work. However, so that they feel safe about reporting these deficiencies, they must be assured immunity from retaliation by the child care facility unless the report is malicious. This immunity is best provided when a state statute mandates it. Individuals who report problems in their own workplace may be known as "whistle-blowers".

States should recognize and develop a system to deal with complaints against a provider that are retaliatory by disgruntled staff or parents. At times these nuisance complaints serve only to harass the provider and expend valuable licensing resources or unnecessary work.

RECOMMENDATION 9.022
PUBLICITY ABOUT REPORTING SUSPECTED CHILD ABUSE

Licensing agencies should publicize the requirements for reporting and methods of reporting suspected child abuse.

DISCUSSION: Child care staff and parents should be aware of the reporting requirements and the procedures for handling reports of child abuse. State requirements may differ, but those for whom reporting suspected abuse is mandatory usually include child care personnel. Information on how to call and how to report should be posted so it is readily available to parents and staff. Emotional abuse can be extremely harmful to children, but unlike physical or sexual abuse, it is not adequately defined in most state child abuse reporting laws. States need to develop procedures for handling allegations of all types of abuse.

Procedures for evaluating allegations of physical and emotional abuse may or may not be the purview of the licensing agency. This responsibility may fall to another agency to which the licensing agency refers child abuse allegations.

For additional information, see Posting Documents, STANDARD 8.077; for training and educational materials, see STANDARD 1.023 and STANDARD 1.036; and Child Abuse and Neglect, STANDARD 3.053 through STANDARD 3.059.

ENFORCEMENT

RECOMMENDATION 9.023
STATE STATUTE SUPPORT OF REGULATORY ENFORCEMENT

The state statute should authorize the suppression of illegal operations and enforcement of child care regulations and statutory provisions.

> DISCUSSION: Without proper enforcement, especially the suppression of illegal operations, licensing could become a ritual and lose its safeguarding intent. Some state laws lack adequate provisions for enforcement.

ADVISORY GROUP

RECOMMENDATION 9.024
CHILD CARE ADVISORY BODY

States should have an official broad-based child care advisory body to deal with a wide scope of both regulatory and policy child care related issues. This advisory body should be composed of public and private agency personnel, child development and health professionals, child care providers including caregivers, parents, and citizens.

> DISCUSSION: A child care advisory board is needed to:
> - Review overall rules and regulations for the operation and maintenance of facilities and the granting, suspending, and revoking of both provisional and regular licenses;
> - Recommend administrative policy;
> - Recommend changes in legislation.

The advisory group may include representatives from the following agencies and groups:
a) Governor's office;
b) Legislature;
c) State agencies with regulatory responsibility or an interest in child care (human services, public health, fire marshal, emergency medical services, education, human resources, attorney general, safety council);
d) Private organizations with a child care emphasis;
e) Child care providers including caregivers;
f) Professionals with expertise in pediatrics, nutrition, mental health, oral health, injury prevention, or early childhood education;
g) Parents who represent ethnic and cultural diversity;
h) Citizens.

The advisory group should actively seek citizen participation in the development of child care policy, including parents and child care providers at the level of administration and one-to-one care to children. One method for encouraging citizen participation is through public hearings. In response to specific issues, it is often effective to constitute an ad hoc group to study the questions and provide input to the regulatory agency.

9.2 HEALTH DEPARTMENT RESPONSIBILITY

HEALTH DEPARTMENT ROLE AND PLAN

RECOMMENDATION 9.025
STATE AND LOCAL HEALTH DEPARTMENT ROLE

State and local health departments should play an important role in the identification, prevention and control of injuries, injury risk, and infectious disease in child care settings as well as in using the child care setting to promote health. This role includes the following activities to be conducted in collaboration with the child care licensing agency:
1. Assisting in the planning of a comprehensive health and safety program for children and child care providers.
2. Monitoring the occurrence of serious injury events and outbreaks involving children or providers.
3. Alerting the responsible child care administrators about identified or potential injury hazards and infectious disease risks in the child care setting.
4. Controlling outbreaks, identifying and reporting communicable diseases in child care settings including:
   a) Methods for notifying parents, caregivers, and health care providers of the problem.

b) Providing appropriate actions for the child care provider to take;

c) Providing policies for exclusion or isolation of infected children;

d) Arranging a source and method for the administration of needed medication.

e) Providing a list of reportable diseases, including descriptions of these diseases. The list should specify where diseases are to be reported and what information is to be provided by the child care provider to the health department and to parents;

f) Requiring that all facilities, regardless of licensure status, and all health care providers report certain communicable diseases to the responsible local or state public health authority. The child care licensing authority should require such reporting under its regulatory jurisdiction and should collaborate fully with the health department when the latter is engaged in an enforcement action with a licensed facility;

g) Determining whether a disease represents a potential health risk to children in out-of-home child care;

h) Conducting the epidemiological investigation necessary to initiate public health interventions;

i) Recommending a disease prevention or control strategy that is based on sound public health and clinical practices (such as the use of vaccine, immunoglobulin, or antibiotics taken to prevent an infection).

j) Verifying reports of communicable diseases received from facilities with the assessment and diagnosis of the disease made by a health care provider and, or the local or state health department.

5. Designing systems and forms for use by facilities for the care of ill children to document the surveillance of cared for illnesses and problems that arise in the care of children in such child care settings.

6. Assisting in the development of orientation and annual training programs for caregivers. Such training shall include specialized education for staff of facilities that include ill children, as well as those in special facilities that serve only ill children. Specialized training for staff who care for ill children should focus on the recognition and management of childhood illnesses, as well as the care of children with communicable diseases.

7. Assisting the licensing authority in the periodic review of facility performance related to caring for ill children by:

a) Reviewing written policies developed by facilities regarding inclusion, exclusion, dismissal criteria and plans for health care, urgent and emergency care, and reporting and managing children with communicable disease;

b) Assisting with periodic compliance reviews for those rules relating to inclusion, exclusion, dismissal, daily health care, urgent and emergency care, and reporting and management of children with communicable disease.

9. Collaborating in the planning and implementation of appropriate training and educational programs related to health and safety in child care facilities. Such training should include education of parents, physicians, public health workers, licensing inspectors, and employers about how to prevent injury and disease as well as promote health of children and their caregivers.

10. Ensuring that health care personnel, such as qualified public health nurses, pediatric and family nurse practitioners, and pediatricians serve as child care health consultants as required in STANDARD 1.040 through STANDARD 1.044 and as members of advisory boards for facilities serving ill children.

DISCUSSION: A number of studies have described the incidence of injuries in the child care settings (23-26). Although the injuries described have not been serious, these occur frequently, and may require medical or emergency attention. Child care programs need the assistance of local and state health agencies in planning of the safety program that will minimize the risk for serious injury(10). This would include planning for such significant emergencies as fire, flood, tornado, or earthquake (27). A community health agency can collect information that can promptly identify an injury risk or hazard and provide an early notice about the risk or hazard (28). An example is the recent identification of un-powered scooters as a significant injury risk for preschool children (29). Once the injury risk is identified, appropriate channels of communication are required to alert the child care administrators and to provide training and educational activities.

Effective control and prevention of infectious diseases in child care settings depends on affirmative relationships among parents, caregivers, public health

authorities, regulatory agencies, and primary health care providers. The major barriers to productive working relationships between caregivers and health care providers are inadequate channels of communication and uncertainty of role definition. Public health authorities can play a major role in improving the relationship between caregivers and health care providers by disseminating information regarding disease reporting laws, prescribed measures for control and prevention of diseases and injuries, and resources that are available for these activities (9).

State and local health departments are legally required to control certain communicable diseases within their jurisdictions. All states have laws that grant extraordinary powers to public health departments during outbreaks of communicable diseases (4). Since communicable disease is likely to occur in child care settings, a plan for the control of communicable diseases in these settings is essential and often legally required. Early recognition and prompt intervention will reduce the spread of infection. Outbreaks of communicable disease in child care settings can have great implications for the general community (6). Programs administered by local health departments have been more successful in controlling outbreaks of hepatitis A than those that rely primarily on private physicians. Programs coordinated by the local health department also provide reassurance to caregivers, staff, and parents, and thereby promote cooperation with other disease control policies (7). Communicable diseases in child care settings pose new epidemiological considerations. Only in recent decades has it been so common for very young children to spend most of their days together in groups. Public health authorities should expand their role in studying this situation and designing new preventive health measures (8).

Collaboration is necessary to use limited resources most effectively. In small states, a state level task force that includes the Department of Health, might be sufficient. In larger or more populous states, local task forces may be needed. The collaboration should focus on establishing the role of each agency in ensuring that necessary services and systems exist to prevent and control injuries and communicable diseases in facilities.

Health departments generally have or should develop the expertise to provide leadership and technical assistance to licensing authorities, caregivers, parents, and health professionals in the development of licensing requirements and guidelines for the management of ill children. The heavy reliance on the expertise of local and state health departments in the establishment of facilities to care for ill children has fostered a partnership in many states among health depart-

ments, licensing authorities, caregivers, and parents for the adequate care of ill children in child care settings. In addition, the business community has a vested interest in assuring that parents have facilities that provide quality care for ill children so parents can be productive in the workplace.

This vested interest is likely to produce meaningful contributions from the business community to creative solutions and innovative ideas about how to approach the regulation of facilities for ill children. All stakeholders in the care of ill children should be involved for the solutions that are developed in regulations to be most successful. For additional information on the training for staff in facilities serving ill children, see STANDARD 3.073; for information regarding health consultants in facilities serving ill children, see STANDARD 3.075.

See also Reporting Illness, STANDARD 3.086 and STANDARD 3.087.

RECOMMENDATION 9.026
WRITTEN PLANS FOR THE HEALTH DEPARTMENT ROLE

The health department's role defined in RECOMMENDATION 9.028 should be described in written plans that assign the responsibilities of community agencies and organizations involved in the prevention and control of injury, injury risk and communicable disease in facilities. The plan should identify child care related risks and diseases as well as provide guidance for risk reduction, disease prevention and control. The health department should develop these written plans in collaboration with the licensing agency (if other than the health department), health care providers, caregivers, and parents to ensure the availability of sufficient community resources for successful implementation. In addition, the health department should provide assistance to the licensing agency (if other than the health department) for the promulgation and enforcement of child care facility standards. These services should be in addition to the health agency's assigned responsibilities for enforcement of the state's immunization and other health laws and regulations.

In addition to Caring for Our Children and Stepping Stones, the following resources should be consulted in the development of the health department plan:

a) Guidelines provided by the Centers for Disease Control and Prevention (CDC);
b) Guidelines from the American Academy of Pediatrics (AAP), including *The Red Book*, the *Report of the Committee on Infectious Diseases: Guidelines for Health Supervision,* and the many other relevant technical manuals on such topics as environment and nutrition;
c) Guidelines from the American Public Health Association (APHA), including *Control of Communicable Diseases in Man;*
d) Guidelines from the U.S. Public Health Service's Advisory Committee on Immunization Practices, as reported periodically in *Morbidity and Mortality Weekly Report;*
e) State and local regulations and guidelines regarding communicable diseases in facilities;
f) *Bright Futures - Guidelines for Health Supervision of Infants, Children, and Adolescents;*
g) *Healthy Child Care America Campaign;*
h) Current early childhood nutrition guidelines such as *Making Food Healthy and Safe for Children.*

DISCUSSION: Written plans help define delegation and accountability, providing the continuity of purpose that helps to institutionalize performance. Contact information for the resources listed above is located in Appendix BB.

RECOMMENDATION 9.027
REQUIREMENTS FOR FACILITIES TO REPORT TO HEALTH DEPARTMENT

The child care licensing authority should require all facilities under its regulatory jurisdiction to report to the health department and comply with state and local rules and regulations intended to prevent injury and infectious disease that apply to child care facilities.

DISCUSSION: State and local health departments are legally required to control certain communicable diseases within their jurisdictions. Legal requirements for the role of health departments and other government entities in control of injuries vary. States may delegate injury prevention duties to agencies responsible for fire prevention, building inspection, transportation safety, environmental health, agriculture, etc. All states have laws that grant extraordinary powers to public health departments during outbreaks of communicable disease (4). Since communicable disease is likely to occur in child care

settings, a plan for the control of communicable diseases in these settings is essential and often legally required. Early recognition and prompt intervention will reduce the spread of infection.

Outbreaks of communicable disease in child care settings can have great implications for the general community (6). Programs administered by local health departments have been more successful in controlling outbreaks of hepatitis A than those that rely primarily on private physicians. Programs coordinated by the local health department also provide reassurance to caregivers, staff, and parents, and thereby promote cooperation with other disease control policies (7). Communicable diseases in child care settings pose new epidemiological considerations. Only in recent decades has it been so common for very young children to spend most of their days together in groups. Public health authorities should expand their role in studying this situation and designing new preventive health measures (8).

RECOMMENDATION 9.028
HEALTH DEPARTMENT ASSISTANCE TO PREPARE PARENT AND STAFF FACT SHEETS

Health departments should help child care providers use prepared prototype parent and staff fact sheets on common illnesses associated with child care. These fact sheets should:
a) Be provided to parents when their child is first admitted to the facility, to staff at the time of employment and to both parents and staff when communicable disease notification is recommended.
b) Contain the following information:
   1) Disease (case or outbreak) to which the child was exposed;
   2) Signs and symptoms of the disease that the parents and caregivers should watch for in the child;
   3) Mode of transmission of the disease;
   4) Period of communicability;
   5) Disease prevention measures recommended by the public health department (if appropriate);
c) Emphasize modes of transmission of respiratory disease and infections of the intestines (often with diarrhea) and liver, common methods of infection control (such as handwashing). See Hygiene, STANDARD 3.012 through STANDARD 3.027, and Infectious Diseases,

STANDARD 6.001 through STANDARD 6.039, for specific diseases that may be asymptomatic in the child but have important consequences for a parent contact (such as hepatitis A virus (HAV) or cytomegalovirus (CMV) including the Centers for Disease Control and Prevention (CDC) guidelines specific to cytomegalovirus (CMV) transmission, exposure, and fetal risk for women providing child care.);

DISCUSSION: Education is a primary method for providing information to physicians and parents about the incidence of communicable diseases in child care settings (11). Education of child care staff and parents on the recognition and transmission of various communicable diseases is important to any infection control policy (11). Training of child care staff has improved the quality of their health related behaviors and practices. Training should be available to all parties involved, including caregivers, public health workers, health care providers, parents, and children. Good quality training, with imaginative and accessible methods of presentation supported by well-designed materials, will facilitate learning. The number of studies evaluating the importance of education of child care staff in the prevention of disease is limited. However, data from numerous studies in hospitals illustrate the important role of continuing education in preventing and minimizing the transmission of communicable disease (11). The provision of fact sheets on communicable childhood diseases at the time their child is admitted to a facility helps educate parents as to the early signs and symptoms of these illnesses and the need to inform caregivers of their existence. Illness information sheets can be assembled in a convenient booklet for this purpose. Health departments may consult or use nationally accepted fact sheets on common illnesses available from such agencies as the Centers for Disease Control and Prevention (CDC), the American Academy of Pediatrics (AAP), and the National Association for the Education of Young Children (NAEYC).

For example, CMV is the leading cause of congenital infection in the United States, with approximately 1% of live born infants infected prenatally (12). Fortunately, most infected fetuses escape resulting illness or disability, but 10% to 20% will have hearing loss, mental retardation, cerebral palsy, or vision disturbances. Although it is well known that maternal immunity does not prevent congenital CMV infection, evidence indicates that initial acquisition of CMV during pregnancy (primary maternal infection) carries the greatest risk for resulting illness or disability (12). With current knowledge about the risk of CMV infection in child care staff and the potential consequences of gestational CMV infection, child care staff should

be counseled regarding risks. However, it is unlikely that many facility directors have access to the information needed to counsel employees, and many health care providers may lack sufficient knowledge in the area. Therefore, state and local health departments should distribute the Centers for Disease Control and Prevention (CDC) guidelines on CMV to providers.

For information on Staff Education and Policies on cytomegalovirus (CMV), see STANDARD 6.021. Contact information for CDC, AAP, and NAEYC is located in Appendix BB.

RECOMMENDATION 9.029 SOURCES OF TECHNICAL ASSISTANCE TO SUPPORT QUALITY OF CHILD CARE

Public authorities, such as licensing agencies, and private agencies, such as resource and referral agencies, should develop systems for technical assistance to states, localities, and child care agencies and providers that address the following:
a) Meeting licensing and certification requirements. See Individual Credentialing/Certification, RECOMMENDATION 9.006 and RECOMMENDATION 9.007;
b) Establishing programs that meet the developmental needs of children;
c) Educating parents on specific health and safety issues through the production and distribution of related material. See Health Education for Parents, STANDARD 2.065 through STANDARD 2.067.

DISCUSSION: The administrative practice of developing systems for technical assistance is designed to enhance the overall quality of child care that meets the social and developmental needs of children. The chief sources of technical assistance are:
a) Licensing agencies (on ways to meet the regulations);
b) Health departments (on health related matters);
c) Resource and referral agencies (on ways to achieve quality, how to start a new facility, supply and demand data, how to get licensed, and what parents want).

The state agency has a continuing responsibility to assist an applicant in qualifying for a license and to help licensees improve and maintain the quality of their facility. Regulations should be available to parents and interested citizens upon request.

Licensing inspectors throughout the state should be required to offer assistance and consultation as a regular part of their duties.

Providing centers and networks of small or large family child care homes with guidelines and information on establishing a program of care is intended to promote appropriate programs of activities. Child care staff are rarely trained health professionals. Since staff and time are often limited, caregivers should have access to consultation on available resources in a variety of fields (such as physical and mental health care; nutrition; safety, including fire safety; oral health care; developmental disabilities, and cultural sensitivity) (13).

The public agencies can facilitate access to children and their families by providing useful materials to child care providers.

TECHNICAL ASSISTANCE FROM THE LICENSING AGENCY

RECOMMENDATION 9.030 LICENSING AGENCY PROVISION OF CHILD ABUSE PREVENTION MATERIALS

The licensing agency should be a resource for or have knowledge of sources of child abuse prevention materials for child care facilities and parents.

DISCUSSION: Centers and small and large family child care homes are good locations to distribute materials for the prevention of abuse.

RECOMMENDATION 9.031 LICENSING AGENCY PROVISION OF WRITTEN AGREEMENTS FOR PARENTS AND CAREGIVERS

The licensing agency or a resource and referral agency should provide guidance, technical assistance, and training to support parents and caregivers in developing the written agreements that are required to be available at the time of an inspection visit based on standard language for agreements.

DISCUSSION: The licensing agency can be a resource to parents and caregivers in locating the appropriate materials and tools.

RECOMMENDATION 9.032 COLLECTION OF DATA ON ILLNESS OR HARM TO CHILDREN IN FACILITIES

The state regulatory agency should have access to an information system for collecting data relative to the incidence of illness, injuries, confirmed child abuse and neglect, and death of children in facilities. This data should be shared with appropriate agencies and the child care health consultant for analysis.

DISCUSSION: Sound public policy planning in respect to health and safety in facilities starts with the collection of epidemiological data.

RECOMMENDATION 9.033 SUPPORT FOR CONSULTANTS TO PROVIDE TECHNICAL ASSISTANCE TO FACILITIES

State agencies should encourage the arrangement of and the fiscal support for consultants from the local community to provide technical assistance for program development and maintenance. Consultants should have training and experience in early childhood education, issues of health and safety in child care settings, ability to establish collegial relationships with child care providers, adult learning techniques, and ability to help establish links between facilities and community resources.

The state regulatory agency should provide or arrange for other public agencies, private organizations or technical assistance agencies (such as a resource and referral agency) to make the following consultants available to the community of child care providers of all types:
1) Program Consultant, to provide technical assistance for program development and maintenance. Consultants should be chosen on the basis of training and experience in early childhood education and ability to help establish links between the facility and community resources;

2) Child Health Consultant, who has expertise in child health and child development, is knowledgeable about the special needs of children in out-of-home care settings, and knows the child care licensing requirements and available health resources. A regional plan to make consultants accessible to facilities should be developed;

3) Nutrition Specialist, to be responsible for the development of policies and procedures and for the implementation of nutrition standards to provide high quality meals, nutrition education programs, and appropriately trained personnel, and to provide consultation to agency personnel, including licensing inspectors;

4) Mental Health Consultant, to assist centers, large family child care homes, and networks of small family child care homes in meeting the emotional needs of children and families. The state mental health agency should promote funding through community mental health agencies and child guidance clinics for these services. At the least, such consultants should be available when caregivers identify children whose behaviors are more difficult to manage than typically developing children.

DISCUSSION: Securing expertise is acceptable by whatever method is most workable at the state or local level (for example, consultation could be provided from a resource and referral agency). Providers, not the regulatory agency, are responsible for securing the type of consultation that is required by their individual facilities.

The mental health consultant for children younger than school-age is the most difficult of the health consultants to locate. Pediatricians who specialize in developmental pediatrics are most likely to be helpful for this type of consultation. Some, but not all, pediatric psychiatrists and psychologists have the necessary skills to work with behavior problems of this youngest age group. To find such specialists, contact the Department of Pediatrics at academic centers. The faculty at such centers can usually refer child care facilities to individuals with the necessary skills in their area.

The administrative practice of developing systems for technical assistance is designed to enhance the overall quality of child care that meets the social and developmental needs of children. The chief sources of technical assistance are:
a) Licensing agencies (on ways to meet the regulations);
b) Health departments (on health related matters);

c) Resource and referral agencies (on ways to achieve quality, how to start a new facility, supply and demand data, how to get licensed, and what parents want).

Providing centers and networks of small or large family child care homes with guidelines and information on establishing a program of care is intended to promote appropriate programs of activities. Child care staff are rarely trained health professionals. Since staff and time are often limited, caregivers should have access to consultation on available resources in a variety of fields (such as physical and mental health care; nutrition; safety, including fire safety; oral health care; developmental disabilities, and cultural sensitivity) (13).

The public agencies can facilitate access to children and their families by providing useful materials to child care providers.

RECOMMENDATION 9.034 DEVELOPMENT OF LIST OF PROVIDERS OF SERVICES TO FACILITIES

The local regulatory agency or resource and referral agency should assist centers and small and large family child care homes to formulate and maintain a list of community professionals and agencies available to provide needed health, dental, and social services to families.

DISCUSSION: Families depend on their child care facilities to provide information about obtaining health and dental care and other community services. A number of communities have Family Resource Centers, which are central points for information. It is important that regulatory agencies and resource and referral agencies have knowledge of family resource centers or can provide a directory of community services to child care facilities.

Partnerships among health care professionals and community agencies are necessary to provide a medical home for all children. The American Academy of Pediatrics (AAP) defines the medical home as care that is accessible, family-centered, continuous, comprehensive, coordinated, compassionate, and culturally competent. The medical home is not a building, house, or hospital, but an approach to providing health care services in a high-quality and cost-effective manner (14, 15, 16). Health care professionals and other community service agencies are beginning to recognize that child care facilities are a logical opportunity to provide health promotion and disease prevention services for children and families.

CONSULTANTS AND TECHNICAL ASSISTANCE FOR CHILDREN WITH SPECIAL NEEDS

RECOMMENDATION 9.035 RESOURCES FOR PARENTS OF CHILDREN WITH SPECIAL NEEDS

The state agency or council of agencies responsible for child care services for children with special needs should provide or arrange for the distribution to parents, printed and audiovisual information about assessment of facilities for care of children who are developing differently from typical children.
In addition, the regulatory agency should refer caregivers of children with special needs to community resources for assistance in development and formulation of the written plan of care.

DISCUSSION: Parents of children with special needs require support to enable their identification and evaluation of facilities where their children can receive quality child care.

Parents should participate in facility evaluation, both formally and informally. Unless the Interagency Coordinating Council (ICC) or some similar body provides materials to parents, they are unlikely to be able to find and evaluate options for child care for special needs children. While the professionals involved with the family may do this for the family, the parents should have every opportunity to play a significant role in the process.

The state licensing agency as well as the state agencies responsible for implementation of Public Law 105-17, known as the Individuals with Disabilities Education Act (IDEA), should assist child care providers to recognize the opportunity they have to participate in the child's overall care planning and to obtain education they need to provide care to the children.

RECOMMENDATION 9.036 COMPENSATION FOR PARTICIPATION IN MULTIDISCIPLINARY ASSESSMENTS FOR CHILDREN WITH SPECIAL NEEDS

The agency (or a council of such agencies) within the state responsible for overseeing child care for children with special educational needs should assure that the Individualized Family Service Plan (IFSP) or the Individualized Education Program (IEP) includes compensation for the hours of time spent by members of the multidisciplinary team and the staff from the out-of-home facility in developing the assessment defined in Assessment of Facilities for Children with Special Needs, STANDARD 7.014 through STANDARD 7.016.

DISCUSSION: Unless there is a source of compensation for the time spent in planning and completing assessments, these requirements cannot be implemented.

Funding under Individuals with Disabilities Education Act (IDEA) makes it possible for the resources and funding for service to follow the child. Traditionally, these funds have paid for individual therapists, and not for involving others who do not receive compensation for the time they spend in the planning process. Tradition and restrained spending by this practice inhibit effective service delivery for children and families.

NETWORKING

RECOMMENDATION 9.037 DEVELOPMENT OF CHILD CARE PROVIDER ORGANIZATIONS AND NETWORKS

State-level agencies and resource and referral agencies should encourage the development of child care provider organizations or networks, to attract, train, support, and encourage participation in facility accreditation, and monitor those caregivers who would like to be part of an organization or system.

DISCUSSION: To enhance staff qualifications and a nurturing environment, child care providers need

support (17). This especially applies to family child care home providers who tend to be more isolated than those employed in centers.

In studies of the quality of care in family child care homes, the caregivers who provided better care were those who viewed their role as a profession and acted accordingly, participating in continuous improvement activities (18). Individual caregivers vary widely in educational background and experience. Participation in a network provides access to education and support for individual caregivers. When possible, these networks should include a central facility for enrichment activities for groups of children and support and inservice programs for caregivers.

See Individual Credentialing/Certification, RECOMMENDATION 9.006 and RECOMMENDATION 9.007.

9.3 TRAINING

RECOMMENDATION 9.038
REGULATORY AGENCY PROVISION OF CAREGIVER AND CONSUMER TRAINING AND SUPPORT SERVICES

The regulatory agency should promote participation in a variety of caregiver and consumer training and support services as an integral component of its mission to reduce risks to children in out-of-home child care. Such training should include mechanisms for training of prospective child care staff prior to their assuming responsibility for the care of children.

Persons wanting to enter the child care field should be able to learn from the regulatory agency about training opportunities offered by public and private agencies.

Training programs should address the following:
a) Child growth and development;
b) Child care programming and activities;
c) Discipline and behavior management;
d) Health and safety practices including injury prevention, infection control and health promotion;
e) Cultural diversity;
f) Nutrition and eating habits;

g) Parent education;
h) Design and use of physical space;
i) Care and education of children with special needs.

DISCUSSION: Training enhances staff competence (17, 18). In addition to low child:staff ratio, group size, age mix of children, and stability of caregiver, the training/education of caregivers is a specific indicator of child care quality (17, 18). Most states require training for child care staff depending on their functions and responsibilities. Staff members who are better trained are more able to prevent, recognize, and correct health and safety problems. Decisions about management of illness are facilitated by the caregiver's increased skill in assessing a child's behavior that suggests illness (19, 20). Training plans should be based on improving performance rather than on a required number of hours.

The National Resource Center for Health and Safety in Child Care maintains a list of training resources as do Healthy Child Care America (HCCA) grantees within each state.

RECOMMENDATION 9.039
CHILD DEVELOPMENT ASSOCIATE TRAINING

Community colleges, vocational schools, and high schools should make training programs available to all child care providers, regardless of setting, to prepare for the Child Development Associate (CDA) credential.

DISCUSSION: CDA training should be offered at times when staff members who are employed fulltime in facilities may attend.

Training of child care staff has improved the quality of their health related behaviors and practices. Training should be available to all parties involved, including caregivers, public health workers, health care providers, parents, and children. Good quality training, with imaginative and accessible methods of presentation supported by well-designed materials, will facilitate learning.

For additional information on training, see also STANDARD 1.023; Continuing Education, STANDARD 1.029 through STANDARD 1.033; and The Health Department's Role, RECOMMENDATION 9.025.

RECOMMENDATION 9.040 PROVISION OF TRAINING TO FACILITIES BY HEALTH AGENCIES

Health departments and Emergency Medical Services (EMS) agencies should provide training, written information, and consultation in coordination with other community resources to facilities, including staff, parents, licensing personnel, and health consultants, in at least the following subject areas:
a) Immunization;
b) Reporting of communicable diseases;
c) Techniques for the prevention and control of communicable diseases;
d) Exclusion and inclusion guidelines and care of acutely ill children;
e) General hygiene and sanitation;
f) Food service and nutrition;
g) Care of children with special needs (chronic illnesses, developmental disability and behavior problems);
h) Prevention and management of injury;
i) Managing emergencies;
j) Oral health;
k) Environmental health;
l) Health promotion, including routine health supervision and the importance of a medical or health home for children and adults;
m) Health insurance, including Medicaid and the Children's Health Insurance Program (CHIP).

DISCUSSION: Training of child care staff has improved the quality of their health related behaviors and practices. Training should be available to all parties involved, including caregivers, public health workers, health care providers, parents, and children. Good quality training, with imaginative and accessible methods of presentation supported by well-designed materials, will facilitate learning.

For additional information on training, see also STANDARD 1.023; Continuing Education, STANDARD 1.029 through STANDARD 1.033; and The Health Department's Role, RECOMMENDATION 9.025.

9.4 PROGRAM DEVELOPMENT

RECOMMENDATION 9.041 TECHNICAL ASSISTANCE TO FACILITIES TO ADDRESS DIVERSITY IN THE COMMUNITY

Technical assistance and incentives should be provided by state, municipal, public, and private agencies to encourage facilities to address within their programs, the cultural and socioeconomic diversity in the broader community, not just in the neighborhood where the child care facility is located.

DISCUSSION: Children who are exposed to cultural and socioeconomic diversity in early childhood are more likely to value and accept differences between their own backgrounds and those of others as they move through life. This attitude results in improved self-esteem and mental health in children from all backgrounds. Facilities can attract participants from different income and cultural groups by locating in areas convenient to low income families and accessible to middle and upper income parents, and by offering programs that are desirable to a range of parents. Possible locations include:
a) Sites close to the edge of, rather than deep within, low income housing areas;
b) Sites near work sites and schools that serve a mix of families;
c) Sites in mixed income housing areas.

RECOMMENDATION 9.042 FOSTERING COLLABORATION TO ESTABLISH PROGRAMS FOR SCHOOL-AGE CHILDREN

Public and private agencies should foster collaboration among the schools, child care facilities, and resource and referral agencies to establish programs for school-age children, ages 5 to 12 and older. Such care should be designed to meet the social and developmental needs of children who receive care in any setting.

DISCUSSION: School-age children who are under-supervised ("latchkey children") are exposed to considerable health and safety risks. Bringing these children into supervised, quality child care is a societal responsibility.

RECOMMENDATION 9.043
PUBLIC-PRIVATE COLLABORATION
ON CARE OF MILDLY ILL CHILDREN

Employers should collaborate with state and regional agencies to facilitate arrangements for the care of mildly ill children in the following settings:
a) The child's own home, under the supervision of an adult known to the parents and the child;
b) A separate area in the child's own facility or in a specialized center, where both the caregiver and the facility are familiar to the child;
c) A child's own small family child care home;
d) A space within the small family child care home network's central place that serves children from participating small family child care homes, where both the caregiver and the facility are familiar to the child.

DISCUSSION: Appropriate care of ill children is preferable to makeshift arrangements that are not in the best interests of the ill child, other children in care, or the family. The most appropriate care of an ill child is at the child's own home by a parent. Businesses should be encouraged to allow the use of sick leave for this purpose. However, when parent care puts the family income or parent employment at risk, the child should receive care that is appropriate for the child. Often, when faced with the pressures of the workplace, parents take ill children to work, leave them in places where either or both the caregiver and place are unfamiliar, or leave them alone. Under the stress of illness, children need familiar caregivers and familiar places where their illnesses and their emotional needs can be managed competently.

See RECOMMENDATION 9.048, regarding paid parental leave to care for ill children.

9.5 REGULATORY COORDINATION

RECOMMENDATION 9.044
AGENCY COLLABORATION TO
SAFEGUARD CHILDREN IN CHILD
CARE

The state health department, Emergency Medical Services (EMS) agencies, regulatory agencies, funding agencies, child protection agencies, law enforcement agencies, community service agencies, and local government should collaborate to safeguard children in child care. The child care licensing, building, fire safety, and health authorities, as well as any other regulators, should work together as a team. The team should eliminate duplication of inspections to create more efficient regulatory efforts. Examples of activities to be coordinated include:
a) Inspection;
b) Reporting and surveillance systems;
c) Guidance in managing outbreaks of infectious diseases;
d) Preventing exposure of children to hazards;
e) Reporting child abuse;
f) Training and technical consultation.

Agencies should collaborate to educate parents, health care providers, public health workers, licensors, and employers about their roles in ensuring health and safety in child care settings.

DISCUSSION: Frequently, caregivers are burdened by complicated procedures and conflicting requirements to obtain clearance from various authorities to operate. To use limited resources, agencies must avoid contradictions in regulatory codes, simplify inspection procedures, and reduce bureaucratic disincentives to the provision of safe and healthy care for children. When regulatory authorities work as a team, collaboration should focus on establishing the role of each agency in ensuring that necessary services and systems exist to prevent and control health and safety problems in facilities. Each member of the team gains opportunities to learn about the responsibilities of other team members so that close working relationships can be established, conflicts can be resolved, and decisions can be reached.

In small states, a state level task force may be sufficient. In larger or more populous states, local task forces may be needed to promote effective use of resources.

9.6 PUBLIC POLICY ISSUES AND RESOURCE DEVELOPMENT

RECOMMENDATION 9.045 STATE-LEVEL COMMISSION ON CHILD CARE

Each state should establish a state-level commission on child care or charge an existing commission with the responsibility for developing a child care plan and facilitating cooperation among government public health, human service, and education departments as well as community-based human services agencies, schools, employers, and caregivers to ensure that the health, safety, and child development needs of children are met by the child care services provided in the state. The commission should include both parents and representatives of agencies and organizations affecting child care. The commission should be mandated by law, and should report to the legislature, to the governor, and to all agencies and organizations represented on the commission no less frequently than once a year. Larger communities should have a local child care advisory body charged with the responsibility of overseeing the development and provision of child care to meet the needs of the particular community with the same broad representation recommended for the state level commission. The state advisory body to the regulatory agency should be a component part of or report to this commission.

DISCUSSION: Coordination among public and private sources of health, social service, and education services is essential, especially when young children are in care. Some states have separate groups that advise the health agency, the social service agency, the education agency, the licensing agency, the governor, and the legislature. Other states have some, but not all, of these advisory bodies; each of which has some relevance to child care, but often with a different focus. National initiatives such as the Healthy Child Care America campaign have done much to encourage effective collaboration among agencies and

organizations with the ability to impact child care within states.

Time limited task forces could be created for specific purposes, but there is a need for one standing commission that addresses child care as its primary responsibility. Mandating the commission by law will reduce the likelihood that the commission will be victimized by changes in political leadership or dissolved when its recommendations are not in agreement with a current administration.

Large municipalities with a similarly diverse group of agencies, authorities, and public and private resources should also have a group to coordinate child care activity. Participation of parent representatives in planning and implementing child care initiatives at the state and local levels promotes effective partnerships between parents and caregivers.

RECOMMENDATION 9.046 DEVELOPMENT OF RESOURCE AND REFERRAL AGENCIES

States should encourage the use of public and private resources in local communities to develop resource and referral agencies. The functions of these agencies should include the following:
a) Helping parents find developmentally appropriate child care that protects the health and safety of children;
b) Giving parents consumer information to enable them to know about, evaluate, and choose among available child care options;
c) Helping parents maintain a dialogue with their caregivers;
d) Recruiting new potential caregivers;
e) Providing training, technical assistance, and consultation to new facilities, and to all caregivers;
f) Compiling data on supply and demand to identify community needs for child care;
g) Providing information to employers on options for their involvement in meeting community child care needs.

DISCUSSION: Resource and referral agencies provide a locus in the community to assist parents in fulfilling their childrearing responsibilities, a mechanism to coordinate and provide the resources and services that supplement and facilitate the functions of the family, and a mechanism for the coordination of services that helps keep children safe and healthy.

RECOMMENDATION 9.047 COORDINATION OF PUBLIC AND PRIVATE POLICYMAKERS TO ENSURE FAMILIES' ACCESS TO QUALITY CHILD CARE

Public and private policymakers should coordinate public and private resources to ensure that all families have access to affordable, safe, and healthful child care for their children. Stabilizing the child care workforce should be a major goal in improving available child care. To the extent possible, communities should coordinate multiple funding streams to support child care.

DISCUSSION: Quality cannot be attained by merely applying standards to caregivers; resources are necessary to meet the cost of quality care at a price that parents can afford. Currently, the low wages and benefits earned by child care staff result in high staff turnover, which adversely affects the health and safety of children. Frequently replaced, untrained, barely oriented, poorly compensated, and overworked staff cannot maintain sanitation routines, be prepared for emergencies, or meet the mental health needs of children for constancy in relationships. Child care is a labor intensive service. Staff wages make up the largest cost in providing care, and caregiver wages in the United States are currently too low to attract and retain qualified staff. Countries that successfully recruit and retain good child care staff pay salaries and benefits equal to those paid to elementary school teachers.

The cost of child care in the United States is currently subsidized by the low wages and benefits of caregivers, who leave their jobs at an astonishingly high rate. Research provides clear evidence that a well qualified and stable staff is essential to the provision of good care for children. Quality care requires not only lower child:staff ratios and smaller group sizes, but also well trained staff to reduce the spread of infectious diseases, provide for safe evacuation and management of emergency situations, and to offer developmentally appropriate program activities. Facilities cannot benefit from training provided to staff if the staff members leave their jobs before the training is implemented (20).

See The Child Care Bureau's *Case Studies of Public-Private Partnerships for Child Care* (21) for examples of successful state-wide collaborative projects.

RECOMMENDATION 9.048 ARRANGEMENTS FOR PARENTAL LEAVE

Arrangements for parental leave should be available to support the ability of parents to take temporary leave from work for up to 3 months after the birth or adoption of a child, or to care for an ill child for whom out-of-home child care is not as safe and healthful as parental care.

DISCUSSION: Safe and healthful child care at times when a child is significantly ill or when the child is a newborn or newly adopted child is usually best provided in the child's home by parents. The Family and Medical Leave Act of 1993 provided a minimum of 12 work weeks of unpaid leave during a 12-month period for the birth of a child, adopting or providing foster care, an illness of a close relative, or a disabling health condition of the employee (22). However, effective implementation of the intent of the law requires employer flexibility about the use of vacation, personal and sick leave benefits to protect parent income when using parental leave.

There is no mandate for paid parental leave in the United States. To be a realistic option for parents whose children need them at home, parental leave should be available on short notice, and parent income should be protected by the parents' sick leave, vacation time, personal leave or other benefits. Ready access to paid leave should include all working parents of young children since for many families, the use of unpaid leave is not a realistic option.

Nevertheless, taking parental leave should be a matter of choice. In some families, two parents can combine their leaves to provide extended care at home for a child who is not ready for group care. In other families, the child and family may benefit from the child's entry into a group care setting early in infancy. This is particularly so with difficult infants or stressed parents for whom child care serves as an extended family, providing respite, comfort, advice and support to parents. Parents in nontraditional families should receive the same leave as parents in traditional families.

REFERENCES

1.   *Licensing and Public Regulation of Early Childhood Programs: A Position Statement, Adopted 1997.* Washington, DC: National Association for the Education of Young Children; 1997.

2.   Newacheck PW, Strickland B, Shonkoff JP, et al. An epidemiologic profile of children with special health care needs. *Pediatrics.* 1998;102(pt 1):117-123.

3.   Finkelhor D, William LM, Burns N. *Nursery Crimes: Sexual Abuse in Day Care.* Beverly Hills, Calif: Sage Publications; 1988.

4.   Grad FP. *The Public Health Law Manual.* 2nd ed. Washington, DC: American Public Health Association, 1990.

5.   *Child Care Center Licensing Study.* Washington, DC: The Children's Foundation; 1999.

6.   Churchill RB, Pickering, LK. Infection control challenges in child-care centers. *Infect Dis Clin North Am.* 1997;11(2):347-365.

7.   Chin J. ed. *Control of Communicable Diseases Manual.* 17th ed. Washington, DC: American Public Health Association; 2000.

8.   Reves RR, Pickering LK. Impact of child day care on infectious diseases in adults. *Infect Dis Clin North Am.* 1992;6:239-250.

9.   *Centers for Disease Control and Prevention (CDC) Child Care Health and Safety Action Plan: Goals, Objectives, and Actions; Public Health Information Systems.* Atlanta, GA: CDC; 1995.

10.   Sacks JJ, Addiss DG. The perceived needs of child care center directors in preventing injuries and infectious diseases. *AJPH* 1995;85: 266-267.

11.   Pickering LK, Peter G, Baker CJ, Gerber MA, MacDonald NA, eds. *Red Book 2000: Report of the Committee on Infectious Diseases.* 25th ed. Elk Grove Village, Ill: American Academy of Pediatrics, Committee on Infectious Diseases; 2000.

12.   Osterholm MT, Reves RR, Murph JR, Pickering LK. Infectious diseases and child day care. *Pediatr Infect Dis J.* 1992;11(suppl 8):S31-S41.

13.   American Academy of Pediatrics, Committee on Early Childhood, Adoption and Dependent Care. Pediatrician's role in promoting the health of patients in early childhood education and/or child care programs (RE9325). *Pediatrics.* 1993;92(3):489-492.

14.   Kempe A, Beaty B, Englund BP, Roark RJ, Hester N, Steiner JF. Quality of care and use of the medical home in a state-funded capitated primary care plan for low-income children. *Pediatrics.* 2000;105(5):1020-8.

15.   American Academy of Pediatrics. Policy statement: the medical home (RE9262). *Pediatrics.* 1992;90(5):774.

16.   *Policy Statement: The Medical Home Statement Addendum, Pediatric Primary Health Care (RE9262).* Elk Grove Village, Ill: American Academy of Pediatrics; 1993.

17.   US General Accounting Office. *Child Care: Promoting Quality in Family Child Care: Report to the Chairman, Subcommittee and Regulation, Business Opportunities and Technology, Committee on Small Business, House of Representatives.* Washington, DC: US General Accounting Office; 1994:Publication No. GAO-HEHS-95-36.

18.   Galinsky E, Howes C, Kontos S, Shinn M. *The Study of Children in Family Child Care and Relative Care.* New York, NY: Families and Work Institute; 1994.

19.   Aronson SS, Aiken SA. Compliance of child care programs with health and safety standards: impact of program evaluation and advocate training. *Pediatrics.* 1990;652:318-325.

20.   Kendrick A, Shapiro. Science, prevention and practice: VII. improving child day care: plenary: training to ensure healthy child day-care programs. [Abstract] *Pediatrics.* 1994;94(suppl pt 2):1108-1110.

21.   *Case Studies of Public-Private Partnerships for Child Care.* Washington, DC: US Dept of Health and Human Services, Administration for Children and Families, Child Care Bureau; 1998.

22. Family and Medical Leave Act, 28 USC §2612 (1993).

23. Chang A, Lugg MM, Nebedum A. Injuries among preschool children enrolled in day-care centers. Pediatrics 1989;83:272-277.

24. Sacks JJ, Smith JD, Kaplan KM, et al. The epidemiology of injuries in Atlanta day-care centers. JAMA; 1989; 262: 1641-1645.

25. Gunn WJ, Pinsky PF, Sacks JJ, et al. Injuries and poisonings in out-of-home child care and home care. Am J Dis Child 1991;145:779-781.

26. Sellstrom E, Bremberg S, Chang A. Injuries in Swedish day-care centers. Pediatrics 1994;94(6 Pt.2):1033- 1036.

27. Certo D. Helping children and staff cope with earthquakes. Child Care Exchange March 1995. Pgs.71-74.

28. Browning KS, Runyan CW, Kotch JB. A statewide survey of hazards in child care centers. Injury Prevention 1996; 2:202-207.

29. Centers for Disease Control and Prevention. Unpowered scooter-related injuries- United States, 1998-2000, MMWR 2000;49:1108-1110.]

Guiding Principles for the Standards

The following are the guiding principles used in writing these standards:

1. Child care for infants, young children, and school-age children is anchored in a respect for the developmental needs, characteristics, and cultures of the children and their families; it recognizes the unique qualities of each individual and the importance of early brain development in children 0 to 3 years of age.

2. To the extent possible, program activities should be geared to the needs of the individual child, as well as to the group as a whole.

3. The relationship between parent and child is of utmost importance for the child's current and future development and should be supported by caregivers. The parent/legal guardian is the primary decision maker regarding the child's day-to-day care. A cornerstone of out-of-home child care is planned communication and involvement between the parent/legal guardian and the child's caregiver.

4. The nurturing of a child's development is based on knowledge of general health and growth and on the unique characteristics of the individual child. This nurturing enhances the enjoyment of both child and parent as maturation and adaptation take place. As shown by recent studies of early brain development, trustworthy relationships with a small number of adults and an encircling, benevolent, affective atmosphere are essential to the healthy development of children. Staff selection, training, and support should be directed to the following goals:
   a) Promoting continuity of affective relationships;
   b) Encouraging staff capacity for identification and empathy with the child; and
   c) Emphasizing an attitude of playfulness while maintaining the stance of an adult.

5. Programs and care should be based on a child's functional status, and the child's needs should be described in behavioral or functional terms. Rigid categorical labeling of children should be avoided as much as possible.

6. Written policies and procedures should identify facility requirements and persons and/or entities responsible for implementing such requirements. Whenever possible, written information should be provided in the native language of parents, in a form appropriate for parents who are visually impaired, and also for parents who are illiterate. However, processes should never become more important than the care and education of children.

7. Confidentiality of records and shared verbal information must be maintained to protect the child, family, and staff. The information obtained in the course of child care should be used to plan for a child's safe and appropriate participation. Parents/legal guardians must be assured of the vigilance of the staff in protecting such information.

8. Health education for the toddler and for the pre-school and school-age child is an investment in a lifetime of good health practices and contributes to a healthier childhood and adult life. The child care setting offers many opportunities for incorporating health and safety education into every-day activities.

9. The facility's nutrition activities complement and supplement those of home and community. Food provided in a child care setting should help to meet the child's daily nutritional needs while reflecting individual, cultural, and philosophical differences and providing an opportunity for learning. Facilities can contribute to overall child development goals by helping the child and family understand the relationship of nutrition to health, the factors that influence food practices, and the variety of ways to provide for nutritional needs.

10. No child with special needs should be denied access to child care because of his/her disabilities, unless the child's extreme special needs make it unsafe for the child to be cared for in a community child care setting.

11. The facility chosen for each child should be one that is geared to meet the developmental needs of that child. Whenever possible, children with special needs should be cared for and provided services in settings including children without disabilities. If care in an integrated/inclusive setting is not feasible (due to the particular nature of the child's needs and level of care required; the physical limitations of the site; limited resources in the community; or the unavailability of specialized, trained staff), a segregated setting is the next best alternative.

12. The expression of, and exposure to, cultural and ethnic diversity enriches the experience of all children, parents, and staff. Planning for cultural diversity and working with language differences should be encouraged.

13. Community resources should be identified and utilized as much as possible to provide consultation and related services as needed.

Major Occupational Health Hazards

Infectious Diseases and Organisms

General Types of Infectious Diseases
Diarrhea (infectious)
Respiratory tract infection

Specific Infectious Diseases and Organisms

Adenovirus
Astrovirus
Caliciviruses
Campylobacter jejuni/coli
Chickenpox (varicella)
Clostridium parvum
Cytomegalovirus (CMV)
Escherichia coli 0157:H7
Giardia lamblia
Hepatitis A
Hepatitis B
Hepatitis C
Herpes 6
Herpes 7
Herpes simplex
Herpes zoster
Human Immunodeficiency Virus (HIV)
Impetigo
Influenza
Lice
Measles
Meningitis (bacterial, viral)
Meningococcus (Neisseria meningitildis)
Mumps
Parvovirus B19
Pertussis
Pinworm
Ringworm
Rotavirus
Rubella
Salmonella organisms
Scabies
Shigella organisms
Staphylococcus aureus
Streptococcus, Group A
Tuberculosis

Injuries and Noninfectious Diseases

Back injuries
Bites
Dermatitis
Falls

Environmental exposure
Art materials
Cleaning, sanitizing and disinfecting solutions
Indoor air pollution
Noise
Odor

Stress
Fear of liability
Inadequate break time, sick time, and personal days
Inadequate facilities
Inadequate pay
Inadequate recognition
Inadequate training
Insufficient professional recognition
Lack of adequate medical/dental health insurance
Responsibility for children's welfare
Undervaluing of work
Working alone

Reference: American Academy of Pediatrics, Committee on Infectious Diseases. *Red Book 2000: Report of the Committee on Infectious Diseases.* Elk Grove Village, Il: American Academy of Pediatrics; 2000.

Nutrition Specialist and Child Care Food Service Staff Qualifications

TITLE	LEVEL OF PROFESSIONAL RESPONSIBILITY	EDUCATION AND EXPERIENCE
Child Care Nutrition Specialist (state level)	Develops policies and procedures for implementation of nutrition food standards statewide and provides consultation to state agency personnel, including staff involved with licensure.	Current registration with the Commission on Dietetic Registration of the American Dietetic Association or eligibility for registration with a Bachelor's and Master's degree in nutrition (including or supplemented by course(s) in child growth and development), plus at least 2 years of related experience as a nutritionist in a health program including services to infants and children. A Master's degree from an approved program in public health nutrition may be substituted for registration with the Commission on Dietetic Registration.
Child Care Nutrition Specialist (local level)	Provides expertise to child care center director and provides ongoing guidance, consultation, and inservice training to facility's nutrition component. The number of sites and facilities for one child care Nutrition Specialist will vary according to size and complexity of local facilities.	Registered Dietitian, as above. At least 1 year of experience as described above.
Child Care Food Service Manager	Has overall supervisory responsibility for the food service unit at one or more facility sites.	High school diploma or GED. Successful completion of a food handler food protection class. Coursework in basic menu-planning skills, basic foods, introduction to child feeding programs for managers, and/or other relevant courses (offered at community colleges). Two years of food service experience.
Child Care Food Service Worker (Cook)	Under the supervision of the Food Service Manager, carries out food service operations including menu planning, food preparation and service, and related duties in a designated area.	High school diploma or GED. Successful completion of a food handler food protection class. Coursework in basic menu-planning skills and basic foods (offered through adult education or a community college). One year of food service experience.
Child Care Food Service Aide	Works no more than 4 hours a day, under the supervision of an employee at a higher level in food service unit.	High school diploma or GED. Must pass the food handler test within 1 to 2 months of employment. No prior experience is required for semi-skilled persons who perform assigned tasks in designated areas.

Gloving

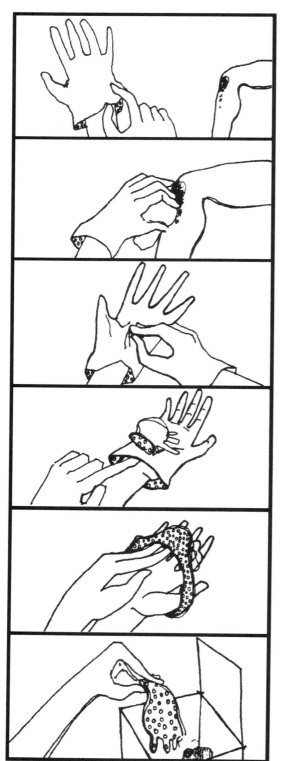

Put on a clean pair of gloves.

Provide the appropriate care.

Remove each glove carefully. Grab the first glove at the palm and strip the glove off. Touch dirty surfaces only to dirty surfaces.

Ball-up the dirty glove in the palm of the other gloved hand.

With the clean hand strip the glove off from underneath at the wrist, turning the glove inside out. Touch dirty surfaces only to dirty surfaces.

Discard the dirty gloves immediately in a step can. Wash your hands.

Reference: California Department of Education. *Keeping Kids Healthy Preventing and Managing Communicable Disease in Child Care.* Sacramento CA:California Department of Education, 1995.

Child Care Staff Health Assessment

********* Employer should complete this section. ********

Name of person to be examined: _____

Employer for whom examination is being done: _____

Employer's Location: _____ Phone number: _____

Purpose of examination: ☐pre-employment (with conditional offer of employment) ☐annual re-examination

Type of activity on the job: ☐lifting, carrying children ☐close contact with children ☐food preparation

☐desk work ☐driver of vehicles ☐facility maintenance

**** Part I and Part II below must be completed and signed by a licensed physician or CRNP. ****
*Based on a review of the medical record, health history, and examination, does this person
have any of the following conditions or problems that might affect job performance or require accommodation?*

Date of exam: _____

Part I: Health Problems (circle)

Visual acuity less than 20/40 (combined, obtained with lenses if needed)?...yes .... no

Decreased hearing or difficulty functioning in a noisy environment (less than 20 db at 500, 1000, 2000, 4000 Hz)? .... yes .... no

Respiratory problems (asthma, emphysema, airway allergies, current smoker, other)?...yes .... no

Heart, blood pressure, or other cardiovascular problems?..yes .... no

Gastrointestinal problems (ulcer, colitis, special dietary requirements, obesity, other)?...............................yes .... no

Endocrine problems (diabetes, thyroid, other)?...yes .... no

Emotional disorders or addiction (depression, substance dependency, difficulty handling stress, other)? .... yes .... no

Neurologic problems (epilepsy, Parkinsonism, other)? ....yes .... no

Musculoskeletal problems (low back pain or susceptibility to back injury, neck problems, arthritis, limitations on activity)?.... yes .... no

Skin problems (eczema, rashes, conditions incompatible with frequent handwashing, other)?.................yes .... no

Immune system problems (from medication, inherent susceptibility to infection, illness, allergies)?.....................yes .... no

Need for more frequent health visits or sick days than the average person?...yes .... no

Other special medical problem or chronic disease that requires work restrictions or accommodation? .... yes .... no

Part II: Infectious Disease Status

Immunizations now due/overdue for:

dT (every 10 years) ....yes .... no

MMR (2 doses for persons born after 1989; 1 dose for those born in or after 1957)...................yes .... no

polio (OPV or IPV in childhood)..yes .... no

hepatitis B (3 dose series)...yes .... no

varicella (2 doses or had the disease) ....yes .... no

influenza ....yes .... no

pneumococcal vaccine ....yes .... no

Female of childbearing age susceptible to CMV or parvovirus?..yes .... no

Evaluation of tuberculosis status shows a risk for communicable TB?...yes .... no

Mantoux test date_____ Result_____

Tuberculosis transmission shall be controlled by requiring regular and substitute staff members and volunteers to have their tuberculosis status assessed with a one-step or two-step Mantoux intradermal skin test prior to beginning employment unless they produce documentation of the following:
a) A positive Mantoux intradermal skin test result in the past, or
b) Tuberculosis disease that has been treated appropriately in the past.
The one-step Mantoux intradermal tuberculin test shall suffice except that for individuals over 60 years of age or those who have a medical condition that reduces their immune response, the use of the two-step method is required. Individuals with a positive Mantoux intradermal skin test or tuberculosis disease in the past shall be evaluated with chest radiographs and shall be cleared for work by their physician or a health department official.

Please attach additional sheets to explain all "yes" answers above. Include the plan for follow up.

MD
DO
CRNP

_____ _____ _____
(Date)   (Signature)   (Printed last name)   (Title)

Phone number of physician or CRNP: _____

I have read and understand the above information.

_____ _____
(Date)   (Patient's Signature)

Reference: Pennsylvania Chapter, American Academy of Pediatrics. *Model Child Care Health Policies.* 3rd ed. Washington D.C: National Association for the Education of Young Children, 1997.
This form was adapted from *Model Child Care Health Policies*, June 1997, by the Early Childhood Education Linkage System (ECELS), a program funded by the Pennsylvania Depts. of Health & Public Welfare and contractually administered by the PA Chapter, American Academy of Pediatrics.

Enrollment / Attendance / Symptom Record

Classroom _____

MONTH

20

NAME	AGE IN MONTHS	DAILY HOURS IN CARE	1	2	3	4	5	6	7	8	9	10	11	12	13	14	15	16	17	18	19	20	21	22	23	24	25	26	27	28	29	30	31

FOR EACH CHILD, EACH DAY CODE TOP BOX "+" = PRESENT or "O" = ABSENT. N = NOT SCHEDULED
CODE BOTTOM BOX "O" = WELL or " " "SYMPTOM CODE FROM BOTTOM OF PAGE.

TOTAL PLACED ON REGISTER

NUMBER OF DAYS FACILITY WAS OPEN

Symptom Codes: 1 = ASTHMA, WHEEZING, 2 = BEHAVIOR CHANGE WITH NO OTHER SYMPTOM, 3 = DIARRHEA, 4 = FEVER, 5 = HEADACHE, 6 = RASH, 7 = RESPIRATORY (COLD, COUGH, RUNNY NOSE, EARACHE, SORE THROAT, PINK EYE), 8 = STOMACHACHE, 9 = URINE PROBLEM, 10 = VOMITING, 11 = OTHER (SPECIFY ON BACK OF FORM)

Reference: Pennsylvania Chapter, American Academy of Pediatrics. *Model Child Care Health Policies*. 3rd ed. Washington D.C: National Association for the Education of Young Children, 1997.
This form was adapted and updated from *Model Child Care Health Policies*, June 1997, by the Early Childhood Education Linkage System (ECELS), a program funded by the Pennsylvania Depts. of Health & Public Welfare and contractually administered by the PA Chapter, American Academy of Pediatrics.

Recommended Childhood Immunization Schedule United States, January - December 2001

Vaccines[1] are listed under routinely recommended ages. [Bars] indicate range of recommended ages for immunization. Any dose not given at the recommended age should be given as a "catch-up" immunization at any subsequent visit when indicated and feasible. (Ovals) indicate vaccines to be given if previously recommended doses were missed or given earlier than the recommended minimum age.

AGE ▶ / VACCINE ▶	Birth	1 mo	2 mos	4 mos	6 mos	12 mos	15 mos	18 mos	24 mos	4-6 yrs	11-12 yrs	14-18 yrs
Hepatitis B[2]	Hep B #1	Hep B #1	Hep B #2		Hep B #3						Hep B[2]	
Diptheria, Tetanus, Pertussis[3]			DTaP	DTaP	DTaP		DTaP[3]	DTaP[3]		DTaP	Td	Td
H. influenzae type b[4]			Hib	Hib	Hib	Hib						
Inactivated Polio[5]			IPV	IPV	IPV[5]	IPV[5]				IPV[5]		
Pneumococcal Conjugate[6]			PCV	PCV	PCV	PCV						
Measles, Mumps, Rubella[7]						MMR				MMR[7]	MMR[7]	
Varicella[8]						Var		Var			Var[8]	
Hepatitis A[9]											Hep A-in selected areas[9]	Hep A-in selected areas[9]

Approved by the Advisory Committee on Immunization Practices (ACIP), the American Academy of Pediatrics (AAP), and the American Academy of Family Physicians (AAFP).

[1] This schedule indicates the recommended ages for routine administration of currently licensed childhood vaccines, as of 11/1/00, for children through 18 years of age. Additional vaccines may be licensed and recommended during the year. Licensed combination vaccines may be used whenever any components of the combination are indicated and its other components are not contraindicated. Providers should consult the manufacturers' package inserts for detailed recommendations.

[2] **Infants born to HBsAg-negative mothers** should receive the 1st dose of hepatitis B (Hep B) vaccine by age 2 months. The 2nd dose should be at least one month (4 weeks) after the 1st dose. The 3rd dose should be administered at least 4 months after the 1st dose and at least 2 months after the 2nd dose, but not before 6 months of age for infants. **Infants born to HBsAg-positive mothers** should receive hepatitis B vaccine and 0.5 mL hepatitis B immune globulin (HBIG) within 12 hours of birth at separate sites. The 2nd dose is recommended at 1-2 months of age and the 3rd dose at 6 months of age. **Infants born to mothers whose HBsAg status is unknown** should receive hepatitis B vaccine within 12 hours of birth. Maternal blood should be drawn at the time of delivery to determine the mother's HBsAg status; if the HBsAg test is positive, the infant should receive HBIG as soon as possible (no later than 1 week of age). **All children and adolescents** who have not been immunized against hepatitis B should begin the series during any visit. Special efforts should be made to immunize children who were born in or whose parents were born in areas of the world with moderate or high endemicity of hepatitis B virus infection.

[3] The 4th dose of DTaP (diphtheria and tetanus toxoids and acellular pertussis vaccine) maybe administered as early as 12 months of age, provided 6 months have elapsed since the 3rd dose and the child is unlikely to return at age 15-18 months. Td (tetanus and diphtheria toxoids) is recommended at 11-12 years of age if at least 5 years have elapsed since the last dose of DTP, DTaP or DT. Subsequent routine Td boosters are recommended every 10 years.

[4] Three *Haemophilus influenzae* type b (Hib) conjugate vaccines are licensed for infant use. If PRP-OMP (PedvaxHIB® or ComVax® [Merck]) is administered at 2 and 4 months of age, a dose at 6 months is not required. Because clinical studies in infants have demonstrated that using some combination products may induce a lower immune response to the Hib vaccine component, DTaP/Hib combination products should not be used for primary immunization in infants at 2,4 or 6 months of age, unless FDA-approved for these ages.

[5] An all-IPV schedule is recommended for routine childhood polio vaccination in the United States. All children should receive four doses of IPV at 2 months, 4 months, 6-18 months, and 4-6 years of age. Oral polio vaccine (OPV) should be used only in selected circumstances. (See MMWR *Morb Mortal Wkly Rep* May 19, 2000/49 (RR-5);1-22).

[6] The heptavalent conjugate pneumococcal vaccine (PCV) is recommended for all children 2-23 months of age. It is also recommended for certain children 24-59 months of age. (See MMWR *Morb Mortal Wkly Rep* Oct. 6, 2000/49 (RR-9);1-35).

[7] The 2nd dose of measles, mumps, and rubella (MMR) vaccine is recommended routinely at 4-6 years of age but may be administered during any visit, provided at least 4 weeks have elapsed since receipt of the 1st dose and that both doses are administered beginning at or after 12 months of age. Those who have not previously received the second dose should complete the schedule by the 11-12 year old visit.

[8] Varicella (Var) vaccine is recommended at any visit on or after the first birthday for susceptible children, i.e. those who lack a reliable history of chickenpox (as judged by a health care provider) and who have not been immunized. Susceptible persons 13 years of age or older should receive 2 doses, given at least 4 weeks apart.

[9] Hepatitis A (Hep A) is shaded to indicate its recommended use in selected states and/or regions, and for certain high risk groups; consult your local public health authority. (See MMWR *Morb Mortal Wkly Rep* Oct.1,1999/48(RR-12);1-37).

For additional information about the vaccines listed above, please visit the National Immunization Program Home Page at www.cdc.gov/nip or call the National Immunization Hotline at 800-232-2522 (English) or 800-232-0233 (Spanish). The Immunization Schedule is updated annually. Please access the current schedule at http://www.aap.org/family/parents/immunize.htm

Reference: American Academy of Pediatrics, Committee on Infectious Disease. Recommended childhood immunization schedule - United States, January - December 2001. *Pediatrics*. 2001; 107: 202-204. Used with permission of the American Academy of Pediatrics, 2001.

Recommendations for Preventive Pediatric Health Care (RE9939)

Committee on Practice and Ambulatory Medicine

Each child and family is unique; therefore, these **Recommendations for Preventive Pediatric Health Care** are designed for the care of children who are receiving competent parenting, have no manifestations of any important health problems, and are growing and developing in satisfactory fashion. **Additional visits may become necessary** if circumstances suggest variations from normal.

These guidelines represent a consensus by the Committee on Practice and Ambulatory Medicine in consultation with national committees and sections of the American Academy of Pediatrics. The Committee emphasizes the great importance of **continuity of care** in comprehensive health supervision and the need to avoid **fragmentation of care.**

AGE[5]	PRENATAL[1]	NEWBORN[2]	2-4d[3]	By 1mo	2mo	4mo	6mo	9mo	12mo	15mo	18mo	24mo	3y	4y	5y	6y	8y	10y	11y	12y	13y	14y	15y	16y	17y	18y	19y	20y	21y
			INFANCY*							EARLY CHILDHOOD*						MIDDLE CHILDHOOD*						ADOLESCENCE*							
HISTORY Initial/Interval	●	●	●	●	●	●	●	●	●	●	●	●	●	●	●	●	●	●	●	●	●	●	●	●	●	●	●	●	●
MEASUREMENTS																													
Height and Weight		●	●	●	●	●	●	●	●	●	●	●	●	●	●	●	●	●	●	●	●	●	●	●	●	●	●	●	●
Head Circumference		●	●	●	●	●	●	●	●	●	●	●																	
Blood Pressure													●	●	●	●	●	●	●	●	●	●	●	●	●	●	●	●	●
SENSORY SCREENING																													
Vision		S	S	S	S	S	S	S	S	S	S	S	O[6]	O	O	O	O	O	S	O	S	S	O	S	S	O	S	S	S
Hearing		O[7]	S	S	S	S	S	S	S	S	S	S	S	O	O	O	O	O	S	O	S	S	O	S	S	O	S	S	S
DEVELOPMENTAL/ BEHAVIORAL ASSESSMENT*		●	●	●	●	●	●	●	●	●	●	●	●	●	●	●	●	●	●	●	●	●	●	●	●	●	●	●	●
PHYSICAL EXAMINATION[9]		●	●	●	●	●	●	●	●	●	●	●	●	●	●	●	●	●	●	●	●	●	●	●	●	●	●	●	●
PROCEDURES-GENERAL[10]																													
Hereditary/Metabolic Screening[11]		←→																											
Immunization[12]		●	●	●	●	●	●	●	●	●	●	●	●	●	●	●	●	●	●	●	●	●	●	●	●	●	●	●	●
Hematocrit or Hemoglobin[13]							←→		★	★	★	★	★	★	★	●	★	★	★	★	★	★	★	★	★	★	★	★	★
Urinalysis		←→											●←→		●				←→										←→
PROCEDURES-PATIENTS AT RISK																													
Lead Screening[16]								★	★		★		★																
Tuberculin Test[17]									★				★		★				★										
Cholesterol Screening[18]													★	★	★	★	★	★	★	★	★	★	★	★	★	★	★	★	★
STD Screening[19]																			★	★	★	★	★	★	★	★	★	★	★
Pelvic Exam[20]																			★	★	★	★	★	★	★	★←→			★
ANTICIPATORY GUIDANCE[21]																													
Injury Prevention[22]		●	●	●	●	●	●	●	●	●	●	●	●	●	●	●	●	●	●	●	●	●	●	●	●	●	●	●	●
Violence Prevention[23]		●	●	●	●	●	●	●	●	●	●	●	●	●	●	●	●	●	●	●	●	●	●	●	●	●	●	●	●
Sleep Positioning Counseling[24]		●	●	●	●	●	●	●																					
Nutrition Counseling[25]		●	●	●	●	●	●	●	●	●	●	●	●	●	●	●	●	●	●	●	●	●	●	●	●	●	●	●	●
DENTAL REFERRAL[26]									▼				●																

1. A prenatal visit is recommended for parents who are at high risk, for first-time parents, and for those who request a conference. The prenatal visit should include anticipatory guidance, pertinent medical history, and a discussion of benefits of breastfeeding and planned method of feeding per AAP statement "The Prenatal Visit" (1996).
2. Every infant should have a newborn evaluation after birth. Breastfeeding should be encouraged and instruction and support offered. Every breastfeeding infant should have an evaluation 48-72 hours after discharge from the hospital to include weight, formal breastfeeding evaluation, encouragement, and instruction as recommended in the AAP statement "Breastfeeding and the Use of Human Milk" (1997).
3. For newborns discharged in less than 48 hours after delivery per AAP statement "Hospital Stay for Healthy Term Newborns" (1995).
4. Developmental, psychosocial, and chronic disease issues for children and adolescents may require frequent counseling and treatment visits separate from preventive care visits.
5. If a child comes under care for the first time at any point on the schedule, or if any items are not accomplished at the suggested age, the schedule should be brought up to date at the earliest possible time.
6. If the patient is uncooperative, rescreen within 6 months.
7. All newborns should be screened per the AAP Task Force on Newborn and Infant Hearing statement "Newborn and Infant Hearing Loss: Detection and Intervention" (1999).
8. By history and appropriate physical examination; if suspicious, by specific objective developmental testing. Parenting skills should be fostered at every visit.

9. At each visit, a complete physical examination is essential, with infant totally unclothed, older child undressed and suitably draped.
10. These may be modified, depending upon entry point into schedule and individual need.
11. Metabolic screening (eg, thyroid, hemoglobinopathies, PKU, galactosemia) should be done according to state law.
12. Schedule(s) per the Committee on Infectious Diseases, published in the January edition of Pediatrics. Every visit should be an opportunity to update and complete a child's immunizations.
13. See AAP Pediatric Nutrition Handbook (1998) for a discussion of universal and selective screening options. Consider earlier screening for high-risk infants (eg, premature infants and low birth weight infants). See also "Recommendations to Prevent and Control Iron Deficiency in the United States." MMWR. 1998;47 (RR-3):1-29.
14. All menstruating adolescents should be screened annually.
15. Conduct dipstick urinalysis for leukocytes annually for sexually active male and female adolescents.
16. For children at risk of lead exposure consult the AAP statement "Screening for Elevated Blood Levels" (1998). Additionally, screening should be done in accordance with state law where applicable.
17. TB testing per recommendations of the Committee on Infectious Diseases, published in the current edition of Red Book: Report of the Committee on Infectious Diseases. Testing should be done upon recognition of high-risk factors.
18. Cholesterol screening for high-risk patients per AAP statement "Cholesterol in Childhood" (1998). If family history cannot be ascertained and other risk factors are present, screening should be at the discretion of the physician.
19. All sexually active patients should be screened for sexually transmitted diseases (STDs).
20. All sexually active females should have a pelvic examination. A pelvic examination and routine pap smear should be offered as part of preventive health maintenance between the ages of 18 and 21 years.
21. Age-appropriate discussion and counseling should be an integral part of each visit for care per the AAP Guidelines for Health Supervision III (1998).
22. From birth to age 12, refer to The Injury Prevention Program (TIPP) as described in A Guide to Safety Counseling in Office Practice (1994).
23. Violence prevention and management for all patients per AAP statement "The Role of the Pediatrician in Youth Violence Prevention in Clinical Practice and at the Community Level" (1999).
24. Parents and caregivers should be advised to place healthy infants on their backs when putting them to sleep. Side positioning is a reasonable alternative but carries a slightly higher risk of SIDS. Consult the AAP statement "Changing Concepts of Sudden Infant Death Syndrome: Implications for Infant Sleeping Environment and Sleep Position" (2000).
25. Age-appropriate nutrition counseling should be an integral part of each visit per the AAP Handbook of Nutrition (1998).
26. Earlier initial dental examinations may be appropriate for some children. Subsequent examinations as prescribed by dentist.

NB: Special chemical, immunologic, and endocrine testing is usually carried out upon specific indications. Testing other than newborn (eg, inborn errors of metabolism, sickle disease, etc) is discretionary with the physician.

The recommendations in this statement do not indicate an exclusive course of treatment or standard of medical care. Variations, taking into account individual circumstances, may be appropriate. Copyright © 2000 by the American Academy of Pediatrics. No part of this statement may be reproduced in any form or by any means without prior written permission from the American Academy of Pediatrics except for one copy for personal use.

American Academy of Pediatrics
DEDICATED TO THE HEALTH OF ALL CHILDREN™

Key:
● = to be performed
S = subjective, by history
O = objective, by a standard testing method
●--→--● = the range during which a service may be provided, with the dot indicating the preferred age.

★ = to be performed for patients at risk

Selecting an Appropriate Sanitizer

One of the most important steps in reducing the spread of infectious diseases among children and child care providers is cleaning and sanitizing of surfaces that could possibly pose a risk to children or staff. Routine cleaning with detergent and water is the most useful method for removing germs from surfaces in the child care setting. However, some items and surfaces require an additional step after cleaning to reduce the number of germs on a surface to a level that is unlikely to transmit disease. This step is called sanitizing. A household bleach and water mixture, or one of a variety of other industrial products can be used.

Sanitizer solutions can be applied in various ways:
- Spray bottle, for diaper changing surfaces, toilets, and potty chairs.
- Cloths rinsed in sanitizing solution for food preparation areas, large toys, books, and activity centers.
- Dipping the object into a container filled with the sanitizing solution, for smaller toys.

The concentration and duration of contact of the sanitizer varies with the application and anticipated load of germs. More chemical is required when a cloth or objects are dipped into the solution because each dipping releases some germs into the solution, potentially contaminating solution. When you apply the sanitizing solution to a surface, follow the instructions for that solution to determine the dilution and minimum contact time.

In general, it is best not to rinse off the sanitizer or wipe the object dry right away. A sanitizer must be in contact with the germs long enough kill them. For example, when you using a properly prepared solution of bleach water applied from a spray bottle to cleaned and rinsed surfaces, the minimum contact time is 2 minutes. For cleaned and rinsed dishes submerged in a container that is filled with properly prepared bleach solution, the contact time is a minimum of 1 minute. The label on industrial sanitizers specifies the instructions for using the special chemicals. Since chlorine evaporates into the air leaving no residue, surfaces sanitized with bleach may be left to air dry. Some industrial sanitizers require rinsing with fresh water before the object should be used again.

Label spray bottles and containers in which sanitizers have been diluted for direct application with the name of the solution (such as Bleach Sanitizer) and the dilution of the mixture. Although solutions of household bleach and water are merely irritating if accidentally swallowed, some other types of sanitizer solutions are toxic. Keep all spray containers and bottles of diluted and undiluted sanitizer out of the reach of children.

Household Bleach & Water

Household bleach with water is recommended. It is effective, economical, convenient, and readily available. However, it should be used with caution on metal or metallic surfaces. If bleach is found to be corrosive on certain materials, a different sanitizer may be required.

When purchasing household bleach, make sure that the bleach concentration is for household use, and not for industrial application. Household bleach is typically sold in retail stores in one of 2 strengths: 5.25% hypochlorite (regular strength bleach) or 6.00% hypochlorite (ultra strength bleach) solutions.

The solution of bleach and water is easy to mix, non-toxic, safe if handled properly, and kills most infectious agents.

- *Recipe for a spray application on surfaces that have been detergent-cleaned and rinsed in bathrooms, diapering areas, countertops, tables, toys, door knobs and cabinet handles, phone receivers, handwashing sinks, floors, and surface contaminated by body fluids (minimum contact time = 2 minutes):*
  ¼ cup household bleach + 1 gallon of cool water
  OR
  1 tablespoon bleach + 1 quart of cool water

- *Recipe for weaker bleach solutions for submerging of eating utensils that have been detergent-cleaned and rinsed (minimum contact time = 1 minute):*
  1 tablespoon bleach + 1 gallon of cool water

A solution of bleach and water loses its strength and is weakened by heat and sunlight. Therefore, mix a fresh bleach solution every day for maximum effectiveness. Any leftover bleach solution should be discarded at the end of the day.

References: Canadian Paediatric Society. *Well Being: A Guide to Promote the Physical Health, Safety and Emotional Well-Being of Children in Child Care Centers and Family Day Care Homes,* 2nd ed. Toronto, ON; 1996
Centers for Disease Control and Prevention. *The ABC's of Safe and Healthy Child Care; 1996*

Selecting an Appropriate Sanitizer

Note: Do not mix household bleach with other household chemicals such as toilet cleaners, rust removers, acids or products containing ammonia. Mixing these chemicals with bleach will produce hazardous gases.

Industrial Products

There are a number of industrial products that are available. Industrial products that meet the Environmental Protection Agency's (EPA's) standards for "hospital grade" germicides (solutions that kill germs) may be used for sanitizing.

Be cautious about industrial products that advertise themselves as "disinfectants," having "germicidal action," or "kills germs." While they may have some effect on germs, they may not have the same effectiveness as bleach and water, or EPA approved hospital grade germicides.

Before using anything other than bleach for sanitizing, consult with your local health department or regulatory licensing authority.

If you use an EPA-approved industrial product as a sanitizer, read the label and always follow the manufacturer's instructions exactly.

References: Canadian Paediatric Society. *Well Being: A Guide to Promote the Physical Health, Safety and Emotional Well-Being of Children in Child Care Centers and Family Day Care Homes,* 2nd ed. Toronto, ON; 1996
Centers for Disease Control and Prevention. *The ABC's of Safe and Healthy Child Care;* 1996

Cleaning Up Body Fluids

Treat urine, stool, vomitus, blood, and body fluids as potentially infectious. Spills of body fluid should be cleaned up and surfaces sanitized immediately.

- For small amounts of urine and stool on smooth surfaces; Wipe off and clean away visible soil with a little detergent solution. Then rinse the surface with clean water.
- Apply a sanitizer to the surface for the required contact time. See Appendix I.

For larger spills on floors, or any spills on rugs or carpets:

- Wear gloves while cleaning. While disposable gloves can be used, household rubber gloves are adequate for all spills except blood and bloody body fluids. Disposable gloves should be used when blood may be present in the spill.
- Take care to avoid splashing any contaminated material onto the mucous membranes of your eyes, nose or mouth, or into any open sores you may have.
- Wipe up as much of the visible material as possible with disposable paper towels and carefully place the soiled paper towels and other soiled disposable material in a leak-proof, plastic bag that has been securely tied or sealed. Use a wet/dry vacuum on carpets, if such equipment is available.
- Immediately use a detergent, or a disinfectant-detergent to clean the spill area. Then rinse the area with clean water.
- For blood and body fluid spills on carpeting, blot to remove body fluids from the fabric as quickly as possible. Then spot clean the area with a detergent-disinfectant rather than with a bleach solution. Additional cleaning by shampooing or steam cleaning the contaminated surface may be necessary.
- Sanitize the cleaned and rinsed surface by wetting the entire surface with a sanitizing solution of bleach in water (1/4 cup of household bleach in 1 gallon of water) or an industrial sanitizer used according to the manufacturer's instructions. For carpets cleaned with a detergent-disinfectant, sanitizing is accomplished by continuing to apply and extract the solution until there is no visible soil. Then follow the manufacturer's instructions for the use of the sanitizer to be sure the carpet is sanitized by the treatment.
- Dry the surface.
- Clean and rinse reusable household rubber gloves, then treat them as a contaminated surface in applying the sanitizing solution to them. Remove, dry and store these gloves away from food or food surfaces. Discard disposable gloves.
- Mops and other equipment used to clean up body fluids should be:
  1) Cleaned with detergent and rinsed with water;
  2) Rinsed with a fresh sanitizing solution;
  3) Wrung as dry as possible;
  4) Air-dried.
- Wash your hands afterward, even though you wore gloves.
- Remove and bag clothing (yours and those worn by children) soiled by body fluids.
- Put on fresh clothes after washing the soiled skin and hands of everyone involved.

References:

Canadian Paediatric Society. *Well Being: A Guide to Promote the Physical Health, Safety and Emotional Well-Being of Children in Child Care Centers and Family Day Care Homes,* 2nd ed. Toronto, ON; 1996.
Centers for Disease Control and Prevention. *The ABC's of Safe and Healthy Child Care;* 1996.
Centers for Disease Control and Prevention. Guidelines for Prevention of Transmission of Human Immunodeficiency Virus and Hepatitis B Virus to Health-Care and Public Safety Workers. *MMWR.* 1989; 38(S-6): 1-36.
Centers for Disease Control and Prevention. Update: Universal precautions for prevention of transmission of Human immunodeficiency virus, hepatitis B Virus, and other bloodborne pathogens in health-care settings. *MMWR.* 1988; 37: 377-382, 387-388.

Clues to Child Abuse and Neglect

Type of Abuse	Physical Signs	Behavioral Signals
Physical Abuse	Bruises or welts in various stages of healing or other visible injuries that appear on a child recurrently and cannot be explained by developmentally expected behavior.	Explanation for a physical injury that is inconsistent with the injury, or the child's developmental age.
	Unexplained or multiple broken bones, especially a broken rib, severe skull fracture or other major head injury.	Persistent or repetitive physical complaints of unclear cause, such as headache or belly pain.
		The parent/caregiver reports that a significant injury was self-inflicted or the child reports being injured by a parent or other caregiver.
	Burns or injuries in the shape of an object used to cause the injury such as bite marks, hand prints, cigar or cigarette burns, belt buckle markings. Burns from immersion in scalding water or other hot liquids.	The parent/caregivers have delayed seeking appropriate medical care.
	Unexplained or repetitive dental injuries.	
	Failure to grow at the expected rate in a child who seems hungry and eager to eat when offered food.	
Sexual Abuse	Pain, itching, bruises or bleeding around the genitalia. Stained or bloody underclothing.	Bizarre, too sophisticated, or unusual sexual knowledge or behavior for the child's age such as asking others to do sex acts, putting mouth on sex parts, trying to have intercourse.
	Venereal disease.	Child reports sexual abuse by a parent or adult.
	Difficulty walking or sitting.	
	Discharge from the vagina or urine openings.	
Emotional Abuse	Delayed physical, emotional or intellectual development that is not otherwise explicable.	Impaired sense of self-worth, depression, withdrawal.
	Habits such as rocking, sucking on fingers in excess of expectation for developmental stage.	Extremes of behavior, such as overly aggressive or passive, apathetic, empty facial appearance, decreased social interaction with others, phobias, generalized fearfulness, fear of parent.
Neglect	Constant hunger, begging for food or hoarding food. Fatigue or listlessness. Poor hygiene such as dirty hair, skin and clothes. Inappropriate dress.	Lack of supervision for long periods of time, inappropriate to the child's age or developmental stage.
	Malnutrition or failure to thrive not explained by physical illness.	
	Delayed seeking of professional attention for physical or dental problems.	
	Impairment of parent or caregiver due to substance abuse, physical or mental illness.	
Any Type of Abuse	Substance abuse. Unexplained absences from the child care program.	Over and under compliance of the child. Lack of selectivity in friendly approach to adults. Developmental regression, such as a previously toilet-trained child reverting to incontinence. Sleep and appetite disturbances. Depression. Self-destructive behavior. Excessive/inappropriate fears.

Adapted from: *Child Abuse Primer for Health Care Professionals* © 2000 Project Child, 2200 West Broad St. Bethlehem, PA 18018-3200.
Phone 1-610-419-4500; Fax 1-610-419-3888; email:projectchildlv@aol.com

Risk Factors for
Abuse and/or Neglect

1. **Child Risk Factors**
   - Premature birth
   - Colic
   - Physical disabilities
   - Developmental disabilities
   - Chronic illness
   - Emotional/behavioral difficulties
   - Unwanted child

2. **Abuser's Risk Factors**
   - Low self esteem
   - Depression
   - Poor impulse control
   - Substance abuse
   - Abused as a child
   - Teenage parent
   - Unrealistic expectations of child's behavior
   - Negative view of themselves and children in care
   - Punitive child-rearing style

3. **Social/Situational Stresses**
   - Isolation
   - Family/domestic violence
   - Non-biologically-related male in the home
   - Unemployment/financial problems
   - Single parenthood

4. **Triggering Situations**
   - Crying baby
   - Child's misbehavior
   - Discipline gone awry
   - Argument, adult-adult conflict
   - Overly zealous toilet learning/training

Adapted from EPIC-SCAN (Educating Physicians in their Communities - Suspected Child Abuse and Neglect), Pennsylvania Chapter, American Academy of Pediatrics, 2001

Special Care Plan for a Child with Asthma

Child's Name:_____ **Date of Birth:**_____

Parent(s) or Guardian(s) Name:_____

Emergency phone numbers: Mother_____ Father_____

(see emergency contact information for alternate contacts if parents are unavailable)

Primary health provider's name: _____ **Emergency Phone:** _____

Asthma specialist's name (if any): _____ **Emergency Phone:** _____

Known triggers for this child's asthma (circle all that apply):

colds	mold	exercise	tree pollens
house	dust	strong odors	grass flowers
excitement	weather changes	animals	smoke
foods (specify): _____			room deodorizers
other (specify): _____			

Activities for which this child has needed special attention in the past (circle all that apply)

outdoors	*indoors*
field trip to see animals	kerosene/wood stove heated rooms
running hard	art projects with chalk, glues, fumes
gardening	sitting on carpets
jumping in leaves	pet care
outdoors on cold or windy days	recent pesticides application in facility
playing in freshly cut grass	painting or renovation in facility
other (specify):_____	

Can this child use a **flowmeter** to monitor need for medication in child care?　　NO　　YES

personal best reading: _____　　reading to give extra dose of medicine:_____

　　　　　　　　　　　　　　　　　　　　　　reading to get medical help:_____

How often has this child needed urgent care from a doctor for an attack of asthma:

in the past 12 months?_____　　in the past 3 months?_____

Typical signs and symptoms of the child's asthma episodes (circle all that apply):

fatigue	face red, pale or swollen	grunting
breathing faster	wheezing	sucking in chest/neck
restlessness,agitation	dark circles under eyes	persistent coughing
complaints of chest pain/tightness	gray or blue lips or fingernails	
flaring nostrils, mouth open (panting)	difficulty playing, eating, drinking, talking	

Reminders:

1. *Notify parents immediately if emergency medication is required.*

2. *Get emergency medical help if.*

- the child does not improve 15 minutes after treatment and family cannot be reached

- after receiving a treatment for wheezing, the child:

• is working hard to breathe or grunting	• won't play
• is breathing fast at rest (>50/min)	• has gray or blue lips or fingernails
• has trouble walking or talking	• cries more softly and briefly
• has nostrils open wider than usual	• is hunched over to breathe
•has sucking in of skin (chest or neck) with breathing	• is extremely agitated or sleepy

3. *Child's doctor & child care facility should keep a current copy of this form in child's record.*

Reprinted with permission from Child Care and Children with Special Needs Workbook.
Wilmington, DE: Video Active Productions, 2001; 302-477-9440

Special Care Plan for a Child with Asthma (Continued)

Medications for routine and emergency treatment of asthma for:			
Child's name _____ Date of Birth _____			
Name of medication			
When to use (e.g., symptoms, time of day, frequency, etc.)	*routine or emergency*	*routine or emergency*	*routine or emergency*
How to use (e.g.,by mouth, by inhaler, with or without spacing device, in nebulizer, with or without dilution, diluting fluid, etc.)			
Amount (dose) of medication			
How soon treatment should start to work			
Expected benefit for the child			
Possible side effects, if any			
Date instructions were last updated by child's doctor	Date: _____ Name of Doctor (print): _____ Doctor's signature:_____		
Parent's permission to follow this medication plan	Date:_____ Parent's signature: _____		

If more columns are needed for medication or equipment instruction, copy this page

Reprinted with permission from Child Care and Children with Special Needs Workbook.
Wilmington, DE: Video Active Productions, 2001; 302-477-9440

Situations that Require Medical Attention Right Away

In the two boxes below, you will find lists of common medical emergencies or urgent situations you may encounter as a child care provider. To prepare for such situations:

1) Know how to access Emergency Medical Services (EMS) in your area.
2) Educate Staff on the recognition of an emergency.
3) Know the phone number for each child's guardian and primary health care provider.
4) Develop plans for children with special medical needs with their family and physician.

At any time you believe the child's life may be at risk, or you believe there is a risk of permanent injury, seek immediate medical treatment.

Call Emergency Medical Services (EMS) immediately if:

- You believe the child's life is at risk or there is a risk of permanent injury.
- The child is acting strangely, much less alert, or much more withdrawn than usual.
- The child has difficulty breathing or is unable to speak.
- The child's skin or lips look blue, purple, or gray.
- The child has rhythmic jerking of arms and legs and a loss of consciousness (seizure).
- The child is unconscious.
- The child is less and less responsive.
- The child has any of the following after a head injury: decrease in level of alertness, confusion, headache, vomiting, irritability, or difficulty walking.
- The child has increasing or severe pain anywhere.
- The child has a cut or burn that is large, deep, and/or won't stop bleeding.
- The child is vomiting blood.
- The child has a severe stiff neck, headache, and fever.
- The child is significantly dehydrated: sunken eyes, lethargic, not making tears, not urinating.

After you have called EMS, remember to call the child's legal guardian.

Some children may have urgent situations that do not necessarily require ambulance transport but still need medical attention. The box below lists some of these more common situations. The legal guardian should be informed of the following conditions. If you or the guardian cannot reach the physician within one hour, the child should be brought to a hospital.

Get medical attention within one hour for:
- Fever in any age child who looks more than mildly ill.
- Fever in a child less than 2 months (8 weeks) of age.
- A quickly spreading purple or red rash.
- A large volume of blood in the stools.
- A cut that may require stitches.
- Any medical condition specifically outlined in a child's care plan requiring parental notification.

Approved by the American Academy of Pediatrics Committee on Pediatric Emergency Medicine, January 2001.

FOOD Guide PYRAMID

for Young Children

A Daily Guide for 2- to 6-Year-Olds

Fats & Sweets — Eat LESS

MILK Group 2 servings

MEAT Group 2 servings

VEGETABLE Group 3 servings

FRUIT Group 2 servings

GRAIN Group 6 servings

Center for Nutrition Policy and Promotion
U.S. Department of Agriculture
Program Aid 1651
January 2000

USDA is an equal opportunity provider and employer.

FOOD IS FUN and learning about food is fun, too. Eating foods from the Food Guide Pyramid and being physically active will help you grow healthy and strong.

WHAT COUNTS AS ONE SERVING?

GRAIN GROUP
1 slice bread
1/2 cup of cooked rice or pasta
1/2 cup of cooked cereal
1 ounce of ready-to-eat cereal

VEGETABLE GROUP
1/2 cup of chopped raw or cooked vegetables
1 cup of raw leafy vegetables

FRUIT GROUP
1 piece of fruit or melon wedge
3/4 cup of juice
1/2 cup of canned fruit
1/4 cup of dried fruit

MILK GROUP
1 cup of milk or yogurt
2 ounces of cheese

MEAT GROUP
2 to 3 ounces of cooked lean meat, poultry, or fish.

1/2 cup of cooked dry beans, or 1 egg counts as 1 ounce of lean meat. 2 tablespoons of peanut butter count as 1 ounce of meat.

FATS AND SWEETS
Limit calories from these.

Four- to 6-year-olds can eat these serving sizes. Offer 2- to 3-year-olds less, except for milk. Two- to 6-year-old children need a total of 2 servings from the milk group each day.

Reference: United States Department of Agriculture Center for Nutrition Policy and Promotion. *Food Guide Pyramid for Young Children*. Washington, D.C; 2000. Chart can be downloaded in color from: http://www.usda.gov/cnpp/KidsPyra/LittlePyr.pdf.

Child and Adult Care Food Program
Child Care Infant Meal Pattern

Age	Breakfast	Lunch or Supper	Snack (midmorning or midafternoon)
Infants Birth through 3 months	4 to 6 ounces formula[1] or breast milk[2,3]*	4 to 6 fluid ounces formula[1] or breast milk[2,3]	4 to 6 fluid ounces formula[1] or breast milk[2,3]
Infants 4 months through 7 months	4 to 8 fluid ounces formula[1] or breast milk[2,3] 0 to 3 tablespoons infant cereal[1,4]	4 to 8 fluid ounces formula[1] or breast milk[2,3] 0 to 3 tablespoons infant cereal[1,4] 0 to 3 tablespoons fruit and/or vegetable	4 to 6 fluid ounces formula[1] or breast milk[2,3]
Infants 8 months through 11 months	6 to 8 fluid ounces formula[1] or breast milk[2,3] 2 to 4 tablespoons infant cereal[1] 1 to 4 tablespoons fruit and/or vegetable	6 to 8 fluid ounces formula[1] or breast milk[2,3] 2 to 4 tablespoons infant cereal[1] AND/OR 1 to 4 tablespoons meat, fish, poultry, egg yolk, or cooked dry beans or peas OR 1/2 to 2 ounces cheese OR 1 to 4 tablespoons cottage cheese, cheese food, or cheese spread OR 1 to 4 tablespoons fruit and/or vegetable	2 to 4 fluid ounces formula[1], breast milk,[2,3] or fruit juice[5] 0 to 1/2 slice bread[4,6] OR 0 to 2 crackers[4,6]

[1] Infant formula and dry infant cereal shall be iron fortified.

[2] It is recommended that breast milk be served in place of formula from birth through 11 months.

[3] For some breastfed infants who regularly consume less than the minimum amount of breast milk per feeding, a serving of less than the minimum amount of breast milk may be offered, with additional breast milk if the infant is still hungry.

[4] A serving of this component shall be optional.

[5] Fruit juice shall be full strength.

[6] Bread and bread alternatives shall be made from whole-grain or enriched meal or flour.

* breast milk is a commonly used term for human milk.

Reference: United States Department of Agriculture. *Building Blocks for Fun and Healthy Meals: A Menu Planner for the Child and Adult Care Food Program*, Washington, D.C; 2000.

Child and Adult Care Food Program
Meal Pattern Requirements for Children Ages 1 through 12 Years

AGE	Children 1-2 Years of Age	Children 3-5 Years of Age	Children 6-12 Years of Age
BREAKFAST			
Milk *	1/2 cup	3/4 cup	1 cup
Vegetable or Fruit or Juice (100%)	1/4 cup	1/2 cup	1/2 cup
Grains/Breads (enriched or whole grain)	1/2 slice* (or 1/2 serving)	1/2 slice* (or 1/2 serving)	1 slice* (or 1 serving)
- or cold dry cereal	1/4 cup (or 1/3 oz.)	1/3 cup (or 1/2 oz.)	3/4 cup (or 1 oz.)
- or cooked cereal	1/4 cup	1/4 cup	1/2 cup
SNACK *(select two of the following four components)*			
Milk *	1/2 cup	1/2 cup	1 cup
Vegetable or Fruit or Juice (100%)**	1/2 cup	1/2 cup	3/4 cup
Meat or meat alternative	1/2 ounce	1/2 ounce	1 ounce
- or yogurt (plain or sweetened)**	2 oz (or 1/4 cup)	2 oz (or 1/4 cup)	4 oz (or 1/2 cup)
Grains/Breads (enriched or whole grain)	1/2 slice* (or 1/2 serving)	1/2 slice* (or 1/2 serving)	1 slice* (or 1 serving)
LUNCH/SUPPER			
Milk *	1/2 cup	3/4 cup	1 cup
Meat or poultry or fish	1 ounce	1 1/2 ounce	2 ounces
- or cheese	1 ounce	1 1/2 ounces	2 ounces
- or cottage cheese, cheese food, or cheese spread	2 ounces (1/4 cup)	3 ounces (3/8 cup)	4 ounces (1/2 cup)
- or egg	1 egg	1 egg	1 egg
- or cooked dry beans or peas	1/4 cup	3/8 cup	1/2 cup
- or peanut butter, soynut butter or nut or seed butters	2 Tablespoons	3 Tablespoons	4 Tablespoons
- or peanuts, soynuts, tree nuts or seeds	1/2 ounce	3/4 ounce	1 ounce
- or yogurt	4 ounces (or 1/2 cup)	6 ounces (or 3/4 cup)	8 ounces (or 1 cup)
- or an equivalent quantity of any combination of the above meat/meat alternative			
Vegetables and/or Fruits (2 or More)	1/4 cup (total)	1/2 cup (total)	3/4 cup (total)
Grains/Breads (enriched or whole grain)	1/2 slice* (or 1/2 serving)	1/2 slice* (or 1/2 serving)	1 slice* (or 1 serving)
POINTS TO REMEMBER: • Keep menu production records. • The required amount of each food must be served. • Use full-strength (100%) juice.	* Or an equivalent serving of an acceptable grains/breads such as cornbread, biscuits, rolls, muffins, etc., made of whole grain or enriched meal or flour, or a serving of cooked enriched or whole grain rice or macaroni or other pasta products. ** For snack, juice or yogurt may not be served when milk is served as the only other component.		

Reference: United States Department of Agriculture, *Building Blocks for Fun and Healthy Meals: A Menu Planner for the Child and Adult Care Food Program*, Washington, D.C; 2000.
* Dry/Reconstituted milk is not acceptable.

Food Storage Chart

This chart has information about keeping foods safely in the refrigerator or freezer. It does not include foods that can be stored safely in the cupboard or on the shelves where quality may be more of an issue than safety.

FOOD	IN REFRIGERATOR	IN FREEZER
Eggs		
Fresh, in shell	3 weeks	Don't freeze
Raw yolks, whites	2-4 days	I year
Hardcooked	I week	Don't freeze
Liquid pasteurized eggs or egg substitutes, opened	3 days	Don't freeze
unopened	10 days	I year
Mayonnaise		
Commercial, refrigerate after opening	2 months	Don't freeze
TV Dinners, Frozen Casseroles		
Keep frozen until ready to heat and serve		3-4 months
Deli and Vacuum-Packed Products		
Store-prepared or homemade egg, chicken, tuna, ham, macaroni salads	3-4 days	Don't freeze
Pre-stuffed pork and lamb chops, stuffed chicken breasts	I day	Don't freeze
Store-cooked convenience meals	1-2 days	Don't freeze
Commercial brand vacuum-packed dinners with USDA seal	2 weeks, unopened	Don't freeze
Hamburger, Ground, and Stew Meats (Raw)		
Hamburger and stew meats	1-2 days	3-4 months
Ground turkey, chicken, veal pork, lamb, and mixtures of them	1-2 days	3-4 months
Hotdogs and Lunch Meats*		
Hotdogs, opened package	I week	
unopened package	2 weeks	In freezer wrap, 1-2 months
Lunch Meats, opened	3-5 days	
Unopened	2 weeks	In freezer wrap, 1-2 months
Deli sliced ham, turkey, lunch meats	2-3 days	1-2 months
Bacon and Sausage		
Bacon	I week	I month
Sausage, raw from pork, beef, turkey	1-2 days	1-2 months
Smoked breakfast links or patties	I week	1-2 months
Hard Sausage-Pepperoni, Jerky Sticks	2-3 weeks	1-2 months

Food Storage Chart

FOOD	IN REFRIGERATOR	IN FREEZER
Ham		
Canned, unopened, label says keep refrigerated	6-9 months	Don't freeze
Fully cooked - whole	7 days	1-2 months
Fully cooked - half	3-5 days	1-2 months
Fully cooked - slices	3-4 days	1-2 months
Fresh Meat		
Steaks, beef	3-5 days	6-12 months
Chops, pork	3-5 days	4-6 months
Chops, lamb	3-5 days	6-9 months
Roasts, beef	3-5 days	6-12 months
Roasts, lamb	3-5 days	6-9 months
Roasts, pork and veal	3-5 days	4-6 months
Fresh Poultry		
Chicken or turkey, whole	1-2 days	1 year
Chicken or turkey pieces	1-2 days	9 months
Giblets	1-2 days	3-4 months
Fresh Seafood		
Fish and shellfish	2 days	2-4 months

*Uncooked salami is not recommended because recent studies have found that the processing does not always kill the E. coli bacteria. Look for the label to say "Fully Cooked."

Reference: Graves, D.E., Suitor, C.W., & Holt, K.A. eds. *Making Food Healthy and Safe for Children: How to Meet the National Health and Safety Performance Standards Guidelines for Out-of-Home Child Care Programs.* Arlington, VA: National Center for Education in Maternal and Child Health; 1997.

Sample Food Service Cleaning Schedule

TASK	HOW OFTEN?					COMMENTS
	After each use	Before & after each use	Daily	Weekly	As necessary	
RANGE						
Clean grill and grease pans	√					
Clean burners	√					
Clean outside			√			
Wipe out oven				√		
Clean edges around hood				√		
Clean hood screening and grease trap				√		
REFRIGERATOR AND FREEZER						Or when more than 1/4-inch frost develops or temperature exceeds 0°F.
Defrost freezer and clean shelves					√	
Wipe outside			√			
Dust top				√		
Clean inside shelves in order			√			
MIXER AND CAN OPENER						
Clean mixer base and attachments	√					
Clean and wipe can opener blade	√					
WORK SURFACES						
Clean and sanitize		√				
Organize for neatness			√			
WALLS AND WINDOWS						
Wipe if splattered or greasy					√	
Wipe window sills					√	
Wipe window screens					√	
SINKS						
Keep clean	√					
Scrub			√			
CARTS (if applicable)						
Wipe down	√					
Sanitize			√			
GARBAGE						Or more often, as needed.
Take out			√			
Clean can					√	
TABLES AND CHAIRS						
Clean and sanitize		√				
LINENS						
Wash cloth napkins	√					
Wash tablecloths and placemats	√ if plastic		√ if cloth			
Wash dishcloths			√			
Wash potholders				√		
STORAGE AREAS						
Wipe shelves, cabinets, and drawers					√	

Reference: Graves, D.E., Suitor, C.W., & Holt, K.A. eds *Making Food Healthy and Safe for Children: How to Meet the National Health and Safety Performance Standards Guidelines for Out of Home Child Care Programs.* Arlington, VA: National Center for Education in Maternal and Child Health; 1997.

Adaptive Equipment for Children with Special Needs

Physical Therapy/Occupational Therapy Equipment

Infants, Ages 0-2

Equipment
Floor mats, 2-3-inch of varying firmness
Therapy balls of varying sizes
Wedges: 4, 6, 8 and 12-inch
Inflatable mattress
Air compressor (for inflatables)
Therapy rolls and half rolls of varying sizes
Nesting benches, varying heights
Wooden weighted pushcart
Toddler swing
Floor mirror

Feeding
Bottle straws
Cut-out cups
Bottle holders
Built-up handled utensils
Scoop bowls
Coated spoons

Toys
Books
Mirror
Ring stack
Container toys
Pegboard
Rattles
Squeeze toys
Tracking toys
Toys for pushing, swiping, cause and effect
Form boards
Large beads
Large crayons

Pre-K, Ages 2-5

Equipment
Floor mats, 2-3-inch of varying firmness
Therapy balls: 16, 20, 24 and 37-inch diameter
Nesting benches
Therapy rolls: 8, 10 and 12-inch diameter
Steps
Floor mirrors
Climbing equipment
Small chair and table
Scooter board
Suspended equipment (see also Adaptive Physical
   Education Equipment, Balance/Gross Motor
   Coordination)
Walkers, sidelyers, proneboards, adapted chairs

Toys
Easel
Tricycles
Ride-on scooters
Wagon
Wooden push cart
Manipulative toys (puzzles, beads, pegs and pegboard,
   nesting toys, etc.)
Fastening boards (zippers, snaps, laces, etc.)
Paper, crayons, chalk, markers
Sand/water table
Play-Doh or clay
Target activities (beanbags, ring toss)
Playground balls (see under Adaptive Physical
Education Equipment, Eye-Hand Coordination)

Adaptive Equipment for Children with Special Needs

Speech and Language Development

Infants, Ages 0-2

Equipment
Mirrors, wall and hand-held
Assorted spoons, cups, bowls, plates
Mats and sheets
Preston feeding chairs
High chair

Toys
Dolls (soft with large features and feeding equipment)
Rattles (noisemakers and easy to grasp)
Manipulative toys (for pulling, pushing,
    shaking, cause and effect)
Assorted picture books (large pictures, one-a-page)
Building blocks
Balls/belts
Telephone
Stacking rings
Shape sorters
Xylophone
Drum

Assessments and Books
Small Wonder Activity Kit
Pre-Feeding Skills by Suzanne Morris
Parent-Infant Communication
Bayley Scales of Infant Development
Movement Assessment in Infants by S. Harris
    and L. Chandler
RIDES
HAWAII HELP
Early Learning Accomplishments
    Profile and Kit (Kaplan)
Rosetti Infant/Toddler Language Scale

Pre-K, Ages 2-5

Equipment
Mirrors, wall and hand-held
Tongue depressors
Penlight
Stopwatch
Tape recorder and tapes
Toothettes
Horns and Whistles

Toys
Dolls (with movable parts and removable clothing)
Manipulative toys (cars and toys for pushing, stack-
    ing, cause and effect)
Building blocks
Dollhouse
Pretend play items (dress-up clothes, dishes, sink,
    food, telephone)
Play-Doh or clay
Puzzles (individual pieces or minimal interlocking
    parts)
Picture cards (nouns, actions, etc.)
Puppets
Animals
Storybooks with simple plot lines (large pictures and
    few, if any, words)

Assessments and books
Clinical evaluation of Language Fundamentals –
    Pre-School
Sequenced Inventory of Communication
Test of Auditory Comprehension of Language
Goldman Fristore Test of Articulation
Pre-School Language Assessment Inventory
Assessment of Phonological Processes
Expressive and Receptive One-Word Picture
Vocabulary Tests

Adaptive Equipment for Children with Special Needs

Adaptive Physical Education Equipment

Pre-K, Ages 2-5

Balance/Gross Motor Coordination
Incline mat
Balance beams, 4 and 12-inch wide
Floor mats, 2-inch
Bolsters
Rocking platforms
Scooters (sit-on type)
Tunnel (accordion style)
Training stairs
Hurdles, adjustable height

Eye-Hand Coordination
Balls (to hit, throw, and catch)
Beanbags and Target
Hula hoops
Lightweight paddles/rackets
Lightweight bats
Traffic cones
Batting Tees
Beachballs

Eye-Foot Coordination
Balls for kicking
Foot placement ladder
Footprints or "stepping stones"
Horizontal ladder

Poisonous Plants and Safe Plants

- Keep all plants away from small children. Teach children never to eat unknown plants.
- Different parts of the plant are poisonous. Phone the Poison Control Center before treating a child who has eaten a plant. Follow their directions. Keep an unexpired bottle of syrup of ipecac in a locked place if your policy allows. Use it **only** if the Poison Control Center or a physician tells you to make a child vomit. In some cases, vomiting may worsen the situation and increase the risk of severe health consequences.

Poisonous Plants*

Flower Garden Plants
Autumn Crocus
Bleeding heart
Chrysanthemum
Daffodil
Four-o'clocks
Foxglove
Hyacinth
Hydrangea
Iris
Jonquil
Lily of the valley
Morning glory
Narcissus
Snow on the mountain

Trees and Shrubs
Black locust
Boxwood
Chokecherry
Elderberry
English yew
Ground ivy
Horse chestnut, buckeye
Juniper
Oak tree
Water hemlock
Yew

Vegetable Garden Plants
Asparagus
Sprouts and green parts of potato
Rhubarb leaves
Green parts of tomato

House Plants
Bird of paradise
Castor bean
Dumbcane (Dieffenbachia)
English ivy
Holly
Jequirty bean (Rosary Pea)
Jerusalem cherry
Mistletoe
Mother-in-law
Oleander
Philodendron
Poinsettia
Rhododendron

Wild plants
Belladonna
Bittersweet
Buttercups
Indian hemp
Jack-in-the-pulpit
Jimson weed
Larkspur
Monkshood
Mushrooms (certain ones)
Nightshade
Poison hemlock, ivy,
    oak, sumac and tobacco
Skunk cabbage

Safe Plants*

African Violet
Aluminum Plant
Anthurium, Taliflower
Aphelandra
Baby tears
Begonia
Blood leaf
Boston fern
Christman cactus
Coleus
Corn plant
Dracaena
Emerald ripple, pepromia
Hen-and-chickens
Hoya
Impatiens
Jade Plant
Parlor palm
Pepronia
Prayer plant
Rubber plant
Schefflera
Sensitive plant
Snake plant
Spider plant
Swedish ivy
Velvet, purple passion
Wandering jew
Wax plant
Weeping fig
Yellow day lily

* Not complete lists.

References: American Red Cross. *American Red Cross Child Care Course.* Washington, D.C: American Red Cross.
    Rocky Mountain Poison Center. *Uh Oh. Poison! Poison Safety Tips.* Denver, CO: Denver Health.

Depth Required for Tested Shock-absorbing Surfacing Materials for Use Under Play Equipment

These data report tested drop heights for specific materials. All materials were not tested at all drop heights. Choose a surfacing material that tested well for drop heights that are equal to or greater than the drop height of your equipment.

Height of Playground Equipment (feet)	Shock-absorbing Substance	Minimum Depth Required Uncompressed (inches)	Minimum Depth Required Compressed (inches)
4	Coarse Sand	--	9
5	Fine Sand	6	9
	Coarse Sand	6	--
	Medium Gravel	6	9
6	Double Shredded Bark Mulch	6	--
	Engineered Wood Fibers	6	9
	Coarse Sand	12	--
	Fine Gravel	6	9
	Medium Gravel	12	--
7	Wood Chips	6	--
	Double Shredded Bark Mulch	--	9
	Engineered Wood Fibers	9	--
	Fine Gravel	9	--
9	Fine Sand	12	--
10	Wood Chips	9	9
	Double Shredded Bark Mulch	9	--
	Fine Gravel	12	--
10-12	Shredded Tires (see note 4 below)	6	--
11	Wood Chips--Double Shredded	12	--
	Double Shredded Bark Mulch	12	--
>12	Engineered Wood Fibers	12	--

Notes:
1. The testing of loose-fill materials was done by the CPSC in accordance with the voluntary standard for playground surfacing systems, ASTM F1292. CPSC reported these data as critical heights for varying depths of material. Since most users of the standard want to know what surfacing is required for a given piece of equipment that has a known fall height, the authors of *Caring for Our Children* converted the CPSC table to start from the known drop height, rather than a specific depth and type of surfacing material. Where CPSC offers no data, the table shows a dash (--). These playground surfacing requirements apply to play equipment whether it is located indoors or outdoors.
2. Fall height is the maximum height of the structure or any part of the structure for all stationary and mobile equipment except swings. For swings, the fall height is the height above the surface of the pivot point where the swing's suspending elements connect to the supporting structure.
3. Protective surfacing recommendations do not apply to equipment that the child uses standing or sitting at ground level like sand boxes or play houses that children do not use as a climber.
4. For shredded tires, the CPSC recommends that users request test data from the supplier showing the critical height of the material when it was tested in accordance with ASTM F1292.
5. Surfacing materials are available as two types, unitary or loose-fill. These recommendations for depth of materials apply to the loose-fill type. For unitary surfacing materials, the manufacturer should provide the test data that show a match between the critical height shock-absorbing characteristics and the fall height of the equipment where the surfacing is used.
6. Since the depth of any loose fill material could be reduced during use, provide a margin of safety when selecting a type and depth of material for a specific use. Also, provide a means of containment around the perimeter of the use zone to keep the material from moving out into surrounding areas, thereby decreasing the depth in the fall zone. Depending on location, weather conditions, and frequency of use, provide maintenance to insure needed depth and loosening of material that has become packed. By placing markers on the support posts of equipment that indicates the correct level of loose-fill surfacing material, users can identify the need for maintenance work.

Reference: United States Consumer Product Safety Commission. *Handbook for Public Playground Safety.* Washington, D.C: U.S. Consumer Product Safety Commission; 1997. Publication 325.

Permission for Medical Condition Treatment

Parent or Guardian signature indicates permission for child care provider to follow these instructions:

_____

(Parent Signature)

TO: Facility name _____ Phone: _____

           Address: _____ Fax: _____

           _____

Child's name: _____ Date of Birth: _____

Address: _____

Medical condition(s) of concern: _____

_____

_____

_____

_____

Signs and/or symptom(s) to watch for: _____

Medications: _____ Dose: _____

How given: _____ When given? _____

Possible side effects: _____

Temporary program adaptations: _____

_____

When to call parent/health provider regarding symptoms or failure to respond to treatment:

_____

_____

When to consider that the condition requires urgent care or reassessment:

_____

_____

FROM: Health care provider: _____ Phone: _____

           Address:_____

           Date of exam: _____

Emergency Information Form for Children With Special Needs

American College of
Emergency Physicians®

American Academy
of Pediatrics

Date form completed	Revised	Initials
By Whom	Revised	Initials

Name:	Birth date:	Nickname:
Home Address:	Home/Work Phone:	
Parent/Guardian:	Emergency Contact Names & Relationship:	
Signature/Consent*:		
Primary Language:	Phone Number(s):	

Physicians:

Primary care physician:	Emergency Phone:
	Fax:
Current Specialty physician:	Emergency Phone:
Specialty:	Fax:
Current Specialty physician:	Emergency Phone:
Specialty:	Fax:
Anticipated Primary ED:	Pharmacy:
Anticipated Tertiary Care Center:	

Diagnoses/Past Procedures/Physical Exam:

1.

2.

3.

4.

Synopsis:

Baseline physical findings:

Baseline vital signs:

Baseline neurological status:

*Consent for release of this form to health care providers

Diagnoses/Past Procedures/Physical Exam continued:

Medications:

1. _____

2. _____

3. _____

4. _____

5. _____

6. _____

Significant baseline ancillary findings (lab, x-ray, ECG):

_____

_____

Prostheses/Appliances/Advanced Technology Devices:

_____

_____

Management Data:

Allergies: Medications/Foods to be avoided and why:

1. _____

2. _____

3. _____

Procedures to be avoided and why:

1. _____

2. _____

3. _____

Immunizations (mm/yy)						Dates					
Dates						**Dates**					
DPT						Hep B					
OPV						Varicella					
MMR						TB status					
HIB						Other					

Antibiotic prophylaxis: Indication: Medication and dose:

Common Presenting Problems/Findings With Specific Suggested Managements

Problem	Suggested Diagnostic Studies	Treatment Considerations

Comments on child, family, or other specific medical issues:

Physician/Provider Signature: **Print Name:**

Reference: American College of Emergency Physicians & American Academy of Pediatrics. *Emergency Information Form for Children with Special Needs* Available at: http://www.acep.org/library/index.cfm/id/1256.pdf. Accessed 2001. Used with permission of the American College of Emergency Physicians and American Academy of Pediatrics, 2001.

Incident Report Form

Fill in all blanks and boxes that apply.

Name of Program: _____ Phone: _____

Address of Facility: _____

Child's Name: _____ Sex: M F Birthdate: ___/___/___ Incident Date: ___/___/___

Time of Incident: ___:___am/pm Witnesses: _____

Name of Legal Guardian/Parent Notified: _____ Notified by: _____ Time Notified: ___:___am/pm

EMS (911) or other medical professional ☐Not notified ☐Notified Time Notified: ___:___am/pm

Location where incident occurred: ☐Playground ☐Classroom ☐Bathroom ☐Hall ☐Kitchen ☐Doorway
☐Gym ☐Office ☐Dining Room ☐Stairway ☐Unknown ☐Other (specify)_____

Equipment / Product involved: ☐Climber ☐Slide ☐Swing ☐Playground Surface ☐Sandbox
☐Trike/Bike ☐Handtoy (specify): _____
☐Other Equipment (specify):_____

Cause of Injury (describe): _____

☐Fall to surface; Estimated height of fall ___feet; Type of surface: _____
☐Fall from running or tripping ☐Bitten by child ☐Motor vehicle ☐Hit or pushed by child
☐Injured by object ☐Eating or choking ☐Insect sting/bite ☐Animal bite ☐Exposure to cold
☐Other (specify):_____

Parts of body injured: ☐Eye ☐Ear ☐Nose ☐Mouth ☐Tooth ☐Part of face ☐Part of head
☐Neck ☐Arm/Wrist/Hand ☐Leg/Ankle/Foot ☐Trunk ☐Other (specify): _____

First aid given at the facility (e.g. comfort, pressure, elevation, cold pack, washing, bandage): _____
_____

Treatment provided by: _____

☐No doctor's or dentist's treatment required
☐Treated as an outpatient (e.g. office or emergency room)
☐Hospitalized (overnight) # of days: _____

Number of days of limited activity from this incident: _____ Follow-up plan for care of the child: _____
_____

Corrective action needed to prevent reoccurrence: _____
_____

Name of Official/Agency notified: _____

Signature of Staff Member: _____ Date: _____

Signature of Legal Guardian/Parent:_____ Date: _____

Reference: Pennsylvania Chapter; American Academy of Pediatrics. *Model Child Care Health Ploicies.* 3rd ed. Washington D.C: National Association for the Education of Young Children, 1997.
This form was developed for *Model Child Care Health Policies,* June 1997, by the Early Childhood Education Linkage System (ECELS), a program funded by the Pennsylvania Depts. of Health & Public Welfare and contractually administered by the PA Chapter, American Academy of Pediatrics.

CHILD HEALTH ASSESSMENT

Parents & Child Care Providers fill-in this part.

CHILD'S NAME: (LAST)	(FIRST)	PARENT/GUARDIAN
DATE OF BIRTH:	HOME PHONE:	ADDRESS:
CHILD CARE FACILITY NAME:		
FACILITY PHONE:	COUNTY:	WORK PHONE:

To Parents: Submission of this form to the child care provider implies consent for the child care provider to discuss the child's health with the child's clinician.

PA child care providers must document that enrolled children have received age appropriate health services and immunizations that meet the current schedule of the American Academy of Pediatrics 141 Northwest Point Blvd., Elk Grove Village, IL 60007. The schedule is available at <www.aap.org> or Faxback 847/758-0391 (document #9535 and #9807). Print copies provided by DPW have the schedule on the back of the form.

Health history and medical information pertinent to routine child care and emergencies (describe, if any): ☐ NONE	Date of most recent well-child exam:
Allergies to food or medicine (describe, if any): ☐ NONE	Do not omit any information. This form may be updated by health professional. (Initial and date new data.) Child care facility needs 2 copies.

Parents may write immunization dates, health professionals should verify and complete all data.

LENGTH/HEIGHT	WEIGHT	HEAD CIRCUMFERENCE	BLOOD PRESSURE
____IN/CM %ILE____	____LB/KG %ILE____	____IN/CM %ILE____	(BEGINNING AT AGE 3) ____/____

PHYSICAL EXAMINATION	✓ = NORMAL	IF ABNORMAL - COMMENTS
HEAD/EARS/EYES/NOSE/THROAT		
TEETH		
CARDIORESPIRATORY		
ABDOMEN/GI		
GENITALIA/BREASTS		
EXTREMITIES/JOINTS/BACK/CHEST		
SKIN/LYMPH NODES		
NEUROLOGIC & DEVELOPMENTAL		

IMMUNIZATIONS	DATE	DATE	DATE	DATE	DATE	COMMENTS
DTaP/DTP/Td						
POLIO						
HIB						
HEP B						
MMR						
VARICELLA						
PNEUMOCOCCAL						
OTHER						

SCREENING TESTS	DATE TEST DONE	NOTE HERE IF RESULTS ARE PENDING OR ABNORMAL
LEAD		
ANEMIA (HGB/HCT)		
URINALYSIS (UA) (at age 5)		
HEARING (subjective until age 4)		
VISION (subjective until age 3)		
PROFESSIONAL DENTAL EXAM		

HEALTH PROBLEMS OR SPECIAL NEEDS, RECOMMENDED TREATMENT/MEDICATIONS/SPECIAL CARE
(ATTACH ADDITIONAL SHEETS IF NECESSARY)

☐ NONE

NEXT APPOINTMENT - MONTH/YEAR:

MEDICAL CARE PROVIDER: SIGNATURE OF PHYSICIAN OR CPNP:	SIGNATURE OF PHYSICIAN OR CPNP:
ADDRESS:	
	PHONE	LICENSE NUMBER:	DATE FORM SIGNED:

Reprinted with permission from Pennsylvania Department of Public Welfare, 2001

Licensing and Public Regulation of Early Childhood Programs

A position statement of the
National Association for the Education of Young Children

Adopted 1987
Reaffirmed 1992, 1997

One of the most dramatic changes in American family life in recent years has been the increased participation of young children in nonparental child care and early education settings. Between 1970 and 1993 the percentage of children regularly attending these types of arrangements soared from 30% to 70% (U.S. Department of Health and Human Services). Much of the demand comes from the need for child care that has accompanied the rapid rise in maternal labor force participation. Increased demand for early childhood care and education services also comes from families who--regardless of parents' employment status--want their children to experience the social and educational enrichment provided by good early childhood programs.

Background

Families seeking nonparental arrangements choose among a variety of options: *centers* (for groups of children in a nonresidential setting), *small family child care homes* (for 6 or fewer children in the home of the care provider), *large family or group child care homes* (typically for no more than 7 to 12 children in the home of a care provider who employs a full-time assistant), *in-home* care (by a nonrelative in the family home), and *kith and kin* care (provided by a relative, neighbor or friend to children of one family only).

The responsibility to ensure that any and all of these settings protect and nurture the children in their care is shared among many groups. Families are ultimately responsible for making informed choices about the specific programs that are most appropriate for their own children. Early childhood professionals and others engaged in providing or supporting early childhood services have an ethical obligation to uphold high standards of practice. Others within the community, including employers and community organizations, who benefit when children and families have access to high-quality early childhood programs--also share in the responsibility to improve the quality and availability of early childhood services. Government serves a number of important roles, including:

- **licensing** and otherwise regulating so as to define and enforce minimum requirements for the legal operation of programs available to the public;

- **funding programs and supporting infrastructure**, including professional development and supply-building activities;

- providing **financial assistance** to help families with program costs;

- supporting **research and development** related to child development and learning and early childhood programs as well as data-gathering for community planning; and

- **disseminating information** to inform consumers, service providers, and the public about ways to promote children's healthy development and learning, both at home and in out-of-family settings.

While many of these functions can and should occur at multiple levels of government, the licensing function is established by laws passed by state legislatures, creating offices that traditionally play the primary role in regulating the child care market by defining requirements for legal operation. States vary considerably in the methods and scope of regulation, using processes that may be called licensing, registration, or certification. These terms can have different meanings from state to state.

The importance of an effective system of public regulation

The primary benefit from public regulation of the child care and early education market is its help in ensuring children's rights to care settings that protect them from harm and promote their healthy development. The importance of these rights is underscored by a growing body of research evidence that emphasizes the importance of children's earliest experiences to their development and later learning (Hart & Risley 1995; Center for the Future of Children 1995; Bredekamp & Copple 1997; Kagan & Cohen 1997). Emerging research on brain development indicates that the degree of responsive caregiving that children receive as infants and toddlers positively affects the connections between neurons in the brain, the architecture of the brain itself (Newberger 1997; Shore 1997). Given the proportion of children who spend significant portions of their day in settings outside their family, ensuring that these environments promote healthy development becomes increasingly important.

Reference: National Association of the Education of Young Children. *Licensing and Public Regulation of Early Childhood Programs: A Position Statement.* Washington, D.C: National Association of the Education of Young Children; 1997.

Research documents that those states with more effective regulatory structures have a greater supply of higher quality programs (Phillips, Howes, & Whitebook 1992; Helburn et al. 1995). Additionally, in such states differences in quality are minimized between service sectors (e.g., nonprofit and proprietary programs) (Kagan & Newton 1989).

Children who attend higher quality programs consistently demonstrate better outcomes. These differences are apparent in many areas: *cognitive functioning and intellectual development* (Lazar et al. 1982; Clarke-Stewart & Gruber 1984; Goelman & Pence 1987; Burchinal, Lee, & Ramey 1989; Epstein 1993; Helburn et al. 1995; Peisner-Feinberg & Burchinal 1997); *language development* (McCartney 1984; Whitebook, Howes, & Phillips 1989; Peisner-Feinberg & Burchinal 1997); and *social development* (McCartney 1982; Clarke-Stewart 1987; Howes 1988; Whitebook, Howes, & Phillips 1989; Peisner-Feinberg & Burchinal 1997). The demonstrated outcomes appear in cross-sectional studies conducted at a specific point in time as well as in longitudinal studies over time (Carew 1980; Howes 1988; Vandell, Henderson & Wilson 1988; Howes 1990; Schweinhart, Barnes, & Weikart with Barnett & Epstein 1993; Barnett 1995). The differences in outcomes occur even when other family variables are controlled for, including maternal education and family income level (Helburn et al. 1995; NICHD 1997).

Research is also consistent in identifying the structural factors most related to high quality in early childhood programs:

- small groups of children with a sufficient number of adults to provide sensitive, responsive caregiving;

- higher levels of general education and specialized preparation for caregivers or teachers as well as program administrators; and

- higher rates of compensation and lower rates of turnover for program personnel (Whitebook, Howes, & Phillips 1989; Hayes, Palmer, & Zaslow 1990; Galinsky et al. 1994; Helburn et al. 1995; Kagan & Cohen 1997; Whitebook, Sakai, & Howes 1997). Many of these factors can be regulated directly or influenced by regulatory policy.

Despite widespread knowledge of what is needed to provide good quality in early childhood programs, many programs fail to do so. Two large-scale studies of licensed centers and family child care homes found that only about 10 to 15% of the settings offered care that promoted children's healthy development and learning. For infants and toddlers, the situation is grave: as many as 35 to 40% of the settings were found to be inadequate and potentially harmful to children's healthy development (Galinsky et al. 1994; Helburn et al. 1995).

Support for an effective licensing system falls short

An effective licensing system minimizes the potential for harmful care, but regulatory systems in many states receive inadequate support to fully protect children's healthy development and learning. The lack of support can be seen in five broad areas: (1) some states set their basic floor of protection too low, failing to reflect research findings about the factors that create risk of harm; (2) a large number of settings in some states are exempt from regulation; (3) the licensing office in some states is not empowered to adequately enforce the rules; (4) multiple regulatory systems may apply to individual programs, sometimes with resulting overlapping or even contradictory requirements; and (5) policymakers may view licensing as unnecessary because they believe it seeks the ideal or imposes an elitist definition of quality rather than establishing a baseline of protection. Each of these issues is discussed briefly below.

1. *Some states set their basic floor of protection too low, with licensing rules that fail to reflect research findings about the factors that promote or hinder children's healthy development.* Clear links exist between the quality of early childhood programs in child care centers and homes and the quality of the public regulatory systems governing these services. The overall quality level of services provided to children is not only higher in states with more stringent licensing systems (Phillips, Howes, & Whitebook 1992; Helburn et al. 1995), but also demonstrable improvements can be seen in program quality in states that have worked to improve aspects of their licensing processes (Howes, Kontos, & Galinsky 1995). Despite such compelling evidence as to the importance of strong licensing systems, a 1997 study looking at grouping, staff qualifications, and program requirements found that "the majority of states' child care regulations do not meet basic standards of acceptable/appropriate practice that assure the safe and healthy development of very young children." (Young, Marsland, & Zigler in press). Similar findings also have been reported on licensing standards for the care of four-year-olds (Snow, Teleki, & Reguero-de-Atiles 1996).

2. *A large number of settings in some states are exempt from regulation.* Many children are unprotected because they receive care outside their families in programs that are legally exempt from regulation. Exemptions affect both centers and family child care homes. Among centers the most common licensing exemptions are for part-day programs (roughly half of the states) and programs operated by religious institutions (nine states) (Children's Foundation 1997). Programs operated by or in public schools are sometimes exempt from licensing, although in some cases public school programs must meet comparable regulatory standards. Many states exempt family child care providers from regulation if they care for fewer children than stipulated as the threshold for regulation. About half of the states set such a threshold that ranges from 4 to 13 children (Child Care Law Center 1996).

Reference: National Association of the Education of Young Children. *Licensing and Public Regulation of Early Childhood Programs: A Position Statement.* Washington, D.C: National Association of the Education of Young Children; 1997.

3. ***States do not always provide the licensing office with sufficient funding and power to effectively enforce licensing rules.*** A 1992 report found that "many states face difficulties protecting children from care that does not meet minimum safety and health standards" (U.S. General Accounting Office, p. 3). According to the report, staffing and budget cuts forced many states to reduce on-site monitoring, a key oversight activity for effective enforcement. These cutbacks occurred during a time of tremendous growth in the number of centers and family child care homes. The number of centers is estimated to have tripled between the mid 1970s and early 1990s, while the number of children enrolled quadrupled (Willer et al. 1991). An indicator of the growth in the number of regulated family child care providers is found in the recorded increase in the number of home-based participants in the USDA Child and Adult Care Food Program (regulation being a requirement of participation) from 82,000 in 1986 to nearly 200,000 in 1996 (Morawetz 1997).

Lack of meaningful sanctions makes enforcement of existing regulations difficult (Gormley 1997). Licensing offices in all states have the power to revoke licenses, but some states have a much broader range of enforcement tools. Others lack funding to adequately train licensing personnel and fail to receive appropriate legal backup for effective enforcement. Although most states require that a facility license be prominently posted, many states do not require prominently posting or public printing of violation notices when facilities fail inspections. Information about licensing violations is only available in some states by checking the files in the state licensing office (Scurria 1994). The high demand for child care and early education services can exert pressures to keep even inadequate facilities open (Gormley 1995).

4. ***Multiple regulatory layers exist, sometimes with overlapping or even contradictory requirements.*** Different laws have created different inspection systems for different reasons, all affecting child care programs. Programs typically must comply with local zoning, building and fire safety, and health and sanitation codes in addition to licensing. A lack of coordination of requirements can frustrate new and existing providers and undermine the overall effectiveness of the regulatory system. For example, state and local regulatory structures sometimes impose contradictory requirements on family child care providers (Gormley 1995). If providers react by "going underground," children suffer.

5. ***Policymakers may view licensing as unnecessary because they believe it seeks the ideal or an elitist definition of quality rather than establish a baseline of protection.*** By definition, licensing rules represent the most basic level of protection for children. Licensing constitutes official permission to operate a center or family child care home; without this permission, the facility is operating illegally. Licensing rules, combined with other regulatory requirements, such as environmental health codes, zoning provisions, and building and fire safety codes, define the *floor* for acceptable care that all child care programs must meet. In the current deregulatory climate, efforts to improve licensing rules and provide better basic protections for children's healthy development have sometimes been misrepresented as attempts to impose a "Cadillac" or ideal quality child care that is too costly and unrealistic for all programs to achieve. When such misrepresentations succeed, the floor or safety net that licensing provides to protect children in out-of-family care is weakened.

Drawing upon a conceptual framework first espoused by Norris Class (1969), Morgan distinguishes multiple levels of standards needed to achieve quality in early childhood programs (1996). As the strongest of governmental interventions, licensing must rest on a basis of the prevention of harm. Other regulatory methods, including approval of publicly operated programs, fiscal control and rate setting, credentialing and accreditation, provide additional mechanisms that, building upon the basic floor of licensing, can encourage programs to achieve higher standards.

Nonregulatory methods can also promote higher quality services: for example, public and consumer awareness and engagement, professional development of teachers/caregivers and administrators, networking and information sharing among professionals, and dissemination regarding best practices. These standards can interact and be dynamic. For example, licensing rules can reference credentialing standards, or fiscal regulation can reflect higher rates for accredited programs. Also, greater knowledge of the importance of various factors in preventing harm to children's healthy development and learning can result in changes in licensing rules so as to raise the level of basic protection over time.

NAEYC's position

The National Association for the Education of Young Children (NAEYC) affirms the responsibility of states to license and regulate the early care and education market by regulating centers, schools, and family and group child care homes. The fundamental purpose of public regulation is to protect children from harm, not only threats to their immediate physical health and safety but also threats of long-term developmental impairment.

NAEYC recommends that states continue to adopt and improve requirements that establish a basic floor of protection below which no center, school, or family child care or group home may legally operate. Basic protections should, at a minimum, protect children by striving to prevent the risk of the spread of disease, fire in buildings as well as other structural safety hazards, personal injury, child abuse or neglect, and developmental impairment.

Licensing rules should be coordinated statewide and streamlined to focus on those aspects that research and practice most clearly demonstrate as reducing these types of harm. Licensing rules and procedures should be developed in

Reference: National Association of the Education of Young Children. *Licensing and Public Regulation of Early Childhood Programs: A Position Statement.* Washington, D.C.: National Association of the Education of Young Children; 1997.

a context that recognizes other strategies and policies that encourage all programs to strive continuously for higher standards of quality. Such strategies and policies include application of levels of funding standards and rates for the public purchase of or operation of services; maintenance of broadly accessible registries of programs or providers who meet nationally recognized standards of quality (such as NAEYC accreditation); provision of a broad array of training and technical assistance programs to meet the varied needs of different types of providers; and development and dissemination of model standards or best practices.

Public regulation of early childhood program facilities, including licensing, represents a basic level of protection afforded to all children in settings outside their family. Additional strategies and policies along with licensing are needed to support the provision of high-quality services for all families who want or need them. These strategies and policies, however, cannot substitute for licensing in providing basic protection.

NAEYC's principles for effective regulation

NAEYC offers the following 10 principles for implementing an effective regulatory system.

1. **Any program providing care and education to children from two or more unrelated families should be regulated; there should be no exemptions from this principle.**

NAEYC believes that all types of care and education programs within the child care market should be regulated to provide basic protections to children. These protections must apply to all programs, without limiting definitions, exemptions, or exceptions. Whenever programs are exempted, not covered, or given special treatment, children are vulnerable and the entire regulatory system is weakened. NAEYC believes that programs should be regulated regardless of sponsorship, regardless of the length of program day, and regardless of the age of children served. NAEYC explicitly opposes the exemption of part-day programs or programs sponsored by religious organizations, because such exemption does not provide an equal level of health and safety protection for all children.

NAEYC's definition of licensed care specifically excludes care by kith and kin when a family engages an individual to care solely for their children. A family support/education model that provides helpful information and support to individuals caring for children is likely to be more effective and meaningful in reaching kith-and-kin providers than a formal licensing model. Programs targeted to parents of young children to help them in their role as their child's first teacher should also be accessible to kith-and-kin caregivers. If kith-and-kin providers are paid with public funds, NAEYC supports the application of funding standards to these arrangements.

2. **States should license all facilities that provide services to the public, including all centers, large family or group child care homes, and small family child care homes (i.e., granting permission to operate).**

NAEYC recommends that all centers or schools (serving 10 or more children in a nonresidential setting) be licensed facilities. Facility licensure should include an on-site visit prior to licensure and periodic inspections to monitor continued compliance. Licensing rules should focus on the aspects deemed most critical to maintaining children's safety and their healthy development, both in terms of their immediate physical health and well-being and their long-term well-being in all areas of development. NAEYC supports the use of *Stepping Stones to Using Caring for Our Children* (National Resource Center for Health and Safety in Child Care 1997) to identify those requirements in the National Health and Safety Performance Standards (APHA & AAP 1992) most needed for prevention of injury, morbidity, and mortality in child care settings.

Licenses are typically granted to privately administered programs rather than publicly operated programs; although some states do require publicly operated programs (such as those administered by the state department of education) to be licensed. If licensure is not required of publicly operated programs, the administering agency should ensure that the program's regulatory standards and enforcement procedures are at least equivalent to those applied to licensed facilities. Such language should be written into law to empower the administering agency to develop statewide policies for implementation.

States currently vary widely in their definitions and procedures for regulating family child care homes. NAEYC recommends the adoption of consistent definitions of *small family child care homes* as care of no more than six children by a single caregiver in her home, including the caregiver's children age twelve or younger and *large family child care homes* as care in the caregiver's residence employing a full-time assistant and serving 7 to 12 children, including the caregivers' children age twelve or younger. When infants and toddlers are present in a small family child care home, no more than three children should be younger than age three, unless only infants and toddlers are in the group and the total group size does not exceed four. Large family child care homes should meet the same ratios and group sizes recommended for use in centers.

NAEYC supports licensing methods for small family child care homes that are designed to achieve full regulatory coverage of all home-based care providers in a state. These methods sometimes do not require an on-site inspection prior to operation. NAEYC believes that such methods—whether called registration, certification, or another form of licensing—are viable ways to license small family child care homes provided that (1) standards are developed and applied; (2) permission to operate may be removed from homes that refuse to comply with the rules; (3) parents are well informed about the standards and the process; and (4) an effective

Reference: National Association of the Education of Young Children. *Licensing and Public Regulation of Early Childhood Programs: A Position Statement.* Washington, D.C: National Association of the Education of Young Children; 1997.

monitoring process, including on-site inspections, is in place. NAEYC believes that large family child care homes should be licensed in the same way as centers, with an inspection prior to licensure.

3. **In addition to licensing facilities, states should establish complementary processes for professional licensing of individuals as teachers, caregivers, or program administrators (i.e., granting permission to practice).**

The skills and qualifications of the individuals working in an early childhood program are critically essential to creating environments that promote children's healthy development and learning. Establishing licenses for the various roles included in early childhood centers and family child care homes not only protects children's healthy development by requiring the demonstration of key competencies but also will enhance early childhood professionalism and career development. In addition, individual licensure holds promise for increasing the compensation of staff (Kagan & Cohen 1997). Licensing of individuals is also a more cost-effective way of regulating qualifications centrally rather than on a licensing visit.

A number of states are implementing career or personnel registries (Azer, Capraro, & Elliott 1997); individual licensure can build upon and complement these efforts. Personnel licensure should provide for multiple levels and roles, such as teacher/caregiver, master or lead teacher/caregiver, family child care provider, master family child care provider, and early childhood administrator. Attaining a license should require demonstration of the skills, knowledge, and competencies needed for the specific role. (For further information, see *NAEYC's Guidelines for Preparation of Early Childhood Professionals* [NAEYC 1996] and "*A Conceptual Framework of Early Childhood Professional Development*" [Willer 1994]).

Multiple licenses are needed because of the diversity of roles and functions fulfilled by program personnel; multiple levels help to establish a career ladder with meaningful opportunities for career advancement, with higher levels of compensation linked to higher levels of qualification and demonstrated competence. In states in which early childhood teacher licensure or certification already exists for public school personnel, early childhood personnel licensing should be coordinated with these efforts. Individual licensure efforts may also be used to provide a form of consumer protection for families using in-home care by enabling them to check the credentials of a potential employee.

4. **Licensing standards should be clear and reasonable and reflect current research findings related to regulative aspects that will reduce the risk of harm.**

Licensing rules reflect public policy not program specifications. Highly detailed descriptions of program implementation are inappropriate for inclusion in licensing

rules. Such areas are better addressed through consumer education and professional development. For example, requiring programs to establish a planned program of activities to enhance children's development and learning would be an appropriate licensing rule, specifying the number of blocks to be available in a classroom would not.

NAEYC recommends that the licensing standards address health and safety aspects, group size, adult-child ratios, and preservice qualifications, and inservice requirements for staff (referencing individual licensing standards). Periodic review and revision (every five years) are needed to ensure that rules reflect current issues as well as the latest knowledge and practice. Licensing rules should be widely publicized to parents and the public; these groups, along with service providers, should also participate in the review and revision of the rules.

5. **Regulations should be vigorously and equitably enforced.**

Enforcement is critical to effective regulation. Effective enforcement requires periodic on-site inspections on both an announced and unannounced basis with meaningful sanctions for noncompliance. NAEYC recommends that all centers and large and small family child care homes receive at least one site visit per year. Additional inspections should be completed if there are reasons (such as newness of the facility, sanction history, recent staff turnover, history of violations, complaint history) to suspect regulatory violations. Unannounced visits have been shown to be especially effective when targeted to providers with a history of low compliance (Fiene 1996).

Clear, well-publicized processes should be established for reporting, investigating, and appealing complaints against programs. Parents and consumers especially should be informed of these processes. Staff should be encouraged to report program violations of licensing rules. If whistle-blowing laws do not exist or do not cover early care and education workers, such legislation should be enacted. Substantiated violations should be well publicized, at the program site as well as in other venues (such as resource and referral agencies, newspapers, public libraries, online, etc.) easily accessible to parents and consumers. Lists of programs with exemplary compliance records also should be widely publicized along with lists of programs that meet the requirements of recognized systems of quality approval, such as NAEYC accreditation.

Sanctions should be included in the regulatory system to give binding force to its requirements. Enforcement provisions should provide an array of enforcement options such as: the ability to impose fines; to revoke, suspend, or limit licenses; to restrict enrollment or admissions; and to take emergency action to close programs in circumstances that are dangerous to children. When threats to children's health and safety are discovered, sanctions should be promptly imposed without a delayed administrative hearing process. The vulnerability of children mandates the highest level of official scrutiny of out-of-family care and education environments.

Reference: National Association of the Education of Young Children. *Licensing and Public Regulation of Early Childhood Programs: A Position Statement.* Washington, D.C.: National Association of the Education of Young Children; 1997.

6. **Licensing agencies should have sufficient staff and resources to effectively implement the regulatory process.**

Staffing to handle licensing must be adequate not only to provide for timely processing of applications but also to implement periodic monitoring inspections and to follow up complaints against programs. Licensing agencies must consider a number of factors in determining reasonable caseloads, for example, program size and travel time between programs. NAEYC believes that, on the average, regulators' caseloads should be no more than 75 centers and large family child care homes or the equivalent; NAEYC recommends 50 as a more desirable number. States that do not make on-site inspections prior to licensing small family child care homes may assume larger caseloads, but allowing for timely processing of licenses, periodic on-site inspections, and prompt follow-ups to complaints.

Regulatory personnel responsible for inspecting and monitoring programs should have preparation and demonstrated competence in early childhood education and child development, program administration, and regulatory enforcement, including the use of sanctions. These criteria should be included in civil service requirements for licensing staff.

7. **Regulatory processes should be coordinated and streamlined to promote greater effectiveness and efficiency.**

Rules and inspections should be coordinated between the licensing agency and those agencies responsible for building and fire safety and health and sanitation codes so that any overlap is reduced to a minimum and contradictions resolved. In many cases coordination will require reform at a statewide level, as different requirements derive from different laws, are implemented by different agencies, and respond to different constituencies (Center for Career Development 1995). Coordination with funding agencies is also crucial. Licensing personnel can provide program monitoring for the funding agency, thus eliminating duplicate visits; funding can be withheld possibly in cases of substantiated violations.

Other methods for consideration in streamlining the regulatory process include (1) establishing permanent rather than annual licenses for centers, allowing for the removal of the license for cause at any time, and conducting inspection visits at least annually to determine continued compliance; (2) coordinating local teams that monitor and inspect for licensing and regulation of health, fire and building safety codes; (3) and removing zoning barriers. NAEYC believes that centers and family child care homes should be regarded as a needed community service rather than as commercial development, and should be permitted in any residential zone. Planning officials should take into account the need for these services as communities develop new housing and commercial uses.

8. **Incentive mechanisms should encourage the achievement of a higher quality of service beyond the basic floor.**

In addition to mandated licensing rules that establish a floor of quality below which no program is allowed to operate, governments can use incentive mechanisms to encourage programs to achieve higher levels of quality. Examples of incentive mechanisms include funding standards, higher payment rates tied to demonstrated compliance with higher levels of quality, and active publicity on programs achieving higher quality. Given the nature of the early childhood field as severely underfunded, these mechanisms should be implemented in conjunction with funding targeted to help programs achieve and maintain higher levels of quality, or else the strategy simply enlarges the gulf between the *haves* and *have-nots*. Differential monitoring strategies, whereby programs maintaining strong track records and experiencing low turnover in personnel receive shortened inspections or are eligible for longer-term licenses, also may serve as incentives to programs for providing higher quality care.

9. **Consumer and public education should inform families, providers, and the public of the importance of the early years and of ways to create environments that promote children's learning and development.**

Actively promoting messages about what constitutes good settings for young children not only encourages parents to be better consumers of services in the marketplace but also, because these messages will reach providers outside the scope of regulation (family members and in-home providers), may help improve the quality of other settings. Public service announcements, the development and dissemination of brochures and flyers that describe state/local standards, open workshops, and ongoing communication with organized parent groups and well-care programs are all excellent ways for the regulatory agency to raise the child-caring consciousness of a community. A highly visible regulatory system also helps to inform potential and existing providers of the existence of standards and the need to comply with the law.

10. **States should invest sufficient levels of resources to ensure that children's healthy development and learning are not harmed in early care and education settings.**

NAEYC believes that public regulation is a basic and necessary component of government's responsibility for protecting all children in all programs from the risk of harm and for promoting the conditions that are essential for children's healthy development and learning, which must be adequately funded. Additionally, government at every level can and should support early childhood programs by ensuring sufficient funding for high quality services, opportunities for professional development and technical assistance to service providers, consumer education to families and the general public, and child care resource and referral services to families.

Reference: National Association of the Education of Young Children. *Licensing and Public Regulation of Early Childhood Programs: A Position Statement.* Washington, D.C: National Association of the Education of Young Children; 1997.

Early childhood regulation in context

An effective system of public regulation is the cornerstone of an effective system of early childhood care and education services, because it alone reaches all programs in the market. But for the regulatory system to be the most effective, other pieces of the early childhood care and education services system must also be in place, including (1) a holistic approach to addressing the needs of children and families that stresses collaborative planning and service integration across traditional boundaries of child care, education, health, employment, and social services; (2) systems that recognize and promote quality; (3) an effective system of professional development that provides meaningful opportunities for career advancement to ensure a stable, well-qualified workforce; (4) equitable financing that ensures access for all children and families to high-quality services; and (5) active involvement of all stakeholders--providers, practitioners, parents, and community leaders from both public and private sectors--in all aspects of program planning and delivery. NAEYC is committed to ensuring that each of these elements is in place. As early childhood educators, we believe that nothing less than the future of our nation--the well-being of its children--is at stake.

References

APHA & AAP (American Public Health Association & American Academy of Pediatrics). 1992. *Caring for our children– National health and safety performance: Guidelines for out-of-home child care programs.* Washington, DC: APHA.

Azer, S.L., L. Capraro, & K. Elliott. 1996. *Working toward making a career of it: A profile of career development initiatives in 1996.* Boston: The Center for Career Development in Early Care and Education, Wheelock College.

Barnett, W.S. 1995. Long-term effects of early childhood programs on cognitive and social outcomes. *Center for the Future of Children.* 5(3):25-50.

Bredekamp, S. & C. Copple, eds. 1997. *Developmentally appropriate practice in early childhood programs.* rev. ed. Washington, DC: NAEYC.

Burchinal, M., M.W. Lee, & C.T. Ramey. 1989. Type of day care and preschool intellectual development in disadvantaged children. *Child Development* 60:128-137.

Carew, J. 1980. *Experience and development of intelligence in young children at home and in day care.* Monographs of the Society for Research in Child Development, vol. 45 nos. 6-7; ser. no. 187.

Center for Career Development in Early Care and Education at Wheelock College. 1995. *Regulation and the prevention of harm.* Boston, MA: Author.

Center for the Future on Children. 1995. Long-term outcomes of early childhood programs. *The Future of Children* 5 (3).

Child Care Law Center. 1996. *Regulation-exempt family child care in the context of publicly subsidized child care: An exploratory study.* San Francisco: Author.

Children's Foundation. 1996. *1996 Family child care licensing study.* Washington, DC: Author.

Children's Foundation. 1997. *1997 Child care licensing study.* Washington, DC: Author.

Clarke-Stewart, K.A., & C. Gruber. 1984. Daycare forms and features. In *Quality variations in daycare,* ed. R.C. Ainslie, 35-62. New York: Praeger.

Clarke-Stewart, K.A. 1987. Predicting child development from child care forms and features: The Chicago Study. In *Quality in child care: What does research tell us?* ed. D.A. Phillips. Washington, DC: NAEYC.

Epstein, A. 1993. *Training for quality: Improving early childhood programs through systematic inservice training.* Ypsilanti, MI: High/Scope Press.

Fiene, R. 1996. Unannounced versus announced licensing inspections in monitoring child care programs. Paper developed for the Cross-systems licensing project, Pennsylvania State University at Harrisburg and Pennsylvania Department of Public Welfare.

Galinsky, E., C. Howes, S. Kontos, & M. Shinn. 1994. The study of children in family child care and relative care. Highlights and findings. New York: Families and Work Institute.

Goelman, H., & A. Pence. 1987. Effects of child care, family and individual characteristics on children's language development: The Victoria day care research project. In *Quality in child care: What does research tell us?* ed. D.A. Phillips, 89 - 104. Washington, DC: NAEYC.

Gormley, W.T. Jr. 1995. *Everybody's children: Child care as a public problem.* Washington, DC: Brookings Institution.

Gormley, W.T., Jr. 1997. Regulatory enforcement: Accommodation and conflict in four states. *Public Administration Review,* 57 (4): 285-293.

Hart, B., & T. Risley. 1995. *Meaningful differences in the everyday experiences of young American children.* Baltimore: Paul H. Brookes.

Hayes, C. D., J.L. Palmer, & M. J. Zaslow, eds. 1990. *Who cares for America's children? Child care policy in the 1990s.* Washington, DC: National Academy Press.

Helburn, S., ed. *Cost, quality and child outcomes in child care centers.* Technical report. Denver: University of Colorado at Denver.

Howes, C. 1988. Relations between early child care and schooling. *Developmental Psychology,* 24:53-57.

Howes, C. 1990. Can the age of entry into child care and the quality of child care predict adjustment in kindergarten? *Developmental Psychology,* 26 (2): 292-303.

Howes, C., E. Smith, & E. Galinsky. 1995. *The Florida child care quality improvement study.* New York: Families and Work Institute.

Kagan, S.L. & N. Cohen. 1997. *Not by chance: Creating an early care and education system.* New Haven, CT: Yale Bush Center for Child Development and Social Policy.

Reference: National Association of the Education of Young Children. *Licensing and Public Regulation of Early Childhood Programs: A Position Statement.* Washington, D.C.: National Association of the Education of Young Children; 1997.

Kagan, S.L. & J.W. Newton. 1989. Public policy report. For-profit and nonprofit child care: Similarities and differences. *Young Children* 45 (1): 4-10.

Lazar, I., R. Darlington, H. Murray, J. Royce, & A. Snipper. 1982. Lasting effects of early education: A report from the Consortium for Longitudinal Studies. *Monographs of the Society for Research in Child Development*, 47: Serial No. 201.

McCartney, K. 1984. The effect of quality of day care environment upon children's language development. *Developmental Psychology* 20: 224-260.

Morawetz, E. 1997. Personal communication in July. Unpublished data, Child and Adult Care Food Program, U.S. Department of Agriculture, Food and Consumer Service, Child Nutrition Division, Alexandria, VA.

Morgan, G. 1996. Licensing and accreditation: How much quality is *quality*? In *NAEYC accreditation: A decade of learning and the years ahead*, eds. S. Bredekamp & B.A. Willer, 129 - 138. Washington, DC: NAEYC.

NAEYC. 1996. *Guidelines for preparation of early childhood professionals*. Washington, DC: Author.

National Resource Center for Health and Safety in Child Care. 1997. *Stepping stones to using Caring for ourchildren: National health and safety performance standards: Guidelines for out-of-home child care programs*. Denver: Author.

Newberger, J.J. 1997. New brain development research--A wonderful window of opportunity to build public support for early childhood education. *Young Children* 52 (4): 4-9.

NICHD Early Child Care Research Network. 1997. Mother-child interaction and cognitive outcomes associated with early child care: Results of the NICHD study. Paper presented at the 1997 Biennial Conference of the Society for Research in Child Development, Washington, DC.

Peisner, E.S., & M.R. Burchinal. 1997. Relations between preschool children's child-care experiences and concurrent development: The Cost, Quality, and Outcomes Study. *Merrill-Palmer Quarterly* 43 (3):451-477.

Phillips, D., C. Howes, & M. Whitebook. 1992. The social policy context of child care: Effects on quality. *American Journal of Community Psychology* 20 (1): 25-51.

Schweinhart, L.J., H.V. Barnes, & D.P. Weikart with W.S. Barnett & A.S. Epstein. 1993. *Significant benefits: The High/Scope Perry Preschool study through age 27*. High/Scope Educational Research Foundation Monograph, no. 10. Ypsilanti, MI: High/Scope Press.

Scurria, K.L. 1994. Alternative approaches to regulation of child care: Lessons from other fields. Working paper prepared for the Quality 2000: Advancing Early Care and Education initiative.

Shore, R. 1997. *Rethinking the brain: New insights into early development*. New York: Families and Work Institute.

Snow, C.W., J.K. Teleki, & J.T. Reguero-de-Atiles. Child care center licensing standards in the United States: 1981 to 1995. *Young Children* 51 (6): 36-41.

U.S. Department of Health and Human Services. no date. Blueprint for Action. Healthy Child Care America Campaign. Washington, DC: Author.

United States General Accounting Office. 1992. *Child care: States face difficulties enforcing standards and promoting quality*. GAO/HRD-93-13. Washington, DC: U.S. Government Printing Office.

Vandell, D.L., V.K. Henderson, & K.S. Wilson. 1988. A longitudinal study of children with day-care experiences of varying quality. *Child Development* 59:1286-92.

Whitebook, M., C. Howes, & D.A. Phillips. 1989. *Who cares? Child care teachers and the quality of care in America. The National Child Care Staffing Study*. Oakland, CA: Child Care Employee Project.

Whitebook, M., L. Sakai, & C. Howes. 1997. *NAEYC accreditation as a strategy for improving child care quality, executive summary*. Washington, DC: National Center for the Early Childhood Work Force.

Willer, B. ed. 1994. A conceptual framework for early childhood professional development. In *The early childhood career lattice: Perspectives on professional development*, eds. J. Johnson & J.B. McCracken, 4-23. Washington, DC: NAEYC.

Willer, B., S.L. Hofferth, E.E. Kisker, P. Divine-Hawkins, E. Farquhar, & F.B. Glantz. *1991. The demand and supply of child care in 1990*. Washington, DC: NAEYC.

Young, K., K.W. Marsland, & E.G. Zigler (in press). *American Journal of Orthopsychiatry*.

This document is an official position statement of the National Association for the Education of Young Children.

Reference: National Association of the Education of Young Children. *Licensing and Public Regulation of Early Childhood Programs: A Position Statement*. Washington, D.C: National Association of the Education of Young Children; 1997.

Contact Information

The Academy of Breastfeeding Medicine
P.O. Box 15945-284
Lenexa, KS 66285-5945
Phone: 913-541-9077
Fax: 913-541-0156
http://bfmed.org

American Academy of Allergy, Asthma, and Immunology(AAAAI)
611 East Wells Street
Milwaukee, WI 53202
Phone: 414-272-6071
Fax: 414-272-6070
http://www.aaaai.org
Email:info@aaaai.org

American Academy of Family Physicians (AAFP)
11400 Tomahawk Creek Pkwy.
Leawood, KS. 66211
Phone: 800-274-2237 or 913-906-6000
http://www.aafp.org

American Academy of Pediatrics (AAP)
141 Northwest Point Boulevard
Elk Grove Village, IL 60007-1098
Phone: 847-434-4000
Fax: 847-228-5097
http://www.aap.org

American Academy of Pediatric Dentistry
211 East Chicago Avenue, #700
Chicago, IL 60611-2663
Phone: 312-337-2169
Fax: 312-337-6329
http://www.aapd.org
E-mail: info@aapd.org

American Alliance for Health, Physical Education, Recreation, & Dance
1900 Association Drive
Reston, VA 20191-1502
Phone: 1-800-213-7193
Fax: 703-476-9527
E-mail: webmaster@aahperd.org
http://www.aahperd.org

American Association of Family and Consumer Services
1555 King St.
Alexandria, VA 22314
Phone: 703-706-4600
Fax: 703-706-4663
http://www.staff.aafcs.org

American Association for Health Education (AAHE)
1900 Association Drive
Reston, VA 20191-1599
Phone: 1-800-213-7193 or 703-476-3437
Fax: 703-476-6638
E-mail: aahe@ahhperd.org
http://www.aahperd.org/aahe

American Automobile Association (AAA)
1000 AAA Dr.
Heathrow, FL 32746
Phone: 407-444-4240
Fax: 407-444-4247
http://www.aaa.com

American Cancer Society
1599 Clifton Road NE
Atlanta, GA 30329-4251
Phone: 1-800-227-2345 or 404-320-3333
http://www.cancer.org

American College of Emergency Physicians
1125 Executive Circle
Irving, TX 75038-2522,
Phone: 1-800-798-1822
http://www.acep.org

American Diabetes Association
1701 North Beauregard Street
Alexandria, VA 22311
Phone: 800-342-2383
Fax: 703-549-6995
E-mail: customerservice@diabetes.org
http://www.diabetes.org

American Dietetic Association (ADA)
216 West Jackson Boulevard
Chicago, Illinois 60606-6995
Phone: 312-899-0040
Fax: 312-899-1979
http://www.eatright.org

Americans with Disabilities Act Accessibility Guidelines (ADAAG)
U.S. Department of Justice
Civil Rights Division
Disability Rights Section
P.O. Box 66738
Washington, DC 20035-6738
Phone: 1-800-514-0301
Phone (TDD): 1-800-514-0383
http://www.usdoj.gov/crt/ada/adahom1.htm

Please note contact information may change. Check http://nrc.uchsc.edu for updates.

Contact Information

American Furniture Manufacturer's Association (AFMA)
P.O. Box HP-7
High Point, NC 27261
Phone: 336-884-5000
Fax: 336-884-5303
http://www.afma4u.org

The American Gas Association
1515 Wilson Blvd.
Arlington, VA 22209
Phone: 703-841-8400
http://www.aga.org

American Heart Association (AHA)
7272 Greenville Avenue
Dallas, Texas 75231
Phone: 214-373-6300
http://www.amhrt.org

American Lifeguard Association
8150 Leesburg Pike #600
Vienna, VA. 22182
Phone: 703-748-4803
Fax: 1-888-432-9252

American Lung Association
432 Park Ave. South
New York, NY 10016
Phone: 212-889-3370
Fax: 212-889-3375
http://www.alany.org

American National Standards Institute (ANSI)
1819 L Street, NW, 6th Fl.
Washington, DC, 20036
Phone: 202-293-8020
Fax: 202-293-9287
E-mail: ansionline@ansi.org
http://www.ansi.org

American Nurses Association (ANA)
600 Maryland Ave., SW
Suite 100 West
Washington, DC 20024
Phone: 1-800-274-4262 or 202-651-7000
Fax: 202-651-7001
http://www.nursingworld.org

American Public Health Association (APHA)
800 I Street N.W,
Washington, DC 20001-3710
Phone: 202-777-APHA(2742)
Fax: 202-777-2534
http://www.apha.org
E-mail: comments@apha.org

American Red Cross (ARC)
4333 Arlington Blvd.
Arlington, VA 22203-2904
Phone: 703-527-3010
Fax: 703-527-2705
http://www.redcross.org

American School Food Service Association
700 South Washington St.
Suite 300
Alexandria, VA 22314-4287
Phone: 703-739-3900
Fax: 703-739-3915
E-mail: servicecenter@asfsa.org
http://www.asfsa.org

American Society of Heating, Refrigerating, and Air Conditioning Engineers (ASHRAE)
1791 Tullie Circle, NE
Atlanta, GA 30329
Phone: 404-636-8400
Fax: 404-321-5478
http://www.ashrae.org

American Society for Testing and Materials (ASTM)
100 Barr Harbor Drive
West Conshohocken, PA 19428-2959
Phone: 610-832-9500
Fax: 610-832-9555
http://www.astm.org

Art and Creative Materials Institute (ACMI)
1280 Main St.
PO Box 479
Hanson, MA 02341
Phone: 781-293-4100
Fax: 781-294-0808
http://www.acminet.org

Association of Home Appliance Manufacturers
1111 19th St. N.W.
Washington, DC 20036
Phone: 202-872-5955
Fax: 202-872-9354
http://www.aham.org

Asthma and Allergy Foundation of America
1233 20th St., N.W.
Suite 402
Washington, DC 20036
Phone: 1-800-727-8462
Fax: 202-466-8940
http://www.aafa.org

Please note contact information may change. Check http://nrc.uchsc.edu for updates.

Contact Information

Boy Scouts
1325 West Walnut Hill Lane
PO Box 152079
Irving, TX 75015-2079
Phone: 972-580-2000
Fax: 972-580-2502
http://www.bsa.scouting.org

Building Officials & Code Administrators International
4051 W. Flossmoor Rd.
Country Club Hills, IL 60478
Phone: 708-799-2300
Fax: 708-799-4981
E-mail: info@bocai.org
http://www.bocai.org

Canadian Paediatric Society
100-2204 Walkley Rd.
Ottawa ON K1G 4G8
Phone: 613-526-9397
Fax: 613-526-3332
http://www.cps.ca
E-mail: info.cps.ca

Canadian Standards Association (CSA)
178 Rexdale Boulevard
Toronto, ON
M9W 1R3, CANADA
Phone: 1-800-463-6727
Fax: 416-747-2510
E-mail: info@csa-international.org
http://www.csa.ca

Center for the Child Care Workforce (CCW)
733 15th Street, NW Suite 1037
Washington, DC 20005-2112
Phone: 1-800-879-6784
Fax: 202-737-0370
E-mail: ccw@ccw.org
http://www.ccw.org

Centers for Disease Control and Prevention (CDC)
1600 Clifton Road NE
Atlanta, GA 30333
1-800-311-3534
http://www.cdc.gov

Child Care Action Campaign (CCAC)
330 Seventh Avenue, 14th Floor
New York, NY 10001
Phone: 212-239-0138 or 1-800-424-2246
Fax: 212-268-6515
http://www.childcareation.org

Child Care Bureau
Administration for Children and Families
U.S. Department of Health and Human Services
Switzer Building, Room 2046
330 C Street SW
Washington, DC 20447
Phone: 202-690-6782
Fax: 202-690-5600
E-mail: ccb@acf.dhhs.gov
http://www.acf.dhhs.gov/programs/ccb

Child Care Law Center
973 Market Street, Suite 550
San Francisco, CA 94103
Phone: 415-495-5498
Fax: 415-495-6734
http://www.childcarelaw.org

Child Care Nutrition Resource System
Food and Nutrition Information Center
National Agricultural Library10301 Baltimore Avenue
Beltsville, MD 20705-2351
Phone: 301-504-5719
http://www.nal.usda.gov/childcare

Children's Safety Network
CSN National Injury and Violence Prevention Resource Center
Education Development Center, Inc.
55 Chapel Street
Newton, MA 02458-1060
Phone: 617-969-7100
Fax: 617-969-9186
http://www.edc.org/HHD/csn

Consumer Product Safety Commission, US (CPSC)
1-800-638-2772
http://www.cpsc.gov

Cooperative State Research, Education, and Extension Service
U.S. Department of Agriculture
Washington, D.C. 20250-0900
Phone: 202-720-4651
Fax: 202-690-0289
E-mail: csrees@reeusda.gov
http://www.reeusda.gov

Dairy Council
10255 West Higgins Road
Suite 900
Rosemont, IL 60018-5616
Phone: 847-803-2000
http://www.nationaldairycouncil.org

Contact Information

Disability and Business Technical Assistance Centers
(American with Disabilities Act Experts)
1-800-949-4232

Early Childhood Education Linkage System (ECELS)
Healthy Child Care America Pennsylvania
Pennsylvania Chapter, American Academy of Pediatrics
Rosemont Business Campus
Building 2, Suite 307
919 Conestoga Road
Rosemont, PA 19010
Phone: 610-520-3662
http://www.paaap.org

The Edison Electric Institute
701 Pennsylvania Ave., NW
Washington, DC 20004-2696
Phone: 202-508-5000
http://www.eei.org

Emergency Medical Services for Children National Resource Center
111 Michigan Avenue, N.W.
Washington, DC 20010-2970
Phone: 202-884-4927
Fax: 202-884-6845
http://www.ems-c.org

Environmental Protection Agency (EPA)
401 M Street SW
Washington, DC 20460-0003
Phone: 202-260-2090
http://www.epa.gov

Federal Bureau of Investigation (FBI)
J. Edgar Hoover Building
935 Pennsylvania Avenue, N.W
Washington, D.C. 20535-0001
Phone: 202-324-3000
http://www.fbi.gov

Food & Nutrition Information Center
Agricultural Research Service, USDA
National Agricultural Library, Room 105
10301 Baltimore Avenue
Beltsville, MD 20705-2351
Phone: 301-504-5719
Fax: 301-504-6409
http://www.nal.usda.gov/fnic
E-mail: fnic@nal.usda.gov

Food Research Action Center
1875 Connecticut Avenue, N.W., Suite 540
Washington, D.C. 20009
Phone: 202-986-2200
Fax: 202-986-2525
E-mail: webmaster@frac.org
http://www.frac.org

The Healthy Child Care America Campaign
American Academy of Pediatrics
141 N.W. Point Blvd.
Elk Grove Village, IL 60007
Phone: 888-227-5409
Fax: 847-228-6432
E-mail: childcare@aap.org

Institute of Electrical & Electronics Engineers (IEEE)
445 Hoes Lane
Piscataway, NJ 08855-1331
Phone: 732-981-0060
Fax: 303-758-1138
E-mail: askieee@ieee.org
http://www.ieee.org

Juvenile Products Manufacturers Association (JPMA)
17000 Commerce Pkwy. Suite C
Mt. Laurel, NJ 08054
http://www.jpma.org

La Leche League International
1400 N. Meacham Rd.
Schaumburg, IL 60173-4048
Phone: 847-519-7730
Fax: 847-519-0035
http://www.lalecheleague.org

Maternal and Child Health Bureau (MCHB)

MCHB Region I
Room 1826
John F. Kennedy Federal Building
Boston MA 02203
Phone: 617-565-1433
Fax: 617-565-3044
States - CT, ME, MA, NH, RI, VT

MCHB Region II
26 Federal Plaza
Federal Building, Room 3835
New York, N.Y. 10278
Phone: 212-264-2571
Fax: 212-264-2673
States - NJ, NY, PR, VI

Please note contact information may change. Check http://nrc.uchsc.edu for updates.

Contact Information

MCHB Region III
Health Resources, Northeast Cluster
Public Ledger Building
150 S. Independence Mall West
Suite 1172
Philadelphia, PA 19106-3499
Phone: 215-861-4422
Fax: 215-861-4385
States - DE, DC, MD, PA, VA, WV

MCHB Region IV
HRSA Field Coordinator, Southeast Cluster
Atlanta Federal Center
61 Forsyth Street, S.W., Suite 3M60
Atlanta, GA 30303-8909
Phone: 404-562-7980
Fax: 404-562-7974
States - AL, FL, GA, KY, MS, NC, SC, TN

MCHB Region V
105 W. Adams Street, 17th Floor
Chicago, IL 60603
Phone: 312-353-4042
Fax: 312-886-3770
States - IL, IN, MI, MN, OH, WI

MCHB Region VI
1301 Young Street, 10th Floor, HRSA-4
Dallas, TX 75202
Phone: 214-767-3003
Fax: 214-767-3038
States - AR, LA, NM, OK, TX

MCHB Region VII
Federal Building, Room 501
601 E. 12th Street
Kansas City, MO 64106-2808
Phone: 816-426-5292
Fax: 816-426-3633
States - IA, KS, MO, NE

MCHB Region VIII
Federal Office Building, Room 409
1961 Stout Street
Denver, CO 80294
Phone: 303-844-7862
Fax: 303-844-0002
States - CO, MT, ND, SD, UT, WY

MCHB Region IX
Federal Office Building, Room 317
50 United Nations Plaza
San Francisco, CA 94102
Phone: 415-437-8101
Fax: 415-437-8105
States - AZ, CA, HI, NV, AS, FM, GU, MH, MP, PW

MCHB Region X
Mail Stop RX-23
2201 Sixth Avenue, Room 700,
Seattle, WA 98121
Phone: 206-615-2518
Fax: 206-615-2500
http://www.mchb.hrsa.gov
States - AK, ID, OR, WA

National Association for the Education of Young Children (NAEYC)
1509 16th Street, NW
Washington DC 20036
1-800-424-2460
http://www.naeyc.org

National Association for Family Child Care (NAFCC)
Sixth Ave., Suite 900
Des Moines, IA 50309
515-282-8192
http://www.nafcc.org

National Association of Child Care Resource and Referral Agencies
1319 F Street, NW Suite 500
Washington, DC 20004-1106
Phone: 202-393-5501
Fax: 202-393-1109
E-mail: info@naccrra.org
http://www.naccrra.org

National Association of Diaper Services
994 Old Eagle School Road, #1019
Wayne, PA 19087
610-971-4850
http://www.diapernet.com

National Association of Governor's Councils of Physical Fitness and Sports
401 W. Michigan St.
Indianapolis, IN 46202
Phone: 317-237-5630
Fax: 317-237-5632
E-mail: info@physicalfitness.org
http://www.physicalfitness.org

National Association of Pediatric Practitioners (NAPNAP)
1101 Kings Highway, North, Suite 206
Cherry Hill, New Jersey 08034-1912
Phone: 856-667-1773
Fax: 609-667-7187
http://www.napnap.org

Please note contact information may change. Check http://nrc.uchsc.edu for updates.

Contact Information

National Association for Regulatory Administration
26 East Exchange Street, Fifth Floor
St. Paul, MN 55101-2264
Phone: 651-290-6280
Fax: 651-290-2266
http://www.nara-licensing.org

National Association for Sick Child Daycare (NASCD)
1716 5th. Ave. N.
Birmingham, AL 35203
Phone: 202-324-8447
Fax: 202-324-8050
E-mail: gwj@nascd.com
http://www.nascd.com

National Association of WIC Directors
2001 S Street, NW
Suite 580
Washington, DC 20009
Phone: 202-232-5492
Fax: 202-387-5281
http://www.wicdirectors.org

National Center for Cultural Competence
Georgetown University Child Development Center
3307 M Street, NW, Suite 401
Washington, DC 20007-3935
Phone: 800-788-2066
Fax: 202-687-8899
http://gucdc.georgetown.edu/nccc
E-mail: cultural@georgetown.edu

National Center for Education in Maternal and Child Health (NCEMCH)
2000 15th Street, North, Suite 701
Arlington, VA 22201-2617
Phone: 703-524-7802
Fax: 703-524-9335
E-mail: info@ncemch.org
http://www.ncemch.org

National Child Care Information Center
(Funded by the Child Care Bureau)
243 Church Street, NW 2nd Floor
Vienna, VA 22180
Phone: 1-800-616-2242
Fax: 1-800-716-2242
TTY: 1-800-516-2242
http://www.nccic.org

National Clearinghouse on Child Abuse and Neglect Information
330 C Street, SW
Washington, DC 20447
Phone: 800-394-3366
Fax: 703-385-3206
http://www.calib.com/nccanch

National Child Care Association (NCCA)
1016 Rosser Street
Conyers, GA 30012
Phone: 1-800-543-7161
Fax: 770-388-7772
http://www.nccanet.org

National Commission for Health Education Credentialing, Inc. (NCHEC)
944 Marcon BLVD., Suite 310
Allentown, PA 18103
Phone: 1-888-624-3248
Fax: 1-800-813-0727
E-mail: nchectce@fast.net
http://www.nchec.org

National Committee for the Prevention of Child Abuse
PO Box 2866
Chicago, IL 60690-9950
Phone: 312-663-3520
http://www.childabuse.org
E-mail: mail@preventchildabuse.org

National Fire Protection Association (NFPA)
1 Battery march Park
Quince, MA 02269-9101
Phone: 617-770-3000
Fax: 617-770-0700
http://www.nfpa.org

National Food Service Management Institute
The University of Mississippi
P.O. Drawer 188
University, MS 38677-0188
Phone: 1-800-321-3054
Fax: 1-800-321-3061
http://www.nfsmi.org

National Heart, Lung, and Blood Institute
Health Information Center
P.O. Box 30105
Bethesda, MD
Phone: 301-592-8573
Fax: 301-592-8563
E-mail: NHLBlinfo@rover.nhlbi.nih.gov
http://www.nhlbi.nih.gov/health/infoctr/index.htm

Contact Information

National Healthy Mothers, Healthy Babies Coalition
121 North Washington St.
Suite 300
Alexandria, VA 22314
Phone: 703-836-6110
Fax: 703-836-3470
http://www.hmhb.org

National Highway and Transportation Safety Administration (NHTSA)

NHTSA Region I
Kendall Square Code 903
Cambridge, MA 02142
Phone: 617-494-3427
Fax: 617-494-3646
States - CT, ME, MA, NH, RI, VT

NHTSA Region II
222 Mamaroneck Avenue Suite 204
White Plains, NY 10605
Phone: 914-682-6162
Fax: 914-682-6239 Fax
States - NY, NJ, PR, VI

NHTSA Region III
10 South Howard Street
Suite 6700
Baltimore, MD 21201
Phone: 410-962-0090
Fax: 410-962-2770
States - DE, DC, MD, PA, VA, WV

NHTSA Region IV
61 Forsyth Street, SW
Suite 17T30
Atlanta, GA 30303
Phone: 404-562-3739
Fax: 404-562-3763
States - AL, FL, GA, KY, MS, NC, SC, TN

NHTSA Region V
19900 Governors Drive, Suite 201
Olympia Fields, IL 60461
Phone: 708-503-8822
Fax: 708-503-8991 Fax
States - IL, IN, MI, MN, OH, WI

NHTSA Region VI
819 Taylor Street Room 8a38
Fort Worth, TX 76102-6177
Phone: 817-978-3653
Fax: 817-978-8339 Fax
States - AR, LA, NM, OK, TX, Indian N.

NHTSA Region VII
901 Locust Street Rm466
Kansas City, MO 64106
Phone: 816-329-3900
Fax: 816-329-3910
States - IA, KS, MO, NE

NHTSA Region VIII
555 Zang Street, Room 430
Lakewood, Colorado 80228
Phone: 303-969-6917
Fax: 303-969-6294 fax
States - CO, MT, ND, SD, UT, WY

NHTSA Region IX
201 Mission Street, Suite 2230
San Francisco, CA 94105
Phone: 415-744-3089
Fax: 415-744-2532 Fax
States - AZ, CA, HI, NV, Amer. Samoa, Guam, Mariana Island

NHTSA Region X
3140 Jackson Federal Building
915 Second Avenue
Seattle, WA 98174
Phone: 206-220-7640
Fax: 206-220-7651
Phone: 1-888-327-4236
http://www.nhtsa.dot.gov
States - AK, ID, OR, WA

National Information Center for Children and Youth with Disabilities
P.O. Box 1492
Washington, DC 20013-1492
Phone: 1-800-695-0285
E-mail: nichcy@aed.org
http://www.nichcy.org

National Institute of Health, National Institute of Child Health and Human Development
P.O.box 3006
Rockville, MD 20847
Phone: 1-800-370-2943
Fax: 301-984-1473
E-mail: nichdclearinghouse@mail.nih.gov
http://www.nichd.nih.gov

National Maternal and Child Health Clearinghouse
2070 Chain Bridge Road, Suite 450
Vienna, VA 22182-2536
Phone: 1-888-434-4624
Fax: 703-821-2098
E-Mail: nmchc@circlesolutions.com
http://www.nmchc.org

Contact Information

National OnSite Wastewater Recycling Association, Inc. (NOWRA)
632 Main Street
Laurel, MD 20707
Phone: 301-776-7468
Fax: 301-776-7409
http:// www.nowra.org

National Recreation and Park Association
22377 Belmont Ridge Road
Ashburn, VA 20148
Phone: (703) 858-0784
Fax: (703) 858-0794
http://www.nrpa.org

National Resource Center for Health and Safety in Child Care
University of Colorado School of Nursing
Campus Mail Stop F541, P.O. Box 6508
Aurora, CO 80045-0508
Phone: 1-800-598-5437
Fax: 303-724-0960
http://nrc.uchsc.edu

National Safety Council (NSC)
1121 Spring Lake Drive,
Itasca, IL 60143-3201
Phone: 630-285-1121
Fax: 630-285-0797
http://www.nsc.org

National Sanitation Foundation (NSF)
PO Box 130140
Ann Arbor, MI 48113-0140
Phone: 800-673-6275 or 734-769-8010
Fax: 734-769-0109
http://www.nsf.org

National School-Age Care Alliance
1137 Washington Street
Boston, MA 02124
Phone: 617-298-5012
Fax: 617-298-5022
http://www.nsaca.org

National SIDS Resource Center
2070 Chain Bridge Road, Suite 450
Vienna, VA 22182
Phone: 703-821-8955
Fax: 703-821-2098
E-mail: sids@circlesolutions.com
http://www.sidscenter.org

National Technical Information Service (NTIS)
5285 Port Royal Road
Springfield, Virginia 22161
Phone: 703-605-6000
Fax: 703-605-6900
E-mail: info@ntis.gov
http://www.ntis.gov

National Training Institute for Child Care Health Consultants
Department of Maternal and Child Health
University of North Carolina at Chapel Hill
116A S. Merritt Mill Rd. Box 8126
Chapel Hill, NC 27599-8126
Phone: 919-966-3780
Fax: 919-843-4752
E-mail: nticchc@sph.unc.edu

National Weather Service
1352 East-West Highway
Silver Spring, MD 20910
http://www.nws.noaa.gov

Occupational Health & Safety Administration (OSHA)
200 Constitution Avenue, N.W.
Washington, D.C. 20210
Phone: 202-693-1999
http://www.osha.gov
(Web site of OSHA Regional Office Contacts)

Office of Special Education & Rehabilitative Services
U.S. Department of Education
330 C Street S.W.
Washington, DC 20202
Phone: 202-205-5465
Fax: 202-205-9252
http://www.ed.gov/offices/OSERS

Oregon Child Development Coalition
PO Box 2780
9140 SW Pioneer Court, Suite E
Wilsonville, OR 97070
Phone: 503-570-1110
Fax: 503-682-9426
http://ocdc.net

Presidents Challenge Physical Fitness Program
400 E. 7th Street
Bloomington, IN 47405
Phone: 1-800-258-8146
Fax: 812-855-8999
E-mail: preschal@indiana.edu
http://www.indiana.edu/~preschal

Please note contact information may change. Check http://nrc.uchsc.edu for updates.

Contact Information

President's Council on Physical Fitness & Sports
200 Independence Avenue SW.
Humphrey Building, Room 738 H
Washington, DC 20201
Phone: 202-690-9000
Fax: 202-690-5211
http://www.fitness.gov

Project Child
2200 West Broad Street
Bethlehem, PA 18018-3200
Phone: 610-419-4500
Fax: 610-419-3888
E-mail: project childlv@aol.com

Seattle King County Department of Public Health
999 3rd Ave. Suite 1200
Seattle, WA 98104
Phone: (206) 296-4600
http://www.metrokc.gov/health

Shape Up America
4500 Connecticut Ave. N.W.
Washington, DC 20008
Phone: 301-493-5368
Fax: 301-493-9504
E-mail: suainfo@shapeup.org
http://www.shapeup.org

Snell Memorial Foundation
3628 Madison Avenue, Suite 11
North Highlands, CA 95660
Phone: 916-331-5073
Fax: 916-331-0359
http://www.smf.org/snell.html

Society for Nutrition Education
1001 Connecticut Avenue, NW Suite 528
Washington, DC 20036-5528
Phone: 202-452-8534
Fax: 202-452-8536
E-mail: membership@sne.org
http://www.sne.org

State and Territorial Injury Prevention Directors' Association
2141Kingston Court, Suite 110-B
Marietta, GA 30067
Phone:770-690-9000
Fax: 770-690-8996
E-mail:
http://www.stipda.org/

Superintendent of Documents
U.S. Government Printing Office
Washington, DC 20402
Phone: 202-512-2000
http://www.gpo.gov

Tribal Child Care Technical Assistance Center (TriTAC)
(Funded by the Child Care Bureau)
Phone: 1-800-388-7670
http://nccic.org/tribal

Underwriters Laboratories (UL)
333 Pfingsten Road
Northbrook, IL 60062-2096
Phone: 847-272-8800
Fax: 847-272-8129
E-mail: northbrook@us.ul.com
http://www.ul.com

US Department of Energy
1000 Independence Ave.
Washington, DC 20585
Phone: 202-586-5000
http://www.energy.gov

US Consumer Product Safety Commission See Consumer Product Safety Commission, US

US Food and Drug Administration (FDA)
HFI-40
Rockville, MD 20857
Phone: 1-888-463-6332
http://www.fda.gov

USDA Food and Nutrition Service
3101 Park Center Drive
Alexandria, VA 22302
Phone: 703-305-2062
http://www.fns.usda.gov

USDA Food Safety and Inspection Service
Room 1175-South Building
1400 Independence Ave. SW
Washington, DC 20250
Phone: (202) 720-7943
http://www.fsis.usda.gov

Visiting Nurse Associations of America
11 Beacon Street, Suite 910
Boston, MA 02108
617-523-4042
http://www.vnaa.org

Contact Information

Wheelock College Institute for Leadership and Career Initiatives
200 The Riverway
Boston, MA 02215
Phone: 617-734-5200 x2211
Fax: 617-738-0643
http://institute.wheelock.edu

YMCA
101 North Wacker Dr.
Chicago, IL 60606
Phone: 312-977-0031
Fax: 312-977-9063
http://www.ymca.net

National Health and Safety Performance Standards

Conversion Table - First Edition to Second Edition

The numbering system for the standards was changed in the second edition to ensure the safety of children by clearly differentiating old standards from those in the new edition. In the second edition, the letter codes for each chapter used in the first edition, have been replaced by numbers such as 1. for Chapter 1; 2. for Chapter 2 and so on. To determine the 2nd Edition and location for Standards that appeared in the first edition of *Caring for Our Children*, you may look up the old number in the left hand column. The new number is in the right hand column. An example: Center child:staff ratios was ST 002 in the first edition, it is now 1.002 in the second edition.

Many standards were merged and thus there are fewer standards in the second edition. If a standard was totally deleted and not merged into another standard(s), the table designates such by the word DELETED in the second column. See Appendix DD for the Conversion Table from Second Edition numbers to First Edition numbers.

Chapter 1 1st Edition	Chapter 1 2nd Edition	Chapter 1 1st Edition	Chapter 1 2nd Edition	Chapter 1 1st Edition	Chapter 1 2nd Edition
ST1	1.001	ST32	1.008	ST63	1.040
ST2	1.002	ST33	1.008	ST64	1.041
ST3	1.004	ST34	1.008	ST65	1.043
ST4	1.005	ST35	1.007	ST66	1.041
ST5	1.006	ST36	1.018	ST67	1.041
ST6	1.014	ST37	1.018	ST68	1.041
ST7	1.014	ST38	1.018, 1.019	ST69	1.041
ST8	1.015	ST39	1.023	ST70	1.041
ST9	1.009	ST40	1.023	ST71	1.045
ST10	1.014	ST41	1.023	ST72	1.045
ST11	1.014	ST42	1.025	ST73	1.045
ST12	1.017	ST43	1.023	ST74	1.045
ST13	1.016	ST44	1.026	ST75	1.046
ST14	1.018	ST45	1.026	ST76	1.047
ST15	1.010	ST46	1.027	ST77	1.047
ST16	1.018	ST47	1.028	ST78	1.048
ST17	1.011	ST48	1.026	ST79	1.049
ST18	1.018	ST49	1.026	ST80	1.050
ST19	1.012	ST50	1.029	ST81	1.050
ST20	1.018	ST51	1.030	ST82	1.051
ST21	1.018	ST52	1.031	ST83	1.053
ST22	1.018	ST53	1.032	ST84	1.054
ST23	1.018	ST54	1.032	ST85	1.055
ST24	1.021	ST55	DELETED	ST86	1.052
ST25	1.021	ST56	1.034	ST88	1.056
ST26	1.022	ST57	1.035	**Chapter 2 1st Edition**	**Chapter 2 2nd Edition**
ST27	1.019	ST58	1.036	PR1	2.001
ST28	1.019	ST59	DELETED	PR2	2.003
ST29	1.019	ST60	1.037	PR3	2.004
ST30	1.009	ST61	1.038	PR4	2.006
ST31	1.020	ST62	1.039		

Chapter 2 1st Edition	Chapter 2 2nd Edition	Chapter 2 1st Edition	Chapter 2 2nd Edition	Chapter 3 1st Edition	Chapter 3 2nd Edition
PR5	2.007	PR49	2.053	HP28	3.014
PR6	DELETED	PR50	2.053	HP29	3.020
PR7	2.010	PR51	2.054	HP30	3.021
PR8	2.008	PR52	2.055	HP31	3.023
PR9	2.011	PR53	2.056	HP32	3.023
PR10	2.011	PR54	2.060	HP33	3.025
PR11	2.012	PR55	2.060	HP34	3.024
PR12	2.013	PR56	2.060	HP35	3.026
PR13	2.014	PR57	2.061	HP36	3.020
PR14	2.015	PR58	2.062	HP37	3.026
PR15	2.016	PR59	2.063	HP38	3.026
PR16	2.017	PR60	2.064	HP39	3.028
PR17	2.018	PR61	2.065	HP40	3.028
PR18	2.019	PR62	2.066	HP41	3.029
PR19	2.020	PR63	2.067	HP42	3.030
PR20	2.005	**Chapter 3 1st Edition**	**Chapter 3 2nd Edition**	HP43	3.031
PR21	2.021	HP1	3.001	HP44	3.032
PR22	2.022	HP2	3.001	HP45	3.033
PR23	2.023	HP3	3.001	HP46	3.028
PR24	2.024	HP4	3.002	HP47	3.028
PR25	2.025	HP5	3.003	HP48	3.028
PR26	2.026	HP6	3.008	HP49	3.034
PR27	2.027	HP7	2.028	HP50	3.036
PR28	2.028	HP8	3.010	HP51	3.028, 3.036
PR29	2.029	HP9	5.095	HP52	3.028
PR30	2.038	HP10	5.095	HP53	3.028, 3.036
PR31	2.039	HP11	3.011	HP54	3.037
PR32	2.040	HP12	3.010	HP55	3.028
PR33	2.040	HP13	3.012	HP56	3.028
PR34	2.041	HP14	3.013	HP57	3.038
PR35	2.042	HP15	3.014	HP58	3.028, 3.039
PR36	2.043	HP16	3.015	HP59	3.028
PR37	2.039	HP17	3.016	HP60	3.028, 3.040
PR38	2.044	HP18	3.017	HP61	3.028, 3.034
PR39	2.044	HP19	3.018	HP62	3.028
PR40	2.045	HP20	3.018	HP63	3.028
PR41	2.046	HP21	3.014	HP64	3.028
PR42	2.047	HP22	3.014	HP65	3.026
PR43	2.048	HP23	3.014	HP66	3.028
PR44	2.049	HP24	3.019	HP67	3.028
PR45	2.050	HP25	3.014	HP68	3.065
PR46	2.046	HP26	3.014	HP69	DELETED
PR47	2.052	HP27	3.018	HP70	3.066
PR48	2.053			HP71	3.067

Chapter 3 1st Edition	Chapter 3 2nd Edition	Chapter 3 1st Edition	Chapter 3 2nd Edition	Chapter 4 1st Edition	Chapter 4 2nd Edition
HP72	3.068	HP116	3.042	NU5	4.005
HP73	3.069	HP117	3.042	NU6	4.008
HP74	DELETED	HP118	3.043	NU7	4.008
HP75	3.006	HP119	3.044	NU8	4.011
HP76	3.006	HP120	3.044	NU9	4.012
HP77	DELETED	HP121	3.044	NU10	4.013
HP78	3.086	HP122	3.044	NU11	4.014
HP79	3.087	HP123	3.044	NU12	4.016
HP80	3.088	HP124	3.042	NU13	4.017
HP81	3.087	HP125	3.044	NU14	4.017
HP82	3.081	HP126	3.044	NU15	4.017
HP83	3.082	HP127	3.044	NU16	4.018
HP84	3.082	HP128	3.041	NU17	4.019
HP85	3.082	HP129	3.064	NU18	4.019
HP86	DELETED	HP130	3.064	NU19	4.020
HP87	3.083	HP131	3.064	NU20	4.021
HP88	3.084	HP132	3.070	NU21	4.022
HP89	3.065	HP133	3.070	NU22	4.023
HP90	3.065	HP134	3.070	NU23	4.024
HP91	3.065	HP135	DELETED	NU24	4.025
HP92	3.085	HP136	3.009	NU25	4.001
HP93	3.089	HP137	DELETED	NU26	4.026
HP94	3.053	HP138	DELETED	NU27	4.027
HP95	3.054	HP139	DELETED	NU28	4.027
HP96	3.057	HP140	3.071	NU29	4.026
HP97	3.055	HP141	3.073	NU30	4.028
HP98	3.056	HP142	3.073	NU31	4.028
HP99	3.056	HP143	3.073	NU32	4.030
HP100	3.056	HP144	3.073	NU33	4.031
HP101	3.059	HP145	3.074	NU34	4.032
HP102	3.058	HP146	3.075	NU35	4.033
HP103	3.059	HP147	3.075	NU36	DELETED
HP104	DELETED	HP148	3.075	NU37	4.034
HP105	3.048	HP149	3.076	NU38	4.029
HP106	3.050	HP150	3.077	NU39	4.035
HP107	3.051	HP151	3.078	NU40	4.036
HP108	3.052	HP152	3.079	NU41	4.037
HP109	3.045	HP153	3.080	NU42	4.038
HP110	3.045	**Chapter 4 1st Edition**	**Chapter 4 2nd Edition**	NU43	4.038
HP111	3.045	NU1	4.001	NU44	4.001
HP112	1.005	NU2	4.002	NU45	4.039
HP113	3.046	NU3	4.003	NU46	4.039
HP114	3.047	NU4	4.004	NU47	4.040
HP115	1.005			NU48	4.040

Chapter 4 1st Edition	Chapter 4 2nd Edition	Chapter 4 1st Edition	Chapter 4 2nd Edition	Chapter 5 1st Edition	Chapter 5 2nd Edition
NU49	4.041	NU93	4.060	FA27	5.024
NU50	4.042	NU94	DELETED	FA28	5.025
NU51	4.044	NU95	4.061	FA29	5.025
NU52	4.044	NU96	4.062	FA30	5.024
NU53	4.043	NU97	4.063	FA31	5.028
NU54	4.045	NU98	4.064	FA32	5.028
NU55	4.046	NU99	4.065	FA33	5.028
NU56	4.045	NU100	4.019	FA34	5.029
NU57	4.047	NU101	4.029	FA35	5.030
NU58	4.047	NU102	4.066	FA36	DELETED
NU59	4.048	NU103	4.067	FA37	5.031
NU60	4.048	NU104	4.068	FA38	5.032
NU61	4.049	NU105	4.069	FA39	DELETED
NU62	4.018	NU106	4.069	FA40	5.033
NU63	4.029	NU107	4.069	FA41	5.034
NU64	4.029	NU108	4.070	FA42	5.035
NU65	4.029	**Chapter 5 1st Edition**	**Chapter 5 2nd Edition**	FA43	5.036
NU66	4.042	FA1	5.001	FA44	5.038
NU67	4.042	FA2	5.005	FA45	5.034
NU68	4.050	FA3	5.005	FA46	5.039
NU69	4.051	FA4	5.006	FA47	5.041
NU70	4.051	FA5	5.007	FA48	5.042
NU71	4.052	FA6	5.008	FA49	5.042
NU72	4.052	FA7	5.009	FA50	5.043
NU73	4.052	FA8	5.010	FA51	5.044
NU74	4.052	FA9	5.011	FA52	5.045
NU75	4.052	FA10	5.012	FA53	5.046
NU76	4.052	FA11	3.059	FA54	5.046
NU77	4.052	FA12	5.013	FA55	5.047
NU78	4.052	FA13	5.042	FA56	5.048
NU79	4.052	FA14	5.014	FA57	5.049
NU80	4.052	FA15	5.015, 5.027	FA58	5.050
NU81	4.052	FA16	5.015	FA59	5.051
NU82	4.052	FA17	5.016	FA60	5.052
NU83	4.053	FA18	5.022	FA61	5.053
NU84	4.053	FA19	5.018	FA62	5.054
NU85	4.052	FA20	5.019	FA63	5.055
NU86	4.054	FA21	5.026	FA64	5.055
NU87	4.054	FA22	5.020	FA65	5.056
NU88	4.055	FA23	5.020	FA66	5.057
NU89	4.056	FA24	5.022	FA67	5.058
NU90	4.057	FA25	5.022	FA68	5.059
NU91	4.059	FA26	5.023	FA69	5.060
NU92	4.060			FA70	5.061

Chapter 5 1st Edition	Chapter 5 2nd Edition	Chapter 5 1st Edition	Chapter 5 2nd Edition	Chapter 5 1st Edition	Chapter 5 2nd Edition
FA71	5.062	FA115	5.092	FA159	5.067
FA72	5.063	FA116	5.093	FA160	5.118
FA73	5.064	FA117	5.094	FA161	5.118
FA74	5.064	FA118	5.096	FA162	5.119
FA75	5.064	FA119	5.096	FA163	5.026
FA76	5.064	FA120	5.100	FA164	5.134
FA77	5.065	FA121	5.101	FA165	5.116
FA78	5.066	FA122	5.102	FA166	5.116
FA79	5.066	FA123	5.102	FA167	5.134
FA80	5.067	FA124	5.103	FA168	5.135
FA81	5.068	FA125	5.104	FA169	5.040
FA82	5.066	FA126	5.104	FA170	5.034
FA83	5.066	FA127	5.104	FA171	5.040
FA84	5.069	FA128	5.100	FA172	5.136
FA85	5.066	FA129	5.105	FA173	5.137
FA86	5.070	FA130	5.106	FA174	5.138
FA87	5.071	FA131	5.107	FA175	5.139
FA88	5.071	FA132	DELETED	FA176	5.137
FA89	5.072	FA133	5.108	FA177	5.140
FA90	5.070	FA134	5.109	FA178	5.141
FA91	5.070	FA135	5.110	FA179	5.141
FA92	5.073	FA136	5.110	FA180	5.142
FA93	5.073	FA137	5.111	FA181	5.144
FA94	5.073	FA138	5.112	FA182	5.144
FA95	5.073	FA139	5.113	FA183	5.144
FA96	5.074	FA140	5.116	FA184	5.144
FA97	5.075	FA141	5.117	FA185	5.144
FA98	5.076	FA142	5.120	FA186	5.147
FA99	5.077	FA143	5.121	FA187	DELETED
FA100	5.078	FA144	5.122	FA188	5.148
FA101	5.079	FA145	5.123	FA189	5.144
FA102	5.079	FA146	5.124	FA190	5.144
FA103	5.079	FA147	5.125	FA191	5.144
FA104	5.080	FA148	5.126	FA192	DELETED
FA105	5.081	FA149	5.130	FA193	5.149
FA106	5.145	FA150	5.131	FA194	5.151
FA107	5.082	FA151	5.130	FA195	5.144
FA108	5.083	FA152	5.127	FA196	5.153
FA109	5.084	FA153	5.128	FA197	5.154
FA110	5.085	FA154	5.132	FA198	5.155
FA111	5.085	FA155	5.126	FA199	5.151
FA112	5.086	FA156	5.133	FA200	5.156
FA113	5.090	FA157	DELETED	FA201	5.157
FA114	5.091	FA158	DELETED	FA202	5.158

Chapter 5 1st Edition	Chapter 5 2nd Edition	Chapter 5 1st Edition	Chapter 5 2nd Edition	Chapter 5 1st Edition	Chapter 5 2nd Edition
FA203	5.159	FA247	5.185	FA291	5.225
FA204	5.160	FA248	5.186	FA292	5.226
FA205	5.005	FA249	5.188	FA293	5.226
FA206	5.161	FA250	5.189	FA294	5.227
FA207	DELETED	FA251	DELETED	FA295	5.228
FA208	5.114	FA252	5.190	FA296	5.229
FA209	5.112	FA253	5.191	FA297	5.230
FA210	5.143	FA254	5.192	FA298	5.231
FA211	5.087	FA255	5.193	FA299	5.231
FA212	5.088	FA256	5.194	FA300	5.232
FA213	5.087	FA257	5.195	FA301	5.233
FA214	5.089	FA258	5.196	FA302	5.234
FA215	5.112	FA259	DELETED	FA303	5.235
FA216	5.112	FA260	5.196	FA304	5.237
FA217	5.114	FA261	5.197	FA305	5.238
FA218	5.115	FA262	5.196	FA306	5.238
FA219	5.162	FA263	5.198	FA307	5.239
FA220	5.162	FA264	5.199	FA308	5.240
FA221	5.163	FA265	5.200	FA309	2.030
FA222	5.164	FA266	5.201	FA310	2.030
FA223	5.165	FA267	5.202	FA311	2.029
FA224	5.168	FA268	5.203	FA312	2.029
FA225	5.116	FA269	5.204	FA313	2.035
FA226	5.169	FA270	5.205	FA314	2.030
FA227	5.170	FA271	5.206	FA315	2.036
FA228	5.171	FA272	5.207	FA316	1.004
FA229	5.172	FA273	5.208	FA317	2.033
FA230	5.173	FA274	5.210	FA318	2.031
FA231	5.174	FA275	5.207	FA319	2.034
FA232	5.175	FA276	5.211	FA320	2.032
FA233	5.176	FA277	5.212	FA321	5.241
FA234	5.177	FA278	5.213	FA322	5.242
FA235	5.178	FA279	5.214	FA323	2.037
FA236	5.179	FA280	5.215	**Chapter 6 1st Edition**	**Chapter 6 2nd Edition**
FA237	5.179	FA281	5.216	ID1	6.014
FA238	5.180	FA282	5.218	ID2	6.014
FA239	5.180	FA283	5.216	ID3	3.005
FA240	DELETED	FA284	5.216	ID4	6.002
FA241	5.183	FA285	5.219	ID5	6.003
FA242	5.181	FA286	5.220	ID6	6.001
FA243	DELETED	FA287	5.221	ID7	DELETED
FA244	5.182	FA288	5.222	ID8	6.006
FA245	5.183	FA289	5.223	ID9	6.007
FA246	5.184	FA290	5.224		

Chapter 6 1st Edition	Chapter 6 2nd Edition
ID10	6.008
ID11	6.008
ID12	3.005
ID13	6.009
ID14	6.010
ID15	6.011
ID16	6.012
ID17	6.013
ID18	6.013
ID19	6.017
ID20	3.069
ID21	6.024
ID22	6.025
ID23	6.023
ID24	6.023
ID25	6.025
ID26	3.088
ID27	3.005
ID28	3.005
ID29	3.005
ID30	3.006
ID31	3.007
ID32	6.018
ID33	6.020
ID34	6.019
ID35	6.020
ID36	6.018
ID37	6.021
ID38	6.021
ID39	6.021
ID40	6.022
ID41	6.027
ID42	6.027
ID43	6.027
ID44	6.027
ID45	6.027
ID46	6.028
ID47	DELETED
ID48	6.029
ID49	6.030
ID50	6.030
ID51	6.031
ID52	6.027
ID53	6.027

Chapter 6 1st Edition	Chapter 6 2nd Edition
ID54	6.027
ID55	6.033
ID56	6.034
ID57	6.027
ID58	6.035
ID59	6.036
ID60	6.034
ID61	6.034
ID62	6.034
ID63	6.034

Chapter 7 1st Edition	Chapter 7 2nd Edition
CSN1	7.001
CSN2	7.002
CSN3	7.003
CSN4	7.003
CSN5	7.004
CSN6	8.013
CSN7	8.016
CSN8	8.046
CSN9	2.053
CSN10	2.053
CSN11	2.051
CSN12	2.057
CSN13	2.053
CSN14	7.005
CSN15	DELETED
CSN16	7.006
CSN17	7.007
CSN18	2.044
CSN19	2.002
CSN20	7.008
CSN21	7.008
CSN22	7.008
CSN23	7.008
CSN24	7.008
CSN25	7.009
CSN26	7.010
CSN27	7.007
CSN28	DELETED
CSN29	DELETED
CSN30	7.007
CSN31	7.007

Chapter 7 1st Edition	Chapter 7 2nd Edition
CSN32	2.058
CSN33	7.007
CSN34	7.011
CSN35	8.053
CSN36	1.014
CSN37	1.003
CSN38	1.017
CSN39	DELETED
CSN40	1.044
CSN41	1.042
CSN42	1.024
CSN43	1.024
CSN44	1.024
CSN45	1.026
CSN46	DELETED
CSN47	1.029
CSN48	1.019
CSN49	2.038
CSN50	2.029
CSN51	2.033
CSN52	2.029
CSN53	5.021
CSN54	5.004
CSN55	5.021
CSN56	5.112
CSN57	5.150
CSN58	5.150
CSN59	5.152
CSN60	5.097
CSN61	4.007
CSN62	4.009
CSN63	4.009
CSN64	4.009
CSN65	2.005
CSN66	2.005
CSN67	3.060
CSN68	3.061
CSN69	3.060
CSN70	3.061
CSN71	3.063
CSN72	1.024
CSN73	5.098
CSN74	5.099
CSN75	1.024

Chapter 7 1st Edition	Chapter 7 2nd Edition	Chapter 8 1st Edition	Chapter 8 2nd Edition	Chapter 8 1st Edition	Chapter 8 2nd Edition
CSN76	1.024	AD26	8.017	AD70	8.062
CSN77	7.012	AD27	8.020	AD71	8.062
CSN78	7.008	AD28	8.021	AD72	8.063
CSN79	7.013	AD29	8.022	AD73	8.064
CSN80	7.007	AD30	8.023	AD74	8.063
CSN81	2.059	AD31	8.024	AD75	8.063
CSN82	8.018	AD32	8.025	AD76	8.065
CSN83	8.018	AD33	8.026	AD77	8.066
CSN84	8.018	AD34	8.027	AD78	8.067
CSN85	8.019	AD35	8.027	AD79	DELETED
CSN86	DELETED	AD36	DELETED	AD80	8.068
CSN87	7.014	AD37	8.028	AD81	8.069
CSN88	DELETED	AD38	8.028	AD82	8.070
CSN89	7.015	AD39	8.030	AD83	8.071
CSN90	7.016	AD40	8.031	AD84	8.072
CSN91	3.049	AD41	8.032	AD85	8.073
CSN92	DELETED	AD42	8.033	AD86	8.074
Chapter 8 1st Edition	**Chapter 8 2nd Edition**	AD43	5.084	AD87	8.075
AD1	8.001	AD44	8.034	AD88	8.076
AD2	8.001	AD45	8.035	AD89	8.077
AD3	8.002	AD46	8.034	AD90	8.078
AD4	8.003	AD47	8.036	AD91	8.079
AD5	8.004	AD48	8.037	**Chapter 9 1st Edition**	**Chapter 9 2nd Edition**
AD6	8.005	AD49	8.038	REC1	9.001
AD7	8.006	AD50	8.040	REC2	9.002
AD8	8.007	AD51	8.041	REC3	9.004
AD9	2.028	AD52	8.042	REC4	9.005
AD10	2.028	AD53	8.042	REC5	9.006
AD11	8.008	AD54	8.043	REC6	9.007
AD12	8.009	AD55	8.044	REC7	9.006
AD13	8.008	AD56	8.045	REC8	9.008
AD14	8.010	AD57	8.046	REC9	DELETED
AD15	8.011	AD58	8.053	REC10	9.009
AD16	DELETED	AD59	8.054	REC11	9.010
AD17	8.012	AD60	8.055	REC12	9.011
AD18	3.072	AD61	8.054	REC13	9.012
AD19	8.013	AD62	8.054	REC14	9.038
AD20	8.013	AD63	8.056	REC15	9.013
AD21	8.013	AD64	8.054	REC16	9.014
AD22	8.014	AD65	8.057	REC17	9.015
AD23	DELETED	AD66	8.058	REC18	9.017
AD24	8.015	AD67	8.059	REC19	9.019
AD25	3.004	AD68	8.060	REC20	9.018
		AD69	8.061		

Chapter 9 1st Edition	Chapter 9 2nd Edition
REC21	9.016
REC22	DELETED
REC23	9.020
REC24	9.021
REC25	9.022
REC26	9.023
REC27	9.024
REC28	9.025
REC29	9.025
REC30	9.027
REC31	9.026
REC32	9.025
REC33	9.026
REC34	9.026
REC35	9.025
REC36	9.025
REC37	9.028
REC38	9.028
REC39	9.028
REC40	9.025
REC41	DELETED
REC42	9.025
REC43	9.025
REC44	9.025
REC45	9.029
REC46	9.029
REC47	9.029
REC48	9.029
REC49	9.030
REC50	9.031
REC51	9.031
REC52	9.032
REC53	9.033
REC54	9.033
REC55	9.033
REC56	9.033
REC57	9.033
REC58	9.034
REC59	9.034
REC60	9.035
REC61	9.036
REC62	DELETED
REC63	9.035
REC64	DELETED

Chapter 9 1st Edition	Chapter 9 2nd Edition
REC65	9.037
REC66	9.038
REC67	9.038
REC68	9.039
REC69	9.040
REC70	9.041
REC71	9.042
REC72	9.043
REC73	9.044
REC74	9.045
REC75	9.046
REC76	9.047
REC77	9.048
Appendices 1st Edition	**Appendices 2nd Edition**
A	1.007 through 1.021
B-1	9.033
B-2	Appendix C
C	8.046 through 8.052
D	Appendix B
E	2.061, 2.064, 2.067
F	Appendix H
G	Appendix F
H	Appendix N
I-1	6.003
I-2	6.006, 6.007
I-3	6.009, 6.010
I-4	6.005
J	Appendix P
K	Appendix Q
L	8.036
M	4.026
N	Appendix U
O-1	DELETED
O-2	DELETED
O-3	Appendix V
O-4	5.180
O-5	5.171, 5.175, 5.181 through 5.186
O-6	5.184

Appendices 1st Edition	Appendices 2nd Edition
O-7	5.173, 5.181 through 5.186
O-8	5.181 through 5.183
O-9	5.181 through 5.183
O-10	DELETED
O-11	5.198
P-1	Appendix G
P-2	Appendix G
Q	Appendix K
R	8.022
S	8.044
T	8.058
U	Appendix Y
V	8.076
W	8.077
X	8.005

Conversion Table - Second Edition to First Edition

The numbering system for the standards was changed in the second edition to ensure the safety of children by clearly differentiating old standards from those in the new edition. In the second edition, the letter codes for each chapter used in the first edition, have been replaced by numbers such as 1. for Chapter 1; 2. for Chapter 2 and so on. To determine what new second edition standards replaced first edition standards, you may look up the new number in the left hand column. The previous number in the first edition will be located in the right hand column. An example: Center child:staff ratios is 1.002 in the second edition; it was ST 002 in the first edition.

Many standards were merged and thus there are fewer standards in the second edition. If a standard in the second edition is new to this edition and not a merged or replacement from the first edition, it will say NEW in the second column. See Appendix CC for the Conversion Table from First Edition numbers to Second Edition numbers.

Chapter1 2nd Edition	Chapter1 1st Edition	Chapter1 2nd Edition	Chapter1 1st Edition
1.001	ST1	1.026	ST44, ST45, ST48, ST49, CSN45
1.002	ST2	1.027	ST46
1.003	CSN37	1.028	ST47
1.004	ST3	1.029	ST50, CSN47
1.005	ST4	1.030	ST51
1.006	ST5	1.031	ST52
1.007	ST35	1.032	ST53, ST54
1.008	ST32, ST33, ST34	1.033	NEW
1.009	ST9, ST30	1.034	ST56
1.010	ST15	1.035	ST57
1.011	ST17	1.036	ST58
1.012	ST19	1.037	ST60
1.013	NEW	1.038	ST61
1.014	ST6, ST7, ST10, ST11, CSN36	1.039	ST62
1.015	ST8	1.040	ST63, ST66, ST67, ST68, ST69, ST70
1.016	ST13	1.041	ST64
1.017	ST12, CSN38	1.042	CSN41
1.018	ST14, ST16, ST18, ST20, ST21, ST22, ST23, ST36, ST37, ST38, CSN48	1.043	ST65
		1.044	CSN40
1.019	ST27, ST28, ST29, ST38	1.045	ST71, ST72, ST73, ST74
		1.046	ST75
1.020	ST31	1.047	ST76, ST77
1.021	ST24, ST25	1.048	ST78
1.022	ST26	1.049	ST79
1.023	ST39, ST40, ST41, ST43	1.050	ST80, ST81
1.024	CSN42, CSN43, CSN44, CSN72, CSN75, CSN76	1.051	ST82
		1.052	ST86
1.025	ST42	1.053	ST83
		1.054	ST84

Chapter1 2nd Edition	Chapter1 1st Edition	Chapter 2 2nd Edition	Chapter 2 1st Edition
1.055	ST85	2.039	PR31, PR36
1.056	ST88	2.040	PR32
1.057	NEW	2.041	PR34
Chapter 2 2nd Edition	**Chapter 2 1st Edition**	2.042	PR35
		2.043	PR36
2.001	PR1	2.044	PR38, PR39, CSN18
2.002	CSN19	2.045	PR40
2.003	PR2	2.046	PR41, PR 46
2.004	PR3	2.047	PR42
2.005	PR20, CSN65, CSN66	2.048	PR43
2.006	PR4	2.049	PR44
2.007	PR5	2.040	PR45
2.008	PR8	2.051	CSN11
2.009	NEW	2.052	PR47
2.010	PR7	2.053	PR49, PR50, CSN9, CSN13
2.011	PR9, PR10		
2.012	PR11	2.054	PR51
2.013	PR12	2.055	PR52
2.014	PR13	2.056	PR53
2.015	PR14	2.057	CSN12
2.016	PR15	2.058	CSN32
2.017	PR16	2.059	CSN81
2.018	PR17	2.060	PR54, PR55, PR56
2.019	PR18	2.061	PR57
2.020	PR19	2.062	PR58
2.021	PR21	2.063	PR59
2.022	PR22	2.064	PR60
2.023	PR23	2.065	PR61
2.024	PR24	2.066	PR62
2.025	PR25	2.067	PR63
2.026	PR26	**Chapter 3 2nd Edition**	**Chapter 3 1st Edition**
2.027	PR27		
2.028	PR28, HP7, AD9, AD10	3.001	HP1, HP2, HP3
2.029	PR29, FA311, FA312, FA316, CSN52	3.002	HP4
		3.003	HP5
2.030	FA309, FA310, FA314	3.004	AD25
2.031	FA318	3.005	ID3, ID12, ID26, ID27, ID28, ID29. ID30
2.032	FA320		
2.033	FA317, CSN51	3.006	HP75, HP76
2.034	FA319	3.007	ID31
2.035	FA313	3.008	HP6
2.036	FA315	3.009	HP136
2.037	FA323	3.010	HP8, HP12
2.038	PR30	3.011	HP11

Chapter 3 2nd Edition	Chapter 3 1st Edition	Chapter 3 2nd Edition	Chapter 3 1st Edition
3.012	HP13	3.047	HP114
3.013	HP14	3.048	HP105
3.014	HP15, HP21, HP22, HP23, HP25, HP26, HP28	3.049	CSN91
		3.050	HP106
		3.051	HP107
3.015	HP16	3.052	HP108
3.016	HP17	3.053	HP94
3.017	HP18	3.054	HP95
3.018	HP19, HP20, HP27	3.055	HP97
3.019	HP24	3.056	HP98, HP99, HP100, HP101
3.020	HP29, HP36		
3.021	HP30	3.057	HP96
3.022	NEW	3.058	HP102
3.023	HP31, HP32	3.059	HP101, HP103
3.024	HP34	3.060	CSN67, CSN69
3.025	HP33	3.061	CSN68, CSN70
3.026	HP35, HP37, HP38, HP65	3.062	NEW
		3.063	CSN71
3.027	NEW	3.064	HP129, HP130, HP131
3.028	HP39, HP40, HP46, HP47, HP48, HP51, HP52, HP53, HP55, HP56, HP58, HP59, HP61, HP62, HP63, HP64, HP66, HP67	3.065	HP068, HP89, HP90, HP91
		3.066	HP70
		3.067	HP71
		3.068	HP72
		3.069	HP73
3.029	HP41	3.070	HP132, HP133, HP134
3.030	HP42	3.071	HP140
3.031	HP43	3.072	AD18
3.032	HP44	3.073	HP141, HP142, HP143, HP144
3.033	HP45		
3.034	HP49, HP61	3.074	HP145
3.035	NEW	3.075	HP146, HP147, HP148
3.036	HP50, HP51, HP53	3.076	HP149
3.037	HP54	3.077	HP150
3.038	HP57	3.078	HP151
3.039	HP58	3.079	HP152
3.040	HP60	3.080	HP153
3.041	HP128	3.081	HP82
3.042	HP116, HP117, HP124	3.082	HP83, HP84, HP85
3.043	HP118	3.083	HP87
3.044	HP119, HP120, HP121, HP122, HP123, HP125, HP126, HP127	3.084	HP88
		3.085	HP92
		3.086	HP78
3.045	HP109, HP110, HP111	3.087	HP79, HP81
3.046	HP113		

Chapter 3 2nd Edition	Chapter 3 1st Edition		Chapter 4 2nd Edition	Chapter 4 1st Edition
3.088	HP80		4.039	NU45, NU46
3.089	HP93		4.040	NU47, NU48
Chapter 4 2nd Edition	**Chapter 4 1st Edition**		4.041	NU49
			4.042	NU50, NU66, NU67
4.001	NU1, NU25, NU44		4.043	NU53
4.002	NU2		4.044	NU51, NU52
4.003	NU3		4.045	NU54, NU56
4.004	NU4		4.046	NU55
4.005	NU5		4.047	NU57, NU58
4.006	NEW		4.048	NU59, NU60
4.007	CSN61		4.049	NU61
4.008	NU6, NU7		4.050	NU68
4.009	CSN62, CSN63, CSN64		4.051	NU69, NU70
4.010	NEW		4.052	NU71, NU72, NU73, NU74, NU75, NU76, NU77, NU78, NU79, NU80, NU81, NU82, NU85
4.011	NU8			
4.012	NU9			
4.013	NU10			
4.014	NU11			
4.015	NEW		4.053	NU83, NU84
4.016	NU12		4.054	NU86, NU87
4.017	NU13, NU14, NU15		4.055	NU88
4.018	NU16, NU62		4.056	NU89
4.019	NU17, NU18, NU100		4.057	NU90
4.020	NU19		4.058	NEW
4.021	NU20		4.059	NU91
4.022	NU21		4.060	NU92, NU93
4.023	NU22		4.061	NU95
4.024	NU23		4.062	NU96
4.025	NU24		4.063	NU97
4.026	NU26, NU29, Appendix M		4.064	NU98
			4.065	NU99
4.027	NU27, NU28		4.066	NU102
4.028	NU30, NU31		4.067	NU103
4.029	NU38, NU63, NU64, NU65, NU101		4.068	NU104
			4.069	NU105, NU106, NU107
4.030	NU32		4.070	NU108
4.031	NU33		**Chapter 5 2nd Edition**	**Chapter 5 1st Edition**
4.032	NU34			
4.033	NU35		5.001	FA1
4.034	NU37		5.002	NEW
4.035	NU39		5.003	NEW
4.036	NU40		5.004	CSN54
4.037	NU41		5.005	FA2, FA3, FA205
4.038	NU42, NU43		5.006	FA4

Chapter 5 2nd Edition	Chapter 5 1st Edition	Chapter 5 2nd Edition	Chapter 5 1st Edition
5.007	FA5	5.051	FA59
5.008	FA6	5.052	FA60
5.009	FA7	5.053	FA61
5.010	FA8	5.054	FA62
5.011	FA9	5.055	FA63, FA64
5.012	FA10	5.056	FA65
5.013	FA12	5.057	FA66
5.014	FA14	5.058	FA67
5.015	FA15, FA16	5.059	FA68
5.016	FA17	5.060	FA69
5.017	NEW	5.061	FA70
5.018	FA19	5.062	FA71
5.019	FA20	5.063	FA72
5.020	FA22, FA23	5.064	FA73, FA74, FA75, FA76
5.021	CSN53, CSN55	5.065	FA77
5.022	FA18, FA2, FA25	5.066	FA78, FA79, FA82, FA83, FA85
5.023	FA26		
5.024	FA27, FA30	5.067	FA80, FA159
5.025	FA28, FA29	5.068	FA81
5.026	FA21, FA163	5.069	FA84
5.027	FA15	5.070	FA86, FA90, FA91
5.028	FA31, FA32, FA33	5.071	FA87, FA88
5.029	FA34	5.072	FA89
5.030	FA35	5.073	FA92, FA93, FA94, FA95
5.031	FA37	5.074	FA96
5.032	FA38	5.075	FA97
5.033	FA40	5.076	FA98
5.034	FA41, FA45, FA170	5.077	FA99
5.035	FA42	5.078	FA100
5.036	FA43	5.079	FA101, FA102, FA103
5.037	NEW	5.080	FA104
5.038	FA44	5.081	FA105
5.039	FA46	5.082	FA107
5.040	FA169, FA171	5.083	FA108
5.041	FA47	5.084	FA109, AD43
5.042	FA13, FA48, FA49	5.085	FA110, FA111
5.043	FA50	5.086	FA112
5.044	FA51	5.087	FA211, FA213
5.045	FA52	5.088	FA212
5.046	FA53, FA54	5.089	FA214
5.047	FA55	5.090	FA113
5.048	FA56	5.091	FA114
5.049	FA57	5.092	FA115
5.050	FA58	5.093	FA116

Chapter 5 2nd Edition	Chapter 5 1st Edition	Chapter 5 2nd Edition	Chapter 5 1st Edition
5.094	FA117	5.137	FA173, FA176
5.095	HP9, HP10	5.138	FA174
5.096	FA118, FA119	5.139	FA175
5.097	CSN60	5.140	FA177
5.098	CSN73	5.141	FA178, FA179
5.099	CSN74	5.142	FA180
5.100	FA120, FA128	5.143	FA210
5.101	FA121	5.144	FA181, FA182, FA183, FA184, FA185, FA189, FA190, FA191, FA195
5.102	FA122, FA123		
5.103	FA124		
5.104	FA125, FA126, FA127	5.145	FA106
5.105	FA129	5.146	NEW
5.106	FA130	5.147	FA186
5.107	FA131	5.148	FA188
5.108	FA133	5.149	SA193
5.109	FA134	5.150	CSN57, CSN58
5.110	FA135, FA136	5.151	FA194, FA199
5.111	FA137	5.152	CSN59
5.112	FA138, FA209, FA215, FA216, CSN56	5.153	FA196
		5.154	FA197
5.113	FA139	5.155	FA198
5.114	FA217, FA208	5.156	FA200
5.116	FA140, FA165, FA166, FA225	5.157	FA201
		5.158	FA202
5.117	FA141	5.159	FA203
5.118	FA160, FA161	5.160	FA204
5.119	FA162	5.161	FA206
5.120	FA142	5.162	FA219, FA220
5.121	FA143	5.163	FA221
5.122	FA144	5.164	FA222
5.123	FA145	5.165	FA223
5.124	FA146	5.166	NEW
5.125	FA147	5.167	NEW
5.126	FA148, FA155	5.168	FA224
5.127	FA152	5.169	FA226
5.128	FA153	5.170	FA227
5.129	NEW	5.171	FA228
5.130	FA149, FA151	5.172	FA229
5.131	FA150	5.173	NEW
5.132	FA154	5.174	NEW
5.133	FA156	5.175	FA232
5.134	FA164, FA167	5.176	FA233
5.135	FA168	5.177	FA234
5.136	FA172	5.178	FA235

Chapter 5 2nd Edition	Chapter 5 1st Edition	Chapter 5 2nd Edition	Chapter 5 1st Edition
5.179	FA236, FA237	5.223	FA289
5.180	FA238, FA239	5.224	FA290
5.181	FA242	5.225	FA291
5.182	FA244	5.226	FA292, FA293
5.183	FA241, FA245	5.227	FA294
5.184	FA246	5.228	FA295
5.185	FA247	5.229	FA296
5.186	FA248	5.230	FA297
5.187	NEW	5.231	FA298, FA299
5.188	FA249	5.232	FA300
5.189	FA250	5.233	FA301
5.190	FA252	5.234	FA302
5.191	FA253	5.235	FA303
5.192	FA254	5.236	NEW
5.193	FA255	5.237	FA304
5.194	FA256	5.238	FA305, FA306
5.195	NEW	5.239	FA307
5.196	FA258, FA26, FA262	5.240	FA308
5.197	FA261	5.241	FA321
5.198	FA263	5.242	FA322
5.199	FA264	**Chapter 6 2nd Edition**	**Chapter 6 1st Edition**
5.200	FA265	6.001	ID6
5.201	FA266	6.002	ID4
5.202	FA267	6.003	ID5
5.203	FA268	6.004	NEW
5.204	FA269	6.005	NEW
5.205	FA270	6.006	ID8
5.206	FA271	6.007	ID9
5.207	FA272, FA275	6.008	ID10, ID11
5.208	FA273	6.009	ID13
5.209	NEW	6.010	ID14
5.210	FA274	6.011	ID15
5.211	FA276	6.012	ID16
5.212	FA277	6.013	ID17, ID18
5.213	FA278	6.014	ID1, ID2
5.214	FA279	6.015	NEW
5.215	FA280	6.016	NEW
5.216	FA281, FA283, FA284	6.017	ID19
5.217	NEW	6.018	ID32, ID36
5.218	FA282	6.019	ID34
5.219	FA285	6.020	ID33, ID35
5.220	FA286	6.021	ID37, ID38, ID39
5.221	FA287	6.022	ID40
5.222	FA288		

Chapter 6 2nd Edition	Chapter 6 1st Edition	Chapter 8 2nd Edition	Chapter 8 1st Edition
6.023	ID23, ID24	8.004	AD5
6.024	ID21	8.005	AD6
6.025	ID22, ID25	8.006	AD7
6.026	NEW	8.007	AD8
6.027	ID41, ID42, ID44, ID45, ID52, ID53, ID54, ID57	8.008	AD11, AD13
		8.009	AD12
6.028	ID46	8.010	AD14
6.029	ID48	8.011	AD15
6.030	ID49, ID50	8.012	AD17
6.031	ID51	8.013	CSN6, AD19, AD20, AD21
6.032	NEW		
6.033	ID55	8.014	AD22
6.034	ID56, ID60, ID61, ID62, ID63	8.015	AD24
		8.016	CSN7
6.035	ID58	8.017	AD26
6.036	ID59	8.018	CSN82, CSN83, CSN84, AD26
6.037	NEW		
6.038	NEW	8.019	CSN85
6.039	NEW	8.020	AD27
Chapter 7 2nd Edition	**Chapter 7 1st Edition**	8.021	AD28
7.001	CSN1	8.022	AD29
7.002	CSN2	8.023	AD30
7.003	CSN3, CSN4	8.024	AD31
7.004	CSN5	8.025	AD32
7.005	CSN14	8.026	AD33
7.006	CSN16	8.027	AD34, AD35
7.007	CSN17, CSN27, CSN30, CSN31, CSN33, CSN80	8.028	AD37, AD38
		8.029	NEW
7.008	CSN20, CSN22, CSN24, CSN78	8.030	AD39
		8.031	AD40
7.009	CSN25	8.032	AD41
7.010	CSN26	8.033	AD42
7.011	CSN34	8.034	AD44, AD46
7.012	CSN77, CSN78	8.035	AD45
7.013	CSN79	8.036	AD47, Appendix L
7.014	CSN87	8.037	AD48
7.015	CSN89	8.038	AD49
7.016	CSN90	8.039	NEW
Chapter 8 2nd Edition	**Chapter 8 1st Edition**	8.040	AD50
		8.041	AD51
		8.042	AD52, AD53
8.001	AD1, AD2	8.043	AD54
8.002	AD3	8.044	AD55, Appendix S
8.003	AD4	8.045	AD56

Chapter 8 2nd Edition	Chapter 8 1st Edition	Chapter 9 2nd Edition	Chapter 9 1st Edition
8.046	AD57, Appendix C	9.008	REC8
8.047	Appendix C	9.009	REC10
8.048	Appendix C	9.010	REC11
8.049	Appendix C	9.011	REC12
8.050	Appendix C	9.012	REC13
8.051	Appendix C	9.013	REC15
8.052	Appendix C	9.014	REC16
8.053	CSN35, AD58	9.015	REC17
8.054	AD59, AD61, AD62, AD64	9.016	REC21
		9.017	REC18
8.055	AD60	9.018	REC20
8.056	AD63	9.019	REC19
8.057	AD65	9.020	REC23
8.058	AD66, Appendix T	9.021	REC24
8.059	AD67	9.022	REC25
8.060	AD68	9.023	REC26
8.061	AD69	9.024	REC27
8.062	AD70, AD71	9.025	REC28, REC29, REC32, REC35, REC36, REC40, REC42, REC43, REC44
8.063	AD72, AD74, AD75		
8.064	AD73		
8.065	AD76	9.026	REC33, REC34
8.066	AD77	9.027	REC30
8.067	AD78	9.028	REC37, REC38, REC39
8.068	AD80	9.029	REC45, REC46, REC47, REC48
8.069	AD81		
8.070	AD82	9.030	REC49
8.071	AD83	9.031	REC50, REC51
8.072	AD84	9.032	REC52
8.073	AD85	9.033	REC53, REC54, REC55, REC56, REC57, Appendix B-1
8.074	AD86		
8.075	AD87		
8.076	AD88, Appendix V	9.034	REC58, REC59
8.077	AD89, Appendix W	9.035	REC60, REC63
8.078	AD90	9.036	REC61
8.079	AD91	9.037	REC65
Chapter 9 2nd Edition	Chapter 9 1st Edition	9.038	REC14, REC66, REC67
		9.039	REC68
9.001	REC1	9.040	REC69
9.002	REC2	9.041	REC70
9.003	NEW	9.042	REC71
9.004	REC3	9.043	REC72
9.005	REC4	9.044	REC73
9.006	REC5, REC7	9.045	REC74
9.007	REC6	9.046	REC75

Chapter 9 2nd Edition	Chapter 9 1st Edition
9.047	REC76
9.048	REC77
Appendices 2nd Edition	**Appendices 1st Edition**
A	Front matter
B	Appendix D
C	Appendix B-2
D	NEW
E	NEW
F	Appendix G
G	Appendices P-1, P-2
H	Appendix F
I	NEW
J	NEW
K	NEW
L	NEW
M	NEW
N	Appendix H
O	NEW
P	Appendix J
Q	Appendix K
R	NEW
S	NEW
T	Appendix Q
U	Appendix N
V	Appendix O-3
W	NEW
X	NEW
Y	Appendix U
Z	NEW
AA	NEW
BB	NEW
CC	NEW
DD	NEW

GLOSSARY

Note: Some of these definitions were contained in the first edition in which they were reprinted with permission from *Infectious Diseases in Child Care Settings: Information for Directors, Caregivers, and Parents or Guardians*, by the Epidemiology Departments of Hennepin County Community Health, St. Paul Division of Public Health, Minnesota Department of Health, Washington County Public Health, and Bloomington Division of Health. Other definitions were supplied by our Technical Panels. Please see the Acknowledgments section for a list of the Technical Panels' members.

AAP - Abbreviation for the American Academy of Pediatrics, a national organization of pediatricians founded in 1930 and dedicated to the improvement of child health and welfare.

ACIP - Abbreviation for the U.S. Public Health Service Advisory Committee on Immunization Practices, which provides general recommendations on immunization against certain communicable diseases.

Acrocyanosis - Blueness or pallor of the extremities, usually associated with pain and numbness and caused by vasomotor disturbances.

Adaptive equipment - Equipment (such as eye glasses, hearing aids, wheelchairs, crutches, prostheses, oxygen tanks) that helps children with special needs adapt to and function within their surroundings. See also Appendix T.

Aflatoxin - Aflatoxin is a naturally occurring mycotoxin (fungus) produced by mold. The mold occurs in soil, decaying vegetation, hay, and grains undergoing microbiological deterioration. Favorable conditions include high moisture content and high temperature (USDA).

AIDS - See Human immunodeficiency virus (HIV) disease.

Allergens - A substance (food, pollen, pets, mold, medication, etc.) that causes an allergic reaction.

Ambient measurements - Measurements that help assess the amount of air pollutants, noise, or lighting within a specific area.

Anaphylaxis - An allergic reaction to a specific allergen (food, pollen, pets, mold, medication, etc.) that causes dangerous and possibly fatal complications, including the swelling and closure of the airway that can lead to an inability to breathe.

ANSI - Abbreviation for the American National Standards Institute, an organization that acts as a clearinghouse for standards, ensuring that any standard that comes out is created by a consensus process.

Andiropometric - Relating to physical measurements of the human body, for example, height, weight, or head circumference.

Anthropometry - The study of human body measurements.

Antibiotic prophylaxis - Antibiotics that are prescribed to prevent infections in infants and children in situations associated with an increased risk of serious infection with a specific disease (Red Book).

Antibody - A protein substance produced by the body's immune defense system in response to something foreign. Antibodies help protect against infections.

Antigen - Any substance that is foreign to the body. An antigen is capable of causing a response from the immune system.

Antisiphon ballcock - An automatic valve in the toilet tank, the opening and closing of which is controlled by a spherical float at the end of a lever. The antisiphon ballcock does not allow dirty water to be admixed with clean water.

APHA - Abbreviation for the American Public Health Association, a national organization of health professionals, which protects and promotes the health of the public through education, research, advocacy, and policy development.

Aseptic technique - The use of procedures that prevent contamination of an object, fluid, or person with infectious microorganisms.

Asphyxial crib death - Death attributed to an item within the crib that caused deprivation of oxygen or obstruction to normal breathing of an infant.

Asphyxiation - Death or unconsciousness due to inadequate oxygenation, the presence of noxious agents, or other obstructions to normal breathing.

Aspiration - The inhalation of food, liquid, or a foreign body into a person's airway, possibly resulting in choking and respiratory distress.

Assessment - An in-depth appraisal conducted to diagnose a condition or determine the importance or value of a procedure.

ASTM - Abbreviation for the American Society for Testing and Materials, an organization that provides voluntary standards through a consensus process for materials, products, systems, and services.

Asymptomatic - Without symptoms. For example, a child may not have symptoms of hepatitis infection, but may still shed hepatitis A virus in the stool and may be able to infect others.

Autoerotism - Sexual self-stimulation through which an individual obtains self-gratification for his or her own body.

Background checks - The process of checking for history of criminal charges of potential child care providers before they are allowed to care for children.

Bacteria - Plural of bacterium. Bacteria are organisms that may be responsible for localized or generalized diseases and can survive in and out of the body. They are much larger than viruses and can usually be treated effectively with antibiotics.

Bacteriostatic - Having the ability to inhibit the growth of bacteria.

Balusters - Vertical stair railings that support a horizontal handrail.

Bleach solution - For disinfecting environmental surfaces. One-quarter (1/4) cup of household liquid chlorine bleach (sodium hypochloride) in one gallon of water, prepared fresh daily. See also Disinfect.

Body fluids - Urine, feces, saliva, blood, nasal discharge, eye discharge, and injury or tissue discharge.

Bottle propping - Bottle-feeding an infant by propping the bottle near the infant's mouth and leaving the infant alone rather than holding the bottle by hand.

Bronchitis - Most often a bacterial or viral infection that causes swelling of the tubes (bronchioles) leading to the lungs.

Campylobacter - The name of a bacterium that causes diarrhea.

Campylobacteriosis - A diarrheal infection caused by the campylobacter bacterium.

Capture velocity - Airflow that will collect the pollutant (such as dust or fumes) that you want removed. Airflow that will collect the pollutant (such as dust or fumes) that you want removed.

Cardiopulmonary resuscitation (CPR) - Emergency measures performed by a person on another person whose breathing or heart activity has stopped. Measures include closed-chest cardiac compressions and mouth-to-mouth ventilation in a regular sequence.

Care coordinator - This term is used by some agencies or caregivers in place of, or in association with, the term case manager. The term care coordinator implies that someone is assigned to work with the child's family or alternative caretaker to assist in coordinating services, either internally within an agency directly providing services or with other service providers for the child and family. The term care coordinator is usually preferred these days over the term case manager, since the latter implies management of a case rather than assistance in ensuring coordinated care.

Caregiver - Used here to indicate the primary staff who work directly with the children, that is, director, teacher, aide, or others in the center and the child care provider in small and large family child care homes.

Carrier - A person who carries within his/her body a specific disease-causing organism, who has no symptoms of disease, and who can spread the disease to others. For example, some children may be carriers of *Haemophilus influenzae* or *giardia* and have no symptoms.

Case manager - See Care coordinator.

Catheterization - The process of inserting a hollow tube into an organ of the body, either for an investigative purpose or to give some form of treatment (such as to remove urine from the bladder of a child with neurologic disease).

CCFP - Abbreviation for the U.S. Department of Agriculture's Child Care Food Program, a federally sponsored program whose child care component provides nutritious meals to children enrolled in centers and family child care homes throughout the country.

CDA - Abbreviation for Child Development Associate, a credential awarded by a program that trains workers in Head Start, centers, and small and large family child care homes to help them achieve professional status in the child care field. The CDA credential is based on the caregiver's ability to work with young children, rather than on formal academic credits.

CDC - Abbreviation for the Centers for Disease Control and Prevention, which is responsible for monitoring communicable diseases, immunization status, injuries, and congenital malformations, and for performing other disease and injury surveillance activities in the United States.

Ceftriaxone - An antibiotic often prescribed for those exposed to an infection caused by *Haemophilus influenzae* type b (Hib) or *Neisseria meningitidis* (meningococcus).

Center - A facility that provides care and education for any number of children in a nonresidential setting and is open on a regular basis (for example, it is not a drop-in facility).

Child abuse - For the purposes of this set of standards, its definition is considered to be that contained in the laws of the state in which the standards will be applied. While these differ somewhat, most of them contain basic elements as follows:

    Emotional abuse - Acts that damage a child in psychological ways, but do not fall into other categories of abuse. Most states require for prosecution that psychological damage be very definite and clearly diagnosed by a psychologist or psychiatrist; this category of abuse is rarely reported and even more rarely a cause of protective action.

    Neglect - Neglect is divided into two categories: general neglect and severe neglect.

    General neglect - Failure to provide the common necessities, including food, shelter, a safe environment, education, and health care, but without resultant or likely harm to the child.

    Severe neglect - Neglect that results or is likely to result in harm to the child.

    Physical abuse - An intentional (nonaccidental) act affecting a child that produces tangible physical harm.

    Sexual abuse - Any sexual act performed with a child by an adult or by another child who exerts control over the victim. (Many state laws provide considerable detail about the specific acts that constitute sexual abuse.)

Child:staff ratio - The maximum number of children permitted per caregiver.

Children with special needs - Children with developmental disabilities, mental retardation, emotional disturbance, sensory or motor impairment, or significant chronic illness who require special health surveillance or specialized programs, interventions, technologies, or facilities.

Childrens Health Insurance Program (CHIP) - CHIP is a state/federal partnership that gives states three options for covering uninsured children: designing a new children's health insurance program; expanding current Medicaid programs; or a combination of both strategies. The CHIP statute expands health insurance to children whose families earn too much to qualify for Medicaid, yet not enough to afford private insurance.

Chlordane - An insecticide that has been used successfully against flies and mosquitoes that are resistant to DDT, and for the control of ticks and mites. Chlordane requires special handling, as it is toxic to humans when applied to the skin.

Chronic - Adjective describing an infection or illness that lasts a long time (months or years).

Ciprofloxacin - An antibiotic often prescribed for those exposed to an infection caused by *Haemophilus influenzae* type b (Hib) or *Neisseria meningitidis* (meningococcus).

Clean - To remove dirt and debris (such as blood, urine, and feces) by scrubbing and washing with a detergent solution and rinsing with water.

CMV - See Cytomegalovirus.

Cohorting toys - Keeping toys used by a group of children together for use only by that group of children.

Communicable disease - A disease caused by a microorganism (bacterium, virus, fungus, or parasite) that can be transmitted from person to person via an infected body fluid or respiratory spray, with or without an intermediary agent (such as a louse, mosquito) or environmental object (such as a table surface). Many communicable diseases are reportable to the local health authority.

Communicable period - The period of time when an infected person is capable of spreading infection to another person.

Compliance - The act of carrying out a recommendation, policy, or procedure.

Congenital - Existing from the time of birth.

Conjunctivitis - "Pink eye"; Inflammation (redness and swelling) of the delicate tissue that covers the inside of the eyelids and the eyeball.

Contact dermatitis - Contact dermatitis is a skin inflammation that results when the skin comes in direct contact with substances that can cause an allergic or inflammatory reaction.

Contamination - The presence of infectious microorganisms in or on the body, on environmental surfaces, on articles of clothing, or in food or water.

Contraindication - Something (as a symptom or condition) that makes a particular treatment or procedure inadvisable.

Contractual relationship - A signed and written contract between parents and child care providers that documents child care agreements involving policies and procedures and educational programming goals.

Corporal punishment - Pain or suffering inflicted on the body (such as spanking).

CPR - See Cardiopulmonary resuscitation.

CPSC - Abbreviation for the U.S. Consumer Product Safety Commission, created in 1972 and charged with the following responsibilities: (1) to protect the public against unreasonable risks of injury associated with consumer products; (2) to assist consumers in evaluating the comparative safety of consumer products; (3) to develop uniform safety standards for consumer products and to minimize conflicting state and local regulations; and (4) to promote research and investigation into the causes and prevention of product-related deaths, illnesses, and injuries.

Croup - Spasms of the airway that cause difficult breathing and a cough sounding like a seal's bark. Croup can be caused by various bacteria and viruses.

Cryptosporidium - A parasite that causes cryptosporidiosis, a diarrheal illness.

Cytomegalovirus (CMV) - A very common virus, which often infects young children. In most cases, CMV causes no symptoms. When symptoms are experienced, they typically consist of fever, swollen glands, and fatigue. CMV can infect a pregnant woman who is not immune and damage the fetus, leading to mental retardation, hearing loss, and other nervous system problems in the unborn child.

Decibel (db) - The unit of measure of the loudness of sounds; one decibel is the lowest intensity of sound at which a given note can be heard. The decibel level is the number of decibels of noise perceived or measured in a given place.

De-institutionalization - This term is commonly used to refer to the process by which persons with mental retardation or mental illness have been removed from large residential facilities and placed in various forms of community-based care.

Demand feeding - The feeding of infants whenever they indicate that they need to be fed, rather than feeding according to a clock schedule.

Dental caries - Tooth decay resulting in localized destruction of tooth tissue. Also known as dental cavities.

Dental sealants - Dental sealants are clear protective coatings that cover tooth surfaces and prevent bacteria and food particles from settling into the pits and grooves. Dental sealants are usually applied after a child reaches the age of six when the first permanent molars come in. Dental sealants last for 4-5 years and can be reapplied when they wear off.

Dermatitis - An inflammation of the skin due to irritation or infection.

Diarrhea - An increased number of abnormally loose stools in comparison with the individual's usual bowel habits.

Diphtheria - A serious infection of the nose and throat caused by the bacterium Corynebacterium diptheriae, producing symptoms of sore throat, low fever, chills, and a grayish membrane in the throat. The membrane can make swallowing and breathing difficult and may cause suffocation. The bacteria produce a toxin (a type of poisonous substance) that can cause severe and permanent damage to the nervous system and heart. This infection has been almost entirely eliminated in areas where standard infant immunizations and boosters are performed.

Disease surveillance - Close observation for the occurrence of a disease or infection. Surveillance is performed to discover a disease problem early, to understand a disease problem better, and to evaluate the methods used to control the disease.

Disinfect - To eliminate virtually all germs from inanimate surfaces through the use of chemicals (e.g., products registered with the U.S. Environmental Protection Agency as "disinfectants") or physical agents (e.g., heat). In the child care environment, a 1:64 dilution of domestic bleach made by mixing a solution of 1/4 cup household liquid chlorine bleach with 1 gallon of tap water and prepared fresh daily is an effective method to remove germs from environmental surfaces and other inanimate objects that have been contaminated with body fluids (see Body fluids), provided that the surfaces have first been cleaned (see Clean) of organic material before applying bleach and at least 2 minutes of contact time with the surface occurs. (Since complete elimination of all germs may not be achieved using the 1:64 dilution of domestic bleach solution, technically, the process is called sanitizing, not disinfecting. The term sanitize is used in these standards most often, but disinfect may appear in other or earlier publications when addressing sanitation in child care. See Appendix I. To achieve maximum germ reduction with bleach, the precleaned surfaces should be left moderately or glistening wet with the bleach solution and allowed to air dry or be dried only after at least 2 minutes of contact time. A slight chlorine odor should emanate from this solution. If there is no chlorine smell, a new solution needs to be made, even if the solution was prepared fresh that day. The 1:64 diluted solution will contain 500-800 parts per million (ppm) chlorine.

Two minutes of contact with a coating of a sprayed 1:64 diluted solution of 1/4 cup household liquid chlorine bleach in one gallon of tap water prepared fresh daily is an effective method of surface-sanitizing of environmental surfaces and other inanimate objects that have first been thoroughly cleaned of organic soil. By itself, bleach is not a good cleaning agent. Household bleach is sold in the conventional strength of 5.25% hypochlorite and a more recently marketed "ultra" bleach that contains 6% hypochlorite solution. In child care, either may be used in a 1:64 dilution.

Bleach solutions much less concentrated than the recommended dilution have been shown in laboratory tests to kill high numbers of bloodborne viruses, including HIV and hepatitis B virus. This solution is not toxic if accidentally ingested by a child. However, since this solution is moderately corrosive, caution should be exercised in handling it and when wetting or using it on items containing metals, especially aluminum. DO NOT MIX UNDILUTED BLEACH OR THE DILUTED BLEACH SOLUTION WITH OTHER FLUIDS, ESPECIALLY ACIDS (E.G., VINEGAR), AS THIS WILL RESULT IN THE RAPID EVOLUTION OF HIGHLY POISONOUS CHLORINE GAS.

Commercially prepared detergent -sanitizer solutions or detergent cleaning, rinsing and application of a non bleach sanitizer that is at least as effective as the chlorine bleach solution is acceptable as long as these products are nontoxic for children, are used according to the manufacturer's instructions and are approved by the state or local health department for use as a disinfectant in place of the bleach solution.

These methods are used for toys, children's table tops, diaper changing tables, food utensils, and any other object or surface that is significantly contaminated with body fluids. Sanitizing food utensils can be accomplished by using a dishwasher or equivalent process, usually involving more dilute chemicals than are required for other surfaces.

Drop-in care - A facility providing care that occurs for fewer than 30 days per year per child either on a consecutive or intermittent basis or on a regular basis.

DTP - Abbreviation for the immunization against diphtheria, tetanus, and pertussis.

Dyspnea - Difficulty in breathing or shortness of breath.

E. coli 015 7. H7 - *E. coli* O157:H7 is one bacterium of hundreds of strains of *Escherichia coli*. Although most strains are harmless and live in the intestines of healthy humans and animals, this strain produces a powerful toxin and can cause severe illness, including bloody diarrhea and abdominal cramps. The organism can live in the intestines of healthy cattle. Meat can become contaminated during slaughter, and organisms can be thoroughly mixed into beef when it is ground. Eating undercooked meat, drinking unpasteurized milk, and swimming in or drinking sewage-contaminated water can cause infection (CDC).

Ectoparasite - An organism that lives on the outer surface of the body.

Emergency response practices - Procedures used to call for emergency medical assistance, to reach parents or emergency contacts, to arrange for transfer to medical assistance, and to render first aid to the injured person.

Emetic - An agent that induces vomiting (such as Syrup of Ipecac).

Encapsulated asbestos - Asbestos fibers that are coated with a material that makes them not easily inhaled.

Encephalitis - Inflammation (redness and swelling) of the brain, which can be caused by a number of viruses, including mumps, measles, and varicella.

Endonuclease tracking - The laboratory process of examining the genetic material of viruses and bacteria, often used to determine similarities and differences among viruses or bacterial strains that appear to be the same.

Endotracheal suctioning - Endotracheal suctioning involves the mechanical aspiration and removal of mucous from a person's airway through a tracheostomy (an artificial opening in the trachea).

Enteric - Describes the location of infections affecting the intestines (often with diarrhea) or the liver.

EPA - Abbreviation for the U.S. Environmental Protection Agency, established in 1970, which administers federal programs on air and water pollution, solid waste disposal, pesticide regulation, and radiation and noise control.

Epidemiology - The scientific study of the occurrence and distribution of diseases.

Epiglottis - Tissue lid of the voice box. When this organ becomes swollen and inflamed (a condition called epiglottitis), it can block breathing passages. *Haemophilus influenzae* that commonly causes epiglottitis. This infection has been greatly reduced in areas where standard infant immunizations and boosters are performed.

EPSDT - Abbreviation for Medicaid's Early Periodic Screening and Diagnostic Treatment program, which provides health assessments and follow-up services to income-eligible children.

Ergot - A toxic fungus found as a parasite on grains of rye and other grains. Consumption of food contaminated with ergots may cause vomiting, diarrhea and may lead to gangrene in serious cases. Chronic exposure through consumption of contaminated food can lead to health complications.

Erythromycin - An antibiotic medication used to treat many upper respiratory illnesses. It is often prescribed for people exposed to pertussis.

Evaluation - Impressions and recommendations formed after a careful appraisal and study.

Exclusion - Denying admission of an ill child or staff member to a facility.

Excretion - Waste material that is formed and not used by the body, such as feces and urine.

Facility - A legal definition. The buildings, the grounds, the equipment, and the people involved in providing child care of any type.

Failure to Thrive Syndrome - Failure of a child to develop mentally and/or physically. This syndrome may be due to a variety of causes, but often is associated with a disturbed parent/child relationship and inadequate feeding and attachment.

Febrile - The condition of having an abnormally high bodily temperature (fever), often as a response to infection.

Fecal coliforms - Bacteria in stool that normally inhabit the gastrointestinal tract and are used as indicators of fecal pollution. They denote the presence of intestinal pathogens in water or food.

Fecal-oral transmission - Transmission of an organism from an infected person's stool (bowel movement) into another person's mouth to infect him/her. This transmission usually occurs when the infected person fails to wash his/her hands after having a bowel movement and then handles things (such as food or toys) that other people subsequently put in their mouths. Many diseases are spread this way, including hepatitis A, campylobacteriosis, shigellosis, and salmonellosis.

Fever - An elevation of body temperature The body temperature can normally be as high as 99.3' oral, 100' rectal, or 98 0 axillary. A fever mists when the body temperature is higher than these numbers. The amount of temperature elevation varies at different body sites, and the height of the fever does not indicate a more or less severe illness. The method chosen to take a child's temperature depends on the need for accuracy, available equipment, the skill of the person taking the temperature, and the ability of the child to assist in the procedure. Oral temperatures should not be taken on children younger than 4 years. Rectal temperatures should be taken only by persons with specific health training in performing this procedure. Axillary temperatures are only accurate in young infants Electronic devices for measuring temperature in the ear canal give temperature results similar to rectal temperature, but these devices require specific training and are not widely available in child care settings.

First aid - See Pediatric first aid.

Fomites - Environmental surfaces or objects that may serve as reservoirs for spreading disease from person to person.

Foodborne pathogen - A germ contained in a food product that is transmitted to persons eating the food.

Footcandles - The amount of illumination produced by a standard candle at a distance of one foot.

Friable - Readily crumbled; brittle.

Functional outcomes - Health status measures that go beyond traditional physiological assessments. By incorporating a multidimensional definition of health that encompasses physical, psychological and social aspects, functional outcome measures can capture the broader impact of disease and treatment on life from a child's (or parent's) own perspective. Such tools enable children and parents to offer input on their quality of life and their capacity to function in normal social roles (AAP).

Fungi (singular fungus) - Plant-like organisms, such as yeasts, molds, mildews, and mushrooms, which get their nutrition from other living organisms or from dead organic matter.

Gastric tube feeding- The administration of nourishment through a tube that has been surgically inserted directly into the stomach.

Gestational - Occurring during or related to pregnancy.

Giardia lamblia - A parasite that causes giardiasis, a diarrheal illness. Commonly referred to as "Giardia."

Gross-motor skills - Large movements involving the arms, legs, feet, or the entire body (such as crawling, running, and jumping).

Ground-fault circuit-interrupter (GFCI) - A piece of equipment in an electrical line that offers protection against electrocution if the line comes into contact with water.

Group A streptococcus (GAS) - Group A streptococcus is a bacterium commonly found in the throat and on the skin that can cause a range of infections, from relatively mild sore throats and skin infections to life-threatening disease.

Group size - The number of children assigned to a caregiver or team of caregivers occupying an individual classroom or well-defined space within a larger room. See also Child:Staff Ratio.

***Haemophilus influenzae* type b (Hib) -** Before introduction of effective vaccines in 1988, Hib was the most common cause of bacterial meningitis in children in the United States. Since 1988, the incidence of diseases caused by Hib have declined by 99%. Other infections caused by Hib include epiglottitis, otitis media (ear infections), sinus infections, skin infections, and pneumonia. When two or more cases of Hib disease appear in a child care center within 60 days, a prophylactic antibiotic and immunization is indicated for all children and employees (Red Book).

HbCV - Abbreviation for the Haemophilus b Conjugate Vaccine, one of the vaccines available against *Haemophilus influenzae* type b (Hib).

HBIG - Abbreviation for hepatitis B immunoglobulin, preventive treatment for those that have been exposed to hepatitis B virus carriers.

HBV - An abbreviation for hepatitis B virus. See also Hepatitis.

Health care provider - A health care professional practices medicine by an established licensing body with or without supervision. The most common types of health care providers include physicians, nurse practitioners, and physician's assistants.

Health consultant - A physician, certified pediatric or family nurse practitioner, or registered nurse who has pediatric or child care experience and is knowledgeable in child care, licensing, and community resources. The health consultant provides guidance and assistance to child care staff on health aspects of the facility.

Health plan - A written document that describes emergency health and safety procedures, general health policies and procedures, and policies covering the management of mild illness, injury prevention, and occupational health and safety.

Hepatitis - Inflammation of the liver caused by viral infection. There are five types of infectious hepatitis: type A; type B; non-A, non-B; C; and D. Hepatitis type A infection has been documented as a frequent cause of hepatitis in child care settings and is often asymptomatic in children. Chronic carriers of hepatitis B may be found in child care settings. Non-A, non-B, and C hepatitis are associated with blood transfusions and intravenous drug abuse, and have not been identified as a problem in child care settings. Hepatitis D occasionally accompanies hepatitis B infections.

Herpes simplex virus - A viral organism that causes a recurrent disease which is marked by blister-like sores on mucous membranes (such as the mouth, lips, or genitals) that weep clear fluid and slowly crust over.

Herpetic gingivostomatitis - Inflammation of the mouth and lips caused by the herpes simplex virus.

Hib - see *Haemophilus influenzae* type b.

HIV - see Human Immunodeficiency Virus disease.

Human Immunodeficiency Virus (HIV) disease - HIV disease leads to a failure of the human immune system, leaving the body unable to fight infections and cancers. It is characterized by a relatively long (up to 10 years) asymptomatic stage and a brief acute stage. Gradually, an HIV-infected person develops multiple symptoms and infections that progress to the end stage of the disease, called acquired immunodeficiency syndrome (AIDS). HIV is transmitted by sexual contact or blood-to-blood contact, or from an infected mother to her baby during pregnancy, labor, delivery, or breast-feeding. Hygiene- Protective measures taken by individuals to promote health and limit the spread of infectious diseases. These measures include (1) washing hands with soap and running water after using the toilet, after handling anything contaminated, and before eating or handling food; (2) keeping hands, hair, and unclean items away from the mouth, nose, eyes, ears, genitals, and wounds; (3) avoiding the use of common or unclean eating utensils, drinking glasses, towels, handkerchiefs, combs, and hairbrushes; (4) avoiding

exposure to droplets from the noses and mouths of other people, such as the droplets spread by coughing or sneezing; (5) washing hands thoroughly after caring for another person; and (6) keeping the body clean by frequent (at least daily) bathing or showering, using soap and water.

IEP - See Individualized Education Program.

IFSP - See Individualized Family Service Plan.

Immune globulin (Gamma globulin, immunoglobulin) - An antibody preparation made from human plasma. It provides temporary protection against diseases such as hepatitis type A. Health officials may wish to give doses of immune globulin to children in child care when cases of hepatitis appear

Immunity - The body's ability to fight a particular infection. For example, a child acquires immunity to diseases such as measles, mumps, rubella, and pertussis after natural infection or by immunization. Newborn children initially have the same immune status as their mothers. This immunity usually disappears within the first 6 months of life.

Immunizations - Vaccines that are given to children and adults to help them develop protection (antibodies) against specific infections. Vaccines may contain an inactivated or killed agent or a weakened live organism. Childhood immunizations include protection against diphtheria, pertussis, tetanus, polio, measles, mumps, rubella, and *Haemophilus influenzae* type b. Adults need to be protected against measles, rubella, mumps, polio, tetanus, and diphtheria.

Immunocompromised - The state of not having normal body defenses (immune responses) against diseases caused by microorganisms.

Immunosuppression - Inhibition of the body's natural immune response, used especially to describe the action of drugs that allow the surgical transplantation of a foreign organ or tissue by inhibiting its biological rejection.

Impervious - Adjective describing a smooth surface that does not become wet or retain particles.

Incubation period - Time between exposure to an infectious microorganism and beginning of symptoms.

Individualized Education Program (IEP) - A written document, derived from Part B of IDEA (the Individuals with Disabilities Education Act—PL 94-142), that is designed to meet a child's individual educational program needs. The main purposes for an IEP are to set reasonable learning goals and to state the services that the school district will provide for a child with special educational needs. Every child who is qualified for special educational services provided by the school is required to have an IEP.

Individualized Family Service Plan (IFSP) - A written document, derived from Part C of IDEA (the Individuals with Disabilities Education Act), that is formulated in collaboration with the family to meet the needs of a child with a developmental disability or delay, to assist the family in its care for a child's educational, therapeutic, and health needs, and to deal with the family's needs to the extent to which the family wishes assistance.

Infant - A child between the time of birth and the age of ambulation (usually between the ages from birth to 18 months).

Infant walkers - Infant walkers, or baby walkers, consist of a wheeled base supporting a rigid frame that holds a fabric seat with leg openings and usually a plastic feeding/play tray. The device is designed to support a preambulatory infant, with feet on the floor, and allow mobility while the infant is learning to walk. Walkers are not safe for infants and children and are not recommended for use.

Infection - A condition caused by the multiplication of an infectious agent in the body.

Infectious - Capable of causing an infection.

Infectivity - The ability to spread infection from person to person.

Infested - Common usage of this term refers to parasites (such as lice or scabies) living on the outside of the body.

Influenza ("flu") - An acute viral infection of the respiratory tract. Symptoms usually include fever, chills, headache, muscle aches, dry cough, and sore throat. Influenza should not be confused with *Haemophilus influenzae* infection caused by bacteria, or with "stomach flu," which is usually an infection caused by a different type of virus.

Ingestion - The act of taking material (whether food or other substances) into the body through the mouth.

Injury, intentional - Physical damage to a human being resulting from an intentional event (one done by design) including a transfer of energy (physical, chemical, or heat energy).

Injury, unintentional - Physical damage to a human being resulting from an unintentional event (one not done by design) involving a transfer of energy (physical, chemical, or heat energy).

Intradermal - Relating to areas between the layers of the skin (as in intradermal injections).

IPV - Abbreviation for "Inactivated Polio Virus," as in the inactivated (Salk-type) polio virus vaccine. The immunization is given by way of a subcutaneous injection.

Isolation - The physical separation of an ill person from other persons in order to prevent or lessen contact between other persons and the ill person's body fluids.

Jaundice - Yellowish discoloration of the whites of the eyes, skin, and mucous membranes caused by deposition of bile salts in these tissues. It occurs as a symptom of various diseases, such as hepatitis, that affect the processing of bile.

Large family child care home - Usually, care and education for 7 to 12 children (including preschool children of the caregiver) in the home of the caregiver, who employs one or more qualified adult assistants to meet the child:staff ratio requirements. This type of care is likely to resemble center care in its organization of activities. Applicable terms are abbreviated here to large family home or large family home caregiver

Lead Agency - This term refers to an individual state's choice for the agency that will receive and allocate the federal and state funding for children with special educational needs. The federal funding is allocated to individual states in accordance with the Individuals with Disabilities Educational Act (IDEA).

Lethargy - Unusual sleepiness.

Lice - Parasites that live on the surface of the human body (in head, body, or pubic hair). Louse infestation is called pediculosis.

Listeriosis - A term applied to the diseases caused by Listeria bacterium. Listeria can cause meningitis, blood infections, heart problems, and abscesses, and can cause a pregnant woman to miscarry These diseases are usually acquired by eating or drinking unpasteurized milk or milk products.

Longitudinal study - A research study in which patients are followed and examined over a period of time.

Mainstreaming - A widely used term that describes the philosophy and activities associated with providing services to persons with disabilities in community settings, especially in school programs, where such children or other persons are integrated with persons without disabilities and are entitled to attend programs and to have access to all services available in the community.

Mantoux intradermal skin test - The Mantoux intradermal skin test involves the intradermal injection of a standardized amount of tuberculin antigen. The reaction to the antigen on the skin can be measured and the result used to assess the likelihood of infection with tuberculosis.

MD - Abbreviation for Doctor of Medicine. An MD is a health practitioner who has received a degree from a college of medicine.

Measles (red measles, rubeola, hard measles, 8- to 10-day measles) - A serious viral illness characterized by a red rash, high fever, light-sensitive eyes, cough, and cold symptoms. This infection has been almost entirely eliminated in areas where standard infant immunizations and boosters are performed.

Medicaid - Medicaid is a program which provides medical assistance for individuals and families with low incomes and resources. The program became law in 1965 as a jointly funded cooperative venture between the Federal and State governments to assist states in the provision of adequate medical care to eligible needy persons. Medicaid is the largest program providing medical and health-related services to America's poorest people (HCFA).

Medications - Any substance that is intended to diagnose, cure, treat, or prevent disease or is intended to affect the structure or function of the body of humans or other animals.

Meninges - The tissue covering the brain and spinal cord. When this tissue becomes infected and inflamed, the disease is called meningitis.

Meningitis - A swelling or inflammation of the tissue covering the spinal cord and brain. Meningitis is usually caused by a bacterial or viral infection.

Meningococcal disease - Pneumonia, arthritis, meningitis, or blood infection caused by the bacterium *Neisseria meningitidis*

Methemoglobinemia - Methemoglobinemia, also known as blue baby syndrome, is a blood disorder caused when nitrite interacts with the hemoglobin in red blood cells and is characterized by the inability of the blood to carry sufficient oxygen to the body's cells and tissues. Although methemoglobinemia is rare among adults, it may affect infants, when nitrate-contaminated well water is used to prepare formula and other baby foods.

Midinfancy - The middle of the infancy period or the first year of life, that is, approximately 9 to 15 months of life.

MMR - Abbreviation for the vaccine against measles, mumps, and rubella.

Monilia - A type of fungus, also know as Candida albicans. The infection may occur in the mouth, lungs, intestine, vagina, skin, or nails. If found in the mouth, it is known as oral thrush.

Morbidity - The incidence of a disease within a population.

Mucocutaneous - Involving the skin and mucous membranes, such as the eye conjunctiva or the mouth.

Mumps - A viral infection with symptoms of fever, headache, and swelling and tenderness of the salivary glands, causing the cheeks to swell. This infection has been almost entirely eliminated in areas where standard infant immunizations and boosters are performed.

NAEYC - Abbreviation for the National Association for the Education of Young Children, a membership-supported organization of people who share a desire to serve and act on the needs and rights of children from birth through age 8.

Nasogastric tube feeding - The administration of nourishment using a plastic tube that stretches from the nose to the stomach.

Nasopharyngeal - Pertaining to the anatomical area of the pharynx and nose.

Neisseria meningitidis **(meningococcus) -** A bacterium that can cause meningitis, blood infections, pneumonia, and arthritis.

Neurotoxicant - A substance or chemical that can damage the nervous system.

NFPA - Abbreviation for the National Fire Protection Association, which provides specific guidance on public safety from fire in buildings and structures.

Nonprescription medications - Drugs that are generally regarded as safe for use if the label directions and warnings are followed. Nonprescription medications are also called "over-the-counter" (OTC) drugs because they can be purchased without a prescription from a health care provider. Foods or cosmetics that are also intended to treat or prevent disease or affect the functions of the human body (such as suntan lotion, fluoride toothpaste, antiperspirant deodorants, or anti-dandruff shampoo) are also considered to be nonprescription medications.

Nonpurulent conjunctivitis - "Pink eye" that is usually accompanied by a clear, watery eye discharge, without fever, eye pain, or redness of the eyelid. This type of conjunctivitis usually can be managed without excluding a child from a facility, as in the case of children with mild infection of the respiratory tract.

Nutrition Specialist - As defined in these standards, a registered dietitian with 1 to 2 years' experience in infant and child health programs and coursework in child development, who serves as local or state consultant to child care staff.

Occupational therapy - Treatment based on the utilization of occupational activities of a typical child (such as play, feeding, toileting, and dressing). Child specific exercises are developed in order to encourage a child with mental or physical disabilities to contribute to their own recovery and development.

OPV - Abbreviation for oral polio virus, as in trivalent (Sabin-type) polio virus vaccine.

Organisms - Living things. Often used as a general term for germs (such as bacteria, viruses, fungi, or parasites) that can cause disease.

OSHA - Abbreviation for the Occupational Safety and Health Administration of the U.S. Department of Labor, which regulates health and safety in the workplace.

Otitis media - Inflammation or infection of the middle part of the ear. Ear infections are commonly caused by *Streptococcus pneumoniae* or *Haemophilus influenzae*.

Parasite - An organism that lives on or in another living organism (such as ticks, lice, mites).

Parent - The child's natural or adoptive mother or father, guardian, or other legally responsible person.

Particulate resilient material - Cushioning material made up of loose surfacing materials (like bark, wood chips, mulch, gravel, sand) designed to help absorb the shock if a child falls off playground equipment.

Pediatric first aid - Emergency care and treatment of an injured child before definite medical and surgical management can be secured. Pediatric first aid includes rescue breathing and first aid for choking.

Pertussis - A highly contagious bacterial respiratory infection, which begins with cold-like symptoms and cough and becomes progressively more severe, so that the person may experience vomiting sweating, and exhaustion with the cough. Although most older children and adults with pertussis whoop with coughing spells (hence the common term whooping cough), infants with pertussis commonly do not whoop but experience apneic spells, during which the infant becomes blue and stops breathing. The cough and apnea may persist for 1 to 2 months. This infection has been almost entirely eliminated in areas where standard infant immunizations and boosters are performed.

Pesticides - A chemical used to kill pests, particularly insects.

Physical therapy - The use of physical agents and methods (such as massage, therapeutic exercises, hydrotherapy, electrotherapy) to assist a child with physical or mental disabilities to optimize their individual physical development or to restore their normal body function after illness or injury.

Picocuries - A measure of concentration of radiation per liter of air.

Pneumonia - An acute or chronic disease marked by inflammation of the lungs and caused by viruses, bacteria, or other microorganisms and sometimes by physical and chemical irritants.

Poliomyelitis - A disease caused by the polio virus with signs that may include paralysis and meningitis, but often with only minor flu-like symptoms. This infection has been almost entirely eliminated in areas where standard infant immunizations and boosters are performed.

Post-traumatic stress disorder - Psychological stress resulting from a frightening or distressing experience (e.g. any kind of injury, a physical or sexual assault, car crash, fire or other disaster) where reactions from the experience last for more than a month and are strong enough to affect an individual's everyday functioning.

Postural drainage - Body positioning resulting in the gradual flow of mucous secretions from the edges of both lungs into the airway so secretions can be removed from the lungs by coughing.

Potable - Suitable for drinking.

PPD - Abbreviation for purified protein derivative, a substance used in intradermal tests for tuberculosis. See also Mantoux skin test.

Prenatal - Existing or occurring before birth (as in prenatal medical care).

Preschooler - A child between the age of toilet learning/training and the age of entry into a regular school; usually aged 3 to 5 years and related to overall development.

Prescription medications - Medications that can only be dispensed by a licensed practitioner (such as a physician or nurse practitioner) because it may be unsafe if not used under professional supervision.

Prodromal - Pertaining to the earliest signs and symptoms of a disease or those that give warning of its presence.

Projectile - A fired, thrown, or otherwise propelled object.

Prosthetic devices - A prosthetic device is an artificial body replacement adapted to reproduce the form and, as much as possible, the function of the missing part.

Pseudomonas aeruginosa - A type of organism that is commonly a contaminant of skin sores but that occasionally causes infection in other parts of the body and is usually hospital-acquired; the most serious infections occur in debilitated patients with lowered resistance due to other diseases and/or therapy.

Psychosocial - Involving aspects of social and psychological behavior (as in a child's psychosocial development).

Purulent - Containing pus, a thick white or yellow fluid.

Purulent conjunctivitis - "Pink eye" with white or yellow eye discharge, often with matted eyelids after sleep, and including eye pain or redness of the eyelids or skin surrounding the eye. This type of conjunctivitis is more often caused by a bacterial infection, which may require antibiotic treatment. Children with purulent conjunctivitis, therefore, should be excluded until the child's health care provider has examined the child and cleared him or her for readmission to the facility.

Radon - A radioactive gaseous element formed by the disintegration of radium that occurs naturally in the soil. Radon is considered to be a health hazard that may lead to lung cancer.

Reflux - An abnormal backward flow of stomach contents into the esophagus.

Rescue breathing - The process of breathing air into the lungs of a person who has stopped breathing. This process is also called artificial respiration.

Respiratory syncytial virus - A virus that causes colds, bronchitis, and pneumonia.

Respiratory system - The nose, ears, sinuses, throat, and lungs.

Rheumatic fever - A severe infectious disease often occurring after a strep infection. Rheumatic fever is characterized by fever and painful inflammation of the joints and may result in permanent damage to the valves of the heart.

Rhinovirus - A virus that causes the common cold.

Rifampin - An antibiotic often prescribed for those exposed to an infection caused by *Haemophilus influenzae type b* (Hib) or *Neisseria meningitidis* (meningococcus), or given to treat an infection caused by tuberculosis. This medication my be prescribed as a prophylactic treatment in a child care setting.

Rotavirus - A viral infection that causes diarrhea and vomiting, especially in infants and children.

Rubella - A mild viral illness with symptoms of red rash, low-grade fever, swollen glands, and sometimes achy joints. The rubella virus can infect and damage a fetus if the mother is not immune to the disease. Also known as German measles, 3-day measles, or light measles. This infection has been almost entirely eliminated in areas where standard infant immunizations and boosters are performed.

Salmonella - A type of bacteria that causes food poisoning (salmonellosis) with symptoms of vomiting, diarrhea, and abdominal pain.

Salmonellosis - A diarrheal infection caused by Salmonella bacteria.

Sanitize - To remove filth or soil and small amounts of certain bacteria. For an inanimate surface to be considered sanitary, the surface must be clean (see Clean) and the number of germs must be reduced to such a level that disease transmission by that surface is unlikely. This procedure is less rigorous than disinfection (see Disinfect) and is applicable to a wide variety of routine housekeeping procedures involving, for example, bedding, bathrooms, kitchen countertops, floors, and walls. To clean, detergent or abrasive cleaners may be used but an additional sanitizer solution must be applied to sanitize. A number of EPA-registered "detergent-disinfectant" products are also appropriate for sanitizing. Directions on product labels should be followed closely. See Appendix I on *Selecting an Appropriate Sanitizer.*

Scabies - A skin disease that causes intense itching and is caused by a tiny parasite that burrows into the skin, particularly on the front of the wrist, the webs and sides of the fingers, the buttocks, the genitals, and the feet.

Scarlet fever - An acute contagious disease caused by a streptococcal infection, occurring predominantly among children and characterized by a scarlet skin rash and high fever.

School-age child - This term describes a developmental period associated with a child who is enrolled in a regular school, including kindergarten; usually from 5 to 12 years of age.

School-age child care facility - A center offering a program of activities before and after school and/or during vacations.

Screening - Mass examination of a population group to detect the existence of a particular disease (such as diabetes or tuberculosis).

Secondary infection - When a person is infected by an organism that had originated from the illness of another person. The first person infected has the primary infection, and any persons infected from the originally infected person is said to have contracted a secondary infection.

Secretions - Wet material, such as saliva, that is produced by a cell or a gland and that has a specific purpose in the body.

Seizure - A sudden attack or convulsion due to involuntary, uncontrolled burst of electrical activity in the brain that can result in a wide variety of clinical manifestations, including muscle twitches, staring, tongue biting, loss of consciousness and total body shaking.

Sepsis - An infection that involves the presence of pathogenic organisms or their toxins in the blood or body tissues.

Seroconversion - The increase in serum antibody against a microorganism that occurs after an infection with the microorganism or after vaccination with all or a part of the microorganism.

Serologic - Pertaining to the study of blood serum.

Seronegative - Refers to the absence of serum antibodies against a specific microorganism.

Seropositive - Refers to the presence of serum antibodies against a specific microorganism.

Serum - The clear liquid that separates in the clotting of blood.

Shigella - A type of bacterium that causes bacillary dysentery or shigellosis, a diarrheal infection.

Shigellosis - A diarrheal infection caused by the Shigella bacterium.

SIDS - See Sudden Infant Death Syndrome.

Small family child care home - Usually, the care and education of one to six children (including preschool children of the caregiver) in the home of the caregiver. Caregivers model their programs either on a nursery school or on a skilled parenting model. Applicable terms are abbreviated here to small family home or family home caregiver.

Small family child care home network - A group of small family child care homes in one management system.

Special facility for ill children - A facility that cares only for ill children or a facility that cares for more than six ill children at a time. This is not the same as child care for ill children provided by the child's regular center, large family child care home, or small family child care home.

Staff - Used here to indicate all personnel employed at the facility, including both caregivers and personnel who do not provide direct care to the children (such as cooks, drivers, and housekeeping personnel).

Standard precautions - Apply to contact with non-intact skin, mucous membranes, blood, all body fluids, and excretions except sweat, whether or not they contain visible blood. The general methods of infection prevention are indicated for all people in the child care setting and are designed to reduce the risk of transmission of microorganisms from both recognized and unrecognized sources of infection. Although Standard precautions were designed to apply to hospital settings, with the exceptions detailed in this definition, they also apply in child care settings. Standard precautions involve use of barriers as in Universal Precautions (see separate definition) as well as cleaning and sanitizing contaminated surfaces.

Child Care Adaptation of Standard Precautions (exceptions from the use in hospital settings):
a) In child care settings, use of non-porous gloves is optional except when blood or blood containing body fluids may be involved.

b) In child care settings, gowns and masks are not required.
c) In child care settings, appropriate barriers include materials such as disposable diaper table paper, disposable towels, and surfaces that can be sanitized in child care settings.
See also Transmission-based precautions; Universal precautions.

Standing orders - Orders written in advance by a health care provider that describe the procedure to be followed in defined circumstances.

Staphylococcus - A common bacterium found on the skin of healthy people that may cause skin infections or boils.

Status epilepticus - A prolonged seizure or a series of seizures that continue uncontrolled for 20 minutes or more.

Streptococcus - A common bacterium that can cause sore throat, upper respiratory illnesses, pneumonia, skin rashes, skin infections, arthritis, heart disease (rheumatic fever), and kidney disease (glomerulonephritis).

Substitute staff - Caregivers (often without prior training or experience) hired for one day or for an extended period of time, who work under direct supervision of a trained, licensed/certified permanent caregiver.

Suction - Most commonly referring to the removal of respiratory secretions or mucous of a child to aid in breathing. This can be accomplished by a handheld suction bulb, or a machine powered vacuum attached to a suction tube. Both devices are commonly inserted into the nostrils and occasionally into the mouth or tracheostomy tub (a tube protruding from the front and center of the neck in children with major respiratory compromise).

Sudden Infant Death Syndrome (SIDS) - The sudden and unexpected death of an apparently healthy infant, typically occurring between the ages of 3 weeks and 5 months and not explained by an autopsy.

Sulfa-drugs - A term most commonly referring to a certain class of antimicrobial medications containing sulfur. The most common childhood prescriptions of sulfa-drugs include antibiotic eye drops for the treatment of pink eye, and oral antibiotics for the treatment of urinary tract, ear and lung infections. This term is very important as it relates to a type of drug allergy that children may have. (It is important to note that other medications may contain sulfur, but are not "sulfa-drugs" and may not cause an allergic reaction in a child with a "sulfa-drug allergy."

Syrup of ipecac - A type of medicine that induces vomiting in a person who has swallowed a toxic or poisonous substance.

Systemic - Pertaining to a whole body rather than to one of its parts.

Tb - See Tuberculosis.

Termiticide - A chemical used to kill termites.

Thermal injury - Bodily injury due to burns.

Toddler - A child between the age of ambulation and the age of toilet learning/training, usually one aged 13 to 35 months.

Toxoplasmosis - A parasitic disease usually causing no symptoms. When symptoms do occur, swollen glands, fatigue, malaise, muscle pain, fluctuating low fever, rash, headache, and sore throat are reported most commonly Toxoplasmosis can infect and damage an unborn child while producing mild or no symptoms in the mother.

Transmission - The passing of an infectious organism or germ from person to person.

Transmission-based precautions - Precautions, in addition to Standard precautions, that are required where airborne, droplet, and contact transmission of infectious organisms may occur. In addition to handwashing, cleaning and sanitation of surfaces, transmission-based precautions include use of a room shared only by those who are infected with the same infectious agent (with negative-pressure ventilation when airborne spread is involved), use of masks for infections spread by the airborne and droplet routes, and use of gowns and gloves for diseases spread by contact. Use of gloves for diaper changing is not mandatory in these circumstances either. Transmission-based precautions are applicable to child care where children are receiving care who would otherwise be excluded because they have a communicable disease See also Standard precautions; Universal precautions.

Tuberculosis (Tb) - A disease caused by the bacterium Mycobacterium tuberculosis that usually causes an infection of the lungs.

Underhydration - A condition of the body that occurs when it does not receive adequate fluid intake. Chronic underhydration can lead to severe problems that affect blood pressure, circulation, digestion, and kidney function.

Under-immunized - A person who has not received the recommended number or types of vaccines for hi/ her age according to the current national and local immunization schedules.

Unitary surface material - A cushioned surface material (such as rubber mats or a combination of rubberlike materials held in place by a binder) for placement under and around playground equipment that forms a unitary shock absorbing surface.

Universal precautions - apply to blood, other body fluids containing blood, semen, and vaginal secretions, but not to feces, nasal secretions, sputum, sweat, tears, urine, saliva and vomitus unless they contain visible blood or are likely to contain blood. Universal precautions include avoiding injuries caused by sharp instruments or devices and the use of protective barriers such as gloves, gowns, aprons, masks, or protective eyewear, which can reduce the risk of exposure of the worker's skin or mucous membranes that could come in contact with materials that may contain blood-borne pathogens while the worker is providing first aid or care. See also Standard precautions; Transmission precautions.

Vacuum breaker - A device put on a pipe containing liquid (such as drinking water) to prevent the liquid from being sucked backward within the pipe.

Varicella-zoster - Varicella (also know as chickenpox) is caused by the varicella-zoster virus and is highly infectious. Transmission occurs from person-to-person by direct contact or through the air. Varicella is characterized by a blister- and pimple-like rash that turns into noninfectious, dried crusts within approximately six days. A person with varicella is contagious from one to two days before the rash appears until all of the lesions have formed scabs.

Virus - A microscopic organism, smaller than a bacterium, that may cause disease. Viruses can grow or reproduce only in living cells.

Volunteer - In general, a volunteer is a regular member of the staff who is not paid and is not counted in the child:staff ratio. If the volunteer is counted in the child:staff ratio, he/she must be 16 years or older and preferably work 10 hours per week or more in the facility.

WIC - Abbreviation for the U.S. Department of Agriculture's Special Supplemental Food Program for Women, Infants and Children, which provides food supplements and nutrition education to pregnant and breastfeeding women, infants, and young children who are considered to be at nutritional risk due to their level of income and evidence of inadequate diet.

A